W9-BWR-665

PRAGUE IN BLACK AND GOLD

PRAGUE IN BLACK AND GOLD

Scenes from the Life of a European City

PETER DEMETZ

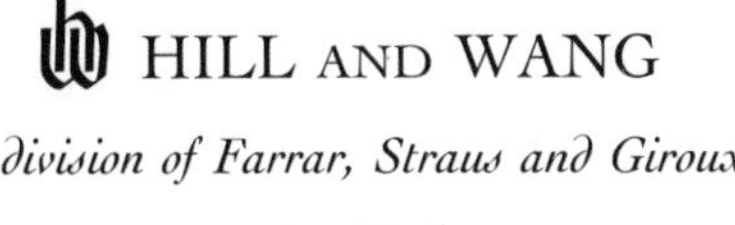

HILL AND WANG

A division of Farrar, Straus and Giroux

New York

Hill and Wang
A division of Farrar, Straus and Giroux
19 Union Square West, New York 10003

*Published simultaneously in Canada by HarperCollins*CanadaLtd
Printed in the United States of America
First edition, 1997

Library of Congress Cataloging-in-Publication Data
Demetz, Peter, 1922–
Prague in black and gold : scenes from the life of a European city
Peter Demetz. —1st ed.
p. cm.
Includes bibliographical references and index.
ISBN 0-8090-7843-0 (cloth : alk. paper)
1. Prague (Czech Republic)—History. I. Title.
DB2626.D46 1997 *96-52216*
943.71'2—dc21

Contents

7. 1848 and the Counterrevolution / 272

8. T. G. Masaryk's Prague / 314

Postscript. A Difficult Return to Prague / 365

Maps

Preface

I love and hate my hometown, and my warring sentiments have not been assuaged by recurrent returns to Prague in the years since the takeover of 1989, sometimes poetically called the Velvet Revolution. My happy memories of long walks among the chestnut trees in May or diving into the Vltava River from the rafts under the National Theater were accompanied by other, more disturbing images. I recall the daily lists of Czech citizens, summarily executed after the Reichsprotektor Reinhard Heydrich had been ambushed, on May 27, 1942, on his way to Hradčany Castle by a commando of Czechoslovak parachutists flown in from London, and I recall an aging woman with sturdy shoes and a full rucksack (my mother) riding a shabby tramcar of the No. 7 line to the assembly hall from which Jews were transported to the camps, never to return; three years later, when Prague had been liberated, German women, children, and old men were taken from their apartments, herded into old cinema halls and sports stadia, and, ultimately, expelled from the city and Czechoslovakia. Many of my European colleagues who like to write about Bohemian affairs have an easier time, unburdened by memories that make the heart ache and the stomach turn; the many coffee-table books now offered in Prague bookshops to tourists do not do much harm, permitting the travelers to come and go, their preconceptions unchanged. In one of his rare lyrical poems, Franz Kafka speaks of walking across the Charles Bridge and softly resting his hands on the old stones, *"die Hände auf alten Steinen."* I always believed that he tried in that gentle gesture to keep the blood of many brutal battles from oozing out.

I am not foolish enough to believe that I can offer a Prague history as it *really* happened, but I hope to counter some of the traditional narratives with other stories that do not hide my polemical intentions. I wish to sketch a few selected chapters of a paradoxical history in which the golden hues of proud power and creative glory, of emperors, artists and scholars, and restive people, are not untouched with the black of suffering and the victims' silence. I have learned a good deal from Czech historiography over the last forty years, but my joys of exploration have been diminished by memories of Charles University in the spring of 1948, when I was a student and could not help watching, immediately after the Communist putsch, some of my most admired teachers instantly revise their ideas rather than risk an honorable place among the hapless opposition. Each of the many learned books published under the party regime has its own story to tell—of eager servitude, of compromise, of self-humiliation, and sometimes of rare resistance.

Multiethnicity, or a livable society made of many different societies, has become a fundamental commitment in political life and in academic studies, at least in the United States. It is sad to see that in the Old World many places of multiethnic traditions have, in the past generation or so, turned to the more solid enjoyments of a single national culture characterized by policies of exclusion and a dash of xenophobia. In this particular moment it may not be useless to explore the history of a European city built over many centuries by Czechs, Germans, Jews, and Italians—though many of the national historians would like to diminish the contributions of one or the other group and often agree only in their efforts to ignore the people of the Jewish Town. Prague has a long history of mass murder, whether triggered by street mobs or organized by bureaucrats, and religious and ethnic "cleansings" that invariably dirtied the hands that "cleansed." Prague had the pogrom of 1389, in which three thousand Jews were killed, Maria Theresa's expulsion of the Jews from their ancient town in 1744, and the Shoah of 1940–45, the transports to Theresienstadt (Terezín) and to the killing camps; Prague historians know the story of the forced expatriation of all Evangelicals, Czech and German, after the Battle of the White Mountain in 1620, and the expulsion of nearly all Germans, whether culpable or not, after May 1945.

Yet there were many moments when Prague societies lived with each other, or at least next to each other, and the names of those who attempted to guide different people to tolerance and sympathy with each other deserve new respect today, whether they are famous or known only to the happy few. I am thinking of the philosopher Bernard Bolzano, of President T. G. Masaryk, his disciple Emanuel Rádl, and the German ministers who served Masaryk's republic loyally in the shared government of 1926–

38. I also think of Franz Kafka's onetime friend Milena Jesenská, who at the time of Munich described, in a series of compassionate essays addressed to her Czech compatriots, the personal and political tragedy of the German Socialists and liberals in the Sudetenland, or the philosopher Jan Patočka, whose lectures I attended before I left Prague and succeeded in crossing the border in the thick of the Bohemian forest. Prague can be proud of these thoughtful citizens.

There is yet another favored narrative that blocks the view of the fullness of Prague history. It has its rather recent origins in the idea that Prague harbors more secrets of the magic, or mystical, kind than any other city in Europe; the new travel industry lovingly cherishes the mystical aura for market reasons. International tourists arrive with images in their minds of the golem, of Franz Kafka (rather simplified), and of alchemists, but they hear little and know less about the mathematicians at the court of Rudolf II, the pedagogical reforms of the stern moralist Rabbi Loew, or the sober philosophy of T. G. Masaryk, and they are led by their guides through the ancient quarters of the city and never set foot in the old proletarian suburbs of Karlín or Smíchov. It is difficult to discover any sustained traces of Prague's alleged mystical ideas in historical documents (though a few may be found by the searching scholar), and it is only fair to assume that stories about "magic Prague" must be ascribed to an early wave of international travelers, mostly from the Protestant countries, who came to Prague and Bohemia in the early and mid-nineteenth century and were struck by its many ancient churches and by the old Jewish quarter. I hope to show, at least briefly, that the images of mystical Prague, created by English, German, and American travelers only a few decades before the Prague city government began in 1895/96 to raze the timeworn Jewish Town and the adjacent Baroque corners, were eagerly developed by Prague Czech and German "decadents" of the *fin de siècle* (among them young René Rilke, as he was called in his youth) and, after the first German golem movie (1914), were amply used by eclectic German writers of varying talents and inclinations, in World War I and later, not by Czechs. Gustav Meyrink's *Golem* (1915), an international best-seller, was not the first to shift the old gothic novel to Prague, but Meyrink combined its conventions with those of early whodunits in a highly effective but kitschy melodrama.

Strangely enough, "magic Prague" and its conventions were brought to new life in the early 1960s when challenging questions of social and cultural importance were asked again in Prague. The idea of "magic Prague" was seized upon by the dissident left, both in Prague and elsewhere, in its protest against the decaying prescriptions of socialist realism, and in an intricate ideological process linked the late-nineteenth-century idea with the revolutionary pleasures of French surrealists, great friends of alchemy. These combinations were codified in the Italian scholar Angelo Maria Ripellino's *Praga Magica* (1973), which aimed to resuscitate the city as an eerie place of mystics and specters, madmen and alchemists, *poets maudits* and soothsayers of occult powers—all in legitimate protest against the boring world of state planning and against the wooden and mercurial apparatchiks who feared change and spontaneity. The new left myth of magic Prague was more productive within the neo-Stalinist regime than after its demise. Before 1989 it helped to undermine an official construction of life and literature, but in the new parliamentary democracy it runs the danger of prolonging yesterday's protest (long turned into a tourist commodity) into a kind of romantic anticapitalism. It is not much of a surprise that Ripellino's *Praga Magica* has been translated into many languages while Karel Krejčí's *Praha legend a skutečností* (*Prague: Legend and Reality*, 1967) has not found many readers beyond the family of his Czech contemporaries. Krejčí, of course, tries to circumscribe the amplitude of Prague's royal, imperial, bourgeois, and plebeian past, and carefully avoids imaginative simplifications. In my own views I find myself closer to Krejčí than to Ripellino, but I have to confess that I have felt most encouraged if not inspired by Ilsa Barea's *Vienna* (1966), which I have often assigned in my undergraduate courses. Ilsa Barea (née Pollak, from Vienna, later married to a general of the Spanish Republican Army) shows with greater precision and yet closer sympathy than anybody else what the traditional versions the history of Vienna hide and obfuscate, and I only hope that I was at least partly able to follow her admirable example.

I owe a heavy debt of gratitude to many people and institutions, and I would like to thank all of them here for patience and encouragement. In the Café Slavia, now dormant, the famous Mánes, the new Savoy, and the little place at the National Library, I enjoyed talking, on post–1989 occasions, to old and new Prague colleagues and friends, who at times prevented me from rushing in with émigré arguments. I am thinking of instructive conversations with Dr. Anna Siebenscheinová, my old friend Dr. Ladislav Nezdařil, and helpful colleagues from Charles University of Prague, including Professor Dr. Kurt Krolop and Professor Dr. Jiří Stromšík, as well as Professor Dr. Josef Kroutvor of the Museum of Decorative Arts, the Kafka scholar Dr. Josef Čermák, and the learned archaeologist Dr. Ladislav Hrdlička of the Czech Academy. Veronika Pokorná, M.A., and Johanka Muchková, M.A., spent much time in Prague providing me with copies of rare articles and newspaper clippings, and, in New Haven, Ms. Jale Okay was untiring in her support of my research. When I began to write the present book, I was afraid that Yale University's Sterling Library, my second home, would not have many of the fundamental monographs I needed, but I soon discovered that the Yale libraries were particularly strong in Slavica and Judaica; and I have to thank here also the Vienna Institute of Human Sciences, where I was able to present a few lectures from my gathering of materials.

I should like to express my gratitude to Ms. Luba Rašínová-Ortoleva, who provided the illustrations, as well as to Böhlau Publishers (Vienna), who permitted me to reprint a sketch of Prague's social topography of 1930 from Elisabeth Lichtenberger's study *Metropolenforschung: Wien/Prag* (1993). I am grateful to Professor Harry Zohn of Brandeis University, who translated my postscript (originally published in German by the magazine of the *Frankfurter Allgemeine Zeitung* and later reprinted in a collection of my essays gathered by Verlag Franz Deuticke, Vienna) into English for publication in *Cross-Currents* (unfortunately defunct) and gave me his permission to use his version here (I could not have done better). I owe a debt of gratitude to my agent, Bill Goodman, who attentively followed my progress and encouraged me when I felt disheartened, and to Ms. Suzanne G. Kelley, actually my first American reader, who brought order to my misplaced commas and to the early version of my manuscript. I was particularly happy in my editor, Elisabeth Sifton, who spent more time on my text than it ever deserved, gently tolerated my idiosyncrasies, and taught me, with an unerring eye, the architecture of effective argument. *Una corona d'alloro* goes to Paola, who for a long time tolerated at her side a writer constantly lost in the dark alleys of Prague (fictional) and yet never ceased to enjoy our walks and a native goulash (real) at the inn "U radnice" (at the Town Hall), not far from where Kafka was born.

New Haven, April 1996

Author's Note

A few suggestions about Czech pronunciation

Czech words are stressed on the first syllable, with the following syllables pronounced clearly and distinctly ("Smetana").

Vowels are short unless marked by a diacritical sign (e.g., á, é, í, or ý); i (í) and y (ý), though different letters, indicate the same sound. These vowels are pronounced roughly as in English, except for long í, which is always pronounced "ee" (as in "meet"). Short u sounds like the vowel in "good." Long u (as in "shoot") can be marked one of two ways: ú at the beginning or in the middle of a word or ů at the end. Vowels in final position are spoken clearly, at least in educated discourse.

Czech č is like the English ch (as in "church"), and the Czech c is like the English ts (as in "bits"). Czech ch should be pronounced in the German way (as in "J. S. Bach"). Czech š is pronounced sh (as in "shoe"); Czech ž is like a soft English s (as in "leisure").

The letter j is pronounced like the English y (as in "yes"). The letter h is always voiced (as in "Hungary") and never dropped. The letters ť, ď, and ň are palatal (the back of the tongue touches the hard palate). The presence of ě (approximately, "ye") and of i (but not y) always indicates the palatalized pronunciation of the preceding consonants t, d, and n—for example, the initial d in "děti" (children) sounds like the one in English "duty," and the n in nic (nothing) like the ñ in Spanish "mañana."

The letters p, t, and k are always without aspiration (Jerry Lewis knew) and never have the tense sound of the English initial consonants in "pass," "tap," or "key."

The ř sound is rather difficult: phonology speaks of a "rolled postalveolar fricative," but it may be easier to approach the sound by pronouncing a trilled r and an ess aitch (as in "shoe") simultaneously, if possible: r/sh. For instance, the composer Dvořák is pronounced "Dvorshak," with the stress on the first syllable and a long vowel in the second.

Here are some examples of common Czech words that you will encounter in the book. The underlined sounds are stressed.

Arnošt (Ernest) = Arnosht
babička (grandmother) = babichka
český (Czech) = chesky, with a long final vowel
Hradčany (the Prague castle) = Hradchany, with a short final vowel
Krč (Prague suburban district) = Krch
Libuše (the Ur-mother) = Libushe
Přemysl (the king) = Pr/shemissle
Trh (market) = trch (ch pronounced the German way)
Újezd (street name, thoroughfare) = Oo-yezd

PRAGUE IN BLACK AND GOLD

1

LIBUSSA, OR VERSIONS OF ORIGIN

What the Schoolchildren Learn

In February 1893, the Czech writer Alois Jirásek, patriot, industrious historian, and late ally of Walter Scott, was preparing a little book for young readers and, in a letter to a friend, expressed his hope that it would make its way without "big band and loud advertising." Jirásek's *Old Czech Legends* first appeared in 1894, and his hopes, and those of his publisher, Josef Richard Vilímek, were fulfilled far beyond their expectations. *Old Czech Legends* has been published and republished for a hundred years now, to be read in and outside school, and every educated Czech remembers at least some scenes and sayings from the book—though perhaps, among the more recent, skeptical generation, not so vividly as those from Jaroslav Hašek's *Good Soldier Švejk.* Making eclectic use of old chronicles, Jirásek described the wandering of the Czechs, their arrival in Bohemia, where they settled after a perilous migration, and the wise Libussa, who, after she married the peasant lad Přemysl (father of future Czech kings), in one of her trances guided the people to a place in the forest where the castle and the city of Prague, of never-ending fame and glory, were founded.

Jirásek's *Old Czech Legends* appeared thirteen years after the premiere of Smetana's patriotic opera *Libuše* (1881), and Jirásek's admiration for Smetana (as a Prague student he liked to go to the old Café Slavia because he could see the composer sitting there) clearly shows. The tales are grand opera, too, highly serious, intentionally archaic in vocabulary and syntax, and written without the slightest trace of irony. The movement of unnamed masses (the chorus) in proper old Czech costumes alternates with ceremonious speeches (or, rather, arias) of the rulers, heroines, and heroes; and the space in which events occur is decorously arranged with a fine sense of symmetry and hierarchical proportions, lighting effects included. In Jirásek's tale of origin a tribe from the east, later named after its leader and patriarch, Czech, moves westward and crosses three rivers, the Oder, the Elbe, and the Vltava, and the people think of the far country which they have left behind and begin to grumble about the perils and the fatigue; "there is no lasting rest for us anywhere." Ur-father Czech, their Moses, ascends a mountain rising from the land, and when he arrives at the top: "Lo and behold! The broad landscape unfolded into the endless distance up to the bluish mountain ranges, easily and freely, forests and thickets, glens and meadows, and through the wild green the rivers shone like silver spilled." The land is empty of other people, "and the rivers well stocked with fish, and the soil fertile," and after three days of meditation, Ur-father Czech tells his people that the "land long promised" was right there and that their wanderings were over for good.

A golden age of love, peace, work, and mutual trust followed, at least as long as Ur-father Czech lived; after his death, his son Krok ruled the tribe, always deeply respecting the assembly of elders (Jirásek wanted to stress Czech democratic traditions), but there was trouble when Krok died without a male heir. Each of his three daughters had particular gifts and virtues: Kazi, the oldest, knew healing herbs and often, by uttering the magic names of the gods, was able to save a life in agony; Teta watched over religious rites and guided the people in observing the rhythm of sacrifices and prayers; and Libussa, the youngest, particularly beautiful, unworldly and serious, was able to see what was hidden from other people's ken and to prophesy. The assembly of elders invested Libussa with the power to rule and to judge, and at first everybody was willing to accept a woman's resolutions. Yet when two neighbors fought over the boundaries of their fields and Libussa resolved the case in favor of the younger man, the older exploded in unseemly anger, condemning her and all women, "long hair, short minds," screaming, the spittle running down his chin, that it would be better to die than to bear with the rule of women, a custom unknown to any other tribe.

Pensive Libussa, far from losing dignity, answered that she was a woman indeed and behaved like one, judging not with an iron rod but with compassion, which was unfortunately taken for weakness. After a night of prayers in her sacred grove, she called a meeting of the elders and warned the assembly that a male ruler would demand service and tribute. The meeting would not nominate a candidate, and she made her own decision with the help of the gods, sent out messengers to be led by her magic white horse to find, near a little river, the plowman Přemysl (the "thoughtful," or even the "cunning"), who was working with his oxen. (For some time he has been reappearing on Czech TV before the evening news.) Libussa duly married Přemysl, invited him to see the treasures and her sacred grove, and he began to rule and to judge in his own male way. Once, on a mild summer night when Libussa, her husband, and the elders stood on a cliff above the Vltava River, while looking across the water to the wooded hills she was seized by the spirit, raised her hands toward the other shore, and uttered her prophecy: "I see a great city whose fame will touch the stars!" She guided her people to find a man there who was busy hewing the threshold (in Czech, *prah*) of a house and asked them to build a castle, to be called Praha, right on the spot. "Just as princes and army commanders bow their heads when they enter a house," she proclaimed, "so will they bow their heads to my city. It will be honored, noble, and respected by all the world."

Not everybody, however, was happy after Libussa's marriage and the prophecy of future glory. Her maidens, who enjoyed high esteem in the time of gynocracy, felt abandoned and "angry when the men held them up to ridicule" and called them "lost sheep." It was Vlasta, Libussa's favorite, who gathered the disconcerted and harassed women; they seized arms, and the "Maidens' War" against the menfolk began. Vlasta deftly organized her army and trained the many women who were leaving their husbands, brothers, and fathers to join the fight; the strong were chosen to lead the attack, and the most beautiful to entice the men away from their battle groups to be killed. Přemysl's male retinue made fun of the armed women, but Přemysl himself warned the men not to underrate the women's strength. In the forest and valleys, much blood was shed mercilessly, hundreds of men died in the field, many were killed in bed, and young Ctirad, strong and handsome—and particularly hated, or perhaps loved, by Vlasta—was lured into an ambush by attractive Šárka, then tortured and put to death. The warriors wanted revenge, and Vlasta, fighting stubbornly, was killed; a counterattack of the maidens failed, all were slaughtered, and the fortified Děvín, or "Castle of the Maidens," was razed. The storyteller would like to side with the young women but finally turns against them because, he says, they had no heart.

What Archaeologists and Historians Believe: Hypotheses and Reconstructions

In the beginning (after firm land had risen for the third time from the primal seas) were the clouds, the sun, the river, and the hills that gently descended to the east and southeast and softly flattened out to the north (at least after the recurrent glaciations of the alpine and northern lands of Europe had come to an end). The region in which, much later, many hamlets, villages, and townships were to constitute the city of Prague was attractive to human beings in search of food and shelter from time without time. A first "flake" of flintstone and traces of campfires, signaling a human presence by 250,000 B.C., have been found at Letky in what is now the north of Prague (a much older site near Podbaba is now being discussed by the experts). After long stretches of inclement climatic conditions, bands of roaming mammoth hunters appeared, as did later settlers, in the Šárka Valley and elsewhere on the west bank of the Vltava River, though always at a respectful distance from the water and, on the east bank, only at higher elevations.

At first, the river was treacherous and deeply cut into the rocks, and hunters and settlers were helpless when its banks were swiftly and recurrently inundated. Much, much later (counting in geological periods rather than historical ages), the river eroded the rocks, the riverbed filled with silt and sediments, and the broadened waters began to flow more slowly and quietly—the composer Bedřich Smetana in his symphonic poem "Vltava" (it is known to many listeners by the river's German name, "Moldau") intoned an almost ceremonial and majestic rhythm to indicate the point when the waters enter the Prague region. The left, western bank was hilly, ascending steeply to a high plateau; the right, eastern bank was flatter, at least close to the river, with the exception of a single cliff, later called the Vyšehrad. A number of tongue-shaped, sandy islands emerged from the placid waters, and, in war and peace, people found a few places where they could ford, crossing over, for instance, from the left bank under the castle to what is now called the Old Town, slightly north of where the medieval stone bridges were later built. Economic historians presume that the flowering of Prague was due to its location at an intersection where an ancient trade route from Western Europe crossed the river to continue to Eastern and Southeastern Europe.

The first farming people, of unknown origin and possibly from the southeast, arrived after 4000 B.C. and settled across a wide arc in the

Prague regions we now know as Liboc, Bubeneč, and, on the east side of the river, Libeň, and Vršovice and Krč, farther south. They worked the soil with wooden and stone implements, and bartered for copper trinkets and shells with other tribes; in their cult, fertility was of prime importance (Neolithic "idols" showed large breasts and heavy buttocks but paid no attention to head or face). Evidently the Šárka Valley, now an idyllic place of cliffs, forests, meadows, and cherry trees, a forty-minute tram ride from the center of the city and much visited on Sundays by families with children and by little old ladies with their walking sticks, was among the oldest and recurrently peopled places of early settlement, and Dejvice and Bubeneč, now districts in which shabby flats for blue- and white-collar workers jostle for space with office buildings of the first Czechoslovak Republic and obsolete industries, have the distinction, unsuspected by the tourists, of being sited on the oldest continuously settled places in Prague, perhaps contemporary with the organization of the Sumer city-states and the unification of Egypt.

The Ages of Bronze and Iron did not much change the patterns of settlement in the Prague region, but it was as thickly settled then, a Czech archaeologist has concluded, as it was in the beginning of "historical" time. Bronze and Iron Age farmers mostly lived and worked on the accustomed grounds of their predecessors and what was later Prague's Minor Town (possibly making the first hesitant step closer to the river); on the east side, they still preferred to cling to higher areas, away from the water. All these settlers were "silent" people who left no trace in writing or stories told in chronicles by others; to name these societies and subsocieties, archaeologists tend to define their cultures by speaking of handmade pottery of diverse ornamentation—linear, spiral, and "stroke" wares; new waves of invaders are known as the people of "corded" pottery (their graves yielded skulls, trepanned to heal headaches or exorcise evil ghosts, or both); and the people of "bell-beaker" pottery, possibly from the Mediterranean, arrived with flint arrows and a knowledge of copper and silver.

The Celts appeared in the Prague region by the end of the fourth and the beginning of the third century B.C., and, for the first time, the "silent" evidence of pottery, implements, and graves is confirmed by stories to be read and words to be heard. Greek and Roman historians, from Hekataeus of Miletus to Herodotus and from Livy to Julius Caesar, told stories of the Celts' homelands and far-reaching exploits, and the Celts themselves gave names to their tribes and rivers (Boii-Boiohaemum-Bohemia, Albis-Elbe-Labe), filtered by later Germanic speakers into Latin and Czech. They were a people of ostentatious warriors who constantly improved their high technology, used the pottery wheel, and produced implements, weapons, and adornments; the older populations continued to farm for their Celtic masters, with increasing yields. In their time the Prague region participated in a cosmopolitan culture of imports and long-distance trade by exchange; the Celts were in contact with Greek colonies, imported their commodities, including metal mirrors and wine amphorae, as well as Macedonian coins, later imitated in Bohemia and Slovakia with the names of the rulers in the Latin alphabet. The Celtic topography of Prague followed the pattern of older settlements: graves of warriors and their wives have been discovered in the districts we now call Bubeneč, Libeň, and (about eight miles farther south) Krč, and Celtic warriors later fortified their villages as *oppida* (so called by Julius Caesar) to concentrate their military power and protect the mass production of weapons and jewelry made by craftsmen affiliated with the princes. The most important *oppidum* in the Prague region was constructed to the south, at Závist, across the river from Zbraslav, and another one at Stradonice, to the west, near Beroun.

In the last century B.C., the glory of Celtic civilization was withering away, and Germanic tribes, ceding to Roman pressure in Western Europe, invaded Bohemia and established dominance for nearly six centuries over a large population consisting of the older farming people and those Celts who stayed on; Celtic pottery patterns, at least, long survived into the Germanic epoch. Nineteenth-century Czech archaeology, no less ideological in its nationalist bent than its German competition, only hesitatingly admitted this Germanic presence and, especially in popular presentations, Czech archaeologists still prefer to speak of the "Roman" period—a label easily fitting the conditions on the south side of the Danube where Roman legions constructed their forts (in Vindobona/Vienna) and garrison towns (Carnuntum) but not really adequate for Bohemia when it was ruled by the Marcomanni and when Roman merchants trekked through the "Hercynian forest" (as ancient writers called the wilderness north of the Danube) to peddle their remarkable imported goods to the Germanic upper class. Political involvement of the Marcomanni with the Roman Empire was close; Marbod, the Marcoman ruler, had been in Rome, admired the efficiency of Roman military administration, and around 18 A.D. had to seek Roman protection when a conspiracy of his underlings forced him into exile in Ravenna and his kingdom collapsed.

Compared with the Celts, Germanic civilization was far from sophisticated; there was no glass or enamel work (though some women were buried with necklaces of imported amber), the pottery wheel disappeared, and agricultural technology fell back to the more basic ways of pre-Celtic times. Germanic graves, male and female, have been found in the Prague region, and there is evidence of a Germanic settlement, in what is now the Minor Town (actually on Malostranský Square, close to the old café where German tourists now rest their feet before ascending to the castle); and though the Germanic tribes preferred to live in lonely hamlets rather than in thick agglomerations, there are strong reasons to assume that a remarkable concentration of small iron smithies, including shaft furnaces brought from the Germanic north, flourished on the grounds of Dejvice-Bubeneč-Podbaba, the center of an iron industry in "Roman" Prague. It is less clear why the Germanic population quickly disappeared in the mid-sixth century A.D. during the Great Migration of the tribes, which lasted from the third century B.C. to the seventh century A.D.—originally caused by the search for new soil and later intensified by pressure from Roman armies in the west and raids of the Huns coming from the east. Some Germanic groups may have joined other tribes on their warpaths, and it is probable that at least a generation of Germanic Langobards moved through the Bohemian lands as well.

Nineteenth-century Czech or German archaeologists and historians have spun fine fictions to strengthen an argument for the historical priority of this or that future nation, useful in the battle for historical rights and political power. There have been Czech archaeologists who discovered a Slavic population living in all the appropriate places *before* the arrival of Germanic tribes; and there emerged, in response, a German theory in the early twentieth century saying that the Germanic tribes, or what was left of them, actually *never* abandoned Bohemia, resisted assimilation, and created a bridge of continuity to the German colonists of the twelfth and thirteenth centuries (we are no latecomers either). In the context of Central European conflicts, it is a miracle of its own kind that conscientious scholars on both sides have come to compatible views and sober give-and-take conclusions about a brief encounter, if not a potential symbiosis, of Germanic and Slavic tribes in the sixth century A.D., the one group being increasingly absorbed, and the other constantly increasing in numbers, wave by wave.

The Slavic tribes (known as Venedi or Venethi and Sklavenoi to Byzantine and Latin historians) probably arrived in central Bohemia in the middle of the sixth century. Some of the first waves certainly settled, for a while at least, close to the remaining Germanic and other populations; in some cases, two villages of different cultures lived side by side, like

Březno near Louny; in others, as for instance, at Baba, Germanic Thuringians held on to a Vltava ford while Slavs settled in the surrounding hills. Ultimately, the Slavs dominated the field(s), as Celtic and Germanic tribes had done earlier. The Slav settlers were, like so many before them, attached to the high ground that had been cultivated ever since the times of the Bronze Age farmers, but they also dwelt in the north and northeast, possibly avoiding the south because the soil was poorer there; it is clear that they later extended their reach beyond what is now the Prague periphery and pushed to the Hradčany plateau and to the slopes descending to the river from it, the expanse of what is now Újezd Street ("the Thoroughfare"), Neruda Street, and possibly Malostranský Square. Slavic presence, archaeology believes, is revealed by a combination of traces: among them the simple but elegant pottery of the "Prague type"; square huts, partly built into the earth and with a little fireplace in one corner; flat pans to dry or roast grain; and a cremation ritual with burned bones and a few gifts, a knife, or a flintstone to start a fire (many pig bones have also been found, and the unhealthy Czech habit of eating too much pork roast, not to speak of dumplings and kraut, may be a very old tradition). In the seventh and eighth centuries, the Slavs (who had risen against the Avars in the east and the Franks in the west) began to build their own fortifications, large burgs protected by wood and stone constructions to house the emerging families of the noble warriors and to protect ancient trade routes and access to the river fords. There were, possibly, five of these burgs in the Prague region, the most important being, once again, close to the Šárka cliffs, at Butovice and, later, at Levý Hradec, north of present-day Prague. In these burgs, archaeologists have found evidence of fine artistry and Frankish coins, suggesting the growing importance of long-distance commerce.

Archaeological discoveries about the ninth and the tenth centuries firmly combine with evidence in written documents, including Frankish annals, Bavarian topographies, Arabic and Hebrew texts, to fix the places and shapes of events, however distant and diffuse. In the ninth century at least a dozen Slavic tribes were settled in diverse regions of Bohemia, in some contrast to more centralized Moravia, and new groups of feudal chieftains and their retinues emerged to make decisions about war and peace and their peoples. Each tribe began to build fortified burgs and communities, and a contemporary Bavarian geographer indicated that the "Beheimare" (whoever that was) had fifteen *civitates* and those of the more powerful "Fraganeo" region forty (he may have overstated the numbers).

It was at Levý Hradec that the family of the Přemyslids began to consolidate its power over the Czechs and pushed its claims from there. Only the Slavníkovci, a clan who later united the tribes east and south of Prague and ruled two-fifths of Bohemia, came to resist the Prague dukes, occasionally allying themselves with Saxons and Poles to do so. But on September 28, 995, their well-built *civitas* Libice fell, and the Slavníkovci and their people, men, women, and children, were mercilessly slaughtered by the Přemyslids, who consolidated their power in the eleventh and twelfth centuries and ruled until 1306.

As happened recurrently in later Czech history, the Přemyslids and other dukes of the Bohemian tribes confronted neighboring realms of greater power and, throughout the melodramatic ninth century, had a difficult time in furthering their interests by military force or, if necessary, by carefully shifting allegiances. Francis Dvorník (born 1893), the grand old man of early Slavic history, deplores that, in matters spiritual, these western Slavs (including those in Bohemia) were faced early with the only recently Christianized young and half-barbarian Carolingian empire, rather than being able to live, as did the southern Slavs, closer to the gates of Byzantium, long Christian and heir to Greek culture. The "Behaimi" were, after protracted resistance to the Carolingian empire, forced to accept its hegemony (806), symbolized by a yearly tribute of five hundred measures of silver and one hundred and twenty oxen (used by Nazi historiography more than a thousand years later as a political argument about the German power in Bohemia); Bohemian representatives appeared at imperial gatherings carrying the appropriate gifts; and on January 13, 845, fourteen Bohemian *duces* (chieftains) appeared in Regensburg, capital of East Franconia and starting point of the missionary expeditions to the east, to be Christianized together with their retinues. Not much later, a Frankish expansion eastward ran against the resistance of the rulers of Great Moravia, which originally united Moravia with central parts of Slovakia, and Frankish armies again and again marched through or close to Bohemian territory to reestablish "law and order."

By the year 862, Prince Rostislav of Great Moravia (after the pope had ignored his wishes) asked the emperor of Byzantium to send teachers of the Christian faith who could make themselves understood to the Slavs of Great Moravia, earlier Christianized by missionaries from Bavaria who taught in Latin. Within a year, Constantin (later called Cyril) and Methodius, two learned brothers of Greek origin, were dispatched to Great Moravia to teach in a Slavic idiom (in practice, the one spoken in the vicinity of their hometown of Thessalonika) and possibly to create a church organization independent of the Bavarian hierarchy. Cyril construed a script, the Hlaholice (or Glagolica), to write down Slavic translations of religious and legal texts, and the Bavarian clerics promptly accused the brothers of the heresy of introducing a fourth language (after Hebrew, Greek, and Latin) to Christian liturgy.

Rome showed unexpected sympathy for the Slavic missionaries, but the conflicts between East Franconia and Great Moravia went on, with many invasions, revolts, cruel betrayals, and sudden reversals of fortune. A kind of temporary balance was restored after the Czech defeat of 872 by the agreements of Forchheim (874), which gave the Great Moravians a chance to extend their power both north and south and (while the Franks were busy with their own internal problems) to make the Czechs accept Great Moravian hegemony. Yet Arnulf, king of East Franconia and last Carolingian emperor, was not willing to accept an erosion of his power; he allied himself with Magyar horsemen who attacked Great Moravia, and it was ultimately destroyed by these invasions and by internal disunity. In the year 895 two Bohemian princes, at least one of them of the Přemyslid clan, again renewed their allegiance to Arnulf and the Franconian empire; Regensburg and Salzburg regained their preeminence in Bohemian church affairs, at least for a while. The collapse of Great Moravia did not, however, end the history of the Slavic rites. The traditions of Cyril and Methodius were preserved among the southern Slavs, and in the first Bohemian churches, in the region of Prague and elsewhere, celebrants of the Slavic rites may have found refuge. An early Church Slavonic legend about the life and death of Bohemia's patron saint—Duke Václav, or St. Wenceslas—was written after he died in 929, and *"Hospodine, pomiluj ny"* ("God, take mercy on us"), a venerable Czech song possibly dating from the tenth century, preserves resounding traces of its Church Slavonic origins. The Slavic rite survived in the monastery at Sázava until the mid-eleventh century.

During these restless years, the life of Duke Bořivoj (c. 852/53–888/89), the first Christian ruler emerging from the Přemyslid clan and, probably, the founder of the stronghold of Praha, may have been more dramatic than the faint traces in legends and chronicles reveal. The writer of the first Bohemian chronicle, composed more than two hundred years after his death, believes that real history commences with Bořivoj's Christian rule; the dukes before him, the learned chronicler says, were "given to gluttony and sleeping" and "lived like animals, brutal and without knowledge." Bořivoj had to cope with Frankish pressures and bloody Czech defeats, and an early legend has it that he accepted Christianity in a rather pragmatic way. Visiting a Moravian prince, he was relegated to sitting in front of and under the table, together with other pagan guests, because non-Christians were not allowed to dine with Christians, and when Methodius, the missionary, explained to him the virtues and, possibly, advantages of the new creed (sitting at the table with others, new might in the field, and so forth), he was duly christened and returned to Bohemia with priests of the Slavic rite; his wife, Ludmila, grandmother of St. Wenceslas who was killed by his enemies when she was sixty-one years old, accepted baptism, too. Bořivoj built a church dedicated to St. Clemens at Levý Hradec (the first Christian church on Bohemian soil), but his more traditionalist rivals, dissatisfied by his new allegiance, rose against him and he had to seek refuge with the Moravians and again returned with their help. He may have decided, right then and there, to build an ex-voto chapel about six miles south of Levý Hradec, dedicated to the Virgin Mary and designed as a mausoleum for his family, and it is perhaps more than a poetic thought that he had it constructed on a place called Gigi (Žiži), on the Hradčany plateau, sacred to the old gods—as if he wanted symbolically to express his triumph over his defeated rivals. Toward the end of his life, possibly in the late 880s, he made a decision of far-reaching strategic, political, and economic implications, and resolved to shift his residence and that of his retinue from Levý Hradec to an eminent place on the Hradčany plateau, close to his new church, and the new castle was called Praha.

The etymology of *Praha* has long been discussed by historians and linguists, and the final results are not in yet. There are, of course, the Cosmas/Libuše people patriotically adhering to the mythological "threshold" (*prah*) idea; a few others believe, as did V. V. Tomek in the nineteenth century, that the word referred to the cleaning of the forest by fire (*pražiti*) or are inclined to derive it from *prahy*, eddies in the river. More recently, interpreters have come to assert that the term originally denoted a barren place on which the sun beat down mercilessly (*na praze*), while still others defend the hypothesis that the ancient speakers meant a knob, a little hill, or a terrace near the river—immediately provoking the question what *Praha* stood for first, the burg or the little market below it, or vice versa.

The important point is that Duke Bořivoj (appearing under the name of Goriwei in the Latin annals of the Fulda monastery in 872) decided to erect the burg of Prague not in the solitude of wild forests but in the elevated middle of a Czech settlement close to the river. Archaeological evidence of Slavic settlements on the left (western) riverbank, including the one at Malostranský Square built in the place of older Germanic hamlets, as well as old Slavic cemeteries on Hradčany Hill and its vicinity, distinctly indicate that Bořivoj and his sons, who continued building, followed the people rather than initiated radical change. The new fortification sat nearly astride an old route from Germany to Russia, which long-distance commercial travelers increasingly used after the Magyars blocked the route along the Danube; merchants went from Mainz to Regensburg and from there north to Prague, where the route reached the fords of the river, and from the other shore on to Cracow and Kiev. The new ducal residence and its *suburbium* attracted barons, artisans, goliards, scribes, ecclesiastics, and merchants of local and international interests; native people still avoided the right side of the river, often inundated, but iron was made there in small furnaces, the smithies plied their trade, and an ancient cemetery at Bartolomějská Street seems to indicate that a settlement of foreign merchants may also have sprung up there quite early on.

The duke and his family lived in a house best described as a magnificent log cabin, but there was ample space for later changes, and the residence was protected by massive earth embankments, natural ravines, stone walls, and mighty wooden beams locked into each other in intricate grids. The burg of Praha protected the left riverbank, and, by economic and military necessity, another fortification, originally called Chrasten and later the Vyšehrad (the "High Burg"), was built upstream on a steep cliff on the eastern, right bank, but not before the first half of the tenth century. Some of the Přemyslid rulers were to dwell there for some time, and another *suburbium*, though of modest size, grew around or below that fortification.

Prague is mentioned as a lively trade center by German chroniclers and Arab travelers in the 940s and 950s, but the first international observer who left an interesting record of his visit to early Přemyslid Prague—that is, to the castle and the *suburbium* on the left bank—was Ibrahim ibn Yaʿqūb, an erudite Jew from Tortosa, in Spain, who wrote in Arabic. It is difficult to say whether he was a slave trader or a scientist, or both, and he showed so many diverse interests in his travelogue that scholars believed that he must have been two persons of the same name; only more recently have they come to believe that he was sent by Caliph al-Hakam II, of noted scientific interests, as a member of a diplomatic mission to Emperor Otto I in Merseburg, and that he wrote his observations on landscapes, plants, commerce, medical problems, and peoples for a brilliant group of Jewish scholars assembled, at that time, at Córdoba who preserved his text for later readers. He probably arrived in Prague in 965,

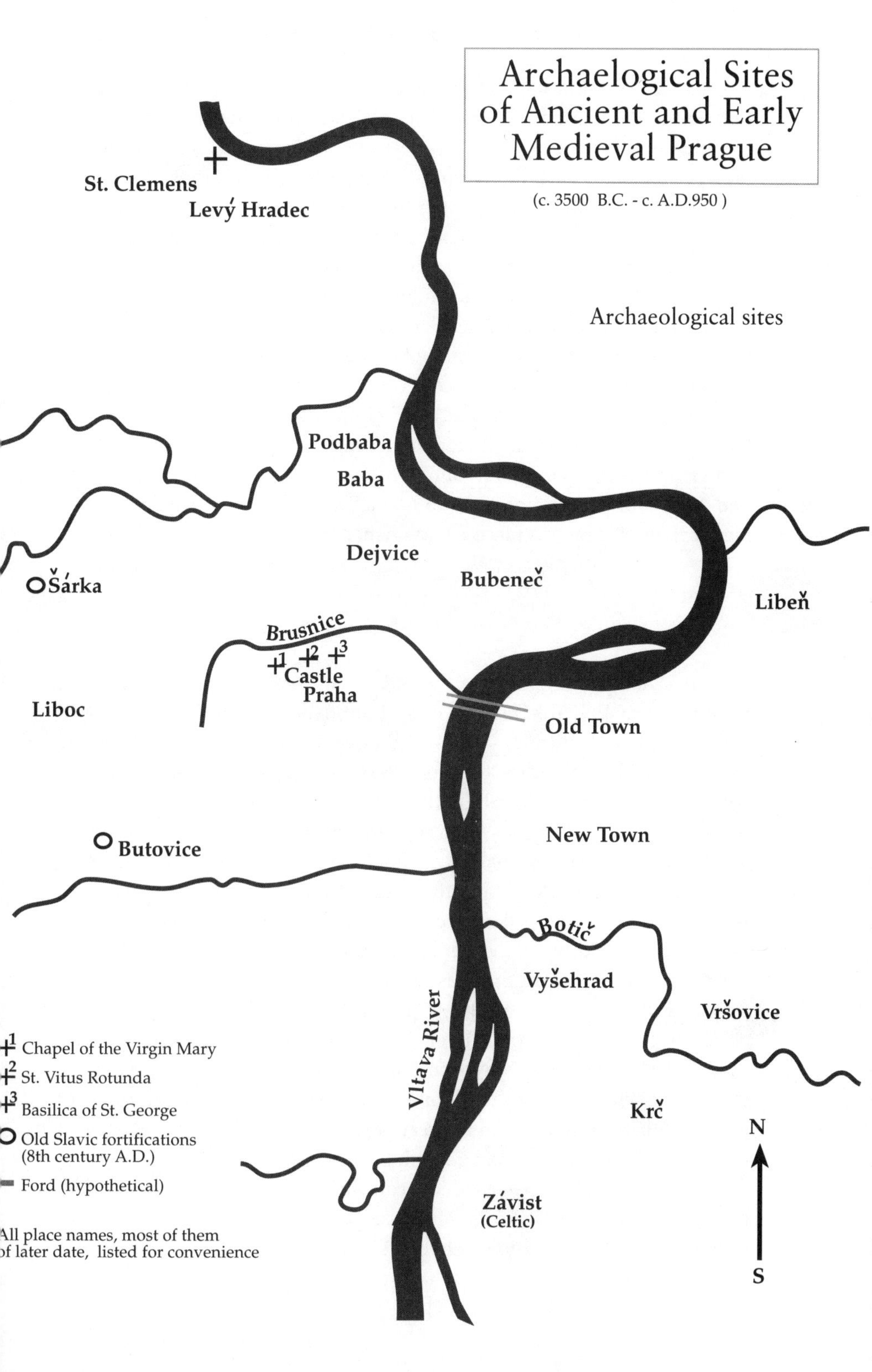
Archaelogical Sites
of Ancient and Early
Medieval Prague
(c. 3500 B.C. - c. A.D.950)
St. Clemens
Levý Hradec
Archaeological sites
Podbaba
Baba
Dejvice
Bubeneč
Šárka
Libeň
Brusnice
Castle
Praha
Liboc
Old Town
New Town
Butovice
Botič
Vyšehrad
Vršovice
Vltava River
Krč
N
S
Závist
(Celtic)
1 Chapel of the Virgin Mary
2 St. Vitus Rotunda
3 Basilica of St. George
Old Slavic fortifications
(8th century A.D.)
Ford (hypothetical)
All place names, most of them
of later date, listed for convenience

when Boleslav I still reigned (according to the legend, he had murdered his brother the sainted Wenceslas), and he was astonished to find "Frága" (or "B.ragha[t]," in a more recently discovered version of his manuscript) built of stone and lime, though possibly he was referring to the new walls and buildings of the castle erected by Bořivoj's sons and grandsons. He noted that many Slavic merchants, Russians and others, were arriving from Cracow and some from Turkey (modern commentators believe he was referring to Hungary), including Muslims and Jews who bought slaves, tin, and furs. Food was inexpensive, and leather saddles and shields were of remarkable quality. He must have looked closely at what was going on at the marketplace on the left riverbank below the castle; people mostly carried light pieces of cloth instead of coin, and though these pieces of textile lacked value in themselves, they were hoarded like money and used to buy "all kinds of things." Even coming from Mainz and Merseburg, he found Prague ("smaller than towns usually are but bigger than villages") a place "made richer by commerce than all others."

The Fortunes of Libussa

The first Latin legend reaching beyond the age of Christianity far into the pagan past of Bohemia offered little illumination about the founding of Prague for later historians, artists, and poets, even if they had trusted the text, which many scholars long considered a later falsification. The tenth-century writer called himself, with a formula of modesty, a "Christian by name only" and, being in sympathy with the Slavic rite, had little use for pagan stories. Christian's narrative about the woman who guided the people to build Prague takes about five lines. The Slavic Czechs (*Sclavi Boemi*), resembling "animals without reason," he says, were hit by a plague, asked "some kind of soothsayer" (*quandam phitonissam*) what to do, and, receiving her advice, built a castle (*civitas*) and called it "Praga." Only after they had done so and the plague had abated did they find a "very clever and cautious" farmer named Přemysl, make him their ruler, and give him the virgin-soothsayer in marriage. Christian was not really interested in what, to more modern ears, sounds like an echo of a distant fertility cult, uniting a virgin of great powers and a tiller of the earth, and he does not even have a name for the "*phitonissa*."

It was Christian's later clerical colleague, the learned dean Cosmas, of Prague Cathedral, who in his remarkable *Chronicle of the Bohemians* (*Chronica Boëmorum*), written between 1119 and 1125, provided names and scenes of unusually colorful detail. He was a loyal defender of the Přemyslid dynasty and made the story of Lubossa (as many manuscripts of the chronicle spell her name) and Přemysl the opening chapter of Czech tradition; patriots have for centuries based their visions and claims on his text. Cosmas was the first Prague intellectual, and his book, full of political analyses, documents, lively and occasionally ribald episodes, and eyewitness reports, or so he tells us, has challenged the imagination of his nation for more than nine hundred years. Born c. 1045, Cosmas came from a fairly well-to-do family of Prague clerics (only a century later a legate from Rome began removing married priests from offices in Bohemia), received his early training in Latin, liturgy, and reciting the psalms at the cathedral school, but left Prague, probably in the mid-1070s, to be further educated abroad, and studied at Liège, then an elite church school with close relationships to Prague. Old Cosmas remembered, with tears in his eyes, his years at Liège as the happiest of his life, studying with Magister Franco, once chancellor of the Liège bishopric, and "gambolling, with the muses, on the meadows of grammar and dialectics." He read widely among the ancient classics and the early church fathers, and evidently acquired a taste for scholarly and elegant prose; as a writer he definitely favored Horace, Ovid, Sallust, and Boethius. He returned to Prague in the early 1080s and was appointed secretary to Bishop Jaromír (1068–90), brother of the duke and king (as of 1085), and chancellor at the court of Emperor Henry IV. In the service of Bishop Jaromír and his successors, Cosmas traveled widely, to Mantua and Verona, to Mainz (on his return, he remembered, he had to sleep in the open because houses and churches were filled, after the plague, with corpses), and to Slovakia and Hungary, where he was ordained a priest by the archbishop of Esztergom (Strigonium) rather late in life (1099). As *canonicus* he ran the economic and administrative affairs of the Prague diocese and once was sent to Moravia to settle a dispute of long standing concerning the market rights of Prague Cathedral and the duke of Olomouc. He was married to Božetěcha, whose unflagging loyalty he praised in his chronicle; their son followed in his footsteps (literally, for he too became dean of Prague Cathedral). Cosmas must have been in his mid-seventies when he began to write his chronicle; he nearly finished three books, and a colleague of his added a note to the manuscript saying that Cosmas had died on October 1, 1125, *Valete fratres!*

Cosmas is not easily given to radical pronouncements. He clearly tries to distinguish, not always successfully, between fictive and true sources (*fabulosa/vera relatio*), and the most nationalist utterances are often ascribed to speakers in dramatic situations and are not, inevitably, his own. He certainly cannot stand well-fed German warriors who are easily defeated by their more nimble Czech opponents; however, when we hear that "asses' shit" (*asini merda*) would be better than a *German* bishop who came to Bohemia "without pants," he puts these words in the mouth of an irascible Czech elder, who is ultimately disowned by the ruler himself (the chronicler sympathizes with the elder, though). Cosmas speaks hardly less favorably of the Poles, these "carpetbaggers with uncircumcised lips," whatever that may mean (yet to this day Polish scholars insist, on the basis of a single disputed line in the text, that Cosmas was actually a Pole).

As far as Prague's Jews are concerned, Cosmas does not usually denounce them in his own voice, but he does not seem to be disinclined to approve of what higher-ups in the secular and clerical hierarchy hold against them. He anticipates the later view that Jews are the personal property of the ruler and therefore are not free to leave the country taking their riches with them (if they do, the ruler is right to punish them); and he reports at some length about the anxieties of his bishop who, on his deathbed, bitterly reproached himself for not doing enough to keep Jews who had been forcibly baptized by roving crusaders from slipping back to the beliefs of their forefathers. In his own voice, though, he unsparingly turns against one Jacob—possibly the first Prague Jew in Bohemian literature mentioned by name—who dared to act in the name of the duke in some financial matter (obviously, his transactions were a failure). Cosmas mobilizes much of the repertory of contemporary anti-Semitism against Jacob: his hand makes dirty whatever he touches, his breath kills by poison, Satan is seen to be his steady companion ("many trustworthy say"), he destroys a Christian altar and throws the holy relics in his cesspool (*cloaca*); yet the Jewish community can ransom his life for three thousand measures of silver and one hundred measures of gold (the duke knows whom he can squeeze); and erudite Cosmas, always ready to serve his ruler, throws in an artful hexameter about Mary Magdalene, on whose day, in the year of the Lord 1124, the entire affair happened. On other occasions, he shows independent and poetic gifts, when writing, for example, about an advancing army in full armor as if made "of translucent ice," or elders at a meeting "confused like fish in turbid waters."

Cosmas is the first who gives the woman who speaks of the glory of Prague the name Lubossa, but he characterizes her ambivalently, as if she were perhaps not entirely explicable by a Christian view of pagan times alone. Her sisters Kazi and Thethka are almost theological allegories of evil: Kazi, compared to Medea, is accused of being a *venefica*, of preparing and administering poisons; and Thethka is simply a witch (*malefica*) eager to return people to the blasphemous rituals of yore. Lubossa is unique; in a narrative designed to legitimize the power of the Přemyslid dynasty, Cosmas cannot but celebrate the future mother of his dukes and the king, yet she remains, in his eyes, a rather disturbing character. He begins his portrait with a catalogue of extraordinary praise: "among women she was especially admirable, circumspect in advice, vigorous in her speech, of chaste body, honest conduct, second to none in resolving the legal affairs of the people, affable with everybody and worthy of love, the adornment and glory of womanhood who took care, with discernment, of the business of men" (I,4). Unfortunately, in the human realm nobody is perfect, Cosmas adds, and Lubossa was, after all, a soothsayer (*phitonissa*); he remarks elsewhere that she and her sisters, through magic art, "played" with the people.

It is during the judgment scene that Lubossa, by her relaxed ways, reveals something of the problems of her character, and the chronicler, or rather the teller of ribald tales, uses words that will be censured by his more spiritual translators and disappear totally from later patriotic legends. In Cosmas's version, Lubossa does not sit on the throne surrounded by the elders (as in later schoolbooks), but receives the plaintiffs in bed. "Resting on her elbow like one who is giving birth, she lay there on a high pile of soft and embroidered pillows, as is the lasciviously wanton habit of women (*lasciva mollicies mulierum*) when they do not have a man at home whom they fear" (I,4). It is an image of impropriety, *déshabillé*, spread legs and sensuous disorder, and the male plaintiffs are not sparing in their insults. Women, they say, have little understanding sitting on a throne, and even less when they are lying in bed, where they should be ready to receive their husbands rather than to resolve a legal case. In matters of men Lubossa cannot speak but deceptively, being a woman of a "fissured" body (*rimosa*).

Lubossa has a difficult time, as is not surprising, when she subsequently warns her people of the dangers of a male ruler; although she proclaims that under male law the new division of labor will change people into those who pay and those who collect taxes, into executioners, cooks, bakers, workers in vineyards and on the fields, furriers and cobblers (to name but a few), they want their duke, whom Lubossa, submitting, provides. Her prophecy of the glories of Prague does not lack a touch of Virgil, provided by the learned chronicler—"Behold, I see a great city whose fame will touch the stars" (*"urbem conspicio, fama que sydera tanget,"* I,7; *Aeneid*, I, 287: *". . . famam qui terminet astris"*)—and her topography of the future castle has remarkable precision. On the west bank of the Vltava River, there is a place protected by the Brusnice brook on the north, while on the south a rocky hill, the Petřín, rises above the land and spins around, as if it were a dolphin, turning toward the brook. That is the place where a man hewing a threshold *(prah)* will be found and the castle of Praga should be built. Paradoxically, Lubossa, the pagan *phitonissa,* continues her prediction by saying that from that castle, one day, two golden olive trees will grow: St. Wenceslas and St. Vojtěch, the famous missionary and first Czech bishop of Prague (she hides the names in a riddle), who will illuminate the entire world by their wonders and miracles. Cosmas enhances the paradox by saying that she would have continued to speak if the hellish spirit of prophecy (*spiritus pestilens et prophetans,* I,9) had not left her body, created by God.

Even in our century of suspicion, old romantic ideas about Lubossa have surprisingly survived, and the cultural policies of the Communist Party insisted that Dean Cosmas carefully preserved the oral traditions of the toiling masses. More independent scholars, who were averse to simplistic, linear, and strictly national ideas of transmitting narratives, were long unable to publish their arguments. After emigrating to West Germany in 1968, the Czech scholar Vladimír Karbusický, with great learning and astonishing tenacity, radically affected, if not destroyed, the ancient dreams about the simple folk and what they told the scribe Cosmas. Karbusický's hypothesis, fully informed by international scholarship, does away with the strictly Czech qualities of the early stories and shows that they consist of wandering motifs well known from the sagas of other peoples. From the romantic debris a new image of Cosmas emerges—a cosmopolitan littérateur easily conversant with the literary canon of his time who takes his cue from the wandering singers, artists, "kitharists" (about whom he speaks himself), and *joculatores* gathered at the contemporary Prague court; the scene shifts from the wretched huts of the illiterate peasants to the court of duke and king, as a splendid place for transmitting what the poets recite; art combines with art, and Cosmas reflects the consciousness of the feudal elite.

In such a view, even Lubossa and Přemysl are deprived of their strongly national character (after all, the plowman as ruler appears in the traditions of many societies, including that of Rome, Hungary, and the Goths); Cosmas particularly is seen to have strengthened and at the same time undermined fictive Lubossa by relating her narrative to that of the historical Mathilda of Toscana (1046–1115), a remarkable woman of his own time, who by her diplomatic negotiations between pope and emperor adversely affected Czech dynastic interests, then allied to the emperor. Both Lubossa and Mathilda were women of extraordinary power, both of them ruled and judged, and both, provoking the male world by their energy and competence, invited courtly *Klatsch* and revealing anecdotes which gave a chance to men of lesser power to take their revenge; it is, indeed, difficult to ignore that, in the entire *Chronica Boëmorum*, they are the only women about whom Cosmas tells risqué stories. Disorderly Lubossa arguing a legal case from her unmade bed has her counterpart, and not only structurally, in Mathilda, who, at forty-four years of age, marries a seventeen-year-old duke and has great trouble, on her wedding night, in arousing the appetites of the suddenly impotent young man. Cosmas coyly regrets that he has to tell the story, and yet he comes up with a good deal of lip-smacking detail; for three nights, the newlyweds strive for happiness and the duke fears that a magic object has been hidden in the bed that makes it impossible for him to perform as the occasion warrants. The enraged Mathilda puts a stool on a table, takes off her nightgown, climbs up, shows herself all naked to the young man, and, as the learned dean says, "wiggled her ass like a goose who wanted to build a nest" (II,32), telling the duke to search her thoroughly for any hidden magic object. (The young man flees the scene.) The marriage was dissolved, historians tell us, only four years later.

In his radical reinterpretation of Cosmas as a writer preserving the poems and narratives of artists, restlessly traveling all over Europe from court to court in search of noble patrons, Karbusický delivers a blow to sentimental traditionalists, including those of the Stalinist *nomenklatura*, but he also suggests the productive idea that it is much more important to know what happens to Libussa (to use her traditional English name) in the rich historiographic and artistic material that came after Cosmas than to ask whether there was ever a real person of her name. Her life in history and the arts, to which different nations in different circumstances contributed, should be more important than the shadow of the *phitonissa*, if there ever was one. Yet intellectual tradition is highly selective, as Karbusický's more conservative colleague František Graus has shown; it forgets, and remembers, whatever it needs. After Cosmas, Libussa asserted her fundamental place as mother of the Přemyslids in the castle of Prague and, as the dynasty died out, assumed a more independent position. The line between the myth and the historical events was increasingly blurred. She was lifted from myth into history; the fourteenth-century Italian Franciscan Giovanni dei Marignolli, who was called to Prague in 1355 (after fourteen years in the Far East) by the Emperor Charles IV to write a world history for him, actually related her to Eliška, of the Přemyslids, that is, to the emperor's mother; in other chronicles, e.g., that of the so-called Dalimil, who wrote earlier in the fourteenth century (c. 1315), she became clearly a woman of the times, keeping her head high at the council of Czech nobility (because Dalimil wanted to stress the importance of Czech barons) and speaking up against the foreigners, Germans, who were flooding the land.

The Renaissance and the Baroque age revived interest in wondrous women of magic powers. The Czech Catholic chronicler Hájek of Libočany, an imaginative sixteenth-century master of poetic inventions, in his own way completed Libussa's historicization by defining abstruse chronologies, and he also followed Dalimil's narrative in offering melodramatic and gory detail about the "Maidens' War," fighting body to body, blood and treachery, eros and thanatos (Cosmos had written about the ancient love game [*ludus*] of Whitsuntide, using the metaphors of war for wooing and submitting). Hájek is responsible for bringing Libussa closer to Czech and German readers of his age (his book was published in 1541) and of successive centuries. His popular book was adorned with expressive woodcuts, and its translation into German, for the first time as early as 1596, gave Libussa an important place in the Central European imagination. In Dresden, a German play about her was staged in 1666, and Italian opera in Prague, performing mostly for aristocratic audiences, provided *La Libussa* (1703). Czech rationalists, however, were definitely not enchanted by her or her forebears, and they tried to explain away her myth by the discourse of reason; while Gelasius Dobner, a scholarly Prague abbé, succeeded in totally discrediting Ur-father Czech, he could not prevent Libussa, surviving the myth and the dynasty, from attracting more attention to herself. She was loved by Czech and German romantics; the Czechs were eager for greatness to compete with German history, and the Germans were charmed by the Bohemian forests and their secrets. In Germany, Johann Gottfried Herder wrote a ballad on Přemysl (1779), which was followed by J. K. A. Musäus's finely wrought and sophisticated rococo fairy tales (1782–86), which spread Libussa's fame among imaginative German and Austrian readers of the 1820s and 1830s. In Bohemia, an old narrative entitled "Libussa's Judgment," in ancient Czech, conveniently emerged in 1818 to provide patriots with a fragment of the epics long missing from Czech literary tradition (unfortunately, these fragments were an ingenious fake).

It would be easy to say that the Great German romantic poet Clemens Brentano experienced Prague through the visions of Libussa when he wrote his "romantic historical" play about the origins of the city, but the workings of his imagination were not so simple. In 1810 he went from Frankfurt, his home, to Bukovany, a Bohemian estate owned by his brother, but he felt ill at ease there. Bukovany was not Arcadia, and the "ugly" Czech peasants were ready "to steal the wheels off the carts." Frustrated, he went to Prague and took long walks under the stars, trying to bring order to the "conglomerate" of Bohemian and Prague images in his mind. He had seen Bohemian glass merchants at fairs in Frankfurt, had heard about the many students at the old university, and had learned of the true "Kabbalah," studied in the Jewish Town more energetically than elsewhere. He had also read about the death of St. Nepomuk, statues of whom he had encountered "on all the bridges of Catholic Germany," about the Hussites and the beginnings of the Thirty Years' War, and he was, being a true lyrical poet, oddly affected by the spectral sounds of the word "*Hradschin.*" To him, Prague was "strangely dark," "adventurously crammed full," "inaccessibly girded," "bridged over and armored"; the intimation of claustrophobia is difficult to ignore. It was the image of Libussa, found in the chronicle of that old (if dubious) storyteller Hájek of Libočany, that fortunately brought serenity, light, and clarity to his mind and prompted him to study the Bohemian past more systematically, in the writings of "lively" Cosmas, whose irony and elegant Latin he admired, and, he claimed, in conversations with the Czech philologist Josef Dobrovský, whose books he bought for his own library. One fine evening in the early spring of 1812 he went up the Petřín Hill, looked over the churches and the river, suddenly felt deeply moved by the vision of Libussa and her city emerging from the forest, and resolved to celebrate her and her prophecy in a play, or rather in an entire series of plays, reaching deeply into the past. He was ready to yield to an image of a magic Prague of his own making, and yet in his notes he continued to see the realities of the provincial Biedermeier town of his time, and she, "the modern," responded to him, the "modern" traveler. People made small talk about the theater, which he abhorred; the many minor civil servants were hardly like Přemysl; and though he toyed with the notion that a few of the Czech girls and women he saw in the street were reminiscent of Libussa and her maidens, his lasting and unfortunate impression was of a Prague mannequin in a millinery shop, "affected, stiff, cold, and ugly."

While living in Prague, Brentano untiringly worked on four versions of his grand drama, *The Founding of Prague* (1815), and the result renders his interpreters, if they remember the play, either speechless or enthusiastic about something unique and strange. It is certainly not a play to be measured by Aristotelian norms of order, plot, and character but, rather, a text that actually feels impoverished by using mere words rather than music, for there are many songs, martial melodies, lyrical moments, trumpet fanfares; in its desire for musicality and its monumental conception, Brentano's text longs for fulfillment in an opera. Libussa's story is set in the context of a mythological spectacle; lacking an orchestra, Brentano uses an abundance of diverse poetic structures and modes, from the solemn to the grotesque, to show how the dark and devilish forces of the past confront the first stirrings of Christianity anachronistically brought to the Bohemian forest from Byzantium. In Brentano's view, Libussa is a plantlike maiden, aware of the divine ground of all being; and though she can be as cold as steel in turning down uncouth suitors, she is graceful and tender when yielding to tradition and her spouse. There is plenty of melodramatic action, which would challenge a postmodern producer to take the play apart and stage, in the creative spirit of romantic irony, a Brentano collage: the Avars are attacking, and the belligerent maidens in the Bohemian forest (with whom the playwright does not really sympathize) occasionally resemble a distaff version of Friedrich Schiller's *Robbers*. Libussa's prophecy about the glories of Prague concludes the play, but the conflict of evil and good will clearly continue; she takes her cue about the name of the place from the people working on a threshold in the woods, and she sees a city slowly emerging on the banks of the river, "the golden city / in the mantle of a king / glides down from throne and promontory" (V,9341–42), and "like a starry cincture / around her solemnly the river Moldau [Vltava] flows." Yet it is a highly ambivalent finale; Libussa collapses in agony, and while Přemysl dryly remarks that he will duly define the borders of the new settlement, his people, unaware of future vicissitudes, automatically repeat what they are asked to repeat by their duke: "Prague! Prague! Thou threshold of our deliverance and faith!" (V,9360).

The first tale to include the Prague Jews in Libussa's world appeared in print in 1847, only one year before the revolution that was to divide Czech and German interests and make life even more difficult for the Jews of Central Europe, who were asked to affirm their national allegiances. Salomon Kohn's narrative *The Jews in Bohemia's Ancient History*, published in German, argued implicitly that Jews were closer to Czechs than to Germans, at least those beyond the Bohemian borders, since before dying Libussa herself prophesies their appearance in Prague, and the narrative makes it clear that they come from the Slavic east rather than from the German west: she proclaims that a "foreign, homeless and endangered" people who believe in one God would seek protection in Bohemia; and when, a hundred and more years later, Duke Hostiwit succeeds to the throne, she appears to him in a dream and tells him about the foreign people who will appeal to him for help and protection. In the year 850, the narrative tells us, the Jews are driven out of Muscovy, for many years search for new homes, finally arrive in Bohemia, and, sending two of their elders to Hostiwit, explain that they are the children of Abraham and ask humbly for a place to stay. Hostiwit immediately recognizes that they are the people announced by his grandmother Libussa, consults his council, and grants their wish. In a formal audience, the Jews declare that they will be "loyal and obedient subjects" who will love their new "fatherland" as much as their forefathers loved the blessed land of Canaan, from which they were expelled because of their sins. Hostiwit gives them a place on the left bank of the Vltava River; it is perhaps of some importance to the message of Kohn's story that the Jews arrive in Prague even before the first Přemyslid is baptized. Later, the Jews strongly support Duke Bořivoj financially and otherwise when he must drive inimical German invaders from the region. Clearly, though Salomon Kohn writes good German, his heart is on the side of a pre-1848 territorial patriotism celebrating the history of a shared ground.

The Viennese playwright Franz Grillparzer came to Prague for only a week on a trip to Germany in 1826, "with a kind of prejudice," he confessed himself, against the town and the "narrow nationalism" (*Nationalsinn*) of its inhabitants. Grillparzer knew much more about the history of the Czechs than Brentano did, and he kept his mind open to the "grandiose impression" of the town, "the advantageous contours, the broad river right through the middle, . . . strange towers and the excellent architecture, and the Hradschin crowning the whole." He compared Prague to Venice in its fusion of ancient and modern, or to Florence, and felt, when he looked down from the Petřín Hill as Brentano had done, something fantastic, "strangely consonant with the spirit of the old history of Bohemia." He felt irritated in the Jewish Town (though a few young women there struck him as more beautiful than any he had ever seen), but Prague had all the marks of "the free creative power of the mind" (*der freien schaffenden Geisteskraft*); and when he left by uncomfortable stagecoach for the north, he felt surprisingly reconciled to the Czechs, whom "he had never really liked" because he had never before had an opportunity to see how they lived in their own ambience. Grillparzer worked on his Libussa play, off and on, hopefully and despairingly, for more than twenty years, from at least 1822, when he jotted down a few remarks about Libussa, to the prerevolutionary time of 1847–48. The first act was performed at a Viennese matinee in 1840, but the completed play did not appear on the stage of Vienna's Burgtheater until 1874, two years after his death, and with indifferent results.

In Grillparzer's play traditional forms uneasily sustain pessimistic views of marriage and the history of humanity; Libussa and Primislaus, as they are called here, after a few wondrous moments of tenderness and anticipation (he saves her from drowning in a swift river) have terrible difficulties relating to each other, man and woman, plowman and princess. He does not want to be at her mercy as humble husband and duke consort, and she (though she loves him) does not want to submit unthinkingly to his wishes and resolves; though she bears his child, they remain an irritated couple, confronting each other in a Strindbergian marriage in which moments of intense if silent love quickly and agonizingly alternate with those of near-hate. (Grillparzer rightly says himself that he endangered the play by an unnecessary intrigue concerning jewels and gold chains.) His Libussa, by loving Primislaus the ruler-to-be, alienates herself from her essential nature, which is, like that of her sisters, one of feeling, solitude, and meditation on a divinely ordered universe; and when she decides that she wants "to be human together with other human beings" (I,405), she takes an irreversible step away from the pure realm of her origins, even though she insists on a matriarchal society inspired by "childlike trust" (I,446) rather than by the "rights" asserted by fierce male litigants:

> wherever I look, I see but kindness, mercy
> in everything that fills the world for all
> Why, right and proof, what are they but the crutches
> that help all lame and crooked causes stand? (II,903–4, 910–11)
>
> *(trans. by Henry H. Stevens)*

It is inevitable that in such a clash of feeling and reason, sympathy and the law, Primislaus's ideas will prevail. He wants to rule by formal order, intends to found the city, cleverly manipulates the elders to agree with his plans as if it had been their idea, and demands of Libussa that she give her priestly blessing to his urban project and "perhaps" provide an artfully arranged prophecy for the astonished nation, to inspire it with "hope of triumph and success."

Grillparzer's productive perversion of the Czech myth keeps Libussa and Primislaus quarreling until she dies; though her husband is ready to cancel the ritual blessing of the future city, which she deeply resents, she insists on going through with it, stamping her priestly foot in a show of stubbornness and declaring that she will be "his obedient wife" again only after the rite. She makes it clear to him that it is his city, not hers; to build a city unfortunately means

> to leave behind your goodly cottages
> where each lived as a man, a son, a husband,
> a being in himself, and self-sufficient. (V,2329–31)
>
> *(trans. by Henry H. Stevens)*

Instead of independence and self-sufficiency in union, labor and society will be divided, people will be "only parts of some large whole" and crave "use and profit," or even leave with greedy zeal to make "a home in alien countries, alien here." Almost condescendingly, Libussa tells Primislaus that his city will, of course, "thrive and prosper," creating a threshold to history—yet history, she feels, will be dark and bloody before the primal conditions of humanity can be restored. Her visions of the great nations of the world, including the Slavs, are melancholy and far from consoling; all "races dwelling on earth" will, in turn, dominate the scene of history—Romans, Gauls, the English, Germans, "that blue-eyed race o'erflowing with rude force: / blind when it acts, inactive when it thinks" (V,2416). The Slavs, "age-old servants," will finally be masters, and their dominance will be "far and wide, yet never high nor deep" (V,2421), like the Vltava River, as Grillparzer had noted in his diary, in a last chapter in the development of a "weary world" far removed from its origins. Primislaus wants to push her from the altar because her words endanger his political intentions, but before dying, she completes her prophecy: history will come to an end, she says, only when the long-lost moment of feeling is renewed; "then will the days return that now are gone, / the days of prophets and of genius" (V,2482–83). Until then, everyone will be alienated from the essential nature of humanity.

Bedřich Smetana's *Libuše*, composed in 1869–72, incarnates, by intent and shape, the force of Czech national tradition without ever deteriorating into mere folklore. It is a festive opera, if not a national oratorio, which took as much of Richard Wagner as Smetana wanted to without being unduly Wagnerian; it was precisely Smetana's attention to contemporary music abroad that made him unwelcome to the conservative "Old Czechs," influential in politics and culture, and an ally to the more radical

"Young Czechs," who were to dominate Czech life in the later 1870s and the 1880s. The problem was that the story of Libuše did not yield sufficient drama for a complete opera, and the libretto, largely based on the fabricated fragment of "Libussa's Judgment," enhanced rather than diminished the problem of the plot. The libretto was first concocted by the Prague pedagogue and Czech patriot Josef Wenzig in his accustomed German, and then translated by Ervín Špindler, a journalist and civil servant, into Czech. In the opera, the litigants, appearing before Libuše, again are brothers, as in many younger versions of the story, but Wenzig and Špindler believed that a love intrigue was needed and introduced Krásava, a rich and somewhat flirtatious Czech maiden who, offended by the elder brother's lack of response to her charms, decides to challenge him by pretending to feel something for the younger. Finally, all is well, the lovers have their happy end, and Libuše proceeds to her prophecy, the culminating scene.

In Smetana's music, Přemysl's arias have a particularly solemn and lyrical charm, and the famous finale for which the opera was written consists of a series of six "pictures" or presentations in which Libuše "shows," as if in a *laterna magica*, the great heroes and two heroines of Czech history from the year 1034 to the sixteenth century (the nearly four hundred years of subsequent Hapsburg rule are simply eliminated). Libuše evokes the historical meaning of the figures briefly and with dignity—Duke Břetislav I and his wife, Jitka, who won Moravia; Jaroslav of Šternberk, who, as it was believed, defeated the invading Tartars; King Otakar II, Eliška of the Přemyslids, and her son, the Emperor Charles IV, three towering figures of medieval imperial glory; the radical Hussites of the fifteen century, including their military leaders Jan Žižka and Prokop the Great, *vivace con fuoco* and with a strong allusion to the great Hussite Battle Hymn; George of Poděbrad, king of peace, elected by his own people in 1458; and, finally, Prague Castle on the hill, "in magic illumination," and a chorus who celebrate the proud nation that never will be defeated, not even by "the horrors of hell."

Contemporary audiences understood very well why the final scene of the opera showed Hradčany Castle, and they were thrilled by the recurrent fanfare signifying the power of the ancient Czech state. In 1867, the monarchy had been divided into Austrian and Hungarian parts; the claims of the Czechs, with their long tradition of power and autonomy, had been ignored; and the emperor in Vienna had not been crowned king of Bohemia at Prague Castle, as tradition required. Smetana had kept his composition in his desk for nine years to save it for the opening of the

National Theater, but general enthusiasm at the opening night on June 11, 1881, was somewhat dampened by the official presence of the Hapsburg crown prince, Rudolf (actually of a progressive cast of mind, and a suicide at Mayerling later). Because of some "Old Czech" intrigue, Smetana had been denied a ticket to his own premiere, but Rudolf invited him to his little salon and there created another difficult situation, because, not knowing that Smetana was hard of hearing (due to a syphilitic infection), he tried to make himself understood by raising his voice. *Libuše* was again performed at the "new" National Theater on November 18, 1883—the original building had been destroyed by fire soon after its opening and rebuilt thanks to the spontaneous financial efforts of the entire nation—but it was a piece too monumental to be performed *en suite*. Smetana survived the opening of the new theater by only a year: he died in a Prague asylum for the insane in 1884. The famous *Libuše* fanfare endures at state ceremonies and on the Czech radio, formally announcing the presence of the president of the republic, though Václav Havel, shy of overstatement, does not always insist on its performance.

Grillparzer's play and Smetana's opera, with their final acts speaking of the glories and the vicissitudes of Prague, show how the ancient myth, first told to legitimize the Přemysl dynasty, was monumentalized or subverted in the nineteenth century. The Czechs used it to evoke national history and, ultimately, for ceremonial celebration of the nation itself. Czech tradition, in the age of emancipatory nationalism, culminated in Smetana's oratorio and the attendant achievements of the great nineteenth-century artists and sculptors, yet the national celebration was only two steps away from the stony gesture, the museum, the patriotic postcard, and Alois Jírasek's narrative, however poetic, for the schools. The German romantics had admired Libussa from a distance until Grillparzer turned his analytical mind to unmasking the implications of the ancient myth pertaining to men and women, male rule and gynocracy, the modern division of labor, and the relative, not absolute, value of nations. Strangely enough, it was this analytical and dyspeptic Viennese who fully revealed the bitter modernity of Prague's ancient myth and, by asking corrosive questions, made it different from all other stories about the origins of cities.

2

OTAKAR'S PRAGUE, 880–1278

From Trading Post to Royal Residence

In the four hundred years between Duke Bořivoj's decision to shift the seat of the Přemyslid family to the Hradčany plateau and the rise of Bohemian royal power in the late thirteenth century, Prague or, rather, its constituent parts approached their modern shape by topographical expansion, social diversity, and architectural transformation, ecclesiastic and secular. The changes were most visible at the ever transformed castle, by the sudden rise and near-fall of the Vyšehrad as residence of the dynasty and, above all, by the new development of town life on the right bank of the river constituting the actual core of historical Prague as it appears to visitors today. The right-bank Old Town, as it is called now, was slowly settled in the eleventh century; it is certainly older than the New Town, founded by Emperor Charles IV in the mid-fourteenth century, though it is younger than the castle and the left-bank settlements in its shadow, or the Vyšehrad with its own small suburb to the south.

The richly structured Hradčany Castle was, from the beginning, conceived as a late Slavic burg protecting, within its ample space, sacred and princely dwellings, constantly built and rebuilt, almost a little town in itself, like Kafka's castle as seen by K. After Duke Bořivoj had built a modest enough little church and his rough-hewn residence in the late ninth century, his sons and daughters in turn established churches and convents on the fortified plateau, especially after 973, when Prague's first bishop was appointed and moved into his own house (a Chapel of St. Maurice, who is usually represented as a black knight, was later built close by); after many sieges by German, Polish, and Moravian armies, the dukes were not remiss in building more substantial fortifications, the white square stones of the walls shining in the light. As early as 920 Duke Bořivoj's son built a basilica dedicated to St. George, and a few years later his son, Duke Václav, the massive rotunda of St. Vitus (possibly employing artisans well informed about Dalmatian Romanesque architecture). Duke Václav—known as St. Wenceslas, patron saint of Bohemia—was later buried there according to his own wishes, and also the mortal remains of St. Vojtěch. For more than a hundred and fifty years, the basilica and rotunda stood side by side; Princess Mlada, returning from Rome, had founded a Benedictine convent there in 973 affiliated with the basilica (to educate Přemyslid princesses appropriately), and the rotunda attracted many pious pilgrims visiting the graves of the Czech martyrs. In 1060, Cosmas reports, the king decided to build another magnificent Romanesque basilica to replace the rotunda, with three naves, three towers, and all in white stone to dominate the castle from above; construction was completed a generation later.

All around the Hradčany plateau, on the hills and also closer to the river, a constellation of new convents and churches emerged: in 993, the first monastery of Benedictine monks, who arrived from Monte Cassino, south of Rome, on Břevnov Hill; in 1140 the new convent of Praemonstratenses from the west of Germany on Mount Zion, later called Strahov; and a third monastery, that of the Knights of St. John, and their Church of St. Mary Under the Chain, closer to the river, in 1169. King Přemysl Otakar II's royal imagination was more challenged than pleased, possibly for military and economic reasons, by the disorderly mosaic of churches, manors, miserable huts, and monastic enclaves on the left bank of the river, and he acted accordingly.

Old chronicles sometimes suggest that the Vyšehrad was fortified earlier than Prague Castle (some assume that Libussa actually resided at the Vyšehrad), but archaeologists assert that this place, on a right-bank cliff where the Botič brook flows into the Vltava, emerged as a fortified place of secular and ecclesiastical eminence only sixty or seventy years after Prague Castle. It grew rapidly for some time when Přemyslid princes quarreled with members of their family residing downstream. A ducal mint was working on the Vyšehrad late in the tenth century, and scholars believed that a ducal residence and a few early chapels were built there and endured the Polish siege of the region in 1000. It was Vratislav II (1061–92), duke and later king, who formally shifted the Přemyslid residence to the Vyšehrad, built there a dwelling for himself and a chapter for his clerics, a Romanesque rotunda of St. Martin (now completely restored) and, close to older church buildings, a Basilica of St. Peter and St. Paul, extended and adorned by his successors and later reshaped in Gothic style. Yet, after this moment of splendor and hope, the Vyšehrad lost its political importance in the later reign of Soběslav I (1125–40), who decided to move to Prague Castle again, and from his time on the Přemyslids and the other dynasties following them resided there. King Přemysl Otakar II did not do anything to revive the royal splendor, and it was only Emperor Charles IV who, in his desire to claim the glories of the Přemyslid dynasty for himself and his house, rebuilt the Vyšehrad to serve as a place of memory and respect for the past, and so it has remained, or what is left of it after the Hussite revolution, until today.

It was advantageous to dwell and do business in the shadow of Prague Castle, but for the humble people life was made more difficult by recurrent sieges, often by stubborn Polish and Moravian princes, as in 1105 and 1142, and by the conflagrations devastating the castle and its *suburbium*. In the late eleventh and the twelfth centuries, as if driven by the impulse of colonization felt in Bohemia if not in Europe in general, people shifted from the left to the right bank more rapidly, particularly after the fire on the left bank in 1142 and the completion of Queen Judith's Bridge in 1172, a structure of red sandstone comfortably crossing the river on twenty pillars, somewhat north of the later Charles Bridge. A number of settlements of Czechs, Germans, Jews, and even Italians emerged on the right bank, only sporadically inhabited before; by 1230 there were eight churches on the left bank in addition to those at the castle and those affiliated with the monasteries, while the right bank and its hamlets had twenty-two places of worship, including the Jewish "Old Synagogue," which, unfortunately, has disappeared without a trace, and the residence of the Knights Templars, who came in 1223. The mendicant friars came early: the Franciscans in the 1220s, during the lifetime of St. Francis, and the Dominicans in 1226, only ten years after the rules of their order had been confirmed by the pope. A marketplace was established as early as 1105, according to Cosmas, as the center of this new settlement, goods were regularly offered and sold on Saturdays, and for the protection of foreign merchants a manor house was built close to the market where they could feel safe. A little later, the dukes or the kings demanded that they stay there at the Týn (a word etymologically close to "fence" or "town"), open their wares for inspection, and pay a market fee, or *Ungelt*, to the authorities. There is documentary evidence that by 1212 a certain Blažej was appointed to supervise market affairs in the name of the king,

Landmarks of Přemyslid Prague

(c.A.D.1250)

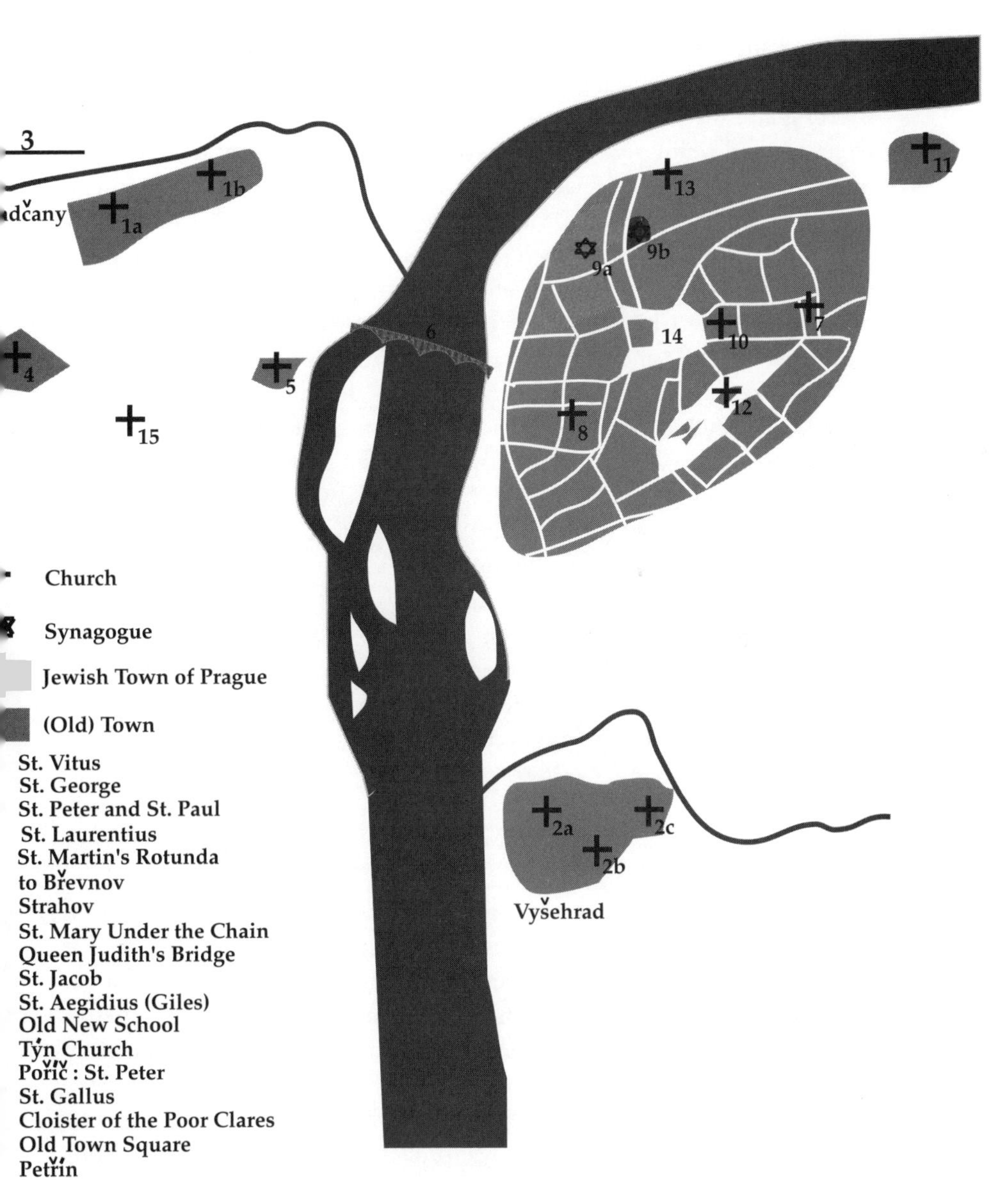

and he functioned as the first town judge or, perhaps, royal sheriff in the urban history of Prague.

Not far from this marketplace, which is Staroměstský Square today, rich merchants built elaborate and massive Romanesque stone houses; recent archaeological research has unearthed nearly seventy of these buildings, rare in Central Europe, which were hidden behind later Gothic and even classicist facades. These houses, most of them on Celetná, Jilská, Husova, and nearby streets, were two stories high, the lower floor being reserved for business, the upper as private space; though there was no heating and the windows were covered in winter with heavy leather, the columns and ceilings were finely structured. The richest of these Romanesque houses, later ascribed to a clan of the Czech gentry, can still be found at Řetězová Street. On the north side of the market, closer to the river, Jewish and German merchants were settling in rather close proximity: the Germans before the end of the eleventh century at the Poříč and around the Church of St. Peter, which they yielded briefly to the Teutonic Knights; and the Jews possibly after fires had destroyed their left-bank neighborhood.

These different settlements were far from constituting a unified city; there was Prague Castle and its *suburbium*, the Vyšehrad and its *vicus*, the new market settlement, nearby the Jewish and German neighborhoods, and all around hamlets and villages. In some Hebrew documents the settlements between the two castles at Prague and the Vyšehrad were called Mezigrady (Between-the-Castles), and it was only during the thirteenth century that the name Prague, first reserved for the castle or marketplace below, began to refer to the settlement(s) on the right side of the river too. About 3,500 people lived here on a stretch of land close to the size of Nuremberg, Ghent, or Bruges at that time.

The Rise of a King

The biographer who wants to know more about Přemysl Otakar II, fifth king of Bohemia and the most powerful ruler of the dynasty, hears conflicting voices among his contemporaries and Otakar's almost condescending silence. He left us not a single line in his own hand, and remains hidden behind the elaborate allusions of Middle High German knightly poems and the rhetorical terms of Latin chronicles or Czech and Styrian texts praising his magnificence or telling us how evil and treacherous he really was. Prince Otakar was born, probably in 1233, at the illustrious

Prague court of his father, King Václav I, and his German mother, Kunigunde, of the noble Hohenstaufen family, granddaughter of an emperor of Byzantium and later closely related through her sisters to the most important European courts, including those of Emperor Otto IV and the king of Castile. Historians have speculated about Otakar's early training and education; at the Prague court, the king and his nobles were committed to the fashionable ideas of chivalry, horsemanship, the hunt and the joust, but it is also suggested that Otakar, as a second son, was, according to tradition, surely trained for a position in the church, at least as long as his older brother Vladislav lived (he died in 1247). At the cathedral or the collegiate school at the Vyšehrad, he may have acquired a smattering of dynastic history, the beginnings of Christian teachings, and a little Latin. Considering the presence at court of German clerics, ladies-in-waiting to the queen, and itinerant poets, his German may have been passable (though I wonder how he really conversed with his Austrian mistress or the German and Austrian poets who rode with him in his wars).

The writer of the *Colmar Chronicles*, an account in Latin composed in the late fourteenth century by a scribe in an Alsatian monastery, describes young Otakar as a "handsome youth, of swarthy complexion [*fusco colore*], middling stature, broad chest, full lips, vivacious and wise," and a wondrous reflection (especially of the *figura mediocriter longa* and the *pectus magnum*) strikingly illuminates the stone effigy with armor and sword which the artist Peter Parler created in 1373 to adorn Otakar's tomb in Prague Cathedral (his worried face was disfigured by irate Swedes who tried to rob his grave in 1648). There is something strangely young and tragic about Otakar; he was fifteen when he revolted against his father, thirty when he was at the height of his power, and forty-five when he was killed, almost like a mad dog, on the fields of Dürnkrut and Jedenspeigen.

Young Otakar entered Bohemian political life by committing a few blunders, but he quickly learned from his mistakes. The noble families were once again dissatisfied with King Václav I; the landed barons felt endangered by his policies, which favored the new towns and a growing money economy. Otakar did not lead the revolt against his father, but was talked into it when it became surprisingly successful at first; and the king, a seasoned diplomat, hesitated in his responses. In July 1248, Otakar, clearly manipulated by his older friends, was proclaimed *rex iuvenis Boemorum* at Prague Castle while his father gathered his forces in the northeast of Bohemia. But the youthful *rex* and the rebels underrated the power of the Roman Curia; the pope intervened, the Prague clerics' support for the revolt faded, and when the wily older king captured the right bank in a surprise maneuver, it was necessary to negotiate. The king took his time, and after some tactical compromises, he imprisoned Otakar for a few days and put two leaders of the revolt to death, one beheaded and the other broken on the wheel, without trial or investigation. In the meantime, the crown prince had died, and the king restored Otakar to the dignity of margrave of Moravia, though with his few privileges diminished and under close supervision.

The first lesson which Otakar learned—perhaps too well, as a Czech historian suggests—was that he had to work with the Curia, not against it. He took his oath of loyalty to the church seriously; two Bohemian crusades against the Prussians on the shores of the Baltic (where he participated in establishing the royal fort of Königsberg, first mentioned in 1256) were certainly undertaken with a view to the Curia, as was his sudden turn away from the Baltic exploits when it became clear that Rome did not have much interest in supporting his plan to make his Moravian bishop responsible for the spiritual administration of the new lands and souls. The other lesson, which he learned not well enough, was to deal adroitly and circumspectly with the great feudal families of Bohemia and elsewhere. Whenever they disputed his royal prerogatives, he was not ready to forgive easily, and more than a trace of impatience and cruelty in his decisions can be found in his tempestuous dealings with the restive nobles, who were to take their bloody revenge.

Young Otakar demonstrated admirable skill and courage, and as margrave of Moravia asserted a Přemyslid presence in Austria, which was on the brink of anarchy after the death of the Babenberg duke Frederick in 1246. The emperor had tried to appoint administrators there, but they could not function, and in 1251 Otakar, who had systematically cultivated close contacts with many Austrian noble families (much to the ire of the suspicious Hungarians and Bavarians), was invited by a gathering of these Austrians to accept the dignity of *dux Austriae*, and he took up residence in Vienna. For political reasons it was suggested that he marry Margarete of Babenberg, heiress to the Austrian lands (the bridegroom was nineteen years old and she, once married to King Henry VII [1211–42], a widow in her mid-forties). This *mariage de raison* was quickly concluded with the approval of the church hierarchy, and Margarete moved to Prague Castle; this did not prevent Otakar from loving young Agnes, of the noble Austrian Kuenring family (he had a son and two daughters with her), and contemporaries recall her as a young woman with hair cropped like a boy's (she must have looked like Jean Seberg in *Au bout de souffle*). In fighting his enemies Otakar showed himself more tenacious than brilliant as a strategist; against the Bavarians he suffered a deplorable defeat at Mühldorf in 1257 because a retreat was badly planned and many heavily armed knights drowned in the Inn River; and in 1260 he turned the battle of Groissenbrunn against the Hungarians (during which he had some difficulties fighting the legendarily ferocious nomad horsemen of the steppe, the Cumans) into a massive defeat of the Hungarian king Béla.

When Otakar wanted to consolidate his realm, he had to ask himself who was to inherit it, and after the Curia denied his request that his children born to Agnes be legitimized, the idea emerged to divorce Margarete, who had been unable to bear him an heir, and to contract a Bohemian-Hungarian marriage to strengthen the peace. This was all done rather speedily; a group of clerics investigated Margarete's past and conveniently discovered that she had, as a widow, entered a Dominican convent in Trier, taking an oath of chastity which invalidated her marriage to Otakar; Otakar married young Kunhuta, granddaughter of King Béla, strikingly beautiful and rich, intelligent, and, possibly, a spoiled brat. On October 18, 1261, Margarete quietly left Prague Castle for a silent old age in Austria, and on December 23, just two months later, Otakar, now twenty-eight, and sixteen-year-old Kunhuta were ceremoniously welcomed to Prague Castle by the archbishop of Mainz, six bishops, and Otakar's princely in-laws from Brandenburg and Poland. After the couple had been crowned in the cathedral, a magnificent feast was prepared, with music, dancing, and rich gifts for the guests, who dined at long wooden tables in a hall constructed for the purpose on Letná Hill.

The archbishop of Mainz had some qualms about the coronation of Kunhuta, not mentioned in the pope's permission, but Otakar's gift, including a hundred measures of gold for his archdiocese and four measures of silver for the adornment of Mainz Cathedral, made him change his mind. There may have been some talk in the wings, for the cleric writing about these affairs in the *Annales Otakariani* was caught between his loyalty to the dynasty and his feeling for the aging former queen. He tried to explain to himself why she had left and sadly remarked, "God knows the reason." Later chronicles, especially those on the Austrian side, suggest that Otakar succumbed to the evil charms of power-hungry Kunhuta; it is true that she was more independent than most, established her own office with a chancellor in charge, and, after Otakar had been killed, married Záviš of Falkenštejn, his archenemy, a leader of Prague's internal opposition to the king, who ruled the country for a time and was put to death by a pro-Hapsburg faction in 1290.

Otakar never won epic battles, but he was accomplished in turning even military half-measures to his political advantage, and in the 1260s and early 1270s he strengthened his power by military expeditions, skillful politicking, and fiduciary arrangements in a way that astonished European observers. By invitation and marriage he had become duke of Austria, and after his expeditions against the Hungarians, he held on to Styria and the land down to Pordenone, north of Venice, until 1276 and acquired Carinthia by bequest (paying off his cousin Philip, the eternal bane of his life, with an empty title and more persuasive subsidies). He ruled Carniola, a region then including Slovene Ljubljana, asserted his power in the patriarchy of Aquileja, an old bishopric (in the northern Italian province of Udine), and prompted other important towns of the Adriatic region to seek his royal protection. Bohemia nearly touched the sea, though not as literally as in Shakespeare's *The Winter's Tale*, and rhetorically gifted contemporaries, at least those in the chronicles, praised his realm extending from "sea to sea" and were able to imagine Přemyslid standards fluttering on the shores of the Baltic and close to the Adriatic. It was a kingdom, a modern Czech historian suggests, that anticipated the contours of the later Austrian monarchy of many nations, and it was ironic that it was to be destroyed by Otakar's enemy Rudolf of Hapsburg, who, in turn, left it to his heirs to build the realm anew, to be ruled later from Vienna rather than Prague.

Otakar's authority was based on personal power and on shifting local alliances at home and abroad; his tendency to centralize administrative decisions alienated many Czech nobles, especially in the south of the country, and many powerful Austrians feared loss of their prerogatives to Otakar's administrators. The Styrian noble Siegfried von Mahrenberg, whom Otakar suspected of disloyalty, was seized, dragged to Bohemia, held in a Prague Castle dungeon, and killed there, provoking his relatives to seek their revenge. Otakar had considerable support in the Bohemian towns and in Vienna but many enemies among Czech and Moravian nobles, as, for instance, Záviš of Falkenštejn and Boreš of Riesenburk; though it is true that many noble Austrian families were loyal to him, especially the Kuenrings (declared to be robber barons by later Austrian historians), it was symptomatic that when he faced ruin, members of the Vienna town patriciate led by Paltram vor dem Freithof conspired to defend him and had to run for their lives when Rudolf of Hapsburg finally and triumphantly entered the city in 1276.

A wise Czech historian has suggested that Otakar's achievements as reformer of the law, innovative administrator, and chivalric protector of law and order were far more important than his ephemeral military exploits. Otakar's administrative and legal initiatives quickened rather than triggered historical developments that had emerged during the rule of his immediate predecessors. These developments included the shift from a feudal to a money economy; internal colonization, with Czech farmers fanning out to grounds never tilled before; and the arrival, in significant numbers, of German farmers, artisans, and merchants, invited by monasteries and by royal power to cultivate new lands and establish new towns to increase the tax base. A chronicle tells us how Otakar withdrew one day to study the corpus of Bohemian and other laws, to identify bad rules, do away with useless decrees, and "transform bad habits into better ones." The presence at his court of Italian notaries and legal experts would suggest that he wanted to follow the splendid administrative example of Emperor Frederick II, without challenging the church, of course, or, at any rate, to apply in his realm administrative and legal norms that had been useful elsewhere—as, for instance, the ones concerning Jews which Otakar lifted, without many changes, from legal documents of the Babenberg duke Frederick the Belligerent. Přemysl Otakar II was unable to protect Prague against recurrent floods, fires, and miserable winters of rising food prices, but he kept away foreign invaders, who respectfully called him *rex ferreus*, the iron king; disciplined predatory nobles; shielded burghers and farmers from exploitation; and made valiant attempts to stabilize the currency and the marketplace by controlling weights and measures. He was the richest ruler in Central Europe, and his income from taxes, *regalia*, and the newly organized Bohemian silver mines was apparently close to one hundred thousand measures of silver per year.

In spite of his innovative administrative ideas, Otakar followed the traditions of early medieval princes in conducting his royal business, and spent much time on horseback, riding with his retinue of knights and notaries and sometimes with the queen, from castle to castle and from town to town rather than luxuriating in his Prague residence. He ruled from Prague but he governed on the spot, be it at his favorite Bohemian castle of Zvíkov or in Vienna or Graz. Yet it is clear that he, being of a pious bent of mind, insisted on regularly spending Christmas and Easter, and the feasts of the Bohemian saints, at his Prague castle. His architectural plans were based on strategic and administrative considerations rather than aesthetic or antiquarian ideas, in a style perhaps more characteristic of Charles IV one hundred years later: at a time when Mongol invasions threatened from the east, massive defense systems of walls, moats, and towers were essential to defend towns; and Otakar not only enlarged the royal residence at the castle but built up the Hradčany fortifications. He continued the initiatives of his father, who, by 1231, had begun to surround the settlements on the right riverbank with defensive walls and high towers, though they excluded a few neighborhoods (for example, the old German neighborhood at St. Peter) and cut others in half, the church within the wall and the others outside. About 1235 Otakar's father had invited South German colonists to establish an autonomous little settlement, under the supervision of Eberhard, master of the royal mint, around the Church of St. Gallus near the core of the right-bank settlement; King Přemysl Otakar II suddenly one day in the spring of 1257 expelled the inhabitants of most of the *suburbium* under the castle and dispersed them in neighboring hamlets while North German colonists were invited to take their place; he surrounded their new settlement with a system of walls and moats. In the late 1270s, then, the Prague region consisted, apart from many hamlets and villages, of this strongly fortified New Town (later it was called the Minor Town, or Malá Strana) in the shadow of the castle; the Old Town on the opposite side of the river, which included the Jewish community and the German neighborhood of St. Gallus (the still older German settlement at St. Peter remaining *extra muros*); the Vyšehrad, with its own suburb; and Prague Castle itself, made impregnable by the king who was to die luckless on the plains of the Moravian-Austrian border.

The Early Jewish Community and the Prague Tosafists

Traveling Jewish merchants were doing business in the Prague and Bohemian regions in the ninth and tenth centuries—coming and going in caravans, selling spices, silk, and other luxury goods to barons, clerics of the upper hierarchy, and the court, and exporting from the Slavic east slaves, weapons, leather goods, and beeswax to Mediterranean and Oriental countries. The most reliable evidence concerning the business activities of Jewish merchants, preeminent among their competitors, can be found in a document called the "Raffelstetten Customs Ordinance" of about 905, which regulated traffic between eastern Franconia, Bohemia, and the greater Moravian realm. In the Prague region, Jewish families may have settled in different spots on both sides of the river in the late tenth and early eleventh centuries; legal documents issued (c. 1080) by Vratislav II guaranteed judicial privileges to resident Italians and Germans, and to Jews as well, and they were confirmed by Soběslav II nearly a hundred years later. Dean Cosmas mentions a rich Jew named Podiva, who bought himself a castle, but he does not say whether he did so before or after becoming a Christian; he also reports that in 1091 the noble Wirpirk, wife of the Přemyslid Prince Konrad of Brno (Brünn) in Moravia, in a dramatic scene told the duke of Prague to desist from attacking and plundering Moravia—it was entirely unnecessary, she suggested, because he could find all the gold he needed in the treasuries of Prague Jews and other merchants; their property was his anyway, and she gave him, in case he did not know, the address of these merchants at the *vicus Vyšegradensis*, a Jewish neighborhood close to Vyšehrad Castle.

Life abruptly changed for the Jews of Central Europe, not only those in the Prague region, when a ragtag army of crusaders, perhaps twenty thousand strong, ready to start a war against the infidels right then and there, in the year 1096 marched from northern France through Germany and Bohemia, plundering (with the enthusiastic help of the townsfolk), setting fire to Jewish neighborhoods, baptizing by force and killing those who resisted. At Mainz a thousand Jews were killed, it is said, and in Prague, while the duke was absent in Poland, the bishop tried to prevent the worst and told the crusaders that they were committing a sin in the eyes of God. Two years later, in 1098, the Jews wanted to leave, and provoked the duke's ire because they tried to take their belongings with them; and for many years, as Cosmas attests, the church authorities were disturbed because Jews baptized by force loyally returned to the beliefs and laws of their forefathers.

The Jewish community of Prague is possibly younger than that of Cologne (which goes back to Roman times), Mainz (first mentioned in 900), or Regensburg (981), but older than the Jewish communities of Frankfurt, Vienna, and Berlin, the last for long nothing more than a Slavic fishing village. In discussion of the early topography of what became Prague, a certain dearth of historical evidence, especially for the earlier centuries, combines with wishful thinking; it cannot be otherwise. Thus most historians assume that groups of Jewish families congregated in two or three different neighborhoods. Originally, Prague Jews lived and moved freely among their fellow citizens, and built dwellings close to the trade routes, on the left bank under the castle, and, as Wirpirk's speech confirmed, on the right bank at the *vicus Vyšegradensis*; a third group, it is suggested, was settled by 1067 at St. Martin's Újezd, a narrow thoroughfare in a rather swampy spot near today's Charvátova and Spálená streets on the right bank; south of this small settlement the Jewish Garden, the oldest cemetery, was located. Tradition has it that the earliest Jews in Prague settled on the left bank; the Sázava chronicler reports that their synagogue (close to a place where later the Knights of St. John settled) burned down in 1142, when the Moravians once again attacked the Prague Přemyslids, and it is believed that they consequently decided, as did so many people at that time, to move across the river. A "Jewish Town" began to take shape on the right bank, rapidly growing with the arrival of Jewish families from southern Germany, following the eastward movement of German colonization or, after the bloody pogroms of 1096, wanting to go further east on their own.

The Jewish Town within the mighty walls protecting the town on the right bank has its own variegated legends of origin, but traces of the original synagogue have been destroyed by incessant reconstruction. The oldest part of the town was possibly established by families of Byzantine origins (though evidence is missing) who moved across the river after 1142 and built a few wooden houses and the "Old School" (synagogue) on the corner of Kozí and Vězeňská streets, but by 1346 the Church of the Holy Spirit was built on an adjacent lot, creating a line of demarcation, unique in medieval Jewish communities; in the place of the Old School, after many devastations and fires, stands a "Spanish" synagogue in late-nineteenth-century "Moorish style" which serves today as a museum of Jewish art.

The actual core of the town was created by Jews from elsewhere, especially from Germany, who built their own "Old New School" and settled along the Breite Gasse (Široká) from which narrow streets fanned out; their original houses and the Old School formed a branch of a settlement that thinned out toward the river (Hampejz Street became the red-light district of Gothic Prague). Historians of art and visitors from all over the world admire the Old New School, the oldest synagogue of Central Europe that has survived terrible catastrophes of nature and history nearly unchanged; though many ages and generations contributed different elements and ornamental shapes to it, including a few added by purist architects in 1863, the synagogue retains in full the somber solemnity of its Gothic structure, one of the earliest in Bohemia. Historians of architecture believe that the building was shaped according to Burgundian concepts and, possibly, after the example of earlier synagogues at Worms and Regensburg; it is possible, recent researchers have come to believe, that skilled artisans who were busy nearby putting finishing touches on the Gothic compound of the convent of St. Francis lent a helping hand with a few decorative details (Jews were excluded from the highly organized building trades). One must remember that these two most magnificent monuments of early Gothic architecture in Prague, the Old New School and the convent of St. Francis, Jewish and Christian, both completed during the reign of King Přemysl Otakar II, stand close by—about twelve minutes' walk apart.

It would be difficult to reconstruct how the inhabitants of the medieval Jewish town felt about being in Bohemia, but an old story, recently rediscovered and brilliantly interpreted by Ruth Kestenberg-Gladstein, suggests that many were conscious, however diffusely, of coming from Ashkenazi Germany by imperial privilege. The story was possibly long current in oral tradition, absorbing many international fairy-tale motifs; it was written down and published in 1705 in Jewish-German by Bella Hurwitz and Rahel Rausnitz, the first Jewish women writers of Prague, under the title *Ein schein Meisse* (*A Nice Story*). The plot is not easy to follow because of its many delightful twists and turns, but the gist is that a spirited and clever young Jew from Frankfurt pleases the emperor and is sent to Prague to establish a community there. His happy end is, of course, delayed for quite a while, and the narrative actually starts at the time when "there were only four Jewish merchants in Prague before Jews were living there," three of them bad, the fourth honest and rich yet, unfortunately, dependent in his business on the dishonest three, who were more mobile and traveled back and forth between Prague and Frankfurt. One day he decides that he wants to do business in Frankfurt himself, puts his gold pieces in a tin bottle, and rides off with the other three to the Frankfurt fair, where they all take lodgings in an inn highly recommended by the evil trio; the innkeeper, in cahoots with them, takes the gold pieces and fills the bottle with wine. When the rich merchant discovers that he has been robbed, he appeals for justice to the imperial court, but he cannot produce witnesses and the impudent innkeeper starts to ask for money because he considers that his name has been stained by an unfair accusation.

In the evening, one of the emperor's advisers, worried about the investigation, rides through Frankfurt, overhears three young Jewish men discussing the now famous case, and one of the lads, Gumpricht, suggesting that the tin bottle should be cut in half to see if any traces of gold remain. The adviser reports this to the emperor, the litigants are brought to court again, and inside the bottle not only traces of gold but three gold pieces are found. The three evil merchants and the innkeeper are instantly beheaded, and the emperor (asking why, if Jews are so clever, so few of them live in Prague) showers young Gumpricht with gifts and sends him off to live in Prague. Yet there is another difficulty to overcome. Gumpricht wants to marry, for he has heard about a beautiful girl in Bumsle (or, rather, Jung-Bunzlau/Mladá Boleslav) but, after a marriage is promised and planned, he runs into trouble with an envious imperial adviser who wagers to woo and win the girl for himself and declares the bet a matter of life and death. The father protects the young daughter, but the adviser bribes the "Shabbesgoyte," the Christian servant girl who works for the family on the Sabbath, and she brings him the daughter's velvet shoes, with pearls, and tells him about a wart on the girl's shoulder. At the court, the imperial adviser boasts about the shoes and talks about what else he knows. Then suddenly a young woman dressed like a princess appears and addresses him familiarly in public; he declares that he has never seen her before. But she is no less ingenious than her fiancé Gumpricht and asks the adviser how he can know about the wart on her shoulder if he does not know her at all; the man is instantly hanged by order of the emperor. Gumpricht and the young woman marry immediately, the emperor gives them gold and pearls and signs a privilege that enables them and a few friends, and friends of friends, to settle in Prague, build a synagogue, and appoint a rabbi. It is, the commentator writes, a story not of need and loneliness, as is Salomon Kohn's later (1847) story of Jews coming to Prague from Muscovy, but of ingenuity rewarded, even if much is wrong historically, given that Jews settled in Frankfurt about a hundred years after they had established a community in Prague. It is not chronology that is at stake but a legal claim for an emperor's privilege.

Later oral tradition may not have been aware of the legal complexities and niceties of early ducal and royal privileges, but the early Jewish community had ample reason to be thankful to King Přemysl Otakar II, whose *Statuta Judaeorum* of 1262 clearly defined the legal norms pertaining to Jewish community life. In his father's and his own time, the Jewish Town and the small Jewish communities in Bohemia enjoyed a moment of peace and intellectual creativity, rare before and after. The *Statuta*, derived from similar documents issued by the Austrian duke Frederick of Babenberg in 1244, fully respects the religious and civil self-administration of the Jewish community and sets forth in exact detail the legal procedures to be followed in their business affairs, essentially consisting of granting cash credit to consumers, including, on certain conditions, the nobility. Jewish civil affairs were to be handled by a Jewish judge, not a Christian town functionary, and appeals were to be directed to the High Chancellor or the king himself. Jews were permitted to transport their dead from place to place for interment without paying a fee, and if a public official should illegally extort money from them, in the way robbers do, he would be punished by the king. Synagogues were protected by law, and whoever violently entered and vandalized a Jewish cemetery would be sentenced to death and his property forfeited to the royal chamber. Jews were not to be harmed bodily; if a Christian killed a Jew, he would be punished according to the law, again forfeiting his property to the king; if he wounded a Jew, he had to pay to the king twelve measures of gold, to the victim twelve measures of silver and medical expenses; if he attacked a Jew but no blood was spilled, he had to pay four measures of gold to the king and four measures of silver to the victim—if he could not pay, his hand would be cut off (*si vero pecuniam habere non poterit, per detruncacionem manus satisfaciat pro commisso*).

Other paragraphs of the *Statuta* regulated the legal and commercial aspects of taking pawns for cash credit, plus interest; while a few commentators suggest that the king was eager to protect this Jewish business in order to be able to extort monies himself more easily, King Otakar cannot be accused of violating his own decree, in contrast to his son Václav II, who readily blackmailed the Jewish community when it was opportune. Jews, the *Statuta* asserted, were permitted to accept any object as security except bloody clothing or church vestments, and Christians were not allowed to force Jews to appear before a court on Jewish holidays. If a Jew was put on trial, whether for commercial or other reasons, it was not sufficient to have only a Christian witness, for Christian and Jewish witnesses were needed; if a Christian accused a Jew of falsely evaluating a pawn, the Jew could clear himself by taking an oath (the wording of which was not prescribed); and if a Jew lost pawns by fire, violence, or robbery, he could clear himself by taking an oath and free himself of future responsibilities.

It is perhaps most important that Otakar's *Statuta* firmly defended Jews against blood libel and stated that Jews resident on royal lands could not be accused of using human blood, for, it said, Jews have no use for blood generally (*. . . ab omni prorsus sanguine se Judei contineant universi*). Six witnesses, three Christian and three Jewish, would be needed to sustain an accusation of that kind, but if they could not prove their allegation, the Christians would be punished and not without justification. Otakar was judicious in quoting papal opinions about blood libel, but in many practical respects his *Statuta* ran counter to the more severe anti-Jewish policies of the church as defined by the fourth Lateran Council in 1215 and in the decrees of Cardinal Guido of Lucino, who in 1267 demanded that they be followed in Vienna and Salzburg, as well as in Prague. Thus in his Jewish policies the king differed from the church hierarchy, whose claims he otherwise fully respected. A scribe who copied the *Statuta* in the sixteenth century added a little note about Otakar, saying, "Either you were a Jew yourself or you had Jewish friends" (*nebo jsi žid byl, a nebos židy přáteli jmíti musil*). The same comment was made much later about T. G. Masaryk, first president of the Czechoslovak Republic, when he argued against blood libel and defended his Jewish fellow citizens against a rising tide of anti-Semitism in a series of famous essays in 1899–1900.

In recent times, the intellectual traditions of the early Prague Jewish community have been rather indiscriminately identified with the speculations of the Kabbalah, but the flowering of Jewish scholarship on Prague in the age of the later Přemyslids, above all Václav I and Otakar II, was characterized by a predominance of lucid legal commentaries of the Talmud, defining the ritual, familial, communal, and economic rules of Jewish experience. The first learned Jews of Prague belonged to the Tosafists of Western Europe, who, after Rashi and his descendants, continued working on "additions" (Tosafot, or metacommentaries) to the inherited Talmud commentaries. They all were a part of a concatenation of schools stretching from Paris and Troyes through Speyer, Worms, and Regensburg to Prague and Vienna. By 1200, Jewish scholarship was firmly established in Prague, even before the Old New School was built; Isaac ben Jacob-ha Laban, Isaac ben Mordechai, and Abraham ben Azriel, author of *Arugat ha-Bosem* (*The Spice Garden*), a scholarly encyclopedia of Jewish knowledge, were well known to their colleagues in France and Germany; intellectual contact between the schools of Regensburg and Prague was particularly close.

One of the renowned Tosafists of the European community was Isaac ben Moses, whose restless life is not easy to reconstruct. We know that he was born in Bohemia or Prague and spent much of his youth in Bohemia (I am following Roman Jakobson's biographical sketch), studied with famous Prague scholars, above all Abraham ben Azriel, but, being very poor, moved around the Tosafists' schools, continued to study in Rhenish communities and in Paris, spent a good deal of time in Regensburg and Würzburg, and returned to Prague, where he possibly did some teaching; when a number of Otakar's officials moved to Vienna, he moved there too, and taught and died there in the 1250s. He was an international scholar who enjoyed the privilege of studying with the most erudite Tosafists of his time; he conceived of his major work, *Or Zaru'a* (*Light Sown*), a compendium of legal comments that is in effect a rich encyclopedia of Jewish life, before 1224 and was still working on it in the mid-1240s.

Medieval Tosafists asserted the tradition of authority and yet questioned interpretative legacies in a continuous sequence of assumptions and arguments. Later Tosafists, among them scholars of the Prague school, were particularly concerned with the hermeneutic process of developing legal interpretations which, in turn, were to be questioned by other interpretations; but if asked about a specific legal problem they did not hesitate to state their judgment unequivocally. Isaac ben Moses's *Or Zaru'a* concentrates, in its first part, on rules of purity and impurity, the temple service, and marriage and divorce; the second part deals with feast and holy days, and the third and fourth with questions of civil and criminal law. On rare occasions, as for instance in the introduction, Isaac ben Moses indulges in theological speculations, uses *gematria*, a cryptic way of dealing with letter combinations, and tells us a spectral story (a dead man appears, with flowers picked in paradise, at the entrance of the synagogue and tells people about the beyond), but these motifs and ideas merely confirm that he studied loyally with Rabbi Jehuda-he-Hasid of Regensburg, a scholar of speculative and ascetic inclinations, and imported what he had learned there to Prague. It may be more characteristic of the peaceful epoch in Bohemian-Jewish experience that Isaac ben Moses felt justified in deciding that it was permitted to sell weapons to Christian soldiers because they defended and did not kill Jews (he might have been thinking of the soldiers of the Přemyslids); "and if they go to fight in other countries, they do so to defend us against our enemies so that the enemy cannot invade our homeland. It is legal for us to sell weapons to our soldiers, for they want to protect us, and it is possible to assume that they are not going to kill Jews" in those other countries. Elsewhere, in response to a question about marriage laws, Isaac ben Moses can be harsh, utterly rejecting more lenient views, as in the case of a girl baptized by force during the Frankfurt pogroms of 1241 who had been promised in marriage but, after what happens, is abandoned by her husband-to-be, who marries another woman and refuses to divorce when the girl returns to the religion of her forefathers. Three rabbis had suggested that the man should divorce and fulfill his first promise, but Isaac ben Moses strongly responded that forced baptism amounted to a kind of rape and the man was not bound to divorce in order to marry his unfortunate fiancée.

The Přemyslid and Czech loyalties of Isaac ben Moses are a matter not of speculation but of fascinating philological evidence which has been discussed for nearly a hundred and fifty years now. When speaking of

Bohemia and the Czech language (or perhaps other West Slavic languages), Isaac ben Moses and other Tosafists of his time use the terms "Canaan" and "Canaanite"; he proudly speaks of "our kingdom of Canaan" and "Canaanite," and Czech glosses, together with a few French and German words, are numerous in his manuscript. Abraham ben Azriel used "Canaanite," or Czech, examples to explicate different questions of grammar and syntax, and Isaac ben Moses, in his glosses on terms of rabbinical Hebrew, prefers to cite things of daily life, for instance *led* (ice), *blecha* (flea), *jahody* (berries), or *motouz* (thread). In one of his most brilliant essays Roman Jakobson has suggested that these Czech glosses belong among the earliest traces of the Czech vernacular in written literature, but it is more difficult to accept his more general conclusion that the "Canaanite" glosses offer incontrovertible proof that the Prague Jews had adopted the Czech vernacular as their idiom of communication *within* their town, whatever language they used earlier or later. I fully understand the reasons why Jakobson, writing during World War II, wished to argue against older German-Jewish scholars who were infected, he thought, by what he rather hastily called Pan-German ideas and therefore could not imagine Prague Jews as early speakers of Czech. But it is a dubious assumption that continued use of Jewish-German, or *daitch*, a medieval German idiom much enriched by Hebrew (only later called Yiddish), binds fourteenth-century Jewish speakers to a later Germany. It is another question entirely whether Jakobson's argument was not really directed against Czech nationalists, who always very much disliked the idea that Yiddish, in its early shape, was spoken in Slavic Prague. The Přemyslid dynasty was Christian and Czech, but their state was not so entirely, at least not in the sense of later nationalists who cultivated ideas of exclusion and "cleansing." Learned glosses are one thing, the idiom(s) actually spoken within a community another, and I am not fearful of the idea of Prague Jews, learned in sacred Hebrew, speaking *daitch* or Czech or any language they wished in a town where many idioms were heard and many cultures thrived.

Czech Saints, Italian Rhetoricians, and German Poets

The real, not fictional, medieval women whose names and distinct lives have been preserved in the history of Prague are all of the Přemyslid family and deeply committed to the spirit of the church. Ludmila educated Duke Václav in the tradition of the Slavic priests who had baptized her; Princess Mlada, sister of Boleslav I, established a Benedictine convent at Prague Castle (after 973) and served as its first abbess; Princess Anežka (Agnes), sister of King Václav I and aunt of Otakar II, moves both in pious legends and on the sober scene of history (the life and death of Blažena, allegedly her sister and suspected of heresy in the Italian Inquisition, is another story entirely).

Anežka, born in 1211, was the third and youngest of King Přemysl Otakar I's daughters from his second marriage, and from early on her father used her as a pawn in traditional intrigues about political betrothals and prearranged diplomatic marriages, projected and canceled as the power plays required. When she was three years old, she was promised to a Silesian prince; as a girl she was sent to the Cistercian convent at Trebnitz (now Polish), but when her fiancé died, she was returned to her family and then farmed out again for nearly two years to the Bohemian convent at Doxany, where she learned how to read. (The magnificent Book of Hours which she used there is now in the Morgan Library in New York.) Again, her father called her back because ten-year-old Heinrich, son of Emperor Frederick II, was to be her next suitor; after this convent childhood, she was sent to the Babenbergs' lively court at Vienna to be educated as queen or perhaps empress. The trouble was that her gracious host, Duke Leopold VI, in the best Viennese manner elegantly undercut her father's plans and married off his own daughter Margarete to Heinrich; the enraged king of Bohemia wanted to attack Vienna, and Anežka had to come home again. The next suitor-to-be was Henry III, king of England (the negotiations dragged on for years, mostly about the dowry); when Emperor Frederick II himself wanted to marry Anežka, first in 1228 and then again in 1231, she turned him down (Pope Gregory IX may have strengthened her resolve).

In 1234, at the age of twenty-three, she entered a convent in the Old Town next to the river, and remained there for almost a half-century (she died in 1282). Anežka had long been an object of dynastic and family politicking, and when she decided to become a bride of Christ she did so on her own terms and with remarkable independence. She wanted her own life in a convent of her own and silently brushed aside the traditional possibility of entering the Benedictine convent of St. George, at the castle. She organized her own hospital in 1233, run by a lay brotherhood later called the Order of the Knights of the Cross with the Red Star (1237), the only monastic order ever to emerge in Prague, and then, when Pope Gregory IX sent her a group of Italian nuns, she founded a convent that she established as a Franciscan cloister, thereby risking a prolonged conflict with the *Fratres Minores*, who had come to Prague in the 1220s and settled, according to the king's will, at St. Jacob in the Old Town. On June 11, 1234, after her hair had been shorn and she had given away her riches, she entered this convent herself (seven bishops officiating and the entire royal family being present), and the pope appointed her, hardly a year later, abbess of the new institution. Soon she left the hospital to the Knights of the Cross and by her own example, as the Latin legend of her life tells us, made the new convent a radiant home of Franciscan spirituality and a magnificent monument of early Prague Gothic architecture. Construction probably went on for nearly fifty years; first, art historians assume, came a Church of St. Francis and convents for the sisters; then, after 1240, friaries were built, and, later, the Church of the Redeemer, to serve as a burial place for the dynasty. The early part still reveals the Cistercian-Burgundian legacy of sacred architecture, but the later buildings are closer to the High Gothic of German and French cathedrals.

"A queen turned servant," the Latin legend suggests, but Anežka was very much concerned about the rules according to which she and the sisters were to live, and for more than twenty years she corresponded and pleaded with Rome about her Franciscan theory and practice; the letters going back and forth between her and Clara (who had established at San Damiano, in Umbria, the first women's convent in the spirit of St. Francis—hence the name Poor Clares for the nuns of this new order) amply suggest that the two women strongly supported each other. They both defended a radical view of poverty which the Holy See, for many pragmatic reasons, did not share. Gregory IX did not wish to see the new monastic orders multiply endlessly, each with a different set of rules and rituals, and he believed that it would be economically more feasible if the Poor Clares' convents shared property rather than depend on the *Fratres* begging in the streets. Anežka and Clara in unison believed in absolute poverty as a way of pious life; it was precisely her belief in poverty which prompted Anežka early to disaffiliate herself from her hospital, which was substantially endowed by the queen mother. Discussion intensified, busy Franciscans carried letters across the rivers and the Alps, and after Anežka sent him a sketch of her own new rules to be approved Gregory IX did not, in response, even bother to hide his iron fist in a glove of velvet rhetoric: he admonished Anežka to distinguish between zeal and expert knowledge and told her in no uncertain terms to follow in God's grace the old rule.

At least he had been willing to listen; Anežka had pleaded for a modification of rules originally written for the sunny hills of Italy, not unheated cloister halls of a Prague winter, and while the pope readily gave permission for his Poor Clares of the north to shorten the times of fasting and wear double tunics, wool stockings, and fur-lined coats, he remained adamant on the central question of the privilege of poverty, which the Curia interpreted as "shared endowment." Anežka relented for the time being, but as soon as Innocent IV was elected in 1243, Anežka wrote again, though modestly speaking only of modifications; the new pope, addressing her as his "peaceful dove" (*columba pacifica*: he had a sense of discreet irony), gently asked her to "quit worrying" and "calm down," and allowed the sisters of the inclement clime to partake of warm food, wine, and eggs. Ultimately, the Roman hierarchy granted the wishes of the Poor Clares; in 1247, the rule of St. Francis was substituted for that of St. Benedict (though shared property was still recommended), and on August 9, 1253, two days before Clara died, Innocent IV confirmed the *privilegium pauperitatis* as she wanted it to be; the Poor Clares in Umbria and Prague rejoiced that their vision had prevailed.

One can point out, of course, that Anežka's convent, the pride of early Gothic Prague, was amply supported by the king and the queen, who were always willing to sell a few villages when architects needed money for expansions and additions (Prague art historians have found the documentary evidence), but it is also true that Anežka, like her friend Clara, also of a noble family, truly lived according to early Franciscan ideals. Her legend, written some fifty years after she died and discovered in 1896 by the scholar Achille Ratti (later Pope Pius XI), praised her simplicity, the humble willingness with which she served the sisters, washed and mended their clothes, lived on a frugal diet of raw onions and fruits with long weeks of fasting, and her joy in the Eucharist. "There she sucked, like a bee, honey from the rock of the sweetest godhead and the oil of compassion from the hardest stone" (*ibi sugebat enim ut apicula mel dulcissime divinitatis de petra et condescensionis humanitatis oleum de saxo durissimo*).

Anežka and Clara belonged to those Franciscans who cherished a radical view of evangelical poverty and anticipated the thought and the protest of later church reformers who argued against a church too deeply involved in worldly power and magnificence. Unfortunately, the Poor Clares of Prague did not have a chance to go on living undisturbed by history. During the Hussite revolution in the fifteenth century, the convent, from which the sisters and friars had escaped, was turned into an arsenal (1420), and though Dominicans and Poor Clares returned for a while in the sixteenth and seventeenth centuries, Emperor Joseph II secularized and transformed it, in his own revolution from above, into a place where the Prague poor lived or set up little workshops; the churches and chapels fell apart. Even in our century, the "Na Františku" neighborhood was a picturesque place for the underprivileged and a few imaginative screwballs (all wonderfully portrayed in the writings of Géza Včelička, who was born there). Czech archaeologists and art historians fought city planners who wanted to do away with the medieval remnants, as they had in the Jewish Town, and insisted on a judicious restoration, which was completed against many odds in the 1980s. "Anežčin Klášter," St. Anežka's convent, now serves as a branch of the Czech National Gallery, elegant concerts are performed in its halls, and during the intermissions chic tourists and those Prague citizens who can afford it have drinks at the little bar built into the old cloister wall.

Anežka, patroness of Bohemia, was canonized in 1990, but neither profane nor sacred history has much to say about her alleged sister Blažena, who, far from Prague, established her own Christian community. One Blažena, or rather Guglielma Boema, appeared with her son in Milan in 1270 and settled there in different neighborhoods until she was given a home in the nearby Cistercian abbey of Chiaravalle. She called herself a widowed daughter of the king of Bohemia, and many people admired her piety, humility, and exemplary other virtues, stayed close to her, and, after she died on August 24, 1292 (only a few months after her sister Anežka), revered her as a saint; the Chiaravalle abbey built an altar and a chapel above her grave, and her followers declared her to be the female incarnation of the Holy Spirit.

The church was uneasy about the Milan "Guglielmites," and the Inquisition established only a few decades before to investigate allegations of heresy and improper doctrine or practice—especially in cities—scrutinized the Chiaravalle abbey. It was satisfied with public acts of recantation and contrition, at least at first, but Andrea Saramita, the convent's business agent, pushed Guglielma's cause and convinced a Milan priest to go with him to Bohemia to notify the royal family of her demise (in vain, because Bohemia was in political chaos); by 1300, the Milan Inquisition had opened formal proceedings against the "Guglielmites," citing Saramita and two women of Milan's Umiliati lay community (the "Humble Ones") for heresy—Maifreda da Pirovene (who was to be Guglielma's spiritual heir and the next incarnation of the Holy Spirit) and Giacobba dei Bassani. (František Palacký, father of Czech historiography, brought back to Prague from a research trip to Italian archives in the 1830s some Latin excerpts of the trial and published them in 1838.) Saramita, probably under torture, ultimately declared that Guglielma herself had believed she incarnated the Holy Spirit; her corpse was disinterred and burned; and Saramita, Maifreda, and Giocobba were sent to the stake. Guglielma/Blažena may have been the first Czech heretic (at least *post exhumationem*), but there is little evidence that she was remembered by anybody in her nation, proud of its Hussite martyrs and the fires in which they died. In Italy, historians and feminists now continue their research.

The first-born daughter of King Otakar II, Kunhuta, born in 1265 and named after her mother, was possibly more docile than Anežka or Blažena. When she was eleven years old, she entered the cloister of the Poor Clares but was removed almost immediately because her father engaged her to a son of Rudolf of Hapsburg as part of his tactical arrangements in 1276; as soon as these arrangements were null and void and Otakar took the field against Rudolf, Kunhuta returned to her great-aunt Anežka but not for long, because her brother Václav II married her off to a Polish duke, with whom she had three children. By 1302, she was divorced and finally entered the Benedictine cloister of St. George to serve God and the arts. She was appointed abbess almost immediately, greatly expanded the cloister's endowment, supported the importation of fine illuminated manuscripts from the scriptoria of Salzburg, Passau, and Bologna, and attracted excellent Czech artists to compose and illuminate manuscripts for her use and that of the sisters. The Dominican priest Kolda of Koldice, of noble Czech birth and a member of the Inquisition, dedicated to her his allegory of the knight-errant (Christ) who succeeds in freeing his love (the soul of man) from captivity; and Beneš, an outstanding artist, illuminated a passion of Christ for Kunhuta that is a work of rare beauty. These early-fourteenth-century manuscripts were written in Latin, but Kunhuta is perhaps better remembered because of a prayer in Old Czech which signals a new strength in Czech writing, its richness of sacred, lyrical, dramatic, and epic forms fully emerging during the last years of her life (she died in 1321).

Inserted into a Latin breviary belonging to a lay sister, Máňa, the Old Czech prayer was written in the hand of a scribe still active after 1310, and it is now assumed that "Kunhuta's Prayer," as the text is called by antiquarians and philologists, was written before the turn of the century to be recited or sung during mass before the Eucharist was celebrated. It is a singular text because the spiritual lyric written in Czech, which was late in joining the liturgical languages of Old Church Slavonic and Latin, here suddenly emerges in a highly formalized structure, with references, terms, and images suggesting a sophisticated way of speaking about communion. "Kunhuta's Prayer" clearly shows that mystical thoughts about the presence of Christ in bread and wine were not absent in the mind of whoever composed it. The text of the prayer welcomes the coming of the all-powerful king and creator, gives thanks for what he has done for mankind, praises the wondrous change (*proměna*) of Christ's flesh and blood into bread and wine, and expresses the belief that Christ is completely present in each single piece of the "living and joyous bread."

The formal analysis of "Kunhuta's Prayer" has been much refined, especially by the Czech linguist Pavel Trost, who places the text close to the hymn "Lauda Sion Salvatorem" ("Praise, O Zion, Thy Redeemer") ascribed to Thomas Aquinas. The mystical core of its argument centers on the One God and the multitudes partaking in communion *sub utraque specie* (receiving both the bread and the wine), as St. Thomas asserts in his hymn (stanza 7). The prayer suggests that God is all-one in all places; even if the bread is broken into small parts, God is present in all of them, just as we see many rays emanating from one sun (stanza 15); the living bread is given completely and entirely, to the first, second, third, fourth, thousandth, even the last who partakes of the Eucharist:

> God hides in the shape of bread
> you hide your divine light there
> entirely you dwell in the host
> entirely in the heavens you dwell.

These poetic thoughts of a mystical Czech scribe in Prague were not surpassed for a long time.

During the thirteenth century, when European life was affected by the great struggle between the Guelf (pro-pope) and Ghibelline (pro-emperor) factions in Italy and in imperial politics, the Přemyslid court attracted a number of highly qualified refugees from the Ghibelline camp who were allied with the Hohenstaufen emperor. These refugees, well informed about the changing situation in Italy and elsewhere, found protection in Bohemia's church (surprisingly enough) and came to serve Otakar II and his son in diplomatic missions and perhaps in his chancellery. Henricus de Isernia, the most outstanding among them, must have convinced his Bohemian contemporaries of his excellent erudition; and when Václav II, Otakar's son, needed a loyal expert to codify a corpus of ordinances pertaining to silver mining, a new industry that had become essential to Bohemia's economy, he invited another Italian, Gozzi di Orvieto, who seems to have been quietly effective in his job.

Henricus de Isernia belonged to the southern Italian partisans of the Hohenstaufen imperial interests and, after the fifteen-year-old Conradin Hohenstaufen was put to death in 1268, faced the wrath of the triumphant Charles of Anjou, who ruthlessly persecuted the Italian Ghibellines. Henricus lost his lands near Naples, had to run for his life, and was advised by Neapolitan friends to go across the Alps to Saxony and Prague to mobilize resistance against the French. After staying a while at the court of the Wettin family in Meissen, Henricus by 1270 went to Prague and tried to find a place for himself and to advocate intervention against the French. Historians agree about his considerable rhetorical and literary talents, but they differ about his sincerity and about whether or not he was actually appointed by the king to an important position; for a hundred years now the experts have tossed the question back and forth as to whether he was really one person or two, the second being a less colorful scribe and notary, Henricus Italicus (Jindřich Vlašský) by name. One eminent Czech historian believed that Henricus de Isernia was, basically, a windy Neapolitan who tried to insinuate himself everywhere, practicing an elegant rhetorical art far too exquisite for his own good; the German historian Jörg K. Hoensch, in an informed book about Otakar II, recently suggested that Henricus actually was Otakar's right-hand man in his administrative reform of the realm. At any rate, Henricus's first protector was Bishop Bruno of Schauenburg, Otakar's most loyal adviser, and although Henricus complained about being kicked out of the Strahov monastery, he probably moved to the Vyšehrad, where he established a private school of rhetoric, and then back across the river to Prague Castle again; he never lacked intimate knowledge of what was going on politically.

Henricus's many elaborate Latin letters and poems, whether penned as stylistic exercises for his tutorials or as official documents, should be read with appropriate caution. He *was* involved: on one war expedition he rode out with the king and a few bishops and a German poet; in the army camp he joined in a discussion about the Ghibelline-Guelf problem or, in more appropriately metaphorical terms, the question whether the pope was the sun, the emperor the moon, or vice versa. He liked to show off his art of composition: to Princess Kunhuta, the later abbess, he wrote a passionate letter about the beauties of Sicily and southern Italy (alas, she was five years old, and the letter was really addressed to her fiancé, whom he was asking to intervene there), spoke of Otakar as "king of kings," and, when Otakar found himself politically isolated, issued a kind of Slavic manifesto appealing to the Poles to give military support to Otakar and speaking of the close relationship between the Přemyslid family and the ancient Polish dynasty of the Piasts, "the consonance of languages," and the need to band together against the German enemy, who, if he defeated Prague, would almost certainly "force Polish freedom into a stern yoke and present the Polish nation with innumerable iniquities." This early appeal to Slavic solidarity, a Czech historian remarks, written in the best *fioritura* style which Henricus had learned at the University of Naples, sounds so convincing that we easily forget that Henricus began his political career in the north trying to enlist German help against the French (and that Otakar himself tried to mobilize at least four German princes against Rudolf of Hapsburg). Yet it seems that his elegant writing style was very much admired by literate people in Prague, and there is evidence to suggest that Magister Bohuslav, the notary in charge of the queen's office, happily imitated his style and included a few of his pieces in his own collection of formulas to be used in diplomatic correspondence. It is a poetic thought that Henricus de Isernia, whose name disappears from the Prague scene after 1278, may have died loyally with King Otakar on the battlefield, while the other Henricus (Italicus) went on serving Otakar's son in an official function for years to come.

The rising political importance of the Přemyslid dynasty in an uncertain age of fierce conflicts between partisans of the empire and those loyal to the papacy, as well as the German presence at the Prague court and in Bohemia's church hierarchy, attracted many German poets who hoped to make a living in Prague entertaining the elite and proclaiming royal views in didactic stanzas, songs, and epic narratives. Elsewhere, the poetry of high chivalry was beginning slowly to wither away; after the demise of Duke Leopold VI in 1230, the court of Vienna offered little support to the gifted singers who had once found it a splendid haven. By 1240, writers began to flock to Prague, and there—though they were not masters of the first rank, as Walther von der Vogelweide, Wolfram von Eschenbach, and Gottfried von Strassburg had been—they sustained a late flowering of chivalric literature. The number of poets who lived at the Prague court to write in the service of the king was smaller than that of itinerant writers who visited at least for a time. The Tyrolean Friedrich von Sonnenburg may have been in Prague in 1250 and then again in 1271, when he joined Otakar's expedition against Hungary. The Tannhäuser, too, on his far-flung journeys through Europe, may have briefly stayed in Prague, which he described as being located close to the Woltach (Vltava)

River, and Ulrich von dem Türlin in the 1260s dedicated an epic narrative to Otakar, perhaps in the service of the Carinthian estates. Others, including Heinrich der Klausner, Heinrich von Freiberg, and Heinrich von Meissen (called Frauenlob), were probably welcome guests at the court of Otakar's son Václav II, to whom three fine love poems are ascribed. After Václav II's death in 1305—a moment nearly coincident with the strong emergence of vernacular Czech writing, including the Czech *Alexandreis* and the chronicle of the so-called Dalimil—Prague ceased to be a gathering place for itinerant German poets, and by the time of Emperor Charles IV of the Luxembourgs in the late fourteenth century, the situation had changed substantially.

The first important poet writing in German (or, rather, an artful and literary Middle High German, not really spoken by anybody) to take up residence in Prague had been Reinmar von Zweter, of middle-class, not noble, origin. He said himself that he was born in the Rhineland, grew up in Austria, and chose to live in Bohemia (*Bêheim hân ich mir erkorn*), not because of the land but because of the king—yet, he added, both king *and* country were good. Whether he came from Vienna or from serving imperial interests elsewhere seems less clear than that he lived in Prague for four or five years (1237–41). He had put great hopes in King Václav I, praising him as the sun that illuminates the day, but there was trouble from the beginning, and Prague's Czech nobles and German clerics were possibly less than enchanted by the itinerant artist who used German and earlier had defended the emperor against the pope. He may have been caught between his pro-imperial past and a Bohemian king who was usually of the anti-imperial party except when he was neutral or wavered for reasons of expediency; using an erudite chess image, Reinmar said that he just held on to the king after losing the knights and the rooks. But then, in growing anger, he turned against his false friends at court, accused them of wickedness, double-talk (*hinderrede*), or simple lying, and left for western Germany, where he died in 1260.

Reinmar von Zweter writes as an upright and honest man who feels disturbed by the decay of chivalric norms, defined by the golden measure and by polite circumspection. He condemns the new brutal way of jousting which makes the noble ladies pale of cheek because they fear their knights being in mortal danger, castigates gambling and (whether or not the poem was written in Prague) heavy drinking that makes people deaf and dumb. He does not beg, as itinerant singers do, but rather works with the art of the gentle hint, suggesting that it is essential to knights and kings to have *milte* (munificence)—yet again, stressing balances, Reinmar believes that true *milte* does not mean wasting what is precious but knowing true value, keeping *and* giving. There is little laughter in his serious, sometimes pedantic admonitions and he became melancholy. In his last elegy, he asks the restless World what reward to expect of her in the hour of death, and he has her respond, "Let go!" (*Ich waene, ez ist niht anders wan "lâ varn"!*). This is his most impressive poem, and it is not surprising that later *Meistersänger* listed him among the twelve great masters of their craft.

Another master, Sigehêr, may have come from southern Germany, as the Bavarian-Austrian coloring of his idiom suggests, and he was of middle-class origins too, speaking ironically about riding through the forest on a horse when he felt especially happy. He was in Prague by 1252, served Václav I and his son, and probably left Prague again by 1256, later acquiring land at Mezzotedesco in the southern Tyrol. He is a more lively and erudite writer than Reinmar (who had left Prague before Sigehêr arrived); he tested new patterns, including political messages shaped as prayers or sayings of the prophetess Sibylla, and he often wished to appeal to connoisseurs by strings of literary allusions. His praise of King "Watzlab" sparkles with biblical references, and he writes that the king was crowned by Solomon the Wise and King Arthur of the Round Table, paragons of chivalry. Sigehêr rode with King Otakar against the Prussians in 1254–55 and made the young king's first and rather modest military undertaking into a melodramatic event, as if Christianity itself was at stake: the din of the battle rages, the Prussians advance, and Otakar's army must fight as valiantly as the crusaders in the *other* Holy Land: "If Otakar does not win, we are all lost!" He compares Otakar to noble Alexander, the famous and just conqueror (as other poets did), and yet he also tells the story of King Belshazzar of Babylon, who does not want to see the writing on the wall and provokes God to punish him for his lawless pride (*unrecht hôhvart*). Scholars still argue as to whether Sigehêr changed his mind about Otakar, whom he once praised so lavishly.

The first native Bohemian writer of the German tongue, residing at the Prague court from the early 1270s to the end of the century, was Ulrich von Etzenbach. His literary language uses elements suggesting that he came from the north of the country: he says that he was born in the Land of the Lion (Otakar's sign), and when the archbishop of Salzburg invited him to join his illustrious court he gracefully declined, adding that he would not leave the lion and, turning to his king, reminded him that now was the time to recognize his true merits and show a "munificent hand." Ulrich knew a good deal of Latin, which he often parodied, and showed a respectable knowledge of his literary predecessors and contemporaries, from Homer (he is the first writer in German to mention him) to Wolfram von Eschenbach, whom he follows poetically, and from Reinmar von Zweter to Ulrich von dem Türlin, who may have introduced him to the court "*ze Prâge*," in the good town. He arrived by 1270 and spent nearly thirty years writing epic narratives in the service of the kings Otakar and Václav II; for a while he was close to the nobleman Boreš of Riesenburk, rich and civilized enough to employ an aging poet who was not averse to writing in favor of a political arrangement based on balances of interest, of king, and of responsible nobility. Etzenbach was of middle-class origin, mocked his own lack of martial courage, and confessed that he favored a good glass of wine and the groaning board, above all juicy roasts and, in true Bohemian fashion, well-prepared *gense* (geese).

Ulrich von Etzenbach's epic poem (more than 28,000 verses) about the life and death of Alexander anticipates the glory of King Otakar. It combines, as in a coat of many colors, numerous and often divergent narrative traditions, religious, historical, adventurous, and, on occasion, a little salacious, to praise Otakar's rising power. Ulrich began to write his *Alexander* about 1270, but work seems to have come to a halt when Otakar II died in 1278, and recent scholarship assumes that he continued to write, perhaps with a new accent on plot and adventure, when Václav, Otakar's son, became king in 1283. Ulrich rededicated the narrative to the new ruler and possibly finished it in the late 1280s, when he began to write another epic in praise of Václav II and his Hapsburg wife. He constantly compares Otakar to Alexander, ascribes Otakar's silver lion to the standards of Alexander, and, rather unhistorically, describes how Alexander defended his frontiers against the Hungarians. Both Alexander and Otakar show *milte*, *êre* (honor), and *wirde* (dignity) in the highest perfection; it speaks for Ulrich's honesty that he remarks that Alexander-Otakar has courage and magnanimity rather than learning—"*von der lernunge was er mager*" ("he had a certain dearth of learning"). These serious matters are, fortunately, counteracted by interesting descriptions of feasts and festivals, of encounters with monsters and dwarfs, and of the rituals of courtly love; even heroic Alexander feels enamored by charming Queen Candacis, to whom he writes a love letter *comme il faut*.

We are also entertained by a daring story about Candacis, who, acting on a wager, efficiently demonstrates that even a famous scholar (in another version, Aristotle) will pay homage, to say the least, to her charms. She puts on a little chemise (*ein cleinez hemde*, v. 23447), wades through the morning dew (in front of the window of the scholar, who tries to keep his eyes on his books), and lifts her little nothing away from her knees (*daz hemdel sie ze berge zôch*, v. 23461); the scene ends with the scholar, who stops reading, on all fours and Candacis riding on his back. Elsewhere, Ulrich creates an interpretative problem by lifting, from one of his Latin sources, the almost Faustian story of Alexander trying to explore the heavens and the deep sea: Alexander binds himself to eagles who carry him beyond the clouds, and, to continue his research, constructs a diving bell made of glass, oil, brick, and cotton and submerges himself in the sea, where he watches strange animals fighting each other (he also suffers a severe case of the bends when he comes up). These actions show him to be a man of *unmâze* (lack of measure), and it is difficult to believe that contemporary listeners, especially after Otakar's death, would not have heard a note of caution, even if Ulrich was more intent on telling an interesting story than in judging his fallen hero morally.

After protracted years of anarchy, the long-postponed coronation of Václav II and his wife, Guta (Czech Jitka), announced, on the sunny day of June 2, 1297, the consolidation of Bohemia in the hands of Otakar's son and his Austrian wife. It was a rare moment of hope for the people in the Prague towns, and Peter von Zittau, a German Cistercian and great territorial patriot, enthusiastically describes in his chronicle the cathedral rites and the public festivities as events that he happily witnessed himself. Two archbishops, those of Mainz and Magdeburg, and seven bishops assisted at the main altar, dukes and princes from all neighboring countries made their ceremonial appearance, and for the elite an elevated wooden banquet hall, richly adorned with tapestries and wall hangings, was erected between the Petřín Hill and the river. On the right bank, wine for everybody in the town flowed from special fountains, and so many people thronged through the streets, the chronicler remarks, that Prague seemed smaller and the streets more narrow than ever. There were public dances—alas, the Czechs on one side of the square and the Germans on the other—and musicians performed on lutes, fifes, drums, kithars, and trumpets. Here, a sportive group of men, all naked, ran a race; there, boxing matches were held; one "jumped in the air," another "walked on his hands," and another "recited poems." Of course, there were many thieves in the crowd, the writer admits, but everybody went home "with a happy heart."

It is said that King Václav, whose unfortunate wife suddenly died three weeks after the coronation, wrote German poems in the intimate tradition of the chivalric love ritual (three of which have been preserved).

The royal poet was well informed about his predecessors and contemporaries, and he handled the traditional possibilities with unusual lucidity and artistic finesse. He is an ingenious traditionalist: "Like a rose thirsting for sweet dew," the beloved offers her lips to him and yet, in melancholy joy, "he did not pluck the rose though it would have been in his power." In a winter poem, the cold and the stillness of forests and meadows invite him "to the better joys" of a lively flirt, "playful glances which prompt mouth to mouth." In his *Alba*, the traditional song of love and the break of day, Václav ironically, if not skeptically, goes a step beyond tradition: the morning dawns, and the watchman, who usually warns the lovers loyally of the end of night, offers a pompous speech about night and day, turns out to be a mercurial fellow who blackmails the lady, who must pay him off richly before she can return to bed and "to the friend of her delights." We have entered a modern world in which protection for love must be bought, and the royal poet assures his listeners that he does not write of fiction but speaks from his own experience.

". . . My kingdom stands on brittle glass"

Many historians have asked why King Přemysl Otakar II did not use the conflict between the Curia and the Hohenstaufen imperial power—a conflict which dominated the last half of the thirteenth century and led to continuing conflict and division—to push his claim for the crown of the Roman king and emperor more energetically; it is possible that his ambition, more secret than revealed, prompted him to look to the Curia first and foremost. He grievously underrated the power of the German prince-electors whom he considered, of course, unequal to him, the mighty king of Bohemia. At the beginning of his reign, Otakar supported the candidacy of Wilhelm of Holland, who was also backed by a league of Rhenish towns, but by 1254 his own chances were propitious: the German princes were not unwilling to consider him, the rich son of a Hohenstaufen princess, secret negotiations were held, and Wilhelm of Holland suggested his willingness to withdraw his candidacy if paid off sufficiently. Otakar, who did not want to offend the Curia, was ready to become a candidate himself, but Pope Alexander IV, newly elected, did not appreciate the idea; Otakar submitted to his decision and lost a unique chance.

By 1272 and the death of another contender, Richard of Cornwall, the field was wide open again. In Prague, court poets and Henricus de Isernia were vying to praise the *emperor* Otakar poetically; Otakar himself, unfortunately, relied on the reports of his diplomatic emissaries, who were far too inclined to read the signs in his favor. He certainly put his Italians to work; Jacopo Robba, son of a Ghibelline exile at the court of Prague, reported wrongly that the pope was ready to accept a Bohemian candidate if the princes elected him; Federigo Spigri, another of Otakar's diplomatic messengers, was to sound out Charles of Anjou, ever close to the Curia; and the indefatigable Henricus de Isernia, possibly on the pretext of his brother's demise, ventured as far as Bologna but had reason to fear the Anjou soldiers there and went back to the Hungarian front to report to Otakar what he had seen and heard. Otakar failed to deal with the German prince-electors, most of whom did not favor him because he was too powerful. For some time, they discussed a Bavarian candidacy and, finally, in 1273 unanimously voted for shrewd Rudolf of Hapsburg, who had patched together his lands in the Swiss and Alsatian regions along the upper Rhine. Otakar, fighting in Hungary, was informed, and with good reasons protested the unacceptable election procedures; the unanimous vote had been achieved by disregarding Bishop Berthold of Bamberg, who represented the Bohemian vote and whose ballot had been divided between two other princes. Otakar's adviser, Bruno, in December 1273 submitted a memorandum to the Curia outlining Otakar's great merits in defending Christendom in the north and the east, but this did not find much sympathy; impatient Pope Gregory X, who wanted to end the imperial interregnum, accepted the election of Rudolf in September 1274, but Otakar continued to insist on the illegitimacy of the results. Nonetheless, Rudolf, crowned Roman king without delay, demanded that Otakar return all lands acquired by his armies and administrators. By 1275 they were set on a course of inevitable collision, and it was prolonged only a little by a war in 1276 and tactical compromises the following year.

In terms of physical and military power, Rudolf's forces were no match for those of the king of Bohemia, but he skillfully negotiated with the Hungarians, fomented anti-Bohemian opposition in the Austrian lands, and was well informed about the Czech *fronde* against Otakar; Rudolf was also able to rely on the families of Styrian nobles whose relatives had been held or killed in the dungeons of Prague. In early 1276, Otakar, on his part, who had now for three years refused to recognize Rudolf's royal rank, arranged a festive meeting of his Austrian allies in Prague, including delegates of the Viennese patriciate loyal to him (Vienna's *Lumpenproletariat* was incited against him by mendicant friars). Later that year, his armies began to march, first as if seeking an engagement on the western frontiers of Bohemia but then going on to the Danube and Vienna, where they came to a diplomatic halt. Vienna was held by forces loyal to Otakar, and Rudolf, on the plain outside the gates, was waiting for Hungarian help. The short war ended when many noble Czech clans revolted against Otakar at home. He was forced to negotiate and to accept the harsh condition of returning to the empire all the lands he had acquired after 1250 and receiving, in turn, inherited Bohemia and Moravia as fief from the emperor (to make his point, the legend asserts, Rudolf accepted Otakar's formal obeisance in a shabby leather doublet). Yet sporadic fighting continued in the provinces before Bohemian garrisons were completely withdrawn and prisoners exchanged; Otakar, unwilling to accept his utter humiliation, used the time to sign additional peace protocols, to retaliate against the Czech nobles at home (Boreš of Riesenburk was put to death, and Záviš escaped to Rudolf's camp), and to prepare for the ultimate battle.

On St. Rufus Day, August 26, 1278, Otakar and Rudolf confronted each other on the plains of Dürnkrut and Jedenspeigen, on the Moravian-Austrian border. Later schoolbooks suggested that it was a confrontation between Czechs and the father of the Austrian monarchy, but it was in fact a fierce, short clash between armies of many nations. Poles, Silesians, Brandenburgians, Thuringians, Saxons from Meissen, and Bavarians were fighting with Otakar's Czechs and Moravians against a strong Hungarian army, mostly Cumans (with their famous horses and deadly arrows), supporting Rudolf's Austrians. Otakar's men shouted "Praha!" and the others "Rome and Christ!" including the Cumans, who were not yet Christians. In the opening engagement, the Czechs and Moravians fighting against Cuman light cavalry were unable to hold their ground; in the second engagement King Otakar himself rode with his heavily armed knights against the Austrians, who began to retreat (this encounter was entirely a matter of Germans versus Austrians). Rudolf, more patient, gave orders that Otakar's forces be attacked by a special group of armored knights whom he had hidden in ambush against all the rules of chivalric warfare (he had considerable difficulties finding a willing commander for that particular group). These horsemen attacked the Bohemian flank, split its ranks in two, and when Otakar's Poles and Silesians could not intervene, the Bohemian forces were overwhelmed by confusion. Many tried to save their lives by escaping to the vineyards or by retreating across the Morava River, but their king went on fighting "almost alone," until, trying to escape, he was brutally killed by personal enemies—possibly by one Offo, sole heir to Siegfried of Mehrenburg, who had been murdered in a Prague prison, or, as later pro-Austrian chroniclers insisted, by the Moravian noble Milota of Dědic. Roving camp followers, Cumans or others, robbed the dead king of his armor and clothes and mutilated his corpse, which was later brought to a monastery and ultimately to Prague, to be interred in St. Vitus Cathedral in 1296. When his tomb was opened in 1976 by a team of scientists, they found traces of the blow that had killed him still visible on his skull.

Otakar II has been strangely absent from the historical imagination of his own people, and his life has not challenged important Czech playwrights and poets, many of whom prefer the condottiere and traitor Záviš of Falkenštejn: Václav Vlček's professorial *Otakar* (1865) is not exactly an impressive piece. Once again, the Viennese Franz Grillparzer, that untiring student of Bohemian history, after studying the (mostly Austrian) sources wrote *König Ottokars Glück und Ende* (1825, *The Fortune and Fall of King Otakar*). In Grillparzer's view, Otakar is a kind of Czech Richard III, especially in his conflict with Rudolf (Richmond), or, in the reverse image, like Napoleon, who divorced Josephine in order to marry the Austrian princess Marie Louise. The enlightened antinationalist Grillparzer came to regret that he had ever written this play, which brought out "the patriotic swine," he said, and mobilized Metternich's police, who insisted that the play fomented unwelcome nationalist conflict. Grillparzer clearly preferred sober Rudolf, characterized as a modest *empereur bourgeois* liked especially by Viennese artisans (among whom we find a child named Kathi Fröhlich, with compliments to Grillparzer's lifelong fiancée), but the play itself sides with Otakar, proud, ambitious, condescending (he treats the lord mayor of Prague like a personal valet), though, in a last monologue and prayer, Otakar is fully aware of his transgressions against the people: "I threw them away by thousands at a time, / to satisfy a folly, please a whim / as one would scatter refuse from a door" (v.2846–48). The playwright ends the tragedy with a patriotic "Hapsburg forever!" yet after the Hapsburgs are gone, it is the defeated and saturnine Otakar who continues to trouble our imagination.

Only Dante, like Grillparzer in his magnificent fifth act, moved away from national feelings. In his *Purgatorio*, canto 7:91–102, he boldly sees Ottacchero and Rodolfo together, in the chorus of souls heavy with earthly burdens and trying to rise to spiritual incandescence. Here the defeated Otakar, who ruled the country "where the waters spring to be carried by the Molta [Moldau] to the Albia [Elbe]," in a moving and thoughtful gesture seems to comfort victorious Rudolf (. . . *che nella vista lui conforta*). Rodolfo does not even care to sing with the rest.

In the wake of the Battle of Dürnkrut, many chronicles tried to account for the fate of the great king; Austrians and Styrians usually take Rudolf's side (especially Otacher oûz der Geul's influential Styrian narrative in verse) and Bohemians the king's, but there are notable exceptions to the rule. Abbot Otto, a German and Bohemian patriot, as well as the Austrian Heinrich von Heimburg, have pro-Otakarian views, and even in the Latin *Colmar Chronicles,* not exactly favorable to Otakar, a moving German elegy on his death is inserted to praise his knightly virtues: "*ez weinet milt und êre / den küng ûz Bêheimlant*" ("munificence and honor weep over the king of Bohemia"). The traditional Czech viewpoint, which is strongly critical of Otakar, was expressed early in the so-called *Dalimil Chronicle* of c. 1315, which lauded young Otakar but strongly argued against him, enemy of Czech barons and friend of the Germans, for he was willing to give villages and towns to the Germans and to build protective palisades around these settlements. Otakar was like a beautiful flower, a "rose in the meadow" ("*jako róži prostřed lúky*"), but later alienated himself from his own people in his "irrational pride," and suppressed the gentry and nobles; even such an honest man as Záviš, Dalimil says, had to seek protection abroad.

Dalimil's view prevailed in many variations in the ideological arsenal of later Czech nationalism and contributed to the essential ambivalence about Otakar (German nationalists of the nineteenth century on their part suggested that the Czech king had fought against the German Reich). The truth is that Czechs have long lacked a clear consciousness of the continuities of their own state, because modern definitions of what it means to be Czech were formed when "the state" was a foreign monarchy and the heroes and heroines of the Czech imagination were, above all, simple people, rebels and heretics persecuted by the foreign state, not the crowned heads of an ancient dynasty. Czech historical consciousness is deeply populist, and it does not really care for kings, lost in the dust and din of battles past.

Even František Palacký (1798–1876), in his dignified and thoughtful analysis, written toward the end of his life, confirms rather than argues against the traditional ambivalence toward the most powerful Czech in Bohemian history. He calls Otakar "an outstanding and particular personality," speaks of his ideas and actions as shaping the Czech destiny, and valiantly defends him against the accusation of being an apostate to his nation (unfortunately, he quotes Henricus de Isernia's Slavic manifesto, which is dubious evidence). Clearly Otakar's invitation to German settlers is foremost in his mind, and he tries to distinguish, as his most enlightened compatriots did later, between two kinds of German, the aggressive and those more peacefully concerned with *Bildung* and economic progress; he says that Otakar was inviting people ready to earn an honest living. Yet Palacký also asserts that Otakar, eager to open new sources of hard cash, invited too many Germans and did not think about the future of his nation. He goes out of his way to describe Otakar's sense of fairness and justice but ultimately suggests in almost metaphysical terms that Otakar's death was a tragic punishment for his sins against his own nation.

From another point of view, freed of the burdens of nineteenth-century nationalism, one could argue that Otakar was the first Prague king who protected the working people and the merchants of whatever nation against rapacious barons of whatever society, and who created an urban conglomerate that gathered together communities of Czechs, Germans, Jews, and Italians—people who were to live, work, and create together, or at least next to each other, peacefully for centuries. It is a pity that Václav Havel, in his inaugural speech upon assuming the presidency of the Czech Republic in 1993, did not list Otakar among the great Czechs from St. Wenceslas to Charles IV and from Jan Hus to T. G. Masaryk and the philosopher Jan Patočka. In his own hometown, King Přemysl Otakar II, the only Shakespearean character of Czech history and the founder of Prague as a European city, has become nearly invisible.

3

THE CAROLINIAN MOMENT: CHARLES IV AND HIS AGE

Burghers, Markets, and Cobbled Streets

After the death of King Přemysl Otakar in 1278, and then again in 1306 after young Václav III, the last Přemyslid king, was for cryptic reasons murdered by an unknown killer, Prague went through terrible years of invasions and foreign occupations, anarchy and revolt, plunder, hunger, and pestilence. To bury the many corpses, big ditches were hastily dug near many parish churches, and near St. Peter's two thousand bodies were thrown into a single ditch; rumors told of a physician who was buried alive and survived, chewing on the flesh of the corpses, until he was saved by the astonished people. Hunger drove people to brutal murder; a needy widow, we are told, lured a well-dressed boy to her hovel by showing him a green apple, and killed him to sell his fine clothes at the market. In the village of Obora, near the town gates, a hungry mother and her son murdered a beggar woman for a few slivers of bread, but when the son dragged the corpse away, he was arrested and immediately hanged, while his mother escaped.

Yet there were glorious moments of peace, and by the turn of the fourteenth century, an emerging Old Town patriciate, really the first wave of Prague's rising bourgeoisie of German origin, began to define its social interests and to enter the larger field of Bohemian politics, demanding, with all due respect and occasionally with economic and political pressure, its share of power. Patriotic schoolbooks usually dwell on the horrors of the Brandenburg invasion of 1278–80 and the undisputed greed of Otto of Brandenburg, who, after having bravely supported his brother-in-law King Přemysl Otakar in the field, briefly held Otakar's son to negotiate a good ransom at the Bezděz fortress in northern Bohemia and later in Spandau, near Berlin. Much less is said, however, about the rapacious Czech barons who used that propitious moment to seize unprotected lands of the king and of the monasteries. In 1280, the Brandenburg garrison at Prague Castle was besieged by a combined force of Czech nobles and Prague burghers, and a year later a gathering of Czech nobles, eminent church dignitaries, and representatives of the royal towns agreed to restore order together and to create a council of regents until the boy king Václav II, Otakar's son, would return to Prague, which he did in 1283.

The Prague Old Town patriciate in its struggles relied on its increasing wealth, derived from far-flung commerce, interests in Bohemia's silver mines, and local real estate. By the late thirteenth century the legal institutions of the Old Town government were firmly in the hands of these patrician families, and they held on to power for nearly a hundred years. From their ranks were appointed the town judge, as the king's legal representative (who actually bought the job at a high price), and members of the town council; only in the most important matters did they consult with a group of privileged citizens, and it was up to the council what advice to seek and when. The king took his time in granting the town council the privilege of employing a scribe; the councillors first submitted their humble petition to have one in 1296, but it was not granted until much later. Among the first known town scribes was Master Peter, who had studied in Italy and lived, to judge from his meager income, on bread and air. In the fall of 1310, in spite of all upheavals, the keeping of an Old Town Book was initiated, and regulations, ordinances, commodity prices, and important town events were faithfully recorded forthwith. His Royal Grace was equally slow in permitting the council to conduct business in a town hall, and for a long time the councillors met in their homes. It was only under the rule of the Luxembourgs that they were allowed to buy a house (1338) on the Old Town Square to use as town hall (the institution has not moved from the spot since). In time, the community developed its own bureaucracy of tax collectors, supervisors of foreign merchants (two as early as 1304), guards of towers and gates, servants of the town judge, constables, as well as a torturer and a hangman. One begins to think of Kafka early on.

Prague's most prominent patrician families, surrounded by bevies of clients and dependent craftsmen, can be first identified during the last decades of the thirteenth century, where their names appear on the list of town judges and town councillors year after year for a long time. Burghers were those in the legal sense who owned houses in the Old Town (never mind the obligatory capital to be eligible for appointment on the town council). The oldest and more prominent of these were the Wölflins, or Wölfels, patrons of the parish church of St. Gallus; among the younger sons, Franz Wölflin was well known as financier to King John of Luxembourg, who never tired of selling a castle or an official job to a German patrician, much to the disgust of Czech nobles. If the Wölflins were the old Prague Capulets, the Olbrams (the name was derived from that of Wolfram, the patriarch's oldest son) were the Montagues, patrons of the parish of St. Nicholas. At times, the Wölflins, favoring Henry of Carinthia as king, and the Olbrams, preferring a Hapsburg candidate on the Bohemian throne, violently opposed each other in matters of grand politics, but more often they loyally served on the town council together. There were other important families too, including the Stucks, the Fridingers, the Rokyzans, the von Steins, and, somewhat later, the Tafelrungs, Geunahers, and Tausendmarks. Václav Vladivoj Tomek, a conservative Czech historian of the nineteenth century who kept close tabs on these clans, believes that only the families of Junoš and Kokot (von den Hähnen) may have been of Czech origin.

It was during the unstable rule of Henry of Carinthia, king of Bohemia and Poland (1307–10), that Prague's German patricians, in alliance with their rich colleagues of the Kutná Hora silver mines, made their first move to force the Czech nobles actually running Bohemia to share some power with them. Jakob Wölflin and Nikolaus Tausendmark, of Prague, together with Peregrin Pusch and his men of Kutná Hora, in 1309 ambushed a group of important Czech nobles and forced them to agree that the merchants would have a voice in the future of the country; the burghers' and merchants' sons were to be permitted to marry daughters of the nobility; brides and bridegrooms (average age, two or three) were selected immediately and brides delivered to their patrician future in-laws for an upright bourgeois education.

Once again, foreign troops intervened in a situation close to civil war, in which Prague's poorest people, who were Czech, sympathized with the Czech nobles rather than with the German patriciate, however progressive these latter may seem to us. It was agreed to send an embassy to King Henry to ask that his young son, John of Luxembourg, marry Eliška of the Přemyslids and become Bohemia's future king. The delegation comprised three representatives of the Czech nobility, three distinguished Cistercian abbots, and citizens from Prague and Kutná Hora. More important, the Prague burghers allied themselves with a pro-Luxembourg faction of Czech nobles to deliver the Old Town to

John, who was approaching with his mostly German army; and when church bells sounded the alarm on December 3, 1310, Prague's burghers, including the nonpatrician butchers, rose in arms and opened, or rather hacked to pieces, a strategically important gate to let in Prince John; King Henry and his brutal Meissen allies left Hradčany by the back door. John of Luxembourg, interested in cash rather early on, immediately demanded a payment of 720 measures of silver to cover the expenses of his coronation, including new jewels. He was, at least, amenable to business, confirmed the rights of Prague's burghers to hold property, and magnanimously transferred to them the excise duties imposed on foreign merchants (the money had to be used to pay for the expenses of the embassy inviting John to come to Prague). But by the summer of 1319, Prague's German patriciate, like the Czech nobles earlier, tired of empty Luxembourg promises and unpaid bills. The people rose in open revolt against the king, who promptly threatened to occupy the Old Town; an uneasy peace ensued.

Prague's artisans and craftsmen, many of them Czech, had reasons to band together to define and defend their particular interests even before the end of the thirteenth century, as craftsmen did elsewhere in Europe. It is believed that artisans formed their organizations for religious and economic reasons; the "brotherhoods" of men working at the same craft collectively participated in religious and festive processions (also providing an early kind of insurance group), but guilds also organized production, set prices, and protected their members against unfair and foreign competition. In developing social conflicts it was a fundamental question whether the authorities, town council or king, would allow artisans to group in mere folkloric brotherhoods or in guilds that were established on the basis of legal statutes. By 1318, the tailors of the Old Town were the first group in Prague allowed to constitute a guild, and they were followed by the goldsmiths (1324), harness makers (1328), butchers (1339), millers (1340), and others. Below these organized artisans were a rather motley, poor group, easily excited and often surprisingly loyal to the king, who eked out dubious livings—among them day laborers from the Czech countryside, impoverished craftsmen, tradespeople, apprentices, servants of many kinds, horse grooms, prostitutes, and beggars. Some historians have said that at least half of Prague's population belonged to this sector, which long lacked any consciousness of its potential strength.

The days were gone when Arab travelers had noticed the sale of slaves, weapons, and inexpensive leather goods in the shadow of the castle. Now, the merchants of the Old Town were dealing, on a European scale, with a wide variety of commodities and luxury goods that satisfied local demand as well as customers in Poland, Hungary, and farther east. Wheat and cattle were brought to Prague from nearby (chicken was duty-free), carp and pike arrived from southern Bohemia, and salted herring from the European north was shipped via the Elbe River. Local peasants offered onions, cabbages, and leeks; saffron was imported from stores in Regensburg, figs and almonds from Venice and the Orient. Bohemian wine was for sale, mostly from north of Prague, but connoisseurs also had their choice of Alsatian, Tyrolean, Frankish, and Italian imports. Beer consumption was, then and now, at a record high (good beer, as a Czech proverb demanded, had to be as "sharp" as horseradish, *pivo jako křen*), and every burgher jealously guarded his ancient right to brew his own kind; imports were strictly forbidden. Fine cloth from Flanders was considered most valuable, but there were also less expensive textiles from Poland, mostly gray, and other kinds woven at home. Linen came from Bavaria and northern Italy, and there is some evidence for an early taste in buckram and loden.

King and town council were unanimous in wanting Prague's townspeople to be peaceful and prosperous, at least in theory; in 1287, a renewed royal ordinance made it illegal to carry arms day or night (unless certain financial preconditions were fulfilled), and illegal to hide knives in shoes or stockings (if you were caught repeatedly, your hand was pierced and you were expelled from town). In the evening, and after the bell of the town judge had rung thrice, everybody was to carry a light in the dark streets; if you were discovered without one, you had to pay a fine or go to prison for a week (first offense). Kaprova Street, where Franz Kafka was born more than five hundred years later, was the first street to be paved, and in 1339 King John turned over the royal fees earned from the import of wine to pay for the paving of others as well. By 1335, the first public bath is mentioned in the Old Town, though history does not disclose what really went on there; five years later the town council awarded a public-works contract to one Heinrich Nithart to clean the streets for a year. It must have been an execrable job to do. A much later Prague anecdote records that an Italian artist by the name of Giovanni Spinelli was convicted of spilling blood in church (during mass, he attacked his girlfriend with a knife) but agreed that his original prison punishment be commuted to a sentence of cleaning Prague streets for three years with his own hands; the story does not reveal whether he regretted his choice.

Prince Václav or, Rather, Charles

The hopes of the Bohemians that young John of Luxembourg would come to love his country and his wife, Eliška, of proud Přemysl origins, were soon disappointed. After raising conflicts with nearly everybody, including the church hierarchy and the Old Town patricians, young King John, intelligent, adventurous, and impatient, roamed around Europe, returning to Prague only to squeeze the burghers for money or to arrange knightly jousts. (Once he fell off his horse, to the great glee of the *vulgares,* into the splattering dirt of Staroměstský Square.) His son Václav, the third child after two sisters, was born on May 14, 1316, and, as crown prince, almost immediately became a pawn in the conflicts between his father, Queen Eliška, an energetic and self-willed woman, and a changing coalition of the king's adversaries, which occasionally even united the Olbrams and the Wölflins. After a wobbly agreement was signed between the king and the opposition (ably led by the Czech noble Jindřich of Lípa), the barons persuaded the king that he should do without the advice of their enemy the queen; John, suspecting, possibly not without some justification, a revolt in support of the queen and his son, took by force the fortress of Loket (in German, Elbogen), where mother and child dwelled. He held his three-year-old son in a dungeon there, "a little light coming in from a hole in the ceiling," and sent his wife off to the town of Mělník. After a new reconciliation and a new revolt, she, disconsolate and tubercular, escaped to Bavaria in 1322; her son Václav never saw her again. Fearing that the opposition would gather around his son, in 1323 King John sent Prince Václav from the castle of Křivoklát, where he had kept him far from Prague, directly to the court of France to be educated there at a useful distance from Bohemia. When Václav returned to Bohemia after more than eleven years, matured by political and military experience in Italy and elsewhere, he solemnly prayed at the grave of his mother, buried at the Cistercian abbey of Zbraslav, just south of Prague, before he, on October 30, 1333, proceeded to the capital.

In France, Václav accepted the name of Charles from the French king, lived at the court, both at St.-Germain-en-Laye and in Paris, and, as a boy, was married to Blanche of Valois; three marriages, all equally diplomatic, were to follow. It is a matter of dispute whether he attended the University of Paris and how much he learned there; both the Austrian historian Heinrich Friedjung and his Czech colleague Josef Šusta seem rather skeptical about his systematic training. His early education had been supervised by Jean and Huetus de Viviers, and in his memoirs Charles writes himself that he learned to read reciting the Hours of the Virgin Mary, repeating these prayers daily. After 1325, his education was supervised by the distinguished diplomat and theologian Pierre de Rosières of the monastery of Fécamp, who was to become his adviser and friend, and later Pope Clement VI of Avignon. Charles notes in his memoirs, written of course many years after the event, that he was greatly moved by one of Pierre's sermons on Ash Wednesday, preached in the presence of the French king, admiring its "beauty of language and art of rhetoric"; he asked himself what it was that made this man of the church radiate such illuminating grace. It was a nice way for an emperor to pay a compliment to a pope.

After seven years in France, Charles was sent to Luxembourg, possibly because King John did not want him in Bohemia, and was involved for three years in his father's northern Italian battles and affairs, during which the prince, emerging from boyhood, began to think and act for himself. Brescia, Parma, Cremona, Pavia, Modena, Lucca, and many other northern Italian towns had been willing to accept King John's "protection" (it cost them a good deal of money), but others, such as mighty Florence and haughty Milan, did not. Representing his father on the spot and often condescending to the role of a royal condottiere, Charles had a good deal of trouble. Once, in Pavia, he was nearly poisoned by a Milanese agent (three nobles in his retinue died, and he escaped only because he did not eat the poisoned breakfast before going to communion), and at the castle of San Felice near Modena he had to fight the armies of the cities revolting against King John's *signoria*, his first, and tough, battle. The horse was killed under him, and just when he thought that all was lost, the Mantuan enemy gave up and left Charles victorious in the field; he ascribed this first great military victory to St. Catherine and later built many shrines to her.

Of the Italian towns given to his care, he liked Lucca most (a lifelong affection), established a princely chancellery there, obviously enjoyed the company of the local young maidens, or *donzelle* (repentance came later), and called a little fortified settlement nearby San Carlo. Ultimately he decided entirely on his own (his memoirs are rather terse about these matters) to disengage himself once and for all from his father's hapless Italian adventures and simply to return to Bohemia, as margrave of Moravia at least, and, somewhat against all expectations, to restore royal power, sadly abused. It was certainly not a return in triumph; he did not encounter in his homeland anyone he would know, "neither father, nor mother, nor sisters, nor any other acquaintances." Hradčany Castle lay in ruins, and he had to take lodgings in the Old Town house "U Štupartů," which belonged to his mother, and later in the household of the Prague burgrave. But he was serious in his intentions, which the Czech barons and his father did not yet entirely grasp, and soon invited his French wife, Blanche, to join him. After she arrived in Prague in June 1334, she showed good sense by sending home her French and Luxembourg retinue and by trying to learn the local languages (quite in contrast to King John's second wife, a Bourbon, who came to Prague and kept her elegant French retinue, making herself vastly unpopular with the locals, high and low).

King John was disturbed by the success of his son, who began patiently to define his position among the baronial factions, favored the important monasteries and royal towns as bases of his power, and repossessed, by ingenious financial transactions, royal property his father had liberally pawned. In a few years King John limited his son's mandate to Moravia again and sent him off, as he had done before, to fight and negotiate elsewhere. After six years the king (who was rapidly going blind) relented once again, the Bohemian nobles confirmed Charles as his future successor, and by 1342 father and son had signed a contract about transferring rule to the younger man, who was to pay 5,000 measures of silver each year to his own father. It may have been symbolic that at the famous Battle of Crécy in 1346, blind King John died with the flower of French chivalry in front of the English positions defended by efficient longbowmen (though he was not chained to two other knights to find his way, as the poet Froissart suggested), while his son, also fighting with the French, was only slightly wounded in a skirmish of the rear guard the next day. Unwavering in his French orientation and shrewd in his dealings with the Avignon papacy, by mid-century, without waging a major war, King Charles was to achieve what the Přemyslid kings had merely dreamed of: he was elected Roman king twice, in 1346 by five out of seven votes, and, after Ludwig of Bavaria conveniently killed himself by falling off his horse or having a stroke, unanimously three years later. He was crowned king of Bohemia in 1347, and not wanting to meddle in Italian affairs, he was also crowned king of Italy in Milan in 1355; two months later, together with his new wife, Anna von der Pfalz, he became emperor of the Holy Realm, in Rome, on April 5. Roman dreamers and Italian patriots urged him again and again to renew the glory of ancient Rome and the true capital of the Christian world, but he had set his mind on Bohemia, kingdom of his Přemyslid mother, and before he died in 1378, he had made Eliška's town, Prague, a wondrous heart of European power, religious feeling, creativity, and erudition. Or so it seemed.

King Charles, Father of His Motherland

Since 973, Prague's bishops had been subordinated to the archbishopric of Mainz, in Germany, and in the spring of 1343 Charles went to the pope in Avignon together with his father to negotiate a possible change, well aware that the kingdom of Bohemia was the last in Central Europe without its own archbishop; he also assumed that a more powerful church organization would strengthen his hand against pressure from the barons. The political circumstances were favorable; the incumbent archbishop of Mainz was a partisan of the excommunicated emperor Ludwig of Bavaria, who had refused to acknowledge the Avignon Curia. On April 30, 1344, the pope issued a bull in which he made the new Prague archbishop independent of Mainz and directly subservient to the Curia, and in some detail suggested the reasons for his decision, among them the geographical distances involved, the days of travel, the difference of languages, and the increasing number of Christians and churches in Bohemia. On the same day, Bishop Arnestus (Arnošt) of Pardubice was appointed archbishop of Prague, and when Charles and King John returned, he was ceremoniously invested with the symbols of his new office on November 21; King John and his son together laid the foundation stone of the new cathedral that was to celebrate the independence of Prague. About the same time, the Prague burgrave, possibly following Charles's wishes, incorporated the houses grouped near the castle around its own *rink*, or square, and the parish church of St. Benedict into the little township of Hradčany. Now its resident nobles, clergymen, craftsmen, and working people were directly dependent on the court.

After Bořivoj's chapel dedicated to the Virgin Mary, the Romanesque basilica, and Duke Václav's rotunda, the new cathedral was the fourth church on Hradčany Hill to attest, by the will of the ruler, to the strength of the Christian tradition in Bohemia. The chief architect of the cathedral was Matthias of Arras, in northern France, who when he arrived in Prague decided on a conservative, if not a little antiquated, structure of High Gothic perfection. It was a project on a grand scale: Matthias, and the men of his construction lodge, together, possibly, with the occasional assistance of his compatriot Jean Deschamps, worked for eight years and completed before Matthias died in 1352 the eastern part of the ambit, eight chapels, with the appropriate supports outside, many pillars of the main nave, and a wall rising to the triforium—all in a linear and somewhat abstract style that Charles may have admired when he lived in France.

In the mid-1350s, Charles appointed as his new architect Peter Parler, born in Cologne, where his father had been among the builders of the cathedral, and this was a first-rate choice. Of the 180 men whom Peter Parler employed in his Prague lodge of builders, twenty-five were Czechs and a few others came from Flanders, Poland, and Hungary; though Parler (the name suggests that he had been a speaker of a lodge, or chief apprentice) may have been a complicated character, involved in a few shady deals and dubious marriages, he was an innovative artist and craftsman of lively imagination, and his clan of sons, nephews, brothers, and grandsons continued to build in his "beautiful style," as it was called in Prague and all over Central Europe even long after he had died in 1399.

Peter Parler did not continue the academic and recurrent patterns of the older design but worked with flying ribs, pendant keystones, and innovative net vaults, derived, as some experts believe, from English cathedrals. He was not averse to returning to earlier elements of Cistercian-Burgundian Gothic style or even to an occasional Romanesque quotation, consonant with the king's historical interests. In his commitment to sparse linearity, Matthias had suppressed ornamentation, but Parler and his gifted collaborators created, on consoles and gargoyles, many grotesque figures and masks, among them Socrates, or the devil violently tearing Judas Iscariot's soul from his mouth, and worked with painters and sculptors (Parler was a master sculptor himself). Many historians agree that Charles probably had a word to say about the construction of the new chapel in honor of Duke Václav, protecting the remains of Bohemia's patron saint. It was to be a "church within the church," and its square shape, radically at odds with the assumptions of the surrounding space, and its fine encrustations of gold and precious stones, which related to earlier Venetian and Byzantine art, expressed, on their own mystical terms, the vision of a "New Jerusalem," as ecstatically described in Revelation 21: 16–19: "foursquare, its length as large as the breadth . . . the city was pure gold, like unto clear glass. And the foundations of the wall of the city were garnished with all manners of precious stones." Similar ideas in Charles's mind possibly determined the location of the tombs of past rulers and queens; the portrait busts of Charles, his four wives, his ecclesiastical friends, and the artisans on the lower triforium; and the images of Christ (exactly above the bust of Charles), Mary, and the patron saints on the highest level. Down in the earth, the past; somewhat higher, the presence of the king and his court; and up on high, the realm of eternity.

In building the castle of Karlštejn, southwest of Prague on a steep hill close to the Berounka River, the emperor had all the authority to insist on his personal preferences in architecture and the arts. It is not known who was in charge of construction, which took place in 1348–67, but it was evidently an architect well aware of French and Italian practices, and the structure and interior of the castle may have been closer to the emperor's curiously mixed, conservatively inclined tastes than any other of his many castles and fortresses; even the residence he built in Brandenburg in the last years of his life was but a pale reflection of the Bohemian exemplar. German and Czech historians have argued whether he wanted his own Montsalvach of the Holy Grail, or a sturdy fortress to protect the imperial and royal crown jewels that were symbolic of his power, or both. Strategically of little importance (though long besieged by the Hussites in a later epoch), austere and strangely impressive, the castle rises dramatically, especially when seen from the Berlin–Prague express train winding its way through the meager forests. Its clean walls and thick towers ascend in virtual terraces of meaning, from the terrestrial (the halls of the staff) to the space of political power (the king's reception rooms on the second level) and, ultimately, on the highest stratum of the highest tower, the chapel of the Holy Cross, again encrusted with gold and precious stones, a mystical Jerusalem of prayer and meditation. There were other chapels, among them Charles's small private oratory, later called St. Catherine's Chapel. Charles employed some of the most important jewelers and painters of his time, local and foreign, among them Tommaso da Modena and Master Theodorik (later much admired by the German romantic writer Friedrich Schlegel), an early expressionist and chief of the Prague guild of artists, to create frescoes and panels, showing the ancestors of the dynasty, beginning with Noah, and the heavens rich with angels, saints, and patrons. The Gothic art of the west and the iconic traditions of the east, possibly transmitted from Venice and Dalmatia, live here in magnificent unison; as in the St. Wenceslas Chapel in the cathedral, the idea of political power and the meditation of transcendence, whence all power comes, are one.

The Founding of the New Town

Young Charles did not reveal much of his plans for Prague as long as his father lived, but eight months after the Battle of Crécy and after he had been crowned Roman king and king of Bohemia, in that order and in record time, he began to issue in quick sequence the first documents announcing the great changes to come. He acted almost like a newly elected American president who, as soon as he arrives in the White House, wants to convince the electorate that he means business. Matthias of Arras had begun on the cathedral two years before King John's death, but then, between April 1347 and April 1348, Charles initiated the construction of Karlštejn Castle, founded a vast New Town, and established Prague University, not to speak of legislative projects and the reorganization of the clergy undertaken by his loyal archbishop. On April 3, 1347, he signed a document at Křivoklát Castle saying that "after mature consideration" and "bowing to the advice and the will of the burgomaster, the town council, and the entire community," he planned to build a New Town adjacent to the Old Town to increase "their honor, freedom, well-being, joy and protect them against all violent conflict." On March 8, 1348, in an exquisitely formulated royal letter he defined the fundamental intentions of the project and the procedures to be followed. Among the foremost worries that burdened his soul, he declared, was the great and essential question how to make certain that Bohemia, his hereditary kingdom, would flourish beautifully in every respect (*ex omni pulchritudine vireat*), constantly enjoy ample peace, increase its riches, and be secure against all attacks by enemies. People who moved into the space of the New Town, an additional ordinance asserted, would enjoy freedom from taxation for twelve years, provided that they finished their houses eighteen months after the building start, and used materials resistant to fire. Christians as well as Jews, given special protection by the king, were invited to come and to settle. The Christians came, mostly artisans from the Old Town, but the Jews, who may have heard the brutal stories of how Charles had handled Jewish property in pogrom-ridden Germany, preferred to stay together in the old Jewish Community close to the river, as before.

Charles had perhaps witnessed the rights and wrongs of urban planning when in Avignon, a small town that haphazardly altered itself to house the pope, cardinals, and the staff of the Curia (not everybody could afford rooms in Avignon and many people lived in the nearby village of Villeneuve-lez-Avignon or at Carpentras, as for instance Petrarch's mother), and his Prague project had purpose and amplitude, but the truth is that it was never completely finished during his lifetime. The new space, defined as lying outside the walls of the Old Town, comprised more than three times the space of the Old Town. Great care was taken to integrate all the hamlets and villages there, including Podskalí and Zderaz, as well as the *extra muros* parts of Poříč and the Újezd of St. Martin, including the "Jewish Garden," Prague's oldest cemetery, and a few Jewish houses nearby. Charles was careful to acquire the necessary real estate by legal measures from the Order of the Knights of the Cross with the Red Star and, in exchange for their compliance, granted important tax reductions to the order and awarded the Prague knights the patronage of the new parish churches to be built. The new town wall, with ramparts and moats, extended for three and a half kilometers from the Botič brook and the Vyšehrad, which formed an element of the new fortification system, in a wide curve north of the Vltava River. The entrance was protected and regulated through a heavily guarded tower and three gates, some of which were strongly fortified too. The entire fortification system was built within two years (1348–50), and Vilém Lorenc, a Czech historian of architecture, has calculated that two hundred masons, three hundred workingmen on the spot, and one hundred thirty in the quarries were needed to do the job, with one hundred carts going back and forth to deliver stone, sand, and water. When the walls were finished, many workingmen were suddenly unemployed, and the ingenious king hired them for further public-works projects, building another wall, this one called the Wall of Hunger, reaching down from Strahov via the Petřín Hill to the river, or happily employing them in the cultivation of Prague's vineyards, which he particularly favored.

New monasteries, parish churches, and markets specializing in particular commodities were to constitute the cores around which wide streets and new housing were planned; the first houses went up on the corner of Wenceslas Square and Jindřišská Street, where people today busily shop at the German Quelle department store. A new Carmelite monastery, with its church of St. Mary of the Snows (never finished in its original grand design) and a Benedictine monastery to house Dalmatian monks were started even before the king laid the foundation stone of the fortifications. To the north of the new space the parish church of St. Henry, and to the south that of St. Stephen, were to be located, and Charles took great pride in building the Karlov, a church dedicated to the memory of Charlemagne, to accentuate the continuity of imperial power. The many markets are still fundamental to Prague topography even after six hundred years: the horse market, now Wenceslas Square; the cattle market, now Charles Square, where they also sold fish, wheat, charcoal, and little articles made of wood; on Ječná Street, close to the fortified gate, where pigs were for sale; and, even closer to the river, at Podskalí, long the home of proud ferrymen and fishermen, where driftwood from the river was offered for kitchen and heating purposes, virtually a Podskalí monopoly.

In renovating or rebuilding the Vyšehrad to be part of the New Town, Charles demonstrated his piety as well as his ideology of power in showing his veneration for the Přemyslid past and expecting that his successors would follow his example: in his Order of Coronation Procedures he prescribed that any Bohemian king to be crowned had to make a pilgrimage to the Vyšehrad, where Přemysl's rustic bark shoes and his peasant pouch were preserved, and ostentatiously went on the pilgrimage himself. When Charles began his rule, the fortified Vyšehrad was mostly fallen in desuetude, the former royal palace uninhabitable, its chapel of St. John desolate. (In a gesture of unusual generosity King John donated its ruins to the dean of the chapter to be used as building material, in case they were needed.) Charles decided that the Vyšehrad should be brought to life again; he constructed a new protective wall with fifteen towers, built a new royal palace (later destroyed by the Hussites), and restored the cathedral of St. Peter and St. Paul, two naves and a side chapel. Not much of that old glory has survived.

The idea of uniting the Old and New Towns to constitute a strong community, well protected and important in international commerce, may have been on the king's mind for a long time, but not until 1367 did he give the order that the fortifications dividing the two towns be destroyed (only a few stretches were) and *one* town be established. It was a useful wish; even after unification, the two towns, different in social structure and distribution of languages, competed fiercely with each other, and after ten years, Charles, who never wanted to waste energy on the irritatingly impossible, ordered the old division to be restored.

It is hard to believe that undertaking to build a new stone bridge across the river, begun in the year of unification, was not part of his original vision of imperial Prague, but the project took a long time, and the bridge was not finished until the turn of the century, many years after his death. Continuities are marked; the old stone bridge (1158–72), named after Queen Judith, the Thuringian wife of King Vladislav II, was damaged beyond repair by ice in early February 1342, and for a while a provisional wooden arrangement had had to serve; the Knights of the Cross with the Red Star, in whose care the bridge was given, collected a fee at the bridge entrances to be used toward the new design. (The pillars of the old bridge can be still seen under the water and in the cellars of a few houses of the Minor Town.) Peter Parler with the occasional assistance of Jan Otlín, a master mason and town councillor of the Minor Town, resolved to build a massive construction much higher than the old bridge and somewhat south of it. The new bridge rested on sixteen pillars without any ornamentation, which was reserved for the bridge towers; there are historians who believe that, ultimately, its most ancient prototype was the bridge built by the Roman legions across the Moselle River at Trier, where, in Charles's time, his favorite great-uncle Balduin, the archbishop, resided; others assume that it was constructed in imitation of the bridge in Regensburg. Visitors to Prague are not always aware that the rich Baroque statuary was installed on the bridge centuries later, and that it was long called simply the Prague Bridge; it was renamed Charles Bridge only in 1870.

The modern demography of Prague in the second half of the fourteenth century rests on ingenious calculations, and a certain patriotism believing that bigger was better is not always absent. The Caroline metropolis consisted of either four or five administrative entities or towns, depending on the method of counting: the Old Town, topographically including the Jewish Town, administered by its own council of elders; the New Town, including the royal Vyšehrad; the Minor or Lesser Town, which did not have equal legal status with the Old and New Towns; and, probably after the mid-1340s, the small Hradčany township near the castle. Estimates vary between V. V. Tomek's total of 100,000 inhabitants and František Graus's recent and more modest 30,000—more than respectable if compared with Frankfurt, Nuremberg, or the somewhat smaller Zurich, though greatly overshadowed by Milan (62,000), Paris (80,000), and Venice the *Serenissima* (90,000 by 1338).

It would be too simple to say that in Caroline Prague the Germans were powerful and rich and the Czechs powerless and poor. It is more probable that more people among the Germans, approximately one-third of the population, were rich and powerful than among Czech speakers. In the Old Town, at any rate, the German patricians held on to power; in the New Town, peopled by a more mobile group and especially by many craftsmen, Czech began to predominate; in the Minor Town, German colonization was progressively balanced by a return of Czechs who were expelled by King Přemysl Otakar; and the small township of Hradčany had, for all practical reasons, a majority of Czech speakers, not to mention the villages and hamlets beyond the walls, constituting the heartland of Czech Bohemia. Inevitably, questions of language were particularly acute in the court and in legal proceedings, especially in the Old Town; though later chronicles and attentive observers, among them Jan Hus, insisted that King Charles himself had commanded the Old Town councillors to learn Czech so that Czechs could use their mother tongue in court and articulate their statements (*aby česky mluvili a žalovali*), a royal document to that effect and signed by the king has never been found, and at least one recent Czech historian has suggested that Jan Hus may have had in mind the temporary situation after the unification of the Old and New Towns, when more Czechs appeared among the members of the town council, previously restricted to German patricians. The first urban legal document in Czech dates from December 12, 1370.

Charles Establishes His University

The early plans for the New Town revealed that Charles wanted to establish a university; he spoke of his expectation that a new institution would attract so many students and teachers to the Old Town that a new area to accommodate these people was needed. It was not a new idea in Prague; among the Přemyslids, Václav II had thought about it before the turn of the century, but the Czech nobility, fearing a diminution of its power by clergy, lawyers, and written documents, had blocked his plans. Of the ten institutions of higher learning which the king and Emperor Charles privileged, Prague's was first and foremost in Central European importance, though Czech and German historians have recently reminded us that Charles was untiring in his efforts to further higher learning not only in Bohemia but also in southern France and northern Italy, where he privileged, among others, the universities of Cividale (1353) and, above all, his beloved Lucca (1369).

The Prague university was authorized on January 26, 1347, by a special bull issued by Charles's friend and teacher Pope Clement VI, who may have wanted to counteract the rebellious Franciscan theologians gathering in Munich around William of Ockham and gave permission to establish a community of students and scholars in Prague, allowing that a theological faculty be established too. Charles issued his own decrees, the first in Prague on April 7, 1348, establishing a *studium generale* offering material security to students and teachers (financed by a special tax on the clergy) and protecting educational travel from and to Prague. In another document of June 14, signed at Eisenach, in Thuringia, he, more as Roman king than as Bohemian ruler, explained that he was bound by his high office to care for all subjects in his realm yet, in founding a university in Prague, was prompted by his particular preference for his native Bohemia. Later fierce disputes about whether he founded the university for Germans or Czechs have not taken into account that Clement VI and Charles himself did not think in these nineteenth- or twentieth-century nationalist terms; the pope had asserted that the university, a clerical institution to be directed by the archbishop of Prague, was to serve the inhabitants of Bohemia and its neighboring countries, and the king was much concerned that his loyal Bohemians, *fideles nostri regnicole,* of whatever language, "who continue to thirst for scholarship, should not be forced to go begging around but should find the tables of plenty ready" in his realm. St. Václav, the patron saint of Bohemia, was to be the patron of the university, and its official seal showed the saint accepting the university charter from the king, humbly kneeling before him.

The university of Prague was to follow the grand examples of Paris and Bologna, both known to Charles, but the royal document of April 1348 revealed in its syntax and imagery that the king's French secretary had made excellent use of the decrees issued by Emperor Frederick II when establishing the universities of Naples and Salerno. The new professors were all loyal to church and Curia; in many cases, they were teachers in the local Dominican and Augustinian monasteries, renowned for scholarship and piety, and scholars of international experience and repute. Among the early appointees were the Augustinian Mikuláš of Louny and John of Dambach, a Dominican of proven loyalty to the pope and yet personally close to the mystics Meister Eckhart and Johannes Tauler; the theologian Jan Moravec, who had studied at Paris and Oxford; the Franciscan Vojtěch of Bluda, certainly of noble and Czech origin, who taught biblical studies; and, among the star appointments, Heinrich Totting of Oyta from Erfurt, who, unfortunately, left soon for Vienna. There were equally remarkable appointments in other fields—e.g., the expert on canon law Buonsignore de Buonsignori from Bologna, or in medicine the Italian Balthasar de Marcellinis. These scholars and scientists were an eminent group, but the initial appointments also show that King Charles, open to intelligence but essentially conservative, and Archbishop Arnestus carefully avoided theologically incorrect choices; they did not dare to consider the colorful bird or the occasional dissident in the cleric's garb. It is a pity that Charles never considered William of Ockham, whose polemic treatise had called him the pope's "errand boy," or, for the faculty of liberal arts, the Roman tribune and archaeologist Cola di Rienzo (instead of imprisoning him), or Petrarch, who would have loved to come as visiting professor with a radically reduced teaching load. Another first-rate candidate would have been the poet Guillaume de Machaut, who also happened to be the most important musician of the age and had served the king's father long and loyally.

In the beginning, lectures and lessons were offered in monasteries and private homes, the more important ceremonies being held at the archbishop's residence or the cathedral, and only in 1360 did Arnestus issue a set of regulations more firmly defining an administrative structure. As in other medieval universities, students and teachers were all organized into four "nations," not according to language but according to the regions of origin along the direction, as it were, of a compass: students and masters all belonged to the Bohemian, Saxon, Polish, or Bavarian "nation."

In 1366, the king established a college for twelve masters of the liberal arts to reside and work together in a house in the Old Town (originally belonging to a well-to-do Jewish merchant named Lazarus, from whom Charles had repeatedly borrowed money). The Carolinum, the oldest university building still functioning today, was originally the stately home of Johannes Rotlöw, master of the mint, and was given to the university by Charles's son in 1383; it was combined with other buildings close to the parish church of St. Gallus to form the university's historical core. In spite of internal tensions (the lawyers broke away in 1372 to create their own institution), the 1370s and 1380s were a lively and productive time for the two hundred docents of different ranks and two thousand students (in the Faculty of Arts). By 1384 the first conflict erupted openly; the Bavarian, Polish, and Saxon "nations" wanted to see their importance reflected in the number of college appointments, and some masters staged their first exodus to Heidelberg and Cologne a few years later, anticipating the momentous and revolutionary events that would transform the university and Prague in only a few decades. King Charles's universalist concept of higher learning was not to survive him for long.

The King's Kitchen Cabinet and the Italian Connection: Cola di Rienzo and Francesco Petrarch

Intending to consolidate royal power, Charles wanted to codify the laws of Bohemia formally and in writing, but an assembly of Czech nobles, unimpressed by imperial power, rejected his *Majestas Carolina* in 1355, and Charles, in one of his shrewdest if not most cynical moments, promptly declared that the sealed codex had been destroyed by fire and did not bind the nobility in any way. Czech barons preferred oral tradition, which, they thought, allowed them more elbow room to handle their affairs than did a written legal code, long researched by the king's office, and, at least in part, written or edited by the king himself.

The *Majestas Carolina*, a massive collection of Bohemian laws, was intended to establish a firm process of justice. It did away with trial by hot iron or cold water as being totally unworthy of a Christian kingdom; landowners were forbidden to blind their peasants and to cut off their noses or ears; and women who had been raped were encouraged to proceed to the place where the crime had happened, tear their veil, and publicly accuse the criminal before taking the accusations to the office of the king (the punishment for rape was death). It also interfered with the joys of playing dice, which, it said, was "apt to leave children impoverished and burdened by heavy shame," and demanded that all people live virtuously and chastely. Section 50 of the *Majestas*, if approved, would have been the first ecological law to protect Bohemia's famous green forests so they would remain "untouched and eternal"; royal power, far from wanting to waste "the beautiful fullness of the forests so much admired by foreigners," wished to protect timber carefully. It was to be cut only by special authorization, and only dry wood or fallen trees could be legally removed for use or sale.

Charles could rely on a number of Czech nobles loyal to or dependent on him, among them Jan of Michalovice, Jan of Veselí, Beneš of Vartemberk, and the brothers Šternberk, but there is little evidence, especially after a short-lived rebellion of the southern Bohemian clan of the Rožmberks (or Rosenbergs) against him, that he surrounded himself with representatives of the nobility as trusted advisers. From time to time he would ask important people for advice (as emperor he also had to consult German and Silesian nobles), but he felt most comfortable with dignitaries of the church. His kitchen cabinet consisted of Archbishop Arnestus (and later his successor, Očko of Vlašim) and the chancellor Johannes Noviforensis (von Neumarkt; in Czech, Jan ze Středy), bishop of Litomyšl and later of Olomouc. Arnestus and Johannes differed in origin and training, Arnestus coming from a family of the Czech gentry in the northeast of the country and Johannes from the provincial Silesian (or north Bohemian) professional class, yet they both served the king self-effacingly almost as long as they lived.

Arnestus was trained internationally; after attending the cathedral school in Prague, he was sent to Padua and Bologna to take up canon law and studied there for fourteen years before he was recalled to be dean of the cathedral and, soon, bishop and archbishop and the young king's counselor and friend. Among his contemporaries, Arnestus was most active, as diplomat, special ambassador, occasional commander of royal troops, and in formulating and executing his king's policy. As a young man, he recalled later in life, he was once disturbed by the vision of the Virgin Mary turning away from him, and he certainly worked hard to do penance. He was a first-rate manager, establishing exact lists of benefices and consecrated priests, and holding regular synods in order to keep in touch with the provinces, praising or harshly exhorting members of the hierarchy if necessary. Yet he was not a single-minded bureaucrat but a cultivated reader and writer, and patron of the arts. He was a protector of young clerics, whom he sent to study abroad with good stipends, and particularly committed to protect and favor the Augustinians involved in the *Devotio Moderna* of introspection, spiritual exploration, and religious feeling.

Somewhat younger than Arnestus, Johannes had been first a parish priest and then made his way up quickly as the king's scribe, notary, court chaplain, and bishop; by 1353 he was protonotary, the first among the notaries in the king's office, and only a year later became the king's chief of office and chancellor to supervise all the king's correspondence. Within a few years, he was traveling to foreign countries for the first time, accompanying Charles to Italy; if he lacked cosmopolitan polish, he amply made up for it by literary talent and eagerness to learn. As anybody else in his position would have done, he collected the best sample letters originating in his office, but he is better known for his important German translations of Latin texts, including "The Soliloquy of a Soul with God" (considered in his time to have been written by St. Augustine himself), a collection of letters about St. Hieronymus (equally spurious), and a remarkable collection of prayers which had an impact on contemporary German prose writing. He knew the German "Lay of the Nibelungs," which was not exactly required reading for the Prague clergy, and was famous for his collections of books, including, possibly, a copy of Dante's Latin works and, as a gift from Petrarch, an edition of Virgil's eclogues. German scholars once overrated Johannes's impact on German writing and believed that he was responsible for a particular brand of Carolinian early humanism, yet even after a more critical generation of younger philologists have shattered many of these illusions, Johannes remains a lively and vulnerable figure, eager to absorb whatever he could from his Italian friends and correspondents. The king's efficient chancellor may also have been a timid poet of the German tongue.

Charles liked to work with well-trained and efficient people of patience and experience and was not fond of enthusiasts or dreamers; to dream, in political matters, was utterly beyond his calculating mind, especially if the dreams touched on relations with the Avignon Curia, which were complicated and pushed him to a participation in Italian affairs that, after his early experiences, he wanted to avoid. His encounter in Prague with Cola di Rienzo—the famous figure made tribune of Rome by the will of its people, self-appointed herald of great changes in church, empire, and the world, an inspired lover of the idea of renascent Rome unifying noble Italy—was not so clean-cut as the chroniclers sometimes described, for they more easily sympathized with the king than with his strange visitor. Charles did not need di Rienzo to achieve any of his plans (though it was possible to use him as a pawn in negotiating with the pope), but his Italian visitor, and later prisoner, in conversations and letters uttered statements about the necessary transformation of the church which in a different idiom resounded in Prague's chapels and streets even before Charles had died; they rang in his son's ears and eventually made Prague, at the time of the Hussite movement, the first scene of a European reformation. It is altogether a different matter that Cola di Rienzo, a theatrical character of high enthusiasm and quick depressions, reinterpreted some of these statements when he found himself in danger of being tried by the Inquisition. For him, Rome was more valuable than a fine point of scholastic theology and ultimately and for all practical purposes he recanted and returned to Rome in the service of the pope whom he had so bitterly attacked.

Charles must have been astonished by this articulate visitor, admitted to his presence by the good offices of the royal pharmacist Angelo in the early summer of 1350, who presented himself after a long journey from the Italian south as the bearer of prophetic messages. He told King Charles about his short but glorious days as tribune of Rome, his escape (after a half-baked putsch by the nobles) to caves in the Apennines, where he dwelled among Franciscan hermits of radical views, and being sent out to the world again by Frater Angelus de Monte Vulcani to present to Charles precious prophecies and tell him that God himself had chosen Charles and "an angelic pope" (certainly not the one residing in Avignon) to undertake a "universal reformation" (*reformatio universalis*). The time of the return of the Holy Ghost was close (*quod tempus instat, in quo spiritus*

Sancti tempus ingreditur), and di Rienzo, his precursor, offered Charles his support for going to Italy to restore Rome to its ancient glory.

Charles perhaps enjoyed di Rienzo's presence; eager to hear more about Italian developments, he invited him for two more conversations, the gist of which di Rienzo summarized in a letter in late July. Yet Charles, a loyal son of the church, was also disturbed by the dire prophecies, so strongly opposed to the present Curia, and by the idea of the imminent coming of the Holy Spirit. Charles asked di Rienzo to repeat his statements to a gathering of dignitaries, including the archbishop; the visitor was promptly taken into custody by the church authorities, held first in Prague and later in the archbishop's residence of Roudnice. He was treated with respect; unlike his servants, he was given wine, since he did not develop a taste for Prague beer; and he untiringly continued to write letters and memoranda to the king, the archbishop, the chancellor, and his Roman friends, to whom he had promised to return in mid-September at the latest.

In his messages to Italy, di Rienzo sounded of good hope, but toward the end of summer he began to feel less certain about the future; the Bohemian authorities did not seem willing to let him go. He was not aware that his detention had been speedily reported to the pope, and the Holy Father had written three return letters to Prague expressing his satisfaction that the "son of Belial" and potential heretic was in loyal hands. Di Rienzo's first two letters to the king—*serenissime Cesar Auguste*—combine a good deal of undiminished pride with an increasing feeling of frustration, fleeting perhaps but noticeable. There are many reasons, he argues, why the king should order his release: the "fear of shame," which he, a true Christian (*fidelis Christianus*), fears more than death; the harm that his protracted stay in Prague would cause the noble people in Rome and Italy, who want to continue fighting tyrants, thieves, and traitors; and, last but not least, his health, which suffers in the constricted space and needs to be nourished by free air (more than a poetic image, for he suffered from epilepsy). He wanted to act as a kind of political St. Francis and, to add weight to his entreaties, revealed to Charles the great secret of his birth: he was, he said, the natural son of Emperor Henry VII and a hospitable Roman woman (*ipsa natura . . . me natum esse fecit . . . gloriose memoriae quondam imperatori Heinrici*). Charles, his close relative by blood, should consider his noble record, described in considerable detail, including the battles against soldiers of the Roman nobility, and the ceremonial embassies from all over the world that had honored him; even the sultan of Cairo, di Rienzo added, had lived in fear of him.

The king's written answer shifted the debate to religious grounds, using an ample number of biblical quotations (in the style of his teacher Pierre of Fécamp) and revealing a good deal of royal irony. Charles had much to say about Christian charity, but when all was said and done he did not give an inch to di Rienzo's wishes. Charles would have nothing to do with prophecies (*fantastica*, he called them), current among spiritualist monks who believed they were extremely knowledgeable in intellectual matters though they had built their edifices on the pillars of pride and vanity; and he especially turned, with some irritation, to predictions concerning the pope and the return of the Holy Ghost to institute a new age. These were completely erroneous and opposed to the truth of the church, he wrote, and it was incorrect to believe that the Holy Ghost had absented himself after he had shown his presence to the apostles and other loyal Christians at Pentecost. As for the great secret of di Rienzo's imperial origins, the king was ready to leave the matter to God (*deo relinquimus*), for, he added, "we only know that we are all created by God, being Adam's sons, and made of the mire of the earth (*limo terrae*), to which we all return ultimately." (He possibly knew that di Rienzo was the son of a tavern keeper and a washerwoman.) Charles distinctly refused to discuss the political implications; if di Rienzo's long absence from Rome set back his cause, that was to be deplored, but God's law was higher than the affairs of Italy and Rome, and it was less dangerous to risk difficulties here on earth than eternal punishment.

Charles, as it turned out, was not satisfied with this one written answer, and in late 1351 he prevailed on his prisoner to write a letter to Italy in his name and communicating his ideas. Di Rienzo's admirer Petrarch, the great and famous poet, had also written to Charles asking him to intervene in Italian affairs, and Charles, being ironic or spiteful or both, now asked di Rienzo (possibly using Johannes, who was always enchanted by good letter writing, as intermediary) to formulate a brief message denying Petrarch's request. The notion was perhaps that the most efficient way to impress his ideas on his Roman prisoner was to ask him to express them himself, in his best style and worthy of Petrarch, and perhaps poor di Rienzo hoped to derive advantage from an involuntary stint as the king's secretary.

He wanted, above all, a fair hearing; and even before he was shifted in September from his Prague prison to the archbishop's residence at Roudnice, where he was held in a prison "of three rooms," he wrote two apologies for his life and ideas, one directed to the archbishop and another one to the king. These longish texts are marvels of discursive energy, precise allusions to a wide array of theological and classical readings, and a courageous resolution to continue his fight. Still unfazed, he told the archbishop that the pope was a private person who could sin and accused the Avignon Curia of dishonesty with the Christian flocks given to its care. Playing on the image of sheep and rapacious wolves, he made the Curia responsible for the tyranny of the Italian nobles, the anarchy in Naples and Rome, and the corruption of justice; it was high time to take the bloody sword from the hands of the pope and return it to those of the king and emperor, where it belonged.

In his treatise addressed to Charles, di Rienzo was no less afraid to take on theological matters, and he demonstrated that he was a fine attorney for his beliefs. Charles had appealed to Christian charity, and di Rienzo (presumably his uncle) promptly addressed him with the informal *tu*, saying that he was following the laws of love, which were desirous of singularity; after all, he wrote, "we even address God who rules us all in the same way . . . and so did the Roman orators when addressing Roman caesars." Invalidating a possible accusation of heresy as if in passing, he also declared that he firmly believed that the Holy Ghost was always active and present, coming and breathing every day; and he taught Charles an admirable lesson in charity, telling him about the humility, poverty, and self-denial of the Franciscan spirituals whom the king had accused of pride and vanity. There was more of the Christian heritage alive in the monks' Apennine caves than in all the glories of Avignon.

Unfortunately, di Rienzo was a volatile man easily fired by enthusiasm and also quickly disconcerted, and as his imprisonment dragged on into its second year and the archbishop's responses to his letters continued curt and impatient, he proposed that he was willing to go to Avignon, which he knew well, and stand trial there, no matter what the outcome. For some time, Charles had actually played a cat-and-mouse game with his irritated friend Pope Clement VI (I'll give you the heretic, and you set the date of my imperial coronation, finally), but then the Curia increased the pressures and Charles finally agreed to deliver his prisoner to the pope—though not without hedging and a few tactical delays, because Charles knew that Clement VI was mortally ill and might die before too much harm was done to di Rienzo. The papal decree excommunicating Cola di Rienzo was read in the churches, and the pope sent the bishop of Spoleto to Prague to read it at St. Vitus Cathedral and take the prisoner away to Avignon. There he was held for another year, recanted (also in a letter to the Prague archbishop, which makes depressing reading), and then, in one of the melodramatic reversals so characteristic of his life, was freed by Pope Innocent VI after the death of his predecessor, and sent to Rome to make it safe for the Avignon hierarchy. Di Rienzo executed a number of noble enemies without hearings or trials, but he was unable to restore his old popularity among the Romans, and when a street demonstration against a newly imposed tax got out of hand, he was brutally murdered by the mob (October 8, 1354), his nearly severed head dangling from his lacerated body. He was hung by his feet (as was Mussolini, another reckless populist, in Milan in 1945), and the Roman Jews were ordered to burn his remains on a stake of thistles and thorns (always a connoisseur of spectacles and emblems, he would have been pleased by the symbolic detail). It is not known whether Charles gave a thought to Cola di Rienzo when he traveled through Italy to be crowned emperor in Rome the following spring.

The king's encounter with Francesco Petrarch, the most renowned man of letters of his age, was a matter of prestige, high decorum, diplomacy, and a little literature. Petrarch, too, dreamed of a *renovatio Romae*, a rejuvenation of Rome, but in literary and historical terms, and he did not conflate his classical utopia with religious ideas on the brink of heresy, as Cola di Rienzo did. Charles, more than willing to entertain a defender of the imperial idea so long as this did not offend the pope, was eager to attract the poet to Prague. If older interpretations of Petrarch's sonnet 238 are legitimate, the Bohemian regent and the Italian poet may have met, or at least observed each other from afar, as early as 1346, in Avignon, for the sonnet describes a festive dance, bringing together many beautiful girls—of course, Petrarch singles out Laura, *"real natura, angelico intelleto,"* of regal nature, angelic intellect—and when Charles enters, "his sound discernment quickly saw/among so many faces the most perfect" (*fra tanti et sì bei volti il più perfetto*): Laura's, as it could not be otherwise. The prince politely approaches Laura "and with kindly expression he kissed her eyes and brow." All the ladies are happy because they consider, or so the poem suggests, that the kisses are compliments to the entire assembly; only the poet, watching from afar, feels a twinge of jealousy and envy (*"me empiè d'invidia l'atto dolce et strano"*). It is a lovely court scene, but the poet never mentioned it later to King Charles and there is little evidence that Charles ever read Italian sonnets, though he could have done so easily.

Petrarch attached his hopes for the rejuvenation of the ancient empire of the Romans variously to the Anjou family and to Cola di Rienzo, whose excesses he viewed with increasing misgivings, and, after a brief visit to desolate Rome, he addressed a stately letter to King Charles urging him to action; in the initial paragraph, he tells him he will spare him flattery and, rather, present lamentations. He entreats Charles not to waste time in superfluous negotiations and to use the time that flies; "what was achieved in the course of many centuries was often destroyed in a single day." Charles should not be distracted by the political problems of Germany or by his love for his sweet Bohemia but hurry to act in Italy, "which has never welcomed with greater joy the coming of a foreign ruler"; after all, he had been educated in Italy and would bring balm to heal its wounds.

In Prague, Charles must have been overwhelmed, or amused, by Petrarch's power of words; he did not immediately dictate an answer, as was his habit, but thought it best to employ his prisoner Cola di Rienzo, ideally qualified to couch a negative answer in an impressive idiom perhaps equal to Petrarch's; it is one of the many ironies of this particular exchange that the king's letter was not delivered to Petrarch until two years later (the poet had changed addresses too often) and he never suspected who had actually written the artful communication. Charles, relying on di Rienzo's *fioritura*, praises Petrarch's letter, adorned by laurel, for its manly courage and compassion but does not hesitate to describe Italian conditions in strong language—"justice sold into the brothel of miserliness" (*ad avaricie lupanar prostituta iustitia*, a master touch by di Rienzo)—and, sighing audibly and referring to a Horatian image, to say that it was more difficult to raise a sunken ship than to restore its sails and ropes. Charles had no quarrel about the glory that was Rome, yet the past was past and the present was different. It was necessary to consider past and present in order to restore honor by honest means; everything had to be tried first before the iron was applied (*omnia nam prius temptanda quam ferrum*), as surgeons and emperors knew. Never was Charles closer to defining the first principle of his diplomacy.

When Petrarch learned that Charles was to cross the Alps to go to Rome to be crowned emperor, he felt immensely encouraged in his hopes. In a new letter, he welcomed Charles descending the Alpine passes, not only for himself but in the name of Italy and Rome; Italy, he wrote, always considered Charles an Italian, wherever he was born, and it was not important whence he came but what he wanted to do. Charles and his retinue settled for a while in Mantua before proceeding south, and by special messenger he invited Petrarch to join him privately as "a friend of peace," not necessarily as a diplomat in the service of the archbishop of Milan, to avoid complications. Petrarch, braving one of the coldest winters ever—"the roads were not so much earth as steel and diamonds"—arrived at

Mantua on December 15, 1354, and stayed there for more than two weeks. We know a good deal about his conversations with the king because he reported about them to his friends; while Charles could not be "more cordial and humane," he clearly skirted the question of his political intentions in Italy and elsewhere, and was not averse to "descending to an everyday level" or kidding (*longis iocosisque sermonibus protracta altercatio*). He asked Petrarch to tell the story of his life, and Charles also wanted to know about work in progress, in particular the book *De viris illustribus* (*On Famous Men*), perhaps in the hope of being included in it. Petrarch, on his part, avoiding a precise answer to the implied question, told him he would receive such a book if he were to join illustrious men not so much "by meaningless diadems" but rather by deeds and by "nobility of spirit." Petrarch also gave Charles a few ancient coins with the image of Caesar Augustus, challenging him symbolically; but when Charles invited the poet to go with him to Rome, politely suggesting that he wanted to see the Eternal City through his eyes, Petrarch declined. There was a later occasion to accompany Charles from Milan, where he had been crowned king of Italy, farther south, but Petrarch stopped at Piacenza and did not ride further.

Charles was crowned in Rome on Easter Day 1355 and left the Eternal City immediately, as he had promised the pope he would. His hasty departure shocked many Italian patriots as an undignified and even dishonorable escape from imperial responsibilities. His Italian joys were not enhanced when, in Pisa, an inimical faction of nobles put the torch to the house where he and the empress rested, and the imperial couple, lightly clad, had to run for their lives before royal soldiers intervened. Petrarch was terribly disappointed (and also knew that Charles had crowned his friend Zanobi da Strada *poeta laureatus*); writing to the emperor in June 1355, when Charles was still on his way to Prague, he did not mince words. Never in the past had any ruler voluntarily discarded such a great hope, but Charles, unfortunately, had only "his desire for Bohemia" in his mind. His august grandfather and his royal father, "hovering over the summits of the Alps," would be shocked. Charles simply "lacked will [*voluntas deest*], the source of all action."

In 1356, Petrarch was sent by Milan's rulers, the Viscontis, who were eager to receive Charles's support against a group of their enemies, on a diplomatic mission to Prague. (It's nice to see Petrarch involved with the powerful ancestors of the film director Luchino Visconti.) Petrarch went via Basel, where he had hoped to meet the emperor, and then through the gloomy and dangerous German forests, and was welcomed at Hradčany as a peerless guest of honor; had he wanted, he could have stayed in Prague for the rest of his life. He was probably not very successful in his mission (the Viscontis had always been a thorn in the emperor's side, to say the least), but everybody, including the empress, the archbishop, and especially his fellow poet and fellow bibliophile Johannes, vied for the honor to make his stay in Prague pleasurable. Charles gave him a golden beaker and appointed him *comes palatinus* (count palatine), a rank which gave him the right to appoint his own notaries and a few other legal privileges; he happily received the appropriate document but refused at first to accept the heavy golden seal, adorned with a panorama of Rome, because he thought it too valuable. He accepted it only later, at the renewed entreaties of the chancellor. As always, Petrarch must have enjoyed his social success among the elite; after returning to Milan, he wrote a polite letter to Arnestus, thanking him for all the encouragement he had received in Prague and assuring him that he remembered the civilized pleasures of the king's metropolis with great affection. Referring to the archbishop's self-deprecatory remark that he must have felt in Prague "among barbarians," Petrarch said that the emperor and a few learned men around him were truly worth remembering, "as if they had been born in Attic Athens" (*si Athenis Atthicis nati essent*). Charles continued to invite the poet to Prague, but he did not accept for a long time, and when he finally did, he was not entirely disconsolate that military complications in northern Italy prevented him from traveling. He met Charles, possibly for the last time, in Udine and in Padua in 1368.

It is not surprising that, among the intellectual elite of the Prague court, the imperial chancellor Johannes was Petrarch's most ardent admirer, enamored as he was by manuscripts, translation work, and the resonance of languages. He confirmed in his first letter to Petrarch that he had heard about him from the king's learned pharmacist Angelo, who had praised the poet's epic invention, his energy of structuring fiction, and his artful style. Johannes longed for a communication from him, perhaps to begin a lasting friendship, but his first letter to Petrarch, written possibly in the early 1350s, was rather strained, amassing learned images and coming close to being a parody of polite Latin rather than an instance of the new Ciceronian elegance (I suspect that Johannes was actually imitating Cola di Rienzo's wilder flourishes). Petrarch must have noticed the somewhat provincial effort, but his response was friendly, even playful, and a true example of spare elegance. He was touched by his admirer from Prague. "I noticed," he wrote, "that my name, however unimportant, already made its way over the summits of the Alps, covered by clouds, and wanders from mouth to mouth, of the most learned people under the Germanic sky. Fame may be something empty and like the wind, and yet it has a certain sweetness which attracts even great minds."

Johannes may have met Petrarch in Mantua, but he certainly had his chance in Prague in the summer of 1356, and again in Udine and Padua when Charles went on a second voyage to Rome. Letters were frequent for seven years; Petrarch had sent him a copy of his *Bucolicum Carmen* (*Bucolic Poem*) and had promised he would deliver an interpretation personally when he came to Prague again. Disconsolate Johannes urged him "to send his interpretation as quickly as possible," confessing that he suffered great pains "reading sentences so resounding and such apt metaphors of delicate things" yet not understanding the intentions of the poet's art. Petrarch certainly had been aware of the gap of learning between northern Italy and Prague, and had touched on it with delicacy, paying a superb compliment to the chancellor. "Born away from the Helicon," he wrote to Johannes, "and educated in a country which dedicates itself to other [theological?] studies entirely, a country in which classical studies are not only not sought after but generally scorned, you have broken through the dense fog of errors which surround you and you have lifted yourself on the wings of the mind and the helpful pinions of study to the lofty tower of truth. . . . We (let me speak in the name of all excellent people of Italy and Greece, past, present, and future) owe your name constant remembrance and the highest praise of unchanging glory, the more so the less we had hoped, in such times and in such a country, to discover a talent, granted by the muses, of such a kind." It was surely an homage to all the learned people who were trying to close the gap between the new humanism of Italy and the late medieval court of Prague.

Charles Builds His Myth

The essential ideological concept, or useful myth, which Charles used to strengthen his power and the dignity of "the Bohemian crown" (which then comprised Bohemia, Moravia, Silesia, Upper and Lower Lusatia, Brandenburg, and paternal Luxembourg) was a confluence of the Carolingian tradition, originating in Charlemagne, and that of the Czech Přemyslids, protected by St. Václav. The prince had been named Charles in France, but he would have certainly preferred to remain Václav, especially after returning to Bohemia. He was constantly concerned, as ruler, writer, and lord of architects, to keep alive the heritage of his Přemyslid mother and the patron saints of the land; after forty years of more or less Marxist scholarship about Charles, at least in Bohemia, psychoanalysts would be amply rewarded by another look at his mother fixation.

Charles himself wrote (c. 1358), in stately though certainly not Petrarchan Latin, a legend about Duke Václav and his grandmother Ludmila, and acknowledged that he was reading the past for his own purpose. Using his knowledge of previous Václav legends, from the tenth century to Dean Cosmas and his own time, he returns to the well-known stories and episodes but sets them firmly in a context that legitimizes the author, who also happened to be king of Bohemia. Once again, Charles tells how pious Ludmila was killed by two men in the employ of Václav's mother, Drahomíra. He described Václav's Christian education and his unique piety, his exhausting deeds of charity offering bread to widows and orphans or buying off the children of slaves, and he writes about the matchless loyalty of his servant Podiven, who on a cold day could warm his feet in Václav's miraculous footsteps (this is a story retained in the English carol about "Good King Wenceslas"). He also told about Václav's last hours, strongly resembling Christ's passion: The duke accepts an invitation from his treacherous brother to an evening meal, prays the night through, and is ambushed in the early morning by Boleslav and his men; when he is only wounded, he offers his body voluntarily to the fatal strike of the sword. The royal author makes his ideological argument at the earliest possible occasion, saying that Ludmila and her husband, Bořivoj, were baptized at the Christian court of Prince Svatopluk of Great Moravia by Bishop Methodius, who came to Moravia and Velehrad from Byzantium. In a single paragraph, not exactly historical in all the details, Charles manages to ignore Přemysl the plowman (a pagan) and the hex Libussa but directly links the Přemyslids with the advent of Christianity from the Slavic and Byzantine east and extends Prague history far into Great Moravia and the Slavic rites.

Charles himself must have felt the irony of writing a Latin legend in praise of the Old Slavonic origins of Bohemian Christianity and the Slavic rites; in his historicism *engagé*, he extended an invitation to Benedictine monks of Slavic origin to settle in Prague and, in opening the view to the southeast, he widened the liturgical and philological erudition of the clergy and renewed the ancient Slavic rites from the time of Bořivoj and Ludmila; even St. Václav, it was thought, was initially educated by a priest of the Slavic mission. Delicate negotiations with the Curia were necessary, but difficulties were avoided by assuming, in Avignon and in Prague, that the learned St. Hieronymus had translated the Bible into Old

Church Slavonic (he came from Dalmatia and was believed to be a Slav): the pope's decree and the king's order unanimously stated that a new monastery and a new church would be dedicated to St. Hieronymus; Charles, in his document, advanced the current idea that "the Slavic language of the kingdom of Bohemia" had emerged from Old Slavonic and that it was only appropriate to return St. Hieronymus "to his nation and country." A contemporary chronicle called the new buildings marvels of architecture; the new church, on a terrace above the river and dedicated to the Virgin Mary, was particularly austere, but the cloister was adorned by more than eighty frescoes, scenes from the Old and New Testaments, painted by the king's most favorite masters who also had worked at his castle at Karlštejn. Most of the Benedictine monks came from Tkon, on the island of Pašman, near Zadar, on the Adriatic, or from Senj, a town on the coast which young Charles had known. These studious Croatians founded a scriptorium to write and copy manuscripts in Latin and in the Glagolica (Old Church Slavonic in its Croatian version), established what one would call today an institute of Slavonic studies (Charles paid for an additional scribe), and celebrated mass according to the Slavic rites. The brothers of the Monastery of the Slavs ("Na Slovanech") were later in sympathy with the Hussites who celebrated their own services there while destroying other monasteries; in the seventeenth century the buildings were redone in the Baroque style and taken over by Spanish and Bavarian Benedictines. The end came swiftly; the Nazis dissolved the monastery in 1941, and on February 14, 1944, church and monastery were nearly destroyed by an American air raid. Reconstruction began immediately after the war but mostly for secular purposes.

Charles believed in the power of the word, and had he ruled in later centuries, he would have made ample use of a few court journalists to justify his rule. He prompted a provost of the Prague Cathedral, who had begun to write a chronicle for the bishop, to work for him; and before he died, he employed at least three more chroniclers, learned amateurs as well as professionals, to narrate the story of his reign and its antecedents. Charles's own writings, whether authentic or merely ascribed to him, show no enthusiasm for the playful refinements of fiction but, rather, a sturdy sense for political necessities and, perhaps, a certain frustration with his chroniclers, who, as hard as they tried, were not up to his lofty aims. Whatever he wrote himself was of ceremonial, legal, and pedagogical relevance, as, for instance, the rules for the coronation of the king and the blessing of the Bohemian queen, compiled from French, German, and Bohemian sources (1347), or the *Majestas Carolina* (1355), to which he certainly wrote the preface himself. Others were policy statements, even if appearing in the guise of the legend of St. Václav; his autobiography, the only one ever written by a medieval ruler (at least Chapters 1–20), was formally addressed to his sons. His pedagogical bent was even more visible in his later years. Both his *Moralitates* (*Moral Sayings*), assembled from snippets of French sources, the Bible, and St. Augustine, and his "Mirror of Princes," which is actually two letters, occasionally using Petrarch, were lessons about pious living and just ruling dedicated to his sons, who later behaved as if they had never read or pondered his well-intended if diffuse instructions. Charles was a writing king and emperor, and though a little schoolmasterish and without much imagination, he was better qualified than any other ruler in contemporary Europe to discuss matters of the mind.

The image of Charles as constant do-gooder, friendly and ceremonious, was carefully burnished by his chroniclers, but it does not coincide with the story of his life, especially the early years. He may have written his memoirs not only to educate his sons but also to tell his chroniclers that he could do a far better job than they. In his youth, he fought in many countries, was lightly wounded at least two times, and succeeded in a few hair-raising cinematic escapes. In Pavia, his breakfast was poisoned; in Dalmatian waters, when his ship was to be seized by pirates (or by Venetian allies who mistakenly thought he was an enemy), he had to escape via the ship's bull's-eyes into a little boat where he hid under fishing nets before reaching port; in Pisa, the irate opposition tried to burn down the house where he and his wife rested; in Poland, he was almost taken prisoner by a treacherous duke but guessed the intention and commandeered assistance at the right spot and hour. Charles was easily offended in his dignity: once, overhearing members of a Florentine delegation exchanging bantering remarks, which he understood perfectly well, he demanded and received an instant apology; and though he was magnanimous, particularly when it served him in the long run, he was also resolute and vindictive: he had Henry of Carinthia's bastard son put on the rack and interrogated him while undergoing torture about other members of an anti-Luxembourg opposition; and he certainly did not hesitate to lay waste to castles and fortresses of rebellious barons, Tyrolean or Czech. He wanted to protect the peace of the land; I do not believe he hanged the Czech robber baron Jan Pancéř by his own hand, as a contemporary source says, but I do not doubt he gave the order for it coolly and without hesitation.

It is a modern attitude to separate the public and private life of a medieval emperor; as we try to do so, it is useful to remember that Charles was educated as a boy at the fashionable court of France and spent his formative years as soldier and prince in the liveliest towns of northern Italy. Bohemian writers assume that he was appropriately chaste and saintly, yet in his memoirs he confesses, in somewhat convoluted terms, that he fell victim to the desires of the flesh; he tries to shift responsibility for this to Satan, his father, and his father's evil advisers, in that order. "The devil," he writes in Chapter 7 of his memoirs, looking back on pleasant days at Lucca, "instigated evil and perverted people who daily surrounded our father, to lure us from the right path into the snare of misery and lust [*libido* is his word]; and seduced by perverted people, we were perverted by the perverts." But he was warned by heaven; on the way to Parma, in Terenzo, near Pontremoli, he had a terrible, unforgettable dream. In his dream, he was watching an army of knights in battle formation; an angel seized him by the hair and dragged him up into the air to behold what was to happen. Another angel descended from heaven with a fiery sword, struck one of the noble knights through the heart and cut off his penis, and the man died in agony.

At any rate, when Charles returned from France and Italy to Prague, he was something of a dandy sporting the most recent chic. He wore a short jacket that revealed much leg, and this promptly offended the virtuous people among the Prague patriciate. In February 1348, the pope, himself well known for his affair with charming Madame de Turenne and his worldly ways, admonished him in writing to wear longer and wider vestments, as was fitting the dignity of a ruler. More than a hundred years later, Aeneas Silvius Piccolomini (Pope Pius II) remarked in his *History of Bohemia* that young Charles had his problems with proper attire.

Charles was always loyal to his four wives, yet each of these marriages, following upon each other in rather hasty sequence, was planned, first by his father and then by Charles himself, to fulfill an important political purpose: to strengthen alliances or territorial interest. The four noblewomen, one from France and three from German-speaking regions, were all the objects of deals, dutiful mothers, and figures of representation. His marriage to Blanche of Valois, the French child bride who bore him a daughter (she, too, was married off to a king), was intended to seal the Luxembourg-France alliance of interest; his marriage to Anna von der Pfalz (of the Palatinate), who gave him a son who died in childhood, was a result of his effort to broaden his base of support among the prince-electors voting for or against the Roman king—a contemporary *chronique scandaleuse*, of course Italian, notes that Anna was not too bright and, feeling neglected (I believe that), prepared a love potion which nearly killed Charles (sober historians speak of a grave affliction in his nervous system in 1350). He married his third wife, Anna of Schweidnitz, mother of a daughter and of the future King Václav IV, to round out his Silesian territories; and finally, Elisabeth of Pomerania, to break up an anti-Luxembourg coalition. She was a girl of sixteen, tall and feisty when she married him, and upon his suggestion would good-naturedly make a show of her strength for visiting dignitaries, bending horseshoes with her bare hands and tearing up coats of mail. When he died, she walked behind his bier, and she survived him for more than thirty years.

Many historians have noted that Charles was a passionate collector of relics; it is difficult to separate in this craving for these objects an archaic kind of religiosity, strangely contrasting with the predominant Augustinian piety of his friends, from a ruler's public interest in surrounding himself with signs of power. A splinter of the Cross and of the lance that wounded Christ had long been among the royal and imperial treasures, but Charles, especially after he became Holy Roman Emperor, developed an ingenious way of pressing, or rather blackmailing, monasteries and friendly allies to contribute to his collection; he had his relics often enshrined in precious vessels of high aesthetic perfection made by the best goldsmiths of Prague. Among the objects of veneration, he acquired part of the whip used in the passion of Christ, two thorns from his crown (donated by the French dauphin), part of the Christ child's swaddling clothes, the bones of Abraham, Isaac, and Jacob (compliments of the emperor of Byzantium), Aaron's staff, the tablecloth used at the Last Supper (from the riches of the Hungarian king), a joint of St. Nicholas's finger, a few drops of the milk from the bosom of the Virgin Mary, one of Mary Magdalene's breasts, and a wooden board from St. Václav's bier. The first catalogue of this collection was compiled only in the eighteenth century; it showed that Charles, otherwise totally pragmatic and a master of financial calculations, in his own way anticipated the later obsessions of Emperor Rudolf II of Prague, who was famous for gathering strange and ghastly items in his seventeenth-century Baroque *Wunderkammer*.

Bohemian chroniclers closely noted the pomp and circumstance of grand events but did not want to write about their personal impressions except in the appropriate clichés; the only snapshot of Charles, as it were, is found in the chronicle of one Matteo Villani, who possibly had a chance to observe Charles on his trip to Rome. What he says does not conflict with difficult evidence of "portrait" paintings or the bust on the Prague triforium, as far as these works of art aim at individuality at all. Charles's eyes were large and dark, his nose delicate, his hair full (he developed a bald spot later), and though he was of more than average height, he seemed short because, if not a hunchback, he craned his head forward (one of his neck vertebrae had been wounded or dislocated by an arrow on the battlefield). He avoided eye contact, it is said, was usually restless and tired, and when receiving someone in audience, he looked into the distance and kept busy by carving wood with a little knife, responding to the visitor quickly and affably but without much warmth. In his later years, he probably did not like people at all.

New Writing in Carolinian Prague

In Prague, the Bohemian metropolis of the Holy Roman Empire, literary tastes and preferences changed during the years of Charles's reign, and the predominant Latin and German of Otakar's time had to compete with a rich Czech literature of many genres, and with sacred scholarship in Hebrew which flourished in the Jewish Town. Charles, who in many of his political and commercial intentions, especially his interest in opening a trade route from Venice via Prague to the northern cities of the Hanseatic League, anticipated many needs of the future, was as a writer a man of the past. Perhaps he was more comfortable with the idioms of architecture and painting, from Peter Parler to Master Theodorik; in his own writings, even in his autobiography, his Latin was definitely medieval compared with that of Petrarch or his own chancellor Johannes, and his choices, or rather nonchoices, of writers to support at his court merely confirm his conservative taste. He invited the Croatian monks to carry on their study of Old Church Slavonic from a combination of antiquarian and ideological interests; in spite of the efforts of Czech philologists to show that the father of the "fatherland" supported native writing in Czech, the evidence is a little thin. His choice of a German poet to be close to his court in the 1350s was less than inspired, and the German poem written by the Saxon Heinrich von Mügeln in praise of his imperial lord has more erudition than life. Mügeln's "The Virgin's Wreath" ("Der Meide Kranz"), dedicated to Charles in the mid-1350s, is far less attractive than the French poem "Le Jugement dou roy de Behaigne" ("The Judgment of the King of Bohemia") written in the early 1340s by King John's loyal secretary Guillaume de Machaut. These poems make both exhilarating and depressing reading because they so amply confirm the traditional clichés about French artistic finesse and German seriousness, devoid of charm.

Both poems are expanded arguments, the French submitted to John of Luxembourg, the German to Charles; the king, after listening to his assembled councillors, was supposed to resolve the problem wisely. In Machaut's poem, a noble lady and a melancholy knight by chance meet in a lovely garden, and the question arises who suffers more—the knight whose ladylove has turned away from him to favor somebody else or the bereaved lady whose friend has died. The poet overhears their conversation and suggests they proceed to the nearby castle where the king of Bohemia happens to hold court. After the king has listened to an elaborate presentation of pro and con in the company of his advisers, all virtues incarnate, he decides that it is the knight who suffers more because the lady, in her bereavement, may be consoled by God. After the argument is decided, he invites the parties to stay, wash their hands, and sit down to a festive dinner. All is *courtoisie* in pastel colors, made lively by a few original strokes (the lady's little dog bites into the knight's coat) and much lyrical finery.

In Heinrich von Mügeln's poem the problem is the pedagogical curriculum and the value of scholarly disciplines (a question certainly of interest to Charles, who had just founded a university), but the procedure is strictly didactic and allegorical: after the liberal arts, all incarnating a central idea, have presented their arguments to the emperor, surrounded by his councillors, once again virtues incarnate, he decides with the support of the German poet that the wreath of excellence goes to theology—and, in another part of the poem, theology immediately demonstrates her acumen by affirming the predominance of virtue over all things natural. One can understand why Charles did not want to continue employing Machaut, who had loyally served his father for more than twenty years (and even paid Charles a few compliments in his last epic poem, "The Conquest of Alexandria"), and yet his support for Heinrich von Mügeln does not show much appreciation of the literary arts, considering the French alternative. Machaut was much admired by Chaucer and Froissart, but Heinrich von Mügeln has disappeared into the dictionaries of medieval writing, perhaps deservedly so.

It is difficult to say why the court did not show any interest in a contemporary Czech writer who wrote the life of St. Catherine. He was Prague's most gifted poet of the mid-1300s, and it is more than probable that he wrote his legend about St. Catherine to attract Charles's attention; the emperor had always believed that his first military victory in the Italian fields was miraculously won by St. Catherine. The writer may have been a priest, knowing a good deal about his predecessors' writing in Latin; and he was fully conversant with the European conventions of courtly love poetry, especially the many stories about Tristan and Isolde. Written for the Czech educated elite, his poem in rhymed verse makes Catherine, the daughter of a good pagan king, a true human being. She is rich, bright, and beautiful, resolutely declines to marry any prince or king not worthy of her, but is instructed and humbled by a wise hermit who tells her about Christ, the glorious king. In a dream vision she lovingly espouses him in a heavenly castle much adorned with gold and precious stones (strictly according to Revelation 21, which also informed the architecture of St. Václav's Chapel at Prague Cathedral and the Chapel of the Holy Cross in the highest tower of Karlštejn). Christ, the bridegroom, and Catherine, the bride, woo each other in songs of lyrical power previously unknown in Czech tradition. After she has convinced fifty of the most learned pagan scholars of the truth of Christianity (she has also read a good deal of St. Thomas Aquinas), the evil emperor Maxentius confronts her with the alternative either to become his son's wife and to honor the pagan gods or to suffer a terrible death. The poet devotes great care to describing the instruments of torture; a grinding mechanism of four giant wheels studded with nails is fortunately destroyed by a divine thunderstorm, but the whips are no less terrible, furnished as they are with little hooks that rip into her flesh. Religious joys are contaminated with sadistic perturbations: the emperor's wife, who had been charmed by Catherine, was hanged on iron hooks piercing her breasts; and after Catherine is whipped, her body mysteriously shows six symbolic colors, the white of her skin, the blue of her lacerations, the red of her blood, the green of shame, the black of the torn flesh, and the gold of her hair spread over her tortured body. Even Karásek of Lvovice, the most daring writer of *fin de siècle* Czech decadence and an expert in tortured ecstasies, at least on the printed page, never wrote such a scene.

It was the new university, rather than the court, which substantially transformed Carolinian literature by bringing together in Prague an international community of scholars, old and young, and educated a new generation of teachers, authors, and native readers. Magister Claretus compiled a number of Latin-Czech glossaries, or rather dictionaries, according to fields of study and interest—theology, botany, zoology, astronomy. They alternate Latin and Czech terms in the rhythmical structure of rhymed hexameters functioning as efficient mnemonic devices (today they resemble samples of concrete poetry). At the end of each section, Claretus usually suggests a source or a collaborator who helped with the materials; in the concluding section 46 of the glossary, listing church holidays, he remarks that he received help from "Carolus King and Emperor," just as he concluded the section on ecclesiastical terms with a reference to Archbishop Arnestus; it would be nice to believe that the verse about the philologically inclined emperor was more than a fine compliment.

Older German scholarship long believed that a new and early humanism emerged from the literary predilections of the Carolinian court, but it is perhaps more appropriate to ask whether another new humanism could not be heard in the writings of the urban clergy, of the lowest ranks, and the university students, well traveled and knowledgeable, and much given to parody, ironic self-deprecation, obscenity, and satire, radically undermining tradition. Even in religious poems, the perspective becomes more urban—God is seen, in pious allegories, as a merchant of pots and a furrier—and students were surely the authors and singers of macaronic verses alternating lines of Czech and Latin, their most explosive effects achieved by surprising rhymes in the two languages, of poems ridiculing brute peasants, and of the self-ironic "Lay of Merry Misery," in which hungry, poorly dressed students greet the cold winter and dream of rich, hot dishes, and lots of cabbage, which will never be served to them.

Prague life of mid-century even invaded the Easter play *The Three Marys*, which had been performed in Latin for a long time at the Abbey of St. George; in the nearly autonomous scene about the "Merchant of Ointments" (*Mastičkář*), it subverts religious tradition, and with a great deal of scatological immediacy. The scene may imitate similar texts of Austrian or French Easter plays, but we are present at the Prague market, hear irreverent Czech spoken by students, customers, and merchants, with a few Latin and German lines thrown in for comic effect. The merchant anticipates Švejk, though he sells strange concoctions rather than dogs with falsified pedigrees, yet most of his work is done by his clever and loquacious Rubín, certainly a student with a part-time job, and a kid named Postrpalk; the merchant's wife has a difficult time making herself heard among so many men. Restless Rubín works as the merchant's barker but constantly runs away to join the crowds; he sets up the stand and praises the all-powerful ointments, one made of the fat of gnats and another one by a monk fornicating with a nun in an outhouse (it gives marvelous erections). The merchant expects good business when the three Marys appear, but they resolutely refuse to buy mere cosmetics and ask, in Latin and in Czech, for oils to anoint Christ in his grave. To demonstrate the efficiency of the ointments, Rubín suddenly appears with a Prague Jew named Abraham carrying his dead son Isaac in his arms. When the merchant pours some of his oils on the corpse, Isaac is suddenly alive and well, and he congratulates the merchant on knowing where to apply the mixture (others, it seems, had aimed at his head rather than his derrière). This comic scene of Isaac's resurrection shows little sympathy for Jews, but it parodies the idea of Christ's resurrection; the merchant's wife, enraged by the low price quoted by her husband to the pious ladies, simply calls them floozies who want a cheap deal. We are far from the Augustinian piety of the elite and the efforts of the court to emulate Petrarch's finesse.

Among the Czech satires of the later fourteenth century, "The Groom and the Student" ("Podkoní a žák") shrewdly views social experience from an ironic point of view. It is, again, a late medieval disputation, or rather a parody of one, and it has moved from the castle or formal garden to a Prague tavern, full of lively conversation and the smell of beer (in our own age, Bohumil Hrabal will still be sitting there to write his gossipy novels). A lazy guest hears a horse groom and a student boasting about their stations in life while actually revealing their everyday misery, the student dressed in shabby gray, with a green cape, a shoulder bag for his books and bread, and a few writing tablets behind his belt, and the groom, not so young anymore, in a courtly but decrepit jacket and elegant stockings full of holes. The groom believes that life at court is the best, and whoever tastes of it will never want anything else—yet he has also to admit that he has been a horse groom for seven years and now hopes to become an archer, mostly because he expects a handsome new outfit to go with the promotion. The student argues that life at court is fine for barons and the rich but not for the poor, and he extols the freedom of university life, though he confesses that he often has to make do with water for a drink—of course, it is good for the brain. Increasingly challenged and irate, the groom condescendingly asserts that students support their freedom by house-to-house begging, but the student, the more articulate of the two, responds with a rich story of how he is usually welcomed on his journeys by big-breasted peasant women eager to fulfill all his wishes, or at least to find a fresh egg for the hungry scholar in the straw of the henhouse, and then plays a trump card by proclaiming to the groom that students become priests, prelates, and bishops who eat hotcakes, so well prepared in Prague. Words do not suffice to resolve the argument, and the two comrades fight it out with their fists, while the fellow who has been quietly drinking at their table goes home for a good night's sleep. In five hundred lines or less, this text shows us glimpses of the plebeian underbelly of royal Prague, and historians are right when they relate these satires to the social and political restlessness articulated, within a generation, in the radical demands of the Hussite revolution.

Cracks in the Facade

The emperor's love for Prague and Bohemia did not deflect him from pursuing his intention to build power bases beyond but contiguous to his native lands; while, in the 1340s and early 1350s, he labored valiantly under political burdens imposed on him by his adventuresome father, he was shrewd enough to cut his inevitable losses, including the Tyrol and Carinthia, leaving them in the long run to Hapsburg interests, and to continue King John's territorial initiatives as long as they were manageable and successful, as, for instance, in Silesia and Lusatia. He was not really interested in Luxembourg, the land of his father, and unwilling to intervene in the treacherous Italian conflicts, though he followed them with a keen eye. Always willing to attune his mind to changing conditions, in the early 1370s Charles shifted his attention to the German north; in the Treaty of Finsterwalde (1373), he bought Brandenburg for the price of half a million gold florins, two hundred thousand to be paid in cash immediately, from Otto of Wittelsbach, who, in turn, agreed to declare his disinterest in the lands of the Bohemian crown. After this, Charles spent a good deal of time in the Brandenburg town of Tangermünde, where he built a little North German residence, employed, to educate his son Sigismund, the learned Italian tutor de Beccari (who promptly wrote a treatise, in Latin, echoing Cola di Rienzo's provocative views), and adorned a new court chapel with encrustations of gold and precious stones, as he had done in Prague and at Karlštejn but nowhere else. Prague may have been closest to him, but he was devoted to other places, for private and political reasons, among them Lucca, from his early years; rich Nuremberg, for economic reasons; and Tangermünde, a retreat for his old age.

In the 1360s, the sweet times of Prague's economic boom had turned sour, and the emperor's chroniclers had a difficult time ignoring its recurrent religious and social conflicts, the first signals of bloody upheavals to come. The patriotic chronicler Peter of Zittau had been disturbed, even in the mid-1330s, by fighting in the Prague streets, caused by differing views about who was to receive payments and fees for religious rites. The Dominicans, Franciscans, and a branch of the Augustinians preached poverty and obedience, yet they challenged the parish priests by preaching at their regular hours and demanding and securing payments for funerals, which often resulted substantial bequests to their monasteries. The Curia had long favored the mendicant monks, exempting them from the jurisdiction of local bishops, but later it changed its mind; in 1334, a gathering of Prague parish priests excommunicated the mendicants by extinguishing candles and ringing the church bells. The friars and their rabid followers in the meantime invaded the churches, screaming accusations against the parish priests, whom they called "drunkards involved in all kinds of crimes, . . . killers of the soul and deceivers of the people." The chronicler, himself a distinguished Cistercian, sadly remarks that he had to see all this with his own eyes: partisans of one side and the other, parish priests often being defended by women, raging against each other, people using fists, knives, and clubs against each other, priests and friars being roughed up, knifed and bloodied, and dragged through the streets of Prague. In the end, the Curia sided with the parishes and against the mendicants, who had to transmit part of their fiscal gains to the parishes.

Earlier in the century, the Prague church hierarchy had had a rather ambivalent attitude toward the Inquisition, not because it wished to side with the heretics, but rather because it felt that this new institution interfered with Bohemia's own administrative habits. It is possible that the emperor's and archbishop's official insistence that heresy in Bohemia must be eradicated mercilessly was both a sincere expression of their orthodoxy and an effort not to allow the flying courts of the papal Inquisition (surprisingly, often manned by Bohemians) to meddle too heavily in the affairs of the Bohemian church. Fourteen heretics were burned at the stake in Prague in 1315, mostly peasants and craftsmen from Lower Austria who had been brought to Prague to be sentenced; as soon as Jan of Dražice, bishop of Prague, was himself called to Rome to answer an accusation of being too lenient about heresy, the Curia established a permanent court of Inquisition housed in the Old Town. It was mostly concerned with the infiltration of heretic ideas across the Austrian frontiers that might affect German settlers in southern Bohemia (many were held in Prague because the southern Bohemian prisons were overcrowded). Citizens of Prague were more directly concerned with the exemption from the rule of secular law of all priests, whether worthy or not, and the affair of the priest Martin taught the town a serious lesson. Martin, a priest at the cathedral, was a professional thief and when he was caught, the town handed him over to the archbishop, who did not take legal action; when, in an economically depressed year (1361), Martin organized a gang of thieves and holdup men, the town councillors caught him again, put him into a sack, and had him drowned in the Vltava River. The emperor, doing business in Nuremberg at the time, was irate and declared that he would not set foot in Prague again until the culprits were punished; the town judge and councillors immediately lost their jobs, and the archbishop sentenced them to deliver two eternal lights to the cathedral and seven thousand measures of wheat to his office, whence he distributed it to the poor. Judge and councillors were expelled from Prague forthwith, and when they were allowed to return later they died early deaths, or so it is said.

The church was the richest institution in Prague, owned more land, not to speak of Prague property, than the Bohemian nobles, and was the most attractive employer for the poor, ambitious, young, and educated; even Jan Hus, martyr of the Hussite revolution, said that "as a little scholar" (*žáček*) he had wanted to become a priest because he hoped for a good roof over his head, a cassock, and the respect of the people. The trouble was that there were too many young clerics and too few benefices; the situation was complicated by the tradition of awarding more than one benefice, or paid position, to a well-connected person who then appointed an easily cowed substitute (there were so many applicants) to fulfill the duties at the altar, or elsewhere. Conditions were particularly bad toward the end of the century; in 1395 there were 980 new clerics but only 204 benefices; in 1399, 1224 against 110, and in 1404, 1,386 young people for 220 positions. The clerical proletariat was on the increase, and those who enjoyed a benefice and their hangers-on were not particularly prompted to be stern examples of ascetic living. The archbishop had to tell the clergy over and over again what its way of life should be, and he often appointed clerical *correctores* to investigate and to punish undisciplined priests. From his irate letters to the bishops, it is evident that many among the Bohemian and Prague clergy were too merry for their own good; spent their time in the taverns drinking heavily, carrying arms, throwing dice, making obscene and "clownish" speeches; dishonored virgins; and committed all kinds of indecencies that asked for immediate arrest and punishment by the ecclesiastical authorities.

The renowned preachers of the 1360s and 1370s, who called for a new purity of Christian living and condemned the role of money in religious experience, were greatly admired as long as they turned to the townspeople, but they inevitably ran into trouble as soon as they touched on the sensitive question of buying and selling benefices and indulgences. Konrad Waldhauser and Milič of Kroměříž, the most famous of these, held on to the truth of the church, yet they were both accused of heresy and were forced to defend themselves before the archbishop or to travel to Rome. Konrad was called Waldhauser because he came to Prague, at the emperor's invitation, from the Augustinian monastery of Waldhaus, in Upper Austria; he preached in German at the Church of St. Gallus and, with ever increasing success, at the Týn Church (he had to speak on the town square just outside, because the sizable church was too small for his audiences, which included the Empress Elizabeth and, it is said, a few Jews from the neighborhood). Patrician ladies took off their high and costly veils and gave away their expensive dresses to indicate their new humility. Mendicants and nuns, whom Waldhauser accused of making money too easily (especially the Dominican nuns of St. Anne, who sold places in their institution to the pious daughters of rich parents), by 1363 united against him and compiled an eighteen-point accusation that was transmitted to the archbishop and a papal delegate, dwelling in Prague. Waldhauser was honest, sober, far from a mystical visionary, and he loved a good fight, particularly with Dominicans, but he never suffered because he had friends in high places, including Pope Urban V, King Charles, and the archbishop (who usually told him that the mendicants were outside his jurisdiction), as well as among the eager students.

Waldhauser's friend and disciple, the Moravian Milič of Kroměříž, was a practical mystic (rare in Prague), precariously hanging on to the accepted truth of the church and yet constantly accused of heresy by his enemies in the mendicant orders. He quickly advanced to notary in the emperor's office and later to a high position at the cathedral. He was among Waldhauser's most impressionable listeners, but suddenly, in 1363, he gave up his cathedral benefice and decided, against the friendly protests of the patient archbishop, to become a simple country priest and preacher. He trained first for six months in the Bohemian provinces and returned to Prague to preach to audiences at the Malá Strana and in the Old Town, initially with limited success, for many laughed at his broad Moravian dialect, but he soon convinced even the most skeptical among his listeners by his fierce earnestness and personal commitment. He was a driven man, given to self-torture, as were so many mystics of his time. He wore a hair shirt under his habit, refused (after a journey to Rome, where Dominicans briefly imprisoned him) to drink wine or to eat meat and fish, preferring instead a steady diet of peas and beans, declined to bathe (when his habit needed cleaning, his friends had to tear it off his body), slept on a wooden board, and often heard the voice of the Holy Spirit telling him what to do and what to say. In Prague, he was difficult to avoid. Speaking for two or three hours in sequence once or twice a day, he was eager to reach all Prague audiences; he preached in Czech at St. Aegid's, in Latin to students and the learned at St. Nicholas, and, after he had brushed up his grammar, in German to the patriciate, at the Týn Church.

Milič preached against pride and luxury, against the dubious fiscal interests of the mendicant friars, and he felt increasingly attracted by the prophecies of the Book of Daniel, which he studied, it is reported, with the help of Jewish scholars. He was obsessed with the idea of the coming of the satanic Antichrist, predicted for the mid-1360s; and during a sermon in 1366 when the emperor himself was present, he pointed his finger at him, telling the people that Charles was the true incarnation of the Antichrist, as prophesied by the Bible. Charles nobly ignored the pious provocation, though the archbishop thought he had to incarcerate Milič at least briefly. Milič was lucky to have friends in Prague, Rome, and Avignon; when he was later called to respond to another catalogue of heresies, he was saved by the shared efforts of the Prague archbishop and one Cardinal Grimaldi, the pope's brother.

Milič's ambitious public project to gather penitent Prague prostitutes in a new Christian community of prayer, communion, and useful work met with an ambivalent response. In 1372 he acquired a vacant house, formerly a well-known place of ill repute run by Madame Keruš Hoffarth (in German, "pride"), who in turn had sold an adjacent building to Prague's executioner (the house was particularly functional because it had a convenient back door opening into the darkness of the small Old Town streets). Milič changed its name from sinful "Venice" to "New Jerusalem," adhering to the emperor's favorite passage in Revelation 21, and offered a home and a Christian haven to Madame Hoffarth's girls and their colleagues. It is said that about eight hundred women went through his New Jerusalem before they either married, were taken home by their parents, or ran away to other brothels (Milič followed them and tried to bring them back). His well-administered project did not long survive him; right after he died, the emperor, uneasy in these matters, dissolved the institution and offered the building to the Cistercians, who made it a college for its novices attending the university (1374). The chroniclers unfortunately do not say anything about what happened to the poor women affected by the emperor's action.

During these uneasy times of religious conflict and increasing social tension, two works of art, one in German and the other in Czech, were created; each in its own distinctive way constituted the highest literary achievement of Prague's Caroline century. They suggest, perhaps with a little delay, the best of an age in which certainties of belief gave way to rising doubt and, looking back to ecclesiastic circumstances and the courtly heritage, show that art can emerge from the study of the educated scribe and the erudite scholar. The Bohemian German Johannes of Tepl, who died as scribe of the New Town of Prague, wrote his *Plowman from Bohemia* (*Der Ackermann aus Böhmen*, 1400) at about the same time as the still unidentified Czech author wrote his *Tkadleček* (*The Weaver*, 1407); past disputes about the chronology of the texts, trying to derive nationalist profit from discovering which came first, long obfuscated the far more important discussion of their literary value. It is possible to assume that both these texts, the most admirable results of a late medieval German-Czech symbiosis, compete to rewrite an older model, perhaps Latin or Old French. This is the working hypothesis by which the American scholar Antonín Hrubý (originally from Prague) accounts for long stretches of textual resemblances, shared images, and analogous references to the authorities, Aristotle among them. Both the Plowman (his plow is the pen, he says) and the Weaver (weaving texts) have suffered grievous losses. The German writer has lost his beloved wife, Margarete, and his Czech colleague his fair Adlička, who turned away from him to favor somebody else. It is as if the protagonists of Machaut's Old French poem "The Judgment of the King of Bohemia" reemerged in a German and a Czech transformation, the plowman arguing against Death himself, and the weaver against Misfortune (*Neštěstí*), both of whom have destroyed their bliss.

In Johannes of Tepl's disputation, man against death, the most provocative sequences are those in which the plowman defends the radiant dignity of his wife, and of all other people, against current ideas of Death, who sees on earth but filth and inevitable putrefaction. Death sings stern songs of condemnation; man is "but a barrel of muck, full of worms, a privy [*ein Stankhaus*], a disgusting slop pail"; he has "nine holes in his body, and out of them all comes loathsome and unclean filth." The plowman extols human beings as God's finest handiwork and enthusiastically praises the earthy virtues of the senses: "in the eyeballs there is sight, the most trustworthy tool, . . . in the ear there is hearing that reaches out into the distance, . . . in the nose there is the sense of smell that goes in and out through the openings, skillfully adapted for the easy acceptance of all pleasurable and delightful perfumes." Yet, ultimately, these intimations of Renaissance transports are silenced by medieval anxiety: between man and death, God is the highest judge, and he accords praise to the plowman for arguing so valiantly, but victory to death, as it cannot be otherwise.

The author of *The Weaver* had been trained at the University of Prague (he says himself that he is Czech in his head but, as far as his feet are concerned, he is from everywhere) and handles his quotations more carefully and ostentatiously than his German colleague, demonstrating that Johannes's alleged quotation of Plato really comes from Aristotle. Earlier critics have suggested that Johannes of Tepl is more sincere because he *really* did lose his wife, while the weaver indulges in a witty and somewhat loquacious exercise, nearly four times longer than the plowman's text. But sincerity of feeling was never a full guarantee of literary quality, and the weaver has his own excellence in the innovative force of his argument, the amplifications of the inherited trial formula, and in the surprising richness of his language (soon to be impoverished by the polemical writing of the coming revolution). The weaver may or may not have lost his Adlička, his lovely *pernikářka* (gingerbread maker), but his work of art, which gathers for the last time the surfeit of older Czech, offers lasting enjoyments.

The Carolinian Jewish Town and the Massacre of 1389

During the reign of King Charles the Jewish Town, the core of which was called *inter Iudeaos* in old documents, was not yet a ghetto (a term that derived from Venice's *borghetto*, a Jewish district, much later). Originally, there had been two settlements closely surrounding the Old School and the Old New one, separated by the Church of the Holy Spirit, its parish, and possibly a small Benedictine convent, established in 1346; another church, that of St. Valentin's, was located close by, and a third one, All Saints, lay almost within its invisible boundary. There were still clusters of Jewish houses elsewhere—a few perhaps in the Minor Town and, though the Jews did not accept the king's invitation to settle in the New Town and enjoy its privileges, the cluster of almost a dozen houses near Prague's oldest Jewish cemetery, which served the Jewish communities of Bohemia for nearly two hundred and fifty years; by 1481, six of the families had left, and nine years later all were gone.

The boundaries of the Jewish Town were rather porous; in some places Jewish and Christian houses constituted a mixed neighborhood, especially if the king had intervened and allotted a Jewish building to a Christian institution (as King Charles did with Lazar's house, later bought back by Jews) or given it to a favorite for excellent services, as King Václav II did when he gave the house of Michael the Jew to his court secretary and in 1404 another one to a gifted artist who illuminated rare manuscripts for his pleasure. There were no massive walls separating the Jewish district from the Old Town, whose own fortification occasionally ran parallel to the Jewish houses, especially near the river, but the Jewish quarter's densely built wooden dwellings, an easy prey to devastating conflagrations, constituted a souk-like district. It could be entered by any of six gates, one close to St. Valentin's near the Vltava ferry, and the others at nearly regular intervals. But the walls did not protect the Jewish settlement when mobs came to rob and kill in 1389.

During the fourteenth century, the chances for Prague Jews to continue in their traditional and various ways of doing business were slowly reduced by the growing competition of Christian capitalists. The German burghers of the Old Town had seized the initiative in long-distance commerce, originally a Jewish sphere of interest; and even in the credit business, Christians circumventing church prohibitions against usury invaded Jewish economic territory. The rich were few and far between in the Jewish Town, though together they possibly commanded more cash than anybody else in Bohemia. Merchants changed currency, lent money, accepted pawns, bought and sold secondhand wares; other Jews, jealously watched by the Christian guilds, tried to shift to crafts, working on their own as tailors, goldsmiths, and later as belt makers and glaziers. A happy few were employed in community jobs, as, for instance, the *shammash*, or janitor of the synagogue, the *shulklopper* who announced when it was time to go and pray, the *mokel*, or circumciser, and the *shochet*, or butcher working according to prescribed rules. By legal definition, and by the consensus of church and empire, Jews were held in "servitude." Church doctrine held that the eternal servitude of the Jews was symbolic penitence for Christ's suffering on the cross, though Jews were also, according to Augustinian thought, necessary witness to the truth of Christianity. The Holy Roman Empire secularized this metaphysical idea and declared that the Jews were *camerknechte*, servants of the imperial chamber or, to call a spade a spade, of the imperial finance office; they were the ruler's personal property, not persons but things, and ruled by the law of objects. Emperor Ludwig of Bavaria spoke of his Jews as belonging "as they do, to the crown and the empire with their body and property, and he could do, act, and proceed with them as he wants and sees fit." Charles may have been an enemy of the Bavarian, but his ideas did not at all differ from Ludwig's concept of the *camerknechte*.

Among the many Jewish scholars of Prague in this time, Jom Tov Lipmann-Mülhausen was long remembered as thinker, interpreter of the

Bible, and keen polemicist. He probably came from Alsatia but spent his most productive years in Prague and by 1407 was appointed *iudex iudaeorum,* judge of the Jews, in the self-administration of the community. Long before the august Rabbi Loew, he was the first philosopher of Prague's Jewish scholars exploring metaphysical questions of faith and free will, but it was always difficult, if not impossible, to reconcile his defense of the rationalist Moses Maimonides, whose ideas he tried to spread as far as he possibly could, with his interest in the Spanish Kabbalah, of the Gerona school, and with his studies in the form and meaning of the letters of the alphabet, as shown in his *Sefer-Alpha-Beta,* of essential importance to writers of sacred scrolls. To his contemporaries and those of the following generation, Jews and Christians, Jom Tov Lipmann-Mülhausen was well known as an energetic polemicist, defending Judaism against apostasy and demonstrating the insufficiency, as far as language and history were concerned, of Christian knowledge of Hebrew sources. His arguments were particularly efficient because he knew Latin and had studied the New Testament and the early church fathers. As a member of the rabbinical court and as a judge, Lipmann-Mülhausen was loyally committed to Prague's Jewish community, but he also traveled widely to study and supervise rabbinical rules and practices, and he headed the council of Ashkenazi Jewry in Erfurt in 1440.

Charles's policies concerning the Jews of his realms have been much discussed by Czech and German scholars, and after abundant evidence has been sifted, it is fair to say that the king of Bohemia benevolently protected his Prague *camerknechte* and those in most other communities of his native kingdom. He made certain that his Prague Jews enjoyed more than thirty years of peace and prosperity, but he also revealed his financial appetite, to say the least, when he failed to protect the Jews in Germany and squeezed them for money, alive or dead, and occasionally just waited in the wings to cash in on a pogrom (foreseen or even organized with his connivance). His statement that his *camerknechte* were "to serve the needs of the ruler when occasion warranted" sounds tolerant enough under late medieval conditions; and though he, at times, formally addressed the Jews as his "*libe* [dear] *camerknechte,*" preferably when imposing new taxes on them, he showed his cold-blooded indifference to human suffering in his financial dealings at the start of his reign when a wave of pogroms was sweeping through Germany in 1348–50 (Prague was spared at that time). Jewish servitude was materially expressed by an ever increasing annual contribution paid to the emperor; Charles, usually strapped for funds, made his income from real or potential Jewish taxes into an instrument of his policies, using it to buy off the towns and territorial princes he needed as allies. There were other sources of Jewish income: as soon as the smoke cleared over a destroyed Jewish community and the burned corpses (in some southwestern German towns Jews were burned alive in their little wooden houses), the emperor fought with the German towns for his part of what was left of the *Judenerbe*, or Jewish property.

The king's record in the German pogrom years of 1348–50, closely studied by younger scholars of the former German Democratic Republic and by František Graus, shows a good deal of financial tenacity and few of the Christian virtues which Charles so praised in his own writings. His involvement in the Nuremberg pogrom of December 5, 1349, in which nearly six hundred Jews were killed and their community destroyed, strikes me as particularly disgusting. When pogroms began to sweep through Germany from the southwest in 1348, Charles was very much concerned with what was to be done with Jewish property left in the ashes, and named his favorite great-uncle, the archbishop of Trier, as chief administrator of all possessions belonging to Jews "who were and are yet to be killed in Alsatia," insisting that everything belonged to the *camer* (the king's chamber); he assured the bishops of Bamberg and Würzburg that he, the king, would not dispose of Jewish property without their consent "in case the Jews of their district would be harmed." In the spring and summer of 1349, Charles began to distribute the property of the Nuremberg Jews, anticipating their possible persecution; on April 6, he gave Arnold of Senckendorf a few Jewish houses "in case the owners would be killed or left town," then transferred ownership of the best Jewish houses to the margrave of Brandenburg, assuming that "the Jews there were to be killed [*nu nehst werden geslagen*] shortly," and finally offered the town council on November 16 the right to tear down the synagogue and a few other buildings to build a new church on the cleared square. In early December the pogrom really occurred as planned by the town council, and Charles, in a letter to the monastery of Waldhausen, had the blasphemous temerity to call it a fateful event sent by God himself.

The Easter pogrom of 1389 in Prague was triggered, eleven years after Charles's death, by an incident, variously described by contemporary reports, in the narrow streets of the Jewish Town. According to a rather dubious story, considering the location of a church within the Jewish quarter, a priest carrying the Host to a sick or dying man was stopped by Jewish adults and children, who badly abused him. Other chroniclers say that the Jews tried to stone the priest; a third narrative suggests that a Jew threw a little stone at the monstrance (*da wart von einem Juden ein klein steinchen geworfen auf die monstrancie*). In the subsequent brawl, the Jews responsible were brought to the town hall to be punished, and fanatical preachers all over town called upon the crowds to revenge the blasphemy lest they be punished by God himself within a year. Inflamed by the sermons, people began to gather, arming themselves and eager to march through the Jewish streets. The council of the Old Town, well aware of the property rights of King Václav IV as the lord of his *camerknechte,* immediately mobilized the privileged citizens to come to town hall to prevent the worst, but in the meantime a man namedJeško emerged as the leader of the people, telling them it would be better to kill all the Jews than to be punished by God. Jews were killed by swords and clubs, fires set to the houses, and those found alive pushed back into the conflagration; only a few children and women were brought to the town hall for Christian baptism by force, as a Latin narrative says. The next morning, the town council met again, ruling that all Jewish property must, under penalty of death, be brought to the town hall for the king, but it did not do anything to punish the people who had broken the laws of the town and of the king. On the third day, three thousand corpses were buried (people feared a pestilence); and since people were digging in the ruins for hidden treasures, the town council had the gates of the Jewish district closed and sealed.

The events of this terrible day were described in a Latin *Passio Judaeorum Pragensium* (*Passion of the Prague Jews*) by a cleric erudite enough to parody the gospels of Matthew and John (the manuscript was published only in 1877). The writer pretended to feel for the Jews but actually gloated over what had been done to them, unsparing in his details of blood and gore, and of how, when everything was over, curious crowds, including thieves and prostitutes, came to see the corpses lying in the streets.

Yet the victims continued to speak, and the renowned Prague rabbi and poet Avigdor ben Isaac Kara, some years later, wrote an elegy that revealed what had happened from the inside, as it were. This learned poet and richly gifted author, whose father had died in the flames, had a clear view of both the political circumstances after Charles's death and the breakdown of authority in Prague. "The order of the world fell apart," he wrote. "Innocence was destroyed by malice for, ach, the power of the state was broken and the royal scepter lost its radiance." He had been enchanted with "magnificent Prague," but he writes of the "muffled and spectral whisper in the streets," "the ghastly gatherings" of the Christians with their arms, axes, and hatchets, "as if they wanted to cut down a forest." Unlike the Christian chroniclers, Avigdor ben Isaac Kara dwells on the courage of the Jews who, like the members of the rabbinate, killed themselves and their families rather than submit to baptism, and he gives an unforgettable account of the brutal plundering of the two synagogues ("Get the gold!" the killers screamed), of the dead, and, finally, of the cemeteries where the graves were opened for spoil. All the Jews killed "were robbed of their garments, and in the dirt of the streets the bloody corpses of babies, men young and old, boys and virgins, were wildly heaped together." When Rabbi Avigdor ben Isaac Kara died in 1439, he was buried at the Jewish cemetery; for centuries his elegy for the dead of 1389 was read in the Prague synagogues on the Day of Atonement. The prayer concluding his text must have resounded with particular urgency far beyond the Middle Ages: "Now . . . Father of us all, it is time to proclaim that the killings must come to an end! Say it now that not a single one will be added to the terrible number of victims anymore! Long enough were they killed and choked to death to the world's derision, long enough!"

4

THE HUSSITE REVOLUTION: 1415–22

The King and the Vicar-General

The wise rabbi Avigdor ben Isaac Kara deplored the radically weakened royal power during the reign of Václav IV, and many contemporaries and later historians share his views. Charles's son Václav assumed power when he was seventeen years old, and it is far more difficult to be fair to him than to his father; contemporary chronicles are sparse, and many later voices speak against him in strange unison—Hussite adversaries, Catholic defenders of the Holy Church, and older German chroniclers who as early as 1400 took their cue from the German princes who had declared him too lazy to run the affairs of Germany. He has come down to us as an irascible if not perverse monster, even though the Prague folk, sympathizing with his fight against the feudal barons, obviously enjoyed stories about his nightly roaming about town, part Harun al-Rashid, part bon vivant. We are told of his rough jokes, his skirt chasing, and many writers like to tell the famous story describing how Susanna, a lovely masseuse, rescued him from the ire of the barons by rowing him in a little boat across the Vltava River. Many people believed that his first wife, a Bavarian princess, was torn to pieces by one of his huge mastiffs when she rose from her bed one night suddenly to avail herself of the Gothic amenities (in fact she probably died of the plague).

King Václav IV had been spoiled by his father, who in his old age was obsessed by the question of succession and dragged his son along on his travels as heir presumptive to whom ceremonious admiration and homage were due. Prince Václav never soldiered in the field as did his father, and though he spoke Czech and German, possibly learned a little

Latin, and may have known a smattering of other languages, he was not particularly interested in literary matters, either privately or at court. Friendly observers describe him, at least in his early years, as a handsome and witty conversationalist, but, as time went on, he withdrew from his royal duties to the hunt in the forests near Prague, carousing with his buddies and often drinking himself into a stupor. (When he was to meet the French king, a festive luncheon had to be postponed for three days because he had to sleep off the results of the first welcome party.) The Czech historian Zdeněk Fiala suggested that Václav lived under the illusion that the administrative machinery of the state would go on working by itself as it had under his father's eyes; and when he ran up against the harsh demands of changing political situations, the enmity of the German princes, and the mutinous barons at home, he was unwilling or unable to cope and slowly drifted along, helplessly and violently, rather than use his considerable intelligence.

Unfortunately, Václav found himself in an uncertain world split by the schism of the church, which ever since 1378 had been divided over two competing popes, Urban VI of Rome, who was supported by the Bohemian hierarchy, and Clement VII of Avignon, who had friends and allies in France and among the German princes. Václav, as young king of Bohemia and the German Reich, showed a great willingness to deal with his tasks; he went to Germany often, as was his duty, intervened in Rhenish affairs, and successfully married off his sister Anne to Richard II of England in 1382. The marriage, incidentally, made it easier for Bohemian students and masters to study at Oxford and bring back to Bohemia the writings and ideas of John Wyclif, who in that same year was declared a heretic, or in doctrinal error, by the church. Yet Václav's royal energies soon lagged; he lingered, procrastinated, lacked the will to make decisions, and by his absences from Germany provoked the princes. After repeated ultimatums, they declared him "totally unfit" to continue as Roman king. In a dubious procedure, they formally deposed him and elected Ruprecht of the Palatinate in his place, the result being that Europe now had two popes and the Reich virtually two monarchs, Václav forever postponing a journey to Rome, where he might have been crowned emperor nonetheless, under reduced circumstances, as it were, by Pope Urban VI or his successor.

At home Václav IV had to contend with Bohemia's powerful barons, who soon sensed his weakness and rebelled against his arbitrary ways and his habit of surrounding himself with favored advisers from the town and gentry. These favorites were quick to claim special prerogatives; they pushed aside the great traditional clans and squeezed the country, the towns, and especially the Jews for ever increasing tributes and taxes. One of these, Sigmund Huler, possibly from a family of German textile merchants from Cheb (Eger), actually ran the financial affairs of the kingdom for many years until it was discovered that he had cleverly put a good deal of money in his own pockets, and the king himself in 1405 sentenced him to death. The baronial opposition, mostly consisting of rich southern Bohemian families who traditionally fought the powers in Prague, established an alliance with the king's restive relatives, including Jošt of Moravia, a serious and effective administrator, and Václav's half brother Sigismund, later emperor, and they imprisoned Václav twice, once in Prague and once in Vienna, while pushing for a settlement of their claims. Four of the king's favorites were murdered in cold blood at Karlštejn, and in the sumer of 1401 the barons joined forces with the Saxon duke Wilhelm of Meissen, whose German armies, plundering and burning, invaded Bohemia and laid siege to Prague Castle.

Charles IV had marvelously succeeded in keeping the barons at bay, at least after the abortive revolt of the southern Bohemian Rožmberks in 1355, by appointing them to high formal offices, as tradition required, while building up his own royal towns and constantly strengthening a loyal church hierarchy. His son was ill advised to challenge Jan of Jenštejn, the third archbishop of Prague and the highest representative of the church in Bohemia. It was clearly a question of predominance, real or imagined, and the dispute was made more corrosive and brutal by the king's irresponsibility, to say the least, and by Jenštejn's rather exalted opinions of his indubitable intellectual gifts and ecclesiastical power. The king and the archbishop had originally worked closely together, but the trouble was that the archbishop was too sensitive to defend himself energetically against the king, preferring to write exquisite Latin poems or a melancholy autobiographical essay, "On Escaping the World"; it is possible that the king and his advisers intentionally provoked him to exaggerated reactions. Jenštejn was a rich youth from an important family in Prague, extremely well connected, and had been a leisurely student at the universities of Padua, Bologna, Montpellier, and Paris, where he declined a teaching position because he did not see himself as teacher or scholar. Rather suddenly he rose in the church to become bishop of Meissen, then archbishop of Prague and king's chancellor, quickly combining in one person the functions that, in the age of Charles IV, had been held by Arnestus of Pardubice and Johannes Noviforensis. He possessed all the intellectual qualifications to check the king's imperiousness and to return a degree of dignity to Bohemian affairs, yet after a grave illness, he underwent great emotional change, turned away from the stage of the world to the inner fire of the "modern devotion," favored the meditative orders of the Augustinians and Carthusians, left his loyal servants to taste the ire of the king, lived in seclusion, mostly away from Prague, and died, lonely, in a Roman monastery in 1396.

The consequences of the king's conflicts with the archbishop were felt for centuries, not because of the power play involved (it was washed away shortly by the Hussite revolution), but because the king was responsible for the death of the vicar-general Johann of Pomuk, canonized by Pope Benedict XIII on March 19, 1729, and one of the martyr patrons of Bohemia. The sordid and confused story about St. John of Nepomuk (as he was later called) combines cynical intrigues in high places with royal brutality and Jenštejn's melancholy inactivity at the wrong time, all in the chiaroscuro of a dark torture cellar and the searing flames of the hangman's torch.

In 1392, when the archbishop sought to discipline one of the king's relatives, Václav IV was deeply offended and, wanting to provoke him, had Jan Čůch, a royal favorite, build a dam on the Elbe River on a spot of land belonging to the archbishop (effectively denying him the payments he had received from passing ships); when the archbishop complained, King Václav IV invited him to one of his castles to talk over matters in a leisurely fashion, while in the meantime ordering Čůch's men to devastate the archbishop's estate. A wise judge restored Jenštejn's shipping rights, but matters went from bad to worse when the king conspired to weaken the archbishop's power by trying to establish a new bishopric in western Bohemia, centered on the monastery of Kladruby. The archbishop and his vicar, the legal expert in matters of the Prague hierarchy, in a quick countermove appointed a new abbot of Kladruby who was loyal to the church, and made it impossible to chip away at the jurisdiction of Bohemia's metropolitan. The king had one of his fits of rage, immediately left his hunting lodge, and rode to Prague to take revenge on the archbishop, who may have been, unsuspectingly, manipulated by his own church dignitaries inimical to the throne.

On March 20, 1393, another meeting of the king and the archbishop, and their retinues, was scheduled for further discussion at the monastery of the Knights of St. John, in the Minor Town, but the king, who had begun to drink early that day, was in no mood for prolonged negotiations. He screamed at the archbishop and his officials, including the vicar, Johann of Pomuk, and two officials named Nicholas Puchník and Václav Knobloch, and commanded the royal guards to arrest all four. In the sudden confusion, the archbishop escaped (he may have been saved by his own men or by reluctant soldiers of the king), and the three remaining prisoners were first dragged up to the cathedral close, where the furious king demanded to hear more about the archbishop's intentions, and later marched down from Hradčany to the Old Town, to the town judge's prison at the corner of Rytířská Street and the Můstek. The king may have hoped that his men would arrest the archbishop (all Vltava ships were checked); when evening came he called for the hangman and had the three prisoners put on the rack. Ultimately, the hangman applied a burning torch to the men, especially their hips and sides, and the king, it is said, took the torch from his hand to continue the torture. Then suddenly he became aware of what he was doing, relented, and gave the order to free the prisoners; a public notary was called, and Nicholas Puchník and Václav Knobloch had to sign a promise that they would never talk about their experience. But it was too late for middle-aged Johann of Pomuk; he expired while being taken from the rack, and his corpse was carried by the hangman and his assistants through the dark Old Town and thrown from the stone bridge into the Vltava River, at about nine in the evening. The heavens remained silent, Vít Vlnas quietly remarks in his recent and finely researched story of Johann of Pomuk and his later cult, and the corpse of the tortured vicar-general was found in the river a few weeks later.

Many stories were told over the centuries about the enraged king and the archbishop's lawyer, especially during the age of the Baroque when the long process of sanctification was going on. Johann of Pomuk was certainly not Queen Sophia's friendly confessor, as was suggested in 1471 by Jan Žídek, a Catholic writer of Jewish origin; it was not his wife's bedroom secrets that King Václav IV wanted to know, but the archbishop's political plans. Johann of Pomuk was tortured and died silently, a martyr of loyalty to his legal office, not to the holy vows of a priest hearing a woman's confession. There is nothing Baroque about his life. Johann of Pomuk was of German origin (his father, Wölfflin, was in the service of the Cistercian monastery of Pomuk, in southwestern Bohemia), and after studying in Prague and Bologna, where he was elected rector and received his doctorate in 1387, he was well qualified as a legal expert and "imperial notary"; he wrote in a wonderfully calligraphic hand. Steadily acquiring benefices and advancements, he held a minor post at Prague Cathedral, was appointed parish priest of St. Gallus, in the Old

Town, the richest and most conservative congregation of the Prague German patriciate, and later, by exchange of benefices, became canon at the Vyšehrad. By 1389, he was vicar-general in the archbishop's office, responsible for all financial and legal matters, and was also involved in supervising the mores of the Prague clergy and investigating preachers accused of heresy and their local supporters and friends. He was, to judge from his benefices and a comfortable piece of Prague real estate which he acquired, not a man of high spiritual intensity, as the archbishop was, but an erudite and loyal lawyer who went about his daily business quietly and punctiliously. He was killed at a moment when the king could not lay hands on the archbishop himself, who escaped to one of his castles most distant from Prague. Jan of Jenštejn, that melancholy and elusive archbishop, may have been (almost) destined to suffer the fate of Thomas à Becket, but it was Johann of Pomuk who died in his stead.

The Advance of the Religious Reformers

Václav IV was not fond of Hradčany Castle, where his father had resided, and construction of a new residence went on at a slow pace. In 1383 Václav IV shifted his residence to the King's Court, a fortified place at the Old Town near the walls, and had two gates opened through the fortifications for easier access to the New Town. The kings of Bohemia were to reside there for a hundred years; Vladislav II, of the Polish Jagiello dynasty, in 1475 asked the Czech architect Matěj Rejsek to build an adjacent New Tower (now called Prašná Brána, or Powder Tower) for reasons of security before deciding eight years later to move back up to Hradčany to be better able to defend the royal residence. The King's Court later became an army barracks and then, at the beginning of the twentieth century, gave way to a mansion for the Prague municipality (Reprezentační dům, or "Repre" for short), built in a graceful Art Nouveau style. Václav IV also disliked his father's ornate Karlštejn and, declaring his independence, built himself a hunting castle at Točník; he did not do much, if anything, to support new architecture or contemporary painters who, perhaps on the archbishop's insistence, excelled in creating late Gothic Madonnas in the "beautiful style."

During the reign of King Václav IV, the question of Czech or German predominance in the Old Town, the most important urban corporation among the towns of Bohemia, for the first time makes political sense—if romantic, or rather metaphysical, notions of nationalities are avoided. We have to accept the limitations of a sober historical analysis based on the count of Czech- or German-sounding names in public documents and also allow for the assumption that many Prague inhabitants then would have found it hard to say whether they considered themselves Czech or German in the modern sense. Over the course of the fourteenth century, the Old Town German patricians tended slowly to disappear from the scene, though it would be wrong to say that poor Czech artisans immediately took their place. The Czech scholar Jaroslav Mezník, who has calculated population changes from lists of taxes and real estate ownership, has shown that of twenty-eight families highly visible in 1325 only four were left a century later. The newcomers were not necessarily Czech; among craftsmen and artisans, those working with metal and wood, furriers, glove and saddle makers were usually German, clothes cutters and purveyors of food mostly Czech.

On the eve of the Hussite revolution, national clusters distinctly appear on a map of the Old Town: Germans are solidly concentrated around the Old Town Square and the St. Gallus parish and radiate in entire blocks of housing to Celetná Street and to the east and northeast. In a few adjacent quarters, Germans and Czechs are still in balance. Czechs are strongly, if not absolutely, predominant toward the periphery—in the northwest, close to the Jewish Town, and in the southwest, where friends of religious reform resided.

Many reasons have been advanced for the withering away of Prague's medieval German patriciate, and the least melodramatic may be closest to the historical circumstances. In business, the old families avoided spectacular risks and preferred stable returns; they began to buy property in the countryside and became landowners, joining the (mostly Czech) rural gentry; or, because of their learning and experience, they were appointed to high positions at the royal or imperial court and were gradually absorbed into the bureaucracy. In their stead, other German families, from Nuremberg and elsewhere, came to Prague, attracted by its commercial opportunities (perhaps more tempting under Charles IV than under his erratic son). Of course, town councils were shaped by the king, who held the undisputed power of appointment; it is possible that Charles strengthened the Czech element when, in 1350, he briefly appointed a majority of guild representatives to the Old Town council (he soon restored the patriciate to power, however) or when, in 1367, he tried to unite the Old with the New Town, in which the Czech element was traditionally very strong. In January 1408 the king appointed, for the first time, an Old Town council with a distinct Czech majority; a year later the predominance of the Bohemian "nation" was decreed at the university; but within five years Germans were prevailing again, which they continued to do until the Hussites profoundly changed all Prague life—religious, social, and national.

Among Prague intellectuals and burghers who longed for a reform of the church, Czech interests, as distinct from the universalist and transnational Caroline ideas, came increasingly to life, but the language of reform changed to the Czech vernacular slowly (even Jan Hus, who preached in Czech, wrote his notes in Latin). After the death of Milič of Kroměříž and the closing of his New Jerusalem, which had brought together repentant women and socially committed young priests and preachers, the reform movement went into organizational decline, for it lacked a firm local center in Prague. Its ideas and claims, however, were strengthened and refined by two thoughtful men, the learned Matěj of Janov and the solitary Tomáš of Štítný.

Matěj was born into a gentry family in southern Bohemia, and like other penniless and brilliant young men, he thought of a comfortable career in the church, which richly rewarded its own. He went to Paris in 1375, received his M.A. after three years, and continued, for nearly six more years, to read for the difficult doctorate of theology. The politics of the schism interfered: at least initially, the University of Paris preferred the Avignon pope, but most Bohemian members of the English "nation" at the Sorbonne (to which Matěj paradoxically belonged) were loyal to Rome, since not supporting the Roman hierarchy would have spoiled their chances for an appointment in Bohemia. Of course, Matěj returned from Paris to Prague via Rome, where he had a chance to acquire a "letter of grace" from the pope, promising a future appointment. When he came to Prague in October 1381, he was appointed to a titular canonry of the cathedral (with no income), made a meager living by occasionally preaching and hearing confession, by the grace of the archbishop, but he felt frustrated. When, in 1388, he was appointed to a poor little parish in a village on the road from Prague to Mělník, his great hopes for preferment were utterly shattered, and he underwent a spiritual crisis as intense as Milič's before him, though for different reasons.

Turning his early foolish aspirations against himself, Matěj began to believe that his failure to be appointed to a comfortable living corresponding to his talents and dignity was a divine sign telling him to choose the path of Christ, of evangelical truth and simplicity. He wrote that it was not an easy question "whether to go after benefices and offices or whether instead to bear the poverty and reproaches suffered by Jesus Christ." His eyes sharpened by lack of success, he turned against prelates and "great canons," castigating their "systematic vanity, their great discrepancy from the virtue and truth of Jesus and from his words and deeds, which they zealously praised with their mouths alone." If Konrad Waldhauser had been an effective preacher and Milič the practical visionary, Matěj was the learned theologian of the growing reform movement in Bohemia, still untouched by the ideas of John Wyclif, later important to the Hussites; and it is probably necessary to distinguish between what he himself wrote and what his willful assistants, Ondřej and Jakub, preached (in Czech) when they served at the church of St. Nicholas as guests of the Old Town parish.

Matěj was well known for asking the pious to come to mass frequently, if not daily, and he did not hesitate to express doubts about venerating pictures, relics of the saints, or miracles caused by material things. However, the Prague synod of 1388 ruled (following the advice of the masters of the university) that frequent communion was in error (once a month was enough) and decreed that images should be venerated as they had always been; a year later, the synod of 1389 ordered Matěj and his two assistants to appear before a clerical assembly gathered at the cathedral. Jakub was forbidden to preach for ten years, but Matěj, who submitted to the better judgment of the Holy Church, was let go more lightly (six months) and was given the friendly advice to concentrate on his job at his little village parish rather than hang around in Prague. Yet he did not change his mind; and in his learned Latin volumes he condemned the church, involved in worldly affairs, as the *mulier fornicaria*, and extolled a poor and simple Church of Christ, free of ceremonies, mandates, decrees, and rules. It is not surprising that the archbishop's office kept a close eye on Matěj: shortly before he died in 1393, he was asked to deliver two books, one in Latin and one in *vulgari Boemico*, or Czech, to the hands of the archbishop's lawyer and adviser Johann of Pomuk, the future victim of royal revenge. F. M. Bartoš, most knowledgeable in Hussite affairs, believes that the Latin manuscript was the *Regulae veteris et novi testamenti*, Matěj's thoughts about the interpretation of the Bible (Matěj assured the office he had not yet corrected them), and the other part of a Czech translation of the Bible to which Matěj substantially contributed. It is a speculative but impressive idea.

Tomáš of Štítný, son of a country squire in southeastern Bohemia, was not particularly radical in his religious reflections, but he was the first layman to write about matters Christian and moral *in Czech*, feeling responsible for the education of his five children and his neighbors who were unable to read Latin. He must have been one of the earliest students at the University of Prague, but he did not seek or receive a degree, and returned to his father's fortified tower to marry, to raise children, and to work the land. He did not bury himself in the countryside, though, for he occasionally traveled to Prague, where he listened to Waldhauser, Milič, and possibly Matěj of Janov. Tomáš may not have changed the canon of accepted ideas, but he single-handedly created a Czech philosophical syntax, making it possible to write in Czech about matters long reserved to the university masters using Latin. After his wife died, he took care of his aging sisters and then in 1381 left for Prague to be close to the scene of religious reform and to live with his oldest daughter, Anežka, who had gathered a group of women trying to live in the Christian spirit. By that time, he was an old man, and he died before revolution erupted in the Prague streets.

Czech historiography, after a long period of considerable isolation, has yet to deal with the record of the medieval Prague communities of pious women who deeply sympathized, to say the least, with the efforts of the time to emulate the life of the early Christians. In their ranks, Czech names of the gentry predominate, and among the first was Tomáš of Štítný's daughter Anežka. Before 1401 she had bought part of a house in the Czech section of the Old Town, not far away from New Jerusalem, and resided there with her friends Ludmila and Catherine; after a number of property deals, the new co-owner of the house, a noblewoman named Střežka of Čejkovice, provided shelter for five more young women. Another pious noblewoman, Petra of Říčan, bought a house in 1410 and lived there together with her friends Markéta of Peruc and Důra of Bethlehem for nine years, praying, attending Czech sermons, and doing good deeds. Such small communities were established elsewhere in Prague too; Catherine Kaplerová of Sulevice, a rich widow, set up a fund to pay for a Czech preacher at St. Vitus Cathedral, and she invited to her comfortable house at Hradčany Square twelve virgins and widows who were willing to leave the temptations of the world and to serve God. The historian V. V. Tomek believed that at least seven other communities of a similar kind were established near various Prague parish churches. Enemies of the reform movement suspected these spontaneously created associations of heresy, called the women *begutae,* to suggest a link to the heretic Beguines of Flanders, and were quick to demonize or ridicule them. In a satirical street ballad of the time, we are told the story of a Czech *beguta* who lured a young man, eager for Christian instruction, to her room, showed him two pear-shaped chapters of the Bible, and more, and soon he and she were singing a *Te Deum laudamus* (*We praise thee, O Lord*) in unison.

Milič's New Jerusalem and its small seminary of young clerics had been the first institution created by Prague Christians for a pristine faith of love; when it was closed by royal decree, its lay congregation may first have thought of legal proceedings to repossess the buildings but ultimately decided to create another institution. We do not know exactly who took charge, but it was possibly the theologian Vojtěch Raňkův of Ježov, who later became the first Czech rector of the University of Paris. Adalbertus Ranconis de Ericinio, to use his Latin name, was in many ways the *éminence grise* of the Prague reform movement, and it was possibly he who brought about an effective coalition of interested people, the commercial middle classes, and the court. In any event the Prague synod of 1389, the one which humiliated Matěj of Janov, seems to have resolved to build a new house of God in which these reform intentions would be continued by young Czech preachers: within three years (1391–94) a new chapel called Bethlehem was constructed not very far from Milič's place in the Old Town Czech neighborhood. Leading Czech businessmen and courtiers worked together to organize the project: the merchant Kříž provided the building lot, a former malt house, and a good deal of money; others, including the cloth cutter Machuta (once investigated by the Inquisition), pitched in. Among the people influential at court, Johannes of Mühlheim was won over to the cause by his wife, Anna, of a Czech baronial family, and contributed considerable prestige and diplomatic skills. It was he who signed the document legally establishing the new chapel; it claimed that the word of God, publicly proclaimed, was foremost in shaping the church and all its members; without God's word, "we would be like Sodom and Gomorrah." Yet a trace of the old was still part of the new, for the merchant Kříž was proud to present to the new institution the bones of a child allegedly killed by King Herod, though such a dubious relic may not have pleased the new congregation's preachers.

This Bethlehem chapel was a large, stern lecture hall, possibly with a low ceiling crossed by strong wooden beams, and a modest pulpit to be entered from the priest's apartment on the upper floor of an adjacent building. Contemporary reports suggest that three thousand listeners flocked to the services, but the number may be hyperbolic. The chapel was certainly built in deliberate contrast with Prague's rich parish churches; its present form, a mid-twentieth-century reconstruction impressively combining architectural erudition and historical imagination (only a few remnants of the original walls, hidden in nineteenth-century apartment houses, could be used), suggests the noble simplicity and the aesthetic space of the original; the reconstructed gables curiously resemble those of the Old New Synagogue in the Jewish Town.

Legally and administratively the affairs of the Bethlehem chapel were far from simple; it was built within the parish district of St. Philip and St. James, and the resident priest, Nicholas Zeiselmeister (later to reappear among the ardent enemies of Jan Hus), had to be compensated for possible loss of fees by a yearly payment; there were to be no festive masses celebrated in the chapel. Two preachers were appointed, one paid by Mühlheim's endowment and the other one by Kříž; these two priests actually received a comfortable living, and if they accrued or earned additional monies, they had to account strictly for the funds and use them solely for the upkeep of the chapel. The number of (frequent) sermons was precisely specified, and to guard against the easy absenteeism so rampant elsewhere, the rules insisted that preachers be in residence and that the archbishop himself approve even a temporary absence.

The Bethlehem chapel was founded by people trying to push Christian reform, and they clearly had the full collaboration of the archbishop, who laid the foundation stone himself. It is also clear that they had close links to the university masters of the Bohemian "nation" (possibly, at that time, a label for Czech intellectuals), for the patrons of the chapel agreed that the masters would recommend clerics for appointment. Jan Protiva, the first preacher at Bethlehem (later to turn against reform), was appointed by the noble patron Johannes of Mühlheim, but the university masters recommended, as Protiva's successor, Štěpán of Kolín, a dean of the faculty of arts. The Kříž appointee, a Cistercian named Jan Štěkna, was also a master and, besides, court chaplain to Queen Jadwiga of Poland; he must have been an effective preacher, for Jan Hus called him a "fiery trumpet" *(trouba zvučná)* or, in another reading, a rather noisy fool.

The middle-class patrons of the chapel took great care to strengthen the institution in the Miličian way: Kříž endowed twelve places for poor students of the Bohemian "nation," probably all Czech, to live and eat at Bethlehem (another adjacent building, called Nazareth, was opened for them), and, through the good offices of Jan Štěkna and Kříž, the Polish queen made plans to endow a college of Lithuanians to study in Prague. She died before the first of them arrived, but fortunately, the legal documents had made provisions for admitting other young men, and now Czech students were invited. Bethlehem and Nazareth became overcrowded, and the Cistercians agreed to house the overflow in a nearby building that had once actually belonged to Milič's New Jerusalem. On

March 14, 1402, another master of the university, thirty-year-old Jan Hus, was appointed preacher and administrator of the Bethlehem chapel. From that moment, the chapel was to be at the heart of Czech history for many years to come.

Jan Hus at Bethlehem

Very little is known about the childhood and the early years of Jan Hus, and all the chroniclers usually repeat the same anecdotes, invented a hundred years later—about the piety of his mother and the goose (*husa*) which she wanted to present to his schoolteacher. Hus was born around 1372 at Husinec, a small village in southern Bohemia; his father was a farmer or village artisan, and his mother wanted Jan to study and to become a priest. Hus received his first education, mostly in reading Latin, in the elementary school in nearby Prachatice, a lively if not rich town run by well-to-do German merchants involved in the transport of goods from Austria and Bavaria to Prague. In 1390, the budding scholar and choirboy arrived in Prague, matriculated at the university as Jan of Husinec, and busied himself with the prescribed philosophical courses, receiving his B.A. (as sixth among twenty-two) in 1393 and his M.A. three years later; by 1400, or shortly thereafter, he was ordained a deacon and a priest. He was serious, averse to wasting time, unlike many of his more relaxed fellow students, and often went hungry and was in ill health (he once made himself a spoon of bread to eat peas, he wrote later, and came to eat the spoon as well). He was happy to be appointed servant at the Carolinum, tidying the rooms of the resident professors and helping in the kitchen in return for a bed and free meals; he must have enjoyed being so close to the famous professors of the Bohemian "nation."

His academic career, at least in the beginning, proceeded with nearly clockwork precision: after the B.A. and M.A., he taught a watered-down version of Aristotle's natural science, then after some time the *Liber Sententiarum* by Petrus Lombardus, required reading in the study of theology; ultimately, he entered the long and difficult course for a doctorate in theology (doctors of theology were the only ones paid for their teaching, their income being derived from the profits earned on a farm in the countryside owned by the university). Word must have spread easily that Hus was eager, loyal, efficient if somewhat plodding as a teacher, not a firebrand in any way. He had good contacts at court (he may have been in the king's retinue on a trip to Germany, where he marveled at the women wearing wigs) and in the Czech business community and among friends of Milič and Matěj; and the young archbishop, Zbyněk, later his enemy, looked upon him with noticeable favor.

Hus never hesitated to engage himself, together with his Czech colleagues, in the discussions and conflicts troubling the Prague faculty at the time. He refrained from challenging authority directly and moved with innate and deliberate caution, but after being appointed to the Bethlehem chapel, he found himself with the leaders of a movement in which the older ideas of Milič and Matěj were more and more combined with the radical new teachings of John Wyclif of Oxford University. The situation was complicated by the diversity of philosophical orientations and nascent national feeling at Prague University. The German masters of the Polish, Saxon, and Bavarian "nations" and a few of their conservative Czech allies were nominalists, believing that things preceded ideas, thus allowing a pragmatic opening to the advances of science and reserving to faith a central role in religious life. This way of thinking had been much domesticated, though, since the time when William of Ockham, its fountainhead, had lived and worked in Munich. Most of the Bohemian (or, rather, Czech) masters, Jan Hus among them, preferred the older traditions of philosophical realism in the tradition of Plato and St. Augustine, which presumed that ideas preceded things, and, above all, John Wyclif's philosophical writings, imported to Prague by Czech students studying in Oxford. (Hus busily copied out Wyclif for himself, and in the margins expressed wonder and astonishment at the new thought.) The German masters and their allies recognized the inherent danger when the older way of thought came newly to life in the minds of their restive Czech contemporaries, and they counteracted it by invoking Wyclif's theology, which an English synod had declared heretical in 1382, against the defenders of his philosophy. The Silesian master Johann Hübner compiled a catalogue of Wyclif's forty-five doctrinal errors and submitted it to the offices of the archbishop, who promptly returned it to the university for an expert opinion. The university meeting of May 28, 1403, the nominalists in the overwhelming majority, easily declared the forty-five articles to be erroneous, false, and heretical; the Czech masters had little choice left but dramatic gestures and the claim that the compilation was partial or incomplete or both.

It was certainly not a matter of mere academic disputation to be accused of Wyclifism or of doctrinal alliance with the famous master of Balliol College at Oxford; though Wyclif had long been protected by Parliament and the powerful duke of Lancaster, the situation in England had changed when the peasants revolted in 1381 and he was forced to retire to his parish of Lutterworth, where he died three years later. (He may have died peacefully, but in 1427 his bones were disinterred and burned, and the ashes thrown into the river Swist.) Wyclif was far more politically minded than Jan Hus; for many years he had been engaged in England's resistance against the French and against the Avignon Curia, he greatly admired the secular power of Kings Edward I and Edward III, and he provided much of the theoretical arguments against the English crown's making payments to the pope. He was a learned theologian in the Augustinian tradition and, through Augustine, closer to Plato than to Aristotle, but his first religious, doctrinal, and social law was the Bible, part of which he rendered into English so that it could be understood by the unlettered; he declared in no uncertain terms that whatever ecclesiastical hierarchies, rites, orders, institutions, and sacraments were not found in Scripture were alien to Christian life. Christ, not the pope (at least not the historical pope, of his time), was the head of the invisible church, and there should be no difference between bishops and priests, who were to roam the countryside in pairs, preaching everywhere. Few of the sacraments were justified by the Bible, he thought, least of all extreme unction, and even in the Eucharist, bread and wine remained mere bread and wine, even after being consecrated, and Christ was received not bodily but "spiritually" by the faithful. Defining his idea of "remanence," Wyclif opposed the orthodox belief in the act of transubstantiation by which the bread and wine, though retaining their accidental forms, were believed to become the true body and true blood of Christ. With increasing fervor, Wyclif demanded that the true church—those predestined for salvation—return to the poverty and pristine virtues of the early days: if the church misused ecclesiastical property, it was the task of the secular powers to right the situation, and the king neglected his duties if he did not intervene.

It has always been difficult to show precisely when and how Jan Hus emerged in the religious life of Prague, where many had long favored him as a loyal if reform-minded son of the church, to defend heresy, as his adversaries insisted on calling it, to claim the essential privilege of all Christians to appeal for ultimate justification to Christ himself, the true head of the church. He was surely a man of quiet decisions, and he was far from being a belligerent radical, even though he looked like one to many. He grew with the events, in which schismatic popes, legitimate and illegitimate kings, comfortable prelates enjoying many benefices and ascetic theologians, the church's legal establishment and the resolution to live in the truth of Jesus Christ, conservative Bohemian patriots and early defenders of the idea of a nation based on language rather than territory—all these were chaotically pitted against each other. Jan Hus had been distinctly reticent at the university discussion about the theological errors of Wyclif in 1403, and Zbyněk of Hasenburk, the archbishop of Prague, wanted earnest Hus to speak to the Bohemian clergy at Prague synods.

Jan Hus may have become aware of his life's truth not in a sudden thrust of inspiration but step by step, feeling after feeling and thought after thought; by 1408, at the latest, he was emerging as a figure of European stature, investigated by papal councils, jeered at and admired at home, and forced to a deeper understanding of himself in his confrontation with the power of the church and the world. The decisions that shaped his life and death were all made within a few years, roughly between 1408 and 1412; when the archbishop, fully supported by the pope, in 1409 appointed a commission to examine Wyclif's teachings and demanded that all copies of his writings be delivered to his office, Hus immediately wrote a short treatise about the study of texts that readers might consider heretical (they do not have to share the author's opinions, after all) and protested to the Curia in a document formulated by his legal adviser, Jan of Jesenice; when, on July 16, 1414, Archbishop Zbyněk, nervous and ill advised, gave the order to burn the collected books, and demonstrating students roamed through the Prague streets singing a ditty about "Bishop Zbyněk ABC / burns books though he / knew not what they contained," Hus, together with five other university masters, organized a learned conference about Wyclif's writing, and coolly ignored the excommunication decreed against him by Zbyněk, who had escaped to his castle at Roudnice, fearing the worst. King Václav IV, however, wrote to the pope to defend Hus, his "faithfully devoted chaplain," and Wyclif's English disciples collected books to send to Prague.

The Prague Wyclifites, Jan Hus among them, were well aware that, in challenging the book-burning archbishop, they were able to rely on the protection of court and King, who had his own ax to grind as far as the archbishop was concerned. The Wyclifites and King Václav IV banded together against the Bohemian church hierarchy and the university enemies of the Wyclifites. It was not clear whether, in this temporary and highly unstable alliance, the Wyclifite masters were skillfully manipulating the king against their university enemies, or whether it was the king who used the Prague Wyclifites and their high moral seriousness to serve his international political aims.

The Decree of Kutná Hora

King Václav IV (definitely not resembling the English king Edward I, whom Wyclif so admired) had been deposed as Holy Roman Emperor by decision of the prince-electors in 1400, and he was not averse to using the conflicts of the schism between Rome and Avignon to undo his humiliation and to strengthen his dignity and international power by recommending himself as a ruler eager to help restore order to the church. The new Roman pope, Boniface IX, had approved Ruprecht of the Palatinate, Václav's German adversary, as emperor (and, after Boniface's death, so did his successors Innocent VII and Gregory XII), and Václav IV had good reason to express sympathy to those cardinals who, weary of the schismatic disorder, wanted to organize a grand council to solve these questions once and for all. His idea was that the council would depose Gregory XII and Benedict XIII of Avignon and elect a single new pope. His problem was that conservatives in the Bohemian church and in the German lands remained loyal to Ruprecht and Gregory XII; in Prague itself, Archbishop Zbyněk, together with his hierarchy, professed the same ecclesiastical obedience and abhorred the idea that the king of Bohemia should move away from it.

Toward the end of 1408, a French delegation of august church dignitaries, committed to plans for a general council at Pisa, appeared in Prague and at Kutná Hora, a rich and proud silver-mining town west of Prague, where the king then resided, and began discussions about Václav's neutrality. The king was eager to seize his chance to enhance his international visibility and, perhaps, to be Holy Roman Emperor again, if Gregory XII's support of Ruprecht would cease to be legitimate. Václav could not hope to be helped by Archbishop Zbyněk, but, needing political support, he intended to enlist the university's many learned masters and doctors, and he shrewdly asked for legal advice from them. It was a diplomatic way to find out how much institutional support he could expect; he could not have been entirely surprised to discover that the Bavarian, Saxon, and Polish "nations" were unshaken in their loyalty to Ruprecht and Pope Gregory XII, and that only the Wyclifites, mostly Czechs of the Bohemian "nation," were willing to support neutrality and the convening of a general council (the less pope, the better).

In turning to Prague University, the king had the international situation in mind, not the squabbles of the local professors, yet it cannot be said that the Wyclifite masters supported him to further the Czech nation in the modern sense. They were passionately engaged in religious reform, ever more radical as the years went by, and first of all they wanted to change the university's power structure, which threatened the advance of their dissenting thought; they also believed—and here the problem of nationality does enter—that this power structure did not entirely correspond to the actual composition of the student body and faculty. King Charles IV had established the university for "loyal inhabitants" (*regnicole fideles*) of the kingdom of Bohemia and for others who wanted to partake of the rich symposia of scholarship in Prague; from the beginning, however, the *regnicole fideles* of whatever language were in a distinct minority while the other three "nations" dominated the examination boards and the most influential university positions. The Saxons (north) comprised students from Saxony, Brandenburg, Frisia, Pomerania, Scandinavia, the Netherlands, and England. The *"natio Polonica"* (east) comprised Poles, Lithuanians, Prussians, Silesians, and Lusatians, whatever their native language. The Bavarian "nation" (south) included not only Bavarians but also Tyroleans, Austrians, Hessians, Swiss, and Lombards. The *"natio Bohemica,"* a rather diverse bunch, included, of course, students from Bohemia and Moravia (both Czech and German speakers), as well as Hungarians, some of whom may have been Slovaks, from the Carpathian countries and the Balkans. At the beginning, the *natio Bohemica*—that is, the *regnicole fideles* addressed by King Charles IV—constituted one-sixth of the total university population, and by the turn of the century, after many students had left for the new universities of Cracow, Vienna, and Heidelberg, the Bohemians increased to at least one-fifth of the academic population. The reformers of the Bohemian "nation" had few chances if the system remained unchanged.

The university's "nations" had quarreled before, but matters had been patched up by administrative compromises, because most of the scholars disliked outside interference in their affairs. The earlier disputes had, of course, concerned appointments, stipends, and benefits—there was not enough money for everybody. Usually, conflicts would erupt about appointments; if the candidate was born in Silesia, for instance, the Bohemians would punctiliously argue that he was not a Bohemian native, but would agree to his appointment provided that any future candidate for the position would be selected from their ranks. In the later 1380s and 1390s, language began to take precedence over territorial place of origin—some scholars may have belonged to the *natio Bohemica* but not all of them were *natione Bohemi* (that is, Czech speakers)—and slowly the principle of national inclusion and exclusion, long opposed by the universalism of the medieval church, began to raise its ugly head. During the reign of

King Charles IV, Archbishop Arnestus had immediately intervened when an Augustinian monastery wanted to restrict its admission of applicants who were Czech speakers, but hardly a generation later, the learned and irritable Adalbertus Ranconis de Ericinio established two fellowships for students in Paris and Oxford but stipulated that they be *natione Bohemi* (that is, Czechs) on their fathers' and mothers' sides.

When the French delegation appeared at Kutná Hora in late 1408, King Václav IV also invited a delegation of distinguished scholars from Prague University to explore the justification for and support of neutrality in the papal schism. He could not have expected a unified vote from the professors, but he must have been quickly disappointed by the differences among them. This university group comprised, among others, the German rector, two conservative Czechs, and, from the Wyclifite faction, Jan Hus's friend the lively Master Jeroným, well known internationally. Václav, who hoped for a majority decision in his favor, first assured the Germans that he would never interfere with their privileges but angrily turned (an anti-Wyclifite writer later attested) on the Wyclifites, whom he held responsible for creating problems and threatened to have them burned. Yet his only hope was in these restless Bohemian Wyclifites, for the other three "nations" were totally unwilling to give up their obedience to the Roman pope. For some days, there was considerable lobbying behind the scenes, but on January 18, 1409, the king issued his decree of Kutná Hora, which radically changed the traditional legal structure of Prague University, giving three votes to the Bohemian "nation" and only one to all the other "nations"—disenfranchising the masters of three "nations" with one stroke and elevating the Bohemians to a dominance that enabled him to claim that a majority at the university fully supported his neutrality and the preparations for the Pisa council.

It cannot be said that King Václav IV, of a Luxembourg family and married to a Bavarian princess, was an ardent Czech patriot, but he needed the support of the *natio Bohemica* as much as the Wyclifites needed his backing, and for a time they banded together. The king was not interested in the quarrels between the masters, and the Wyclifites were not chiefly concerned with French cardinals or the election of a new pope. The decree moved between old and new ideas and implications. It may be true that all human beings must love all other beings, the initial sentences say, but necessary love should proceed from well-ordered care, *ex ordinata caritate*, inspiring the king to favor his own before extending his love to others. His own was the *natio Bohemica*, the true heir of the kingdom (*regni iusta heres*), or the legal inhabitants of his kingdom, but these

Bohemians were confronted in new ways *not* with the three traditional "nations" but with one unified "*natio Theutonica*" consisting of "foreigners and immigrants" (*externi et adveni*). In later Czech history *natio Bohemica* was translated as *český národ* (Czech nation), reminiscent of if not coinciding with nineteenth-century terminology, but in the historical context of 1409, a double reading of the term was still possible, I believe—the old legal way, relating it to the *incolae* (inhabitants of the kingdom of Bohemia), not excluding speakers of German who had been born and bred in the country; and a new linguistic way, meaning Czech speakers whose parents on both sides were Czech. The text of the decree leaves the interpretation wide open; if it is true that the writer was Jan of Jesenice, the Wyclifites' legal expert and legal adviser to Jan Hus, it is possible to assume that he deftly addressed the legal and territorial meaning to the ears of the king and the new linguistic interpretation to his own friends in the reform group.

On January 26, the decree was read out at the university, but the Bavarians, Poles, and Saxons were unwilling to give up without a fight. In subsequent negotiations, they suggested that the *natio Bohemica* secede and establish a university of its own (something like this happened in a different situation, when Prague University was divided into two institutions, German and Czech, in 1882), and both sides seriously entertained the possibility that the university could be run by alternating teams of different "nations," half the year by the Bohemians and the other half by representatives of the others. Pressed for time and suspicious of professors, King Václav IV was not really interested in continuing the debate; his delegates and a few town officials forced the rector to hand over the insignia of the university and, by the king's order, Zdeněk of Laboun and Šimon of Tišnov, a friend of Hus, were appointed rector and dean of the faculty of arts. The German-speaking masters and students in the other "nations" had vowed not to submit, and after May 9 in solemn exodus left the university, town, and country. The Prague merchants complained about the loss of so many customers, whatever their language or country of origin. Historians have long discussed the number of those who left Prague; and the old suggestion of thousands of masters and students may be more hyperbolic than precise. Heinrich Denifle, researching the matriculation books of Erfurt and the then newly founded university at Leipzig, where most of the German masters and students were said to have gone, came up with statistical evidence not exactly demonstrating an exodus en masse; recent calculations speak of six hundred or six hundred and fifty people. Yet it is also true that by the exodus Prague University lost much of its international function and, like many other European universities at the time, became local and national, though not entirely and not in the simple nineteenth-century sense.

Later German and Czech nationalists constantly looked back at the decree of Kutná Hora to nourish their belligerent feelings with melodramatic images of Czech and German villains and heroes. The question always hinges on the changing meaning of the term *natio Bohemica*; in later Hussite documents, the term *jazyk* (*linguagium*, or language) is frequently used to denote nationality. But to speak of a total and radical break between Czechs and Germans in 1409 is to be distinctly premature, if not demagogic; in any case the students and masters of jurisprudence in Prague, who since 1372 had been independent of the university, went on in their accustomed ways, untouched by the king's decree, and there is strong evidence that even among the German professors not everybody joined the exodus (e.g., Johannes Hildesen of Hildesheim); new German masters, inclined to religious reform, returned to or newly joined the Prague faculty, as did Friedrich Eppinge from Dresden, a scholar particularly dear to Hus. Nor did all the masters interpret *natio Bohemica* in the new linguistic manner but preferred its traditional territorial meaning. This complexity helps to explain why, after Hus served as rector for half a year in 1409–10, he was followed, as the historian Ferdinand Seibt has shown, by Andreas Schindel, a Bohemian German from Duchcov (Dux).

Czech and German historians, for different reasons, were rather fond of the idea that Jan Hus himself had played a dominant role, heroic or villainous, in the issuance of King Václav IV's decree and the exodus of the Germans, an early "ethnic cleansing," but recent scholarship tends to stress that his concerns were religious rather than national. He certainly participated in presenting the necessity of change to the royal court, together with his Wyclifite friends, but he became ill at the most decisive moments of the negotiations; it is more probable that his friend Jeroným, who in the best humanist way praised the Slavs as descendants of the ancient Greeks, and his legal adviser, Jan of Jesenice (who also provided the court with a legal brief), were the most active in pushing the change. At any rate, the German students, shortly after leaving Prague, were singing a political ditty in which they named Jeroným and Jan of Jesenice as responsible for their migrations but did not mention Hus at all. At the Bethlehem chapel, Hus, in turn, praised Nicholas Augustin, often called "the Rich," as an influential court counselor who had been instrumental in the king's decision; the possibility that Nicholas was of German origin only complicates the situation even more. He was not the only Prague

German who, in restless times, felt closer to his fellow Czech citizens than to the Germans coming from abroad.

Jan Hus at Constance

The alliance of the Wyclifites and the king that produced the decree of Kutná Hora was in danger of breaking asunder three years later. It was the issue of indulgences sold in the streets that now increasingly isolated Jan Hus from many of his fellow masters, including some of his oldest friends, who were willing to support the hierarchy and the king, eager to rid Bohemia of all dangerous aspersions of heresy. The occasion was the war of the pontiffs: the Avignon pope deposed by the Council of Pisa, together with King Ladislas of Naples and Hungary, occupied Rome and drove Pope John XXIII to exile in Bologna. From there, Pope John XXIII exhorted all faithful Christians to come to the defense of his church and promised everybody who would take up arms or equip a soldier for one month "remission of such of their sins of which they were heartily contrite and which they had confessed." In practice, people believed that if they simply paid, their sins would be forgiven.

In May 1412, the pope's special envoy and commissioner, Wenzel Tiem, actually a southern Moravian German from Mikulov (Nikolsburg), arrived in Bohemia, ingeniously set up a network of subagents to sell indulgences, organized festive Prague propaganda processions with fifes and drums, and placed huge coffers at the churches of St. Vitus, the Týn, and St. Jakob to protect the incoming monies. In Prague, where the practice of indulgences had been opposed as early as 1393 by the German Dominican Heinrich of Bitterfeld, nearly everybody was appalled, but in private rather than in public; after all, the sale of indulgences had been fully approved by the king, who was expecting his appropriate cut. But Jan Hus condemned the sale of indulgences, saying they were "not in harmony with the apostolic mandate," challenged the authorities of church and kingdom, and once again strongly articulated the conflict between Wyclifites and church loyalists, mostly doctors of theology on the faculty of arts. The university resolved to bring the problem to the attention of the king, who in turn, after meeting a few dignitaries, officially confirmed that the earlier condemnation of Wyclif was legitimate and that all public demonstrations against the sale of indulgences were forbidden.

The council of the Old Town, once again dominated by a German majority, was set to follow the king's wishes loyally and strictly when, during mass on Sunday, July 10, 1412, three young men by the names of Jan, Martin, and Stašek, all Czechs and artisans, demonstratively raised their voices at St. Vitus, the Týn, and St. Jakob against the sale of indulgences; they all were quickly arrested and dragged to the Old Town prison. Early next morning, a restive crowd gathered at the Old Town Square to demonstrate in favor of the prisoners. Jan Hus, together with a few masters and students, appeared at the town hall to put in a good word for the young men, proclaiming that it was actually he who was responsible for their deeds. The cunning town councillor assured him that the prisoners would be treated gently, but as soon as he had left, the three young men were marched out of the prison and beheaded. It was the first blood shed in the Hussite revolution.

The townspeople in the square put the corpses on white linen (later adversaries of the Hussites suggested that pious "*begutae*" licked blood from the cobblestones) and carried them in solemn procession through the Old Town to the Bethlehem chapel, where a fiery young preacher intoned the "Isti sunt martyres" ("These are martyrs"). Soon, a militant squad of armed church loyalists attacked the Bethlehem chapel but was repulsed by the virtually bare-handed followers of Hus; King Václav IV, who wanted peace, told Hus to leave town. A royal commission convened to negotiate between the factions failed miserably, and the king, in a curious decision, then exiled four of Hus's most bitter enemies, doctors of theology, ordering them to leave Prague and Bohemia and to cease disturbing the peace at once (most of them went to Moravia). But Prague did not quiet down, and the exiled Hus, living under the protection of Czech nobles at the castles of Kozí and Krakovec, used the opportunity to preach to the country people and to write his most important theological and moral essays in Latin and Czech.

The accusations leveled against Hus by Archbishop Zbyněk, his onetime friend and ally, in a document presented to the Roman Curia in 1410, triggered investigations and proceedings that continued, as it were, on their own, independent of the incumbent pontiffs and cardinals entrusted with the matter, in this respect strongly resembling Kafka's court, ever awake even if apparently dormant, and always watching the Prague lawyer K. The Curia worked with all possible speed (a papal order signed in December arrived in Prague only in March, due to snows on the Alpine passes); the commissions were able to rely on denunciatory information submitted from Prague by the Czech priest Jan Protiva, the local inquisitor, Maurice Rvačka, and the odious Michal, a Prague parish priest who made it his true vocation to denounce Hus in the most strident terms (he was called "de Causis" because of his zeal for legal procedures). Considering the vulnerability of the Roman hierarchy in the years of the schism, the Curia was surprisingly successful and violent in fighting Hus's allies when they began arriving in Italy for various reasons; Jan of Jesenice was imprisoned and barely escaped; Štěpán Páleč, once the fellow student closest to Jan Hus and shortly to be one of his main accusers, was arrested and robbed of his belongings by Cardinal Baldassarre Cossa (soon to be Pope John XXIII). By the time of the indulgences controversy, the Prague "heresy" had become an international problem: the famous Paris theologian Jean Gerson admonished Archbishop Zbyněk to proceed against the sinners, and the pope wrote to King Václav IV in similar terms. Something had to be done. When Sigismund—Václav's half brother and heir presumptive, king of Hungary and, since 1411, Roman king as well, a man of large ambitions—prevailed on John XXIII to call a grand council at Constance, on the border of southern Germany and Switzerland, to reform the church, Jan Hus and his ideas were high on the agenda, though not the most pressing business.

Jan Hus went to Constance with hopes and fears, yet strangely, if not naively, believing that he would be able to convince the council by rational discourse that he was not a heretic in light of the Bible. He seems to have assumed that the council would be, essentially, another Bethlehem gathering, more adversarial perhaps but open to argument, and before leaving he prepared two personal statements which he, the excommunicated B.A. from the Bohemian provinces, proposed to present to the world's most famous experts on canon law, trained in Bologna and Paris. He left the castle of Krakovec on October 11, 1414, with a group of friends and escorts in wagons and on horseback, wended his way to Nuremberg and, stared at by friendly crowds, through southern Germany. He reached Constance on November 3 and, together with his friends, took lodging at the house of Fida, a pious widow living on St. Paul's Street. Much has been made of the safe-conduct promised him, in earlier negotiations, by Emperor Sigismund, but the document, delivered to him considerably later, turned out to be a laissez-passer rather than a letter of protection; it is possible that, in the exhilaration of the journey, Hus did not want to concern himself with its exact wording, since the document would have been worthless anyway if the traveler were condemned as a heretic. Sigismund was far more concerned with his political ambitions than with Hus, and when the council asked him to allow Hus to be formally arrested he consented (sending a letter by special messenger). On a pretext, Hus was prompted to leave the widow Fida's house and shifted under guard to the local Dominican monastery (now a luxury hotel), where he was put in a narrow cell close to the cesspool; he promptly came down with a high fever and other ailments. The council did not procrastinate; the pope named a special commission to continue and conclude the investigation of Hus; work began immediately, relying on the documents earlier prepared by Hus's Prague enemies, above all his former buddy Štěpán Páleč and Michal de Causis.

In Constance, Hus's noble Czech and Moravian friends were unwilling to take his arrest idly. Jan of Chlum put up public notices against the flagrant violation of his friend's safe-conduct, Italian guards were bribed to allow letters to pass from Prague to Hus and back (his friend Jakoubek of Stříbro had begun to offer the chalice of wine as well as bread in communion, though Hus advised delay on this practice); and Moravian noblemen, led by Kravař of Lacek, pressured Sigismund to remember his promise that Hus would have a public hearing. At the Dominican monastery, in the meantime, the investigative commission, demanding in vain that Hus submit, confronted him once again with Wyclif's forty-five articles, long condemned, and paraded before him a procession of star witnesses, including Štěpán Páleč and none other than Nicholas Zeiselmeister, the German priest of St. Philip and St. James, who had long felt shortchanged by the proximity to his parish of the Bethlehem chapel and the success of its preacher.

Still, at moments in the late winter of 1415 Hus may have held high hopes of becoming free again. Pope John XXIII, after festively resigning to make way for a new election, tried to escape to his friends in France (he never made it across the Rhine), Hus's Italian guards left to join the fugitive pope, now again merely the fat Neapolitan Baldassarre Cossa, the council was in danger of falling apart, and the Czech and Moravian nobles would have had an easy time of organizing a commando raid to save their man. Yet the council's bureaucratic machinery went on functioning; after an evening without guards, Hus was taken by local soldiers to Gottlieben, the castle of the bishop of Constance, where he could move more freely by day but was chained to the wall by night (Baldassarre Cossa was imprisoned there too in early June). The council and Christianity were without a pope for the time being, the investigating commission had to be changed to include a number of theological and legal experts, and they all continued to insist that Hus give up the idea of a public hearing, but he persisted. Sigismund, under increasing pressure from the Czech and Moravian nobles, was unable to ignore the demand, and it was decided to shift Hus from the castle of Gottlieben to the Franciscan monastery at Constance, where the public hearings were to be held.

Unfortunately, the hearings were not what Hus had hoped for, but we are lucky that a young Moravian, Peter of Mladenovice (who rode with Hus from Bohemia to Constance and stayed with him to the bitter end), reported about them in a trustworthy account, long and rightly cherished as a unique document in Hussite history. Peter was excluded from the first hearing, but the noise of the chaotic shouting could be heard outside the hall, and it seemed that, once again, Wyclif was on the agenda; only the dean of Cracow University raised his voice to encourage the accused. Peter was present at the second and third hearings, however, chaired by King Sigismund himself on June 7 and 8, 1415. He clearly heard the questions asked by the haughty French Dominican Pierre d'Ailly, who headed the Inquisition at Lille and Tournai, and heard the cries of the prelates unwilling to listen to what Hus wanted to say about the testimony of witnesses and his treatise *De ecclesia* (*About the Church*), passages of which had been torn out of context by his Czech enemies. The procedure was so disorderly that a master from Oxford, otherwise quite reticent, felt it necessary to intervene to guarantee at least a modicum of procedural fairness. The result was predictable, but it cannot be said that the council did not try, for many days, to convince Hus to recant and to abjure his ideas (as interpreted by the learned *doctores*) or at least to accept a prudent face-saving formula. Delegates and older friends came and went, legal statements were tested, but Hus steadfastly refused all offers and suggestions, insisting that he would betray God and "fall into perjury" if he recanted; he knew that submission would be rewarded by lifelong imprisonment in a far-off monastery and would be used by the ecclesiastical and secular hierarchies to destroy the faithful trust of his friends in Bohemia and elsewhere.

The council's final judgment declared Hus to be "a veritable and manifest heretic," to be degraded and delivered up for inevitable punishment to the secular authorities; all his writings, in Latin and in Czech, which few members of the council could have read or understood, were to be burned. After the judgment was passed, the cardinals and bishops prepared for the theatrical scene of degrading the heretic. Hus was first clothed in ceremonial vestments, as if he were to celebrate mass, and then, after another exhortation to submit, the vestments were taken from him one by one while the prescribed curses were uttered. Next, his tonsure was obliterated (there was a short discussion whether to use a razor or scissors, and the scissors won), and a paper hat, eighteen inches high, with images drawn on it of three devils seizing an unfortunate's soul, was put on his head. He was handed over to the secular power, represented by Duke Ludwig of the Palatinate, who in turn formally entrusted him to the executioner and the guards, who marched him off to the place of execution, passing by the cemetery where his books were being burned.

Intent upon finishing the investigation, begun in 1410, the council members had been more eager to demonstrate that their prisoner was a Wyclifite than to listen to his responses, counterarguments, and thoughtful statements. In many theological respects, Hus was not a Wyclifite at all, or an extremely conservative, if not circumspect, one. Unlike many of his more radical Prague friends, he never accepted Wyclif's idea of remanence, and he also did not accept Wyclif's radical idea that bishops and priests "in mortal sin" could not consecrate or baptize; he clung, long before and during the investigations of the council, to the distinctly softer view that sinful bishops and priests might not act "worthily" but what they did was spiritually valid because God was acting through them and they were merely his instruments. The theologians at Constance were possibly more deeply shocked by the full meaning of his largely Wyclifite concept of the church, and his moral opposition to the absolute claims made upon Christian believers by church powers which, he thought, were long alienated from Christ's truth, an opposition strongly nourished by the Czech reform movement of Milič and Matěj. His distinction between the universal church, composed of those predestined by the inscrutable will of God and headed by Christ, and the church militant, made up of the good and the bad ruled by cardinals and the pope, hardly veiled his idea of who was the true head of the church. Ecclesiastical traditionalists and learned theologians had reasons to be disturbed by his insistence that "obedience should be rendered to pope and cardinals as long as they taught the truth according to God's law," and his unshakable belief that all claims and decisions of the church were to be measured against what the Scriptures had to say. When it came to the ultimate choice, Hus sincerely wanted to obey Christ rather than the church, and he calmly held his ground, hoping against hope that the noble assembly would come to understand the veracity of his beliefs.

The place of execution was on the road to Gottlieben (today close to the municipal gasworks) and stank execrably because the burghers used it as a dump for the carcasses of dead animals. Hus prayed, the crowd gawked, the executioner put a rusty chain around his neck and fastened him to an upright pole, put two bundles of wood under his feet and placed other bundles, interspersed with straw, around his body up to his chin. An imperial delegate once again asked Hus to recant; Hus refused, the delegate clapped his hand, and the wood was lit. Hus began to sing aloud, but when the flames blew in his face, he only prayed silently and, after a while, died. The executioners broke his bones and his skull with clubs, received payment from the imperial delegate for his vestments and shoes (usually theirs to sell but thrown into the flames too in order to deprive loyal Bohemians of relics), and carefully searched for his heart, which they put on a sharpened club to "roast" in the flames. Finally, they swept up the ashes, carried them to the Rhine, flowing nearby, and threw them into its waters. It was July 6, 1415.

The Beginnings of Hussite Resistance

When the news from Constance reached Prague and within a few weeks spread through Bohemia and Moravia, friends and foes of Jan Hus gathered to protest the council's sentence or to uphold its legitimacy. Fifty-eight Hussite barons converged on Prague to hold a protest meeting and on September 2 ceremoniously signed and sealed a forceful document that defended Hus and declared that the accusation of heresy had dishonored the entire land; whoever, of whatever station in life, held that there was heresy in Bohemia was "a son of the devil and the father of lies." (Eight copies of the document were sent to Constance with 452 seals affixed.) Three days later, on September 5, fifty-five barons (three had evidently changed their minds) agreed to form a league to defend "the law of Christ," as theologically defined by the masters of Prague University, and a week later the masters, for their part, issued a public statement praising the innocence of Jan Hus. King Václav IV was irresolute, as usual, but it was well known in town that important persons at court favored Hussite ideas and demands, including some of the king's councillors, Queen Sophia (his second wife, another Bavarian princess), and a group of pious women of considerable political influence who had gathered around her, among others, Anna of Frimburg, wife of the master of the mint, Eliška of Kravař, and Anna of Mochov, whose husband had once offered Hus asylum at his castle of Kozí Hrádek.

The Constance council, continuing in session, called the protest of the Hussite League a sorry and grotesque spectacle and demanded that everybody who had signed appear before the cardinals to be investigated. Orthodox opposition against the Hussites stiffened when the council sent Jan Železný, bishop of Litomyšl and an ardent defender of the church, to

Prague (he felt unsafe there, for good reason) to make sure that King Václav's court declare itself unmistakably in its support and that the heretics submit more speedily. A group of fourteen Catholic nobles gathered on October 1, in response to the Hussite League, to declare its loyalty to king, church, and hierarchy, and the archbishop, under pressure from Constance, a month later renewed a strict interdict on Prague—citing, of all reasons, the continued presence there of Jan of Jesenice, Hus's onetime legal adviser and, possibly, organizer of the Hussite League. The archbishop's decree inevitably backfired and, instead of strengthening the Catholic cause, played into the hands of the Hussite clergy. Since masses were not to be celebrated in Prague or sacraments administered, the Hussite clergymen, supported by demonstrative townspeople, immediately moved into the churches and took over the parishes, freely preaching and offering communion *sub utraque specie*—that is, giving both bread and wine to the communicants. The Catholic clergy was forced to seek refuge in the suburbs and orthodox Christians walking there were called "Mohammedans" by the Prague Hussites because, it was said, they were going from Mecca to Medina. The conflict was not made less corrosive by reports from Constance that the council had arrested Master Jeroným of Prague, a flamboyant and tremendously gifted ally and friend of Hus, and tried him for heresy too. Jeroným first recanted, then, in his own melodramatic way, recanted his recantation, and died in Constance at the stake on May 30, 1416.

Among the close friends of Hus and the masters of the university, Jakoubek of Stříbro emerged as the most energetic adversary of the Constance council and for some time the undisputed leader of the Hussite reform movement. He was a saintly and often stubborn man of wide-ranging ideas on divinity and politics and faced the uneasy task of keeping together the many factions of the movement, from the conservatives who hoped for an ultimate conciliation with church and emperor to the radicals impatient to break with pope and emperor as soon as possible. Howard Kaminsky, an American historian, believes that the Hussites would not have survived the onslaught of their many enemies had Jakoubek not tried to define a middle course, often against himself. His personal views were radical, yet he felt the necessity not to alienate the more traditional Hussites in the baronial league and among his university colleagues. The chronology of his training runs almost parallel to that of Hus, who was fond of calling him "Kuba," but he differed intellectually from his friend by his early commitment to the native ideas of Matěj of Janov. Returning to the Ur-church, as Matěj and Wyclif had done, Jakoubek had rediscovered, or was prompted to rediscover, the tradition of the Eucharist *sub utraque specie* and first began, against Hus's hesitations, to offer the parishioners communion in the shape of simple bread and wine at the Church of St. Martin in the Wall; Hussite priests at the churches of St. Michael, of the Old Town, and of St. Vojtěch followed his example. The Constance council declared this to be heretical in 1415, and the Hussite movement made a chalice its first symbol, proudly showing it on its standards.

Jakoubek was not a tribune of the people, and he increasingly disliked those of his clerical brethren willing or even eager to exercise worldly power more legitimately represented by the king, town, university, or Hussite gentry. He was a scholar who had to speak and act politically; he seems to have lacked the popular appeal of Jan Hus, whom he also succeeded at the pulpit at the Bethlehem chapel, and only later in life he shifted to writing in Czech rather than in his accustomed and scholarly Latin. Though Jakoubek was resolute in defending the most radical demands of Matěj of Janov and Wyclif, in practice he disliked the sectarian and outlandish beliefs often adopted on the Hussite left; when the radicals did away with most of the mass and elected their own bishop, irrevocably breaking with the church, Jakoubek openly resisted the move for both theological and pragmatic reasons. At one time, the radicals dominant in Prague forced him to leave town to repent under the supervision of radical priests, and a few revolutionaries may have even conspired to kill him, but he died peacefully on August 10, 1429, back in Prague and among his friends and disciples, still unwavering in his willingness to bring together the diverse followers of his friend Jan Hus. He did not want to see Bohemia totally alienated from shared Christian traditions.

Prague Attracts the European Dissidents

The stories about the life and death of Jan Hus and his friend Jeroným, as well as the strongly organized Bohemian opposition against the Constance council and the Roman church, made Prague a wondrous haven for European dissidents, seekers of truth, itinerant prophets, and religious visionaries. The Holy Inquisition had closed its Prague office in 1415 (it was reopened two centuries later), and while the university had long attracted dissident theologians from Saxony and elsewhere in Germany (never mind the decree of Kutná Hora) there were also other newcomers, individuals from England and an entire group from France, seeking asylum, an opportunity to join the good fight, or simply wanting to live in peace in a new Christian world. In the Bohemian provinces, radicals often combined Hussite ideas with much older habits of protest against the church and social authority. Long-submerged ideas of a Christian fundamentalism, originally ascribed to the Lyon merchant Peter Waldes, appeared among the Hussites of southern Bohemia, and recent scholarship assumes that the Czechs learned about Waldensian attitudes and ideas (for instance, the denial of purgatory and the unwillingness to take any oath) from German-speaking peasants living along the Austrian-Bohemian border and long persecuted, for their heresies, by the flying courts of the Inquisition. In the southern Bohemian forests, little communities of Adamites were established but quickly destroyed—the men, women, and children killed—by radical Hussites who were revolutionaries but also deeply puritan. Their legendary military leader Jan Žižka reported to Prague that these bestial people believed that God resided in each and every one of them, went about naked or nearly so, danced orgiastically around their fires, and made love when and with whom they wanted. The women tore off the men's loincloths and screamed, "Let out your prisoner, give me your soul, and accept mine!"

Peter of Dresden and Friedrich Eppinge, the first German or rather Saxon dissidents from the Dresden school of the Holy Spirit, came or returned to Prague in 1411, even before Hus had broken with King Václav IV, and were given refuge at the house of the Black Rose on Příkopy, the center of the Bohemian "nation" at Prague University. (Ultranationalist interpreters of the Hussite movement have yet to deal with the ready welcome the Czech masters extended to their German colleagues.) Of Peter of Dresden not much can be said for certain; he was among the early defenders of communion "in both kinds" with communicants being offered the chalice as well as the bread; when he later went on a missionary voyage to Germany, as did so many of his brethren, he was arrested by the Inquisition and put to death. Friedrich Eppinge, who was personally close to Hus, publicly defended Hus's ideas about the need to study Wyclifite writings in depth before judging his ideas, but he died in 1412 and was not alive to support his friend in the difficult times thereafter. After Eppinge's death, Master Nicholas of Dresden emerged as the most important and active theologian of the Black Rose school; he was possibly better qualified than any of his friends to grasp fully the complexities of the Prague situation. He was first trained in Dresden but had studied at Prague University since 1400 and may have heard Hus's sermons at the

Bethlehem chapel in 1402; as Amadeo Molnár suggests in his story of the Waldensian movement, Nicholas had independently studied the history of the church and at Wildungen, in Germany, had offered communion *sub utraque specie* on his own because he believed that it was essential to accept what Christ had done at the Last Supper.

Czech, German, and American scholars of Nicholas and his unusual fate must confront the question whether he was actually a Hussite or a Waldensian, or both. He certainly was a highly gifted theologian and Latin writer and, after the death of Hus, the only person in Prague to compete intellectually with Jakoubek; it is not surprising that for a few years Jakoubek and Nicholas, the Czech and the German, closely collaborated in defining the shared heritage of Hus. Jakoubek, who had to keep in mind his allies among the nobles, the masters, and the patriciate, was eager to temper his radical leanings with appropriate qualifications and pragmatic recommendations, but Nicholas was not burdened by second thoughts about the local political situation or by a need to soften his views. The parting of the ways came, as has been suggested, after the Hussite League was formed in the early fall of 1415—Jakoubek fully aware of the inevitable and practical boundaries of his radical theory, Nicholas now going far beyond Hussite ideas to involve himself in a new belligerence, more than once tinged by a Waldensian fundamentalism which he may have learned earlier in Germany; his total aversion to the idea of purgatory, to the taking of any oath, and to making any distinctions between priests and bishops was unacceptable to the university masters. Jakoubek and his allies wanted a constitutional structure of religion and political life in Bohemia, but Nicholas, not bound by loyalty to the king of Bohemia, lived and was to die for a permanent Christian revolution beyond the confines of any one country. The masters, and Jakoubek, must have felt relieved when he went to Germany in 1416, possibly to work for a union of Hussites and Waldensians. He fell into the hands of the Inquisition, and was burned at the stake in Meissen in 1417.

By that time, the increasing tension between moderates and radicals weighed heavily on the minds of the Prague University masters, and the Prague burgrave, Čeněk of Wartenberk, believed it was necessary to ordain young and older priests to strengthen the cause and to integrate those with Waldensian leanings more fully. The archbishop, loyal to the Roman church, could not be approached in the matter, so Čeněk, being a man of action, simply kidnapped one of the archbishop's assistants, brought him to the castle of Lipnice, and told him to ordain the candidates gathered there, including a few German Hussites from the Black Rose.

Among them was Bartholomäus Rautenstock, who first preached to a group of Prague German Hussites but later lived in a little town near the Bohemian border under the protection of the Hussites, and traveled through Germany in the manner of itinerant Waldensian preachers. His friend Johannes Drändorf, of a rich family but choosing voluntary poverty in the name of Christ, was first trained in Saxony and left with the dissidents in 1411 to study at the Black Rose for ten years. He too was ordained at Lipnice, preached in Prague, and was sent to southern Bohemia to work among the German peasants there; long of Waldensian persuasion, he went on missionary trips to Germany like many of his brethren. Peter Turnow, another dissident theologian at the Black Rose, originally came from East Prussia and Saxony, but he left Prague in 1414 for Bologna, where he studied for a while before going on to Greece, then returning via Venice to Prague, much changed by 1423. He wrote a treatise on the rites and teachings of the Greek Orthodox Church, of great interest to his Prague Hussite brethren, and went to teach in Germany too. The Inquisition had been watching these German Hussites closely and, unable to lay hands on them while they worked in Bohemia, caught up with them when they came to preach in Germany. Rautenstock, Drändorf, and Turnow were executed in 1425, but in different German towns. In spite of its medieval bureaucracy, the Holy Inquisition worked quite efficiently.

The English connection had been established early by Czech students and docents who trained at Oxford and brought Wyclif back to Prague; English Wyclifites, materially and politically supported by the magnanimous Sir John Oldcastle, sent copies of Wyclif's treatises to Prague to replace the ones that Archbishop Zbyněk had burned. Among the admirers of Wyclif and Sir John was Peter Payne, the principal of St. Edmund Hall, Oxford, who was investigated for his links to Sir John and accused of sedition and high treason; Sir John managed to escape from the Tower of London and hide in the countryside, and Payne left England for Germany, where he was welcomed by the Waldensians; later, after Sir John had been imprisoned again to be executed, Payne went to Prague, where he was welcomed among the masters and taught at the Black Rose. Payne, called "Master English" by his new Prague friends, supported Jakoubek in his earliest fight for the chalice and was quickly entrusted with high functions in which his Wyclifite learning, his disinclination to identify fully with the radicals, as well as his international perspective were of importance. He had difficulties learning Czech and spoke Latin with a strong Oxford accent, yet he was put in charge of important embassies to the court of Poland, to Emperor Sigismund, to the Council of Basel, to

Romania, and, in his old age, to Constantinople; he clearly served the Hussite cause loyally as its minister of foreign affairs. Payne survived all revolutionary changes, wars, and tiring disputations (often lasting three days and longer), and died peacefully in Prague in about 1456 in the Monastery of the Slavs, founded by King Charles IV.

In 1418, the people of Prague were astonished to see a group of Christians from the north of France arrive in town—fewer than fifty men with their wives and children. It turned out they had been persecuted by the church and had chosen to come to Bohemia, where the word of God was more freely preached than anywhere else. They were welcomed and assisted by Queen Sophia and her women and a few rich people, who visited them to dispense help; the difficulty was that nobody spoke their language and they had among them only a man trained in Latin (*vir latinus*) who read to them from Scripture in their own idiom. However, people soon noticed that the newcomers had strange religious habits. They did not go to church often, did not take communion *sub utraque specie* or were outright indifferent to the Eucharist; the university masters would have been even more dumbfounded if they had been fully aware that these "Picardians" (as they called them) did not believe in the virginity of Mary or in the divinity of Christ, and had totally broken with the doctrine and rites of the church. People in Prague were suspicious, and a moderate Hussite chronicler suggested they were actually "wild wolves in the disguises of sheep." Ultimately the unwelcome guests left town—nobody really knew when and how—but some of their ideas survived for many years with the Hussites in the countryside and on distant mountains and in remote valleys of Bohemia. It is even less clear whether Gilles Mersault, a cloth cutter from Tournai, came with them then or only two years later, when the Prague radicals were in the ascendancy. But he took it upon himself to return to his Christian brothers at Tournai and Lille to inform them about Hussite Prague, and distributed his own samizdat leaflets at night, challenging the church authorities. He was arrested, tried for heresy, and burned at the stake in 1423.

The Revolt of the Prague Radicals

Increasing international pressure exerted by the church and by Emperor Sigismund threatened the Hussites' advances just at the time when their attitude and doctrines began distinctly to diverge. Hussite conservatives and moderates, mostly in Prague, and radicals, mostly in the countryside but with an important stronghold in the New Town, tried to patch up the divergences in theoretical disputes and many meetings, for there was danger of military intervention from abroad. A royal attempt to restore the old order, as the church demanded, noticeably failed in the fall of 1416, yet the enmity of the church was unchanged, and the university masters had good reasons to reaffirm their alliance with the Hussite nobles, who were, however, disturbed by the actions and doctrines of the Hussite left emerging so forcefully in the countryside.

The trouble was that King Václav IV feared that his half brother Sigismund, heir presumptive to the Bohemian throne, who had begun to negotiate with Czech Catholic nobles, would supplant him with the help of the church. So he once again revised his policies in order to show that he did not want to tolerate religious unrest. He sent ambassadors to Rome and to Sigismund, and in 1419 issued a number of decrees suggesting that he meant business. The Catholic parish priests returned with a vengeance, or so it seemed to the Hussite parishioners. They started to clean the churches and wash the altars as if they had been infected by the plague, little choirboys had to repent if they had served the Hussites, members of the reform movement were excluded from the celebration of mass, and extreme unction was refused dying Hussites unless they recanted their beliefs. After the Prague towns lodged a protest at court, King Václav IV relented a little, once again saying that he wanted only peace; he confirmed that communion *sub utraque specie* was to be offered in eight places, among them St. Ambrose, St. Mary of the Snows (in the New Town), and St. Benedict (in the Old Town). This was not enough to placate the ire of the people. Reform was turning to revolt and revolution, and while Jakoubek and the masters fell silent, unwilling as ever to break totally with legitimate secular authority, Jan Želivský, a preacher at St. Mary of the Snows who actively sympathized with the rural radicals, quickly emerged as the first political leader of Prague's Hussite left.

In the countryside, peasants, craftsmen, and their preachers left their villages and small towns (especially after the churches had been restored to the returning Catholic priests) and began to assemble en masse on mountains and hills to hear the word of God and to receive communion *sub utraque specie*. The Hussites were particularly strong in the south, at Ústí on the Lužnice River, Písek, and near Bechyně, and they gathered demonstratively at Easter 1419 on a hill called Tábor, after the place where Christ transfigured had appeared to three of his disciples (Matthew 17: 1–8). Chroniclers say that they "built tents in the manner of a chapel" and held services, the men separate from the women and children, divided among themselves the food they had brought, serenely and calmly addressed one another as brother and sister; gaming, drinking, dancing, and dicing were severely frowned on. Later, other groups gathered on hills they called Mount Horeb or Mount Olivet, and as young preachers, the disciples of the Prague masters, exhorted the crowds to resist the royal decrees, evangelical love of peace rapidly gave way to new belligerence, a growing enmity to the Prague masters, and adventist and chiliast ideas of the coming of the Lord to change the world once and for all. On July 22, 1419, a mass meeting was held on Tábor Hill of tens of thousands of enthusiastic and armed radicals from all regions of Bohemia and Prague, especially the New Town. The militants were out in force, and it is more than probable that among the assembled preachers was Jan Želivský, eager for political resistance and discussion of a plan to rise against the king, or at least by limited action to signal that the moment of rebellion was near.

On Sunday morning, July 30, a week later, people of the Prague Hussite community gathered at St. Mary of the Snows to hear Jan Želivský preach and, once again, to march through the streets in procession to defend the chalice, though the town magistrate had forbidden street demonstrations; many of them carried weapons in case they should meet any opposition. Želivský first preached a provocative sermon on a text from St. John's Revelation, lamenting the fall of Prague and calling for punishment of the unjust (the notes for his sermon have been preserved); then, holding the Eucharist high in his hands, he led a procession up along the Horse Market (now Wenceslas Square), turned into Štěpánská Ulice and onto St. Stephen, where mass was being celebrated by a priest of the order of the Knights of the Cross with the Red Star. The demonstrators broke down the door and chased away the priest, nearly tore the building down and held their own simple service; this being done, the demonstrators turned down the street, quickly reached the hall of the New Town, and demanded that the councillors release the prisoners recently arrested in street violence. It was 9:30 a.m., and the councillors who, together with a few anti-Hussite burghers, had locked the portal talked to the crowd from the windows above and angered the demonstrators. One chronicle has it that they threw stones, one of which hit Želivský's monstrance (the same reason given many years before when mobs had invaded the Jewish quarter).

Historians still discuss the question whether Jan Žižka, later the strategist of the Hussite army, was in the crowd by chance or by intention; at any rate, the crowd stormed the tower, took the aldermen and threw them from the high windows down to the square. Those who did not die when they fell onto the lances and pikes were finished off by clubs, swords, and knives, and their corpses were disfigured; it was said that Jan Želivský stood by with the monstrance held high, urging the killers on. Twelve or thirteen men died, among them the New Town burgomaster and a few councillors and patricians; one man was killed in the torture chamber of the town prison. A royal subchamberlain led three hundred cavalry from Hradčany Castle to intervene but arrived too late and immediately withdrew from the superior mass of Hussite demonstrators. A proclamation was issued by the insurgents, four urban directors were speedily elected to administer town business, men of means and not necessarily Želivský's followers, and the seal and chains of office taken from the killed councillors were duly delivered to these newly elected magistrates; royal councillors of Hussite sympathies tried to persuade King Václav (when in his first rage he threatened to kill all the Wyclifites) that he should forgive what had happened. The king complained of pains in his left hand, was unable to take communion because he could no longer swallow, and died of a stroke on August 16, 1419, roaring like a lion, contemporaries assure us.

The death of the king a few days after the brutal revolt of Jan Želivský's radicals in the New Town raised anxious questions about the future of Bohemia and the course of the reform movement; in Prague, the conflict between those seeking a constitutional resolution and the radicals who were willing to trust their visionary preachers more than the learned university masters spilled out into the streets immediately. In the early morning after the king's death, unruly crowds, among them the poorest people of the Prague towns, roamed through the streets, devastating churches and chapels almost at random, destroying paintings, organs, and relics. In the afternoon, they set out over the stone bridge to turn their rage against the church and the monastery of the Carthusians, who had been tipped off and were trying in vain to save their books and treasures. The rebellious mob broke into the church, tore up the pictures of Christ and the saints, dispersed the relics, invaded the monastery to ransack its reserves of food, clothes, and wine, and forced the assembled monks to march to the Old Town as a column of prisoners. Dire threats were uttered, especially when the monks dragged themselves over the stone bridge, yet nobody was really hurt, and the priests and monks were delivered into the hands of the Old Town magistrates, who, after some delay, again marched them off, under military guard, to a Cistercian monastery in the countryside.

Not all the crowds had left the Carthusian monastery, though. They continued reveling through the night and the next day set the buildings on fire. One of the men, totally drunk, had clothed himself in church vestments, but aldermen arrested him for blasphemy and immediately put him to death. The magistrate in charge was possibly more concerned with political negotiations than with the violence in the street, and the aldermen did not intervene when lusty crowds plundered the Jewish Town on August 19 and turned against the Prague bordellos in the Old (Hampejz) and the New Town (Krakov). (Today's Krakovská Street, right off Wenceslas Square, reveals nothing of its boisterous past.) The crowds drove out the madams and the women, set fire to the buildings, and literally tore down the houses in the red-light districts. On September 1 the people were angry again (over rumors about a confrontation with Sigismund), invaded the monasteries of St. Francis, so gloriously founded by St. Anežka, and of the Holy Spirit and drove out the nuns, but without doing bodily harm to anyone. In the provinces, excited crowds began to attack and destroy churches and monasteries as their brethren had done in Prague, especially in Plzeň (Pilsen), where the Dominican monastery was devastated; at other places too, churches of the Dominicans, the "hounds of God," were among the first to be attacked.

The fall of 1419 was a season of troubling unrest and incipient civil war. The Hussite moderates, led by Čeněk of Wartenberk, burgrave of Prague, once again prepared for negotiations with King Sigismund, while radicals inside and outside Prague exerted their own political pressure by continuing the mass meetings; an effort to call these meetings on mountains ever nearer to Prague revealed something of their strategic intentions. On September 7, they congregated on Bzí Mountain, and two weeks later at U Křížků (At the Crosses), close to the road leading to Prague, where they listened to the radical preacher Václav Koranda; a big group of country and town radicals marched on to Prague and passed through the gates of the Vyšehrad without difficulty. The guests were welcomed to lodge at the cloister of St. Ambrose, in the New Town, and the next meeting was scheduled for Prague itself in early November. The radical guests promptly devastated the Church of St. Michael, in the Old Town (the radical Koranda had an ax to grind with its moderate priest), but open conflict between factions was postponed. The burgrave, wanting peace in order to be able to negotiate with Sigismund from a position of strength, increased the number of troops at Hradčany Castle and the Vyšehrad; this promptly triggered a violent counteraction by the New Town crowds, which on October 25 stormed the Vyšehrad. If all the Hussites from the countryside had reached Prague for the scheduled meeting of early November, Hradčany Castle (where the widow of the king still resided) and the moderates would have been in grave danger, but a commando of Sigismund loyalists ambushed the radicals approaching Prague from the south in a bloody attack. However, many radicals from western and northeastern Bohemia had reached Prague in the meantime, expecting the meeting to take place, and they immediately attacked the royal positions, guarding the stone bridge at the Minor Town, so that radicals could cross the bridge to either the Old or the New Town. In the course of three days and nights, November 4–6, much of the Minor Town was destroyed in a pitched battle between royalists and radicals; for the first time in Prague, artillery pieces, mostly fired from Hradčany Castle, were used. The Minor Town and the stone bridge were of importance for any river crossing: royalists and radicals clashed at the very point where, two hundred years later, in 1648, the Swedes, in the last battle of the Thirty Years' War, kept trying to cross the bridge into the heart of Prague.

The Hussite crowds first attacked the fortified dwellings on both sides of the bridge tower, the palace of the archbishop and the so-called Saxon House, and forced the royalists to withdraw to the castle, leaving their horses and weapons behind. Church bells rang all night; the queen decided to leave and handed over power, for all practical purposes, to burgrave Čeněk. The next day, a Sunday morning, the Hussites attended mass but in the afternoon marched against Minor Town royalists who, after setting fire again to many buildings, retreated once more while the Hussites savaged the archbishop's palace. On November 6, about four thousand more Hussites from the south who had survived the ambush crossed the river Sázava, near Prague, and were enthusiastically welcomed in the Old and the New Town; the royalists massed new troops at the castle and in regions outside Prague. The warring factions, now aware of a stalemate of forces, agreed to an armistice to extend to the spring of the following year; the burgrave and his party, pledged to respect Hussite religious practices and "the community of Prague," was to refrain from further attacks on churches and monasteries and, voluntarily, return the Vyšehrad to the royal troops. The provincial radicals, feeling *de trop*, angrily left town but not before burning the rest of the Minor Town; they marched off to Plzeň, which now became the center of radical resistance. Increasingly, violence was answered by violence; in Catholic Kutná Hora, the mostly German miners were eager to take Hussite prisoners, not only clergy but also artisans and peasants. They tortured and decapitated them or flung them alive into the deep mine shafts; if a Catholic baron wanted to get rid of Hussite prisoners, he could sell them to Kutná Hora to be taken care of. More than 1,600 people perished in that way.

Holding court in the capital of Moravia, Brno (Brünn), Sigismund first refrained from revealing the full intensity of his feelings about the "Wyclifites," but, moving to Breslau, in Silesia, he made his views perfectly clear. Upon his wish, Pope Martin V had issued a bull against the Bohemian heretics and had invited all Christians to join a crusade against the Hussites; even before the bull had been read from the pulpits of the Breslau churches, Jan Krása, a patrician Prague merchant visiting the Breslau fair who did not hide his Hussite ideas, was denounced to the church authorities and, after he had refused to recant, by Sigismund's order was dragged through the streets by four horses and burned. The Bohemians had little to hope for, as far as Sigismund was concerned, and even less to negotiate about. In Prague, Jan Želivský preached belligerent sermons, and in the countryside, fired by visionary priests who spoke of the coming of the revenging Lord, the peasants sought protection in towns dominated by Hussites.

In the south, the radical Hussites left Ústí, at the Lužnice River, when it became militarily untenable, and established a new, fortified settlement not far away. They laid siege to the castle of Hradiště, returned it to its rightful lord, *sub utraque specie*, and founded, on the fundaments of an older village, a new community called Tábor again. It attracted peasants, artisans, and radical gentry from all over the region and quickly gained in strength and respect when the radical Hussites and Jan Žižka, leaving Plzeň to the royalists, marched south and joined the brethren and sisters at the new place. Being the New Jerusalem of radical and militant Hussites, Tábor was run by priests eager to denounce and persecute deviationists on the right and left, and by military commanders in charge of several thousand soldiers; even though the early communism of "common chests" did not survive for long, Táborite religious fervor lived on in many shapes and forms for centuries—even though the Tábor armies were defeated by moderate Hussites in 1434 and never reasserted their might in the field again.

The Crusaders Arrive: The Battle on Žižka's Hill

The announcement of the crusade and the death of the Prague merchant Jan Krása in Breslau made the situation more volatile than ever, with

Catholics scurrying for protection and Hussites girding for the ultimate battle. The Catholic clergy, high and low, and well-to-do patricians, many of them German, as well as a few conservative town councillors, ran for cover to the royal castles at Hradčany and the Vyšehrad, which they thought to be more secure; the Hussites, on April 3, 1420, gathered at the Old Town hall to take a solemn oath to defend the chalice against all enemies, reminded everybody of the "ancient Czech forefathers and St. Wenceslas," and ordered that a long, deep ditch be dug to defend the New Town against royalists from the Vyšehrad. Work on the ditch lasted for five days, and even the Jews, the chroniclers remarked, participated in the common enterprise.

On April 15, the burgrave Čeněk of Wartenberk, who had long hoped to negotiate, returned from Breslau, where he had had a chance to watch the emperor at close range and, to the great joy of the Hussites, organized a revolt of his own: after taking command of Hradčany Castle he arrested all Catholic priests who had sought refuge there, drove out the patricians and their families (keeping their possessions), and assured the town councillors that he was on their side, commanding the castle in the name of the Hussites.

Čeněk as a politician was good on momentary decisions but rather irresolute in being loyal to himself. Perhaps he was horrified by news from the provinces, where his new radical allies had attacked royal castles, killing and burning, or perhaps his feudal mind was disturbed by the newfangled demands made by the lower gentry, burghers, artisans, and peasants. In any case, three weeks after he had declared himself against the emperor, he abruptly reversed himself and tried to negotiate a private deal with Sigismund. Čeněk suggested that he and his family be granted the privilege of communion "in both kinds" for life, and handed over the castle to two royalist nobles closer to Sigismund, who was to arrive soon.

The Prague crowds were enraged by Čeněk's betrayal and on May 8 immediately tried to storm Hradčany Castle, but they succeeded only in breaking through one of the outer gates. They were ineffectively organized, and while Čeněk made his exit out one of the back doors (not the first or last resident of Hradčany to do so), the royalist regulars repulsed the Hussites, who suffered heavy losses and withdrew to Strahov, burning the ancient monastery there and destroying its ancient art treasures. For strategic reasons, the Hussites decided to move all the inhabitants of the Minor Town elsewhere and, after the people had left, carrying with them their few belongings (the Catholics going to the castle, the Hussites to the

Old and New Towns), set fire to the church of St. Mary Under the Chain (of the Knights of St. John), to the chapel, still standing, in the archbishop's devastated palace, to the parish church of St. Nicholas, and to those Minor Town dwellings that were still intact; it was a vigorous application of scorched-earth policy. The mood of Prague was somber and adamant, and as the crusaders drew closer under the command of Sigismund, many Bohemian nobles and knights, committed more deeply to legitimacy than to the Hussite cause, formally renounced their allegiance to the defenders of Prague. These last appealed for military help to all Hussite towns and, in the south, to the well-organized army of Tábor. Allies from Hradec Králové, the so-called Horebites (because they gathered on a hill which, quoting the Bible, they called Horeb), were already in Prague, and the Táborites—men, women, and children on horses and on their wagons—reached the city by May 20, again enthusiastically welcomed by the clergy and the crowds; the Táborite women were lodged at St. Ambrose, now a regular guest barracks for visiting groups from the provinces, and the men in tents on a large island in the river near the Poříč Gate. Other armed Hussite groups from Žatec, Louny, and Slané followed. There was some irritation when these rough country allies, disgusted by Prague elegance, accosted some of the townspeople, pulling their mustaches, cutting off the virgins' braids, tearing apart the ladies' elaborate veils. Their commanders told them to relent, and fifteen hundred Táborite women began to dig yet a new defense ditch against the Vyšehrad, stretching from the river up to the Church of St. Catherine. They started, it seems, with the church itself, taking apart its roof first and then working their way down.

To confirm the ideological unity of the defenders of Prague, a shared (minimum) platform was defined (later known as the famous Four Prague Articles); it included "the ministering of the body and blood of the Lord to the laity in both kinds," the "free preaching of the word of God," the demand that "all priests, from the pope on down, should give up their pomp, avarice, and improper lordship," and the "purgation of and cessation from all public mortal sins" (an article clearly directed against the Babylonian mores of Prague). The Hussites also agreed on a number of stringent security measures that have a distinctly modern flavor, trying, as they did, to prevent the emergence of a fifth column. Hussite delegates visited all families not known to take communion *sub utraque specie* and offered them the choice of accepting the chalice or of leaving; the historian V. V. Tomek believes that among those who left Prague at that time were at least seven hundred well-to-do German Catholics in whose houses soldiers lodged. Wives and children of men who had left earlier were also asked to go unless they showed good reason that they were above suspicion. All people in town, except those in the Jewish district, had to affirm formally that they were ready and willing to fight the enemy, and committees were formed which investigated people of doubtful allegiance. Those who had to go were not hurt bodily, but Táborites were quick to strike back demonstratively in response to royalist terror in the provinces. When royalists killed prisoners at Slané and drowned seventeen Hussites at Litoměřice (Leitmeritz), the Táborites retaliated in full view of Hradčany Castle: four men, two of them monks, were burned in front of the castle walls, and a few days later four more Cistercian monks who had fallen into Hussite hands. Royalists and Hussites fired at each other, the royalists from Hradčany with artillery pieces, the Hussites stationed at Pohořelec mostly with catapults. The battle for Prague was near.

In early July, the armies of the crusaders—a motley crew of Germans from Meissen, Austrians, Silesians, Hungarians, and 16,000 royalist Czechs—surrounded Prague on three sides. Both Sigismund and Jan Žižka, commander in chief of the combined Hussite forces, inevitably had to turn their attention to the long, narrow Vítkov Hill, which dominated access to Prague from the east. This access was still open, which made it possible to provide the defenders of Prague with sufficient provisions (only salt slightly rose in price during the siege). On July 13, Sigismund had a small force probe the readiness of the Hussites and sent a few detachments of cavalry to the so-called Hospital Fields (now Karlín) at the bottom of Vítkov Hill; the result showed the Hussites were ready; and he scheduled the beginning of the operation for Sunday afternoon, July 14, at 5 p.m., leaving only four or five daylight hours to fight what was to be a decisive battle. He stationed his reserves along the left bank of the river, where Bubeneč and Holešovice extend today, and ordered a strong army of Meissners, Austrians, Hungarians, and a battalion of Silesians to take Vítkov Hill. The tough and inventive Jan Žižka had fortified the hill as effectively as possible in a relatively short time. There were three ditches, the last of which was reinforced by a strong wall, a few bunkers of timber and stone, and an old vineyard tower, all ready to be defended by Táborites, including a few fighting women. A synchronized attack against all of their defense lines was well within the possibilities of the crusaders, and it would have created terrible difficulties, but the emperor wanted Vítkov first without engaging Hussite forces elsewhere. It was not his only blunder.

The crusaders rode up the hill on the most easily accessible southeastern side (where Libeň and Vysočany are today). At the ridge, they crossed the first and second ditches without difficulty and seized the old vineyard tower. It was more troublesome to deal with the reinforced third ditch and the blockhouses, which would have been easier to take by foot soldiers; the defenders, among them two women and a girl, fought tenaciously with pitchforks and stones to the end, and one of the dying women was remembered for her last words, that a true Christian would never cede to the force of the Antichrist. It was a decisive moment: the cavalry attack lost its drive, Žižka appeared with a small group of his men, and time was gained for the defenders of Prague to send out a strong column of marksmen and people armed with deadly flails to challenge the crusaders from the left. The heavily armed knights were confused by this unexpected counterattack and could move in only one direction. Caught between the blockhouses and the Táborites on the left and the mass of following cavalry columns of their own behind them, they were pressed forward onto the hill's narrow ridge, which did not allow for a broader unfolding of the attack. The knights tried to disengage themselves by riding to the steep, clifflike northern side of the hill. Some of them were killed in the fall, others tried to escape on the more gentle eastern slope and cross the river, but not knowing where the fords were, many drowned in the Vltava waters. The entire engagement, of about a thousand Hussites against an army of crusaders later estimated to be ten or twenty thousand strong, was over within an hour; more than three hundred of the attacking knights died in the field, among them their commander, Heinrich von Isenburg. Sigismund, who had watched the battle from the other side of the river, silently withdrew to his tent and gave no further orders that day. People spoke of Vítkov as Žižka's Hill from that evening on.

The Hussites believed that the emperor would immediately renew the battle, and so they quickly built fortifications, but in the Prague towns the old tensions between radicals and moderates once again intensified, and in the camp of the crusaders individual army groups accused each other of irresponsibility. Sigismund was advised to use artillery against the Prague defenders, but did not want to do so, some saying because the Catholic German patricians in his camp were not eager to see their homes totally destroyed, others believing that he did not want to devastate his own future metropolis. (A few artillery barrages were fired from Letná Hill against his will and did some harm to the Jewish district and the parts of the Old and New Towns along the river.)

Frustration and brutality were the order of the day. Crusaders roamed around the countryside, plundering and burning Czech men, women, and children whether or not *sub utraque specie*, and the victorious defenders, on their part, put sixteen prisoners in barrels and burned them in full view of the emperor's camp. At Hradčany Castle, Sigismund quickly arranged for his coronation as Bohemian king, a strange and fugitive affair attended by a few of his loyalists, and down in Prague the Táborites presented a catalogue of twelve articles to the university masters, listing their traditional demands for more evangelical discipline and Christian modesty. Offended by the citizenry, they once again made preparations for a demonstrative exodus and, in doing so, they destroyed the old Church of St. Paul and St. Peter at the Poříč and, somewhat later, the monasteries of St. Clemens in the Old Town, of the Servites, and of St. Ambrose (mostly demolished by the Táborite women who were lodged there). When the Táborites prepared to take on the Franciscan monastery and Church of St. Jacob, the Old Town butchers mobilized, took out their long knives and axes, and prevented further destruction. In other cases, the aldermen were sufficiently ingenious to employ effective ruses; the Gothic Church of St. Francis was made an arsenal, the Dominican nunnery of St. Anne was used to house nuns exiled from other places (they each had to take the Eucharist *sub utraque specie*), and the church and monastery of the Holy Spirit were turned over to Prague's German Hussites, congregating there to hear their own preacher in their own language.

Yet there was nobody to prevent the priest Václav Koranda, by now a hard-core radical and experienced Prague hater, from gathering an excited crowd and marching to the noble old Cistercian monastery at Zbraslav, long the burial place of Přemyslid and Luxembourg kings and queens, including Eliška, mother of Charles IV, and, more recently, Václav IV. The crowds did their usual job of plundering and destroying, but also proceeded to pry open the royal tombs and rob the graves. We are told that they put the corpse of King Václav IV, not yet entirely decomposed, on an altar with a crown of straw on his skull, and poured beer over the rotting flesh, saying, "If you had been alive, buddy, you would have been drinking with us anyway!" They left the body there, set fire to the building, and marched back to Prague, parading in monks' habits and sporting broken paintings and fragments of altarpieces as a sign of victory. Jan Želivský, the Táborites' most reliable ally, engineered another revolt in the Old Town, but the Táborites, sensitive as ever to theological niceties, were disappointed by the university masters and left town once again.

Landmarks and Battlefields of Hussite Prague

The Battle for the Vyšehrad and the Death of Jan Želivský

By September 1420 the Prague Hussites felt strong enough to take the Vyšehrad, held by a rugged garrison of Czech and German royalist knights, and they established a military camp high on a nearby hill, looking down on the castle and offering a good view of what was going on inside its walls. Hussites and royalists used artillery and catapults to harass each other; extended artillery duels, often at close range, went on for days and weeks. The Hussites placed one of their cannons in the walls of the Church of St. Mary on the Lawn (which they had destroyed and used as a kind of bunker), but royalist artillerymen responded with considerable precision. Royalists at Hradčany Castle also fired into the Old Town, in support of the Vyšehrad, one missile landing at the fish market, killing five women (one of them pregnant) and a man. Once again, the Prague Hussites appealed to the provinces for help, and allies from Hradec Králové, Louny, and Žatec came by the thousands (but only forty horsemen from Tábor, saying that Tábor could not spare troops at the moment). Hynek Krušina of Lichtenburk, the military leader of the Hussite force, surrounded the Vyšehrad on all sides, cutting off all lines of communication except on the steep side of the Vyšehrad cliff facing the river; military action inevitably concentrated on that spot. The starving garrison of royalists organized a courageous sortie and sent requests to Sigismund, who was roaming the countryside north and east of Prague, for more provisions to be shipped down the river; the Hussites tried to blockade the river and keep boats from slipping through. By the end of October, the situation of the royalist garrison had turned critical; food reserves were exhausted, and Sigismund had sent only fine dispatches about the necessity of holding the fort until he arrived. Jan Šembera of Boskovice, captain of the royalist garrison, met with Hussites to work out a rather complicated agreement to hand over the Vyšehrad on October 31 at 9 a.m., provided that the dearth of provisions continued and that the imperial army did not arrive before that hour. When the agreement was signed, a wonderful rainbow was seen over the river at the Vyšehrad, and the university masters, expert in interpretation, thought that it was a good omen.

Sigismund, who had procrastinated, waiting for his rather self-willed Moravian allies, arrived on the Prague scene on October 31 at noon—that is, three hours too late. The Vyšehrad captain, punctiliously adhering to his agreement with the Hussites, had closed the Vyšehrad gates, declared himself a noncombatant, and even kept his German knights from riding out to support the emperor. Sigismund, with his army of twenty thousand Czechs, Moravians, Germans, and Hungarians, was forced to confront the main Hussite encampment on his own, and in the action his Czech and Moravian knights had to ride across a difficult and swampy terrain while the Germans and Hungarians easily descended from above.

The Prague Hussites first gave way to the heavily armored Germans and Hungarians, who threw them against the walls of a church, but Krušina, appealing to Hussite tenacity, personally led the counterattack. Mikeš Divůšek, a royalist knight, quickly turned to flight with all his men as the Hussites attacked them with deadly flails, tearing into the flesh of horses and men. Again the encounter was short and bloody, like that on Žižka's Hill, and when it was all over, royalist Czechs and Moravians had suffered most. Radical priests gave the order that corpses of the fallen enemy be left in the fields to rot for three days, but many in the Prague army disregarded it. The emperor, who had previously proclaimed that he would "shit into the faces of the Hussites" rather than cede the castle, had to accept the fact that the Vyšehrad garrison had handed over the castle to the Hussites and gone off; for three days or more, the Prague citizens vented their rage on the fallen royalist stronghold, totally disregarding its proud past. First they invaded the chapels and churches to destroy altars, adornments, pictures, and organs; on the next day the dwellings of the prelates were plundered, with people scurrying back and forth between the town and the hill with their spoils; and, lastly, the crowds turned against the palaces of the Czech dukes and kings, leaving them in sad ruins, and tore down, for military reasons, the walls that separated Vyšehrad Castle from the New Town. All the pious efforts of King Charles IV to restore the Vyšehrad to its ancient grandeur were undone. In the absence of the imperial army and on the basis of an agreement with lords and knights, the Prague Hussites occupied Hradčany Castle on June 7, 1421; the invading iconoclasts began to burn paintings and to destroy other works of art, but the worst was prevented by resolute knights and burghers—if they had not intervened, the chronicler (himself a moderate Hussite) remarks, these madmen would have blasphemously destroyed the castle and the cathedral of the Czech patrons.

Whenever dangers ebbed, the conflicts between the Prague moderates and the radicals, allied to Tábor, usually increased. By early 1422, negotiations between the Prague Old Town, mostly moderate if not conservative, and the New Town, mostly radical, were controlled by an administrative group of nineteen men, consisting of many Hussite knights and also Jan Žižka himself. In early March 1422 resistance to Želivský and his faction on the part of the Prague moderates, including the university masters, noticeably stiffened; Master Jakoubek of Stříbro himself presented to the Old Town magistrate an accusation making Jan Želivský responsible for much unrest and the spilling of blood. (Somewhat earlier, the radicals had arrested Jan Sádlo, a Hussite military commander of moderate persuasion, allegedly because of dereliction of duty, and put him to death without a trial.) The Old Town aldermen conspired to get rid of Želivský and his supporters once and for all, and invited him and his most important friends to the town hall on March 9 on the pretext that they wanted to hear his advice about the war. They sweetly pretended to listen to his words, but suddenly the doors swung open, the executioner and his men entered, and the radicals were arrested and put in chains. Jan Želivský behaved with great dignity, knelt down and prayed, confessed to a priest, and, at the head of his group, walked to the courtyard, where all nine men (twelve, according to other reports) were immediately beheaded. His followers had gathered at his church, and it was the blood mixed with water flowing from the town hall gutters into the Old Town Square that revealed to the people what had happened.

Slaughter was answered by slaughter. Surging crowds entered the courtyard and discovered the corpses; and Jan Želivský's severed head was first shown by one of his men from a manure heap on the square to his raging followers and later, in an expression of savage grief, put onto a dish by a priest and carried through the streets of the towns, while church bells rang alarms. Two aldermen were killed immediately, and after a new radical town government had been established, five or six magistrates were discovered, hiding, and put to death, their dwellings ransacked. Želivský's followers then turned against the colleges and university, destroyed the masters' collections of books and much of the university library, and arrested the masters who had not yet escaped. In the traditional ways of the Prague *Lumpenproletariat,* the mob finally invaded the Jewish Town looking for spoils. The arrested masters were exiled to Hradec Králové, where they were supposed to repent under the guidance of radical priests. Jan Želivský was buried under the pulpit of his Church of St. Mary of the Snows; in the funeral oration, interrupted only by the weeping and the sighing of the congregation, his *adlatus* Vilém accused Jakoubek of Stříbro of being fully responsible for the murder of Želivský.

In May, the situation changed abruptly again: the radical aldermen handed over the keys and the insignia of Prague to Prince Sigmund Korybut, who arrived in Prague in the name of his uncle, Grand Duke Witold of Lithuania, who had been elected king of Bohemia by moderate Hussites and was shortly to take up the reins of power (actually, he never did), and the moderates, under his protection, proclaimed a time of reconciliation. Radicals and Táborites later attempted a few times, by stealth or by military force, to take the Prague towns again, but they never succeeded, and Prague, throughout the later Hussite wars, remained a moderate town of Utraquist lords, burghers, and university masters longing for peace and, as the conflict dragged on, for a compromise with the church. Today, tourists are reminded of Jan Želivský by a small plaque on the tower of the Old Town city hall, put there by the Stalinist authorities and explaining that he was a "victim of the bourgeoisie." It is a rather simple view of a radical priest of considerable political and spiritual gifts, and of the vicissitudes of his time.

Hussites and Jews, and a Coda

In a world of increasing brutality, the Prague Jews went on living in their own community, blessed with the traditions of internal self-rule; though theoretically the absence of a central authority protecting its financial interests may have contributed to legal uncertainties, the barons and the towns were disinclined for economic reasons to change Jewish policies radically. King Václav IV was called by many of his enemies a "king of Jews," because he and his middle-class advisers were interested more in successful financial transactions than in endangering an important source of needed cash. But though the king could not be held responsible for the terrible pogrom of 1389, he had listened to the accusations that Prague Jews were blaspheming Christ, and as a result, eighty representatives of the Jewish community were put to death in 1400.

The people of the Prague reform movement held ambivalent views about Jews; in spite of all the insults they hurled at Jews, the Hussites were awed by the Maccabean nation of the Bible and the fierce morality of their prophets. They did not belligerently intervene in Prague Jewish life, but it is also true that in other Bohemian places, and during armed conflict, Jews were given the choice of accepting Christianity *sub utraque specie* or dying: this happened in Chomutov (Homotau), where Jews preferred to die. Yet it has to be said that during the restive Hussite years, Prague Jewry, as if living on an island of tradition, suffered far less (even when the Prague *Lumpenproletariat* invaded the Jewish Town in 1420 and 1422) than Jews in Austria, for instance, where the entire Viennese community was killed off or driven into exile, accused by the Austrian authorities of selling weapons to the Hussites raiding Austrian territory.

In the early years of the Czech reform movement, theologians raised the question of how the coming, or virtual presence, of the Antichrist (a certain sign of the millennium or the fullness of time) related to Jewish history. Milič of Kroměříž believed that the Antichrist was of Jewish origin and that, after the destruction of the first and second temples, he would build a third temple for the Jews; clearheaded Peter Payne rejected such mystical speculations. Matěj of Janov made evil a thoroughly Christian problem, radically severing any link between Jews and the Antichrist; he insisted that the Antichrist was but the totality of all bad Christians wherever they were (one of them being, of course, the highest Antichrist). Others, including Jan Hus himself, believed that in the fullness of time, Jews, who were not at all the people of the Antichrist, would freely convert to Christianity, fervently embrace their new religion, and serve, before the coming of Christ, as an example to others.

Averse to an economy of credit and money, Hussites were brave moralists rather than theological hairsplitters, and early on they turned their attention to the question of Jewish and Christian usury. Both Nicholas of Dresden, the German Hussite, and his Czech colleague Jakoubek of Stříbro wrote pamphlets against usury in 1415. The German radical inveighed against both Jewish and Christian usurers, and he raised his energetic voice against Christian princes who, ultimately, derived substantial income from Jewish taxes and contributions (a point well understood by his contemporaries: King Václav derived one-fifth or perhaps one-fourth of his income from Jewish sources). Jakoubek of Stříbro often alluded to St. Thomas Aquinas in suggesting that Christian society carried its own heavy burden of responsibility by forbidding Jews to do anything except lend money for interest. He believed that the practice of lending money in its own way guaranteed the survival of Jewish tradition; if, he believed, Jews would work, as did the Christians, "in the fields, in the forests, on rivers, on crafts, and profane commerce," they would be easily converted to Christianity; people, he added, were "made for work as flies were made for flying," and shared labor was essential to end the Jews' social and religious isolation. Also, he added with a dash of naiveté or cynicism, "if Jews worked more, they would have less time to study the Talmud and, in consequence, would be less qualified to argue against Christian theologians." Jakoubek was not at all fond of Jews, whom he called "pigeon shit," making the soil fat but not fertile, or "excrement of the patriarchs," but he had little sympathy for Christian usurers either, perhaps even less.

Many Czech historians, among them František Palacký, justly believed that the Hussite movement was strongest, if not invincible, as long as Prague and Tábor lived and fought together, but Palacký was also aware that many Prague citizens, even in times of common campaigns, were uneasy about the alliance with the radicals, who were uncontrollably split into groups and ferocious factions, and were unwilling to consider political and religious solutions to end the splendid isolation of Prague and Bohemia. Jan Želivský, who overreached himself more than once, had uneasily tried to establish a radical stronghold among the moderates, but as soon as his dictatorial power was broken in the Hussite Thermidor of 1422 (the Hussite revolution too devouring its children), Prague preferred the possible election of a king of Polish-Lithuanian origins, joint responsibility for destroying the radical army once and for all (this happened at Lípany field in 1434), and protracted negotiations with the church at the Council of Basel. It is easier to sympathize, for romantic reasons, with the desperate radicals, who suicidally fought to the bitter end, than with the Prague moderates, who were concerned with the devastation of Bohemia and tired of the ossified liberation theology that had been originally so eager to spread freely the word of God. They wanted to return to the European community rather than see Bohemia turn irrevocably into, to speak in more recent terms, a sullen and sectarian Albania.

Hussite Prague was a modern laboratory of religious and social ideas and attitudes, as T. G. Masaryk suggested, and a grand theater of European history, like Paris in the 1780s or Petrograd in the 1920s. There were heroes and cowards, barons and radical poor, pious women and men fighting in the field, inventive theologians and brutal iconoclasts, English Wyclifites, German dissidents, French "Picardians." There was Jan Hus, still strongly hesitant about the more radical beliefs of his followers; his gifted friend Jeroným, the true Renaissance man among the Hussites; studious and politically shrewd Jakoubek; bold and fiery Želivský; harsh Jan Žižka, who saved the Prague towns when the mighty crusaders attacked; and even Peter Chelčický, the fiercely independent Christian thinker and pacifist who preferred to live and write in a lonely southern Bohemian village, who had been attracted to the Bethlehem chapel in his young days and may have returned to Prague occasionally to discuss his ideas (later much admired by Tolstoy) with the learned theologians of his age. Some called Prague a New Jerusalem, others a sinful whore of Babylon; and proud of its new political strength, the community unabashedly asked the Venetian Republic to come to its support.

In the course of events, new administrative structures developed; for a short time, the Old and New Towns united spontaneously, not by decree as had happened under King Charles IV, and essential affairs were decided by direct vote of the "Velká Obec," the great community, bringing together all residents in open town gathering, foreshadowing the direct democracy of Switzerland or of New England town meetings. Yet it is also true that throughout the 1420s and early 1430s, Prague was a place of iron, alarms, and puritan discipline rather than laughter, playful art, exuberant sympathies, and joy. The Hussites collectively created magnificent songs of piety and war, but they raided and ransacked the royal palaces and destroyed and burned many churches and cloisters (if they did not turn them into arsenals). (On their scorched earth, triumphant Catholics of the seventeenth century built many Baroque marvels.) In an age of ideas tensely watched and of literature subservient to theology and teaching, it was one Master Laurence of Březová who retained at least a frail trace of an aesthetic, a rhetorical commitment largely absent in the stern writings of his time. He first translated a Latin book on the interpretation of dreams and a popular travelogue for the king; preferring a secular life to the priesthood, he showed himself in his *Hussite Chronicle* and *Victory Song* a man of moderate persuasion and unusually sensitive to the human suffering of a fratricidal age. He definitely disliked the radicals and, in turn, was disliked by their later defenders, but he kept his mind open and sober. As one of Prague's talented and fragile intellectuals in a difficult time, he deserves to be translated and read with patience and care.

5

RUDOLF II AND THE REVOLT OF 1618

Praga Mystica?

At the turn of the sixteenth century, the parish of St. Apollinaris, on a little hill of the New Town (close to where the medical schools are today), was administered by Jan Bechyňka, *sub utraque specie.* In the last years of his life (he died in 1507), Bechyňka, the son of a tailor, composed a little essay in Czech about his hometown; and while he insisted on calling it *Praga Mystica,* it was actually a highly polemical piece on the local sociology of the Christian religions, full of provocative if partisan insights and earthy views about social life in the age of the Polish kings who ruled Bohemia between 1471 and 1526. He was definitely not a man of mystical feelings, and his first sentence declared that all things should be made clearly known; even Gypsies, he suggested, had after all developed intriguing ways to find out what people wanted to hide in their thoughts. The Gypsies gaze at people's palms, foreheads, faces, and at their dress and gait, and thus come to know more about the invisible stirrings of their hearts. God the omnipotent reveals to everybody who has eyes to see the invisible city of virtue and sin "in the material and visible architecture and landscape of Prague." Jan Bechyňka, a theological Gypsy, reads the urban topography as a text about its spiritual life. In doing so, he unfortunately also shows the limitations of an Utraquist point of view that was quickly hardening into a new orthodoxy.

Bechyňka looks at Prague's three towns—Old, New, and Minor—and argues that they form a trinity of communities believing in the essential importance of the Eucharist, and yet it is clear that he much favors the first two because they are both Hussite, solidly middle-class or artisan, well built, and with a historical dignity all their own. He has misgivings about the strongly Catholic and German Minor Town, which has still not been entirely restored after the battles and ravages of the Hussite revolution (besides, there was a new fire as recently as 1503). Later Czech patriots, including the nineteenth-century composer Bedřich Smetana, would have been shocked by Bechyňka's deprecation of the Vltava River, which he considers evil and poisonous. It flows from the south—that is, from the pernicious direction of Rome and the pope—and cannot bring anything good, quite apart from the bad habits of the Prague burghers, who, in spite of all city ordinances, throw their refuse into it and infect the water and the clime. Bechyňka knows that the city has recently begun to introduce a new system of pipes and water towers to combat epidemic diseases feared by everybody, but, being conservative, he is not fond of newfangled technological developments; besides, he fears that new water taxes will be levied on his parishioners.

The preacher of St. Apollinaris has many reasons to speak of the Vyšehrad, not too distant from his little church, and Hradčany Castle, both marked by the course of history. The Vyšehrad, already in disrepair and once so glorious, has not been demolished by an emperor or the devil but by the very people of Prague, and what is left of it is not pleasing to the eye. There are ruins and some shabby and widely dispersed wooden huts, and a few people, in rags, like peasants in a miserable village, all on the dole—a challenge to Christian charity. Hradčany Castle offers at least a sign of hope. Some construction is going on, it is beautiful to look at, "bright, colorful, well built," and yet since the Polish dynasty has moved its residence away from Prague, it is "empty without a king," and the rather dubious members of the resident administrative council are not a real substitute for royalty. Devastated churches and monasteries are still to be seen here and there but, unfortunately, many returning monks are again welcomed by the people. Yet Prague citizens overwhelmingly lack religious feeling, have nothing on their minds but shady deals, and are busy filling their insatiable bellies from morning until late at night.

Bechyňka intensely dislikes Prague's Jews and the Bohemian Brethren. The Brethren live in tightly organized communities, descendants of radical Hussites who, in love with the simple and spiritual life of early Christianity, had congregated in Prague and in the countryside since the 1450s and 1460s. He constantly praises Utraquist tolerance, but he does not show much willingness to understand Brethren or Jews; in his belligerent statements he relies on the most vulgar arguments against usurers and heretics and uses them interchangeably. Like the Jews, he says, the

Brethren, who want to separate themselves from the Catholics and from the Utraquist establishment, are intent upon robbing their fellow Christians (if these last should be ever foolish enough to trust them) of their souls and their spirituality. The Jews live in their own isolation in a corner of the Old Town, and so do the Brethren, at least in their theological introversion; if the Jews are busy devaluating precious coins by diminishing their weight in gold and silver, so do the Brethren devaluate the ideas of faith, charity, and love on a spiritual level: the Jews suck blood, the Brethren the soul. There is a strong note of envy in Bechyňka's diatribe against the Brethren, who, in spite of many royal edicts, steadfastly attract a loyal following from the ranks of theological dissidents, and in their conventicles and schools constitute an intellectual challenge to Utraquists and Catholics alike. Bechyňka knows even less about the strong traditions of Prague's Jewish community, which would flourish in spite of all danger toward the end of the century. He has little sense of the future.

After the Polish Kings, the Hapsburgs Again

The last Polish king of Bohemia, Louis, died in the Battle of Mohács in 1526 fighting the Turkish armies, and the Bohemian Estates, the representative parliament, or diet, of barons, knights, and towns, proudly insisting on their power to elect the country's monarch, were confronted with a wide array of distinguished candidates, including kings and dukes from Bavaria, Saxony, Poland, and France, and a few powerful Czech nobles. After a relatively short discussion, they unanimously elected as king the twenty-four-year-old Ferdinand of Hapsburg, younger brother of Emperor Charles V and husband of King Louis's sister Anna. Among the candidates, ambitious Ferdinand was closest to imperial power, and the members of the diet may have hoped that they could handle him as long as the Turks continued to put pressure on the Hungarian and Austrian fronts; in 1529, the Turks besieged Vienna for the first time, and indeed the pressure continued for more than a century.

Born in Spain of an Austrian father and a Spanish mother, Ferdinand was more Spanish than Austrian, vivacious, intelligent, and well educated; and people in Prague, where he was to reside for twenty years before shifting his court to Vienna, gladly noted that he understood Czech, though he usually answered Czech questions in Latin or German. In the first years of his reign, the Bohemian Estates underrated his outstanding political skills, his artful ways of hiding his iron fist in a glove of fine velvet (at least as long as Bohemian funds were needed to fight the Turks), and his ability to bear long grudges, finely honed by a spirit of revenge. Hapsburgs had fleetingly appeared on the throne of Bohemia before—in 1306, 1437–39, and 1453—but Ferdinand established himself as the first in a long succession of Hapsburg kings who energetically pursued absolutist policies, issued increasingly from Vienna, against the Bohemian nobility, the Prague towns, and the guilds.

The towns of Prague had been run for some years by a conservative coalition of Catholics and Utraquists, but the opposition—consisting of the Bohemian Brethren, who had completely broken with the church, and, beginning in 1521, German and Czech Lutherans—was gaining in strength; and ancient fires of religious dissent were smoldering in the memory of the people as well as new Reformation ideas. Only a short time after the election of the new monarch, three Praguers, among them a woman "called Martha," from Poříč, were taken by the executioner beyond the Prague gates to be burned at the stake for heretical beliefs. Martha had publicly declared that Jesus Christ in his true substance and nature was indeed sitting in heaven on God's right, as Christian religion asserts, but also that he was not to be found in the Eucharist and only mad people believed otherwise. She seemed to mix radical Wyclifism with the ideas of the early Anabaptists (dissenters favoring adult baptism). Many women had fought in the Hussite ranks of old, but she was the first woman rebel theologian, courageously defending her ideas against all the refined arguments advanced by the masters who visited her in prison; when a Utraquist scholar threateningly told her to get herself a white shirt and to prepare for death, she quietly asked for a coat and said she was ready to die immediately.

The town authorities were so angered by her "masculine" reasoning, as the chronicle puts it, that she had to languish in prison for fifty weeks before she was handed over to the executioner, and his assistants explained to the crowds that she had not only denied Christ's presence in the Eucharist but also received a second baptism by a heretic who had used a rough-hewn wooden vessel in the shape of a chalice. Going to her death through the Prague streets on December 4, 1527, she did not deny the accusations but turned to the people and told them not to believe the priests—"these liars, impostors, loafers, sodomites, ruffians, and seducers"—and said that if she had accepted a second baptism, she had done so because the power of the first had been destroyed by the vices of the priest. When, passing by a church, she was asked by the town judge to kneel down and pray, she did so, turning her eyes to heaven and her backside, demonstratively, to the church. A short time later, Martha died in the flames, and the executioner put her wooden chalice in the fire too.

Ferdinand I, who began the re-Catholicization of Bohemia, was a pioneer patron of Renaissance art and architecture. The summer palace which he built for his beloved wife, Anna, was not Prague's first Renaissance project (that was a small southwest wing of Hradčany Castle, built by Benedikt Rieth under the Polish kings), but, rising on Letná Hill (on the west bank) and surrounded by formal gardens, it was a widely visible instance of the new art, foreign and strange on the crowded and dark medieval scene. Queen Anna's pleasure castle, later often called Belvedere, finished only in 1563, was spacious and airy, with loggias open to sunlight and sky; it enormously pleased the eye with its noble horizontal lines, harmoniously shaped green copper roof, and figural reliefs celebrating the heroines and heroes of ancient mythology. Privileged Prague residents had access to the pleasure gardens (which had been paid for by Jewish contributions) and to nearby greenhouses, where figs, oranges, and lemons grew. The Arcadian simplicity of the summer palace does not reveal the fierce intrigues among architects and master masons—among them Giovanni Spazio, Paolo della Stella, Giovanni Mario Aostalli, Hans Tirol, and Bonifaz Wohlmut—for royal favors and for financial support from the buildings committee of the Bohemian Estates, concerned with every groschen spent. The charm of the building persists, oblivious to the fate of the queen and to the conflicts among Italians, Bavarians, Czechs, and Austrians who collaborated and fought to create its sober grace.

As long as the Turks attacked in the southeast, Ferdinand I was careful to deal ceremoniously with the Estates, for they were paying nearly two-thirds of the war costs. He reconfirmed the Basel Agreements, which had been negotiated between the Catholics and Hussites in 1436, giving them equal rights in determining liturgical practices in their Bohemian churches, for both Catholics and Utraquists were long supportive of his policies; but increasingly he interpreted these old agreements to exclude all other religious groups, including reform-minded Utraquists, Bohemian Brethren, and Lutherans, from legal participation in Bohemia's religious and political life. In Ferdinand's push for autocratic power and administrative centralization, advanced by his new offices in Vienna and his appointees in Prague, political and religious issues were far more important than questions of language or nationality; when in 1528 he removed Jan Pašek, the self-willed Prague mayor, from office so as to appoint functionaries more subservient to the crown, refused legal recognition to the

Brethren, and successfully counteracted an ingenious Lutheran drive to gain hold of the Utraquist church council, he was set on a collision course with the Estates, who now defended their ancient prerogatives, and with the Prague towns, which were unwilling to submit to a king who proclaimed that he disliked "all these new things" causing so many conflicts.

The Estates and the Prague towns had to learn the hard way that their fortunes depended increasingly on the international situation. In 1545, Ferdinand I concluded a kind of armistice with the Turkish sultan, and he felt free, as did his brother the emperor, to turn his attention to Central Europe and to join the war against the Protestant German princes, above all the elector of Saxony, Johann Friedrich. The trouble was that when, on January 12, 1547, the king demanded a mobilization of troops to operate not only within but beyond Bohemia's frontiers with Saxony, irritation and resistance in Prague quickly changed into open revolt. The opposition promptly declared the order illegal, and after the Prague towns had formally protested it, their representatives, together with the nobility, began to assemble in Prague to articulate the legal basis for resisting royal interference in matters traditionally reserved to the Estates. Prague citizens and guild masters calling for an immediate restoration of the great town meetings (the Velká Obec of Hussite tradition) were joined by many nobles, mostly Lutheran or leaning to the Bohemian Brethren. On March 17, a meeting was convened at the university more than three hundred strong (though comprising only one-sixth of the Estates' legitimate representatives) to discuss shared ideas and action to be taken. Conventional in its outlook and oriented toward the past, the final resolution was, nevertheless, an incisive rebuke of the king's idea of centralized personal power. The meeting appointed an executive committee, mobilized its own army to march against the enemies of the country (it strongly implied that these were the royal armies operating on the Bohemian-Saxon borders), appointed a Lutheran commander in chief (who later paid dearly for his inefficiency), and established contact with King Ferdinand's Saxon enemies. Unfortunately, the opposition did not do much more.

When King Ferdinand defeated the German princes at Mühlberg in April and captured the elector of Saxony, most Bohemian nobles quickly submitted again and did not join the Prague towns in their last, desperate attempt to defy him. When royal mercenaries occupied Hradčany Castle and the Minor Town, Prague troops crossed the bridge to fight them and artillery pieces were hauled out of arsenals to be fired from the right bank of the Vltava against the royal position on the other side. Yet the king would not get involved in a battle for Prague and refused permission to his generals to counterattack. They did not have to: the town magistrates, afraid of royal retribution, did not want to go on fighting, and the towns capitulated on July 7, to await the punishment to be meted out by royal power.

The Czech historian Josef Janáček suggests that Ferdinand I had watched the humiliation of the Flemish town of Ghent, which had revolted against the imperial government and had been punished by Charles V with executions and expropriations, and when he arrived in Prague he was ready to follow suit and take his revenge in a theatrical performance of justice, or rather in a series of show trials, to use the modern term. In July and August 1547, he presided over four trials in the Vladislav Hall at Hradčany Castle, sitting on a wooden platform among a hastily convened group of assessors, including the bishop of Olomouc and a few Silesian and Lusatian nobles. Acting both as chief prosecutor (the accused were not allowed to respond to the accusations) and as high judge, who handed down the sentences, the king considered first the citizens of Prague, whom he regarded as the principal offenders, and only after he had done with them did he try the members of their executive committee, elected in March, and the nobles involved in the revolt. All in all, sixteen barons, nineteen knights, and twenty-eight representatives of the towns were put on trial and ten sentences of death were pronounced; ultimately, the executioner beheaded only four on Hradčany Square. A few of the accused had escaped, among them Albin Schlick, of a distinguished German Lutheran family, and since the king did not want to alienate the powerful and well-connected noble families, the four put to death were mostly second-stringers of the gentry or middle classes, including a royal agent who had been remiss in his duties. The king was far less forgiving toward the towns and guilds; many Prague citizens were publicly whipped and exiled; privileges and prerogatives were declared invalid; all weapons, whether in private or in public possession, had to be handed over to the royal army; and country property owned by citizens of the Prague towns was forfeited to the king. (The king made a good deal of money from these confiscations and penalties, as well as a newly imposed permanent beer tax.) The nobles of the opposition were badly wounded but not totally defeated, but the towns of Prague, which together had emerged from the age of the Hussite revolution as a virtually independent city-republic, lost their prerogatives forever, never to be restored to their old glory.

Though involved in war against the Turks again in the 1550s, Ferdinand I felt strong enough to persecute the religious groups that had been active in opposition to him, and he resolved to reinvigorate Bohemian Catholicism. The Lutherans once again had to seek the protection of the Utraquists, whose practices were sanctioned by law, and the king's renewal of the 1508 mandate against the Bohemian Brethren, as well as the arrest of their bishop, Jan Augusta, forced them to leave Prague and Bohemia en masse and to settle in Moravia, rapidly becoming a haven for Jews and Christian dissidents. Ferdinand invited members of the new Jesuit order to Prague, and in April 1556, a group of twelve (mostly Flemish) Jesuits under the guidance of their director, Ursman Guisson, settled in the once Dominican monastery of St. Clemens, in the Old Town. Within six years they had been granted a royal privilege to expand their excellent school—which, ironically, was often attended by sons of the Protestant elite—into a full-fledged Collegium Clementinum, which began to compete with the Utraquist old university, or Collegium Carolinum. Prague had been without an archbishop since the Hussite revolution, when the last incumbent, the Westphalian Konrad of Vechta, had joined the Utraquists in 1421; the pope now appointed Antonín Brus of Mohelnice, Czech grand master of the Order of the Knights of the Cross with the Red Star, though he had long favored the chalice and the importance of Czech, much to the displeasure of Rome.

Once he had defeated the uprising of the Prague towns and the Protestant Estates, Ferdinand I left Bohemian affairs in the hands of his second son, Ferdinand, who settled at Hradčany Castle as royal governor for seventeen years before he shifted his residence and his famous art collection to Amras Castle, near Innsbruck, in the Tyrol. He was there to see to it that Vienna's orders were implemented in Prague, but, excluded as he was from accession to the throne, he was not particularly eager to commit himself to far-reaching quarrels and was not averse to fulfilling the wishes of the Estates—the exception being Jewish policies, since the Estates rigidly opposed Jewish business while the royal governor was far more tolerant for economic reasons. Archduke Ferdinand was internationally known for his secret marriage to beautiful Philippine Welser, daughter of the famous Augsburg banker and one of the richest capitalists in Europe; though she disliked gloomy Hradčany and preferred to live at Křivoklát Castle in the romantic forests (in 1834 extolled by the Czech poet Karel Hynek Mácha), her husband, who spoke fluent Czech and had access to Welser money, was gratefully remembered for releasing from prison the bishop of the Bohemian Brethren and for his intelligent interest in international art and local Czech painting. He had to have his castle and his hunting lodge too: Hvězda, or Villa Star, was built in 1555–65 in the royal game park near Prague according to his ideas by the Italians Giovanni Mario Aostalli and Giovanni Lucchese, with local supervision provided by Hans Tirol and Bonifaz Wohlmut. Hvězda (much admired by the French surrealist André Breton) was designed in the shape of a six-pointed star lacking any outside adornment, but in the true mannerist way it surprises and astonishes the visitor with its surfeit of elaborate stuccos (by Antonio Brocco and collaborators), a magnificent vault rising from the central rotunda, and complex subsidiary spaces on all sides; the ascetic outside reveals nothing of the inside, precious and rich.

When Maximilian II was crowned king of Bohemia in 1562, two years before his father died, Protestants in Prague and elsewhere had high hopes and dared to breathe more easily. He had been educated in Vienna in the Spanish way, but it was known that he sympathized with the Protestant cause and was, perhaps, a Protestant at heart (his father had to remind him that Protestants were excluded from access to the throne). Maximilian II, an avid art collector, mostly resided in Vienna, but he learned his Czech too; when a delegation of Brethren appeared before him in Vienna and discussed their grievances in German, he told them that German, on that occasion, was not needed. He declared in 1575 in rather general terms that he would fully respect the "Bohemian Confession," a religious protocol compiled by all Protestant groups, but later he reneged on his promise. It has always been difficult to say whether he had a bland or an enigmatic mind, but when he lay in agony he refused to confess or accept the sacraments of the Catholic Church. His funeral in Prague on March 22, 1577, was suddenly disrupted by the panic fear that Catholics and Protestants were ready to kill each other in the streets. The cortege barely made it to St. Vitus Cathedral.

Rudolf in Ascendance

Many historians have loyally worked to establish a sober and balanced account of the achievements of Emperor Rudolf II, but the legends prevail. He has come down to us with the image of a royal Faust or as the mad alchemist on the Bohemian throne; historians are first to admit that his commitment to the arts and his wide philosophical and scientific concerns make him particularly dear to poets, novelists, and expressionist film producers—the legend of "magic Prague," prepared by English, German, and American writers on their grand tours in the nineteenth century, richly cultivated by Czech and German writers of the *fin de siècle*, and later renewed first by French surrealists and then by Czech dissidents under neo-Stalinist rule, largely rests on diffuse clichés about Rudolf's life and his court. The difficulties of penetrating his mind are forbidding; as ruler, he intended to do good, rarely succeeded, and, ultimately, madly destroyed himself, yet there must be some reason why he invited to Hradčany so many excellent painters, artists, musicians, and scientists, and why, being a devout Catholic, he welcomed at his court Francesco Pucci, a heretic who roamed all over Europe, Jacobus Palaeologus, a former Dominican, and, above all, Giordano Bruno—all later burned by the Inquisition.

Rudolf, son of Maximilian II and his Spanish wife, Maria (whose mother had died stark mad), did not enjoy a carefree youth. When he was eleven years old, he was sent, together with his brother Ernst, to the Hapsburg court in Madrid to receive his education there (a triumph for his mother and the Spanish faction at the Vienna court). He stayed in Madrid until he was nearly twenty, receiving an excellent training in languages and rhetoric from his mostly Spanish tutors. His household, which may have comprised close to one hundred persons, was supervised by the Austrian noble Adam of Dietrichstein, who wrote glowing letters home to Vienna—one argument he made for keeping Rudolf in Madrid was that he would be in line for the Spanish throne if Prince Don Carlos, who showed signs of mental instability, or so they said, would be unable to reign. For years Maximilian tried to get his son home, and in 1571 he finally succeeded; in a magnificent arrangement, Rudolf and his entourage were brought to Genoa by a flotilla commanded by Don Juan of Austria, who had just smashed the Turkish forces at the celebrated Battle of Lepanto in October, and from Genoa he wended his way home to Vienna. It was not an easy time for Rudolf; his father, hesitant in religious policies and trying to avoid open conflict, and his fiery mother, deeply committed to the Catholic cause, were at odds; he may have rightly felt that he was repeatedly sent to Prague to discuss matters of taxation with the recalcitrant Estates because his father wanted to avoid an outright confrontation with these powers and was using his son as a cover-up in his policy of procrastination. A compromise was reached when Maximilian came to Prague himself and the Estates accepted Rudolf as king of Bohemia. He was crowned on September 22, 1575, at the cathedral, a festive but not particularly glorious affair for either Catholics or Protestants, both well aware of undignified deals and broken promises.

Rudolf was twenty-four years old when he became king of Bohemia, and the eyes of Europe were upon him. He was an excellent linguist, speaking and writing Spanish, German, French, Latin, Italian, and a little Czech (he had had a Czech tutor, Sebastian Pechovský), but he affected, all his life, the distant and stiff Madrid court manner which Austrians and Bohemians alike found cold and unfeeling. Initially, he seemed willing to enjoy the grand life in Vienna and Prague, and took part in elaborate tournaments, balls, and festive dinners arranged by ambitious Austrian and Czech nobles. However, he had to face many suspicions: the Protestants were appalled by his education at the court of Philipp II while not perceiving its virtues; and the Spanish "party," including his mother and the papal diplomats who were active again in Vienna and Prague politics, were never fully satisfied by his less than perfect commitment to the Catholic cause and by his attempts to disengage himself cautiously from strict Madrid policies, especially with an eye to restive Protestants in Bohemia and Hungary. The king and the Bohemian Estates for many years showed cautious restraint with each other, avoiding corrosive words and actions; while the king had come from Madrid with strong ideas about the power and majesty of the absolute monarch, the members of the Estates wisely avoided provoking his vulnerable sensibilities. In 1580 he became seriously ill, the court physicians feared the worst, but he slowly recuperated, and in 1583 decided to move his court to Prague. By then he had changed much.

The historian R. J. W. Evans has suggested that Rudolf continued Maximilian's policies, if they could be called that, for a considerable time when he took over his father's state machinery. Rudolf diligently attended meetings of the Estates, attempted to liquidate royal debts, tried to revive Bohemian silver mining, and worked to stabilize prices. His religious habits were Catholic in the Spanish way, but he did not want to be dependent on the Spanish party (in response, his mother had left Vienna in a huff for Madrid in 1581, never to return), and, like his father, he preferred the virtues of procrastination, diminishing the possibilities of open conflict. As tradition required, Rudolf accepted the Basel Agreements' political covenant of Catholics and Utraquists, but he twice renewed the old royal edicts against the Brethren (though the worst was prevented by unified opposition in the Estates) and, in his own way, politically favored the Catholic cause in a country in which 85 percent of the inhabitants were now non-Catholic and five-sixths of the seats in the Estates were held by Protestants. He was adamant as far as his personal royal power was concerned: when the Catholic noble Jiří Popel of Lobkovic wanted to establish himself as a kind of dictator in the shadow of, or perhaps competing with, the crown, Rudolf had him arrested and sentenced him to prison for life and loss of all property, without mercy; at about the same time, he favored the Protestant Kryštof Želinský of Sebuzín as vice-chancellor of Bohemia, much to the consternation of the papal ambassadors. In 1598, when renewed war against the Turks for a change went well for Rudolf's generals, the papal nuncio in Prague, Filippo Spinelli, convinced Rudolf, who now saw himself as Christianity's imperial savior, that the Protestant administrators had to go, and in 1599 the king appointed a team of Catholic lords, many of the noble Lobkovic family, to run the country, which deeply offended the Protestant majority.

Many darkly attractive stories have been told about Rudolf the magnificent patron of the arts and sciences, yet, among the Hapsburgs, Rudolf was not alone in favoring artists and collecting curiosities. His grandfather Ferdinand I had established the first art collection (*Kunstkammer*) in Vienna; his uncle, the lieutenant general at Hradčany, had moved his collection of art and armor from Prague to his Tyrolean castle; and his father, Maximilian II, had tried hard if in vain to entice the famous architect Palladio to work in Vienna and had gathered a group of important Italian artists, including Giuseppe Arcimboldo, to work for him as portraitists and architects. Maximilian bequeathed, as it were, his Italians to Rudolf, who continued to support them in Vienna and Prague.

In time, however, the older Italians retired or wanted to go home again, and in the early 1580s, when moving to Hradčany Castle, Rudolf began to invite to Prague younger Dutch and German artists, all well trained in Italy. Among them, to name only the most important, were Bartholomäus Spranger from Antwerp, Hans of Aachen (actually born in Cologne), the Swiss Joseph Heintz; in time they were joined by Dirck de Quade van Ravesteyn, Roelandt Savery, the engraver Aegidius Sadeler, and others. By the turn of the century, the group was firmly established at Hradčany and in the Minor Town, constituting its own little aesthetic universe with close personal ties to Rome, Florence, and Amsterdam. By a special letter of majesty in 1595 they were exempted from the rules of the Prague guild of painters, and received yearly stipends, with all commissions extra. True, the imperial offices were always strapped for cash or late in payments, but when Spranger died in Prague in 1611, he left to his heirs five downtown houses, among other valuables.

The style of Rudolf's Prague painters has been usually called "late mannerist" to indicate something of their shared interests and techniques—allegorical celebrations of Hapsburg power (Rudolf, who never went to the front, crushing the Turks under his horse's hooves), encounters of ancient goddesses and gods, heroines and heroes, their stories derived from Homer and Ovid, the women and men in stark and naked contrast, mild and harsh, sweet Venus and hairy Hephaestos, elegant and oblong bodies of expressive if not serpentine gesture, garlanded by emblems of peace, passion, and poetry. Contemporary observers, especially among the ambassadors from Italy, suggested that Rudolf had a certain taste for the lascivious; in a neo-Latin novel of the time, written by John Barclay, an unfriendly Scottish author, Rudolf appears under the name of Aquilius as a dirty old man shuffling back and forth (*fluxis et titubantibus vestigiis*) in his apartment, the walls of which are decorated with pictures usually ascribed by the ancients to the genre of "Prostitute Paintings." Yet the paintings done by his group were fully consonant with international taste; even Dirck de Quade van Ravesteyn's unveiled beauties, in the near absence of anything else, are adorned by chains of dark and precious stones, happily separating their proud breasts. They remain perhaps more alive than Spranger's exquisite theatrical allegories.

The scholar Thomas DaCosta Kaufmann, most knowledgeable about Rudolfine arts, provides rich evidence that the emperor's court painters did not merely concentrate on images of imperial power or mannered erotic scenes. Those who preferred to paint *naer het leven*, or "close to life," possibly anticipated more of the future than the masters of courtly allegory. Hans Hoffmann, Georg Hoefnagel, Roelandt Savery, and Pieter Stevens were painters of "nature and landscapes" in the understanding of their age. Hoffmann adored Dürer (particularly dear to Rudolf), and the emperor was fascinated by the precision and neatness of Hoefnagel's flowers, insects, and traditional ornaments. Savery walked through Prague and Bohemia; Rudolf sent him off to the Tyrol in 1607 to bring back sketches of Alpine scenes; though some of them are peopled by peasants in distinctly Bohemian costumes remembered from earlier travels, these forest and mountain scenes show he was impressed by the ordered confusion of broken trees and new vegetative life, by dramatic rocks and magnificent mountain vistas, and they offer a first glimpse of the romantic sublime. Savery and his colleague Pieter Stevens sketched many corners of Rudolfine Prague too, decrepit homes and approaches to Charles's great stone bridge. Savery was a sharp and untiring observer: when he attended religious services at the Old New Synagogue, he sketched a group of elderly men and explained, in marginal notes in Dutch, what clothes they wore and in what color.

Later surrealist poets and critics have always loved the idea that Giuseppe Arcimboldo most essentially represents the mystical world of Rudolf II, as if Joseph Arcimboldus Midiolanus, as he officially called himself, was not just one among many interesting court painters. Arcimboldo, born in 1527, worked first under the supervision of his father at Milan Cathedral doing minor ornamentation and stained-glass windows; he was attracted to Vienna by Ferdinand I, Rudolf's grandfather, and was appointed *Hof-Conterfetter* (court portraitist) by Maximilian II, to whom he devoted his famous allegories of the four elements and the four seasons, made up of their vegetative symbols. He was also active in Vienna and, occasionally, in Prague as a *maître de plaisirs* and fashion designer of inventive costumes for balls, banquets, masks, and tournaments. Arcimboldo was among the Italian group that Rudolf continued to employ; in 1582, Rudolf sent him to Germany to buy antiques and rare animals; but in 1587, when Rudolf consolidated his German and Dutch team in Prague, Arcimboldo asked for and received permission to return to his native Milan, whence he continued to send paintings and sketches to Rudolf, who made him count palatine two years before his death in 1593; Rudolf perhaps remembered that Emperor Charles IV had awarded a similar, largely symbolic, title to Petrarch. More recently, Oskar Kokoschka, Roland Barthes, and Salvador Dali have come to admire Arcimboldo, and his popular fame largely rests on his portrait of Rudolf as the ancient god Vertumnus, a witty montage of fruits, flowers, and vegetables of all seasons (the hair of millet, grapes, and sheaves of wheat; the nose a pear; his forehead a melon; and his beard consisting of nuts and chestnuts), done in the same *ghiribizzate* (curlicue), or rather wittily allegorical, style in which he had done his "Jurist" with law books in his stomach and his "Librarian," entirely consisting of closed and open books, many years earlier. The surrealists' glorification of Rudolf as Vertumnus must take into account that the painting, showing the royal magnificence by other means, was inspired by the Latin poet Propertius celebrating Vertumnus as a god of change and permanence, done in a manner that Arcimboldo developed long before he entered the service of the melancholy emperor, and was not even painted in Prague but in Milan, Arcimboldo's true home.

Rudolf spared no expense to attract famous jewelers and stonecutters to his Prague court and to provide them with the gold, the silver, the diamonds, and other precious stones they needed for compositions they created solely to please his lonely sensibilities. It is an open question whether painters or goldsmiths were closer to his heart. Goldsmithing had flourished in Renaissance Augsburg, Nuremberg, Milan, and Florence, but Rudolf was not content to place his orders there; in the late 1580s, he invited to Prague several masters whom he chose with a supreme understanding of their craft, above all Anton Schweinberger Augsburg, Jan Vermeyen from Brussels, his disciple Andreas Osenbruck, and the Dutch Paulus van Vianen, who had had difficulties with the Inquisition when he was trained in Rome. The imperial and royal crown, created by Jan Vermeyen (never actually used by the emperor and now in Vienna) is the most perfect, most cryptic, and most valuable work of art ever made at the Rudolfine court. Each of its traditional components—coronet, miter, and arch—symbolized complex meanings of dominance, power, and magnificence, as did the eight big and the one hundred and eighty-six small diamonds (bought all over Europe by Rudolf's special agents), the strings of pearls, the rubies, and the large and luminous sapphire on top, imported from far Kashmir. The art of cutting stones, or glyptics, had been traditionally cultivated in Milan; Rudolf succeeded in bringing from Milan to Prague Ottavio Miseroni and his brothers, and from Florence Cosimo Castrucci, who excelled in *commessi in pietre dure*, or the art of creating pictures from finely polished jasper, agate, and carnelian, a kind of stone intarsia. Italian and German tourists who now line up every day in Prague to buy crystal glass probably do not know that it was one Caspar Lehmann from Westphalia, a talented stonecutter, who in 1601 was appointed stonecutter of the royal chamber (*Kammeredelsteinschneider*) and in royal service shifted his attention from working with mountain crystals to high-quality glass, perfecting his personal technique to an incredible finesse that became fundamental to an entire Bohemian industry.

It cannot be said that the emperor did not support court architects who were kept busy building magnificent halls for his collections and stables for his Spanish stallions, but it would be difficult to show that he was as obsessively committed to their art as he was to painting, jewelry, and glyptics. For reasons of ceremony, he also continued to employ distinguished musicians and singers, among them two castrati, to perform at the cathedral and at Hradčany at state banquets and dances. He was proud to be the patron of Philippe de Monte, a Neapolitan from Holland (Rudolf never permitted him to return home and he died in Prague), Jacques Renart, and Camillo Zanotti, noted and much admired composers of motets and villanelles (their music often printed in Prague).

The most remarkable cavalier involved in composing and performing at the court at that time was Kryštof Harant of Polžice and Bezdražice, who came from the provincial Catholic gentry. He had been educated at the court of Archduke Ferdinand in the Tyrol, fought in the Turkish wars for four years, and later gone out with another Czech noble on a voyage to the Holy Land and the Near East. He described his experience in Jerusalem (where he wrote a motet, "They who trust the Lord") and Egypt in a highly interesting report written in Czech in 1608, and he was welcomed home by the emperor, who bestowed on him the honorific title of chamberlain, or imperial valet. He was one of the few Czechs active in the arts at Rudolf's court. His later life was of more political than artistic importance: he was one of the generals of the rebellious Estates who fought the Hapsburg regime (artillery being his specialty) after 1618 and was put to death in Prague when the victorious dynasty took its revenge in 1621.

Poets and writers have always done a good deal for Rudolf, telling entertaining stories about him, but he did not do much for them. He had little interest in contemporary poetry. He did not show any commitment to the remarkable German poetry written by Theobald von Höck (who was employed by a southern Bohemian baron), remained insensitive to the new strength and purity of the Czech literature emerging in the many activities of Daniel Adam of Veleslavín, who owned the famous Melantrich printing press, and showed no interest in the inspired philological work of the Brethren, who translated the Bible in a six-volume edition (1579–94) that remained the standard of language in Bohemia, Moravia, and Slovakia for centuries to come.

The Rudolfine Prague elite—Czech, German, Italian, Silesian, and Dutch—swarmed with educated people writing in late humanist Latin, and even those who were made *laureati* (the nice title did not carry any emoluments) are largely forgotten today. Jakob Typotius (Dutch) was employed as court historiographer; Jan Campanus (Czech) taught at the university and converted to Catholicism in 1622; and Michael Maier, a court physician and student of the Rosicrucians, wrote a funny ornithological poem—each speaker, or rather bird, uses different meters or forms, the cuckoo staying phonetically close to his nest (. . . *sum cuculus cuculi cuculo* . . .) while geese prefer clumsy hexameters. Visiting British writers, intellectuals, and diplomats, Catholic or Protestant, came and went. The English poet Edmund Campion, who, after a novitiate in Brno was ordained in Prague in 1578, taught for six years at the Jesuit school (he was later hanged and quartered in England), and Sir Philip Sidney came to Prague twice, once in 1575 on a grand tour and again in 1577 to offer to the new emperor Queen Elizabeth's condolences upon the demise of his father, Maximilian; his report about Rudolf was not very friendly, saying that the new ruler was "extremely spaniolated." Among the English in Rudolfine Prague, young Jane Elizabeth Weston, who wrote in Latin too, was encouraged by the imperial councillors rather than by Rudolf himself (she may have been fortunate, considering the rumors about his disorderly affairs); born in Sussex in 1582 she had left her native country together with her Catholic parents and came via France and Italy to northern Bohemia, where her father suddenly died and left the fate of his family in the hands of his Catholic friends. Miss Weston's poems, printed in Frankfurt in 1602 and Prague in 1606, were praised by such European luminaries and influential critics as Heinsius and Scultetus. By 1598 she was settled in Prague, where she married John Leon of Eisenach, agent of the duke of Brunswick at the imperial court, gave birth to two daughters, and died at the early age of thirty. She was buried in the cloister of St. Thomas, in the Minor Town, where thousands of foreign visitors, among them many English, now quaff the famous dark beer oblivious to historical reminiscences.

Scientists in Prague: Tadeáš Hájek, Tycho Brahe, Johannes Kepler, and Jessenius

Emperor Rudolf gathered distinguished people and preciosities of art and nature around himself to create a *cordon sanitaire*, or, rather, *esthétique*, to protect his sensibilities against the treacherous world. In the sciences at least, perhaps in alchemy as well, local scholars and faculty members of the Carolinum were important in linking the artifice of the court with the rapid and contradictory developments downtown. One Tadeáš Hájek of Hájek, called Hegecius in the scholarly parlance of the time, brought to the emperor's attention what was going on in the Utraquist Carolinum (the emperor did not show much interest in the doings of its Catholic counterinstitution), was responsible for convincing him to bring to Prague the Danish mathematician Tycho Brahe, considered the most outstanding astronomer of the age, and personally intervened in the ever renewed quarrels between Tycho Brahe and his younger assistant, Johannes Kepler, who fully agreed on the importance of a systematic observation of the heavens but, unfortunately, on little else.

Tadeáš Hájek came from an old Czech family that resided near the Bethlehem chapel; his father, Šimon, a Prague B.A. of 1509, collected rare manuscripts, wrote a treatise on correct Czech usage, and kept his library and the house open to traveling intellectuals, including a few disreputable alchemists. Tadeáš first went to Vienna to study music and astronomy, received his Prague B.A. and M.A. in the 1550s, and immediately went again to Vienna, then Bologna and Milan, to continue his studies. He was not a sedate scholar, at least not in his early years; in 1555 he taught mathematics for a while at the Carolinum and in the 1560s joined the imperial armies, fighting the sultan on the Hungarian front as a military doctor. As personal physician to Maximilian II and Rudolf II, he traveled a good deal between Vienna and Prague before settling in his father's house, U Hájků. He certainly was not the comic busybody of wrinkled face who appears in Max Brod's novel *Tycho Brahe's Path to God* (*Tycho Brahes Weg zu Gott*, 1915), which though based on legitimate source materials is all too eager to cook up melodramatic scenes.

Tadeáš Hájek was the most eminent Prague scholar and scientist of the 1570s and 1580s, but since professors were still supposed to be celibate he did not really aim at an academic career and, indeed, married three times. The emperor assigned him to examine all the alchemists wanting to work in Prague, and, as a noted astronomer of European rank, he developed his own theory of the comets. He was also an expert in land surveying, much needed by the Bohemian mining industry (Kafka's learned land surveyor in *The Castle* comes from good Bohemian stock), began to work on a topography of the Prague region, and walked through the countryside studying plants and flowers with a botanist's eye. A true citizen of Prague, he also wrote a scientific treatise *De cervecia* (*On Beer*, published in 1564) and developed an early theory of oxidation. When he attended Rudolf's coronation at Regensburg in 1576, he met there the young Danish aristocrat Tycho Brahe, who had not wanted to miss that chic event either, and gave him a folio of Copernicus's *Little Commentary*, copied from a manuscript in his father's Prague library. It was the beginning of a long friendship that, by 1600, made Rudolf's Prague the world's center of scientific astronomy.

Tycho Brahe came to Prague because he had decided to leave his native Denmark in protest against king, church, and society and was happy to accept the emperor's invitation, ingeniously managed by Hájek through the chancellery. A scion of one of the most prominent families of the Danish kingdom, Tycho, haughty, condescending, and rich, was used to doing whatever he was doing in grand style; he once fought a duel with a fellow student (later Denmark's royal chancellor) who had doubted his mathematical skills, and when part of his nose was cut off during the fight, in darkness and close to a cemetery, he had the missing part restored in gold and silver and attached to his face with a salve, which he always carried in a little pouch (that valuable part of his nose was missing when a scholarly commission opened his Prague tomb in 1901). He gave a brilliant account of the new star appearing in 1572, and the king of Denmark, who wanted to keep the famous man at home, in a magnificent gesture gave him the island of Hveen and ample subsidies to build a castle there—the Uraniborg Astronomical Institute—in which Tycho housed his growing family, his fool Jepp, his assistants, library, laboratory, a printing press, and his famous instruments, big and small, made by the best craftsmen of Europe. In Hveen, he devoted himself for twenty years to a continuous and surprisingly precise observation of the stellar skies, the last prince of astronomy without a telescope.

Tycho Brahe's downfall was mostly of his own making; he had provoked the nobility by marrying a poor peasant woman named Kirstine, who bore him eight children and was to die in Prague; he never attended church services and dealt with his parsons as if they were his chattel; when the Hveen peasants, mistreated by him and sometimes put in chains, publicly protested, a court of nobles sided with the peasants and against him. Young King Christian IV, strapped for money and offended by his manners, canceled some of his privileges and substantially reduced his subsidies to Uraniborg; Tycho responded in an arrogant letter and the king never forgave him. In a fit of rage, Tycho packed a cumbersome wagon train with his family, friends, smaller instruments, books, and paraphernalia and, on April 9, 1597, left Hveen forever. He went into exile in Germany and then to Prague.

Tycho arrived in Prague in June 1599 and was lodged in the house of the vice-chancellor near Hradčany Castle. Rudolf, not exactly known to be easily accessible, immediately received him and offered him a salary far in excess of what artists and other scientists received, along with a choice of three Bohemian castles to substitute for Uraniborg. Tycho selected Benátky, on the Jizera River northeast of Prague, which was well fitted, at least potentially, to serve as a new astronomical institute. Tycho praised the splendid and comfortable building, but it had to be altered, of course, to his scientific specifications, and he found himself promptly embroiled in a protracted conflict with the imperial administrator, who absolutely refused to spend money on the costly alterations; Tycho had to learn the difficult way that funds promised by the emperor were not automatically disbursed by the bureaucracy. His most important instruments, large and fragile, were still at Hveen, and not all the assistants showed up in time.

On a few occasions, Tycho was happy to accept the help of David Gans, a Prague Jewish scholar (who wrote about his visits at Benátky), yet he grievously underrated Gans's scientific qualifications and thought he needed the help of a professional astronomer to take over specific tasks, collaborate with a team, and write, on his behalf, a few poisonous pamphlets against his scientific enemies, especially "the Bear," or Ursus, one Reymers Baer, once a North German swineherd and now a self-taught and eminent scientist who happened to be the emperor's court mathematician. The only candidate for the position was, in Tycho's mind, a young Protestant mathematics teacher in Graz in Austria who had impressed the lord of Hveen by sending him an interesting treatise on planetary orbits, written without the use of sophisticated instruments. His name was Johannes Kepler, and when he came to Benátky and met Tycho, he immediately wanted to leave but did not know where to go.

Kepler was ill fitted to deal with tyrannical colleagues of high birth working in the light of the imperial sun. He was born in 1571 in the small Swabian town of Weil der Stadt (it was saved in May 1945 from Allied artillery fire thanks to the intervention of an erudite French officer who did not want to see Kepler's birthplace destroyed) to a family that, according to his own views, was an odd bunch of misfits: his vicious father was a mercenary who ultimately left his family in the lurch; and his mother, garrulous and nosy, was, when she was seventy-three years old, accused of being a witch and was barely saved from burning by her son. Frail of health and strikingly intelligent, Kepler received a fellowship to train for the Protestant ministry, first at Maulbronn (like a character from a Hermann Hesse novel) and later at the University of Tübingen, where he studied with Martin Mästlin, who privately introduced him to the heliocentric ideas of Copernicus (Lutherans still violently opposed these, on biblical grounds). He never finished his theological studies, though he remained a theologian or rather a Pythagorean at heart, dreaming of God and the harmony of the universe; instead of becoming a minister he accepted a position as a teacher of mathematics at a Protestant school in Graz, in Catholic Styria. There he married Barbara Mühleck, "simple of mind and fat of body," as he himself wrote, but well-to-do and of a respected family; though he did not have any students of mathematics, he made himself useful teaching rhetoric and Latin and yearly published popular calendars with meteorological advice for the peasants and a few prophecies about war, conveniently fulfilled by the Turks.

Teaching a class on July 9, 1595, he felt suddenly illuminated about the order of the universe and put down his ideas in a rambling treatise entitled *Cosmic Mystery*, in which he tried to suggest that the arrangement of the five planetary orbits could be explained by inscribing, into the spheres, the three-dimensional shapes of the five regular solids known to ancient philosophers. He felt so enthusiastic about his discovery that the divine order could be defined in these terms that he sent copies of his book to Galileo Galilei, who did not bother to respond, and to Tycho Brahe, who hastily answered, saying that he hoped to meet the young scientist one day. By 1598, Archduke Ferdinand of Austria decreed that all Protestants in Graz must get out within eight days, and though Kepler won a temporary reprieve, possibly because the Jesuits kept an eye on him as a potential convert of importance, he was happy to be invited to come to Benátky. He joined the retinue of a friendly Bohemian baron, left Graz on January 1, 1600, and, after a few days in Prague, was brought to Benátky by Tycho's eldest, "not so much as a guest," as his host wrote, but "as a welcome friend and colleague in the exploration of the skies."

On February 3, the two exiles met for the first time face to face at Benátky Castle and, both sensitive to the uncertain circumstances in a foreign country, were immediately irritated by each other, the lord by the self-assurance of the poor colleague and the math teacher by Tycho's overbearing manner. They both played their own games: Tycho expected to employ a scientist who would help him in his observations, mostly of the planet Mars, and support him in the construction of a geocentric system of his own (modified, of course, with the sun turning around Earth and the planets around the sun); Kepler, hungry for reliable data and the precision instruments dangled by Tycho before his myopic eyes, hoped to be able to show the heliocentric motion of the planets, including Earth, all arranged in harmonic concert by God. After a few days at Benátky, Kepler wrote to a friend that "old age was creeping up on Tycho, enfeebling his spirits and his forces"; he had gathered rich observations but needed "an architect" (namely, Kepler) to make appropriate use of all the materials. Life at the castle was chaotic if not "insane," Kepler observed: builders were all over the place, the imperial administrator protested, and Tycho's senior Danish assistants and a young Westphalian nobleman (who was to marry Tycho's daughter Elizabeth to have a quick career at court) joined forces in an obvious intrigue to get rid of the new man as quickly as possible. The most important instruments were still on their way from Hveen via Hamburg and down the Elbe River to Litoměřice, and Kepler, desperately thinking of returning to Graz or going to Tübingen, wrote himself a little memorandum "on staying in Bohemia" (Tycho ultimately read this document), cataloguing in a rather miserly way what he wanted, paragraph by paragraph—a self-contained apartment, a bath, a kitchen, a chamber for his family, dry wood for the winter, sufficient food including meat, fish, wine, and bread, and permission to go to

Prague whenever necessary, among other things. In early April tempers flared; Kepler raged "with the vehemence of a mad dog," Tycho reported, and, on April 6, after a new outburst, Kepler returned to Prague to lodge with the friendly baron who had brought him there. However, he soon wrote a letter of apology to Benátky and waited for Tycho, who graciously came to Prague and took him back to the castle. All was forgiven. Kepler liked Prague now, "the eager contact of nations" and a neighborly feeling among people speaking German, "important to his wife." Yet Prague was too expensive, and it was "impossible to live there."

Kepler wanted to avoid Tycho as much as he could, and he spent many more months away from him than in his company. That summer he went again to Graz to settle his family affairs, but he was expelled in early August without further reprieve. Tycho once more implored him to return, and when he did so, everything had changed, for Emperor Rudolf had expressed the wish that Tycho work closer to the imperial residence. Tycho dutifully moved his entire establishment to Prague, first at a noisy tavern at the Nový Svět, and by mid-February 1601 to the vice-chancellor's house, which the emperor bought for him; Kepler was supposed to live there too. In the meantime, the instruments had arrived and were put in the loggias of Queen Anne's summer castle, now to be an observatory. Kepler, who with his family moved in with Tycho's clan, promptly had a nervous breakdown and a few psychosomatic complications as well; recuperating, he made another trip to Graz (his wife's father had converted to Catholicism to save the family real estate), but when he returned to Prague there was not much time left for shared studies and observations. On October 13, 1601, Tycho Brahe was brought home in agony from a banquet at the town house of Petr Vok of Rožmberk. It was rumored that his bladder had burst because he did not want to leave the table before the host, and Kepler confirmed in his notes that the rumors were not far off the mark: Tycho held back his water beyond the demands of courtesy and "put politeness before his death"; when "he got home he was scarcely able to urinate." Tycho was delirious for five nights with his uremia, and died on October 24, after he had composed his last words in flawless Latin: *ne frustra vixisse videar* ("let me not seem to have lived in vain"). He was buried, with pomp and circumstance, at the Týn Church, and a few days later Kepler was notified that he was appointed mathematician to his imperial majesty. He could not bear Tycho Brahe while he was alive, but he remained loyal to him and to his research for the rest of his life.

Emperor Rudolf granted his new court mathematician privileged access to all of Tycho's papers and instruments, but Tycho's family energetically staked out its own claims, especially the son-in-law, who sensed the financial possibilities. Kepler had to litigate and, often, to compromise. He had hoped that his salary would be equal or close to that of Tycho, but he had to do with less than a third, the exchequer was always in arrears, and the *mathematicus* was desperate for cash. The Keplers did not live in palatial splendor; after Tycho died, they moved to dwellings close to the New Town cattle market, definitely not a good address, and Kepler rightly complained of having to spend an hour walking to Hradčany Castle. He later resided, possibly free of charge, in a university college at Ovocný Trh (Fruit Market) and, ultimately, in the Old Town in the Karlova Ulice close to the entrance to Charles's stone bridge.

Kepler did not neglect his aristocratic connections, occasionally even condescending to deliver a horoscope, and made friends among Czech scientists and instrument makers who had been attracted to Prague. He probably did not have any opportunity to work with Tadeáš Hájek, who had died in 1600, but Martin Bacháček, rector of the Carolinum, and the physician Jessenius, who were involved in a tardy university reform, both sought his friendship and advice; he also knew Václav Budova of Budovec, political chief of the Czech Brethren in the Estates, who had traveled widely in the Near East and written a number of astronomical essays. Among other members of the Prague scientific community close to Kepler was the Swiss Jost Bürgi, who studied techniques of mathematical computation and early compiled tables of logarithms—unfortunately Lord Napier published his in 1614, six years before Bürgi followed with his own in Prague. Kepler was less happy with Galileo Galilei, whom he deeply admired. He had endorsed his telescopic discoveries enthusiastically and sight unseen, but when he implored him to let him work with one of his telescopes, Galileo did not answer his request; Kepler had to turn to the visiting elector of Cologne, who had received one from Galilei, and was allowed, at least from August 3 to September 9, 1610, to use the elector's instrument. (Twentieth-century admirers of Galileo who take their information from Bertolt Brecht's play might do well to read Arthur Koestler, who closely analyzed Galileo and Kepler's relationship in solid and devastating detail.)

Kepler's twelve years in Prague may have had their financial problems, but they were the most productive years of his life, and the emperor could well have been satisfied with a court mathematician, driven by an appetite for constant work, who published thirty treatises. It is possible that, in Prague, Kepler, who considered himself Tycho's heir, put off at least for a time his Pythagorean visions about the harmony of the universe (he was to return to them when he moved to prosaic Linz, in Upper Austria) and followed, more intensely than in his early and later years, the essential necessity to observe and to calculate rather than to dream; his Prague research about physical astronomy and the fundamentals of optics contributed more substantially to the development of modern sciences than to a magical vision of the universe. In Prague, he articulated two of his planetary laws—about the planets traveling in elliptical orbits and about the variations of their speed—and by asking questions about the cause of their movement made astronomy the physicist's realm, preparing the way for Sir Isaac Newton's universal laws of gravity.

Tycho Brahe and Galileo Galilei had used their instruments without systematic study of their efficiency, and Kepler, perhaps because he was born with impaired eyesight, was the first to develop a theory about the rays of light, the workings of refraction, and the function of the human eye; informed by his Prague colleague Jessenius about human anatomy, he sensed the structure of optical nerves. In a world in which astronomers sold horoscopes as a matter of course, Kepler declined, as early as 1601, to be an astrologer of the traditional kind who ascribed to planets an unmediated influence on man's fortune, though he still believed that planetary aspects molded the human condition. Kepler did not want to get involved, and when he was asked by intermediaries to advise the emperor, he distinctly refused and insisted that "astrology should be kept away from the emperor's mind." It was the tragedy of Kepler the scientist that he had to accept employment late in life by General Wallenstein, who was not at all interested in scientific observation but eager only to enjoy prophecies of future victories.

The physician Johannes Jessenius de Magna Jessen has a special place among the scientists who, in difficult times, wanted to restore the ancient excellence of Prague's Carolinum. He was a true Renaissance scholar, whom Czechs as well as Slovaks counted among their own, for more or less legitimate reasons. Jessenius came from a middle-class family originally in central Slovakia (then part of Hungary), but he was born (in 1566) in Silesian Breslau, where his father owned a tavern and married a local Silesian woman. In various university documents, the student was said to belong to the Polish "nation," being a Silesian by birth, or, in Italy, to the "natio Germanorum"; often, when it was a matter of prestige, he called himself a "Hungarian knight" (so much for Mitteleuropa). Jessenius pursued his early philosophical and medical studies at Wittenberg and

Padua, where he received his doctorate in 1591 after defending a thesis on afflictions of the gallbladder; being well trained and highly ambitious, he returned to Wittenberg as professor of anatomy and became rector of the university later. He too felt attracted to imperial Prague (though the nearly dormant university had little to offer); after placing his bets well by entertaining Typotius, the imperial court historiographer, and Tycho Brahe, in mid-June 1600 at the Carolinum he publicly dissected a male corpse delivered to him from the gallows. This was not the first Prague dissection but certainly the most formal and festive one, judging from the serried ranks of dignitaries and fashionable people who attended his performance, in which he proceeded, according to tradition, from the abdomen to the brain, occasionally praising the cool weather which fortunately diminished the stench of the rotting flesh.

Jessenius described this feat in a longish Latin treatise which includes a marvelous Baroque dedication to nearly everybody who could be helpful in Prague. It includes a few hexameters in praise of Bohemia and the emperor, and a few pages of glowing praise of Prague, not only a city but "a world." The emperor promptly requested the prince-elector of Saxony to let Jessenius come to Prague, but he stayed there only for six years (1602–8). He may have felt frustrated because the university did not offer sufficient possibilities for all his talents or because he felt uneasy about the distinct predominance of the Catholic faction at court. He transferred to Vienna to serve Matthias, Rudolf's brother, perhaps feeling more at ease with a protector who, at that time, was supported by the Protestant Hungarian and Bohemian Estates. Jessenius published a good deal, both in Prague and in Vienna, especially on anatomy and the blood vessels, and when in 1617 he was offered the rectorship of the Carolinum he readily accepted and returned to Prague. He was deeply involved in the rebellion of 1618 and the conflicts between the Prague Estates and Vienna, as both university rector and diplomat seeking international support for the rebels, and he was the prominent academic among those executed in the Old Town Square in 1621. Nearly three hundred years later the Prague physician Jan Jesenský (father of Milena, dearly beloved by Franz Kafka), a Czech nationalist and pioneer stomatologist, proudly derived his ancestry from Jessenius, and I do not know whether he was aware that his Baroque forebear had done excellent work in stomatology too.

The Alchemists Come to Prague

To separate the scientists at the imperial court from the alchemists who flocked to Prague is to use anachronistic norms to define two distinct groups which, to their contemporaries, probably were but one. Some of them preferred systematic observation of natural phenomena while others, strongly believing in the unity of all creation and the necessary correspondences among its constituent parts, experimented with the transmutation of elements or, in the service of the great and the wealthy, hoped to make gold, silver, and precious stones, or to distill a few gulps of *aurum potabile,* fluid and drinkable gold that was said to guarantee eternal youth. Astrology was just beginning to be disreputable to professional astronomers, and the dividing line between chemistry and alchemy was uncertain and diffuse; in Prague—at the court, in the Minor Town, and downtown—there lived as many scientists trying to emancipate solid knowledge from vague Egyptian and Alexandrine traditions as traveling charlatans who, quoting secondhand Trithemius or Agrippa, tried to sell their tricks to the highest bidder, whether the emperor or somebody else. Learned court physicians, among them Tadeáš Hájek and Michael Maier, who had strong interests in pharmacology and chemistry, were not averse to studying the traditional texts of alchemy, but they usually kept apart from the self-assured amateurs, con men, and swindlers who appeared from nowhere, sought the protection of the court, the barons, or gullible rich patricians in the Old Town, took the money, and ran, if they could. Emperor Rudolf, extolled by his admirers as the second Hermes Trismegistos (the magical Egyptian king who had writ the secret of alchemy on sapphire), was rather lenient to the traveling alchemists. Under pressure from the law courts, he occasionally imprisoned an alchemist for debts or banned him from the country (unless a powerful baron intervened), but he never had one executed, as was the habit of the German princes beyond the Bohemian borders. Philipp Jakob Güstenhofer, after some éclat in Prague, was hanged in Saxony; the false Greek count Marko Bragadino, who had astonished Prague citizens while walking with his devilish black hounds at his side, was executed in Munich, clad in an elegant suit adorned with false gold; and the evil Italian Alessandro Scotta, first a great sensation in Prague but later forced to show his art in a little wooden booth in the Old Town Square, on his further journey by less than magic means impregnated the duchess of Coburg, who craved a child, and he would have been killed if he had not succeeded in disappearing. The unfortunate woman was sentenced to life in a nunnery and died twenty years later.

The most famous, or infamous, purveyors of the occult arts appearing in Prague in the early 1580s were John Dee and Edward Kelley, two Englishmen who offered their services to the emperor and to powerful nobles. Prague contemporaries and later Czech historians took a dim view of that traveling pair (not entirely undeserved), but a spate of recent studies about Dee has clearly shown that the two radically differed in character, learning, and attitude, to say the least: the scholarly and earnest John Dee was "a unique intellectual force in Elizabethan England," Peter J. French has argued, and Edward Kelley an imaginative fraud with a criminal record and a lusty eye for profits of all kinds. It is impossible to say with any certainty why Dee, a scholar of high achievements and independence of thought, for many years joined his and his family's life to that of Kelley, an unscrupulous adventurer of the occult; in his thirst for knowledge he may have really believed that Kelley, and nobody else, was capable of understanding the pure language of Adam and would translate to him what the angels said in long magical séances. From 1582, when Kelley first appeared in Dee's study, they traveled and worked together in Poland, Bohemia, and Germany, and parted ways only in 1589 in Prague, when Dee, upon Queen Elizabeth's request, returned to England and Kelley preferred to stay on in Bohemia. Dee died in utter penury in England, forced to sell his books one by one, and Kelley came to a bad and bitter end in Bohemia.

John Dee (born in 1527), son of a vintner who may have been employed in a minor function at the court of King Henry VIII, was early seized by an intense longing for universal knowledge; at St. John's College, Cambridge, he studied for eighteen hours a day, he said, and was among the original fellows of Trinity College. He traveled twice to Louvain to take up mathematical and cartographic studies, lectured on Euclid in Paris, but turned down academic appointments because he wanted to be left to his independent work. His religious principles came under suspicion early; when he suggested to Queen Mary that a royal depository of books and ancient manuscripts be established, there was no official response; he then built his own library, which became one of the most famous in Elizabethan England, at his home at Mortlake, on the banks of the Thames River in Surrey. Queen Elizabeth favored his services and consulted him about naval affairs and her toothaches; he was invited to Richmond to see the queen, who, in turn, visited with all her official retinue at his Mortlake home. He had concentrated on mathematics as informing all creation, but in the early seventies, dissatisfied with the rhetorical canon of the universities, he shifted his interests to the occult meaning of numbers and, by 1581, held his first séance, trying with the help of a "skryer," or translator, to bring down the angels to his study and to understand what they said; unlike Faust, who tried in vain to force the restive *Erdgeist* to speak up, Dee believed the angels were ready to talk if only confronted with a translator of unusual gifts. Unfortunately, on March 10, 1582, a young man appeared at Mortlake, trying to convince Dee that he was heir to occult knowledge and formulae, saved from a bishop's grave (desecrated by iconoclasts); the visitor quickly succeeded beyond his wildest dreams. It was Edward Kelley, or Talbot, a trained apothecary's apprentice, who had briefly gone to Oxford, worked for a time as a scribe, falsified official documents, and been punished by the Lancashire authorities, who cut his ears off (he wore his hair long or had a black cap with flaps to give him a scholarly appearance). Dee had found his disreputable Mephisto.

It may have been Kelley's idea to go to Eastern Europe to sell occult knowledge for profit and preferments; in any case, on the invitation of a Polish nobleman close to the Polish Hapsburg party, they first went to Cracow, then on to Prague, the new Mecca of alchemists. It was the influential Spanish ambassador Guillén de San Clemente who arranged for an audience with the emperor, not an easy feat, but the meeting, on September 3, 1584, was not a success, possibly because Dee, too self-assured, indulged in prophecies of a new age and the defeat of the Turks if only Rudolf would mend his sinful ways; even a subsequent letter addressed to the emperor hinting at the success of occult experimentation and the transmutation of metals did not entirely convince Rudolf, who appointed a senior secretary to find out more about the English visitor. Dee was quick to endear himself to the emperor's trusted physician, Hájek, but papal diplomats persuaded the court to expel the English gentlemen from Prague and Bohemia; the emperor signed the required mandate.

Dee and Kelley were saved from further wanderings in Germany and elsewhere by the southern Bohemian Vilém of Rožmberk, who protected them at his residence of Třeboň, where they went on with their experiments. The foreign correspondents watching from Prague were astonished at the monies Vilém of Rožmberk invested, and wild rumors circulated about Dee's crystal ball and his famous black mirror, made of a polished stone brought from Aztec Mexico, with which he claimed to look into the future (the crystal ball and the mirror are loyally preserved at the British Museum). However, Dee and Kelley began to fight, as Kelley did not want to go on translating angelic messages, all in numerical code. Dee could not do without him, and he finally submitted to Kelley's blackmail and signed a formal statement, on May 3, 1587, declaring that they would own everything in common, as the angels required of them, including their wives. Fortunately, Queen Elizabeth requested Dee's return to England, and he left Bohemia, where his intellectual importance has never been recognized.

After the departure of Dee, Kelley (totally unburdened by scholarly seriousness) dominated occult studies both in Rožmberk's Třeboň and in Rudolf's Prague, and went, at least for a while, from success to success. He seems to have convinced his protectors of the efficacy of his tinctures, acquired Bohemian citizenship, and was knighted by the emperor, accepting the title "de Imany," referring to his alleged distant Irish forebears. He married a rich and well-educated Czech woman who gave him, apart from her opulent dowry, a daughter and a son; soon his brother arrived from England and married a rich Czech girl too. From his Rožmberk protector Kelley received, in 1590, the burgh of Libeřice, the estate of Nová Libeň, and about nine villages, peasants included; from his Czech dowry he bought a brewery, a mill, and a dozen houses at Jílové, well known for its gold mining, and two stately houses in the New Town of Prague, one of them not far from the Monastery of the Slavs. The home was famous in Prague as "Faust's house"—though Faust never resided there. Kelley did, and later, in the enlightened eighteenth century, the home was owned by Mladota of Solopisky, the last Czech alchemist.

Kelley was his own worst enemy. The emperor had strictly forbidden dueling (what duels there were usually took place on the hospital fields, outside the Poříč Gate), but hot-blooded Kelley killed an officer in a duel, was intercepted by imperial agents while trying to escape to southern Bohemia, and imprisoned at Křivoklát Castle. Rudolf's agents were ready to question him, under torture, about his tinctures, the drink of eternal youth, and the strange numbers in symmetric arrangements found among his papers (the results of the angelic séances, now at the Ashmolean Museum in Oxford). He tried to escape but fell from the window and shattered his leg on the rocks below; when he was released for medical treatment, he had to borrow money to survive. In 1596, Emperor Rudolf renewed the mandate against him, and Kelley was imprisoned at the castle Most (Brüx), in northern Bohemia. Again he wanted to escape, but the cripple (the leg had been amputated) took another fall from on high, possibly into the carriage in which his son wanted to spirit him away, and he hurt his other leg. Facing a long prison sentence, perhaps for life, he took poison (he was a trained apothecary) and died. It is a matter of historical record that his unfortunate family was deprived of all property, and his son John Adam was last heard of in Most twenty years later, when he made himself a public nuisance.

But there were others. Among Kelley's guests in Bohemia was the Polish alchemist Michael Sedziwój, or Sendivogius, who impressed his contemporaries as a man of integrity, though he accumulated enormous debts for which he was imprisoned when he could not pay. Kelley tried to keep him in the provinces in order to have the Prague scene for himself, but Sendivogius, who gave himself the air of belonging to a noble family, traveled a good deal between Cracow and Prague and, in the name of alchemy, explored the chemical properties of sulfur and mercury; the scientific results were published from his papers. Emperor Rudolf liked him and made him a *Hofrat*; when Sendivogius, on one of his trips from Prague to Poland, was ambushed by an importunate Moravian knight who wanted to know how to make gold, the emperor imposed a heavy fine on the eager Moravian. Sendivogius much suffered from the envy of his German competitors, but he remained employed by Ferdinand II and probably died in Poland in 1636. His *Novum Lumen Chymicum* (*The New Alchemical Light*) was in its twelfth edition as late as 1702.

The "Golden Age" of Prague's Jewish Community: Rabbi Judah Loew and His Golem; Jewish Tradition and the New Sciences

Prague's Jewish community in the mid-sixteenth century, caught between the interests of the Estates and those of the king, again faced near-extinction but within a generation consolidated its economic energy and intellectual power, and in the last decade of the century entered on what was called its "Golden Age." King Ferdinand I had been educated at the Spanish court shortly before the expulsion of the Jews from Spain, but the Bohemian Estates, fearing competition, were far more eager to get rid of the Jews than he. In the 1530s and 1540s, the Prague citizens, especially of the well-to-do Old Town, were less than tolerant, and Christian merchants and craftsmen busily accused the Jews of illegally dealing with coins, spying for the Turks, and being responsible for the fire of 1541 which destroyed much of the Minor Town and Hradčany, including the state archives (the Estates needed the ancient documents there to defend their old privileges against the king). Under torture, a Jew arrested on charges of arson confessed to the crime; during the spring session of 1541 the Estates demanded the immediate expulsion of the Jews from Bohemia, and pogroms spread through the countryside. They were barely avoided in Prague, and the king ultimately granted the demands of the Estates. Jews had to leave immediately.

Many Jews went to Poland and others settled in nearby Moravia under the protection of the local gentry, who felt independent of Prague or Vienna. It was a time of brutal trouble; many Jews were robbed on their way by villagers, or killed by soldiers accompanying them to the frontiers. Yet economic considerations prevailed again: important Jewish families received letters of exemption enabling them to order their business affairs, while others were allowed, for the same reasons, to return to Prague at least for a short time. To the despair of many, letters of exemption were bought at high prices, but the Hapsburgs' economic needs in their war against the German Protestants forced the king within a few years to rescind the expulsion mandate, at least for the few Jews still living in Prague and in the country; Jewish merchants were important for delivering provisions for the armies. The king reversed himself once again as soon as economic pressure ceased. Mordecai Zemach Kohen, publisher and Jewish community leader, courageously went directly to Rome at the head of a Prague delegation to ask Pope Pius IV to intervene (he did, in a way), but legal uncertainties continued for years after the death of Ferdinand I.

Finally, on April 4, 1567, Maximilian II, Ferdinand's son, revoked all the expulsion orders, confirmed the Jews' ancient privileges in Bohemia, and on a cloudless summer day of 1571 walked "in all his glory and power," accompanied by his wife, Maria (daughter of Emperor Charles V), and the nobles of the realm, "through the jubilant streets of the Jewish Town of Prague to show his royal favor." The Jewish privileges were also confirmed by Rudolf II in 1577 and by his brother Matthias in 1611. Rudolf also protected the self-rule of the Jewish Town by a number of legal measures: he made it incumbent on the imperial judge, not the Prague town authorities, to function as highest legal adviser in Jewish matters, exempted the Jews from paying fees to the townships (rather than to the crown), and went on to protect the community against continuing attacks by the Christian guilds. In his time eight to ten thousand people may have resided in the Jewish quarter, more than ever before, and it was proudly praised as "the mother-in-Israel," the most populous Jewish community in the Diaspora.

The richest and most eminent man of Prague's Jewish community was Mordecai Maisel, and many fairy tales were told about the magical origins of his wealth. Maisel came from an old Prague family that had resided in the Jewish Town for two centuries or more, and he was deeply concerned with the well-being of all its members; politically skilled and with excellent contacts at court and internationally, he did much to consolidate community developments after 1567, and we are told that his residence in Prague attracted many other Jewish families to settle there again.

He was the right man to be in charge of Prague's Jewish community in the age of Rudolf II, who made him his privileged *Hofjude*, and over the course of the centuries he was always remembered as a farsighted and honest benefactor, humble and extremely generous. He made loans, interest-free, to the Jewish poor, gave financial support to suffering communities elsewhere, and, in Prague, built a magnificent Jewish town hall (still standing and in use), a hospital for the old and the sick, a synagogue, ritual baths, and schools, and he supported private scholars who did not yet have a community appointment. Actually, he provided much of the financing of Rudolf's war against the Turks, and Rudolf decreed that Maisel would be free to do with his money and his properties exactly as he liked in his last will and testament. But the truth was that Rudolf could not resist the lure of cash: a few days after Maisel's death, he reneged on his formal assurances, had Maisel's house searched, and immediately impounded what was found in the name of the crown. It was a Prague scandal that in reports of correspondents and embassies reverberated throughout Europe.

The intellectual golden age of the Jewish community did not dawn overnight but was long anticipated by a learned consortium of scholars who, by 1512, began publishing Hebrew books of prayers, blessings, and commentaries for the first time north of the Alps (sharing financial responsibility for their projects); and their activities were continued by Gershom ben Salomon ha-Kohen, who came to Prague from Verona and, after 1527, and by imperial privilege, began publishing the most elaborate volumes, among them his renowned *Story of Passover* with its sixty woodcuts (reproduced as late as 1960 in Jerusalem and in New York); one of Gershom's sons (the one who traveled to Rome to see the pope) revived this publishing business after the expulsion, and the family continued to print for hundreds of years. The rabbis of Prague were all eminently learned men who, far from being backwoods provincials, had been studying in yeshivot in Germany, Egypt, or Poland before settling in Prague and, at times, going on to Verona, Venice, or Cracow. It is easily forgotten that

Rudolf's Prague had many centers of higher learning—the scholars at court, the Utraquist university of old, the new Jesuit school at St. Clemens, and the yeshivot of the Jewish community—yet it has to be said that they were more often than not isolated on their islands of religions; it was difficult to transcend the late medieval boundaries, and the exceptions are all the more glorious.

Rabbi Judah Loew ben Bezalel (later called the august Maharal) is better known to the world as a magician who created the mysterious golem rather than as the most original and intense mind of the Jewish community of Prague. The many attractive legends have done little to define his noble and lonely achievements, which rest on his many books and commentaries, among them *Netivot Olam*, on ethical questions; *Tiferet Yisrael*, on the Commandments; or *Be'er ha-Golah*, on the dignity of the Torah (published in Prague in 1598). We have come to accept, perhaps too easily, that Rabbi Loew symbolically incarnates mystical and Kabbalistic Prague. Actually, he was not born in Prague; many scholars believe that he came from Worms (not from Polish Poznań, which has also been suggested) and he was born in 1520 (rather than 1512, as others assume). He never said anything about his early training and his teachers, whom he intensely disliked, and it is assumed that he studied for a long time at Polish yeshivot. He may have come to Prague to marry Pearl, after a long engagement, but we know for certain that he was rabbi of Mikulov (Nikolsburg) and chief rabbi of all Moravian Jews for twenty years (1553–73), though there was nothing mystical about the town or his activities there. On the contrary, he was well known as a superior administrator and legal expert, who unified the statutes of the Moravian Jewish community, introduced new tax reforms, regulated the election of the country elders, all the time insisting on the dignity of religious services (no conversation allowed), and challenged many by rejecting wine for religious services that had been handled or produced by gentiles (in the midst of the Moravian vineyards, certainly a tough demand).

Rabbi Judah Loew returned to Prague when he was more than sixty years old, teaching at the "Klaus," a school built and privately financed by Mordecai Maisel. He seems to have been respected in the community but was not given an official appointment; informally, he established groups for the study of the Mishnah and was called to draft the statutes of the Hevra Kaddisha, the lay group that prepares the dead for burial. On the Sabbath of Repentance in 1583, he was asked to preach at the Old New Synagogue, but his stern views did not endear him to the elders, who rejected him as a candidate for the office of chief rabbi of Prague.

He left the town, served three years as chief rabbi of Poznań, and though he may have returned to Prague to continue teaching, the Prague elders rejected him again, after a sermon on the great Sabbath before Passover in 1589; again he left for Poland and returned to Prague only in 1597; after some delay he was finally appointed chief rabbi, being eighty years old. He served for nearly ten years, died on August 17, 1609, and was buried at the old cemetery, where his grave has attracted much attention through the centuries. Judah Loew's wife, Pearl, who gave him many daughters and a son who died early, followed him after ten years and was buried at his side. Their daughters, in turn, were the mothers of many distinguished scholars and rabbis: learned Vögele married Isaac Katz, who became chief rabbi of Moravia; Gittel, the third daughter, married Rabbi Samson Brandeis—she and her husband may have been distant forebears of Adolf and Frederika, who were born in Prague but left after the revolution of 1848 for Indiana and Kentucky, where their son Louis Brandeis was born, the U.S. Supreme Court justice, after whom Brandeis University was named.

In the view of his contemporaries, Rabbi Judah Loew was an intransigent scholar who, after twenty-five years and more in Moravia and Poland, became firmly devoted to necessary reforms of ritual and pedagogy. He was a radical conservative, if not a fundamentalist, whose harshness offended Prague's elders, more comfortable with inherited attitudes rarely questioned. His conservative ideas and communitarian engagement made him dear to the later Hasidim, and in the twentieth century he is seen through their eyes by his great defender Gershom Sholem. Rabbi Loew's disgust with wine handled by gentiles was but one highly characteristic symptom of his severity; he was similarly unwilling to tolerate his colleagues' habits of accepting gifts for fulfilling ritual duties or of appointing rabbis with the support of outside authorities (he believed it was a matter for the Jewish community and the community alone). His reform plans, above all, included changes in education; teaching, as the later Czech pedagogue Comenius demanded, should take into account the age and the grasp of the young people, and Rabbi Loew energetically argued against "pilpul," long dominant in Prague, which gave the highest rewards to sophisticated casuistry in handling commentaries and metacommentaries, appreciating cleverness rather than wisdom, and disregarding the fundamental sources. As if inspired by the tenets of the Renaissance, Rabbi Loew demanded an immediate return to the sources—that is, to the Torah, the central text revealed to the Jewish people, and in Talmudic writing to the Haggadah, to those narrative texts that had been unfortunately neglected by the legal inquiry of the Tosafists and especially the pilpul teachers.

The demands for a rigorous reform of the rabbinate, strict education of young people, and a turn away from pilpul to the more rewarding study of the Torah and Haggadah are intimately related to Rabbi Loew's idea that the Jewish people should not, in a late moment of their history, encounter the coming of the Messiah unprepared. It is curious that he expressed these ideas, ultimately aiming at self-assertion, in Aristotelian terminology. To Rabbi Loew, the non-Jew is but unformed matter, but the Jew is form; and from these assumptions (and after the Jews had been cruelly persecuted and expelled from Spain in 1492) he derived other definitions that elevated the Jew above the non-Jew. For him the non-Jew, biblically incarnated in Amalek (the Israelites' first enemy after their crossing of the Red Sea, Exodus 17:6–7, 8–16), is but matter, water, accident, and history; the Jew, incarnated in Israel, lives in the sphere of form, fire, the necessary, and eternity; it follows (though not all Jewish contemporaries were ready to accept these deductions) that the non-Jew can become a Jew, matter seeking its form (as woman, or matter, longs for man, the principle of form). Jews, even those who converted to Christianity, as happened during the expulsions in Spain, cannot be disloyal to form and remain Jews. Anticipating the ideas of the German philosopher Johann Gottfried Herder (later used in the defense of the Slavic peoples), Rabbi Loew declares that each group of people is called to fulfill its own and proper tasks; each must remain pristine and unsoiled in its beliefs, idiom, ways of behavior, even its code of dress. A cohesive community cannot be of evil but, on the contrary, constitutes the precondition of all integrity.

The question discussed for now more than two hundred years as to whether or not Rabbi Judah Loew was a Kabbalist of the mystical kind often coincides with the popular belief that "magic Prague," or its mysterious Jewish community, has been an eminent and unique place of mystical practices and speculations. In the history of the Kabbalah, however, Prague never had the same importance as Safed in Israel or Gerona in Spain, and in Moshe Edel's modern history of the Kabbalah, Prague does not appear at all. Rabbi Loew, who was chief rabbi in Moravia and Poland for many more years than he was chief rabbi of Prague, cannot be considered an incarnation of a Kabbalistic tradition in Prague, much as the recent tourist trade would like to sell him that way—quite apart from the historical circumstance that the traditions of rabbinical Prague were predominantly Tosafist or pilpulist, of the highest exegetic perfection. It is also true, however, that many of the Prague Tosafists—including Isaac ben Moses, in the Přemyslid period, as well as Jom Tov Lipmann-Mülhausen, the most prominent scholar of the post-Carolinian period and a valiant defender of the rationalist Maimonides—played speculative games with numbers and letters or both; it cannot be said that Rabbi Loew did not intimately know the Jewish mystical tradition (perhaps with the exception of books written by his contemporary Luria). The drama of new Renaissance ideas and Jewish tradition was played out in Rabbi Loew's mind, and he did not hesitate to refer to the mystical tradition whenever he defended the old purity of the Torah against recent scientific doubts. When the Jewish Renaissance scholar Azariah ben Moses dei Rossi demanded that the truth of the Torah be tested against the new knowledge developed in many nations, Rabbi Loew angrily argued that scientific knowledge, though legitimate in itself and worthy of being known, could not touch the Torah, which was radically different. He used the Zohar (a collection of mystical texts written in 1270–1300) to show that, in contrast to the developing knowledge of nations, the Torah was totally above all history.

Rabbi Judah Loew's intellectual independence clearly emerged in the way in which he handled the concepts of the Sefirot, fundamental to Jewish mysticism. At the core of their teachings, the Kabbalists believed that God the invisible turned to the world of visibility in ten Sefirot, or "powers," "energies," and in various ways they defined these "powers"—e.g., knowledge, glory, or majesty—as essences, elements, or revelations of a divine unity-in-itself. Insisting on the invisibility and the distance of the Highest, Rabbi Loew argued against the Sefirot as concepts about the being of Being and accepts them in a mere anthropological sense—in a Kantian way, as it were. They have nothing to do with the Highest, and are only categories of human perception which are of help to our knowledge. He saw the only possibility of coming closer to God or "clinging" to him in the study of the Torah (not in pilpul casuistry) and in active fulfillment of the Ten Commandments. Later Prague Kabbalists, and the Hasidim particularly, attached themselves to Rabbi Loew's active "clinging" to the divine, and in their stories and legends changed the learned scholar into a Zaddik, one of the miraculous and exemplary men of extraordinary power who performed many miracles and had the unusual ability to call God's blessing upon a pious and closely knit community.

The story of the golem (Psalm 139:16, an "embryo" in the appropriate commentaries and "imperfect matter"), or the Jewish Frankenstein, has done much more to strengthen the legend of mystical Prague than all of

Rabbi Loew's treatises and books about Jewish tradition put together. Yet the first creation of a golem antedates its appearance in Prague by many hundreds of years. A Hebrew commentary, written at Worms at the end of the twelfth century about the mystical treatise *Sefer Gezirah*, suggests that a golem can be created by a magic ritual in which gestures are as important as combinations of letters and numbers; such *gematria* was studied by the rabbis of Worms and Regensburg. Subsequent legends attach a golem to rabbis of mystical powers as proof positive of their skills, and in the late sixteenth century an early golem was ascribed to the great Rabbi Elijah Baal Shem of Chelm by the Christian writer Christoph Arnold. Rabbi Loew's contemporaries did not speak of a Prague golem, though the situation may have changed a few generations later: in 1725, the Loews' gravestone was piously restored, his descendants suggested that a memoir of his life and achievements should be published, and gentle hints about his more than intellectual powers began to appear in letters and *responsa* (no golem yet). Within a few decades the Jewish community was disturbed, if not rent apart, by conflicts between traditionalists and the followers of Shabbetai Zevi, a self-appointed Messiah and, later, of Jakob Frank (who claimed to be Shabbetai Zevi reincarnated), and everybody was eager to appropriate the heritage of Rabbi Loew, especially the later Hasidim of Eastern Europe. We cannot but speculate; at any rate, the first printed evidence of a Prague golem narrative, possibly long in oral circulation in Yiddish, is to be found only in the year 1841 in *Panorama des Universums*, a popular Prague German periodical. There, the story is told by the German-Czech journalist Franz Klutschak, who made a later career in Bohemian politics; he was not of Jewish origin himself and simply wanted to tell an exotic story.

In 1838, Klutschak had published in the *Panorama des Universums* a few stories relating to the old cemetery and Rabbi Judah Loew, and he called his two-column contribution "The Golam [sic] and Rabbi Loew." The rabbi created "by his magic powers" a near-human being, made of loam, Klutschak writes, and employed this golem as a servant in the Old New Synagogue. Unfortunately even Rabbi Loew was distracted by his scholarly studies at times and had forgotten a particular prayer while creating the golem. As a consequence, the golem, at least potentially, was more powerful than his creator, and the only way to discipline him was to slip an amulet into his mouth, every day of the week, and keep him, by that magic sedative, quiet and intent upon doing good. One day, the rabbi's daughter Esther fell ill and her father's magic powers were insufficient to alleviate her sufferings. It was near the evening of the Sabbath, and the rabbi decided to stay and pray with his daughter, but suddenly the cantor came running from the synagogue, all in terror, screaming that the golem was loose and raging. The rabbi had forgotten to put the Sabbath amulet in the golem's mouth, and when he arrived at the synagogue the raging golem was shaking the old walls and the lights were tumbling down "as if the world had come to its end." The rabbi immediately commanded the prayers to cease (as long as they had not been completed, the Sabbath had not begun), the earlier amulet in the mouth of the golem regained its original power, the golem turned docile again, and the community prayed in unison for the rabbi's daughter Esther, who was soon healthy again. The golem, or what was left of it, was put in storage in the attic of the synagogue, Klutschak writes, a remark that later prompted Egon Erwin Kisch, when he was an eager local reporter and not yet star journalist of the Communist International, to write an entertaining story about how he put up a ladder and searched the attic of the synagogue for the golem but, alas, in vain.

Klutschak's story of the golem has long been forgotten, and now most scholars wrongly assume that the first printed narrative about the golem appeared in *Sippurim*, or "stories," published in German in Prague in 1847. The *Sippurim* merely retell the Klutschak story in a simplified form, together with other legends about Rabbi Loew, and yet they are of essential importance in the cultural history of Prague because they constitute the first volume of a local Jewish literature written in German, not Hebrew or Yiddish, and prepare the way for future generations of Jewish authors writing in German, including Franz Kafka. The *Galerie der Sippurim* was a collection of fairy tales, legends, and biographies of famous Jews, published by Wolf Pascheles, an innovative Prague bookseller and printer who, sensing a change in the marketplace, was rightly convinced that there was a growing Jewish audience for texts in literary German, printed in German letters, not in Hebrew type. His project, later continued by his son-in-law, was eminently successful; the last popular edition of the *Sippurim* appeared in the early twentieth century. Pascheles, who had begun by selling prayer books from his *Pinkel* (backpack), employed young intellectuals of the first Jewish generation trained in philosophy, literature, and the law at Prague University (medical studies had been opened to Jews earlier) and, being rationalists, they all had a difficult time telling interesting stories of mystical purport in which they had long since ceased to believe. They belonged to a generation enchanted by Moses Mendelssohn's Berlin Jewish Enlightenment, the Haskalah, and argued against the mystical and Kabbalistic aura that darkened the image of the Maharal and his contemporaries. The writers of the *Sippurim* distinctly favored enlightened rabbis; the ideal was not a scholarly pedant, living in clouds of dust and hidden behind "the entrenchments of the Talmud" (*Talmudschanze*), but a teacher of humane engagements. They argued "against a mysticism that contradicts common sense, and, like a Chinese wall, stands in the way of all progress, all culture, all science." Divesting Rabbi Loew of mystical glory and speaking of Jewish community life in surprisingly unsentimental, often even self-ironic terms, the *Sippurim* are fully satisfied with a brief narrative reference to the golem (he is, evidently, below the dignity of an enlightened writer and reader), and, in a didactic story, Rabbi Loew warns a nobleman not to study the Kabbalah and practice magical arts. Another story (later used by Alois Jirásek in his famous *Old Czech Legends* and in Paul Wegener's expressionist film *The Golem*) shows Rabbi Loew, at the emperor's wish, magically conjuring up the patriarchs of Jewish history. The writers of the *Sippurim*, however, did not believe in this magic and dryly remarked that he had simply used a *laterna magica*, possibly being the imaginative inventor of that technological toy.

The *Sippurim* view of Rabbi Judah Loew as an enlightened philosopher avoids the question of Loew's unshakable insistence on the sacred primacy of the Torah and his difficulties with the claims of the new Renaissance science, especially mathematics and astronomy, which were being tested and defined, by the grace of the emperor, not far from the Jewish Town. Rabbi Loew did not deny the usefulness of scientific study—e.g., in the calendar calculation of Jewish holidays and in the effort to know more about divine creation—yet he absolutely and coldly rejected any potential transition from the sciences to the wisdom of the Torah, and categorically separated the secondary realm of natural sciences, concerned with a merely fragmentary view of matter, from the sacred essence of the Torah, which would yield to the pious student a total grasp of all existence.

Among the Maharal's disciples there was a man who began to disagree, modestly and hesitatingly. David ben Salomon Anza, also called David Gans, born in Westphalia, was the scientist of Prague's Jewish community; he had studied in yeshivot in Bonn, Frankfurt, Cracow, and Prague, and it is more than probable that he followed the example of Rabbi Moses Isserles of Cracow, a renowned philosopher, mathematician, and astronomer. Gans distinctly praised the Cracow rabbi because, in trying to reconcile the sciences and Jewish sacred tradition, he had suggested possibilities of theoretical compromise presented as attractively as "oranges in a silver basket." In particular, Gans studied Euclid with great enthusiasm, praising him as the most celebrated genius among the nations, and believed that his teachings created a "ladder thrown between earth and heaven." He went pretty far: "Take away Euclid's book, and it will be impossible for you to mount heavenwards." To Rabbi Loew's sensibility, these must have been nearly blasphemous statements.

David Gans, an expert historian, geographer, and astronomer, lived quietly in Prague, and among the many treatises published during his lifetime, his *Zemah David* (*A Branch of David*, 1592), a chronicle of the Jewish and non-Jewish worlds, and *Magen David* (*The Shield of David*, 1612), a critical and illuminating panorama of astronomy past and present, are of particular importance and interest. The first describes in individual entries Jewish events from the creation until his own time and, in a second part, the corresponding events of Christian history; he relies on wide readings of Jewish authorities, German chroniclers, as well as Cosmas and his Czech followers. Prague, he assumes, was originally founded before Troy, and a Prague Jewish settlement existed at the time of the Second Temple; Libussa came much later and actually restored Prague to the Slav people. David Gans is an ardent local patriot; he praises Prague as a "great, splendid, and populous city"; as if cribbing from Cosmas, he proudly describes the Bohemian opulence of fish, pastures, and forests, and speaks in perhaps more modern terms about the precious minerals of the land and the healing waters of Karlsbad and Teplitz (he uses the German names). As astronomer, Gans combines his enthusiasm for Tycho Brahe's and Kepler's investigations—which he had witnessed at close range—with a good deal of reluctance to sacrifice Ptolemy's grand view of the universe, which corresponds to Jewish tradition; when confronted with the new sciences emerging everywhere, he ultimately if grudgingly sympathizes with traditional options. His report about Tycho Brahe and his team at Benátky has the ring of authenticity, both in his feelings and in the precision of the description: "I was there among them in the rooms used as observatory, and I saw with my own eyes the marvelous work that was carried on there . . . there were three instruments, each operated by two scholars, who took the astronomical determination of the star at the very moment it passed the line of midnight." It is the professional astronomer who understands the methodological detail; "each night they would observe each of the six planets in the same way, recording their position in longitude, in latitude, their height in the sky, and the approximate variations in their distance from the earth. . . . I had the privilege of being there three times, each time for a period of five consecutive days."

One of the renowned events of the 1590s was the meeting of Emperor

Rudolf and Rabbi Judah Loew, and if it is not merely a useful fiction to enhance the Rabbi's authority, it is more probable that it happened as David Gans reported in his chronicle rather than in the ceremonious and theatrical arrangement later described by Isaac Katz, the Maharal's son-in-law. Gans greatly respected tradition and yet cherished evidence and experience; in a brief entry for February 13, 1592, he remarks that the emperor himself, "a just ruler, the source of good and light," invited the Maharal to his residence "and received him most graciously." The rabbi and the emperor conversed "face to face" as "a man speaks to his equal," but after the interview they were both unwilling to divulge what they had been talking about. Such a meeting was not at all impossible; Emperors Maximilian I and Charles V had set precedents by personally discussing with Rabbi Jossel of Rosheim, an untiring defender of German Jews, "legal matters of mutual interest"; and, by 1592, Rudolf was still willing and able to welcome visiting scholars (his saturnine isolation commenced only after 1600); it has often been remarked that the scholarly Johannes Pistorius, later his father confessor, was an excellent Christian student of the Kabbalah in the tradition of Johannes Reuchlin. Isaac Katz, who assures us that he speaks as an eyewitness, sets the date of the interview a week later, on February 20, and tells us that the Maharal was allowed to speak only to a courtier, while the emperor listened behind a closed curtain; as far as the discussion was concerned, Katz speaks of "*nistarot*," or secrets, which he promises to reveal later (he never did). By the time of the rabbi's great-great-great-grandson, we hear that the Maharal wrote a number of magic incantations on amulets before setting out to see Rudolf; the story of a remarkable meeting, originally a sober report, has long since deteriorated into a gothic narrative with mystical allusions.

The Jewish intellectual most openly sensitive to the new scientific thought of the Renaissance was Joseph Salomon Delmedigo, who spent his last years in Prague and was buried at the old cemetery in 1655. The inscription on his gravestone praises the many achievements of the "glorious rabbi, scholar, and philosopher, and one mighty among physicians." His life symbolizes the all-embracing thirst for knowledge that fired Muslims, Christians, and Jews alike in the mid-seventeenth century, and his life was more restless and productive than most. Born on Crete to a family of renowned rabbis, he was admitted to the University of Padua when he was fifteen years old; among others, he worked with Galileo Galilei, who allowed the young Jewish student to observe the stars through his telescope, the favor never extended to Kepler. By 1613, Delmedigo returned to Crete as a practicing physician, only to leave again, perhaps frustrated by an unhappy marriage or the island's narrow world. He traveled most of his life, briefly settling in Cairo, Constantinople, Poland (where he was appointed private physician to Prince Radziwill), Hamburg, and Frankfurt; he probably arrived in Prague by the mid-1640s and died there ten years later. He was a rather controversial figure, disliked by the orthodox (possibly because of his friends among the Karaite groups opposed to the rabbinical tradition), and, being able to study and converse in eight languages, he felt inspired to widen the intellectual horizon of the Jewish communities; he was certainly not averse to disputing ideas with Arab and Christian colleagues. Preferring Plato to Aristotle, Copernicus to Ptolemy, a critical reader of the Kabbalah and an untiring author of thirty or forty scientific and philosophical books, he is said to be a forerunner of the Jewish Enlightenment. Emperor Rudolf, if he had had a chance to talk to him (he died as Delmedigo concluded his studies in Padua), would have found him a wide-ranging and tolerant partner in dialogue.

Picaresque Prague and the Case of Baron Russwurm

Rudolf's Prague was not an idyllic place of peace and quiet but, rather, a European metropolis of great splendor and much dirt, with hordes of foreign travelers, a few of them knowledgeable and many of them condescending (as today), boisterous soldiers and maidens raped, and a steadily rising rate of robberies and unsolved murders; the terms *bambitka* (handgun) and *banditi* made their appearance in spoken Czech. Fynes Moryson, an English traveler of cosmopolitan tastes, immediately noticed the terrible stench in the streets, penetrating enough "to put the Turks to flight," as he wrote, and yet, in May or June, men wore little wreaths of roses on their hats and women garlands of flowers on their left shoulders, a French traveler noted. There was always something sensational going on; the arrival of a Persian or a Russian embassy (bringing thousands of precious furs, which Rudolf immediately sold abroad), or other foreign delegations of minor importance, cooling their heels as they waited for months for audiences. Elegant people always had a chance to go to Vladislav Hall at Hradčany Castle, a kind of fair where luxury goods were sold and a *corso* was held: everybody who was anybody met everybody else to exchange political news and court gossip, or to flirt with the well-protected daughters of better families who perambulated there, stiff-necked in their costly embroidery. It was always possible to find ready money (putting up a good family name for collateral) and to buy the favors of willing women or minor jobs; the young officers who came to Prague from the Turkish front for a few days of rest and recreation were short-tempered, ready to draw at the slightest provocation, and willing to disturb the good sleep of the burghers with their nightly revels.

Later writers like to indulge in spectral stories about the magic of Rudolf's Prague, but the first modern Prague prose novel in any language tells us about petty street crime and funny picaresque characters who develop a good sense for the realities of contemporary society, high and low. In 1617, the Augsburg writer Nikolaus Ulenhart's *Wondrous Tale of Isaac Winckelfelder and Jobst von der Schneid* was published, and though it was shown later to be a German adaptation of Cervantes's *Novela de Rinconete y Cortadillo* (written in 1613), Ulenhart knew his Prague topography well, carefully listened to spoken German, Czech, and Rotwelsch, or "thieves' Latin," and it would be impossible to dispute his authenticity. He writes of two young men, one the son of a Calvinist, the other from an Anabaptist family, who roam the countryside and try to make a meager living by thievery and playing with marked cards. After they tell each other their miserable autobiographies, with almost Spanish *grandeza*, they rob a foolish German and a friendly Italian and enter the big city with great hope and some initial success (they cut the purse of an Augustinian monk buying provisions for the monastery of St. Thomas in the Minor Town). Yet they are observed, in flagrante delicto, by a Czech colleague who warns the freelancing country bumpkins (his flawless Czech is incorporated into the German prose text) that thieving in Prague is "not only prohibited" but "outright dangerous," if you do not join the professional guild. He brings them to see the renowned Zuckerbastl ("Sugar Cake"), who runs the guild of the underworld with competence and energy; he anticipates the London beggar king in John Gay's *Beggar's Opera* and Brecht's *Threepenny Opera*. Zuckerbastl welcomes the two heartily and immediately notices that, though young, they are masters of practical experience. At the ensuing Sunday dinner, Isaac and Jobst meet other guild members, including assorted Italian rogues, a few whores with golden hearts and exposed breasts, and Maruška, a former madam who has taken to the Catholic religion and puts up ex-voto candles in all the churches, especially at Anežka's nunnery, and they all mightily cope with a heavy Czech Sunday meal of goose, calves' liver, and *Kolatschen*. Zuckerbastl explains the laws of the organization, praises the self-policing of crime because conflicts with the (paid off) town authorities can be avoided, and suggests that everybody share his profits with the organization. Isaac and

Jobst are formally accepted as full-fledged members, do not have to serve as apprentices, and are assigned an excellent district to work, running from Hradčany Square and the archbishop's palace to Strahov cloister and down the hill. They could not have done better, and it is unsurprising that they are ready to settle in hospitable Prague to avoid being hanged, at least for a while.

In 1655 a rich chapter in Prague's chronicle of scandals and crime was written, in his *Journal de ma vie*, by François Bassompierre, field marshal of France. He had been kept for twelve years at the Bastille upon the order of Cardinal Richelieu and had ample time to recall his youthful adventures (some readers of his memoirs believed he talked too much). He was a twenty-four-year-old officer returning from the Hungarian front when he arrived for the carnival in Prague to dance and to seek command of a cavalry regiment, and though he stayed only a few weeks, from the end of January to the beginning of April 1604, he did not miss much. It was well known that he was greatly favored by Christian Hermann Baron Russwurm, war hero and commander in chief of the imperial troops fighting the sultan; and immediately the two officers, the older and the young one, attended the right parties and dances, and more. They were happily welcomed at the noble house of the Vřesovec family (unmarried daughters again), the skirt chaser Russwurm cast an experienced eye on Esther, eighteen years old and already a widow, and young Bassompierre fell in love, or so he said, with Sybilla (her name was really Sabina but he never had a good memory for names). Yet elegant and fine feelings did not prevent the two chevaliers, immediately after the Vřesovec party, from seeking out, together with a Czech footman as translator, a certain New Town innkeeper who had promised to deliver to them two young girls, both virgins still, for a hundred ducats each. They found the innkeeper in his back room, sitting with his two daughters, who were doing needlework, but when they announced that they had brought the money and wanted the girls, the innkeeper declared he had never agreed to such a deal; Russwurm quickly drew his dagger and held it up to the father's throat, telling Bassompierre to start in on the astonished girls. The young officer answered that he was not willing to rape a girl, and in the presence of the father, at that; Russwurm ordered him to change places with him. The innkeeper, emboldened by anger, opened the window and screamed murder, neighborhood crowds gathered, and the officers had to beat a quick retreat, holding their daggers against the father's wide dark cloak, using him as a hostage to reach the street and their carriage. But there the innkeeper screamed again, the crowd began pelting the two intruders with stones, Russwurm was hit in the kidneys, and Bassompierre had to take him to the carriage. The next day, the emperor himself, from a secret window, watched them playing tennis at the new sports hall at Hradčany Castle.

The rise and fall of Generalissimo Russwurm was one of the grand affairs of Rudolf's monarchy, and it is difficult to recount his story in an orderly way. Baron Russwurm, born a Saxon Protestant in 1565, as a soldier had a deserved reputation for recklessness and cruelty, but he was also a brave commander and an efficient organizer of his troops, and the emperor visibly liked him, much to the chagrin of his fellow officers; Rudolf also feared him, being suspicious of his potential power. The imperial army was run by German-speaking commanders, in council represented by Russwurm, and by an Italian group, including Giorgio Basta and Count Barbiano de Belgioioso, well favored, in turn, by Rudolf's brother Matthias (despite the fact that Belgioioso's soldiers had so terrorized the local populations of Slovakia and Hungary, whether Catholic or Protestant, that in 1604 they rose in armed revolt against the army). The Italians concocted various accusations against Russwurm, but the charges were dismissed in Prague; when Russwurm, after taking Buda from the Turks, was directed to head a commission to investigate Belgioioso's actions, the Italians agreed that he had to go.

The conspiracy against him deserves the attention of a Jacobean playwright, with the Italians as villains in their appropriate places, the fatal chiaroscuro of narrow Prague streets of the Minor Town, and the emperor isolated in his chambers. Enter one Giacomo Furlani, a Milanese living in Prague who wants to eat his cake and have it too (an inappropriate image). Furlani knows that General Belgioioso's brother Francesco, who lives in splendor in Prague, is sought by the Milanese authorities, who have put a price of thousands of ducats on him, alive or dead, because he has abducted a lawyer's wife. Furlani conceives a brilliant plan to have quick-tempered Russwurm kill Francesco and be accused of murder; Furlani will deliver the dead Belgioioso to Milan and receive the tracker's reward. With the help of the willing Italian party, Furlani spreads the rumor, possibly not far from the truth, that the Prague Belgioioso has been responsible for all the false accusations against the generalissimo reaching the court and then, at the right moment, tips off Russwurm that Belgioioso and his entourage are lying in wait to ambush him in a narrow street in the Minor Town (Belgioioso is on hand to serenade a young woman). Russwurm falls into the trap, rushes there with his men, but in the inevitable fight Belgioioso proves to be the better swordsman and wounds Russwurm gravely; Furlani, afraid of losing his precious quarry, fires three pistol shots and kills Belgioioso with a bullet through the head. A court-martial is immediately convened; Furlani is arrested, jailed, sentenced to death, and quartered; the war hero Russwurm is accused of murder and also sentenced to death (it is said that the Spanish party handsomely pays off Rudolf's servants and butlers not to allow anybody with a good word for him into the emperor's presence). The place of the execution is ruled to be the Old Town Hall, and though Russwurm pleads for a public execution, the judges insist on the letter of the sentence.

At 6 a.m. on November 29, 1605, the famous executioner Jan Mydlař—a long-surviving figure in Prague popular ballads—enters the room and, after Russwurm prays, severs his head from his body in one swift motion and with a "whistling sound," as a witness remarks. The emperor's reprieve arrives an hour later. Russwurm's head is sewn to his body, the corpse is put in a wooden coffin to be briefly exhibited to the Prague citizens, and buried at St. Mary of the Snows. The grave has never been found.

The Last Years of Rudolf

Rudolf had been always proud and stiff when dealing with people, and after his terrible crisis, lasting nearly two years (1598–1600), he increasingly withdrew from public view, immuring himself at Hradčany Castle except when he periodically fled outbreaks of the plague. He was a strangely changed man, and his Hapsburg brothers, foreign ambassadors, and his councillors seriously discussed whether he might be possessed by evil spirits or by the devil himself; when he was told that the Infanta Isabella of Spain (whom he had selected to become his wife), after more than twenty years of frustrating negotiations, had decided to marry one of his brothers, he exploded in a tantrum of lèse-majesté, and in desperate fits turned against himself and others. He was said to have tried to commit suicide with curtain cords or splinters of glass, and in a mad moment he chased from the court both Wolf Rumpf and Paulus Sixt of Troutson, both of them long his loyal chief administrators. Access to him and correspondence was controlled for many years by a motley gang of butlers and lackeys, including the Calvinist Hieronymus Makofský; the infamous Philipp Lang, who fell from grace in 1608 and was interrogated under torture and tried on criminal charges; and later a minor painter named Daniel Fröschel.

In his time of rage and self-laceration, Rudolf was fortunate to enjoy the support of his confessor, Johannes Pistorius, who may have had particular sympathies for Rudolf's search for ultimate spirituality beyond all historical religions, for Pistorius himself had a rich history of conversions—from Luther to Calvin and then to the Holy Church—and it was Pistorius who calmed the fears of the Vatican, telling Rome that Rudolf was not obsessed but laboring under the burdens of a heavy melancholia; as Rudolf's master psychiatrist, he turned Rudolf's self-centered mind back to the arts and to his dazzling collections. Another close friend of Rudolf during these doleful years was Heinrich Julius, duke of Braunschweig, whom the emperor looked on almost as a son. The duke came to Prague on a diplomatic mission and, having amassed what was to become the largest library in Europe and being interested in rare books, the arts, and the occult (at home, he sternly persecuted women accused of witchery), stayed near Rudolf, settled in a home not far from Hradčany, and ministered to him both politically and diplomatically, even when it became clear that nobody could prevent Rudolf from destroying himself. I wonder whether many Prague literati knew that the duke was a playwright of note, composing plays in both Latin and German, and was the first to invite to his court English comedians to perform Shakespeare in Germany. The earliest German audiences of Shakespeare at least enjoyed the colorful melodrama, even if much of the language escaped their understanding.

In his disturbed mind, Rudolf came to care more about his extensive collections than about people; recent scholarship has shown that these collections were not merely a hodgepodge of curiosities but also expressions of a philosophical idea about the universe in which all things and corresponding human affairs had their proper place. The first inventory, as early as 1611, suggested that Rudolf's mind, mortally tired of the chaotic world, found refuge in this private cosmos of precious objects, neatly ordered in categories of *naturalia, artificialia,* and *scientifica*. Rudolf's grandfather, father, and uncle had had collections of precious paintings and objets d'art that represented their dignity and power, but Rudolf went much further, and it became impossible to separate his delight from outright obsession. There was a strongly conservative strain in his taste. He much admired Albrecht Dürer, as had his forebear Maximilian. Dürer's great painting "Celebration of the Rosary," or "Rosenkranzfest," had to be carried from a Venice church to Prague by four strong men traveling on foot over the Alps to make sure that the canvas was held in an upright position untouched by the snow; and Rudolf fully shared in the fashionable aristocratic appreciation of Titian, the older Brueghel, Parmigianino, Hieronymus Bosch, and Caravaggio, relentlessly using state funds to buy the paintings of these masters for his private collections. To begin with, the paintings filled seven halls at Hradčany, but he wanted more and other *artificialia*, and his agents traveled all over Europe and the Near East to discover and buy for him (making considerable commissions).

Apart from paintings, sculptures, and precious stones, Rudolf particularly collected clocks, *perpetua mobile*, rare books, ancient manuscripts, ancient coins, exquisite plants cultivated in botanical gardens, and exotic animals kept in a menagerie close to the castle. He also amassed most unusual bric-a-brac, including Přemysl's peasant cap, two iron nails from Noah's Ark, a jaw of one of the sirens from Homer's *Odyssey*, the horn of a unicorn, and wondrous figures formed by mandrake roots. A few thieving servants were caught red-handed when their master was ill, but the great plundering began a few years after his demise when Bohemian rebels sold his jewels to Nuremberg merchants in order to finance their armed revolt against Vienna. During the Thirty Years' War, both Catholics and Protestants were fairly equal in looting without shame. After the Battle of the White Mountain, Maximilian of Bavaria left Prague with 1,500 wagons of precious trophies—his contribution to Munich's famous art collections—and when the Saxons came to Prague for a few weeks in 1631, they carried fifty wagons back to Dresden. For a few days before the Westphalian peace treaties were signed in 1648, the Swedish chancellor gave secret orders to an army group quickly to occupy Hradčany Castle and to confiscate what remained of the imperial collections; Queen Christina duly received an itemized inventory of the loot, dated August 31, 1648. Next came Frederick the Great's Prussians in 1757 and, ultimately, Emperor Joseph II, the enlightened philosopher on the Hapsburg throne, who wanted to transform Hradčany into a useful artillery barracks, and appointed a commission to evaluate and sell what was left. Two centuries after Rudolf's death, Prague's junk shops were still full of the lesser stuff.

Rudolf's collections were administered for more than thirty years by the Stradas—Jacopo, the father, and Ottavio, the son. The Stradas probably came from the Mantuan gentry; Jacopo studied the ancients at the University of Pavia and early discovered the highly profitable market for Italian art and artifacts north of the Alps, where princes, emperors, and early capitalists wanted to establish representative collections; he was the Bernard Berenson of the Renaissance. Being an expert on numismatics, ancient sculpture, and architecture, he first served the Fuggers at Augsburg, among the earliest financiers of the modern world, and then by way of good connections found his way to the Vienna court, where he was employed as architectural adviser and "court antiquary" (appointed in 1556) to Maximilian II. He wrote imposing books on numismatics, expanded scholarly knowledge of Roman history, and was among those few Italian professionals at the Vienna court whom Rudolf continued to employ. By 1577, Jacopo had settled in Prague together with his German wife, Ottilie Schenk von Rossberg (of a Frankish family of robber barons, we are told), and was asked by Rudolf to consolidate and supervise the collections; when he died in 1588, his second son, Ottavio, who had published impressive collections of symbols and emblems, took on his father's job and, by 1600, shared his duties with an Italian colleague, Daniel Miseroni, in charge of precious stones and jewels. Later he relinquished the job altogether, went on to become a highly respected courtier, and loaned money, at steep interest, to proper people high in the imperial hierarchy.

A Venetian competitor accused Jacopo Strada of "unbearable arrogance," and his portrait painted by old Titian shows a well-dressed social climber with all the appurtenances of his courtly station. In the revealing gestures of Jacopo's hands, offering a little silver statue of Venus to a noble customer, Titian may have suggested something about his life. It might have been mere rumor that Jacopo offered Rudolf the favors of his wife, Ottilie, but it is difficult to believe that he did not know what he was doing when he invited the emperor to his luxurious quarters and presented to him his young daughter Catharina—charming, well educated in Vienna, intelligent—on a silver platter, at least if we accept the assumptions of older research (D. J. Jansen has more recently suggested that it was, rather, Jacopo's illegitimate daughter Anna Maria who was introduced to the emperor). Rudolf was well known for his sexual appetites, to say the least, and for quickly changing desires. "He prefers free love to marriage," an unfriendly novelist remarked when speaking of his "troops of concubines" and "virgins who greatly valued their chance to be deprived of that title." The father may have been surprised by Catharina's (or Anna Maria's) loyalty to the aging emperor, who had other favorites, but she was probably the mother of his three sons and three daughters—he legitimized them as far as was legally possible, but they were an unhappy group nevertheless. Carolina d'Austria, the oldest daughter, managed to make a respectable marriage, but her two sisters disappeared into nunneries in Vienna and Madrid; of the younger sons, one died early and another perished in the wars. Julius Caesar, Don Juan d'Austria, the oldest, who was clinically mad (the heritage of his Spanish great-grandmother), was exiled to Krumlov Castle in southern Bohemia, where he killed a young girl named Maruška, disfiguring her corpse with his hunting knife. He lives on in the best of Rainer Maria Rilke's Prague stories, about the first stirrings of desire of a young Czech girl from the provinces. In her feverish dreams she fears Don Juan d'Austria, who, like a wild animal, follows her up the stairs of a high castle tower, and, when he tears her blue silk dress to pieces; she jumps to her death from high up. Catharina (or Anna Maria) Strada was not untouched by scandal in her own life (evil tongues accused her of conspiring with a butler to steal from the collections), and it is truly deplorable that, whoever she really was, she did not find a poet or a historian to speak of her thirty years of loyalty, suffering, and silence.

After the cabinet changes of 1599–1600, the Catholic nobility dominated the administration of Bohemia and, as long as the war against the Turks went well, Prague Protestants had reasons to fear the worst. In many Austrian lands, including Styria and Upper Austria, Rudolf's brothers brutally persecuted Evangelicals; in Prague, the emperor renewed the mandate against the Czech Brethren in 1602 and closed down many of their schools and chapels. The situation rapidly changed in 1604, mostly because the imperial army and Italian Catholic generals indiscriminately terrorized Slovakia and Hungary, and the Hungarian Protestant nobles rose in anger against the empire and appointed István Bocskay as their efficient leader of the revolt; his light cavalry devastated Moravia and threatened Vienna too. It was Matthias, Rudolf's ambitious brother (by now officially head of the Austrian Hapsburg family), who, fully confirming the privileges of the Hungarian Estates, concluded a peace agreement with the Bocskay rebels as well as an armistice with the Turks and created a confederation of the Austrian and Hungarian Estates to protect the peace. Brother stood against brother; Matthias, commanding a confederate army, quickly marched on Prague to make certain that Rudolf and the Bohemians did not sabotage the peace arrangements and did recognize his privilege of being heir to the throne. Rudolf, appearing sick and pale, came to a meeting of the Bohemian Estates for the first time in years; they decided to fight the invaders and mobilized an army of their own. This military stalemate prompted Matthias, a political realist, to sign an agreement in 1608 in the village of Libeň (now an industrial suburb of Prague on the west bank) according to which Matthias was to rule most of Austria, Hungary, and Moravia, while Rudolf was left with Bohemia, Silesia,

Lusatia, and the imperial crown. Rudolf had been saved by the Bohemian Estates, but now they wanted a reward for their support, and immediately.

The Estates presented the first draft of their demands while Matthias was still close to Prague, but Catholics—including the papal nuncio, the Spanish ambassador, Zdeněk of Lobkovic, and his Catholic friends—convinced the emperor that he should postpone discussion to a later date. The final document (actually written by Václav Budova, of the Czech Brethren) was ready for signature on the eve of July 9, 1609. It was basically the earlier draft with a few changes (the Estates wanted to call themselves "evangelical," but the emperor insisted on the more traditional terms of *sub utraque specie*); fortunately, the internal tensions between Lutherans, or Neo-Utraquists, and Czech Brethren, who by now were closer to John Calvin, were calmed by the diplomacy of two German Protestants, Joachim Schlick and Matthias Thurn, and did not endanger the unity of the Estates. The trouble was that the intransigent Catholics refused to sign ex officio as they should have, especially Bohemia's high chancellor, but the declaration was signed after all by the Prague burgrave Adam of Sternberg and deposited in the state archives at Karlštejn Castle. The "Letter of Majesty" of 1609, as it is called, was the most advanced and enlightened statement of Bohemian religious tolerance yet, at least as far as Christian groups were concerned, and the fulfillment of many Renaissance dreams about the interdependence of all religious beliefs. The document guaranteed freedom of religious belief and practice to all Christian groups of the *Confessio Bohemica* (as it had been defined in 1575) and stated that the old university would be administered by the Estates, who were responsible for the appropriate appointments; a number of *defensores*, totally independent of imperial authority, would see that all groups respected each other's rituals, possessions, and claims. New schools and churches were to be built freely, and not even peasants could be forced by barons or any other authorities to change their personal religious beliefs. Bohemian Protestants, even the heirs of the radical Hussites, could take a deep breath but, unfortunately, not for long.

In his earlier years Rudolf certainly wanted to establish a Society of the Wise (as the Czech pedagogue and philosopher Comenius believed), but in his later years an unquenchable thirst for revenge destroyed the last noble gifts of his unbalanced mind. He wanted to strike back at the Estates, who had forced his hand, as he believed, and at his brother Matthias, but lacking substantial support and possibly against his better judgment, Rudolf involved himself with an irresponsible adventurer of high birth and a colonel of mercenaries. Only a madman would have entrusted his future, and that of the kingdom, to his twenty-three-year-old nephew, Archduke Leopold, hungry for glory but devoid of political and military experience. Leopold had gathered at his residence in Passau, in Bavaria, a force of ten thousand men, under the command of one Colonel Ramée, allegedly to fight the Protestants in western Germany but actually poised to march on Prague to fight the Estates and force Matthias to return power to Rudolf. This was to be a banana-republic putsch, and even the papal nuncio and Spanish ambassador in Prague recoiled from the idea that the Catholic cause might be won by such a haphazard band of mercenaries. Nonetheless, the Passau soldiers wended their way through Upper Austria, turned suddenly north to Bohemia, took Budějovice and Tábor easily, and on February 15, 1611, occupied the Minor Town despite the bloody resistance of the local citizens (many stories were told of resident Italians firing at Protestants from the windows). Prague plunged into a brutal war again.

The first action of the Passau soldiers was, of course, to plunder the rich palaces of the nobles and town houses of the patriciate. The Passauers held the Minor Town but in vain tried to cross the stone bridge to take the Old and New Towns; when a Passauer cavalry fought its way across the bridge to the Old Town Square, the soldiers were pulled off their horses and killed, man by man. Protestant defenders of the Old Town proceeded to set fire to monasteries; they killed many monks, though the Jesuits were saved by their noble patrons; the Jewish Town was promptly invaded and pillaged.

Time went against the Passau army; Matthias and his forces were near, the Estates consolidated their defenses, using artillery, and on the night of March 10 the Passauers left town, taking with them irresponsible Archduke Leopold. Hradčany Castle was occupied by armies of the Estates and Matthias, a criminal investigation was started against local allies of the Passauer mercenaries, and Matthias was crowned king of Bohemia on May 23, with the full support of both Catholic and Protestant Estates. Matthias agreed that Rudolf was to go on living at Hradčany Castle, receive an appanage of one hundred thousand taler a year, and remain emperor as long as he lived. Nothing was to disturb the solitude that Rudolf had craved for so long, but in January 1612 his physician found his lungs seriously damaged, his liver inflamed, and putrefying wounds appearing on his body. He died, peacefully, on January 20, and his burial was a very decorous and quiet affair.

Rudolf has not left us any stately buildings for posterity to admire, and the citizens of Prague have never thought of erecting a monument to his memory; his collections are gone, and there is nothing tangible in the city to hold on to his moment in its history. Many Czech, German, and Jewish writers have told colorful legends about him, but among poets and playwrights it was only the sober and irritable Franz Grillparzer, that untiring Viennese student of Bohemian history, who in the last years before the revolution of 1848 deeply sympathized with Rudolf's desire for solitude and tried to understand his self-destruction. Unfortunately, Grillparzer's *Ein Bruderzwist in Habsburg* (*A Conflict of Hapsburg Brothers*), first performed in Vienna in 1872, in the habit of the post-Schiller historical play spreads out a vast canvas of events extending from the Hungarian plains to Hradčany Castle; only in its most magnificent scenes, in the second and fourth acts, in which Rudolf bares his soul to Duke Heinrich Julius, do we come close to the heart of the matter. Rudolf calls himself "a weak, ungifted man," but he adores the order of nature manifesting the divine will to people who boast of their spirituality while brutally "cleansing" entire populations for religious reasons. Foreign tribes have not destroyed what is most noble in the world but, rather, the "barbarians in ourselves who push down everything" to the level of our own vulgarity. Rudolf even comes to have ambivalent feelings about his beloved Prague, that "malicious city" (*die arge Stadt*), and though he has long tried to protect Prague from murder and fire, he speaks of the savageries of the coming war that will engulf all of Europe, and utters a prophetic and merciless curse upon treacherous Bohemia and Prague. Grillparzer has not sketched a historical portrait but rather defined the Platonic idea of a ruler who believes that in a world in which spiritual conflict has turned into a battle for political power, procrastination is better than action. In a note in the margins of his manuscript, Grillparzer expressed a view of Rudolf's age that did not lack either precision or insight. Rudolf's "inertia," he wrote, "would have created happiness but the actions of the others destroyed everything."

The Revolt of 1618 and the Battle of the White Mountain

The intransigent Catholics had refused to sign any document that extended equal privileges to all Christian confessions, and when Matthias, the new king of Bohemia, moved the imperial and royal court back to Vienna after Rudolf's death, the Prague Catholics, firmly supported by the Spanish party in Vienna and the new Prague archbishop, Johannes

Lohelius, began to increase pressure on the Protestants. Inevitably, they provoked a radical group among the Bohemian Estates to think of violent solutions, all other means failing. It was almost a civil war by attrition. Protestants were deprived of traditional offices, the self-rule of the Prague towns was diminished by decree, and tempers ran especially high when two newly built Protestant churches, erected on land belonging to a Benedictine monastery and the archbishop, were razed. The Catholics thought the Protestants were wrong to build their chapels on ecclesiastical ground, while the Protestants, in turn, assumed that all church lands belonged, ultimately, to the king (a difficult question never elucidated by earlier documents). The non-Catholic Estates immediately convened a meeting at the Carolinum to address their grievances to the king, yet a group of radicals, among them Václav Budova, of the Czech Brethren, and the impetuous Count Matthias Thurn, met at the town house of Jan Smiřický of Smiřice in the Minor Town to plan the murder of the royal administrator at Hradčany Castle. When the members of the Estates learned of the king's uncompromising response to the Bohemian grievances, they decided to march to the castle to confront the royal administrators whom they thought responsible for the condescending tone of the king's answer. It was just the occasion for which the radical conspirators had waited.

The towns were restive when, on the morning of May 23, 1618, the members of the Estates went to the castle and, exactly as the radical group had planned, seized the staircase and the offices of the royal administrators and their staff. Six of the officials, sensing something in the air, had left for Vienna on sudden business, and the angry Protestant representatives confronted Adam of Sternberg, Děpold of Lobkovic, Vilém Slavata of Chlum, and Jaroslav of Martinic, who tried to explain that they were not personally responsible for the king's answer. (True, the document had been mainly composed by Melchior Cardinal Khlesl, the *éminence grise* of Matthias's court.) The radicals did not want to listen to these protestations, but at least they had the good sense to spare two of the moderate royal officials, who were shoved into an adjacent chamber and let go. That left Martinic and Slavata, who had been among the most active of the intransigent Catholics for twenty years. An exchange of views, if there ever was one, had long ceased; Count Thurn, the military man, demanded (probably in German) action not speeches, and many hands seized Slavata and Martinic and threw them out of the window. Slavata, calling for the presence of his father confessor, clung to the window until somebody hit him on the hand with a dagger hilt and he fell out too; when the conspirators noticed that Johannes Fabricius, a secretary, quietly wanted to leave the room, they seized him for good measure and tossed him out also. A few random pistol shots were fired after them, but fortunately all three survived the fall; the Protestants claimed that this was because they fell on a dunghill, while the Catholics argued that the Virgin Mary had miraculously spread out her celestial mantle to break their fall. Fabricius hobbled away and escaped; he was later ennobled by the emperor and awarded the title of "von Hohenfall" (of High Fall). Slavata, who badly hurt his head, made his way to the house of the imperial chancellor and, personally protected by the chancellor's courageous wife, Polyxena of Lobkovic, stayed there until his wound had healed. When the news about the defenestration reached the towns, people (much aware of the Hussite precedents) went wild, ransacking and setting fire to churches and monasteries once again; Franciscan monks were killed; and, as usual, the mob invaded the Jewish Town to rob and pillage. People felt that something important had happened, and they were not wrong.

The Estates elected thirty directors, ten each for barons, knights, and towns, and, though these were headed by radicals, the majority was moderate and believed that the new situation should be handled by old-fashioned negotiations (after all, in the summer of 1617 the Estates had accepted Archduke Ferdinand as king of Bohemia without much resistance). In Vienna, Emperor Matthias himself, hesitant as ever, wanted to give negotiations a try, while the Spanish party and Ferdinand wanted to crush any Protestant opposition without mercy. At the same time, both Prague and Vienna began to mobilize international support and consolidate the first army corps clashing in southern Bohemia; Count Thurn operated near Vienna but had to withdraw again.

When Matthias died in 1619, he was succeeded on the imperial throne by Ferdinand, and Catholics and Protestants prepared for an international conflict: the Austrian Hapsburgs sought the support of Spain, Bavaria, Saxony, Poland, and Tuscany, while the Prague Estates, who rightly believed they could not go it alone, discussed financial and military help from Holland, England, Venice, and the Italian Piedmont; though their inexperienced diplomats were astonishingly skillful, they also had many illusions, and few people wanted to fight, or die, for Prague. In the summer of 1619 the Bohemian Estates (joined by the Protestant Estates of Lower and Upper Austria) constituted a confederation of all the enemies of Hapsburg in the crown lands, expelled the Jesuits from Prague "for all time," and confiscated Catholic property to pay for the war. Ferdinand was formally dethroned, and the Estates offered the elected crown of the lands to Friedrich, Calvinist prince-elector of the Palatinate, a young and prominent German Protestant ruler married to Elizabeth, daughter of King James I of England; it was clear that the choice was dictated by the hope for international support.

Friedrich and Elizabeth would have made an exemplary and decorative royal couple at the best of times, but not at the beginning of a war that was to devastate Europe for thirty years. He was twenty-three years old when he accepted "the divine call," as he declared it, to legitimize the revolt of the Bohemian nobles. Well educated by French Calvinists, slim, elegant, serious, and totally green in war or diplomacy, Friedrich lacked energy and judgment; the best one could expect of him, his French educator once remarked, was that he would duly follow honest advice. His wife, Elizabeth (among whose earlier suitors had been the French dauphin and the Swedish crown prince Gustavus Adolphus), did not lack high intelligence and wit—Ferdinard would "make a lousy emperor," she said—but, constantly pregnant, she was too well bred not to accept happily whatever her husband resolved to do; since they were essentially spoiled children who liked to entertain, to ride, and to hunt, they were at the mercy of events. In late September 1619, they left Friedrich's residence in Heidelberg with a train of 153 wagons, hundreds of servants, and a thousand soldiers, and were welcomed at the Bohemian border in Latin; they entered jubilant Prague on October 21, 1619, to be crowned king and queen at St. Vitus Cathedral in festive and separate ceremonies.

While the armies of the Catholic "League" and the Protestant "Union," mostly made up of mercenaries, began to organize on a large scale, Friedrich and Elizabeth played the royal couple with dedication; they were welcomed by everybody at first, but they were also different and it showed; when they asked the Prague burghers for a personal loan to pay for the army, they were brusquely refused. Friedrich spent his time inspecting his (mostly unpaid) troops and dealing with ambassadors; Elizabeth, celebrated in famous poems by John Donne and Sir Henry Wotton, tried to be nice and yet irritated the Bohemians with her expensive dresses, her outlandish hairdo, and her plunging décolletage. (Her court chaplain, Scultetus, in the meantime, almost caused a popular revolt because he tried to transform St. Vitus Cathedral into a Calvinist chapel.) King and queen conversed in French, did not try to learn the languages of the land, and when in early November 1620 the Catholics were preparing to enter Prague, they left in such an undignified hurry that the queen absentmindedly (her biographers hope) left her youngest baby untended at the castle; and it had to be handed over to her by Baron Christopher Dohna, in a bundle, through the windows of the departing coach.

They were without a home and a country; after a long pilgrimage via Küstrin and Berlin, they settled in Holland, where Friedrich continued to call himself king of Bohemia (he died in 1632); Elizabeth returned to England only a year before her demise. "A debonair but plain woman," Samuel Pepys noted when he caught a glimpse of her in London.

Protestants of the Union and Catholic armies of the League engaged in bloody confrontations in the provinces in the course of the year and circumspectly marched on the Prague region, where they inevitably clashed in a fierce short battle—the saddest day in the Czech tradition (to be compared only with that other melancholy day when, after the Munich conference of 1938, President Eduard Beneš decided not to engage the German armies, and ordered Czechoslovakia's mobilized soldiers, willing to fight, to go home). On November 8, 1620, the tactical advantage was on the side of the Protestants, with about 21,000 men, who occupied the flat top of a low hill called the White Mountain (now easily reached by tram number 22). The Catholics, about 28,000 strong, had the numerical advantage, but they were below the hill and had to fight upward. Still, the Protestants had arrived on the White Mountain only after long marches, were exhausted by lack of sleep, and failed to prepare entrenchments for their artillery pieces as they should have done. The Union armies, comprising Czechs, Moravians, Austrians, Germans, and Hungarians, were arranged in the "Dutch" manner, considered by military doctrine more flexible: three columns of three lines of mixed infantry and cavalry companies (the king's guard taking positions in the garden of the Villa Hvězda). The Catholics of the League, an equally international group of Bavarians, Spanish, Walloons, Germans, and French (among them the future philosopher René Descartes), preferred the "Spanish" way, thought to be more stable: four square infantry formations in the middle of their ranks, supported by infantry and cavalry on the side, a strong lateral concentration of Lothringians and Germans facing the right wing of the Protestants, commanded by brave Joachim Schlick.

The battle started with a probing movement of the Catholics against the Protestant left wing—the imperial general merely wanted to assess the strength of the enemy—but it quickly developed into a fierce fight when the Hungarians turned to run and Thurn's more experienced men were exposed to a cutting attack. The Protestant counterattack tried to pierce the Spanish center, while the courageous Moravians attacked the Catholic right wing; the League's Lothringian and German troops, held in reserve, were ordered to intervene. Now the tide turned against the Protestants, and the king's guard in the Hvězda garden was massacred by Italian troops. Within an hour, more than two thousand soldiers on both sides were dead; while the Moravians and Austrians fought a last rearguard action to save the Protestant cause, their companions tried to reach Prague, and the victorious armies of the Catholic League rested on the field. At Hradčany Castle, a nightlong discussion of the war council was held. Count Matthias Thurn and the Austrian Calvinist Georg Erasmus Tschernembl demanded that Prague be defended, but they were turned down, and in the morning the royal couple and the leaders of the revolt packed their bags. The imperial army entered Prague without a shot being fired, and within the day the Protestants formally submitted to Maximilian of Bavaria, who accepted their humiliation in the name of Emperor Ferdinand II.

Maximilian of Bavaria left after a week, with his long wagon train of loot, and the emperor, disregarding the moderate Prague Catholics and relying on the Spanish party, appointed Karl of Liechtenstein, a convert, as eager to make a profit as he was newly ardent in his religion, to chair the commission charged with prosecuting those responsible for the revolt. The Viennese offices and the Prague commission proceeded quietly and deliberately, knowing only too well who had escaped abroad (in the best NKVD manner, a Colonel Tiefenbach was abducted from Switzerland and executed on Austrian soil) and who believed, naively, that their lives would be spared. The order to arrest people on the commission's list was given only in late February 1621, and prisoners were meanwhile held at the Hradčany White Tower or in the Old Town hall. In order to avoid examination under torture, Martin Frühwein, an articulate magistrate of the Old Town who had written a treatise on the defense of the Estates, committed suicide by jumping to his death from the window, but his body was quartered and the pieces of his corpse exhibited at different town squares, his head and one hand nailed to the gallows. In late spring, the Prague commission made its recommendation to Vienna; it was accepted quickly enough, with a few brutal changes, and the executions of twenty-seven barons, knights, and burghers, old and young, Czech and German, Protestant and (one) Catholic, were set for June 21, 1621.

The town was full of soldiers, thirty-nine workers had erected a huge scaffold against the wall of the Old Town hall, black cloth was laid out theatrically, and drums were rolling; an eyewitness remarked, "You couldn't understand your own word or anybody else's." The sequence of the executions was by rank. Joachim Andreas Count Schlick was beheaded first (his Lutheran forebears had been among the leaders of the revolt of 1547) and, after him, seventy-four-year-old Václav Budova, patriarch of the Czech Brethren, Kryštof Harant of Polžice and Bezdružice, famous musician at the court of Rudolf II and artillery commander when Count Thurn lay brief siege to Vienna. Among the many knights were eighty-six-year-old Kašpar Kaplín of Sulevice, Bedřich of Bílá, Otto of Loos, Bohuslav of Michalovice (whose right hand was cut off before he was beheaded), and the Catholic Diviš Černín of Chudenice, who had made the fateful mistake of opening the gates of Hradčany to representatives of the Estates on the morning of the defenestration. There were three German civil servants, Leander Rüpel, of the Palatinate, Georg Hauschild, of the appellate courts, and Dr. Friedrich Georg of Oldenburg. Among the burghers of the Old, New, and other towns, Valentin Kochan was executed because he had raised his voice against Ferdinand at the meeting of the Estates in 1617; Johann Kutnauer, the youngest of the townspeople, was hanged on a beam jutting out of the town hall window. In the case of Jessenius, his majesty the emperor revised the commission's recommendation—his tongue was cut off (he had negotiated on behalf of the Estates with the Hungarians in Bratislava) and then he was beheaded and quartered, rather than the other way around. Minor offenders were dealt with later: a few burghers publicly whipped, those sentenced to life carted away to Castle Zbiroh, and Mikuláš Diviš for two hours nailed by his tongue to the gallows because he had had the temerity to welcome Friedrich and Elizabeth to Prague at the head of a joyful group of people dressed as Hussite peasants who had made a great deal of noise with their flails, or so Queen Elizabeth thought. The severed heads of twelve were carried in iron baskets to the tower of the stone bridge and exhibited there. Only in 1631, when Saxons briefly occupied Prague (among them the indefatigable Count Thurn), were they taken down and buried at the Týn Church, where they were found in 1766.

After the executions, confiscations and expropriations went on for two years or more, and substantially changed Prague's social scene. The emperor gave vast stretches of land, forfeited by Protestant nobles, to his Spanish generals and Austrian advisers (the Eggenbergs were awarded the Rožmberk lands in southern Bohemia), and the new archbishop of Prague and other church dignitaries who demanded restitution of everything the Hussites of old had taken had little reason to be dissatisfied. The imperial commission condemned 680 persons and fifty towns all over Bohemia to loss of property and possessions, and those who were spared outright confiscation and were allowed to sell their belongings were paid in coin that was low in silver—virtually robbed. All non-Catholic clergy had to leave; Lutherans, being protected by the emperor's Saxon allies, were allowed to stay for a year. In 1622, the Jesuits, who had taken back St. Clement, united the old Carolinum and the Clementinum in a single new university institution and were given supervision of all schools and printing presses in Bohemia; it so happened that Bedřich Bridel, chief Jesuit censor, turned out to be the most gifted metaphysical poet of the Baroque Czech tongue. By 1624, the Catholic religion was declared to be the only legal one, with a special commission overseeing forced conversions (six months or else), and a new wave of exiles—German Lutheran burghers and Czech Brethren, among them the philosopher and pedagogue Comenius—left to work, pray, teach, and die abroad: all in all, about 36,000 families. In 1627, the imperial offices issued new administrative rules, the Verneuerte Landesordnung, actually a new constitution, which declared Bohemia to be a land of the Hapsburg Empire ruled by inheritance (not election), in its religious life exclusively Catholic, and yielding to the Estates only those rights that did not clash with the intentions and demands of the Viennese court. The question who, or what, was responsible for the defeat of the revolt of the nobles, was answered as early as 1620 by the sharp-eyed Austrian Tschernembl, who deplored that his brothers in arms the Bohemian nobles had been unwilling to arm the peasants (whom they feared) against the imperial power, to mobilize a *levée en masse*, in the ancient Hussite way. Palacký, the father of Czech historiography, advanced a similar idea two hundred years later.

In an age of executions and confiscations, the Jewish community was distinctly favored by imperial policies, and Prague's Jews, who had few illusions about the Bohemian Estates, felt increasingly loyal to the dynasty, much as Viennese and Prague Jews did in the later nineteenth century. When the Catholic armies were permitted to loot and rape the helpless towns immediately after the Battle of the White Mountain, army guards protected the Jewish community; Ferdinand II confirmed and expanded Jewish privileges by two edicts in 1623 and 1627. The bonds between Prague's Jews and the dynasty were tested in 1648 when Swedes occupied the Minor Town and Hradčany Castle and threatened the Old Town with artillery fire and a fierce attack across the stone bridge. The town was defended by soldiers from a small garrison, students of the university led by their Jesuit teachers, and members of the Jewish community, who helped to extinguish fires, cared for the wounded, and joined in the fighting. Twenty-two Jews died, many more were injured, and the Swedes did not cross the river.

It was Goethe who described the episode, in which the Thirty Years' War at its very end returned to its place of origin, in a piece of ceremonious prose, but he was happily unaware of what it really meant that the inhabitants of Prague courageously fought against a Swedish army in which many distinguished Czech exiles continued to serve; after thirty years of brainwashing, the valiant defenders did not know exactly who was friend or foe. The Hapsburg dynasty was tremendously pleased; Ferdinand III gave the Jewish community a festive banner with the Star of David and a Jewish hat, and graciously allowed the Old Town to modify its coat of arms: traditionally, it had shown three towers and an open, empty town gate, and now in the gate appeared a powerful arm drawing an unsheathed sword against the enemy. Franz Kafka wrote a thoughtful short prose meditation about this revised Old Town coat of arms and revised it once again, speaking of a fist (not a sword) and, whether he knew of the historical circumstances or not, suggesting that a giant fist one day would smash the city whose inhabitants were so fickle and inconstant.

The most powerful man of Prague's Jewish community was, after Mordecai Maisel's demise, the financier Jacob Bassevi, who, together with his brother, had arrived in Prague from Verona in 1590. Taking many more risks than conservative Meisel, Bassevi served three emperors well and enjoyed more privileges than anybody else ever did; in 1622, he was the first Prague Jew to be ennobled, and duly received a coat of arms and the title "von Treuenburg" (of Loyalburg). He built himself a palatial dwelling, the pride of the community (it was razed three hundred years later), but he was also viewed as warmhearted and compassionate, providing his fellow citizens with a new bathhouse, a hospital, and the Grossenhof Synagogue (destroyed by urban modernization in the late nineteenth century). His power was the ultimate cause of his downfall: when the emperor needed cash for his armies, he sold the royal right to coin silver money to a consortium of powerful Bohemian nobles chaired by Karl of Liechtenstein, who had been in charge of the tribunals of revenge, the Dutch economist Hans de Witte, and Jacob Bassevi of Treuenburg; these last two were asked to take care of the economic and technical procedures. The price of silver rapidly rose, and the consortium interpreted the original contract in a way rather convenient to its own interests: it issued infamous "long coins," short on silver, resulting in catastrophic private losses (especially catastrophic when one was forced to sell for religious or political reasons) and public bankruptcy. As long as Liechtenstein lived, Bassevi was protected, but when Liechtenstein died in 1627, the Jew Bassevi became the fall guy and spent many weeks in prison. He was fortunate to be able to escape to the Bohemian territories of the duke of Wallenstein, who immediately made him his efficient minister of finance. But Wallenstein, who had conspired against the emperor, was murdered by a gang of loyalist killers, and Bassevi died in the same year (1634). It took another 150 years before a Hapsburg ennobled a Jewish financier again.

The Prague Baroque

The magnificence of Prague Baroque architecture, perhaps more noticeable to travelers from the north, west, or overseas than to those from Rome, Naples, or Venice, has often been related, especially by later Czech patriots, to the military victory of the Hapsburgs, the terror of the re-Catholicization, and the taste of Jesuits and foreign noblemen building new town residences in a more or less occupied territory. But the contradictions of a historical moment cannot be so easily defined by these nineteenth-century simplifications. It is true, of course, that the victory of the Hapsburgs, the triumph of Spanish imperial policies, favored the immigration of Catholic nobles who had served the Viennese court well, but it is equally true that the outstanding military leaders of the Bohemian revolt—the Schlicks, Count Thurn, and the South Tyrolean Colonna of Völz (who died of a wound in the field)—were not exactly Czechs; of the immigrant nobles settling in Prague and Bohemia in the decades after 1620, many distinguished families, for instance the Schwarzenbergs, came fully to share the historical vicissitudes of the ancient Czech nobility; centuries later the Nazi occupation was an acid test of its loyalties. The label of "foreign nobility" (*cizácká šlechta*), extremely convenient when dispossessing real estate or refusing restitution of old property rights, is less useful in looking at Baroque Prague.

Historians of Prague architecture agree that the Italian Baroque arrived in Prague before the Battle of the White Mountain, and that its French and Austrian versions flourished far into the eighteenth century. The first constructions in the new style were the oval-shaped Italian chapel in the Jesuit Clementinum, the Church of the Holy Trinity, probably built by Giovanni Filippi (1611–13) and originally used by German Lutherans and later by the Carmelite order, and, most visible, the elaborate Gate of the Emperor Matthias (1614), through which nowadays most tourists enter Hradčany Castle. Not long after the executions and expropriations, a new wave of Baroque construction began in Prague and changed many medieval squares and streets in a monumental way. It was sustained by the new most powerful and richest nobles and by the commitments of returning Jesuits and other, newly arrived orders; they all competed for the services of Carlo Luragho, Francesco Carrotti, Domenico Orsi, and others, as well as their clans of architectural assistants and expert plasterers. Albrecht of Waldstein, later to be Generalissimo Wallenstein, still favored by the emperor, immediately wanted a representative palace in the Minor Town, and he razed twenty-six old houses, three gardens, and a brick factory to create enough space for an imposing building; it hides a graceful loggia with many artistic features behind a forbidding facade that recalls a stern military barrack. He was impatiently followed in 1631 by Pavel Michna of Vacínov, who had made a fortune supplying the imperial army and decided to transform a small villa near the river into a huge, unwieldy palace to satisfy all the wishes of a nouveau riche. It was planned on such a grandiose scale that its artful interior was not yet finished a generation later (the building now houses the gymnasts' association).

At about the same time, the Jesuits began to transform the old Clementinum into a large compound of churches, chapels, libraries, colleges, a theater, an observatory, printing shops, and a magnificent refectory (later the main reading room of the National Library, in which I have spent many pleasant months as a young student and as an old professor). They also settled in the Minor Town and in the New Town, where they built the imposing church of St. Ignatius and another college (destroyed by an American air raid in February 1944). Among the early and exquisite achievements of the Prague international Baroque is the Loretto, a pious Prague imitation of the Santa Casa, the holy habitation in which Mary lived and received the Annunciation (miraculously transferred from Palestine to Loreto, in Italy); the Prague shrine was later surrounded by a cloister, a church of the Nativity, and many chapels. By the later 1650s and 1660s, the noble families, old and new, joined the Baroque construction boom and built their town palaces at Hradčany or downtown—the Nostitzes, the Kolovrats, the Czernins (the original plans possibly sketched by the great Roman architect Bernini), and at least forty others. Among the experts, architects of other nations begin to appear—Jean Baptiste Mathey from Dijon, who built the castle at Troja and had great troubles with the masons' guild because he did not speak Czech; and František Maximilián Kaňka, a gifted Czech born in the Old Town. In the mid-1680s, the Dientzenhofer family, originally from Aibling in Bavaria, settled in Prague, and Kilian Ignaz Dientzenhofer finished the Church of St. Nicholas (originally begun by his father), among other distinguished projects, and crowned it with a magnificent dome, considered by many, including the young poet Rainer Maria Rilke (who otherwise did not have much of a historical sense), to be the true symbol of Baroque Prague.

Rudolf II had always hesitated to ally himself too closely with Spanish intransigents, but his successors, especially Ferdinand II, had fewer qualms, and Spanish orientations were all the rage among the victorious. Fashion long preceded politics; the *gorguera*, or the artfully folded white collar, had been worn by elegant people since the mid-sixteenth century, and Prague tailors had to learn how to make a black *capa*, kept longer in Prague than in Madrid because of the unfriendly weather. The Spanish party had long congregated in the salon of Maria Manrique de Lara, who, in spite of some family trouble with the church (the Inquisition condemned her Italian mother because of her contacts with Neapolitan heretics), married Vratislav of Pernštejn, high chancellor of the kingdom of Bohemia after 1565, and her palace was always open to traveling Catholic dignitaries, successive Spanish ambassadors, and scions of the Czech nobility. There were a few scandals and a good deal of flirting; of the eleven living daughters of the house, only four married according to their station (important because their mother later faced financial ruin), and the Spanish ambassador Guillén de San Clemente, a lean Catalan, reported in a nice letter to his sovereign that in de Lara's salon "his sensualities were pulled hither and thither, and he was rescued only by his reason."

Maria's extraordinary daughter Polyxena had inherited her mother's fine political sense, and even Protestant observers were willing to remark on her independence of mind, keen insight, and unusual courage when it came to expressing her views shared by a few friends and opposed by many. She married twice, both times to the most powerful men of the realm: in 1587 Vilém of Rožmberk, owner of rich lands in southern Bohemia, friend of artists and supporter of traveling alchemists including Dee and Kelley; and then Zdeněk Popel of Lobkovic in 1603, high chancellor, moderate leader of the Catholic party for at least two decades, but not necessarily popular in Vienna after 1618. We know deplorably little about Polyxena's experiences, ambitions, and frustrations, but her sympathies for the Order of the Spanish Barefoot Carmelites who came to Prague in 1624 are irrevocably inscribed in the Baroque traditions of Prague.

Ferdinand II had promised Dominicus à Gesù Maria, general of the Carmelite order (who had preached to the imperial troops on the White Mountain), that the Carmelites, of the new and stricter branch, would be welcome in Vienna and Prague, and he stood by his word punctiliously.

In Prague it was, as usual, a matter of confiscation; the Lutheran clergy had been expelled in 1622 and their Church of the Holy Trinity in the Minor Town was now handed over to the Spanish newcomers. Paradoxically it was one of the first Baroque churches in Prague, built with the financial support of Rudolf's Protestant friend Duke Heinrich Julius of Braunschweig. The Carmelites moved in on September 7, 1624, and rededicated the edifice to St. Mary of the Victory and St. Anthony of Padua. A new facade was constructed, and a year later a cloister was added, financed this time by the Spanish army general de Huerta.

Polyxena of Lobkovic may have supported the Jesuits early in her life but in her later years she favored the Carmelites, who lived an ascetic life of silence and solitude; when, after the death of her second husband, she went north from Prague to Roudnice Castle, on the Elbe River, she gave to the Barefoot Carmelites a sculpture of the infant Jesus, an heirloom of the de Lara family, which became one of the glories and wonders of Catholic Prague. It was a wood-and-wax copy (the lower part protected by plates of silver) of a little statue of the infant, created after an original in a cloister somewhere between Córdoba and Seville; it had been acquired by Polyxena's grandmother and then passed on as a wedding gift from mother to daughter. When Polyxena donated it in 1628 to the Carmelites at St. Mary of the Victory, she wrote that she "was giving to them what was most precious to her"; she added that as long as it protected the little statue, the order had nothing to fear. It was true, or so it seemed: the church and the cloister were spared the worst when Saxons and, later, Swedes occupied the Minor Town; and though the Carmelites made a sufficient living by producing an *aqua melissae* (useful against aches and pains) and noble benefactors were not lacking, the little dresses made of gold thread and decorated with pearls that were donated in adoration, and the many miracles, private and public, reported, helped the cult of the infant to spread from Prague to Catholic Austria and, in the course of the nineteenth century, to Spanish America. The German Lutherans of Prague would have been appalled to know that their church became the cradle of a Catholic cult radiating through the Hapsburg lands, to Europe and overseas, through the ages.

The Baroque mysticism of the Prague Counter-Reformation has not been long and widely studied. The spiritual and secular literature of the seventeenth-century Baroque was the international discovery of a generation preceding World War I, and Czech historiography, with strong Protestant and liberal traditions, was not particularly eager to explore the Spanish strain in sixteenth-century Bohemian society and culture. Bohdan

Chudoba, one scholar who did so, died in exile, and the historian Zdeněk Kalista was sentenced to fifteen years in prison for "high treason" in 1951. The mystical Prague Baroque has its most legendary figure in Maria Electa di Gesù, or Caterina Tramazolli from Terni, in Italy, who became a Carmelite nun when she was twenty-two, served her order for twenty-seven years in Vienna and Graz, and in 1656 was charged by her superiors to establish a cloister of women in Prague; she served the new institution as its prioress until she died in 1663 and was long venerated by the Carmelites and their friends. Many stories preserved in Italy and in Prague attest to her strict obedience to the rules given by Theresa of Avila, responsible for the reform of the order, and Maria's ecstatic prayers expecting Christ in the Eucharist show the fervid intensity of her feelings. "Come, O good Jesus! Come, my beloved! . . . Come thou whom my soul loves; *toties te intra me sumere decidero. Inveni quem diligit anima mea . . . tenebo eum et nunquam nunquam nunquam dimittam!* I want to keep him . . . and I will never never never let him go!" The Carmelite sisters so much revered Maria Electa that they exhumed her body and placed the corpse (not much changed, it is said) on a chair at the common table and, later, in a little attic (they had trouble with the head because, when exhuming the body, they had broken her neck). The pious, especially women of the nobility, came from near and far to see the miracle, and it was, perhaps, less than miraculous that the memory of the Prague Carmelite nuns survived in the poems and stories of two decadent Prague writers of the *fin de siècle*: Rilke and Jiří Karásek of Lvovice, the one writing in German and the other in Czech, were attracted by the silent nuns, and sensed in their speechless ecstasies sweet and untold sexual repressions. These feelings may have been, largely, literary inventions (Rilke was about twenty-five years old and Karásek worked at the post office dreaming up rare orgies), but fashionable audiences liked that, around 1900.

6

MOZART IN PRAGUE

Gli Italiani a Praga

Aging Czech intellectuals occasionally speak with a certain nostalgia about the melancholy secrets of a city of three nations, Czech, German, and Jewish, but it is rare that anybody except professional art historians recalls that many Italians lived and worked in Prague for centuries. Cultural history prefers high visibility, happily remembering Cola di Rienzo and Petrarch, and tends to ignore the Italian merchants who were busy in Prague by the end of the twelfth century, or the Ghibelline refugees who served the Přemyslids loyally and well. The history of an organized Italian community, fully and collectively participating in the social and creative life of Prague, begins after these early chapters with Hapsburg rule and the economic boom of the mid-sixteenth century, for the Italians in Prague particularly flourished then—parallel to the "Golden Age" of the Jewish Town, in Rudolf's time—and continued as a more or less formal community almost to the end of the nineteenth century. In the beginning, the Jesuits may have distinctly favored, if not manipulated, the Italian Catholic traditionalists in the service of the early Counter-Reformation, but in any case after the Catholic triumph of 1620 and thereafter, assimilation became easier for Italians who wanted to work and stay in Prague, join the local guilds, or even become town councillors. The merchant Pietro della Pasquina became a Minor Town councillor as early as 1611, and by 1622 he was followed by the candy maker Francesco Cortesi, who was appointed a councillor of the Old Town.

The great majority of the Italians arriving in Hapsburg Prague came from the mountains and the lake regions of Lugano and Como and also from the Ticino; their native regions at that time belonged to Milan or to the Venetian Republic; a few also came from southeastern Switzerland and spoke Romansh rather than Italian (in Prague, people had not developed a fine ear for these difficult linguistic differences). It was the old story: too many people in small villages, with the mountain soil incapable of feeding them. These mountain Swiss and Italians mostly belonged to the building trades, sought seasonal employment north of the Alps, and fanned out to the east and to the northeast; Italian architects and stonemasons were active in Poland and Moscow (where Aristotele Fieravanti and Pietro Antonio Solari had a hand in building the Uspensky Cathedral and the Spassky Tower of the Kremlin) nearly a century before they arrived in Bohemia. By the time of Ferdinand and Rudolf, at least a third of all people engaged in the building trades in Prague came from northern Italy, and even a century later, when Czech, Bavarian, and French architects were taking on Prague projects, the art and craft of stucco remained an exclusive Italian domain. The Aostallis, Bossis, Luraghos, and Spinellis, to name just a few, came in entire clans; the younger sons or apprentices may have regularly returned to their native valleys, at least in the long winter months when construction stopped, but the *Capomaestri* (or chiefs) kept an eye on Prague real estate; Italians settled in two clusters in the Minor Town, near Petřín Hill and around St. Thomas, the most populous parish of the district.

The economic boom of the mid-1600s also attracted a new generation of merchants who were able to continue the fragile traditions of the Italian import-export business, which had been interrupted by the Hussite revolution. Some of the merchants too came from northern Italy—for instance, Federico Troilo, from Trento, and Pietro Olgiato, from Como—but there was at least one from distant Naples; others had earlier established branches at Nuremberg (as the Beccaris had done) and opened offices in Prague as well. Another group of Italian merchants, of Jewish origin, threatened by new persecution in northern Italy, left Milan and Verona and settled in the Prague Jewish Town.

Italian commerce certainly made life more pleasant for those who could afford imported commodities. Silk and lace, olives and wine, the more refined kinds of candy and other foods were now available to Prague customers; ingenious merchants like Ercole da Nova of Mantua specialized in dealing with rich aristocratic customers and extended ready credit, if it was needed, to powerful families. Czech Protestants were not particularly pleased by Catholic immigrants (who were accused of most crimes in the book, as the Roma are in Prague today), but the court and the barons were delighted by the welcome and proficient services of experts in savoir faire—tailors, hatters, cooks, carpenters, tennis and dance instructors, butlers, and footmen. The guardian of the royal lions, kept in a grove near the castle, came from Ferrara, and for many generations all the Prague chimney sweeps were Italians. But for a cup of real coffee, Prague connoisseurs had to turn to Georgios Deodatus, from Damascus, who, clad in an Arab burnoose, walked through the city streets offering hot coffee, and it is to his never-ending fame that he bought himself a house on Karlova Street in the Old Town and established the first coffeehouse there in 1713—exactly at the moment when Prague was visited (for the last time) by the plague, which killed thirteen thousand people.

Organized Italian community life was, for a considerable period, under the protection of Prague's Jesuits. An Italian preacher was appointed as early as 1569, and members of the community gathered for church services at the Italian (*vlašská*) chapel, at first a rather unassuming place at the Clementinum. In 1593 the Italian brotherhood of the Ascension of the Virgin Mary was organized under the supervision of one Father Biaggio Montagnini (undoubtedly S. J.) at the chapel. The brotherhood was quite modern and efficient; its table of organization comprised a rector, usually a well-known architect or merchant, and an administrative committee of assistants, secretaries, and financial experts. By 1590, construction had been initiated on a new, more representative chapel, oval-shaped and architecturally much advanced; it was consecrated (though much had still to be done on it) on August 9, 1600, in the presence of the papal nuncio and the ambassadors of all Catholic nations accredited to Rudolf's court. In the same year, the congregation resolved to build its own hospital (it was to be open to Utraquists too), and after the builders had acquired a garden and a few surrounding houses, as a special favor from nearby Strahov Monastery, an orphanage and a cemetery were also established and a hospital church built during the restive years 1611–17 (the building materials were donated to the congregation by Emperor Matthias himself). After the triumph of the Catholic cause, a modest Italian school was opened in 1622, and, somewhat later, Giovanni Domenico Barifis, among the most important Prague architects of the time, in his last will and testament left one of his houses in the St. Castallus parish to the Italian community to serve as trattoria and social club "for all times."

In the eighteenth century, when Ignacio Giovanni Nepomuceno Palliardi constructed a number of buildings in the late Baroque style, Italians came to contribute to Prague's cultural life in yet another way: as the theater slowly shifted from the court and the town palaces of nobles to public institutions, Italian professionals—organizers of stylish entertainments, impresarios, painters of stage scenery, conductors and singers—were on hand to give the theater, old and new, experience, splendor, quality, and cohesion. Two months after regular lamps were installed in the way leading from Hradčany Castle down Neruda Street (as it is called today) to the Old Town, and after Charles VI was crowned king of Bohemia in 1723, the festive opera *Costanza e Fortezza* (*Constancy and Courage*) was performed near the castle on an open-air stage; its elaborate arrangements of scenes, costumes, and special effects were designed by Giuseppe Galli di Bibbiena, and for nearly a century Italian opera directors skillfully served changing patrons, including Counts Sporck, Thun, and Nostitz, and the Bohemian Estates. When Wolfgang Amadeus Mozart and Lorenzo da Ponte, his gifted and adventurous librettist, came to Prague they came to a place well known for the enthusiasm for the theater of its nobles and educated middle classes, only too proud to compete with imperial Vienna.

It is curious to note how the Italians who contributed so much to Bohemian's artistic life survived in later literary images. Once more, the cliché triumphs, and what remained of all these architects, musicians, and opera singers was but the Italian flunky or bureaucrat chasing blondes and gaining access to important people. A professional Italian manservant employed by a local noblemen in Božena Němcová's *The Grandmother* (1855), the first novel of the modern Czech prose tradition, rather indiscriminately harasses the Czech village girls (totally unaware that the Bohemian flirting code differs from the Tuscan one), and the young men terribly humiliate him by dunking his naked feet in stinking pitch. Unfortunately, he has the ear of the castle steward and can, and does, create real trouble for the upright lads defending village innocence. In *The Trial*, written in 1914–15, Kafka confronts his K. at least with the Italian painter Titorelli, rather eclectic in his art, as the name implies, and yet an important character because he has good connections among judges (needless to say that he happens to be protected in his atelier by a gang of lascivious Prague Lolitas). In Kafka's *The Castle*, we are told the tragic story of Amalia, who has rejected the offensive advances of the castle bureaucrat Sortini (not to be confused with his colleague Sordini with a *d*), a powerful and cunning *donnaiuolo* but also a distant cousin to the Italian lackey in Němcová's novel, which, as Max Brod often assured us, Kafka sincerely admired. Unfortunately, the bureaucrat Sortini is beyond revenge.

A Third-Rate Place: War and Peace in the Provinces

After the Thirty Years' War, the cosmopolitan and imperial glories of Emperor Rudolf's years were gone forever, and Prague became a wounded, impoverished, and provincial town that lost many and attracted few. In the last years before the Protestant revolt in 1618, the Prague towns may together have held 50,000 people, but a generation later, in 1650, only 26,000 were left, including the people of the Vyšehrad and the Jewish Town, and only by 1705 did the number of inhabitants slowly climb to 40,000. Most were Catholic (though a few Evangelicals may have continued to meet clandestinely), and Jews constituted almost one-quarter of the total. Emperor Matthias had moved the court to Vienna again in 1612, and with it went the papal nuncios and accredited ambassadors, the imperial civil servants, and the ambitious young people eager to make a career; Czech sociologists have shown that the number of persons admitted to Prague citizenship distinctly declined during the war—though it is easy to assume that, after the devastations in the countryside and the Saxon and Swedish invasions, the towns were full of vagrants, invalids, beggars, and marauders not appearing on the tax lists. Most Czechs dwelt, even after the emigration of the Evangelicals, in the New Town; the Old Town was half Czech, half German; most foreign residents lived in the Minor Town and on Hradčany Hill, clinging, as it were, to the echoes of the court and the embassies. Among European cities at the beginning of the eighteenth century, Prague was in serious danger of becoming a third-rate place, with little to offer.

After the peace treaties had been signed in 1648, the Hapsburg emperor officially and by decree magnanimously forgave the Prague towns for their participation in the revolt of 1618 (they had, after all, fought valiantly against the Swedes), and to symbolize the final triumph of the Counter-Reformation and the Hapsburg dynasty, a Baroque column dedicated to the Virgin Mary was erected on the Old Town Square. (It was destroyed by a patriotic mob in the fall of 1918, and Ladislav Šaloun's massive monument to Hus and his followers now dominates the square without Catholic competition.) Emperors and kings visited when it was convenient, but they also continued to chip away at the privileges of Prague's towns and the Bohemian Estates; in 1624 a Bohemian chancellery was established in Vienna, which in Prague was represented by a governor and later a *gubernium*; as time went on and Hapsburg centralism intensified, this Bohemian chancellery was combined with its Austrian counterpart, only to yield, in due course, to a central Viennese office that transmitted decrees to Prague—it was so unwieldy, of course, that it had to be separated into three branches, dealing with military, financial, and administrative affairs. As energetic reform proceeded, mostly for military reasons after the loss of Silesia to the Prussians, the Estates were asked to agree on a tax budget for ten years in advance to make military planning easier; in contrast to the Hungarian nobles, who proudly defended their privileges, the Bohemians yielded, grumbling but without much fuss. They even lost the right to initiate meetings without approval from Vienna, and Emperor Joseph II, who declined to be crowned king of Bohemia, cynically remarked that the Bohemian Estates merely performed "peasant dances on an operatic stage."

The invasion by the Saxons in 1631 and the Swedish attacks on Prague in 1639 and 1648 had demonstrated that its old town walls, going back to Charles IV, were now insufficient in the new warfare dominated by artillery, and over seventy-five years (1645–1720) a new state-of-the-art fortification system was constructed beyond the fourteenth-century walls. Military experts and civil architects, among them again members of the Luragho and Bossi families, built a new network of walls, with forty bastions and eleven gates that opened in the morning and closed at night; high on the ancient Vyšehrad cliff, the old buildings were razed again (with the exception of three churches), and architects constructed a Baroque citadel and arsenal to take command of Prague's entire range of defenses. Yet the new system was not invulnerable; mid-eighteenth-century Prague was twice occupied by enemies of the Hapsburgs and barely escaped a third occupation by the victory of the Austrians on a nearby battlefield.

When Empress Maria Theresa assumed the reins of power in 1740, an alliance of her enemies was ready to divide her empire, and among other lands at stake was Silesia, for four hundred years a province of the Bohemian crown. Fierce battles were fought in Silesia, where Frederick and the Prussians triumphed; and in November 1741, their Bavarian, French, and Saxon allies moved on Prague, defended by a garrison of 5,000 men, including a student battalion. Sweeping down from the White Mountain once again, the French pretended that the incisive attack would concentrate on the Strahov Gate; the defenders promptly fell into this trap; the Bavarians and Saxons opened the Bruska Gate, marched into the city, and forced the Austrian commander in chief to surrender on November 26. Bavaria's prince-elector, Karl Albrecht, had his moment of triumph when the majority of the Bohemian Estates, in their own act of revolt against Vienna's centralization, paid homage to him, declaring him Charles III, king of Bohemia; the French occupation force of 10,000 (later 20,000) was besieged by an Austrian army appearing somewhat late on the scene. Meanwhile, the French army devastated Břevnov Monastery as thoroughly as any Hussite army might have done, and Praguers had to share the vicissitudes of a prolonged siege, typhoid fever, dysentery, and nightly alarms. Ultimately, the Austrians were successful on the western front, and the French marshal Charles Duke of Belle-Isle and his force abandoned the city almost secretly at dawn on January 2, 1743, leaving their sick and wounded in the town hospitals but taking a number of prominent hostages to ensure the safety of the French left behind.

In the summer of 1744, Frederick of Prussia, who had entered into a new alliance with Bavaria against the Hapsburgs, marched his armies through northern Bohemia; the Prussian siege of Prague began on November 1, 1744. General Schwerin, famous for his exploits, commanded the Prussian force; the Austrian army was busy on the Rhine, and Prague was defended by 2,000 men, including the indefatigable students. Prussian artillery stationed on the hills wreaked much havoc; after two weeks of the bombardment the Prague commander signed a surrender, and King Frederick and his generals rode into the city. Frederick stayed but a single day (he was not impressed by its historical charms), and a small occupying force was put in place, commanded by Christoph von Einsiedel. (A later member of his family was a Wehrmacht general who, after the Battle of Stalingrad, worked closely with the Soviets against Hitler's regime.) The town was pillaged by the Prussian soldiers, then had to pay high war contributions and deliver horses and food to them; the occupiers felt unsafe, possibly because they overrated Prague's spirit of resistance. By the end of November, Austrians again fought Prussians on Bohemian fields, and Einsiedel had to leave Prague, planning his departure with Prussian meticulousness: before leaving he took the last cash from the town coffers. Following the French example, he thought of making a quiet exit through the Charles Gate, but the Austrian vanguard was close and Hungarian hussars suddenly turned on the departing Prussians in the street, with the Prague militia, emboldened by the regular army, joining in. In a moment without law and order, Prague's mobs once again invaded the Jewish Town, plundered and killed, leaving thirteen dead and three hundred wounded. Prague mobs never lacked poisonous reasons for invading the Jewish Town: it was rumored that the Jews had a secret understanding with the Prussians, and Maria Theresa herself took note and sent a decree from Vienna to expel all Jews from Prague.

Few Bohemians may have known that Prussia's war against Austria, renewed for a third time in 1756, was but part of a world conflict that also involved Britain, Frederick's friends, Russia, and France, which was now allied to Austria. Against all assumptions of international law, Frederick in a preemptive strike occupied neutral Saxony, whence he marched an army of 100,000 to Prague. The Prussians entrenched themselves in a wide angle around the city, but the adamant Austrians engaged the Prussians in heavy battle at Štěrbohol, a village near Prague, in May 1757. Both armies suffered grievous losses, General Schwerin was killed, and the Austrians sought protection in Prague to organize and provide for the many wounded. The Prussians took Žižka's Hill, of Hussite glory, but the Austrians stubbornly defended Letná Hill, strongly fortified. During May, both armies prepared for the final assault, the Prague commanding officer turned down a demand to surrender, and on Whitsuntide Prussian artillery began firing a shattering barrage to weaken the defenders; they continued to fire relentlessly for several days. On June 18, another Austrian army, commanded by General Gideon Ernst Laudon, victoriously fought a Prussian force at Kolín, not far from Prague to the northeast; the siege had to be abandoned, and Praguers had a chance to take care of the wounded and the sick (nine hundred houses had been destroyed). More than a hundred years later, in 1866, Prussian forces occupied Prague for a second time, and then the Wehrmacht came, unopposed, in March 1939.

The Age of Reforms: Mother and Son

Whether Empress Maria Theresa, the only queen of Bohemia who was willing and able to take her responsibilities seriously, was as popular in Prague as she was in the Austrian crown lands remains an open question, and it is easy to see that many of her Prague contemporaries had ample reason to feel rather ambivalent about her—nobles, Jews, and the nascent bourgeoisie, whether Czech- or German-speaking. Pride of family and person were essential to her; as true Magna Mater Austriaca, she had sixteen children (ten of whom survived), and honestly loved her husband, Francis Stephen of Lothringia, a noted ladies' man and financial genius, working mostly for his own pocket. Later nationalists among the many societies of the Austro-Hungarian Empire had few arguments to advance against her personally. The dynasty was her nation; she corresponded with her children in French; as for her German, she spoke it with the sophistication of a plebeian Vienna wet nurse, as a popular ditty of her time suggested, and wrote the language of Klopstock and Lessing quirkily and according to French syntactical rules (only Frederick of Prussia's German was worse, but he was, after all, a French writer of note). The trouble was that she had reasons to like Hungarians more than Bohemians; when Frederick struck against her in December 1740, she presented herself, not yet twenty-four years old, to the gathering of the Hungarian Estates at Poszóny (Bratislava), in a first-rate public relations performance, as a hapless woman and unfortunate mother, with a few Magyar ribbons added. Enthusiastically, and in official Latin, they responded to her pleas and promised an army immediately. The Poszóny melodrama strongly differs from the events in Prague when it was occupied by her enemies only a month later: a majority of the Bohemian Estates paid homage to Karl Albrecht of Bavaria as their new king (he was not actually anointed but he received Duke Václav's sword from the hand of the archbishop). After the occupation force was gone and Maria Theresa came to Prague and was legitimately crowned queen of Bohemia at St. Vitus Cathedral on May 12, 1743 (not as *regina* but as *rex femina*), she had considerable difficulties in forgiving the treacherous Estates, but she at least banished the archbishop.

When Frederick of Prussia—"the monster," she called him—had taken away her Silesia, she was ready to change her half-paralyzed Baroque monarchy into an efficient state rather than to forgive the personal insult. In politics, she was a gifted pragmatic with an eye on the future of her state, and it was fortunate that few people in Prague could have known that, in correspondence, she called the sacred crown of Wenceslas, in one of her more sprightly moods, a *Narrenhäubl* (a clown's cap) before taking that precious piece of jewelry back with her to Vienna.

Maria Theresa was particularly intelligent in selecting her advisers, among them Frederick Wilhelm Count von Haugwitz, who had arrived in Vienna as a refugee from Silesia, for matters of internal administration; and Wenzel Anton Count Kaunitz, efficient and inventive, for international affairs; her new mercantile policies, trying to increase commerce and for the first time industrial production from above, began to invigorate Prague's economic life. In 1754, the city had still only 40,000 inhabitants, but by 1784, when her son came to power, there were 78,000, and Prague was the second most populous city of the Hapsburg monarchy, shorn of political power but of considerable intellectual and artistic importance.

In 1753 a commission for commerce and manufacture was established, and Prague entered, slowly and by a combination of private initiative and government support, its earliest years of industrialization. There were a few establishments for spinning and weaving cotton (among them the town prisons, where labor was especially cheap), printing calico, and producing fustian and gloves; after guild restrictions were lifted, a number of paper mills in and around the city developed quickly. It is interesting to know that as early as 1771, young František Ringhoffer, just after his guild examination, opened a copper workshop in the Old Town; in modern times, the Ringhoffer metal works became one of the most important of the monarchy and the Czechoslovak Republic.

Yet Maria Theresa undercut the early success of her economic reforms by her visceral dislike of Jews, and she used the rumors, spread by the conservative Prague guilds, that Prague's Jews had collaborated with the Prussian armies to justify her edict of December 18, 1744, that the entire community must be removed from its ancient town, almost *stante pede*. A commission to investigate treasonous collaboration with the Prussian enemy sentenced ten Jews to death (though not a single Bohemian baron was ever convicted for having paid homage to Bavaria's prince), but she suspended the sentences, wanting, in her impeccable anti-Prussian rage, to punish *all* Jews, without evidence or exception. So Prague's Jews, 10,000 in number, one-quarter of the city's inhabitants, had to leave for the countryside, at least a two-hour distance from the town line. The first exiles holed up in the villages of Holešovice, Libeň, and Karlín, now Prague suburbs, and in other nearby towns, where they were ordered to wind up their affairs, private and economic, before leaving Bohemia altogether.

Maria Theresa had no idea of the economic consequences of her edict, and she underrated the vocal opposition to her policies of ethnic "cleansing." Opposition brought together an unlikely group of institutions and people: the Bohemian chancellery in Vienna; the Bohemian Estates (for once); the army, wanting well-organized deliveries; the pope and the sultan; the embassies of England and Denmark; and her own economic advisers, who began to grasp the interlocking problems of credit and capital, badly needed at a time of slow reconstruction. In September 1748, Maria Theresa, always the practical administrator, finally reversed herself and allowed the Jews to return to Prague at the price of nearly 300,000 gold pieces (camouflaged as a "toleration" tax). The dangers to the Jewish community had not ended yet; a terrible fire, probably caused by arson, devastated much of the Jewish quarter on a Sabbath night in May 1754, destroyed hundreds of dwellings, and left many families homeless. But the new mercantilism had its distinct virtues too: the Jewish community appealed for credit to a powerful Viennese bank, and twelve years later its town hall, synagogues, hospital, and many private buildings had been restored. Czech historians believe, however, that interest payments to the Vienna bank were so burdensome that they slowed the economic progress of the community for decades.

There was not anybody in Prague, baron or beggar, Christian or Jew, untouched by the policies of Maria Theresa's son Joseph II, the most enlightened despot on the Hapsburg throne, who wanted to change the state radically within ten years (1780–90) to achieve "the general good of the greatest number"; and yet, when he died and the ceilings of the monarchy were caving in, he felt bitterly offended that he had worked so hard day and night only to make so few people happy and so many ungrateful. For fifteen years, he had been his mother's co-regent, and when he came to power alone he was middle-aged, plagued by eye trouble and loss of hair, woefully impatient, obsessed with the first principles of good government, inspired by Lodovico Antonio Muratori's *Della pubblica felicità oggetto de' buoni principi* (1748) and his own admiration of Frederick of Prussia, and incapable of true compassion. In the course of his rule, he issued more than 2,600 edicts, some of which anticipated the most essential civic achievements of the liberal revolution of 1848, but he was also an amateur administrator who hated to delegate responsibilities. He constantly interfered with the work of his bureaucrats, whom he distrusted, and endlessly wrote little notes to the appropriate officials exhorting them to arrive punctually at committee meetings, to do away with the female fashion of tight bodices, unhealthy and therefore harmful to the state, or to prevent too much masturbation, which weakened the flesh, in the military schools.

Joseph was a terribly honest man and a deeply unhappy human being. His first wife, the young and highly talented Infanta Maria Isabella of Parma, whom he passionately adored, barely tolerated him; she was carried away by a strong affair with his sister Mimi (their ardent love letters have been preserved). He brutally ignored his second wife, the Bavarian princess Josepha Maria, whom he had married only because his mother had wished him to; he did not even attend her funeral. His brother, the future Emperor Leopold, chided him for chasing the servant girls at Schönbrunn Castle, and though he later demurely flirted with the Princess Eleonore of Liechtenstein, he mostly relied on his manservant to bring to his bed prostitutes from the Vienna streets (their services, as those of the court artists, had to be inexpensive). He wanted a rational and abstract efficiency, and he inevitably ran afoul of the growing opposition defending regional particularity and the older principle of the many national and territorial interests within the monarchy.

Maria Theresa had been a Baroque Catholic at heart, and she would have continued her intermittent policy of religious "cleansings" had her filial co-regent not interfered. Evangelicals in Austria and Bohemia were arrested in the 1770s, and she renewed an old edict against heretics, but when confronted by the rage of her son, she once again artfully reversed herself, and the Protestants were given the possibility of nonpublic worship. Joseph's own "patents of tolerance," a series of legal documents differing from land to land but all based on his handwritten billet of October 13, 1781, were announced in Prague a week later: they granted Lutherans, Calvinists, and Greek Orthodox equality before the law, admission to educational institutions and town functions, and the right to own houses and other property; Roman Catholicism was still to be "the dominant religion," but wherever one hundred Evangelical families lived in proximity they could build their own house of worship (it could not have either a tower or a direct entrance from the street), choose their own pastor, and establish a school. After long persecution and illegality, people were not easily willing to leave their Protestant closets. In the entire monarchy, only 2 percent of the population declared to be of Protestant faiths, and in Prague, once a Hussite bastion, and in the nearby country a meager one hundred and six families had the courage openly to claim worship in the Protestant way. Dissident groups were not covered by the new rules; when the authorities discovered a group of Bohemian Deists who did not believe in Christ or the sacraments, they mercilessly punished them; children, to receive a Catholic education, were separated from their parents, who were shipped in chain gangs to do forced labor at the Turkish frontier, where they perished. Only later did Joseph stop the deportations, though he ordered at least twenty-eight lashes applied to any Deist because they did not know what to believe. He was not beyond enlightening poor people by the whip.

When Emperor Joseph II declared that Catholicism would be predominant in the monarchy, he had a religion of his own on his Jansenist mind—not linked to Rome, useful to the state, and possibly closer to the tradition of the early Hussites than he ever knew. He did not start his church reforms from scratch, but radicalized those of his mother: Maria Theresa, prompted by her scientific and legal advisers (including the Dutch physician van Swieten and the lawyer Joseph von Sonnenfels, whose grandfather had been a Moravian rabbi) and supported by a reform movement within the church, had made a few reluctant if essential steps to secularize education and, with an eye to economic development, to limit the excessive number of church holidays and the founding of new cloisters. Joseph II continued her reforms with doctrinal zeal—closing churches, dissolving orders and monasteries, abolishing church fairs and pilgrimages, dear to many peasants, and interfering with the rites of the church (the dead had to be buried in linen sacks, in order to save timber). In the entire monarchy four hundred monasteries and cloisters received liquidation orders; in Prague, the "Rome of the North," of one hundred thirty-one churches and chapels in 1770 only fifty-seven remained open after his edicts, and of forty monasteries and seminaries only fourteen were left after his commissions had delivered the notifications; in many cases, the numbers of monks and nuns were radically reduced (no novices could be accepted). Theoretically, his intentions were simple: only monastic orders serving the sick and the poor or contributing to the education of the people were to be tolerated, but in practice it was difficult to make the necessary distinctions. The emperor was particularly insensitive to institutions long important in Bohemian history, and though their assets were carefully transferred to a religious trust fund to be used for educational purposes or to pay lump sums for modest pensions to departing monks or nuns, he worked with a heavy hand and challenged many, not only friends of Czech ecclesiastical antiquities.

The Jesuits left in 1773—by papal rule, reversed only in 1814—and others, by edict of the emperor, followed in the early and mid-1770s: the silent and mystical Carmelites, both shod and barefoot, the learned Augustinians of all branches, the Poor Clares for whom St. Anežka had fought so hard, the venerable Benedictines, the Ursulines, in spite of their devotion to good teaching, the Cyriaks (long forgotten), the Irish Hibernians, the ascetic Capuchins, the Trinitarians, the Servites, the Barnabites . . . and on March 20, 1782, a court edict was read to the thirty-seven Benedictine sisters resident at St. George, near Hradčany Castle, the most ancient of all Bohemian cloisters, established by the Přěmyslid princess Mlada in 973. The nuns received a gift of money and went home (the last of them, Maria Fiedler, died in northern Bohemia in 1841), and their invaluable manuscripts and books were transferred to the university library; in decades to follow, the buildings served as army barracks, as a home for old priests, and, after the revolution of 1848, as a prison for hapless liberals and radicals sentenced by military tribunal. On November 11, 1785, it was the turn of the Karlov Augustinians, whom Charles IV had originally invited from France in 1350 in memory of Emperor Charlemagne. A last mass was celebrated, attended by many people of the New

Town, and the last abbot found refuge first in the Old Town and later with his Bohemian family. The trust fund did not know at first what to do with the splendid buildings; the bells were sold at public auction, the army used the empty spaces to store supplies and provisions, but it was ultimately decided four years later that in the old monastery a hospice for the incurably ill and mentally disturbed should be established (ironically, the church to serve the hospice had to be reconsecrated). Prague topography changed: churches and chapels were torn down, among them the Chapel of the Body and Blood of Christ, established in 1382 in the New Town, the Bethlehem chapel—on the emptied space, building materials were stored—and St. Martin in the Wall, established in 1187; refectories and halls were handed over to military schools, state offices, occasional tenants, factories, stables, theaters, printing presses (for storing paper reserves, as happened at St. Michael in the Old Town, where conservative and radical Hussites had fought again and again). A statistical document of 1884 notes that in that year, Prague had seventy-one churches and chapels again, as well as twenty-six residences or houses of older and new religious orders. We do not yet have a historical report on the changes brought about by the Stalinist years.

Joseph's edicts concerning the Jews were part of his general reforms of 1781, signaled by his patents of tolerance and the abolition of ancient serfdom. They reflect both his filial opposition to his mother's anti-Semitism and his surprising willingness to accept the late Baroque familial law of 1726, which limited the Jewish presence in Bohemia to 8,541 families (Prussia had 1,245) and that of Prague to 2,335 family "spots"; in each family, only the oldest son was allowed to marry and to vote in the community. (Conservatively estimated, Prague still had a Jewish population of 10,000, compared with 2,000 in Frankfurt and 3,000 in Vienna.) Joseph's Jewish legislation commenced on October 19, 1781, and continued almost to the end of his life; though it has been argued that his reforms were of great advantage to the rich but not to the many poor Jews, it is also true that, ultimately, in all economic and social matters, the future of the entire community was involved for better or worse. Joseph's order abolished all badges, signs, and special kinds of clothing earlier worn by Jews, male or female, allowed Jews to leave their houses on Sunday morning (when masses were celebrated), eat in taverns, and attend the theater and other public entertainments. He also did away with demeaning special taxes and made it possible for Jews to be trained in all trades and crafts (so far, a little more than half of Prague's Jews had been active in commerce, and only 27.5 percent were artisans, who worked mostly but not exclusively for Jewish customers). Jews were encouraged to establish factories, to rent land from the domains (not from peasants), and to work the soil if they employed Jewish help; those who could afford it were encouraged to attend institutions of higher learning, although not the faculties of theology. Joseph II certainly did not want to create a new generation of intellectuals—he closed five universities during his monarchy as useless—but he wanted army doctors and civil servants, and these hopes were fulfilled beyond expectation.

Other demands in Joseph's Jewish legislation were far less easy to accept, because they threatened the community's traditional cohesion and autonomy. Maria Theresa had suggested that a *Normalinstitut* be established, offering instruction in German for Jewish children, but the Prague community elders refused to do this, claiming religious reasons; Joseph's insistence split the community—the friends of Moses Mendelssohn's enlightened views on Joseph's side, the traditionalists on the other. Yet Ezekiel Landau, Prague's revered chief rabbi, to everyone's great surprise and in close cooperation with Ferdinand Kindermann, then Bohemia's most outstanding pedagogue, opened a "normal" preparatory school with a secular curriculum taught in German on May 2, 1782 (fireworks in the evening); a corresponding girls' school, with extra hours in home economics of course, was established three years later. The problem was that these schools lacked pupils for decades because well-to-do Jews, distrusting secular education, had their children educated by private tutors as they had before. Technical knowledge of German was to be of importance soon, however: in 1784, Joseph II issued an order that all legal and commercial documents and correspondence of the Jewish community were to be written in "the language of the land"—that is, German—and three years later required that all Jews accept German names (even the occasional Czech first name had to disappear). Given the historical context, these measures cast a long shadow; when, in the revolution of 1848, the question was asked whether Jews were on the Czech or the German side, the results of Josephine legislation created heavy burdens. Czech patriots and later nationalists believed that Jews, who they believed had originally spoken Czech, had switched allegiance under Joseph's rule and sided collectively with Vienna to Germanize Prague. In the shuffle, the question of how the Prague Jews lost their ancient Yiddish was not asked.

For a long time Bohemian grandmothers told stories about the good emperor who made the life of the peasant more humane, who in disguise rode through the provinces ("you shall never know my name—I am the Emperor Joseph") and certainly twice took a plow from the hands of a

Moravian peasant to till the soil himself, at least briefly. In later Czech historical consciousness, Joseph II survives as a Germanizing ruler, whatever else he may have done, and in the modern Prague memory, his language decrees are recalled more than what he did to eliminate church censorship and return a measure of dignity to the Czech peasants (whose sons and daughters, after all, created a modern, educated Czech nation).

Joseph's mother, as was her habit, had wavered a good deal in the matter of national languages; in her earlier years, she had carefully recommended that Czech be taught in the schools, being the language of the Bohemian majority, but later, when Joseph was co-regent, she endorsed a school reform that, if fully realized, would have granted little space to Czech. Joseph II was concerned with the modernization of the state and, thinking of France and England, decided in the mid-1780s that the administrative language of written communications in the empire (with the exception of the Netherlands, the Italian regions, and Galicia) was to be German; when the Magyars, though not the Czechs, violently protested, he responded, totally oblivious to historical circumstance, that one language would create "a sense of fraternity." He was, personally, far from being a rabid German *Kulturträger*; his spoken idiom was the Viennese dialect, he corresponded even with members of his own family in French, and he liked to speak Italian. But he wanted an efficient means of communication "*zur Führung der Geschäfte*" (to conduct business), and if Esperanto could have been used, he would have used it. He disregarded history and yet could not escape it; Joseph II's famous equality before the law was rather fragmentary when the law spoke German and the defendant had to rely on Czech or other translations.

The responses of the Bohemian patriots to the challenges of Emperor Joseph's reforms are not easy to describe, and they are certainly more intricate than later nationalists assume. A strong beginning of a new Czech intellectual renaissance would have been impossible without his abolition of censorship and his imperial preference, adverse to Baroque hierarchies, for rationality. There was much agreement with Joseph's rationalist views but at the same time much opposition to his centralizing policies, which again triggered a rising interest in the history of Bohemia and a rediscovery of the privileges and riches of the Czech language (the first university chair of Czech was established in Vienna in 1775, and another one shortly after Joseph's demise, at Prague University, in 1791). University professors were important: in Prague, above all, the Saxon-born Karl Heinrich Seibt, the first non-Jesuit professor of belles lettres, introduced young Germans, Czechs, and Jews to the most recent achievements of German philosophy; he certainly prompted a few Czech intellectuals to believe it was nigh time to compete once again.

The aristocrats, troubled by restless peasants, increased taxes, and their loss of ceremonial positions, had particular reasons to push for Bohemian special privileges. Franz Joseph Count Kinsky wrote a lively defense of Czech and recent German writing, and the lord burgrave Franz Count Nostitz opened his Prague town palace to learned scholars of the Piarist order and to ex-Jesuits who were busy excavating forgotten documents of Bohemian history, publishing authentic editions of chronicles, and defining the nature of the Czech language. Many of the scholars were elective Czechs, who were born of German-speaking parents but learned Czech in the schools. Gelasius Dobner wanted to do away with the false and "ridiculous fables" of Bohemian history and published an essential edition of historical sources; Mikuláš Adaugt Voigt, an open enemy of Germanization, compiled portraits of exemplary Czech artists, scholars, and humanists; and František Martin Pelcl enthusiastically praised Rudolfine Czech as a perfect language that did not need any correction or addition. Abbé Josef Dobrovský, an ex-Jesuit and trained missionary (he was to go to India), was hired on Seibt's recommendation as tutor to the Nostitz family. He was a scholar of genius who, turning from Oriental to Slavic studies, in his treatises, grammars, and histories established the foundation of Slavic philology, though mostly writing in Latin and German and never relinquishing his rational and skeptical views. Dobrovský was suspicious of the advancing romantic generation, who, after studying the German enthusiast Herder, considered only language "the true character and the community spirit of a nation"; though they may have been inspired by the most noble sentiments, they prepared the ground for ethnic belligerence, which was foreign to the circle of Bohemian nobles.

While patient patriotic scholars were discussing the etymology of the terms *Čech* and *Slovan*, questions loaded with ideological preconceptions, many quarters of Prague lay desolate and in ruins after all the battles and sieges and the closing of churches and cloisters. Yet Praguers now for the first time enjoyed a few modern urban amenities. A special committee appointed by the emperor and charged with beautifying the disheveled city filled the moats between the decaying fortification walls of the Old and New Towns, planted decorative trees, and created the New Alley, or today's Národní třída, an elegant boulevard of fashionable shops, traditional bookshops, and overpriced restaurants leading from the City Center to the National Theater and the Café Slavia. The university library, enriched by books and manuscripts from the abolished monasteries, was opened to the general public, including Jewish readers, and a private postal service (later integrated with the state) operated in a frequent and orderly way. An enterprising lending library of 8,000 volumes opened its door to a new middle-class readership, and the first horse-drawn cabs, or *Fiakers*, according to Viennese lingo, were for hire. More importantly, publication of Czech newspapers was resumed—first by the Schönfeld family, who also owned a flourishing printing press, and later by Václav Matěj Kramerius, a Czech patriotic publisher of note; his Česká Expedice, or Czech book distribution, was essential to readers and writers of the Czech eighteenth-century renaissance and functioned well into the 1820s.

It did not escape the emperor's attention that administration of the Prague towns was a Baroque hodgepodge of colorful and conflicting competencies, and by his court order of February 12, 1784, all the dignities, functions, and privileges of the four towns—Old and New, the Vyšehrad, and Hradčany—were abolished, the legal autonomy of the Jewish community was abrogated (only decisions concerning religion and civic matters remained to the elders), and a central and unified magistrate of the city of Prague was appointed, with a mayor and two assistants. City affairs were to be considered by three senates, for legal, criminal, and financial matters, members of which were elected by a body of worthy citizens appointed, however, by the imperial authorities; later, even that last trace of an elective process was obliterated and all civil servants were appointed from above. It may have been Prague's first efficient city administration, but it was put in place by court decree, at least until the revolution of 1848.

Mozart at the Bertramka

To sustain a theater was an expensive affair, and since the court resided in Vienna, itinerant Italian opera companies sporadically performed at the Prague baronial town palaces for fashionable audiences from which mere bourgeois were largely excluded. Franz Anton Count Sporck was the first to operate a private theater, in the garden of his New Town residence at Hybernská Street, and he opened it to a wider audience. A restless parvenu of wide philosophical and aesthetic interests (suspicious to the authorities), he soon recognized that he needed the help of an expert impresario. In 1724, he invited the Italian Antonio Denzio, who shifted the repertory to mostly opera—not for long, unfortunately, because Count

Sporck lost interest in his theatrical hobby and Denzio lacked other financial support.

In the late 1730s, Prague was again without a theater, though the appetites of the nobility and the patricians had been whetted. An Italian musician, Santo Lapis, born in Bologna and stranded in Vienna, sensed the potential market for opera, and he appealed to the lord burgrave to allow him to run a few seasons at the Sporck theater. He quickly discovered that it was technically too small and too primitive to serve his new purposes; ingeniously, he turned to the patrician magistrate of the Old Town and suggested that a more modern theater was needed to satisfy everybody. After an exchange of letters in wonderful Baroque German, the Old Town council, enjoying its new role as patron of the arts, resolved that the upper floor of an ancient market hall in the quarter of St. Gallus would be appropriately reconstructed (patriotic women, among them the wife of the lord mayor and her friends, invested a good deal of money) and rented to Santo Lapis. A sharp protest from the Carmelite convent nearby was gracefully accepted and, for all practical purposes, totally ignored. Santo Lapis proudly called his institution *"il nuova teatro della communità della reale città vecchia in Praga nel loco della Kotzen,"* this noble Italian phrase barely camouflaging the fact that downstairs, in the little booths and cubicles (called *Kotzen* or *kotce*), clothes cutters and fur merchants went on with their business as they had since the reign of King Charles IV. The term *Kotzen* originally referred to rough wool cloth sold at that particular place, and the people had no qualms about speaking of their new institution as the Kotzen Theater or Divadlo v Kotcích.

In its history of more than forty years, the market-hall theater reflected the vicissitudes of Prague during the Prussian sieges and bombardments, as well as the many interests of its successive impresarios wishing to serve all audiences, high and middle, German and Czech. (When they thought that ticket sales were decreasing, they applied to the magistrate for permission for Jews to attend but were turned down regularly.) These impresarios mostly came from Italy and northern Germany (among them Barbara Schuh, wife of an important German theater producer and an emancipated entrepreneur in her own right), but there were also Josef Kurz, from Vienna, famous in his role as the articulate clown Bernardon whose improvised language games would have pleased Wittgenstein, and, from Prague, Johann Joseph Brunian, who charmed audiences throughout the monarchy with his performances in drag (as Demoiselle Brunner) and who, as director, surprisingly preferred German plays of the most literary kind. The theater had to compete constantly with other spectacles in town: magicians, troops of acrobats, and tightrope walkers performed in the public squares, and on a nearby island in the Vltava regular *Hetzen* or *Štvanice* were held in a popular baiting place; fiery bloodhounds tore bears, stags, goats, and innocent does to pieces, and the audience roared.

It was good business practice to offer an eclectic repertoire at the theater. It included burlesques, ballets, and sentimental comedies, popular with audiences in Vienna and Leipzig, but the Prague public had also had an opportunity to listen to music by Pergolesi as early as 1747, Christoph Willibald von Gluck, and the Czech composer Josef Mysliveček (*"il divino Boemo,"* the divine Bohemian, of course, resided in Italy) or to attend new plays by Goldoni, Diderot, Lessing, Beaumarchais—all in German, to be sure. At the end of the 1771 season, the first play was given in Czech and, judging from the reviews, it is still difficult to say whether the performance was an unmitigated disaster or a praiseworthy demonstration of patriotic importance, or both. The text of *Kníže Honzík* (*Duke Johnny*) was adapted from a successful little German comedy, but in the absence of professional Czech actors it was performed by the same people who had previously done the German presentation, and their Czech was not beyond criticism. It was a play about a poor farm lad who dreams of being suddenly rich and noble (his fiancée, Dorka, suspects that Anička, another village girl, has put these wild ideas in his head). Fortunately there is a happy end: Honzík, as if waking from a dream, embraces Dorka and honestly praises her: "You are my dukedom, my beer, and my pot roast." Even the learned patriot František Martin Pelcl liked this pioneering piece because the Czech text was close to the spoken idiom of country people.

In the later 1770s the impresarios of the market-hall theater ran into financial problems again, and a competing Italian opera group from Dresden regularly performed at the Thun Palace in the Minor Town. Even the honest efforts of Carl Wahr, a professional from Hungary, were not sufficient to solve the complications at the market-hall theater. At that time Franz Anton Carl of Nostitz-Rieneck, a rich friend of the arts, Freemason, lord burgrave, and in loyal opposition against too much Vienna centralization, conceived the idea of building, out of his own pocket, a new "national theater" to please and enlighten his Bohemians and to compete with the Viennese institutions as well. The announcement of his project (to be built at the later Ovocný trh, or Fruit Market) revealed that he used the term "national" in the territorial sense used at the moment and by his class, not yet in the linguistic meaning of a later romantic generation.

What he had in mind (as did Lessing, whom he admired) was an institution independent of the court and serving, if not creating, a civil society at large, and he insisted that he was not opposed to a performance of any legitimate play in any language; after all, Pelcl, an important scholar of the Czech renaissance, was chief tutor to his family. The town magistrate, patron of the old market-hall theater, was not particularly pleased, and the university protested, rightly feeling that a high building in the neighborhood would darken the lecture halls nearby, but Nostitz had an imperial letter of endorsement and all opposition ceased. Construction started on June 7, 1781, and finished two years later (enemies of the project hired gangs who often destroyed by night what was built by day). The original plans may have foreseen a late Baroque building but the Prague architect Anton Haffenecker ultimately preferred a classical style, with striking symmetries, four Corinthian columns, and the crest adorned with the words in gold "*Patriae et Musis*" (to the Fatherland and the Muses), an inscription never changed by any later regime. On April 21, 1783, the splendid new theater was opened with a performance of Lessing's tragedy *Emilia Galotti*, in which an enraged father kills his daughter in order to protect her virtue (endangered, he believes, by an amorous prince); the choice of the play clearly indicated that the aesthetic intentions of the new theater were independent and high.

Count Nostitz wanted to run his theater with Carl Wahr and his troupe (using the market-hall theater merely as storage space for costumes and painted scenery), but the shift was difficult; when the emperor briefly attended a performance and suggested that the count hire the more experienced impresario Pasquale Bondini, a singer and producer well known in Prague since the mid-1760s, his advice was quietly taken. Nostitz appointed Bondini as his "*Impresario theatralischer Spektakel*" in 1784, and it was an excellent choice—mostly because Bondini, who had far-flung interests in Dresden and Leipzig, relied on the loyal Domenico Guardasoni, a distinguished singer and opera producer, renowned in Venice, Prague, Vienna, and Warsaw.

Bondini and Guardasoni were most attentive to opera production, and they left comedies and plays to Franz, or František, Bulla, a director born in Prague and intrigued by the possibility of producing Czech plays for a widening audience of enthusiasts. He was encouraged by his brother Karel, who translated from German, and by the Czech poet Václav Thám, possibly the first of the passionate language romantics (in spite of his rococo verse), and in the 1780s five Czech plays were performed and often repeated to sold-out houses. These plays, mostly adaptations from the contemporary German repertory, included a maudlin comedy about an army deserter who, out of filial love, is saved in the end by the gracious emperor himself, and the drama *Štěpán Fedynger aneb sedlská vojna* (*Stephan Fadinger and the Peasant War*). It represented the peasant revolt in Upper Austria, possibly reminding the Prague audiences of the march of peasants on Prague in 1775, their defeat by the army, and their four leaders being hanged by the Prague town gates; in the play, peasants and the enlightened emperor turn against the cruel nobles. The first original Czech historical play, "*Břetislav [and] Jitka*," written by Václav Thám himself, celebrated the manly virtues of a mythical Czech ruler and his modest Jitka, whom he rescues from a cloister and marries, regardless of the difference of class. The remarkable ensemble of Czech plays, and their social implications, may have challenged a few of the nobles and perhaps some German burghers as well, for pressure on Bondini increased, and the Italian impresario, to his regret, on March 1, 1786, fired the Czech-speaking actors. They did not want to leave Prague and petitioned the authorities for permission to establish a German-Czech theater, but were repeatedly turned down. Finally, they decided to appeal to the emperor personally (who in so many plays sided with the peasants and the oppressed) and speedily received his express approval to perform in a theater of their own. A rough wooden construction was built on the square later called Václavské náměstí; it opened on July 8, 1786, with the Czech adaptation of a patriotic German play, preceded by a prologue praising the emperor and concluded with a pantomime about Prague women cooks. When Joseph himself, a few months later, attended a performance of the new Imperial and Royal Patriotic Theater (called Bouda, or hut, by its Czech friends), he created a sensation among Czechs and Germans, if perhaps for different reasons. Not much later Mozart came to Prague, and I wonder whether he ever sensed that the Czech and German theaters had institutionally just parted ways.

Mozart did not have an opportunity to attend the performance in Prague in 1782 of his comic opera, or *Singspiel, The Abduction from the Seraglio* by the Carl Wahr troupe at the Nostitz theater, but he was pleased to report from hearsay to his father that it was a success; Franz X. Niemetschek, his friend and first biographer, who attended the premiere, later confirmed that the audience was overwhelmed, especially by the bold harmonies of the score and the use of the woodwinds, particularly dear to Bohemians. Four years later it became known that Mozart's opera *The Marriage of Figaro* had not been received in Vienna without reservations, so his Prague friends and admirers banded together to invite him to attend, or even to direct, one of the Prague performances scheduled by Pasquale Bondini's cast. In Vienna the opera had been performed against considerable resistance only nine times (twenty constituted a success), and there may have been many reasons why it was received so coolly—Franz Xaver Count Rosenberg-Orsini, director of the Vienna opera, and many of his Italian singers did not like Mozart's sympathies with the German *Singspiel*; subscribers to the elegant boxes, all aristocrats, were offended by the political implications (though Lorenzo da Ponte had much softened the challenge to the *ancien régime* implicit in Beaumarchais's play on which the opera was based). The music, with its sudden shifts from heated emotion to cool restraint, as well as da Ponte's sophisticated text, often employing his Venetian idiom to hide the barbs, may have been simply offensive to the Viennese nobles, who certainly believed that Mozart and da Ponte were rather too close to the emperor's egalitarian reformist spirit.

In Prague, the reasons for coolness were as many as arguments for enthusiasm, but it was an oversimplification to welcome Mozart, as it happened, with a German ode distributed at the theater, as a "German Apollo." Mozart often wondered why the Germans did not create a German national opera of their own, and he wrote witty German *Singspiele* in unison with the emperor's oscillating tastes. But he liked Italian and Italian-trained singers and was, in alliance with da Ponte, opposed not to *Italianità* as such but rather to the conventions of the dominant Neapolitan theatrical style, much favored by Count Rosenberg-Orsini and his crew in Vienna.

In late 1786, Mozart was not having an easy time financially (though he had made good money before) and was thinking of a concert tour in England, usually monetarily rewarding, and the invitation to Prague by a "society of connoisseurs" lightened his burdens, or so he hoped, at least for the time being. His friends in Prague were many and of different walks of life: as early as 1777 (when he was twenty-one years old) the Prague musician František Dušek and his wife, Josefa, a well-known singer, had visited his father in Salzburg and told him that Wolfgang would be welcome in Prague anytime. Among theater professionals there were Pasquale Bondini and, perhaps even closer to Mozart's music, Domenico Guardasoni, as well as Johann Josef Strobach, long active in Prague church music, now director of the orchestra; and there was, last but not least, Count Thun, in whose town palace in the Minor Town Italian opera had been cultivated for many decades. (Where the tenors and divas once clamored for attention, the Czech parliament now holds its sessions.) Count

Thun's wife, née Wilhelmine von Uhlfeld, knew Mozart from Vienna, where he had attended her musical soirées; and he once wrote his father that she was "the most charming *liebste* lady whom I have ever encountered." In the absence of the Dušeks, who were on a German concert tour, she was to be his hostess in Prague, where he duly arrived on January 11, 1787, in the late morning, accompanied by his wife, her brother Johann Hoffman, Mozart's friend and clarinetist Anton Stadler, a servant, and the family dog Gauckerl, all claiming hospitality. Opera buffs still discuss the question whether Mozart stayed at the Thuns' through his entire Prague sojourn or whether he moved his whole kit and caboodle to the Nová Hospoda (the New Inn) in the Old Town close to the theater; we assume that his rooms were furnished with a pianoforte.

We know a good deal about the nearly four weeks of Mozart's first stay in Prague, in particular the first ten or fourteen days, well documented in his correspondence, memoirs of contemporaries, and newspaper reports. (The German newspapers in Prague spelled his name "Mozard," the consonants *d* and *t* being undifferentiated in Prague German.) After his arrival, Mozart enjoyed a late luncheon with the Thuns, the *Hauskapelle* fiddling away, and at six in the evening he was picked up by Count Canal, a fellow Freemason, who took him to an elegant ball in the house of Baron Bretfeld. Mozart did not dance but enjoyed the music, which echoed motifs from his *Figaro*; "nothing is played, sounded, sung, or whistled but . . . Figaro," he said in his correspondence. On January 12 he was tired, a clear case of stagecoach lag, and spent the day with his wife and the Thun family; on the third day he behaved as any fashionable tourist would—visiting the ancient university and its library, lunching again with Count Canal, and in the evening attending a performance of Giovanni Paisiello's *Le Gare Generose* (*Generous Competitions*) at the Nostitz theater, talking all the time to his friends rather than listening to the (Neapolitan) music. During the second week, he was kept busy: greeted by much applause, he came to see his *Figaro* at the theater; on January 19 a festive concert was arranged (his new symphony in D major, Köchel 504, later called the *Prague Symphony*, was performed, and he improvised for a considerable time on the pianoforte); on the following night, January 20, he conducted his opera himself. This was the grand event of the season, and he had a good chance to evaluate the baritone Luigi Bassi (as Count Almaviva), the basso Felice Ponziani (Figaro), and the renowned Caterina Bondini (Susannah), all of whom were to take major parts in the future *Don Giovanni* production. Madame Bondini was the diva of the evening; at an earlier occasion, an Italian ode celebrating her had been distributed in the theater, "Caterina stupì" (Catherine astonished), *"la Moldau 'onda[sic] oggi t'appresta il verdeggiante alloro"* (the waves of the Moldau present to you today the evergreen laurel). It was her husband, the impresario, who offered Mozart a welcome contract for a new opera to be performed in the next season, and it is more than possible, as da Ponte wrote in 1819, that Guardasoni, Bondini's executive director, suggested that it should be an opera dealing with the legend of Don Juan.

Many stories and anecdotes relate to Mozart's early days in Prague, and even if they may not be all exactly true, they reflect some of his habits and the admiration of his contemporaries. One of the stories belongs to the Mozart-promised-but-did-not-deliver kind. Mozart had promised a few light pieces for ballroom dancing to Johann Count Pachta, a local connoisseur, and when he did not deliver on time, the count invited him, we are told, to a dinner preceding the dance but about an hour earlier than usual. Mozart arrived to find he was the only guest; he was shown into an empty room, where, on a table, a pen, ink, and notepaper were neatly arranged. The maestro, aware of his unfulfilled promise, promptly sat down and composed a few dances in time for the entertainment (K. 509), and to these compositions another series of six German dances, all written in Prague (K. 510), may belong. Another anecdote tells about Mozart's chance encounter with a poor harp player at the Nová Hospoda pub. When Mozart went downstairs for a drink, he heard an old man improvising from *Figaro* and was so pleased with his untutored art that he invited him upstairs and challenged him to elaborate on a theme which he played to him on the pianoforte. The old man wanted to hear it twice but then freely responded on his harp, and was rewarded richly by the composer. That is where the complications of the story really begin; later reports do not agree on the person of the harpist (there may have been two), but one of them was often invited by the dean of the Academy of Music to play Mozart's "theme" for the students, and the virtuoso F. W. Pixis claimed in the later nineteenth century that he was in possession of a legitimate transcription—thirteen bars, *andante* and melancholy, in D minor. By 1890, street and pub harp players in Prague were all gone, or so the Czech writer Jakub Arbes writes in a moving story, but it is sweet to believe that street musicians long played a piece not recorded in Köchel's repertoire.

During his earliest years in Vienna, Mozart had lived in the house of the financier Adam Arnsteiner, alone among Vienna Jews to live at the fashionable Graben; it is possible that he met his librettist da Ponte at the residence of the banker Raimund Wetzlar von Plankenstern, of Jewish origin but ennobled after he was baptized. When Mozart returned to Prague from Vienna in February 1787, da Ponte was much in demand (due to the Italian repertoire of Vienna's Burgtheater) and had told the emperor, who always meddled in theatrical affairs, that he intended to write three libretti at the same time; when the emperor suggested that it was impossible, he answered that he wanted to satisfy all his customers, writing for Mozart at night, for the Spanish composer Vicente Martín y Soler in the morning, and for Antonio Salieri in the evening.

Writing his memoirs in New York many years later, da Ponte saw himself as a character in a comic opera: he holed up in his apartment, working "at his desk twelve hours without a break" every day, a bottle of Tokay on his right, inkwell in the middle, and a reserve of Seville snuff on his left. To complete the opera buffa, there was a sixteen-year-old girl in the house who would bring him coffee and sweet biscuits when he rang a little bell (dreams of an old man in Manhattan). Da Ponte went on saying that she would sit close to him, "absolutely still, without opening her mouth or blinking an eyelid . . . smiling cajolingly, sighing, and now and then seemingly on the verge of tears." As usual, his memoirs are somewhat contradictory; to the emperor he had said that he would read Dante's *Inferno* while working on Mozart's libretto, but he seems to have been more pleased with his young Calliope (later he did not ring the bell so often because her presence would have disturbed him, he said), or studying the new *Don Giovanni* opera by Giovanni Bertati, written for a performance in Venice just a year earlier. He may have also been thinking of his friend Casanova and his servant Costa. Miraculously, he wrote an astonishing text, which was still studied decades later by the German romantic E. T. A. Hoffmann and by Søren Kierkegaard, the Danish father of existentialism.

When Mozart came to Prague for the second time, to put *Don Giovanni* on the stage of the Nostitz theater, the Dušeks had their chance to live up to their promise to his father that Wolfgang would always be welcome in their house, and they must have been particularly pleased that they were able to invite him to their new Villa Bertramka, with its pleasant garden. František Dušek, a poor boy from the Czech countryside who with the support of the noble Sporck family had become a master of the pianoforte and a successful music teacher with a wide following, and his wife, Josefa Dušek (her Czech friends called her, of course, Dušková as grammar required), had enjoyed their new property only since 1784, when she had inherited some money; at their villa gathered, at regular soirées and teas, a loyal group of music lovers, noble, bourgeois, and professional, and all were happy to welcome the star composer, to play games, to sing, to flirt, and as far as the members of the cast were concerned, to intrigue against each other.

La Dušek, seventeen years younger than her husband and a former pupil of his, traveled a good deal to give concerts at the courts of Dresden, Weimar, Berlin, Vienna, and Warsaw where she was feted by the aristocrats but not always by the intellectuals; her husband, hobbled by an unfortunate fall in his youth, liked to accompany her on her trips. She was praised for her *portamento* (read: her statuesque figure), and a contemporary etching suggests that she had an elegant thin nose in a rather broad face, a receding chin, and strong and somewhat protruding dark eyes. Most people agree that her voice was powerful rather than lyrical; a few critics, among them Mozart's father and the poet Friedrich von Schiller, who heard her at a Weimar concert, were close to saying that she screamed too much. She liked to be coquettish and easily offended people by her impolite remarks (a Weimar duchess called her a *maîtresse* in retirement); it was whispered in Prague that her favorite lover was Christian Count Gallas, who lavished a good deal of money on her and on the Bertramka. In her role as concert singer and fashionable hostess, she was a lovable or rather dutiful flirt; since Mozart addressed her with the intimate *du*, gave her a little ring, and composed for her (with the usual delay, or rather under duress) the aria "Bella Mia Fiamma!" (K. 528), rumors were ripe that illicit passions had flared at the Bertramka with poor Constanze, highly pregnant again, in the background. Later, the German and Austrian film industry knew a good story when it saw one, and a popular movie of 1940 shows Mozart, played by the blond Hannes Stelzer, a Hitler Youth matinee idol, deeply attracted in the Bertramka park to a young countess, played by Heli Finkenzeller, who was more Bavarian than delicate. La Dušek, being Czech, was deleted from the story. *The New York Times*'s film critic innocently declared on March 2, 1940, that the movie was "a joy to the eye and the ear."

Mozart probably arrived in Prague on October 1, 1787, and together with Constanze took lodgings at the inn U tří lvů (At the Three Lions) in the Old Town near the theater, as guaranteed by his contact; da Ponte, who joined him for eight days to help with the rehearsals, was put up at the Platýz Inn, not far away—indeed the buildings were so close to each other that the composer and his librettist could talk to each other from window to window. Putting the finishing touches on the score, Mozart spent much of his time at the Bertramka, where two rooms on the garden side were reserved for him. He preferred the one with the green wallpaper, a large mirror, and the ornate chimney (the composer Louis Spohr wept in the room when he visited it decades later); we also hear that Mozart liked to walk late at night from the Old Town to the Bertramka via the stone bridge (the ferries did not work in the darkness); he usually had a cup of strong coffee at the Steinitz Café, to the left of the bridge at the Old Saxon house in the Minor Town. The lively parties at the Bertramka were the talk of the town, and many stories were told about Mozart's cavalier attentions, possibly under the scrutinizing eyes of La Dušek, to the ladies of the cast. When Teresa Saporiti (playing Donna Anna), a fragile and elegant blonde who lived to the age of a hundred and two and died in Milan in 1869, announced that the maestro was too short to be impressive, Mozart (always trying to to appear taller than he was) forthwith concentrated his attentions on Madame Bondini (Zerlina) and Caterina Micelli (Donna Elvira). The male singers had their own problems: the twenty-two-year-old Luigi Bassi (Don Giovanni), extremely handsome but stupid, as a contemporary observer remarked, was dissatisfied with the duet "Là ci darem la mano," and Antonio Baglioni (Don Ottavio) complained that he did not have enough material to show all his talents. There were, in the group, only a few Czech compatriots of the Dušeks, and they have come down in the history of music with their names spelled in German, which they possibly preferred: Johann Baptist Kucharz (Kuchař), a noted organ player and later in charge of the opera orchestra, and Franz Xaver Niemetschek (probably born František X. Němeček, but I accept his spelling of the name because he used it when publishing his biography of Mozart), a music fan and philosophy professor, never wavering in his admiration. A contemporary Prague German novelist, usually unreliable, reported that at these parties da Ponte was seen in animated conversation with his friend Casanova, but there may have been more *Dichtung* than *Wahrheit* in the story.

Rehearsals were not easy, Mozart wrote in a letter, because the Prague singers were not so well trained as those in Vienna, and the overture was not yet written. Madame Bondini was not dramatic enough, and the maestro had to teach her how *really* to scream on stage; one of the trombone players made mistakes and refused to be instructed, and the opera's entertainments, including the few quotations from *Figaro*, were probably added as a last-minute improvisation. The first performance was scheduled for October 14 in celebration of the marriage of the archduchess Maria Theresa and a Saxon prince, but the cast was not yet ready, and Bondini resolutely announced that, instead of the new opera, *The Marriage of Figaro* would be presented, again conducted by the composer himself; the princely couple had to make an early start for Dresden and left the performance long before the end anyway.

Experts are still discussing the question how and when Mozart completed the overture, but nowadays most of them accept Constanze's account that he wrote it while she served strong coffee and, as a latter-day Scheherazade, told him entertaining anecdotes to keep him awake during the night of October 27–28, just in time for the copyists and for distribution to the orchestra. On the evening of Monday, October 29, Mozart, appearing somewhat late at the clavier to conduct the orchestra, was greeted by waves of applause, and the premiere of *Il dissoluto punito ossia Il Don Giovanni* (*The Libertine Punished, or Don Giovanni*) went off without a hitch. Afterward, Mozart was reported to say, "*Meine Prager verstehen mich*" (My Praguers understand me), and the newspapers reported that, in the opinion of the connoisseurs and the general audience, nothing like it had ever been seen in Prague before. The Viennese were much less enchanted when *Don Giovanni* was presented there in May 1788; the emperor told da Ponte that while the opera was "divine," perhaps "better than *Figaro*," yet it was "not quite the right kind of food for the teeth" of his Viennese. "Give them time to chew on it" (*lasciam loro tempo da masticare*), Mozart allegedly told da Ponte when he heard about this conversation with the emperor; the Viennese, slowly chewing, changed their views in time.

It is another question whether the changes da Ponte and Mozart made to the Prague version in order to have *Don Giovanni* more attractive to the Viennese audiences served the opera well, and on many occasions and at different times, producers and music lovers have wanted to return to the Prague "source," the original performance. Da Ponte's problem was that he had taken a good deal from Giovanni Bertati, his immediate predecessor, above all in the first act, and then needed to expand the plot in the second act. Hence, his uncertainty: he introduced a rather cumbersome burlesque in which Zerlina mistreats Leporello, ties up his hands with her kerchief, and binds him to a bench, forcing him to make an escape, with the help of a peasant, dragging the bench noisily behind him. Mozart, at least, took into account Don Ottavio's Prague complaints and added (in Act I, Scene 14) two splendid lyrical stanzas to his aria, "Dalla sua pace, / la mia dipende" (On your peace mine depends). Karl Maria von Weber was the first who, in Prague in 1814, wanted to return to the original production (the management refused to pay for the musicians on stage in Act II, and Weber threatened to pay expenses from his own pocket before the management relented). Ninety years later, Ernst Possart, famous director of the Royal Opera in Munich, also wanted to reconstitute the Prague performance, and experts discussed whether the orchestra, as prescribed by Mozart, would do under modern circumstances. The performance was conducted by Richard Strauss, and it must have been a holiday for opera lovers.

Mozart briefly visited Prague again on a concert trip to Dresden, Leipzig, and Berlin in the spring of 1789, but the days were not particularly productive. On the way to Saxony and Prussia, he spent forty-eight hours at the inn called the Unicorn, in the Old Town, but it was Eastertide and most of his friends, including Count Sporck and Count Canal, were in the countryside; when he went out to the Bertramka as usual, he was told that La Dušek had just gone to sing in Dresden, and he took at least a letter from her husband and duly delivered it to her a few days later when he met her at a Dresden party of "ugly" but polite ladies, as he noted in his correspondence. He did not have a chance to meet his friend Guardasoni, who had taken on sole responsibility for managing the opera (Bondini had retired and died unexpectedly in a small South Tyrolean town on his way home to Italy). Guardasoni discussed a promising contract for a new opera, as yet unspecified, but the agreement was not signed. On his return trip from Berlin, Mozart was again in Prague for a day on June 1, Guardasoni was away, possibly in Warsaw, and the new opera contract was never finalized. If Mozart was disappointed, he did not show his feelings, and the letters he wrote to ailing Constanze from Germany and Prague were among his most loving and sprightly.

Mozart's fourth and last excursion to Prague, in the summer of 1791, was more rewarding than his third trip, yet he had, increasingly, to share the attention of the audience, gathered for the festive coronation of Joseph's brother Leopold as king of Bohemia, with local and Viennese competitors of lesser talent. The Bohemian Estates, now proud owners of the National Theater, which they had bought from the heirs of Count Nostitz, had asked Guardasoni to provide a dignified opera in celebration of the grand event, and it may have been Count Thun or Guardasoni himself who suggested that Metastasio's well-known *La clemenza di Tito* be set to music once again. The choice fully reflected the new emperor's conservative tastes, returning to the Neapolitan opera seria. It may have also offered a challenge to Mozart, who certainly knew that Gluck, among others, had used Metastasio for an opera of his own, first performed in Naples in 1752. In Vienna, Mozart had been working on *The Magic Flute* and the *Requiem*, but he was willing to suspend work on these compositions and, by mid-August, he traveled to Prague, accompanied by Constanze (barely recuperating from the birth of her sixth child) and his friend Franz Xaver Süssmayr, who was to write the *recitativi* of the opera. The invitation to Prague had been delayed, and *La clemenza di Tito* had to be written and rehearsed within three weeks (the usual anecdotes about La Dušek trying to push the maestro to finish the overture once again abounded). On September 2, a special performance of *Don Giovanni* was presented as part of the ongoing celebrations; the imperial family attended, and a number of exiled French aristocrats, among them dukes and counts sporting the white royal cockade, were seen in the boxes; people believed they also saw the young Swedish Count Fersen, Marie Antoinette's last lover and organizer of the desperate attempt of the French royal couple to escape the revolutionaries. There was also one Franz Alexander Kleist, an officer and civil servant (and relative of the Prussian poet) who, in a travelogue published later, gave a vivid description of the evening and noted that Mozart was "a little man in a green frock and only his eyes revealed what was hidden in his modest demeanor." It was rumored that Empress Maria Ludovica, who was offended by da Ponte's *iocoso* libretto, was heard to shout, "*Una porcherìa tedesca!*" (a German Schweinerei!)—others believe that it all happened when she listened to *La clemenza di Tito*, but Metastasio was virtue itself and there was not the slightest reason to be offended.

Mozart had to work with a group of singers whom he did not know (only Antonio Baglioni, once Ottavio, was singing the role of Tito Vespasiano), and the opera celebrating the magnanimity of the Roman emperor who forgives his enemy was not received with the acclaim Mozart's friends had hoped for. Newspaper reviews were sparse, and even Kleist, the faithful admirer, briefly noted that the opera was "worthy of its master, especially in the *andante* passages." The official court circular did not mention the coronation performance at all (only saying that the imperial family had taken their seats in the boxes punctually), and the pro-Mozartians ascribed the Prague audience's cool response to their being almost deafened on that occasion by spectacles, fireworks, balls, concerts, and an industrial exhibition; and in the Jewish Town, a "Turkish" band was entertaining.

Other Mozart enthusiasts suspected intrigues by the anti-Mozart faction in Vienna, present in Prague upon the invitation of the emperor and in full force, Salieri conducting the music of the coronation mass at Hradčany Cathedral, and Mozart's Czech adversary Leopold Koželuh presenting an official coronation cantata. Koželuh, who came from a Czech village and had studied law at Prague University, had decided, after a success with a ballet composition in 1771, to change his life: in Vienna he was appointed by Joseph II to be music teacher to a princess and joined in the intrigues of the Italian group, although his colleague Salieri, usually cast as the villain of the piece, was mostly trained in Vienna and was closer to Gluck than to the Neapolitan tradition. It was believed in Prague that Koželuh was dead set against Mozart, and it remains to be explained why La Dušek sang the solo part of Koželuh's coronation cantata. Koželuh's famous concert at the Palais Czernin, with an orchestra of a hundred and fifty, preceding a glamorous ball, was certainly considered a distinct anti-Mozart demonstration by people in the know.

Among Mozart's Czech friends, F. X. Niemetschek was the most loyal and not only as the author of the earliest biography, "describing" Mozart's life "according to the original sources." After Mozart's death, and when Constanze had to travel to earn a living on her own concert tours, Niemetschek was a second father to Mozart's sons. Karl, the older one, lived in Niemetschek's house in the Minor Town for several years (until 1797), was educated by the Niemetscheks, and together with them spent many a carefree summer at their summer house at Sadska. Only after his fifteenth birthday was he sent to Livorno in Italy to learn the principles of commerce, and even in his later years, when he was a quiet civil servant in the administration of Milan (he died in 1858), he remembered Niemetschek with feeling and gratitude. Franz Xaver Amadeus, the younger son (only two of the six children survived), was left in Niemetschek's care when Constanze gave a concert in Prague and he did not return to Vienna for a year and a half, to be trained as a concert pianist (he died in Karlsbad in 1844). Niemetschek did not want to believe that the thirty-five-year-old Mozart died of natural causes and, unwittingly, gave rise to many stories when, in his biography, he quoted melancholy Mozart saying to Constanze in a late Vienna conversation that "he was surely given poison" and "could not let go of that thought." Niemetschek did not suggest anything about who could have done the deed, but in the minds of many scandalmongering contemporaries it could only have been Antonio Salieri, thought to be the *capo* of the Vienna Italian opera mafia. Rumors quickly spread among music enthusiasts in the European cities, and denials in newspapers and in other early biographies—for instance, that of Ignaz Ferdinand Arnold of 1803—only enhanced the belief that the stories were true. Unfortunately, Salieri suffered a nervous breakdown, and it is said that in his confusion he accused himself of murdering Mozart—in other, clearer moments, he just joked about the rumor. Yet the melodramatic story was the not easily forgotten; Karl Maria von Weber believed it when he was in Vienna in 1803, Alexander Pushkin in 1830 wrote a short piece about Salieri pouring the poison, and, more than a century later, Peter Shaffer's play *Amadeus* and the colorful film by Miloš Forman made from it took a different version of the story back to location in Prague, where it all had begun. F. Murray Abraham, in the role of the Italian irrepressibly hating the genius of Mozart, was, of course, more demonic than Salieri had ever been.

Prague Mozartians may owe a particular debt of gratitude to the maestro's librettist Lorenzo da Ponte, one of the most gifted and adventurous characters of the later eighteenth century—Catholic priest, *dissoluto*, collaborator, friend of Mozart, Salieri, and Casanova, to name only a few, and later grocer, *en gros et en détail*, in Pennsylvania, and in New York self-appointed ambassador of Italian culture at large. He was born in 1749 Emmanuele Conegliano, son of a Jewish leather merchant in the Veneto, and accepted the name of Lorenzo da Ponte (that of the bishop of Caneda, and his benefactor) when he was baptized at the age of fourteen. As a young man, he was a successful teacher of Latin and the humanities at ecclesiastical seminaries, gambled a good deal, had a passionate affair with a patrician girl, was ordained (1773), wrote an elegant political satire, and was expelled, for adultery, from Venice for fifteen years. Undeterred, he set out on his life's pilgrimage, which took him to Dresden, Vienna, Trieste, London, and ultimately the United States. He came to Prague for the first time to assist Mozart with rehearsals of *Don Giovanni* in 1787 and once again in 1792, together with his common-law wife, Nancy Grahl (from a Trieste Jewish family converted to the Anglican Church), and on that occasion he visited his friend Casanova, who lived in northern Bohemia in the castle of Count Waldstein. One of da Ponte's Vienna enemies, an Irish tenor named Kelly, described him as vain, affected in his gait, and speaking with a heavy Venetian accent and a lisp. He was certainly resilient; after many bankruptcies on both sides of the Atlantic, he continued to impress his American contemporaries, especially those in Manhattan, with his commitment to poetry, rare books, and opera. He convinced the García troupe to come from Europe to New York to present a full repertoire of Italian opera, including the first American performance of *Don Giovanni* in 1825 (somewhat of a disaster), and spent a good deal of money to pay for the passage of his grandniece Giulia, a gifted singer, or so he was told, to come to New York too—unfortunately, she was not a great success, but da Ponte may have been attracted by the thought that her music teacher was none other than Antonio Baglioni, Prague's first Don Ottavio, who had always complained to Mozart (or Mozzart, as da Ponte spelled it). Never tiring, a little garrulous as an old man, da Ponte graciously accepted the honor of being named the first professor of Italian language and literature (unpaid) at Columbia College in 1825.

Mozart's visits in Prague have left their traces on many minds but most impressively in the literary imagination of Eduard Mörike, an intriguing German writer of the mid-nineteenth century, and of the Czech poet Jaroslav Seifert, who, at some distance from the official writing in his homeland, received the Nobel Prize in 1984. Mörike's novella *Mozart auf der Reise nach Prag* (*Mozart on His Journey to Prague*, 1855) exquisitely combines a dark view of the genius with many lively historical details, nearly constituting a playful little biography. The events are relatively simple (Mozart and Constanze as chance visitors at a castle on the Bohemian-Austrian border, where he plays *Don Giovanni* to the astonished guests) but they are shot through with Mozart's memories of absolute beauty (a water ballet in the Bay of Naples) and anticipations of death; when the composer comes to the spectral appearance of the stony Commendatore, "the notes came . . . as falling through the blue night from the orbits of far distant stars . . . fierce trumpets, ice cold, piercing through heart and marrow." The young countess, speaking for the narrator, distinctly feels that Mozart "would be swiftly and inevitably consumed by his own inward fires"—rococo images of the provincial nobility's happy life contrasted, abruptly and painfully, with thoughts on the cruel burdens of being creative.

Jaroslav Seifert, one of the most important Czech poets of our age, always loved Mozart, as he assures us in his memoirs, and when the conductor Václav Talich asked him in 1946, just after World War II, to write a sequence of poems to be read at a chamber concert, Seifert wrote thirteen rondels for him. (Unfortunately, plans were changed, and the verses were not read publicly.) Reminiscences of long-lost love are closely linked to images of a wintry season, of rare melodies of sweet flutes, of Mozart's death and shabby funeral, while Vienna furiously dances on; a tender panorama of Prague emerges into the rosy light of an early morning "like a painted vase." In the final lines, however, Seifert has to concede in bitter melancholy that his poems, read against the master's music, are leaden (*"mé verše však jsou z olova"*). Yet there are other moments; in his memoirs, Seifert speaks of a walk through the narrow streets close to the Nostitz theater and senses the fragrant powder of Mozart's wig still floating over the roofs of Prague. It is, and not only to him, a consolation and a joy.

7

1848 AND THE COUNTERREVOLUTION

The Travelers, and What They Did Not See

Provincial, quiet, and darkly dominated by its historical monuments, early-nineteenth-century Prague began to attract many travelers, most of them from the north rather than from the east or south. A century before, fashionable aristocrats like Lady Mary Wortley Montagu had made brief appearances, but now travelers were of the gentry and the well-to-do middle classes. Writers, musicians, and diplomats began to arrive in Prague and often stayed for weeks. The hot springs in western Bohemia, long considered of restorative beneficence, also increasingly attracted travelers from abroad. Europeans always believed more than Americans in the medical virtues of taking the waters: in the later eighteenth century, the ailing, the bored, and the fashionable, among them many mothers with eligible daughters, gathered at the chic places, including Teplitz (for those afflicted by rheumatism) and Karlsbad and Marienbad (prescribed for digestive problems). Prague profited from the new "tourists" (the term was first used in English around 1800); a sober observer remarked that Prague had approximately 80,000 inhabitants but 100,000 during the spa season, when people traveled to and from western Bohemia.

Political affairs were also of importance: when Napoleon defeated Prussia in 1809, many patriotic Prussians came to Prague to organize political and intellectual resistance to him. Among them were the diplomat and writer Varnhagen von Ense, with his lively wife, Rahel (busy going to the theater and, together with other Jewish and Czech women, helping wounded soldiers brought to the city from the battlefields); Baron Heinrich von Stein, formerly Prussian minister of finances and later to reform the Prussian state; the poet Heinrich von Kleist, sick, feverish, and hypochondriac; and the linguist and diplomat Wilhelm von Humboldt. Foreign, Catholic, ancient, and strange, Prague was felt to be an eminently romantic place by the romantics Clemens Brentano, Ludwig Tieck, Josef von Eichendorff, and, somewhat later, young Richard Wagner, who was a shrewd observer of his own enchantments and believed that he was so overwhelmed by exotic Prague because everything there seemed to happen on a stage.

German and Austrian travelers did not have much time to learn what was really going on in Prague's towns (especially when they did not understand the languages), and yet a few of them found their way to pay respects to renowned Czech scholars, who still published mostly in German: the philologist Abbé Dobrovský, the historian Palacký, and—visited by the historian Leopold Ranke and a few visitors from Poland and Moscow—the librarian Václav Hanka, famous far beyond Bohemia because he had found (or rather forged, as it turned out) ancient Czech epic songs. In the early 1830s, another group of political travelers, French and monarchist, came to Prague to demonstrate their allegiance to their former king Charles X, who had been dethroned in the 1830 revolution and was living on the second floor of Hradčany Castle with his family and a few servants. Among the French visitors to Prague were, above all, diplomats, generals, and the romantic poet Chateaubriand, who appropriately thought of the "concatenation of history, human fatality, the fall of empires, the intentions of providence," when gazing from Hradčany Hill down to the roofs and towers of Prague's towns. Joachim Barrande, loyal to the exiled king (he was tutor to the king's grandson, the duke of Chambord), stayed on in Prague, worked as engineer and paleontologist, published a monumental work about Bohemia's Silurian formations, closely collaborated with Czech scientists, and left his manuscripts, his library, a good deal of money, and his collections of trilobites to the Bohemian Museum. (On rainy Sundays, I was among the kids who were supposed to admire his collection at the museum, and I was bored stiff.) To Praguers, the name Barrandov has a more modern ring, for it refers, above all, to Prague's film studios, which in the 1930s were as innovative and powerful as the ones in Rome's Cinecittà and Berlin-Neubabelsberg.

Travelogues and reports about journeys to exotic Bohemia and fascinating Prague were a virtual literary genre of German Biedermeier writing, and most tourists from the north on the Dresden road early established a sightseeing route that is closely followed even two hundred years later. Approaching Prague from the northeast, they admired the historical panorama from the right bank of the river, crossed over the Vltava on Charles's stone bridge (invariably compared with the bridge over the Elbe at Dresden but found more interesting), went up to see Hradčany Castle and its art galleries (Hegel admired the old German paintings), spent some time in one of the many cafés on Celetná Street in the Old Town, imbibed a lot of bad punch, then in vogue, and downed a few refreshing beers; waitresses made a little cross on the wooden top of the mug, the assumption being that nobody would be satisfied with one beer alone and that it would be difficult later to account for the many consumed (the custom has endured: present-day waiters make pencil marks on the round cardboard coasters for the beer glasses). Travel reports never missed out on the ladies; Prague women were charming and vivacious but used too much makeup, in spite of their impeccably pale skin, and they were obsessed with lottery games and dancing. Few were slim, and all travelers unanimously noticed the full curves of their seductive bodies. In an elaborate comparison with women of Berlin, Munich, and Vienna, they came out first because in their eyes a flame burned that was both mystical and sensuous, insisted Heinrich Laube, a young German liberal and later director of the Vienna Burgtheater.

Of course, romantic Prague had bad plumbing and a few other problems; the narrow streets were muddy, street lighting, if any, was dubious, and bathrooms primitive. Caroline Pichler, a Vienna society lady of note, complained about the absence of hot water for her bath; it had to be brought in from a nearby brewery. The ladies of the world's oldest profession were usually out in force in the streets, or served beer in the little taverns around the Meat Market (Masný trh) near the Old Town Square—simple pleasant girls who plastered the walls of their little rooms with pictures of Bohemian saints and the Virgin Mary, and covered an occasional crucifix with a veil before joining their customers in bed. What the travelers did not discover easily was the harsh presence of Austria's well-organized and oppressive police state: spies and paid informers were everywhere—at the hotels, in the cafés and inns, and especially in the university library and the bookshops, where they noted the books that people read and bought. Karl Postl, an ex-monk and later known as the American writer Charles Sealsfield, noted in his clear-eyed analysis, *Austria As It Is* (1828), that the police were interested not so much in the traveling foreigners as in the local people who dared to talk to them.

Many German romantics came to Bohemia and Prague, but local German writing was, for a considerable time, rather provincial and conservative. Varnhagen von Ense, from his Berlin point of view, rightly felt that Prague German writers were really quite Bohemian (*recht eigentlich böhmisch*) by inclination and by their constantly going back to what was "ancient and national" in the Slavic manner; they were territorial patriots in the supranational eighteenth-century sense. The most prominent among these was Karl Egon Ebert, who was born in 1801 and died in 1884, the year after Franz Kafka was born; polished and learned, he was, to his contemporaries, well known for his popular ballads and patriotic verse epics celebrating Czech mythical heroines, such as *Wlasta* (1829), about ancient Amazons. Goethe made a few approving noises about his nature descriptions but failed to see Ebert's formal paradox of telling Czech sagas in the German Nibelungen stanza (four long lines, rhymed in pairs, with a sophisticated use of accents and alliterations), a courageous and desperate effort to bind together Czech myth and German art. (Needless to say, neither German nor Czech scholars have touched on Ebert's efforts since 1900.)

Admired by all Prague writers, Goethe came to Bohemia seventeen times between 1785 and 1827 to take the waters in the company of Europe's most fashionable society, and he kept many Prague correspondents on tenterhooks, always promising a little excursion to "majestic" Prague but hesitating at the last minute; he never came. Among Goethe's Prague correspondents was Karl Ludwig von Woltmann, a professor of history, who had removed himself from Napoleonic Germany to Prague, and his wife, Caroline, author of many novels and editor of a literary periodical as well as a remarkable collection of Bohemian folktales, unfortunately long forgotten today. Prague writers and readers competed in writing to Goethe; Leopoldine Grustner von Grussdorf, seventeen years old, initiated a poste restante correspondence behind the back of her grandfather, sent Goethe her sketches, and prompted him to tell her to concentrate on "the moving, active, strong, and consequential" in art; art should first grasp a "strong reality" (*eine kräftige Wirklichkeit*), Goethe wrote to her, before ascending to the ideational realm (*das Ideelle*) and religion. Alas, when Leopoldine suggested that she wanted to come to Weimar to work under his very eyes, seventy-seven-year-old Goethe answered that an excursion to a Bohemian spa would be more appropriate and then ceased to write. She was the only Prague woman to exchange letters with Goethe; as Johannes Urzidil has ascertained, she later switched from drawing to ballad writing and died in utter poverty.

The most independent mind to write in German was Bernard Bolzano, an ordained priest, mathematician, theorist of science, and social philosopher; he was to pay dearly for his quiet courage and intrepid thought. His father was an Italian art dealer from the Como region, his mother a Prague German, but he called himself a "Bohemian of the German tongue" (*ein Böhme deutscher Zunge*); though he did not know much Czech himself, Bolzano always encouraged Bohemians of the Slavic tongue to do their best to develop their own culture and individuality. His superior gifts as scientist, lecturer, and philosopher were evident early; as soon as he had submitted his dissertation on a mathematical problem and had been ordained, he was appointed in 1805 to teach philosophy of religion, which he defined, a true disciple of the eighteenth century, as "the quintessence of such truths as lead to our virtue and happiness." Almost immediately he was denounced as a freethinker, and he had constantly to defend himself against investigative commissions, secular, legal, and even papal, until, in 1819, he was accused of heterodoxy and of being a danger to the state, was publicly rebuked and deprived of his teaching post. Fortunately, a middle-class benefactor invited him to an estate in southern Bohemia where he had a chance to go on with his scientific studies; he spent the last years of his life under the protection of Count Thun, who took great care to provide him with all the books needed for his work.

Bolzano was, at heart, a Catholic radical who believed in the equality of all people; his own territorial patriotism, differing from that of the Bohemian nobility, who mainly fought Hapsburg centralism by allusions to their independent past, insisted on a present and *future* fatherland, with the people engaged both in cultivating their own aspirations and in learning to see why they should look beyond their egotistic concerns. In his sermons, regularly attended by German and Czech students, Bolzano turned against romantic visions imported from Germany, where people, he said, had ceased to think. He suggested that people should first of all try to acquire more knowledge about their own language and culture, in order to understand more of other communities' languages and cultures; self-definition was only productive when looking at what was not the self.

Anticipating the assumptions of modern linguistics, Bolzano told his audiences that words and their meanings were arbitrary, originating in social agreements rather than in romantic nature, and declared that in Bohemia any involvement with only one language would "obfuscate" (*verdunkeln*) the fundamental equality of all citizens, whatever language they spoke. Differences of languages were "the most insubstantial of all" (*die allerunwesentlichsten*), distrust in the equality of all people was high treason to humanity, and what was needed was a communal spirit reaching out beyond nationality to other and higher values; national consciousness was but a means of acquiring something that went beyond all nationalisms. Unfortunately, the revolution of 1848 swept away Bolzano's urgent appeal to communal and transnational obligations; and while in earlier times many Prague citizens (except in the Jewish Town) would have called themselves "Bohemians," now they wanted to identify with a language nation forthwith. Bolzano's efforts to reconcile nations were as quickly forgotten as his astonishingly modern social engagement—he developed detailed plans for inexpensive housing developments and urged that an organization be instituted to take care of the two thousand waifs living in Prague's streets. But he was later rediscovered as a philosopher of science by Edmund Husserl, and again, somewhat later, by the Czech philosopher Jan Patočka, who in 1969 suggested that the Bohemian nations should have gone Bolzano's way rather than that of his romantic adversaries.

Bolzano may have been the first social philosopher of a multiethnic European community to come, and his noble idea of a "Bohemian community" inspirited by shared social tasks may have found sympathy among the nobles, the older Czech generation of enlightened intellectuals, and the Prague German patriciate. But younger Czechs of romantic inclination held different views. In their minds, shaped by the experiences of the Napoleonic Wars from which so many national aspirations had emerged, and by study of Herder's philosophy of individual nations with their inalienable languages, questions of nationality and idiom were far more important than the abstract dictates of an unloved polyglot state; to this new generation, mostly of the modest bourgeoisie and still firmly bound to their fathers and mothers in Bohemian villages, speaking and writing Czech was a fundamental commitment that defined all others.

It was the philologist Josef Jungmann who, in a new Czech periodical first appearing in 1806, published two seminal essays about the Czech language. He excluded the Bohemian nobility from the nation, for they usually did not speak Czech fluently (never mind what they had done in support of the first generation of learned Czech patriots), and went on to create the figures of Protiva (the "fiend," representing many of Bolzano's ideas) and Slavomil (the etymology suggests love of the Slavs), who condemns all those who publish in languages other than Czech and do not believe in the splendid future of their own nation competing with all the other nations of Europe. Jungmann himself turned into a magnificent Slavomil in his literary and scholarly publications; he demonstrated the importance of being Czech by showing the unusual riches of the language, past and present. Distrusting the all too civilized and orderly idiom of the European Enlightenment, he looked to the opulence of the seventeenth century, and in order to display the full potentialities of Czech translated John Milton's *Paradise Lost* (he also translated Dryden, Goethe, and excerpts from *Hamlet*). His most magnificent achievement was his Czech-German dictionary, published with the help of a supporting team in five volumes in 1834–39; when he died, his dictionary was carried in front of the funeral procession in which thousands demonstratively marched. The question of what Bolzano would have said about Jungmann's idea of the supreme value of national language has but a symbolic answer. In the 1840s, Bolzano, ravaged by a respiratory disease, was able to communicate only by signs and gestures rather than by articulate words, and he died a year after Jungmann, in the year of revolution (1848). It must have been a quiet funeral.

The intellectual shift from territorial patriotism to a revolutionary Czech consciousness was rapidly accompanied by a transformation of older institutions and the establishment of new ones, designed to emancipate a Czech civic society proud of its own culture. The old Bohemian nobility had been politically and financially prominent in the established scholarly and scientific groups—such as the Royal Bohemian Society of Science of 1774—but when a distinguished group of scientists and scholars, among them the botanist Caspar Count Sternberg and his cousin, an expert in numismatics, founded a Bohemian Museum in 1818 to serve all the inhabitants of the land, the young historian František Palacký, who had just come to Prague, shrewdly initiated a more modern national orientation at the museum by suggesting that it publish separate journals in German and Czech (1827); it turned out that the German publication, much favored by Goethe but few other readers, ceased publication within four years, while the *Časopis Českého Musea* (*Journal of the Bohemian Museum*) in scholarly and literary matters flourished throughout the century and beyond. A similar and perhaps even more efficient method was used to change the Society for the Promotion of Industry in Bohemia, established in 1833 by the nobility: in 1843 the original charter was modified to allow middle-class membership, Czechs (all future politicians of note) virtually took over the section for economics and research, and the demand for founding a Czech industrial school appeared high on the list of its new plans. Redirection of older institutions proceeded in synchrony with the foundation of these new bourgeois and distinctly Czech organizations. In 1831 the untiring Palacký initiated the Matice Česká (Czech Foundation) to support the development of Czech culture by subventions for the publication of important books; in the first year, the foundation had 35 members, and 2,329 by 1847. Czech was "going public"; the first Czech ball was held on February 5, 1840, and after some difficulties with the authorities the Měšt'anská Beseda (the Citizens' Club) was established five years later, to gather the new Czech middle-class elite for polite conversation, dances, concerts, literary discussions, and scholarly lectures. Prague Czech culture had found an alluring home.

Czech patriots of the 1830s, especially among the teachers, did not know exactly what to think about Karel Hynek Mácha, a student, amateur actor, and writer of romantic verse, but later generations came to believe that he was the first creator of modern Czech poetry, suddenly and inexplicably surging from his lyrical "novella" *Máj* (*May*), written in 1836. Mácha was born and bred in Prague, which he described as a silent city of the dead: "everything is desolate and barren / doors ajar to every silent dwelling, / and the rooms stand open and unguarded." His father worked for a miller, his talented mother was the daughter of a musician, and the family had to move, in search of ever cheaper lodgings, from the Minor Town to the district of St. Peter and later, when the father acquired a small shop, to the Cattle Market (now Charles Square), where the student lived in a shabby little room, attending prescribed courses of philosophy and, finally, law school. He was freely involved in the student life of his time, going on long walks with his many friends, singing Czech folk songs (proscribed by the police) in the open fields, and showing his histrionic talents by playing heroic roles in Czech performances at the Theater of the Estates, scheduled only on Sundays from 4 to 6 p.m., and with other amateur groups in the Minor Town. Yet people also noticed his sudden bursts of cold despair, a certain theatricality that extended beyond the stage, and an inclination to play the Byronic dandy, which patriots disfavored. Tall, handsome, and sad, he liked to walk around in a light greatcoat with a conspicuous red lining and made people stare. A military guard once presented arms to him, assuming that he was a visiting Hapsburg prince. He restlessly marched through Bohemia from castle to castle, making precise lists of all the ruins he visited, and with a friend walked the entire way from Prague to Venice, Trieste, Ljubljana, and then Vienna, occasionally rolling in the hay with Austrian peasant girls. Yet he was also energetic enough to conclude his legal studies and to take a job with a Litoměřice (Leitmeritz) lawyer—doing so largely because he planned to marry his

Lori, a Prague girl, pregnant with his child. In 1836, twenty-six years of age, three days before he was to go to the altar he died of an infectious disease, listed in the parish register as cholera, and he was buried at the local cemetery. His bodily remains were disinterred in 1938, shortly before the Wehrmacht occupied Litoměřice (now in the Sudentenland); his bones were put in a small coffin and buried at the Prague Vyšehrad, pantheon for the great sons and daughters of the Czech nation.

Mácha had to pay for the printing of *Máj* himself (600 copies, of which he sold nearly 350), and contemporary patriots were disturbed by the poem—arranged in four cantos and two intermezzi—one, though acknowledging his talents, declared it was "un-Czech." It was certainly difficult to grasp the text, especially if read literally; whether Mácha was making use of the many Gothic novels which he read voraciously or was recording a Bohemian event of distant times, he suggested in his poem the story of a young man early abandoned by his family who becomes "terrible lord of the forests" and chief of a robber gang. In a fit of fatal jealousy (not foreign to the author) he kills the man who has seduced the girl he loves; the man was, *pace* Oedipus, his own father. The murderer is thrown into prison, accused of patricide, and, in a public execution, broken on the wheel; before he dies, he thinks of his guiltless guilt and—this was particularly shocking to the patriots, and one hundred years before existentialism—of the metaphysical void (*nic*) that he is about to enter, "an endless silence: not a voice / an endless space: night and time."

Mácha himself wrote in a commentary, perhaps addressed to the censor, that he wanted to celebrate the jubilant life force of spring as contrasted to the wild, impassionate, and restless love of human beings. But it may be more useful to explicate the poem—if music has meaning at all—from the penultimate canto, in which a young traveler passing the hill of the execution wonders about his own life, turning the entire poem, in which even clouds, spirits, and a skull sing their own songs, into an objective correlative of dire feelings about childhood loss and innocence gone:

> Far as the dying thoughts of those who have long been dead,
> Far as their names, far as the ancient battle's ring,
> The bygone northern lights, the glow they once had shed,
> The tones of battered harp, the sound of broken string,
> The deeds of a vanished age, the dying star's last glow . . .
>
> *(trans. by William E. Harkins)*

Czech scholars and critics have analyzed *Máj* more closely than any other text, and the ongoing discussion has been complicated by the publication of Mácha's fragmentary *Diary of 1835*, long decoded but withheld by puritan editors from Mácha's audience; it is certainly painful to many who honor Mácha as the supreme singer of love that he describes his relationship with Lori in such a matter-of-fact way, registering when and how he *fucked* her (his Czech street terms are far more vulgar), as if he wanted to punish her for not living up to his vision of the sublime woman, and she submitted to his despotic whims without much protest. The diary also reveals that his and Lori's pillow talk, if it can be called that, was in German because she was more used to it than Czech. Fortunately, the Czech surrealists, experienced in defending antibourgeois sentiments, long ago warned against using Mácha in the service of national or political interests and suggested, even without knowing about the diary, that he should be accepted as the guardian genius of Czech poetry that he was. It is sound and memorable advice.

Neither Germans, whether they came as tourists or lived in Prague, nor Czechs knew much about the intellectual and linguistic developments in the city's Jewish community. There were at least three groups that argued against each other: first were the older Jewish traditionalists, then the mystical believers in the messianic promises of Josef Frank (who died in Offenbach in 1791), and third the younger readers of Moses Mendelssohn, the Berlin philosopher of the Jewish Enlightenment and Lessing's friend.

Frankists believed that the soul of God had lived on in Shabbetai Zevi and in the messianic Josef Frank, who had announced that within the traditional Torah a more spiritual revelation was yet to be found; Frankists in Poland and elsewhere had challenged and enraged the traditionalists by converting to Christianity and by seeking the protection of Catholic bishops and kings. In the last years of the eighteenth century and the first years of the nineteenth, the Prague Frankists, most prominent among them the distinguished Wehle family, were as ardent in their commitment as their brothers in Poland and Moravia; though they all carried "the burden of silence" and denied, in public, that they were mystical dissidents, most of them did not feel bound anymore by Jewish law.

The Prague elders were disturbed by the stubborn survival of Frankist ideas in their community, and when Rabbi Eleazar Fleckeles preached a sermon against them in 1799 and the traditionalists could not understand why the Frankists continued in their utopian beliefs (since the promises of their erratic leader had remained unfulfilled), unrest swept through the Jewish Town. In the fall of 1800 suspected Frankists were insulted in schools and at funerals, and the warring factions even denounced each other to the Austrian authorities; Chief Rabbi Fleckeles was under arrest for a few days. Twenty years later, Frankism had faded away, and the last sympathizers may have joined the first Prague Reform Temple, established in 1833. Few friends of "magic" or "mystical" Prague have ever studied these events closely.

The young readers of Moses Mendelssohn were inevitably philosophical adversaries of the mystical believers, and yet their principal difficulties were with the older generation of traditionalists, or their fathers. In an age of advancing secular education, many of that generation feared for the legacy of Judaism and yet much admired their learned sons, who studied medicine, theology, and philosophy, wrote and published poems and essays in different languages, and declared that the Prague Jews, a nation among other nations, should know more about their neighbors and about the gentile world. It was the renowned Jeitteles family who came to support these innovative Enlightenment ideas more strongly than any other. Jonas Jeitteles went to study medicine at Halle and Leipzig, even before Joseph II's patents of tolerance, and as chief physician of the community defended vaccination against smallpox, inoculating four hundred patients, including his own daughter, with remarkable success. His older son, Baruch, published a timely pamphlet against the Frankists as well as treatises on Moses Mendelssohn in Hebrew and in German, but it was Baruch's son Ignaz, whom the historian Ruth Kestenberg-Gladstein has called "the first modern Prague Jew."

Ignaz Jeitteles was educated in Prague's best secular schools and at the university and, versatile in his languages, contributed to the short-lived Prague journal *Jüdisch-Deutsche Monatsschrift* (*Jewish-German Monthly*, 1802), in which German texts were printed in Hebrew letters, following the example of Moses Mendelssohn, and published after 1806 in the Dessau journal *Sulamith* (German, published in German lettering). Going to Vienna, he made a good deal of money in commerce and continued there to write on history, statistics, and philosophy; later in life, when he parted ways with Judaism, he edited his famous *Ästhetisches Lexikon* (1835–37); in 1838 he was honored by the University of Jena with a doctorate in philosophy. The story of his life and his writings, which were never collected, symbolically reflects the career of many Jewish Prague and Bohemian writers who, whether they remained loyal to their religion or not, moved from the narrow streets of their hometown (increasingly involved in German-Czech conflicts) to imperial and liberal Vienna, at least until the time when Dr. Karl Lueger, a selective anti-Semite, long opposed by the emperor, took over municipal politics there. By the late 1880s, Prague's intellectual Jewish migration shifted to Berlin, metropolis of publishing, lively stock exchange of new ideas, and dominated by the liberal Freisinnige Partei, strong in the city government.

Perhaps of greater importance, the changing writing practices of Ignaz Jeitteles and his friends reveal an age of cultural transitions in which Prague's Jewish-German literature, so famous later, begins hesitatingly to form itself; even before the revolution of 1848, it constituted a first body of writings that were continued for more than three generations. A radical process of transformation, set into motion by Joseph II's policies and Prague's students of Moses Mendelssohn, accelerated in 1867 when Bohemian Jews were on the way to full citizenship in the Austrian monarchy, and it affected the languages of communication used inside the Jewish community and outside it. It also changed the way in which literary and scholarly communications appeared in print. To simplify one of the most complex Central European linguistic questions, it is probably appropriate to say that in eighteenth-century Prague, and long before, the language of communal and intimate communication among Jews was the old "Jewish-German" (later a branch of Yiddish), brought by Ashkenazi Jews from medieval western and southern Germany and over the passing centuries enriched by Hebrew, Latin, and ultimately Czech elements; the language of scholarship and ritual was Hebrew, accessible to educated males, while the underprivileged women, if they wanted to read, had to do with Jewish-German texts printed in an alphabet of simplified Hebrew letters (often called Weiberdeutsch, or Women's German, typography).

Young early-nineteenth-century Jewish intellectuals in Prague, following the examples of Moses Mendelssohn, developed a new practice in writing in eighteenth-century literary High German printed in Hebrew letters (for the learned elite), while the less privileged continued to read Jewish-German in Weiberdeutsch lettering, which Moses Mendelssohn and later Zionists considered undignified. Transition was not easy; and in the 1790s Isaac Landau argued that it was in the essential interest of the Enlightenment to reach out for a wider audience and to continue publishing Jewish-German texts printed in the traditional way. Yet the young students of the Enlightenment insisted on literary German (as written in Leipzig and Berlin) printed in Hebrew typography; only slowly did they begin to write in German and print in German letters. Ignaz Jeitteles's poem in praise of Emperor Franz I, written and printed in German in Prague in 1804 by the publisher Gottlieb Haase, may have been the first signal of what linguistic choices were to be made in the future; and the *Galerie der Sippurim* (*Gallery of the Sippurim*), an anthology of stories incorporating old Prague tales, was written by Jewish writers of the 1840s and first published by Wolf Pascheles in 1847. They amply documented that, to a new group of Prague Jewish readers, German texts printed in German had become more easily accessible; Hebrew remained the idiom of ritual, and Jewish-German receded even among the privileged members of the community. Subsequent editions of the *Sippurim* indicate by their increasing number of annotations of Hebrew and Yiddish terms that the new reader, enchanted by German *Bildung*, was quietly losing an understanding of the older idioms.

There was at least one young Prague Jew, however, Siegfried Kapper, who decided to write and publish his poetry in Czech (1846), but Czech liberal opinion did not cherish the idea of a Jew appropriating Czech for poetic purposes. A German literature written by Jews was continuously developing, but Czech distrust of "Germanizing" Jews delayed the full emergence of a Jewish-Czech literature for at least a generation, if not more.

Stormy Interlude: The Strikes of 1844

There are many reasons why industrialization developed in Prague so slowly. The nobles who owned land, forests, and money preferred to invest in coal, iron, and, somewhat later, sugar refineries in the countryside; the middle classes of any language usually lacked capital and interest in technological innovations; and the Jewish entrepreneurs, essential to Prague's industrialization, at least until 1848 faced too many rules, prohibitions, and regulations. In industrial production, Prague was definitely behind the German areas of northern Bohemia (which quickly made up for the lost Silesian textile plants) or the leading city of Moravia, Brno (Brünn), infamous as the Manchester of the Hapsburg monarchy. By 1840, Brno had at least 10,000 workers out of 45,000 inhabitants (a century later, when the Nazis came, there still existed in Brno a genuine German proletariat of the left); Prague had only 5,000, at most, out of more than 100,000 citizens. As early as 1791, when the first industrial exhibition was held in Prague to celebrate the coronation of Leopold II, the silks of Joachim Lederer and the fashionable corsets of Messrs. Popper and Fränkel received special awards; Jewish entrepreneurs invested in the cotton-printing industry, which was freed of guild restrictions early, or took over smaller firms ruined by foreign competition. By 1830, two steam engines were functioning in Prague's suburbs, and two years later the first machines to print cotton. But famous travelers usually ignored these new factories in Karlín, Libeň, and Smíchov. At about the same time, the English engineer Edward Thomas established, at the fringes of Libeň, the first machine shop to provide or to repair steam engines for the local market. Technology began to invade towns and communications; early in the 1830s, the steamer *Bohemia*, first of its kind and built by the industrialist Vojtěch (Adalbert) Lanna and the English John Andrews, chugged north along the Vltava River, and people began to discuss the opening of a railway line connecting Prague and Vienna via Olomouc. It was opened in 1845, and was of some importance in the revolutionary events three years later.

The first riots and strikes of working people in Prague in the summer of 1844 were directed against the mostly Jewish early industrialists, and they combined a Chartist rage against the new machines with traditional anti-Semitism. Social historians discuss these events with much discretion; the Prague proletariat does not appear in Hegelian splendor. These riots were sudden explosions of desperate anger; they were triggered on June 15, in the mill yard of Porges and Sons, where it was announced without warning that (because of the efficiency of the new printing presses) wages would be lowered. Over the weekend, the workers promptly elected a delegation of ten, which presented their demands that the old wages be restituted and work proceed without the machines; and when the demands were turned down, they were repeated a day later. The strike was led by one Josef Ulbrich (who had earlier organized a mutual-aid association among his friends), rapidly spread to five other factories, all owned by Jews, and on June 18 the strikers systematically smashed machines at the Porges, Epstein, Brandeis, and Dormitzer works. The army moved in when the strikers demonstrated at the residence of the imperial governor, and when the working people marched to the Old Town to pillage Jewish shops and to attack the merchants, they were dispersed by troops, not a shot being fired (yet). On June 24, over five hundred cotton printers were arrested and let go later, possibly because the magistrate did not want the riot to spread.

The situation was unstable; 20,000 workers employed to complete the eastern branch of the railway line to Olomouc had difficulties with the subcontractors and foremen, who submitted false reports that reduced wages. In early July a group of brickyard and construction workers rioted at the Karlín Viaduct demanding higher pay. They were immediately transferred to other work sites, but they came back on Monday, marching together with other workers from down the line, one thousand strong, and on July 8 reached Libeň at the Hospital Gate, where army grenadiers blocked their path. The men tried to push their way through the gate, bricks were thrown at the soldiers, who nervously opened fire (mostly into the air but hitting onlookers in the windows of nearby houses). Five people were killed, including a little girl in the embrace of her nurse, eleven soldiers were wounded, and a troop of hussars cleared the gate by evening. Two days of anti-Jewish rioting in the Old Town followed, and General Alfred Prince Windischgrätz, in charge of the Prague military, had his chance to show that he was ready to suppress disorder by force. Four years later his artillery was to bombard Prague and defeat the revolution.

Revolution and Counterrevolution: 1848–49

Early in January 1848, spring expectations stirred the wintry Prague air. Prominent nobility met in their salons in the Minor Town, and, across the river, young law and medical students, budding philosophers, and a few radical artisans huddled together in the usual pubs to drink beer and to develop plans for great changes, especially at Petr Faster's inn on what was later called Wenceslas Square. Elsewhere, at the Golden Scale (now 3 Havelská Street), the innkeeper had reserved a small room under the roof for the Repeal Club, whose members sympathized with the Irish opposition to English rule and were fond of new if somewhat confused ideas. In an age of close police surveillance, precise information from restless Italy, Hungary, and France was not easy to come by: the telegraph served the authorities, the new railroad line from Prague to Vienna made a detour overnight, and the only foreign newspaper available to a few subscribers was the mildly liberal *Augsburger Allgemeine Zeitung*. At 10 a.m., when coffeehouses were full of people waiting for the latest issue of this Augsburg newspaper (one per coffeehouse), the owner of the place made a dash to the post office in the Minor Town to pick up his copy and hastened back clutching the paper in his hands. Josef Václav Frič, later a young radical, usually set up a chair on the billiard table in his favorite café, U Rytíře (At the Knight), and by 11:30 a.m. read the paper from his elevation to the assembled guests, including informers. News about revolutionary changes in Italy and the demise of the monarchy on

February 24 in France reached Prague on February 29; it quickly spread among fashionable people gathered at a masked ball at the Theater of the Estates and from there all over town. There was suddenly much curiosity and hope; supporters of the *ancien régime* were fearful of how events would affect Vienna, and others felt it was high time to act in some way or other, rather than to talk. Strangely enough, even the opposition of whatever kind looked to Vienna, hoping that the Viennese authorities could be convinced to permit change in an orderly way, and it turned out that in the spring days of 1848 revolutionary Vienna was really far ahead of Prague.

The first initiative was taken by representatives of the Estates, long experienced in watching changes of policy in Vienna, yet by now incapable of pushing innovative demands energetically. A meeting was called by Count Albert Nostitz and Count Friedrich Deym to discuss the possibility of recommending to Vienna that a gathering of the Estates, extended by members of Prague's patriciate, be called. The petition had to go through channels, of course, never reached the proper people in Vienna, and the Prague citizens did not know for a long time that the nobles had at least tried. It was the hour of the young radicals of the Repeal Club and other discussion groups. On March 8, posters unauthorized by the police appeared all over town admonishing the citizens to shake off their lethargy, to commit themselves to the cause "of a patriotism of intelligence and morality" (a formulation of genius), and to attend, on March 11 at 6 p.m., an open meeting at the St. Wenceslas Bath in the New Town to consider urgent questions of political reform. The organizers of the meeting were mostly young people, but there was also the popular innkeeper Petr Faster, a number of artisans, a tailor and a coppersmith, as well as the gifted writer Karel Sabina, later turned by the police into an informer.

The organizers had diligently worked on a petition of twenty paragraphs to be read at the meeting and then submitted to the emperor. After a long period of political silence, the petition touched on the most urgent and various demands of the moment (freedom of the press and of association, municipal self-rule, an assembly to represent citizens and peasants), with a brave quotation from the French socialist Louis Blanc about the "organization of labor and wages" (the first socialist demand to be heard in Prague). Very little was said about questions of nationality and language, except the rather modest wish that Czech be used in the schools. It was a text noble in spirit yet innocent of legal and administrative sophistication; fully aware of these shortcomings, the young people asked Dr. František August Brauner, a noted liberal who had defended the Polish revolution, to edit it for another scheduled meeting. It was the first step in surrendering radical intentions to a middle-class intelligentsia concerned, above all, with the history of the Bohemian crown and issues of nationality, and it was not the last.

The experienced lawyer Dr. Brauner changed the unruly and rather pragmatic text of the petition into a formal document of historical, national, and liberal aspirations. His revisions demanded the administrative restoration of the Bohemian crown lands, including Moravia and Silesia, a common diet, and the complete equality of the Czech and German nations in all Bohemian schools and offices. Some problems were underplayed; peasants were to be freed from serfdom by paying an indemnity to their landowners, but issues of wages and labor were not mentioned at all; a national guard was to be established to protect law, order, and property. While Brauner was busy working on the text, the authorities and the radicals tiptoed around each other, anxious to avoid violence, and on the rainy evening of March 11, about eight hundred people arrived at the appointed place—Czechs and Germans, many young people, and a few police informers. Members of the nobility were distinctly absent; even Brauner, whose text was to be presented, called in sick, and other Czech notables, including the historian Palacký and the journalist Karel Havlíček preferred not to attend; there was not a single woman among the men.

The meeting was presided over by the innkeeper Faster, of the Zlatá Husa (Golden Goose), but actually run by Alois Pravoslav Trojan, a young lawyer with good contacts in Prague industry. The first item on the agenda was a reading of Brauner's version of the petition, in Czech and then in German: the radicals, to save some of the original demands, suggested changes from the floor, especially about labor and wages. No final vote was taken, but a committee of twenty was appointed to handle the final version of the petition to be voted upon later. This St. Wenceslas Committee, as it was called, was inclusive rather than all radical. There were shopkeepers and artisans, a liberal Jewish banker, and, for the Repeal Club, the Czech Vilém Gauč and the German student Ludwig Ruppert. A prominent lawyer, Dr. Adolf Maria Pinkas, was asked to work on version no. 3. The chair did not want to continue discussions, and by nine o'clock the orderly meeting was over; since it was raining, Prague's inns and cafés were livelier than ever that evening; police informers handed their reports to the burgomaster, the chief of police, and the governor, Count Rudolf Stadion.

The following days were full of meetings, rumors, and unrest. The

St. Wenceslas Committee went into session the very next day, Sunday, March 12, elected Count Deym as president, and entrusted the writing of the ultimate version of the petition to a subcommittee of three, headed by Dr. Pinkas. Workers demonstrated in front of bakeries against the high price of bread, students prepared to hold their own grand meeting, and the burgomaster, eager to sabotage the committee, gathered forty rich and conservative members of the German Casino to present their own counterpetition. They recognized, however, almost immediately, that they would be totally isolated, and since they could not fight the St. Wenceslas Committee, they asked for permission to join it (all too readily granted). By March 14, the radicals had decided that they were going to present the urtext after all rather than the still more diluted and submissive Pinkas version (no. 3), and while discussions about the text were going back and forth, travelers from Vienna arriving on the evening train brought astonishing news about what happened there.

On March 13, the Estates of Lower Austria had met in central Vienna, a demonstration was held at the Ballhausplatz, grenadiers fired into the crowd, and the demonstration had flared into open revolt. The working people set fire to suburban factories and streamed into the inner city, barricades went up, and when the fighting was over, thirty people were dead in the streets; Metternich the all-powerful was in flight; and the emperor had declared he was ready to appoint a constitutional government, the first ever in Austrian history. In Prague, Count Stadion officially announced that the emperor had gracefully granted Bohemia a constitution, censorship was immediately abolished, and the citizens were permitted to form national guards. Public celebrations began without delay. It was a gift from the thirty dead Viennese to the Prague revolutionaries, who had not yet gone very far.

Prague celebrated happy days of an easy revolution (for the time being). But in Berlin, after fierce street fighting, one hundred and eighty-three dead revolutionaries were buried, drums rolling; and in Milan, the citizens rose for their *cinque giornate*, the famous "five days," to fight for liberty, to disperse the Austrian regiments, and to establish a revolutionary government. The citizens of Prague illuminated their windows and peacefully marched through their city; fashion merchants and others quickly discovered the market value of patriotism and the constitution, whatever it was to be, for ladies bought parasols in red and white (the Bohemian colors), men sported red-and-white cravats, and there were constitutional dances and balls, hats and croissants; the students (who held a meeting in the afternoon of March 15 to discuss a petition of their own) began to sport imaginative outfits and paraded through town. More significantly, Czech and German writers published a joint declaration put together by the learned university librarian Pavel Josef Šafařík, saying that all Prague writers of the Czech and German languages felt truly elevated by the new feeling of freedom and the new unity of Czech and German wishes, recently so evident. They expressed their hope that the "happy relationship," based on equality, would not be disturbed but sustained in the future; in matters of state, the writers clearly favored the union of the Bohemian crown lands under a new constitution. The signatories included the most prominent figures in Prague's intellectual and literary life; on the Czech side Palacký, the playwright Josef Kajetán Tyl, the journalist Karel Havlíček, the writer Karel Sabina, the philologist Hanka; and, on the German side, among others Karl Egon Ebert and Moritz Hartmann (who, shortly, shifted his radical allegiance to the German revolutionary parliament). The cautious authorities announced that a few cavalry units had been shifted to the Prague industrial suburbs, especially Karlín and Smíchov, of 1844 memory, simply to check on the excited country people, who were eager to see what was going on.

Within a week, armed citizen battalions and political clubs were forming, and when there was not sufficient initiative from below, the imperial authorities, encouraged by the emperor's proclamation of March 15, busied themselves organizing the national guards. It was of advantage to the conservatives that the authorities incorporated the traditional town militia into the new guards, trained by retired or, later, active army officers. There were about 3,500 Czech and German men in more or less improvised uniforms, usually married and not particularly fond of being shot at by anybody (in contrast, the Vienna national guard joined the popular uprising there). The students had decided as early as March 15 to establish their own Academic Legion, following the example of their brave Viennese colleagues; at least in the beginning, it was a dashing if mixed corps of approximately 3,000 Czechs and Germans, conservative, liberal, and radical, according to faculty and academic interests. Philosophers wore green caps, students of the polytechnic blue (both with red and white stripes), and lawyers red caps with white stripes—the caps and ribbons did not exactly indicate that the lawyers were mostly German and conservative, the philosophers nationally mixed and tending to radical ideas, the medical students German, and future engineers overwhelmingly Czech and, possibly, the most belligerent of the lot. In other organizations, national interests soon emerged; from the three-hundred-strong Czech-German corps Concordia, which was formed to protect

Prague's historical monuments and ancient art treasures, a Czech unit, the Svornost (Concord), split off as early as March 18 (many of its founders had also signed the proclamation of supranational happiness three days earlier). It was supported by Slavia, a kind of political and literary club, and Slovanská Lípa (Slavic Linden Tree), founded in late April to defend the constitution, the Czech language, and a few Pan-Slavic mythological ideas. At the moment, the Prague revolution (if it could yet be called that) could count on an armed "force" of approximately 7,000 people, but the real question was how many were able and willing to fight.

On Sunday, March 19, the Prague delegation took the train for Vienna (many students, eager to exercise their new constitutional rights, joined for a free ride), and on Monday they were duly received by the emperor; they submitted their petition to Count Pillersdorf, the new minister of the interior, who had been in office for only about forty-eight hours. It is difficult to say how the members of the delegations spent their days in Vienna: patriotic reports indicated that they discussed questions of mutual interest with representatives of liberal and radical opinions; other reports suggested that considerable drinking and eating were going on while the petition circulated among third-level court counselors, who prepared a rather evasive response signed by the emperor on March 23. The delegation returned, frustrated, to Prague.

Great celebrations had been prepared but they were immediately canceled in anger. People were rightly impatient, an angry protest meeting was held, with a good deal of shouting and screaming, and the St. Wenceslas Committee worked yet again on another version of the petition (no. 4), far less submissive in tone. The delegation's second departure was delayed because of conflicts within the committee, but when the delegates got to Vienna, the situation had totally changed. Lombardy, Venetia, and Hungary were in open revolt, and Pillersdorf, newly appreciating Prague's willingness to submit a petition to imperial authorities to seek legal redress, actually suggested submitting it in a way that could form the basis of an imperial response; the emperor signed a compromise text on April 8, and the imperial letter was carried home in triumph.

Some members of the delegation had wanted to return to Prague wearing Bohemian national dress, a painter suggested a few outlandish outfits, but only the innkeeper Faster had the courage to put on one of these ancient theatrical costumes. Vienna's response pleased the liberals in Prague and, to some degree, the radicals too: a Bohemian diet, not the ancient Estates, was to be elected on a broad basis to deal with all pressing matters, especially that of nations and languages, and the reference to *robota* (the duty to work for the landowner) being abolished by the decree of March 28 was well received. Though the administrative unity of the ancient Bohemian crown lands had not been approved, there were good reasons to celebrate again, and Prague's first elected mayor took office on April 9, 1848.

It was important to consolidate constitutional authority in Prague against any attempt by the entrenched bureaucracy to sabotage the new order, and Karel Havlíček shrewdly suggested that the St. Wenceslas Committee, to be a truly national committee, should include sixty more noted citizens, Czechs and Germans, to constitute a representative body. Though the original members of the committee had been mostly younger people and artisans of the Repeal Club, later members included merchants, industrialists, booksellers, and—by the elections of April 10, in the last wave, as it were—many well-known Prague citizens, including the enlightened theologian Bernard Bolzano, the editor Franz Klutschak (who had been the first Prague writer to publish a golem story), František Palacký, the counts Buquoy and Deym, and all German and Czech writers who had signed the March 15 declaration of happy and equal nations. For more than two months, the National Committee bravely tried to function as a kind of local and provincial government, but centrifugal energies, and German and Czech nationalism invariably feeding upon each other, increasingly threatened Bohemian solidarity and cohesion. German radicals of the left began to look to revolutionary Germany, romantic Czechs to Pan-Slavic unity, and within a week or so of the foundation of the National Committee, Czechs and Germans had to make difficult and, as it happened, long-range decisions.

In restless Germany, a gathering of five hundred notables on March 31, 1848, in Frankfurt, had prepared the grounds for a national parliament, and a subcommittee of fifty discussing election procedures had invited a few Austrians, as well as František Palacký, to join its deliberations. They assumed, rather theoretically, that the Bohemian crown lands, as part of the Hapsburg monarchy, belonged in the German Confederation (Bund) established after the fall of Napoleon and were part of the territories that once were included in the Holy Roman Empire. Articulating the consensus of his Czech compatriots, Palacký politely refused the invitation and, in a famous letter dated April 11, and first read by him personally to the members of the Prague Měšťanská Beseda before it was published in most of the major newspapers, suggested his personal, historical, and political reasons for considering it totally inappropriate to join the Frankfurt discussions. Playing the national card from the top of his deck, he declared in a now famous phrase, "I am a Czech of Slavic origins" (*jsem Čech rodu slovanského*), and modestly added that he had dedicated himself to serving his nation. The historical questions were more complicated, he said, and though some believed that the Bohemian lands were once bound to the German empire by feudal liens (Czech chroniclers denied this), the feudal relationship had never affected Bohemia's internal sovereignty and its autonomy of laws (*svézákonnost*). Palacký firmly believed that the aims and the intentions of the Frankfurt Assembly would endanger the independence, preservation, integrity, and consolidation (*upevnění*) of the Austrian monarchy and open the door to Russia, which was thirsting to become a universal monarchy ruling over the many nations along the Danube and southeastern Europe. This would be a deplorable "evil and a misfortune," even if the universal monarchy declared itself Slavic. "If the Austrian state had not already existed for so long, it would have been in the interest of Europe, and of humanity itself, to try to create it as soon as possible—a federal society in which there were neither domineering nor submissive nations." (Thirty years later the aging Palacký confessed that his hopes for a just and federalized Austria had been a grievous mistake.)

Palacký's letter to Dr. Alexander von Soiron, chair of the committee of the fifty, was far more than a personal communication. Prague's Czechs and Germans began to divide along national lines again, the Czechs committed to developing their cultural and political life within a revitalized Austria, and many Germans, particularly those living in northern Bohemia, looking to Frankfurt and newly sporting the black, red, and gold colors of revolutionary Germany. Havlíček's suggestion in his newspaper that Czech merchants hang out their shingles in Czech did not do much to strengthen Bohemian solidarity (he quickly corrected himself and recommended that the signs be in both languages), and on April 19 an anti-Czech Prague German Constitutioneller Verein (Constitutional Club) was established; it opposed the Czech majority in the National Committee, from which German members began to withdraw.

It was not easy for the radical writers Alfred Meissner and Moritz Hartmann, who in their German poetry had praised the underprivileged and the Czech Hussite heroes, to leave the National Committee in order to support the Frankfurt Assembly. Hartmann especially, who came from a small Jewish community near Prague, long and honestly debated with himself what the choices were; it was his radical commitment, which had once prompted him to write the Hussite poem "Kelch und Schwert" ("Chalice and Sword"), that made him choose the Frankfurt Assembly, where he took his seat on the radical left; it may have occurred to him that the national conflicts in Prague were less important than the more essential, far-reaching social actions possible in Frankfurt.

At the beginning of May, a small Frankfurt delegation, including Ignaz Kuranda, a German nationalist from a Prague Jewish family, arrived in Prague to proselytize among the Germans and to work with the Constitutioneller Verein to prepare elections on the local level. On May 3, a joint meeting of the delegation and the Verein was violently broken up by Czech nationalists, and the date may be symbolic as a signal of the end of the short-lived revolutionary solidarity of the two nations, so promisingly demonstrated in early March. It was a perturbing spring; the working people again went on a rampage against bakeries and Jewish shops, attacking their owners. In the elections for the Frankfurt Assembly, first opposed and then tolerated by the government, on May 23 and 24, after all these many discussions only a handful of citizens cast their votes for Frankfurt; in only nineteen districts, of sixty-eight in Bohemia, did people bother to vote. There was much to fear: Vienna was in open revolt against the emperor, who had escaped the wrath of Viennese radicals, all committed to Frankfurt, and gone to Innsbruck, in the Tyrol. Those who abstained from voting may have believed that Bohemia's problems were at least their own, and the majority of Prague German nonvoters probably did not want any threatening changes anymore.

By that time, preparations to challenge the Frankfurt Assembly by a representative gathering of Slav people were energetically proceeding in Prague. Many Slav students and politicians in Vienna wanted to come, as well as many of their colleagues and friends in Bohemia, Poland, Slovenia, and Croatia. The first newspaper article to suggest a countermeeting to Frankfurt appeared in a Croatian newspaper in Zagreb and was immediately reprinted in Prague. On April 20 a private meeting of Czechs, Slovaks, and Poles in the Prague apartment of the philologist Jan Erazim Vocel, and later that day another meeting at the Prague Czech Citizens' Club resulted in the appointment of a preparatory committee, including František Palacký, the lawyer F. L. Rieger (later the commanding figure of Czech parliamentary politics in Vienna), three nobles, and a number of writers and librarians; the chairmanship was offered to the Bohemian patriot Count Josef Matthias (Matyáš) Thun, who accepted the honor only to absent himself quickly from the deliberations (he was later investigated by a counterrevolutionary military commission). Invitations were issued in eight languages, including French and German, and an announcement accompanying the invitations spoke of the dangers of an *Anschluss* to

Germany, which would threaten not only the integrity of Austria but also the "cohesion of the Slavic nations." All were invited to come to "ancient Slavic Czech" Prague to defend their national aspirations; even Slavs from outside the Austrian orbit would be welcomed as honored guests (this was soon a matter of dispute).

On June 2, the Slav Congress was opened, Palacký chosen to preside, and immediately three working sections were constituted to deal with fundamental questions, a Czech-Slovak group (237 in number), a Polish-Ruthenian one (61 delegates), and one for the South Slavs, including Serbs, Croats, Slovenes, and Dalmatians (41). Most of the delegates had come via the new railways, and their number fluctuated a little day by day; officially there were at least 340, mostly professors and intellectuals, in analogy to Frankfurt, but also thirty-five nobles, among them a Polish prince, and sixteen clergymen. Delegates of the Russian people were, officially, absent (the roving revolutionary Mikhail Bakunin came on his own), and Montenegrins, Bulgarians, and Lusatians were missing as well. In Germany, Friedrich Engels ridiculed the meeting, and most German newspapers attacked the congress as "Russist"—in spite of the congress's assurances that it was above all concerned with transforming Austria into a federal state (*spolkový stát*) to give equal opportunity to all its nationalities. Palacký did not have an easy time keeping all the different Slavic ideas and aims, within and without Austria, under the Austro-Slav hat, or responding to those critics who pointed out that many guests, among them Bakunin and a few Poles from Russian territory, had been appointed to official congress functions.

Palacký's idea of a Slavic role in a federalized Austria was shared by most of his Czech friends, including Karel Havlíček, who wanted the Slavs more equal than others by virtue of their numbers. The Slovak L'udovít Štúr was dissatisfied with Palacký's professional abstractions and his silence about Slovak vicissitudes under Magyar rule; the Ukrainians were angry with the Poles and vice versa; and the Poles insisted on an independent Poland again and had little patience with any solutions keeping the Austrian monarchy intact. Palacký's real adversary was the Polish philosopher Karol Libelt (a guest from Poznań, yet a member of the Polish-Ruthenian section), who had studied Spinoza and Hegel in Berlin, fought in the Polish uprising against Russia in 1830, served time in Prussian prisons, and, more recently, lived in Paris in exile, and possibly knew more about the intellectual situation in Western Europe than Palacký, who was constrained to learn about the outside world in the pages of the *Augsburger Allgemeine Zeitung*. Libelt was a Catholic philosopher and a socialist, arguing that the Slav sense of community came from their old communes of sharing, and publicly insisted on the restored integrity of Poland, against Russia, Austria, and Prussia. The Slav meeting wisely declared that countries in which two or three "nations" were living together should not be broken up according to ethnic norms, yet there was not sufficient time to ponder all the suggestions. At last, Palacký was able to read a "Manifesto to the European Nations," edited from his own texts and from competing versions by Libelt, Bakunin, and others. Rather than reveal disunity among the delegates, he preferred to be, on that occasion, a dubious historian, going back to Herder's romantic celebration of the peaceful Slavs who "since time immemorial had been on the side of the law and had rejected and held in contempt every domination by mere force." On June 12, however, all hell broke loose in the Prague streets, the congress was hastily adjourned, and the more radical among its younger members left the conference hall and went straight to the barricades.

While the philologists and scholars had made preparations for the congress, riots and demonstrations had continued in the streets. On May 1 and 2, the Jewish neighborhoods were once again invaded by mobs on a rampage, but the national guard and army intervened only when the working people attacked the bakeries; demonstrations and strikes of the cotton printers and textile workers promptly followed. Reasonable people were appalled when they heard that Alfred Prince Windischgrätz, odious to so many after having ruthlessly smashed the workers' demonstrations in 1844, was promoted to commander in chief of Bohemia's armed forces, and when he arrived in Prague on May 20, he did not hesitate long to show his iron fist. He shifted troops from provincial Bohemian garrisons to Prague, held a grand parade in the suburb of Karlín (to provoke the proletariat), and had his soldiers patrol the streets day and night. The National Committee, by now entirely Czech, asked that Windischgrätz be replaced; public protest meetings were held, increasingly dominated by the radical Repeal Club people again, but Windischgrätz grimly refused to hear their delegates. On Sunday, June 11, a red poster appeared in the Old Town to protest the army presence, and on Whitsun Monday, instead of another public meeting, a festive mass was planned to be celebrated in the Horse Market (later Wenceslas Square) as a gesture of civic solidarity. It was organized by the students; in columns streaming through the center of Prague came young girls in white, matrons in national costumes, writers in dark suits, and people in their Sunday best. A priest of liberal sympathies was the celebrant, and by noon the people quietly marched down the square to salute Petr Faster at his Golden Goose. Then shouts were heard that people should march en masse to the army high command on Celetná Street.

On the squares and streets close to the army headquarters, the situation was tense and confused. Two columns of demonstrators marched to Celetná Street, where a change of guard was just underway; when a company of grenadiers from the nearby barracks arrived, the demonstrators and soldiers moved off in almost an elaborate dance to avoid a showdown. Then, unfortunately, the crowds caught sight of Windischgrätz himself, who was accompanying a delegation of conservative Germans to the portal of the building, the mood turned ugly, and the grenadiers were ordered to load their guns. The first shots were fired near the headquarters, and fighting rapidly spread to the student-occupied Carolinum, to the Old Town Square, and to other places on the way from the center of Prague to the bridges. Barricades went up quickly, and though the army took the Carolinum, floor by floor, armed resistance was strong at the Perštýn and Bethlehem Square, where the people were commanded by the playwright Josef Kajetán Tyl. It was of initial advantage to the students that they arrested Governor Count Thun (recognized, in his elegant coat and shining black hat, as he was climbing over the barricades to reach the town hall), but Windischgrätz never lost the initiative. At 4 p.m. he assembled a few artillery pieces and grenadiers to shoot his way through the most important barricades. By 6 p.m. he had cleared the major route to the river; not to disperse his manpower, he left the barricades in the narrow medieval streets on either side untouched. Both his troops and the insurrectionists, who lacked a clear command structure, spent the night in the streets and at the barricades, bivouac fires burning.

During the forty-eight hours that followed, both the army and the insurgents consolidated their positions and mobilized support from the Bohemian provinces. Army units from the northwest arrived without delay, but the students sent out emissaries to the country with little success: the peasants were indifferent to what was going on in Prague, and the provincial national guard was hesitant. Fighting went on sporadically, and the barricades were strengthened on the Old Town Square and elsewhere; reports said that patriotic schoolgirls provided classroom furniture, thrown out of school windows, and Franciscan friars helped too (though they later disclaimed all Franciscan support of the revolt). In the town hall, negotiations went on continuously; Palacký shrewdly convinced the students to let Count Thun go on the grounds that otherwise power would be totally in the hands of Windischgrätz, prisoners were exchanged, and a two-man commission was speedily sent from Vienna to prompt rigid Windischgrätz to pass on his command to another general. Windischgrätz had little sympathy for the Vienna constitutional government, and played his own cat-and-mouse game with the Viennese delegates, resigning in one moment and promptly resuming his function, telling the delegates that he did so at the wishes of his officers. In their enthusiasm, the insurgents, who held on to considerable parts of the Old and New Towns, did not grasp in time that Windischgrätz had isolated Prague by encircling it with troops (though the trains were running on time) or that the national guard on the left bank had decided to support the regular army and was occupying Malostranský Square together with the soldiers who dominated Hradčany Castle and the nearby barracks. On the night of June 14, Windischgrätz continued his operations, and under cover of darkness quietly withdrew all his troops and his artillery from the right to the left bank. When the exhausted insurgents awoke, the soldiers were gone, and Windischgrätz had entrenched all his fieldpieces on the rising hills of the Minor Town.

Precisely at 8 a.m. on June 15, his artillery opened fire across the river, and the bombardment, lasting four hours, immediately deepened the rift between the radicals, who finally held a staff meeting at the Clementinum, and the liberals, who wanted to end the bloodshed immediately. The beginning of the end came on the evening of Friday, June 16. The town council resolved to clean up the barricades, many willing workingmen were paid to do this tough job, and the radicals at the Clementinum, resisting Bakunin's abstract suggestion to proclaim a revolutionary city government with dictatorial powers, made another brave attempt to send out emissaries to appeal for help from the countryside. By 9 p.m. Windischgrätz, reasserting his authority, gave the order to bombard the Old Town again; he concentrated the artillery fire on the Old Town water tower and the right bank. Large flour and wheat magazines burned through the night while the bombardment continued, illuminating the sky over Prague and striking the burghers with fear and feelings of utter helplessness.

On Saturday, June 17, the mayor hastened to Hradčany Castle to announce the municipality's unconditional surrender. The isolated radicals dispersed, army columns marched across the bridges to occupy the Old and the New Towns, and Windischgrätz immediately imposed military rule and, not much later, established a commission to investigate who was responsible for the insurrection (he believed, of course, that it was a vast conspiracy). Twenty thousand Praguers left in a panic to escape the military courts. One train, crammed full of students, members of the Slav Congress, and provincial guards who had come to Prague on a belated and useless excursion, was stopped at Běchovice train station, the first out of Prague, by nervous army units, who killed and brutalized in cold blood: ten people were shot and more than fifty wounded. Still, there were rare pockets of resistance in the New Town, and the proud fishermen of Podolí, close to the river, under the Vyšehrad, were the last to put down their arms. Later historians believed that Windischgrätz's army of more than 10,000 had been opposed by 1,200 barricade fighters, two-thirds of them students, supported by artisans and workingmen, and 500 national guardsmen; when everything was over, forty-six had died in the Prague streets, ten at Běchovice station, and hundreds were wounded, among them three servant girls and a young boy caught in the cross fire. Among the victims was Windischgrätz's wife, Eleonore, who was killed by a ricocheting bullet while she was standing near a window at the high command. In the Vienna insurrection of October 1848, the third of the revolutionary year, Windischgrätz's army units had to fight from house to house, and Vienna's lovers of wine, women, and song fought as fiercely as the Social Democrats of Floridsdorf were to do in February 1934; 5,000 revolutionaries and 1,000 soldiers died in the streets.

Yet the young Prague radicals, at least, wanted to continue their fight, and it was almost inevitable that they threw in their lot with Mikhail Bakunin, a noble revolutionary by profession, who in December announced to his friends the attractive idea of a federation of Slavic republics with Prague as its capital. In Leipzig and Dresden, he talked about Czech conditions with Adolf Vilém Straka, a former theologian (later to be sentenced to death), established contact with Josef Václav Frič and Emanuel Arnold (later to emigrate to the United States), who had been prominent among the June insurgents, and even went to Prague secretly, in March 1849, to inspect the scene; he did not seem to notice that the Prague mood was certainly less than revolutionary. In Saxony, great plans for an uprising in Dresden and Prague were made, to be prepared by *anciens combatants*, and Prague German students organized in Moldavia and Hilaria fraternities. Frič and his group were to occupy Smíchov and others the Old Town hall; a number of hostages were to be taken immediately, among them former Emperor Ferdinand, who was slightly retarded and had recently been pensioned off at Hradčany; he liked to go on long walks without a bodyguard, smiling beatifically. This revolution was scheduled for May 12, but the Dresden conspirators, the young composer Richard Wagner among them, started out too early, on May 3; in

Prague the efficient police had long infiltrated their groups and during the night of May 9 arrested nearly everybody. Military rule was imposed and regular army units occupied Prague.

The trial of the conspirators, half of them Czech, half German, and none older than twenty-six, lasted for four years; twenty-eight were sentenced to death (all the death sentences were commuted to life imprisonment), fifty-one received long sentences, (474 years in all) and the rest were forced to join the army. Frič, a talented and elegant member of the incipient *jeunesse dorée,* was sentenced to eighteen years in jail; amnestied in 1854, he was arrested again, and sent into exile. He lived in London and Paris, but when Prussians occupied Prague in 1866 he returned, then left for Berlin and Zagreb. He ceaselessly wrote plays about political heroes and indefatigably tried to explain Czech affairs to the European public; he was allowed to return in 1879. Bakunin was caught in Saxony, and the Prussians and Austrians handed him over to the tsarist police, who sent him to Siberia. From there, he made a spectacular escape to New York and London, only to be ostracized in the international workers' movement by Karl Marx. He died in 1876, a bitter and disappointed man, in Switzerland.

Three Lives in the Shadow of the Revolution

Karel Havlíček was the first Czech intellectual in the modern sense, bridging the gap between literature and political activism, and in his own way he anticipated the realist T. G. Masaryk, professor of philosophy and founder of the Czechoslovak Republic. (Masaryk, of course, wrote a lively volume about his predecessor.) Patriots of earlier generations had devoted their energies to the study of Slavic archaeology and history, but Havlíček lived in the present, as satirist, literary critic, newspaper editor, and member of committees and the Austrian parliament; one of his recent biographers has raised the legitimate question whether Havlíček suffered more in exile, controlled by the Austrian police, or when he returned home six years after the revolution and found only silence, indifference, and very few friends.

Havlíček's father was a village merchant from the hills on the Czech–Moravian border, and Karel, one of seven children, was the ugly duckling, stubborn, wild, and unruly, and yet a gifted student in the provinces and in Prague, where he attended the archbishop's seminary—though only for one year because he changed his mind about his vocation, and his superiors did not like his epigrams or his Pan-Slavic ideas. He spent much of his time at the university library, and its director recommended him for a position as tutor to the conservative Russian historian Mikhail Pogodin, who passed him on to his learned colleague Stěpan Petrovich Shevyrov, professor of Russian literature at Moscow University and head of a Slavophile group of poets and scholars who were committed to the ancient virtues of Orthodox Mother Russia. At first, the twenty-two-year-old Havlíček felt in an all-Slav heaven, tutoring Shevyrov's son Boris for five hours a day and spending the rest of his time in Shevyrov's rich library or exploring Moscow's street life, admiring the wonderful Russian folk. Unfortunately, the family took him in late May 1843 to its vast country estate, and his Russian illusions were abruptly shattered when he saw the poverty of the villages, the way in which the estate owners dealt with their "souls," dead or alive, and the unemployment that prompted hundreds of thousands of village lads to seek work in the cities, leaving behind their poor sisters and wives, or rather, as he put it, "fifty thousand whores." He learned a lesson about the realities of Slav life, left his employers more or less in a huff, and announced to his friends that he was going home to write in a different style. He did not know yet that he was closely watched by the Austrian police, who believed that he was a Pan-Slav radical, pro-Russian, and dangerous to the state.

Arriving in Prague, Havlíček wasted no time in establishing himself as a new kind of literary critic of political interests, showing little patience with sentimentality and patriotic oratory. In an essay in the widely read *Česká Včela* (*Czech Bee*) he deplored the "irritating truth" that in his homeland every writer was also a praiseworthy patriot, making it difficult to criticize anyone because immediately the nation itself felt offended; frank literary criticism was simply impossible. Havlíček did not have an easy time defining his personal position; he clearly did not like literature without a message because he believed that people living in an important moment of history could not and should not enjoy timeless beauty closed upon itself, and he insisted that poetry with a message (he used the Young German term *Tendenzpoesie*) was simply better than poetry without one—the assumption being, of course, that it was real poetry, and Havlíček was willing to speak on that occasion of a meaning or direction of literature rather than mere tendentiousness.

In practice, Havlíček selected two victims to demonstrate what he had in mind, the popular playwright and novelist Josef Kajetán Tyl and the young Jewish student Siegfried Kapper, who had dared to write poetry in Czech (Havlíček's anti-Jewish arguments showed the limits of his liberalism). Tyl had just published *Poslední Čech* (*The Last Czech*, 1845), a novel of sentimental twists and highfalutin political oratory; Havlíček challenged most of the Prague Czech literati, saying that "it was high time that our patriotic talk moved from our mouth to our head and to our body," for, constantly talking about patriotism, people "forgot the education of the nation." It was certainly easier, he added, and "more sweet to die for the nation than to read all these kitschy books about being patriotic." Opening the way for a down-to-earth literature rather than mere sentimentalism even before the revolution, Havlíček had high praise for his compatriot Mrs. Božena Němcová, who had written "true pristine poetry," and he encouraged her to continue in her admirable way.

Havlíček's brash criticism offended many of the older generation but not the more thoughtful conservatives and liberals, among them the historian Palacký, who quickly recognized the critic's unusual gifts. With their recommendation, twenty-four-year-old Havlíček, to his own surprise, was appointed editor in chief of the government-sponsored *Pražské Noviny* (*Prague News*) and its literary supplement, where he continued to startle his audience with provocative articles; even his friends spoke of his "somersaults." One piece, "Slovan a Čech" ("A Slav and a Czech," 1846), created a political sensation. He disliked Poland, he declared, and his Russian experience had extinguished in him the last spark of all-Slav enthusiasm; when he returned to Prague he came no longer as a dreaming Slav but as an adamant Czech who believed that Czechs were living in a powerful realm (*mocnářství*) which, in time of need, would defend Czech interests. His Austro-Czech sentiment may have pleased Palacký and the more liberal statesmen in Vienna, but the Austrian authorities were less pleased by Havlíček's articles about Ireland and Daniel O'Connell's opposition to London centralism (an allegory of Czech problems which had provided the Prague radicals with their Repeal slogan).

During the spring and summer of 1848, Havlíček was among the reformists; he disliked armed revolutions, preferring "revolutions of the head and the heart," and he joined Palacký, who was defending legality, on the St. Wenceslas Committee and as a member of the imperial Austrian parliament, bitterly opposing the elections to the Frankfurt Assembly. In April he decided to establish an opposition newspaper, *Národní Noviny* (*National News*), and in his declaration of his program demanded "the real equality of the nations, the union of the Bohemian crown lands, the abolition of feudal privileges, . . . a general national parliament, and an incisive reform of all schools and state offices." He was appalled by the June insurrection and the Bakunin conspiracy, accusing them of "playing a lottery game with the future of the nation"—though in his articles he himself became more radical in defining the civil and constitutional liberties that the counterrevolution diminished. He quickly ran into difficulties with the government; the Vienna and the Prague authorities wanted to silence his voice and accused him of defaming the constitution, but two juries declared him not guilty, and when a military court sentenced him to prison, he walked away free, since five Bohemian regions had elected him to represent them in the imperial parliament. The new absolutism, emerging from the defeat of the revolution, used other means. On December 13, 1851, young Emperor Franz Josef I signed a cabinet order to exile Havlíček, and in the early morning of December 16, the police agent Franz Dedera, accompanied by constables and local officials, knocked at Havlíček's door at Německý Brod (Deutsch Brod, later called Havlíčkův Brod), where he had taken refuge with his wife, Julie, and their daughter, Zdenka. He was formally charged and taken in a special coach, which the police had brought from Prague to Německý Brod by railway, on a long trip to picturesque Brixen, in the Tyrol, selected as his place of confinement.

Later in the century a patriotic holograph could be seen on the walls of nearly any Czech village inn, showing Havlíček taking leave of his wife and daughter, stern gendarmes standing by; many largely maudlin stories were told about his confinement in the distant Austrian Alps. The historian Jiří Morava, himself a dissident and far from his homeland, devoted nearly ten years of his own recent exile to historical research about Havlíček in the Tyrol, and his brave book, published in 1991 for the first time, tells, on the basis of authentic police documents, a mixed story of melancholy, a few happy moments, and an entire family killed by a vicious disease after their return to Bohemia.

Havlíček did not resist his arrest (it was too late to use a forged passport for England which he had in his desk), and he was sent via southern Bohemia and Upper Austria to Salzburg, where his transport was checked by a police commissioner named Le Monnier (later police president of Brno and Vienna, gratefully employing the scholarly young T. G. Masaryk to educate his son). From Salzburg, the coach wended its way to Innsbruck, then Brixen, a small town and residence of a bishop, proud of its cathedral, twelve churches, and five cloisters—just the place for a liberal to be confined. Havlíček was put up at the White Elephant, the region's most fashionable hotel then and now, all expenses paid; later he moved to a small apartment, where two sisters cooked for him and did his laundry. In 1852, his family joined him, and they all lived together in a *dépendance* of the hotel. He did not know that police offices in Prague and Vienna fought over him, trying to define their policies, but the local Tyrolean authorities, respecting his calm and self-discipline, were rather friendly. He usually spent his day writing, with a picture of Jan Hus above his desk, going on long walks with Julie, who hoped to strengthen her "weak lungs," and Zdenka. He also talked to a few new friends, among them a postal clerk who had been transferred to the provinces because he was considered a red republican of the Frankfurt variety, and a gentleman who happened to speak Czech and had retired to the Tyrol, telling everybody that his beautiful wife was Italian and wanted to be closer to home; actually he was afraid of his creditors. The Havlíčeks employed a servant girl, Julie baked cakes for their friends, there were little trips to a nearby spa, and a good deal of correspondence, neatly registered and read by the police.

In September 1854, his family chose to return home, Julie fearing that the winter would weaken her fragile health, Zdenka ready for school in Bohemia, and Havlíček was alone again, translating, writing sad poems and modern verse epics, and drinking beer in the evening with the Tyrolean peasants, who remained foreign to him. He was bitter and weary, and he tried to convince the authorities that he was ready to go home to Bohemia to settle on a little rented farm in the countryside. On April 15, 1855, the imperial authorities in Bohemia relented and he was allowed, renouncing all political activities, to return home.

No holograph has ever shown the tragedy that followed as soon as Havlíček crossed the frontier from Austria to Moravia. He expected that his brother-in-law would be waiting for him at Jihlava (Iglau), but they missed each other and only met, by chance, on the road; Havlíček, speechless and confused, had to learn that his wife had died in Prague of her tuberculosis, which had been consuming her body for a long time. She had been buried some time ago, a few friends and the inevitable police informers attending. In Prague, he quickly discovered that his former friends and acquaintances were afraid to talk to him; one of the exceptions was Božena Němcová, by now a prominent writer, who greeted him warmly in the street, saying she did not care what the government thought of her. The problem was that his plans to buy a shop or rent a little farm had been illusions, for his brother-in-law was unable to return the money which Havlíček had lent him to invest in his business. Without reserves or income, Havlíček had to place his daughter with friends, live with his mother in the country, and petition the police in vain for permission to settle in Prague, where he hoped to find "legal employment" (read: not one depending on his pen). Early in 1856, he felt tired, suffered from a severe cough, and two doctors, friendly patriots, told him that his lungs and glands were tubercular and gave him little hope. Friends sent him for a short while to a little spa, but he had to be brought back to Prague in agony, and he died in the apartment of his brother-in-law, opposite the railroad station, on July 29. Now that he was dead, the patriots made his funeral a national affair, but his poor daughter, Zdenka, was passed first to her father's in-laws, who went bankrupt, then from family to family as a "daughter of the nation"; a lottery was arranged which brought her a considerable sum of money to be her future dowry. People did not like the idea of Havlíček's daughter being wooed by an officer (an early suitor), but when the right Czech from the provinces came along, she died of her mother's and father's tuberculosis, in 1872, being twenty-four years old.

In 1843, a group of students from Prague studying in Vienna, Czechs and German-speaking Jews, believed that the time had come to bring Slavs and Jews closer together. The young Czech poet who first advanced this idea was Václav Bolemír Nebeský (who had just left Božena Němcová's embrace), a melancholy Byronist and also ardent defender of liberty and emancipation, only later a stuffed shirt in the service of the Prague Museum. Among his colleagues were David Kuh, from a famous Prague Jewish clan (later a German nationalist much hated by the Czechs), and the medical student Siegfried Kapper, son of a Jewish glazier from Smíchov and a particularly gifted translator of Czech poetry into the German tongue. The friends regularly met at the Slavic café at the corner of Währingerstrasse and Berggasse, not far from Sigmund Freud's later home; Nebeský and Kuh wrote articles and essays in support of a Slavic-Jewish rapprochement which were published in Czech and German periodicals in Prague and Germany; and Kapper's contribution to the cause was a slim volume entitled *České Listy* (*Czech Pages*, 1846). This is the first book of Czech poems written by a Prague Jew; and later critics discussed it from different political perspectives but rarely was it read as a lyrical confession of a young man who did not know where he belonged. Kapper's ambivalence clearly emerges from his allegiance to his Czech, not Bohemian, homeland (*česká vlast*), where the romantic outsider, as Jew, seeks intimacy and consolation among the carefully trimmed Slavic linden trees; in Czech nature, he finds the "Zion of his desire, the Canaan of his thought," while the Czech foliage whispers and the Czech rivers gently flow. Yet he knows himself that his praise of the Czech landscape does not articulate all his feelings; in many poems he pushes aside the props of third-rate national poetry and longs for the biblical land of his ancient origins, with its fierce sun, roses of Sharon, and mysterious cedar trees in the mountains. One set of motifs clashes with the other and, ultimately, young Kapper honestly accepts the pain of his divided self: "I am the son of Jews! I love my country, and yet I am a foreigner."

A few reviews were friendly, yet, unfortunately, it was Karel Havlíček himself, the most intelligent of the liberals, who in a longish article turned against Kapper's poetry and, more essentially, against any Jewish writer claiming allegiance to the Czech nation. It was not, he wrote, a matter of religion but of "origins and nationality," of belonging to a particular "tribe." Jews are of "Semitic origin," and Germans, Englishmen, or Spanish could become Czechs more easily than Jews, who, coming from a totally different tribe, "only accidentally live among Czechs" and "occasionally understand and speak Czech." Havlíček's argument comes close to being racist; if a Jew wants to become a Czech, he has to "cease to be a Jew" (Havlíček does not explain how to do that, in view of the immutable tribal origins), and he cynically suggests that Jews wishing to give up their nationality and language should join the Germans and write in their language, as they do elsewhere. Literary questions are subordinate; Havlíček admits that Kapper has succeeded in writing a few interesting stanzas, but he cannot stand what he calls his "screaming style," with its overdone images so disproportionate to the banal thoughts. The realist Havlíček was never willing to tolerate big political phrases instead of the far more necessary patient social action of the moment, and if the sentimental and loquacious patriot is but a Prague Jew, *tant pis*. It is a pity that Havlíček did not write about Kapper again, when he returned, two years after the revolution, to the Jewish question, a much wiser and perhaps more isolated man among his compatriots, and welcomed the legal emancipation of Jews as an integral event in the emancipation of all nations of mankind. Perhaps he had come to see that Jews cannot be denied those civic privileges that Czechs were so urgently claiming for themselves.

It was impossible to argue against Havlíček's authority. Kapper continued his medical studies and received his Vienna doctorate in 1847. He settled as a young physician in a small town of Croatia, traveled a good deal in Serbia and Bosnia, and quickly returned to revolutionary Vienna in the spring of 1848. He joined the Academic Legion, treated wounded students in the courtyard of the university, published bad German poetry saying that political action, not empty verse, was the order of the day, and wrote regular reports for important German newspapers. In 1853 he moved to Dobříš, a small town not far from Prague, married the daughter of the exiled radical Moritz Hartmann (earning himself the close attention of the Austrian secret police), edited a German yearbook of literature, and became so bored that, in 1859, he joined the Austrian army in Italy as a volunteer and worked in a field hospital in Verona. A year later he tried to settle in Bohemia again, this time in Mladá Boleslav (Jungbunzlau), and within a short time he succeeded in provoking most people there, the Germans because he supported Czech candidates in any election, and the Jewish traditionalists because he was never seen in the synagogue.

In 1867, Kapper finally returned to Prague, opened a physician's office at the corner of Wenceslas Square and Vodičkova Street, announcing that he was welcoming patients with "secret diseases"; every day he worked five hours in his office and devoted the rest of his time to writing. He may have been a rather restless and irritable character, as attested by his contemporaries, but he was not easily deflected from his literary interests. Early in his life, he had begun to study South Slav literature, or rather ancient Serb heroic poetry, and encouraged by the philologist and poet Štefan Vuk Karadžič, he translated many old epic songs into German and Czech, or imitated them in his own way. His German stories and novels are forgettable, but he was a first-rate travel writer, in his admiration of the Serbs often anticipating Rebecca West's classic account of a century later, *Black Lamb and Grey Falcon*; his reports of the brutal Hungarian-Slav battles of 1849 deserve to be reread, and not only by historians. It is interesting that he always considered himself a Czech when traveling (never mind Havlíček), and when, one evening, in a cosmopolitan group in Belgrade, everyone was asked to sing a song close to his heart, he intoned the old Hussite battle hymn "Kdož sú Boží bojovníci" ("Those who are soldiers of God . . .").

In his Prague years, Kapper loyally participated in the cultural life of the Czech middle class; he did not entirely cease to publish in German, but he mostly contributed to important Czech periodicals, joined the Měšťanská Beseda, where he met Jan Neruda, the most important Czech author of the later nineteenth century. Kapper continued to translate Serb heroic poetry, mostly into Czech, published artful Dalmatian fairy tales, and his yearly lectures on his South Slav researches, presented to the literary section of the Beseda, were well attended. His quarrel now was with the Prague Jewish community; he did not want to pay the community tax, complained to the government in Vienna, and finally left the community—only to return to it, humbly and quietly, when he was gravely ill. He spent his last two years in Italy hoping against hope to cure his tuberculosis and died on June 7, 1879, in Pisa, where he was buried at the Jewish cemetery.

Kapper would have been immensely pleased to know that the Prague Czechs did pay homage to his literary achievements; Neruda himself, in a two-part necrology in the *Národní Noviny*, the organ of the dominant Young Czech party, praised his lyrical talents and untiring efforts in the service of the Slavic cause. Earlier, in 1869, Neruda had published an essay in which he had argued against Jews, who, he said, constituted a "polyglot" and "international nation" that watched Czech striving with "icy coldness." Kapper, however, was different—"he felt a Slav and remained a Slav"—and though Neruda had once quoted Richard Wagner's diatribes against Jewish sterility in the arts, he now spoke highly of Kapper's unusual gifts and falconlike thought. He passed over Kapper's German publications, about three-quarters of his production, in a single sentence, and insisted that Kapper was the first Jew to take his rightful place on the Slavic Parnassus, the seat of the muses. Then times changed (somewhat); in 1876, a Spolek Českých Akademiků-Židů (Club of Czech-Jewish Professionals) was established in Prague, and by 1919 it changed its name to commemorate Siegfried Kapper, who had never feared to challenge his fellow citizens.

Many generations of admiring poets, patriotic critics, and, at times, official propagandists have long transformed the bitter life of Božena Němcová, the first Czech woman writer of importance, into a cherished national myth. Critics traditionally incline to read her more sentimental novellas as if they were biographical testimony, and in a recent spate of books and essays tell us that she was really of high aristocratic origins; in these genealogical fantasies the adventurous duchess of Sagan and none other than Metternich, the imperial chancellor, figure prominently. All talented Czechs of the past century, including T. G. Masaryk, came from rather humble circumstances—it could not be otherwise sociologically—and Božena Němcová, christened Barbora, was the daughter of a Czech servant girl working, as thousands of others did, in Vienna, and Johann Pankl, an Austrian *feschak* and horse groom, who legitimized his relationship and his newly born daughter in 1820 after a brief delay. He was honest and faithful in the service of his master, moved his family to the Bohemian estate of Ratibořice, where he was put in charge of the stables while his wife worked as manorial laundress, insisting that she belonged to the higher servant ranks. She preferred to speak German and looked askance at her Czech family, all poor weavers originally. The stable master spent the winter season in Vienna and returned to Ratibořice in the late spring, fathered twelve more children, of whom six survived, and overworked Frau Pankl, as she called herself now, invited her widowed mother to help with the children. The old woman could not stand her daughter's cantankerous ways, moved to another daughter, living in Vienna with a herring merchant, died there, and was buried at the Matzleinsdorfer cemetery in 1841. In Božena Němcová's novel *The Grandmother* (1855), she lives on as the true incarnation of Czech folk wisdom and kindness, forever surrounded by sublime forests and green meadows.

Barbora attended the local elementary school and was later, after the grandmother had left, sent by her ambitious and impatient mother to live with the family of the steward of nearby Chvalkovice Castle to refine her manners, to perfect her German, and to play the piano. In a fashionable way, people called her Fräulein Betty, which she enjoyed, and as time went by she preferred the admiring glances of men, among them the steward himself, to the company of boys. There was flirting, whispers, and first kisses, and long hours of reading Schiller and Wieland, but also a good deal of third-rate German trash nourishing her dreams about the fairy-tale prince to arrive; yet Betty had also a sharp eye for the tangible social world, and at another time described the married life of the steward and his older wife with devastating precision: "in the evening, when she went to bed, she rigged herself out like a wagoneer who wants to go to Amsterdam, with flannel drawers, a skirt, a bodice, and stockings; and above all that she put a warm corset and a shawl around her neck." The many-layered lady, who had served in Vienna, was jealous, so Betty returned home to her mother, who had her hands full and did not know what to do with her lively and imaginative seventeen-year-old daughter; when a member of the border guard revealed that his chief, a man with prospects, was looking for a young wife, the family was more than willing to arrange the marriage.

In due course Josef Němec, of military bearing, rather educated and coarse, presented himself to the parents and to Barbora. At first she was not ready to take the talk of marriage seriously, but she had no other choice and married Josef (twice her age) in a formal ceremony, she in a pale blue dress, he in his Sunday uniform, on September 12, 1827. They both came to regret the day.

There is not another marriage in Czech intellectual history that has been more closely scrutinized by biographers and literary critics than that of Josef Němec and Barbora Panklová. The bridegroom had been a student of philosophy when he was accused of participating in a silly street demonstration and, as punishment, forced to join the army (the regular term of service was fourteen years). Being a proud patriot, he refused to swear the oath of allegiance in German (his officer accepted the Czech version), served many years in Italy, carrying Professor Jungmann's famous book on Czech rhetoric in his pack, perhaps the reason why he never had anything to say about the glories of Italy. When his time of service was reduced, he joined the financial, or border, guards, organized to levy food taxes and fight smugglers of tobacco and cheap cotton. He was a stubborn and pugnacious man, often in conflict with his superiors, and made a slow and meandering career through the ranks. In early June 1853, he was officially notified that he was suspended from the service, confined to a little Hungarian town (which he had chosen to speed up his promotion), and investigated as an *enragé* Czech of republican sentiments, especially dangerous because of his influence on his wife, the writer Božena Němcová, who in turn enjoyed considerable prestige among Czech intellectuals (one of her women friends was a spy in the service of the police, elaborately trained for the job). For brief periods Josef, a man of the barracks, and Božena felt close to each other, especially in the Bohemian provinces, where they were both active in Czech civic life, or when they organized Karel Havlíček's funeral in 1856; though it is impossible to say that he did not know the importance of literature (as correspondent of Czech newspapers he wrote more than sixty articles himself), he did not wish his wife to be a writer—wanting her to be a devoted and practical housewife as were the other petit bourgeois women of Prague. He certainly knew something about Božena's passionate affairs, and there is evidence that he crudely mistreated her (she had to run for protection to the nearest police precinct) or locked her up in her room (she had to escape through the window). Marital rape has a variety of methods.

When Josef married Betty, he was proud of her beauty, and her later friends and enemies speak of her raven-black hair of metallic luster, dark eyes under strong brows, and a high seriousness of feeling. In Prague, scandalized mothers and adamant wives were quickly jealous rather than hospitable to the remarkable newcomer from the countryside; her free way of moving, talking, and conversing with the young did not endear her to the people in conservative salons (she may have occasionally smoked cigars, as did George Sand when she visited Prague). She loved to love, absolutely and in total disregard of the conventions, and when as a married woman and caring mother of four, she chose a man, she abandoned herself to her desires and in her letters, almost blindly. Her *grands amours* tended to follow a recurrent and depressing scenario: "a night of nightingales," or a one-night stand on a Prague hill or in a newspaper office, then painful absence and renewed embraces, confessions and correspondences; finally, fiery demands on the men who, usually, feared her sudden passions and were unwilling to become prisoners of her almost masochistic surrender. At least one of them, a physician who was also a translator of Boccaccio, in a cynical communication to a friend called her "the Spleen," alluding to her many health problems (she was to die of uterine cancer). All these men belonged to patriotic circles or were well-educated medical students or doctors, but none had the courage to confront her expectations, and what remained to her was, again and again, bitterness, silence, and despair. In a letter of searing honesty of June 13, 1857, when Josef wanted to return to her, she told him what she thought of modern marriage—"the deceit, the privileged slavery, duty enforced"—and confessed all her disappointments to him. "They possessed my body but my action, honesty and desire looked into a far distance, which I did not know myself. . . . I thought I could fill the emptiness of my feelings only loving a man but now I know that it was not so. . . . I wanted to be better, live in truth, and the world forced me to lie."

Strangely enough, it was the gruff patriot Němec himself who had greatly strengthened his wife's renewed interest in Czech life and literature, dormant as long as she satisfied her emotional needs by reading sentimental German novels. Her grandmother had told her old Czech peasant stories, but it was her self-consciously Czech husband who prompted her to read Prague newspapers and Czech books, and even before she laid hands on Tyl's sentimental prose, she perused as her first Czech text a local translation of a novel by the American writer Washington Irving, who had visited Prague too. After they moved to Prague, Němec introduced her to the family of Dr. Josef Frič, the well-known lawyer and father of the radical, and at the Fričes' home she met all the important people of Czech polite society in the 1840s, including the young poet and medical student Nebeský, her lover, who corrected her first poem "To Czech Women!," published to great acclaim. She enjoyed herself among her new friends and admirers, attended dances, balls, and patriotic picnics, which were then *en vogue*; "like a queen / you came," Nebeský wrote in one of his ardent poems before he escaped to Vienna to continue his studies.

Another, perhaps more important mentor was František Matouš Klácel, an Augustinian priest who had been reprimanded for his Hegelian views and had conceived the idea of trying to organize ideal humanity from scratch, as it were, by founding a "Czech-Moravian brother- and sisterhood" of the happy few. Božena Němcová, whom he called "Sister Ludmila," was among the charter members of this small group, and Klácel addressed a series of letters to her, published in 1849 as a book on the origins of modern socialism and communism, the first treatise on these matters written in Czech. Klácel, too, admired her from afar, but when she slept with another brother, everybody was jealous and the brother- and sisterhood came to a premature end before it had really flourished. Klácel submitted to the ecclesiastical authorities again but later left for the United States, where he edited a number of Czech liberal newspapers for the poor people who had left their Bohemian homeland.

She had little patience with poetry, and by the mid-1840s she joined those romantic philologists and writers, German, Czech, Slovak, Hungarian, and Serb, who collected and retold fairy tales and the stories current, as they thought, among simple people—efforts intended to strengthen the national self-consciousness of societies still, or once again, deprived of states of their own. She was not, as the brothers Grimm and their Czech ally Karel Jaromír Erben had been, predominantly concerned with folk authenticity, and in the Slovak fairy tales and legends she gathered on many field trips to Slovakia, she magnificently played with the idiomatic potentialities of combining Czech and Slovak vocabulary, probably appreciated by modern readers even more than by her own contemporaries. *Babička* (*The Grandmother*), written at a time of despair and misery, intimately relates to her earlier anthropological interests in the service of national reawakening, but fortunately goes far beyond these restraints. She recalls the idyllic days of her childhood at home in northeastern Bohemia and the old woman closest to her heart; though she looks back at these serene days through tears, her evocations of peasant costumes, local habits of speech, and recurrent feasts and pilgrimages are remarkably precise. Portraits and scenes, not plots and counterplots (though more rapidly developing in the final chapters), predominate; the life of her grandmother, symbolic of strong vitality, loving wisdom, and the Czech plebeian tradition, distinctly emerges in confrontation with that of the duchess living in the nearby castle and poor Viktorka, a half-mad peasant girl roaming through the forests. Her social station has kept the duchess from living close to nature and people; and if the grandmother likens herself to a gnarled pear tree that has survived many a storm, the duchess enjoys but a collection of stones and desiccated plants on her shelves (she has no children of her own, only an adopted daughter). Critics and film producers have long felt that Božena Němcová hid many of her own passions in Viktorka, the girl seduced by a soldier and left with a child, whom she drowns. Viktorka lives in a cave, wanders through the woods, gathers berries, and snatches pieces of bread left for her on the windowsills by peasants—until she is killed in the woods by lightning. (The real Viktorka was an alcoholic mother of two, who miserably died on the road not long after the novel was published.) It is the grandmother whom people call a truly "happy woman" without doubts or hesitations.

For more than a hundred years now, *Babička* has been fundamental to the Czech prose canon, dear to any child and adult, and the long efforts of official critics to celebrate Němcová as a socialist realist, relying on folk types and the optimism of the people, prompted an opposition that accentuated her romanticism, early stressed by the critic F. X. Šalda. Yet this debate about generalities has obfuscated the more difficult question of how Božena Němcová used the literary conventions of her moment for her own purposes and where she fell victim to them. Czech feminists are lucky that the modern Czech prose tradition begins in her writings; instead of trying so hard to demonstrate that her father was Metternich or another prince, it is far more important to grasp her pride and her thirst for independence, her plea for women's education (she had almost none), her defense of Jews in the words of an old Czech peasant in her reports from southern Bohemia, and her sudden decision to come, in the disguise of a countrywoman, to the help of the Prague insurrectionists of June 1848 (too late, of course). Even before the Velvet Revolution of 1989, critical interests began to shift, and, as is suggested by a challenging inquiry undertaken by the Swiss scholar and translator Susanna Roth, among Czech writers at home and in exile Božena Němcová is now being read and thought about in many different ways, and not only in response to the political correctness of yesteryear. Attention reaches out for the masterpieces among her smaller prose pieces, for instance, *Čtyři Doby* (*Four Seasons*), revealing in a few veiled pages the trauma of love defiled by marriage, or *Divá Bára* (*The Wild Bára*), celebrating innocence and energy. Important artists like Jiří Kolář and many writers, among them Eva Kantůrková, have rediscovered Božena Němcová's correspondence, and a new chapter of our response to her has just begun.

8

T. G. MASARYK'S PRAGUE

A Modernized City and a Literature of Ghosts

As for other European cities, modernization for Prague was closely bound to advances in industrialization, long delayed, to new networks of communications, and to the economic boom of the 1850s and then again toward the end of the nineteenth century. The first to modernize, in his own way, had been Emperor Joseph II, who by his transformation and destruction of many monastic and ecclesiastical institutions and buildings, had greatly changed the historical charms of Prague's ancient towns. In the 1830s and 1840s, the Prague burgrave Count Karl Chotek energetically pushed for a productive collaboration of urban architects and new industrialists, built new avenues, initiated a society to construct a second bridge over the river (the one that goes from the National Theater to Smíchov), reorganized the quay on the right riverbank, and yet also protected old gardens, parks, and churches against developers.

Another, far more incisive phase of urban modernization began in the mid-1880s, when a proud city government, by 1888 entirely Czech, suggested a radical plan to "sanitize" the most decrepit parts of the Old Town and a few other corners; in 1895 (after the plan had been approved by the Vienna authorities) the old Jewish quarter—with the exception of a few historic synagogues, the cemetery (though narrowed), and the old Jewish town hall—was totally razed, as was the northern side of the Old Town Square and at least three old churches together with adjacent buildings. The rubble was transported in 21,700 wagonloads to be used as landfill in a district still endangered by frequent inundations from the river. Neither the Hussite civil wars nor the enlightened policies of Emperor Joseph II had so massively threatened the historical shape of Prague, and while poets, artists, architects, and students voiced their protest in newspapers and in mass meetings, the city government did not substantially yield. International travelers who visit the Prague Jewish Town today walk in the ancient grid of streets, but all the apartment buildings, left and right, reflect *fin de siècle* middle-class tastes. Pařížská Street, now a concatenation of international airline offices, violently and destructively intrudes into the old street structure.

Yet the advantages of modern *asanace* (sanitation) did not primarily affect Jews, because in the fifth district, newly incorporated into Prague's union of towns in 1850 under the name of Josefov ("Joseph's Place"), Jewish civic life no longer prevailed and only 10 percent of its residents were still Jewish. The emigration of rich Jews to other parts of the city had started well before the revolution of 1848; a year later the familiant's law was annulled; by 1852 Jews were allowed to acquire housing wherever they wished; and in 1867 they were assured all civil rights equal to those guaranteed to Czechs and Germans. Even the less well-to-do tried to find apartments somewhere else, especially in the New Town and at bourgeois Vinohrady (a little east of the New Town), although some families, like that of Franz Kafka, restlessly moved year by year, in a circle around the old ghetto. The shabby old houses in the Jewish Town had become the last refuge of the poorest of the poor; contemporary reportages by the Czech realist Jan Neruda described them as havens of unsavory crime, pimps, and low prostitution (the better places, like the famous Goldschmidt salon, were located elsewhere in the Old Town). Contemporary studies prepared by Dr. Václav Preininger were discouraging; by 1885, the Josefov district, or Prague V, with 186,000 inhabitants, was the most overpopulated of all Prague quarters; in the Old Town, 644 people lived on one hectare of housing space, but 1,822 in Josefov, and even in proletarian Žižkov the number had been 1,300. Overall in the city the proportion of one-room apartments was 53 percent, which was bad enough, but in Josefov it was as high as 64 percent; in one small house more than 200 people were found living together. On the average, one toilet served five to ten apartments. The mortality rate for infectious diseases in the Old Town in 1895 was 18.13 per thousand, in the Minor Town 20.61, and in Josefov, a quarter without clean water, sunlight, or gardens, however small, 30.61. So there was ample need for "sanitation" in the strict sense, but there was another reason too, less often discussed publicly. This was the age in which representative public buildings for the new Czech middle class were being constructed in grand neo-Renaissance style along the Vltava embankment and elsewhere—the National Theater (1881–83), the Rudolfinum concert hall (1884), the School of the Applied Arts (1884), the new National Museum (1885–90), and the Museum of the City of Prague (1898). Prague wanted to rise and shine, preparing for three international exhibitions in the 1890s to show its material and intellectual achievements, and the poor of Josefov were barely hidden by the surrounding new splendor.

The decisions of the magistrate to change so much of Prague provoked the opposition of many organizations, including the Czech Club of Architects and the German Club for City Affairs, yet people were not concerned about the disappearance of the former ghetto, though they helped to protect the streets nearby, the churches of the Old Town, and a few old buildings in the New Town—for instance, the "Faust" house—endangered by city planners. In 1895, the Czech Club of Architects and the Měšt'anská Beseda submitted a memorandum reminding the city fathers of the ancient history of Prague, and soon artists and intellectuals were on a collision course with the powers that be. The distinguished novelist and playwright Vilém Mrštík (a Moravian) unsparingly attacked Prague's urban renewal, speaking against the "blindness" and "ignorance" of the few people robbing Prague of its "most precious treasure," and in yet another, even more belligerent essay (1896–97) called those responsible for the cleanup the "*bestia triumphans*," a term derived from Friedrich Nietzsche to denote the absolute victory of brutal power over sensible intelligence.

One of the old palaces people fought about was the late Baroque Benedictine prelacy originally built by Kilian Ignaz Dientzenhofer in 1730 to be affiliated with nearby St. Nicholas. In that prelacy, secularized by Joseph II, Franz Kafka was born in 1883, but the original building was destroyed by fire (1897) and a new construction, in style and adornment imitating the old prelacy, was built on the spot in 1902. In 1966, after considerable conflict with the Communist authorities, people were able to affix a plaque to the house saying that Franz Kafka was born there—true, in a purely topographical sense—and international pilgrims deciphering the Czech inscription have to learn that in the Old Town, as in Kafka's writings, things are not always what they seem.

In the time of the *asanace*, continuing into the first year of World War I, Prague advanced, as if with a sudden leap of energy, to being a modern city, massively industrialized, especially in its expanding suburbs, and run by a new strong Czech middle class legitimately proud of its splendid cultural and economic institutions, the Czech University, and new banks and insurance companies. Germans had been defeated in the city council elections of 1861 and, increasingly excluded from the political administration of the community, tried to balance their political losses by much attention to their theater, a flowering literary life, and innumerable social clubs. Since the new industries attracted a continuous immigration from the Czech countryside, the number of German speakers in Prague quickly decreased (in 1880 to 15.5 percent, and in 1900 to 7.5 percent).

The four original Prague towns grew constantly; not only was the Jewish community incorporated as Josefov (Prague V) but the Vyšehrad district and Holešovice-Bubny, a mighty bastion of the Czech proletariat, followed in 1901. Other suburbs did not want to be incorporated into the city; they were afraid of its special tax on rents (approximately 14 percent) and enjoyed being favored by the government, which readily granted them the privilege of being imperial and royal towns on their own, as was Vinohrady and Žižkov; Vienna recognized, of course, that rapid incorporation of so many Czechs into Prague would wash away the last vestiges of German entitlements there.

Matters were complicated even more by the social transformations of Prague's Jewish community, which demographically held its own, though its members were now dispersed, predominantly all over the Old and New Towns. An increasing number of families, though continuing to send their sons to German schools and the German university, preferred to declare during statistical inquiries that their language was Czech; by 1900, 14,576 Prague Jews declared themselves to be speakers of Czech, while the number of German speakers had dropped to 11,599. The reorientation of language did not immediately affect the community's religious life; administrative functions were in the hands of well-to-do German-speaking liberals, and the major synagogues, including the Old New and the Pinkas synagogues, retained the old Hebrew rites. Mixed marriages, in spite of the advancing acculturation to other language groups, were surprisingly rare (in 1894, 1 in 655, rising to 4 in 684 in 1895 and 21 in 676 in 1897). (The corresponding numbers in Vienna and especially Berlin were twice as high.) The notion of Jews as a "nation among nations" had been current among the young writers of the *Sippurim* in 1847, and yet the first Zionist student group was not established until 1893, renewed as Bar Kochba (bilingual) in 1899, while the Czech Theodor Herzl group suffered from a dearth of Jewish students at the Czech University (by 1911, there were only 101, and even by 1921, only 469, as compared with 1,400 Jews studying at the German university).

As Prague increasingly modernized, a special literature about it began to emerge internationally, insisting on its magic if not mystical image. Contemporary Czechs, concerned with commercial, technological, and political advances, celebrated Zlatá Praha, the golden Slavic city of past and future achievements, yet English, German, and American writers on the grand tour once again became enchanted by the metaphysical, strange, and spectral town of ancient cathedrals and synagogues, and dutifully wended their way through the old streets to the famous old Jewish cemetery. The walk itself followed literary convention; ever since the later eighteenth century, cemeteries had been sweet places of melancholy reflections about frail life and sublime death, and Prague's Jewish cemetery exerted a strong pull on minds shaped by Christian tradition. Uncertain feelings of otherness, history, and eerie portents curiously mingled; it is not difficult to understand why English and American travelers, who are more substantially responsible for the literature of magic Prague than we perhaps assume, were ready for supernatural experiences, and they wrote stories of hypnosis, strange blood transfusions, ghosts, and weird revenants. The *asanace* ordered by the city magistrate may have razed much of the Jewish Town, but the many stories about magical Prague kept alive the literary image of a topography long gone.

George Eliot, accompanied by her devoted friend George Henry Lewes on a trip from Vienna to Dresden, spent July 16, 1858, in Prague, walked through the Old Town, kissed "a lovely dark-eyed Jewish child . . . in all its dirt," looked at the "somber old synagogue with its smoky groins," and never forgot her impressions. Publishers and critics were confused about the immediate result of her first trip to Prague, a story called "The Lifted Veil," written in 1859, and later she was inclined herself to hide it in a volume of other stories rather than risk independent publication again. She defended it by saying she had written "a *jeu de melancholie*," an "*outré*" story. That much is true: an aging Englishman who always wanted to be a poet but lacked inspiration confesses that instead he received the gift of "prevision," the ability to look forward in time and into people's secret thoughts. Strangely enough, it is the word "Prague" (where his father wants to go on a trip) that, for the first time, triggers a precise vision of a future moment; though he has never been in Prague or seen a picture of it, he suddenly sees "a city . . . in the summer sunshine of a long-past century arrested in its course . . . and the dusty, weary, time-eaten grandeur of a people doomed to live on in the stale repetition of memories, like the past and superannuated kings in their regal gold-inwoven tatters," and as he walks he passes "under the blank gaze of blackened statues" along "the unending bridge."

On a later trip to Prague, he discovers his extraordinary vision fully confirmed, but he also begins to feel how difficult it is to live on. He recognizes in one of his visionary moments that his late wife, whom he truly loved, had been possessed by an uncaring and dangerous egotism: her maid dies, and a medical friend by a rather unorthodox transfusion of blood brings the dead woman to life again and she confesses, in a hypnotic state, that she helped her lady in an effort to poison her husband (who is not totally surprised). Prague, "prevision," and the occult sciences combine here, and yet it is less obvious that this man, burdened with his knowledge of the future, has become one of the denizens of the deadly city himself, "urged by no fear or hope . . . but compelled by this doom to be ever old and undying, to live on in the rigidity of habit . . . without the repose of night or the new birth of morning." With the future known, time paralyzes the mind and petrifies the body, like the statues on the Charles Bridge. Only a few years later, George Eliot turned her attention to contemporary Jewish problems, and after she had met Rabbi Emmanuel Deutsch in London (1866) and taken Hebrew lessons, she returned to Prague in April 1870 (visiting the Old New Synagogue again) and reread Leopold Kompert's Jewish stories in the original German, in preparation for her novel *Daniel Deronda*, in which Jewish Prague, among other cities, reappears.

In May 1859, not long after George Eliot's first visit, the North German writer Wilhelm Raabe came on an excursion to Prague, although he had wanted to go to Italy; four years later his "Holunderblüte" ("Lilac Blossom") appeared, a story that is late romantic in mood and yet a provocative signal of strong, ambivalent feelings laboriously repressed. In it a traveling medical student encounters a fifteen-year-old Jewish girl, a kind of Mignon of Prague V, but he tells of their meetings at the old Jewish cemetery at a distance twice removed—by time and by another story about a life cut short. It is not easy for him to speak of Jemima Loew, and of how they walk hand in hand among the graves, clouded over by lilacs, and how the dead, among them Rabbi Loew, one of her ancestors, come to life in what she tells him. Raabe remarked, as did other writers of the time, on the "incredible dirt" of Prague's narrow streets, but he also showed much compassion for the Jewish people, "so maliciously tormented, mistreated, scorned, and burdened by fear." His traveler does not really want to speak about his most intimate feelings, tries to assure himself that he does not love young Jemima, yet spends his days in Prague almost paralyzed and feverishly driven by the expectation of seeing her again. He refuses to call his enchantment by its name, but later, in a suburban crowd in Berlin one day, he suddenly feels that Jemima has died, as she predicted she would, rushes back to Prague, and hears she was buried eight days earlier. Raabe barely skirts sentimentality, and yet Jemima, in spite of a few "exotic" elements, asserts herself as an astonishing figure, full of honest feelings, coquettish, loving, talking, and teasing. She does not hesitate to taunt her wide-eyed visitor with that famous Czech line without any vowels whatsoever and beyond the phonetic possibilities of any German visitor, "*strč prst skrz krk*" (put your finger down your throat). No wonder that he is smitten.

Only a few years later, as the American scholar Jeffrey L. Sammons has shown again, modern anti-Semitism seized on the motif of the Prague Jewish cemetery as the spectral place where Jewish world domination is plotted. Herrmann Goedsche—once an employee of the Prussian postal service, dismissed because of his involvement in an unsavory forgery case, and later a co-owner of an ultraconservative Berlin newspaper—among other sensational novels wrote a historical potboiler entitled *Biarritz*, dealing with Bismarck and Napoleon III. As early as in Volume 1 (published in 1868), he showed, in the eyes of a secret witness, how the delegates of the twelve tribes of Israel, with the Eternal Jew as an extra, meet in enclave at the Prague cemetery at midnight to consider the Jewish past and to discuss conspiratorial plans for the future domination of the world (the representative of the Prague tribe demands that all management positions in law and education be given to Jews). Goedsche published this popular historical novel under the name of Sir John Retcliffe, and the improvised alias served well when the Prague chapter was separately published in Russian translation (possibly by members of the tsarist secret police in Paris), losing its fictional character on the way and alleged to refer to incontrovertible facts. Sergei Nilus, a homespun Russian mystic and predecessor of Rasputin, added a text based on a French version (which has its own complicated history) to one of his own books; *The Protocols of the Elders of Zion*, thus born, was used by the tsarist secret police, French anti-Semitic groups, German proto-Nazis in the 1920s, and in Henry Ford's newspaper, *The Dearborn Independent*. (Though in 1927 Ford disavowed personal responsibility for the publication, other right-wingers, and not only in the United States, continue to believe the stuff.) Hitler, of course, referred to the *Protocols* in *Mein Kampf*—the most notorious poison flower of magic Prague and, to this day, an underground best-seller of the extreme right in many countries.

At the time when much of the old Jewish Town and other ancient quarters had been destroyed by city planners, the myth of Prague the fantastic city went on crystallizing. A small library of *fin de siècle* novels is built on this theme. The earliest example was *The Witch of Prague* (1890), written by Francis Marion Crawford, an American expatriate who otherwise preferred to write successful novels about Renaissance history; he was followed, in Prague, by Rilke's *König Bohusch* (1899), Jiří Karásek of Lvovice's *Gothic Soul* (*Gotická Duše*, 1900), Guillaume Apollinaire's *Le Passant de Prague* (1903), a witty novella which impressed French and Czech surrealists. After the stories and novels written by Anglo-Saxon and German authors and the publications by Prague "decadents" of both languages, the first German golem movie by Paul Wegener, in 1914, triggered a third and eclectic wave of darkly occult Prague novels. Gustav Meyrink, born in Vienna, in his own golem novel of 1915 concocted a European best-seller made up of mystical and whodunit elements; Paul Leppin liked to add erotic spice; and Leo Perutz, later, stuck to the traditional Baroque sets. It was not difficult to shift the conventions of the old gothic novel to Prague as long as it was considered an eerie place and a repository of eerie tales, with well-defined specters and dramatis personae—the golem, the Eternal Jew, Rabbi Loew, and Rudolf II—seen at particular places, on weird streets, in half-ruined churches, ancient synagogues, cemeteries, or prisons, and, of course, with melodramatic fatalities, creeping disease, Baroque miracles, occult power, and a "Jewish" exoticism that even the anti-Semites did not want to miss.

Crawford's *The Witch of Prague* was in its time unusually popular in England and America (reprinted four times in 1891–92) and available to continental readers in an inexpensive Tauchnitz paperback edition. Much happens in this novel and most of it far beyond the ordinary: a traveling gentleman of artistic leanings and independent income roams all over Europe to find his Beatrice again, once loved and lost, and in his search for her stumbles into the arms of a Prague Czech femme fatale called Unorna. She comes to know that Beatrice lives in a Prague convent, yet charms the gentleman herself, in a hypnotic séance, in the shape of his lost love. Matters are made even more complicated by a dwarfish talkative Arab who experiments with mummies and revivifies the dying, and by Israel Kafka, young and handsome, who passionately loves Unorna. She, in turn, taps his blood to use in the strangest experiments (Kafka has the unfortunate habit of hiding behind gravestones in the old cemetery and surprising her when she walks nearby). The American author was not entirely happy with his occult Prague lore, and in one of his expansive footnotes tells us that Unorna's hypnotic techniques can be fully explained scientifically by reading Professor Krafft-Ebing's recent study, second edition. Yet Crawford, who usually lived in Italy or Munich, had spent some time in wintry Prague, had a good ear for Czech and the meaning of Czech history—"an ardent flame of life hidden beneath the crust of ashes"—and of course offered his readers a long set piece on the ancient Jewish cemetery. His Prague descriptions can amply compete with those of Gustav Meyrink, who transferred to his golem novel pictures of the London slums taken from his own excellent translations of Charles Dickens, done under contract for a German publisher, to serve as visions of magic Prague. "The winter of the black city that spans the frozen Moldau," the American author wrote, "is the winter of the grave, dim as the perpetual afternoon . . . cold with the unspeakable frigid mess of a reeking air that thickens as oil but will not be frozen, melancholy as a stony island of death in a lifeless sea." There are reasons why the witch incarnating the city calls herself Unorna or, translating from the Czech stem of the word, Februaria.

The Republic in Its Monday Best

When World War I entered its third year, Prague was a haggard, cold, and hungry city, and people moved in a gray zone of daily compromises, anger, and hidden hopes, trying to think of the future. Czech soldiers fought on both the Austrian fronts (as conscripts) and on the Allied side (as legionnaires); Hapsburg military tribunals harshly persecuted and imprisoned Czech politicians of note. Only a few courageous men and women knew exactly what Professor T. G. Masaryk and his friend Dr. Eduard Beneš were doing abroad, and they secretly collected information about events in Vienna and Prague to transmit to them in order to support Masaryk in his discussions with the Allies. The majority of the representatives of the Czechs elected to the Vienna parliament for a long time expressed satisfaction with the successes, if any, of the imperial armies, closely watching, all the time, the eastern and southern fronts; they adjusted the tenor of their opportunistic declarations to a rapidly changing situation. It was not a particularly dignified spectacle; in May 1917 Czech writers and intellectuals issued a manifesto, actually written by Jaroslav Kvapil, dramaturge of the National Theater, strongly rebuking these parliamentarians, who had been elected to defend national interests, the writers said, and should renounce their mandates if they thought they could not do so. After the Russian Revolution in October 1917, the Dual Monarchy itself began to explore the possibilities of making a separate peace with the Allies, regardless of Germany; parliament was called into session again; Emperor Charles, definitely not an ardent militarist, amnestied the imprisoned Czech leaders; and even regular publications were allowed to speak of national self-determination—within the Dual Monarchy, of course.

Within a year, the situation had changed. In Rome, the Congress of Oppressed Austrian Nationalities met in early April 1918 to declare their right to self-determination, the Allied War Council at Versailles two months later fully supported these aspirations, and the governments of the Western Allies, including the United States, confirmed that a "state of belligerence existed between Czechoslovakia and the German and Austro-Hungarian Empires." Later that spring, delegates of all the Czech political parties from left to right met in Prague, and on July 13 constituted, once again, a National Committee to prepare for the future. What the committee members had in mind was not a bloody revolution but administrative and economic blueprints for a new state once the Austrian monarchy had collapsed under the weight of its own burdens. The Socialist members, distrustful of middle-class liberals, wanted to have their own piece of the pie but, on October 14, went too far in trying to organize a general strike to protest the export of grain and coal from suffering Bohemia: Prague was immediately occupied by regular army units—for the last time, however—and, after some discussions, the Socialist organizations submitted to the discipline of the National Committee. Dr. Karel Kramář, a distinguished Young Czech of conservative leanings, who had visions of a Bohemian kingdom under the aegis of the Romanovs, was chairman of the committee; at his side were Antonín Švehla, of the Agrarian Party, a patient negotiator; Alois Rašín, an experienced economist; the National Socialist Vilém Klofáč; and the Social Democrat František Soukup. These five men emerged as the National Committee's most important members and formed a de facto government of the new state; they were later to serve the Czechoslovak Republic long and in prominent functions.

In the course of September and October, the monarchy, in order to save itself, in rapid sequence offered more radical concessions to the Czechs than it had done in the last century, but it was too late. The Czechs, encouraged by the United States, which had recognized the Czechoslovak National Council organized in Paris, told Vienna that the Czech cause would depend more on international agreements than on arguments between Vienna and Prague about the extent of its new autonomy. On October 16, Emperor Charles published his last manifesto to his "loyal Austrian nations," calling on them to transform the monarchy into a federation of national states (Palacký's grand vision of 1848); in Prague it was noted immediately that the federalization would not affect Hungary, with its Slovak, Serb, and Romanian citizens. The Prague National Committee felt more in consonance with the Czechoslovak Declaration of Independence that T. G. Masaryk issued in Washington on October 18, followed by President Woodrow Wilson's note of the following day stating that it was not enough any longer to discuss the future of the Dual Monarchy on the basis of his earlier Fourteen Point program; the Czech and the Yugoslav nations would themselves have to determine which way they wished to go. Within a few days, the Italian front collapsed, the Austrian armies retreated, and Count Gyula Andrássy, the empire's last minister of foreign affairs, addressed a polite communication to President Wilson asking, in the name of the Dual Monarchy alone, for a speedy discussion of an immediate armistice. The monarchy, Andrássy said, "by offering federalization to Czechs and Yugoslavs" was, after all, in full compliance with Wilson's program (Point 10) that had demanded the "freest opportunity of autonomous development" for the peoples of Austria-Hungary. Even the brand-new Austro-Hungarian government headed by the pacifist Heinrich Lammasch clearly underrated Wilson's change of mind and foolishly hoped that there might be negotiations between Vienna and the White House. When the Andrássy note was made public in Prague, under great red headlines, in the display windows of newspaper offices at Wenceslas Square by 9:45 a.m. on Monday, October 28, people decided to read the text in their own and perhaps slightly anticipatory way, and began to celebrate the demise of the empire on the spot.

October 28 was a day of immense joy and grand illusions, of little planning and many improvisations, of an astonishing lack of communication between Czechs at home and those abroad (acting, nevertheless, in surprising accord); historians even of the most patriotic kind rightly hesitate to call these events a revolution but call them, rather, a *převrat*, a takeover of power. Since both the Austrian authorities and the National Committee were, after so long a war, concerned with preserving law and order, not a drop of blood was spilled. On the evening of October 27, a Social Democrat named Vlastimil Tusar, who was in close touch with the new Lammasch government, telephoned the National Committee from Vienna to say that, in view of the Austrian defeat on the Piave River earlier in the summer and the breakthrough of the Italian armies in September, Austrian surrender was possibly imminent; the gentlemen of the National Committee agreed to meet the next day at a leisurely nine o'clock in Švehla's apartment to discuss the new situation and to prepare for the hour of Austria's capitulation, which would also be the first hour of a new state.

The Czechs decided that it was important, first of all, whatever the future might bring, to send a delegation to the War Economy Grain Institute, responsible for the distribution of food to civilians and the army, and request that its officials take an oath of allegiance to the National Committee; this was not at all a revolutionary act, for the Vienna government was expecting that its administrative institutions would work with the National Committee; the gentlemen of the committee did not care to go into lengthy legal discussions about what kind of state they had in mind, a federal territory within Austria or an independent body politic. The takeover of the grain institute was ceremoniously brief and polite, and after handshakes all around, the delegates left the Lucerna building, where the institute was housed, and entered Wenceslas Square—suddenly to face a jubilant mass of singing and marching citizens and of red-and-white flags, swiftly appearing from nowhere.

At 11 a.m. the National Committee's executive task force met at Prague's Municipal House, but not even the experts knew exactly how to interpret Andrássy's note. Alois Rašín (later Czechoslovakia's efficient minister of finance, before being killed by an anarchist) suggested that a council delegation ask the governor's office whether instructions or news about the capitulation had arrived from Vienna and announce that responsibility for civil affairs now rested with the committee. At noon, the delegates had made their way to the office of the imperial governor and were told by his (Czech) deputy that Count Max Coudenhove had left on the morning train for Vienna to receive instructions from the new government; the delegates, unable to learn more about what was going on in Vienna, simply recited their declaration that the National Committee was taking over, and departed; the deputy immediately informed the Vienna government on the phone about the visit and implied that he had not been willing to offer resistance. The delegation, in an almost experimental mood, next went to the offices of the Bohemian diet, where they politely asked Count Adalbert Schönborn, chief of its administrative commission, to swear an oath of allegiance to the National Committee, which he readily did, assuming that he was loyally complying with the emperor's federalization manifesto.

In the city, the semiotic transformation went on; people sang a new national hymn ("Kde domov můj," "Where Is My Home," originally a song in a popular play of 1834 by Josef Kajetán Tyl), tore the Austrian signs from the uniforms of officers, adorned policemen with new red-and-white cockades, and watched as the imperial and royal eagles on official buildings came crashing down. Popular speakers addressed the milling crowds at the traditional places: at the St. Wenceslas monument Isidor Zahradník, a patriot priest, was speaking; members of the National Committee orated at the corner of Wenceslas Square and Jindřišská Street; and from a balcony at the National Theater the popular song writer Karel Hašler, long persecuted, was heard, but what he had to sing and say was definitely not gentle. Alois Rašín, who knew his fellow citizens only too well, had few illusions that the jubilations of the crowd would not turn into ugly and destructive anti-German and anti-Jewish demonstrations, and according to earlier plans, the National Committee requested Dr. František Scheiner to mobilize his Sokol (Falcons), a national gymnasts' organization established in the nineteenth century in imitation of the anti-French German *Turnverein*, to make certain that triumph did not change into chaos. The military members of the Mafie, Masaryk's secret organization that had been working for a free Czechoslovakia, all of them Czech officers and soldiers in the Austrian army, made clumsy preparations to neutralize the army command; unfortunately, the chief conspirator lived in a suburb and did not hear until 2 p.m. what was happening in the city, and by that time Magyar units of the army, fully armed and with machine guns, were taking strategic positions all over Prague—at the upper end of Wenceslas Square, close to the Café Rococo, at the Old Town Square, and elsewhere. By three o'clock, a clash between loyal army units and the people seemed almost inevitable.

One participant in the events later noted that on that afternoon the National Committee was still unsure of the Austrian army (though army units were melting away rapidly while the National Committee played for time). The army command in the Minor Town was headed by General Eduard Zanantoni, of an Italian family of soldiers, Paul Kestřánek, a Prague German in spite of his name, both somewhat beyond their prime but experienced bureaucrats, and Colonel Viktor Stusche, a younger man who was politically more acute and had not yet ceased to make fine distinctions between the necessities for Austrian federalization and what the National Committee really had in mind. Orders from Vienna were that bloodshed must be avoided, and when the Social Democrat Soukup, of the National Committee, called General Zanantoni and guaranteed that the committee would keep order in the streets, Zanantoni ordered the Magyars to return to their barracks. Further discussions between the high command and the committee were scheduled for the evening, and it says something about the residual civility of the moment that at 8 p.m. the generals and their entourage came downtown to the offices of the National Committee, where a complicated arrangement was reached: the National Committee and the Sokols would guard factories and ammunition depots, officers were no longer to be insulted in public, and the National Committee would be responsible only for civil affairs while the army command would not yet relinquish its formal military authority. At about the same time, the military experts on the National Committee, including Dr. Scheiner of the Sokol and Jaroslav Rošický of the Mafie conspirators, began organizing a military command post of their own on Žofín Island, and all Czech army personnel on leave in Prague were notified to assemble there to form a first unit of volunteers. They came, ragtag, and were joined by about eighty highly qualified Czech sailors and officers from the imperial navy (then rather decorative among Prague landlubbers), ordinarily stationed at Pola and Cattaro, on the Adriatic Sea, and by an entire Romanian unit that had left its Magyar regiment.

Even if the generals negotiating with the National Committee had known of the committee's political proclamation (they probably did not), they would have noted that the committee painstakingly avoided speaking of military matters. At 6 p.m. (that is, two hours before its discussions with the army command) the National Committee had issued its first Law Concerning the Establishment of an Independent Czechoslovak State, which, resolutely going beyond all previous statements, cut all links between Vienna and the new Czechoslovakia, and declared that the National Committee now had legal responsibility for all administrative affairs. It was left open exactly what this new state would be and all military questions were carefully kept in abeyance—quite apart from the sobering circumstances that the new state, de facto, could not extend farther than fifty or sixty kilometers to the north of Prague, because Germans there were asserting their own self-determination, and Slovak patriots, still under Magyar domination, were represented in Prague by lonely Vávro Šrobár, M.D., whose welcome presence had not much more than symbolic importance.

On October 29, additional imperial offices, including that of the police, were taken over without many complications, but the National Committee still had to deal with the imperial governor, who had returned from Vienna, and with the army command, increasingly showing signs of stiffening resistance, especially after the war ministry in Vienna admonished it for being too soft in its arrangements with the National Committee. By noon the usual delegation paid a call on Count Coudenhove, explained to him the ongoing process of takeovers and, ignoring its own independence resolution of the preceding evening, surprisingly agreed to a principle of co-administration in civil affairs—until Coudenhove, speaking of Bohemia's German citizens, uttered the word *Deutschböhmen* (German Bohemians), which irritated Dr. Rašín, who said he did not want to hear the term again. Then the delegation left, and Coudenhove, no less irritated, called Vienna to report about the meeting, handed in his resignation, and left the field to the National Committee.

The last nest of loyalty to the emperor was, of course, the army command, where the generals began to have second thoughts and yet did not exactly know that many in the Prague garrison were simply going home. On October 29, the German Eger infantry regiment decided to depart, and most of the Magyars assembled at the railroad station. The National Committee conveniently organized trains to get the Magyars out, but the Sokol guards saw to it that each Magyar could leave with only one uniform and one set of underwear; if a Magyar soldier was found to have two, he had to yield one to the new republic. The Czechs and Romanians gathered at Žofín Island waited for orders; by evening, the Austrian command prepared for a last stand and pushed the Sokol guards out of its building, and challenged the National Committee to order its units to block the surrounding streets. Once again, a delegation arrived at the Minor Town to discuss matters of mutual interest, and when the generals noted that the last Maygar troops were fraternizing with the Czechs, they simply gave up and went home; a few officers were put under house arrest for the time being. By the evening of October 30, power was in the hands of the National Committee in Prague and in the Czech regions of Bohemia, and everybody waited for the return of a delegation which had gone to Geneva to discuss the organization of the new state and its future government with Dr. Eduard Beneš of the Czech National Council in Paris and his diplomats.

The Vienna government still wanted to demonstrate that it meant federalization seriously, and to create goodwill among the Allies, the emperor had directed that passports be handed out to a group of Czech representatives to travel to Switzerland to meet Dr. Beneš for a discussion of the future (Beneš himself was rather surprised). On October 25, a delegation of seven had left Prague, among them representatives of the National Committee, Czech members of the Vienna parliament and two directors of important Czech banks; another passport was given to a Catholic delegate, who was, however, shunned by the group and did not participate in the conversations. Beneš welcomed the delegation, headed by

Dr. Kramář, at the five-star Hotel Beau Rivage (a brilliant choice), and although nobody really knew what was going on in Prague, there was unanimity of views. Beneš told the Prague politicians what the Allies believed and expected, and the delegation was at times overwhelmed by the thought that their interests had been so efficiently defended on the international scene (they also enjoyed the clean tablecloths, the excellent food, and the perfect service). Beneš, who shared certain didactic inclinations with his mentor, Masaryk, spoke with the authority of a man who had been active in Europe's capitals and was able to relay the wishes of the Czech legions now fighting on the Allied side in France, Siberia, and Italy; discussions centered on the republican shape of the future state (Kramář sacrificing his views of a royal Bohemia). The legions had elected Masaryk president, and agreement was now reached on a cabinet in which both the National Committee and the National Council would be represented. Kramář was to be chief of government, Beneš minister of foreign affairs, the Slovak Milan Rastislav Štefánik minister of war, Rašín minister of finance, Švehla minister of agriculture, and there were places for three Slovaks and one German "to defend the interests" of their countrymen. (In fact, the first German minister entered a Czechoslovak government only in 1926). On October 30, when the delegates finally heard what had happened in Prague, they tried to get home as quickly as possible—Rašín later wrote that he felt as if "intoxicated by hashish"—and they arrived by train on November 5, welcomed by thousands of citizens. Not many days afterward, the National Committee issued a proclamation asking for citizens to stop singing and celebrating and to start working again. Yet eight weeks later, there was another grand cause for celebration and parades: T. G. Masaryk himself returned home after four years of absence.

Masaryk Returns to Prague

After seeing President Wilson once again, Masaryk started on November 20 on a long trip home from New York via London, Paris, and Italy, accompanied by his younger daughter Olga. He had heard that he was badly needed in Prague to fulfill the most varied expectations; during his ocean voyage on the SS *Carmania*, he was in a pensive mood; "I did not want to speak to anybody," he wrote later, "and for many days I walked back and forth on deck, my eyes roving over the the seas, and in my heart the hammering of future tasks." He came to Bohemia from Italy, where he had been welcomed by the king and watched a parade of Italian soldiers and Czech legionnaires who had fought on the Piave; when his special train wended its way through Austria, he had time to talk to his entourage, the white-haired Italian General Piccione (later to command Czech units against the Hungarians), the British military attaché, Colonel Cunningham, M. Clement-Simon, France's first ambassador accredited to the new republic, and Masaryk's own military adjutant (clad, as we are told by malevolent tongues, in the tsarist uniform of a crack Cherkassian unit). Another special train had been dispatched from Prague to meet Masaryk at the border, carrying his son Jan and an appropriate delegation; at Horní Dvořiště, the border station, when the trains moved up alongside each other, Jan had to tell his father that his mother, Charlotte Masaryk, sinking into melancholy again, had been committed to a Prague institution for the mentally ill. Next day, a cannon shot announced the arrival of the train at Prague station, and a long day of ceremonies immediately commenced. Present were Alice, Masaryk's older daughter (who had been imprisoned in Vienna and let go only upon American intervention), Dr. Kramář and the entire government, officers, poets, and diplomats. Speeches on the platform and in a waiting hall were mercifully short, even that of Alois Jirásek, the most famous writer among the patriots. Masaryk looked ill and feverish, was moved to tears, and stubbornly refused to take a seat in a horse-drawn imperial coach when asked; he rode in an open automobile. Surrounded by flowers, flags, and units of the Russian, French, and Italian legions, his car slowly moved down Wenceslas Square (with the cinematographic cameras rolling). He paused at the Old Town Square to look at Ladislav Šaloun's new Hus monument, which he had not yet seen, and proceeded to the National Assembly in the Minor Town, to take his oath of allegiance in a brief ceremony, and then went up to Hradčany Castle, a rather disheveled and gloomy place at that time.

In the afternoon, Masaryk immediately went to see his wife at the Veleslavín institution, where she was being treated with indifferent success (she was to return to live with him a few times, only to be committed again); it is curious that Masaryk's biographers are very reticent about Charlotte's and his intimate tragedy. Later in the day, we are told, Masaryk in his warm winter coat with a fur collar was seen in the streets of Prague on a leisurely walk with his friend J. S. Machar, a poet and colleague of his Vienna days.

Masaryk had invited members of the National Assembly to visit him at Hradčany next afternoon, but the time of revolutionary improvisations had passed, and he had to learn the hard way that the provisional constitution had defined his prerogatives rather narrowly; it was more than polite conversation when Kramář, as chief of government, told him "to stay above the clouds" as president, for everyone who was immersed more deeply in Czechoslovakian political life would have to defend himself against mudslinging and loss of authority. (Masaryk nonetheless managed to have his prerogatives widened, while Václav Havel seventy years later went the other way.) The National Assembly, newly picky about constitutional niceties, did not wish to be at the president's beck and call, yet resolved to go to the castle not collectively and as an institution but, as it were, altogether privately—in spite of the fact that Masaryk had earlier submitted, by special courier, the text of his first political speech to the government, which promptly cut two paragraphs from it—one suggesting amnesty for wartime collaborators with Austrian power and another one warning against anti-Semitic emotions. As later events showed, Masaryk's warnings were legitimate, and the government was wrong.

Masaryk's speech of December 22 was political (when he wanted it to be), unusually frank, and, as far as Czechoslovakia's Germans were concerned, distinctly contentious; members of the assembly recognized that the president did not intend at all to stay above the clouds. In his speech, he developed a concept of democracy in which he skillfully combined his habitual respect for daily work with the preferences of Czech civil servants: democracy was essentially, he insisted, a workaday matter of justly administering human affairs ("justice as the mathematics of humanism"); he added, possibly with a glance at Kramář and the last Pan-Slavs, that the Russians unfortunately had never learned how to administer and the new democracy was *logically* bound to the traditions of the West. He freely admitted that he had been antimilitarist for a long time, yet the republic needed an efficient army, not to indulge in military adventures but for reasons of defense (Slovakia was still held by the Magyars). Speaking to Bohemia's Germans, Masaryk firmly declared that the state would not be divided, reminding his listeners that the United States had risked civil war rather than tolerate the seccession of the southern states; Czechs and Slovaks had created a new state, defining by that act the legal position of the Germans who "had originally come to the country as immigrants and colonists" (here he sounded like Palacký in one of his more irritable moments). In that one relative clause, quoted for decades by his friends and adversaries, Masaryk chose to break a good deal of political china; even Ferdinand Peroutka, a political analyst who cannot be accused of anti-Masaryk sentiments, in his essential books about the founding of the republic (1934), skeptically asked how many centuries immigrants and colonists would have to live in a country before they ceased being immigrants and colonists. The sociologist Masaryk, usually more ready to defend the natural rather than the historical rights of people, kept his own counsel. Three days after his speech, he attended, together with members of the government, a festive performance at the Prague German Theater and, on that occasion, thanked the Prague Germans for the trust they put in him; he expressed his hope that his presence at the theater was but a "prologue" to the grand drama that Czechs and Germans were now called on to perform. It was an appropriate metaphor, before the curtain rose. Few people in the audience knew in what forms and scenes the drama would develop—creative, conciliatory, and brutal—in the years to come.

From the Coachman's Cottage to Prague Castle: A Modern Fairy Tale

The story of Masaryk's rise from the plebeian cottage of his birth to the castle of the Bohemian kings sounds like a modern fairy tale (he used the term himself), and though he came to enjoy a few surprising and happy turns of fortune, he never ceased to speak of the necessity of hard work, and he knew why. He was born in 1850 at Hodonín (Göding), the son of a Slovak groom and coachman, later a bailiff on an imperial estate in southeastern Moravia, and a Moravian mother who was educated in German and spoke the local Slovak only later in her marriage. It may be said of Masaryk that he did not have a mother tongue (though his mother taught him to count and pray in German), and he grew up with the Slovak-Moravian dialects spoken in the villages near the border. Unfortunately the family was continually transferred from village to village, the result being that the student and scholar Masaryk had considerable trouble with the literary Czech and educated German in which he was to teach and publish. In village schools, some Czech and more German were taught; after he had attended a Catholic *Hauptschule* with good success, his father sent him to Vienna (where his mother had worked as a cook) to be apprenticed to a locksmith; in practice, he had to operate a primitive contraption to punch out heel protectors; after running home from Vienna, he was put up with a local blacksmith in order to learn how to shoe horses and in the hope that the blacksmith would reveal to him something of his art in healing animals and people. A former teacher and an honest village priest, who taught him Latin, told his parents that he should go on to school; after preparing for an entrance exam he entered the *Gymnasium* in Brno (Brünn). He had to tutor to eat and, in a surprising chain of events, was hired by Brno's chief of police, Le Monnier, the very man who had once checked on Havlíček's passage through Salzburg, to tutor his son; he also had a good chance to learn French and to read the German classics, including Lessing and Goethe, which stayed with him all his life. When the strong-willed lad from the provinces almost came to blows with the headmaster and was told to leave, Le Monnier, now appointed police chief in Vienna, welcomed him in his home; young Masaryk was accepted into the elite *Akademisches Gymnasium*, where among his fellow students were three future Austrian ministers and the later president of the Republic of Austria. Masaryk did excellent work in religion, German, and Greek, less so in history and philosophy, and passed his final examinations in the summer of 1872.

After his youth of dire poverty, Masaryk's years as a student at the University of Vienna were free of difficult financial problems, and he devoted most of his time to classical philology and later to philosophy. He was also active in the Czech Academic Union and wrote his first essays, which editors in Prague usually turned down because of his "crabby Czech" (actually, a Slavic language he concocted out of Russian and Slovak elements). He lived as resident tutor in the opulent home of Rudolf Schlesinger, director of the Anglo-Austrian bank, teaching his oldest son, also interested in philosophy; he had no reason to complain either about his open-handed employer or his new academic friends. His early love for Plato prompted him to study Latin and Greek and to attend the lectures of the famous scholar Theodor Gomperz (from a Brno Jewish family), who kept an eye on the young and serious Moravian; Gomperz's colleagues were pedants, however, and Masaryk, perhaps seeking consolation after the death of his younger brother, turned from classics to philosophy. He was attracted by Franz Brentano, ex-priest and newcomer to the university, who urged him to read Aristotle and to study the British skeptics and the French positivists; following Brentano's ideas and Vienna tradition, Masaryk early turned away from Kant, Hegel, and the idealist tradition. But he never resolved, in his own mind, the conflict between his Platonic aspirations and British empiricism, and (as it would appear later) his sincere religiosity, ever in search of a fitting church, and his sociological view of a world accessible to reason and patient research.

In 1876, Masaryk submitted his doctoral dissertation, in German, on the essence of the soul as defined by Plato, and his *Doktorvater*, Brentano, though somewhat puzzled by his written German, which obscured the argument, readily accepted the dissertation, saying, "The labor expended on the thesis must be rated higher than the thesis itself." After passing his oral examination in mid-March 1876, Masaryk received his Ph.D. in philosophy and left for Italy with his student Alfred Schlesinger, all expenses paid by Schlesinger *père*. It was resolved that later they would go to Leipzig to continue their studies in philosophy. Arriving there on October 15, 1876, they rented rooms with Mrs. Augusta Goering (no relative of Hermann) in a little *pension* in which many American visitors also stayed. Masaryk liked Leipzig, attended lectures by Wilhelm Wundt, and enjoyed conversations with his fellow Moravian Edmund Husserl, but in the summer of 1877, studious Masaryk, twenty-seven years old, turned away from the abstractions of philosophy to the enchantments of life. He met Charlotte Garrigue, a young American student of music, who took lodgings at Frau Goering's too.

Masaryk is often described by his biographers as a Victorian and a puritan, and he certainly was (not only judging from his literary opinions about European "Decadents"), but in the summer of 1877 it must have dawned upon him that something was missing in his experience. Curiously, he felt what was coming; he read more voraciously than ever (three novels a day), went to the opera to immerse himself in Richard Wagner, and perused a spate of sociological and anthropological studies about women. When Charlotte turned up with her grave eyes, energetic nose, firm chin, and the bearing of an independent young American woman, his awkward hesitations were gone; he wrote to a friend that the idea had occurred to him that he might be capable of cherishing affections for Charlotte. She was giving English lessons to the landlady's handicapped daughter, Masaryk joined the ladies (who were reading Lord Byron), and upon his recommendations they went on to study Henry Thomas Buckle's *History of Civilization in England*, not exactly a literary aphrodisiac; when Masaryk, on an excursion, helped to save Frau Goering's life (she had slipped and plunged into the Elbe River) he came down with a cold, so the English reading lessons decorously shifted to his room. Romance was in the air.

When Charlotte went to the little Thuringian spa of Elgersburg, Masaryk sent her a letter proposing marriage (she must have thought he was out of his mind), then shortly appeared in Elgersburg himself, and after a few days of walking and arguing, the two announced their engagement on August 10. Charlotte then returned to Brooklyn and Masaryk to Vienna to work on his treatise about the principles of sociology, which was to be submitted to the university. Perhaps it is not impossible to assume that

Charlotte's father—a Huguenot by extraction, of Danish birth, a Leipzig bookseller by training, and more recently director of the Germania Insurance Company—and her midwestern mother wanted to meet her fiancé personally; they wrote to him that she had suffered a little accident and wanted to see him, and in February 1878, T. G. Masaryk went aboard ship in Hamburg. Seventeen days later in New York he found Charlotte much improved (if there had been any danger to her health at all). Young Masaryk expected, perhaps in the European way, that Garrigue Sr. would financially contribute to setting up the new ménage, and he sulked around Brooklyn when his father-in-law refused, but on March 15 Charlotte and Thomas were married nevertheless. Garrigue Sr. then relented as far as financial matters were concerned, and the two newlyweds immediately sailed back to Europe, where they eventually settled in a spacious apartment in Vienna. Their daughter Alice was born within the year, and later Herbert, Olga, and Jan.

Masaryk did not have an easy time trying to fulfill the requirements for his appointment as university lecturer. His disquisition on the principles of sociology was not accepted, and his manuscript "Suicide as a Collective Social Phenomenon" barely squeezed through, a curious and yet remarkable mixture of a romantic philosophy of culture and statistics that ascribed modern frustrations to the loss of religious certainties; his amiable professors argued that their positive evaluation was based on his personal commitment rather than on the manuscript's intrinsic merits. He was duly appointed lecturer, teaching Plato, while Charlotte tried to make ends meet, and when it became known that Prague's Czech University was to be established formally, he applied there, though he had qualms about Prague, which he did not know well, and about his Czech. Charlotte did not like Vienna and welcomed the possible move.

In the fall term of 1882, Masaryk gave his first lecture in Prague, entitled "Hume and Skepticism," immediately challenging his older colleagues by turning to British and French thinkers, by inviting his students to his home on Friday evenings, and by speaking, in a special lecture series for young lawyers, about problems of the state, morality, and prostitution (he was the first professor to utter that terrible P-word, though he abhorred the phenomenon, in the hallowed halls of the university). There were many reasons why the conservatives disliked the newcomer; when in February 1886 the distinguished philologist Jan Gebauer, in a periodical Masaryk edited, again raised the question whether the famous *Rukopisy* were authentic (those allegedly ancient manuscripts, falsified by Václav Hanka in 1817–18, to make certain that the Czechs had an older literature than that of the Germans) and Masaryk in a friendly editorial letter revealed that he too did not believe in the authenticity of the documents, nearly everybody turned against him, accusing him of nihilism. But the young philosopher merely insisted that, from a moral point of view, it was important that national consciousness was not mired in fabrications lacking real historical existence. People called him an abominable traitor to his nation, and the worst was yet to come.

Yet younger intellectuals, scholars, and professionals were attracted by Masaryk's honesty and sobriety. Together with Masaryk himself, they formed a political alliance with the Young Czechs; from 1891 to 1893, Masaryk commuted from Prague to Austria to serve in the Vienna parliament, where he learned fast; his maiden speech touched on the academic problem of reforming the study of the law; later he resolutely condemned the Austrian occupation of Bosnia-Herzegovina in 1878 and turned his attention early to Slovak and South Slav problems.

When the alliance Masaryk had made with the Young Czechs not surprisingly broke down, he returned to his studies, published a series of temperamental books—e.g., about Jan Hus (he could not bear the Young Czechs' disregard of his religious engagement) and Karel Havlíček—and in 1896, after thirteen years of near-disgrace, the associate professor was finally promoted to a full professorship, with a somewhat higher salary. Again, he was not a man to withdraw to his library and to learned discussion; when a young Bohemian Jew was accused of ritual murder and Masaryk fought against the ancient superstition, even his students revolted against him. He thought of going to America until Charlotte, now almost Czech and in strong sympathy with the Social Democrats, encouraged him to fight his adversaries vigorously.

On March 29, 1899, the seamstress Anežka Hrůzová had been found murdered in a little forest near Polna, a provincial Bohemian town, a terrible gash through her throat, and since there was, or seemed, so little blood on the corpse (which had been dragged from another spot closer to the road), local people began talking about ritual murder, and twenty-two-year-old Leopold Hilsner, unemployed and of uncertain means, was arrested on suspicion of murder; after a first trial in Polna based on circumstantial evidence, he was sentenced to death by a second Bohemian court (though found not guilty of another murder which had been thrown in for good measure). The trial of Leopold Hilsner was a European cause célèbre; the emperor commuted the death sentence to life imprisonment, of which Hilsner served twenty-eight years in an Austrian prison.

Masaryk at first did not want to participate in public discussion of the case, but Sigismund Münz, a former Vienna student, asked him about his views, published them in the Vienna liberal *Neue Freie Presse*, and prompted Masaryk to investigate the legal procedures against Hilsner; by 1900, Masaryk had published a number of analyses of the trial and its implications. At that time, many Jewish families in the countryside (among them my Jewish grandfather) fled to Prague because their shops and homes were being attacked by local patriots, and the government persecuted Masaryk for allegedly interfering with the process of justice. Jiří Kovtun, curator of the Slavic division of the Library of Congress, who recently has written the definitive story of the Hilsner case and its repercussions, comes close to saying that Masaryk did not really care about Hilsner personally but only about the principles involved; it is certainly true that he did not have a high opinion of the young Polna drifter, who had never held a regular job (a cardinal sin in Masaryk's view)—and yet, studying the Talmud and the Zohar, Masaryk was fighting a "European disease" for the sake of his own nation, which he wanted to be untouched by intellectual perversions. Leopold Hilsner had a sad life; after the Austrians let him go, against the wishes of a Czech court, he sold needles, beads, and combs from house to house, married, and died in Vienna in 1928. The historian Wilma Iggers reminds us that a Czech newspaper, on May 4, 1968, reported that Anežka Hrůzová's brother on his deathbed in 1961 confessed that *he* had killed his sister: he had not wanted her to have the dowry she asked for.

In later conversations with his friend the writer Karel Čapek (published under the title "Masaryk Tells His Story"), Masaryk tried to suggest that he was, fundamentally, a shy man who disliked being in the limelight. He did not resist his friends, however, when they wanted to establish a political party of high intellectual standards in the wake of the Hilsner affair and make him its leader; it was to stand on its own feet rather than be dragged along by Young Czech or Agrarian organizations. The new group was called the Czech People's Party, or rather Realists, and when general suffrage (for which Charlotte Masaryk demonstrated in the Prague streets) was granted in 1907, Masaryk, with the help of a few sympathetic Social Democrats, was elected to the Vienna parliament from a district in eastern Moravia together with another Realist from Bohemia; after new elections in 1911, when his colleague lost his mandate, he remained the one and only Realist in the Vienna Reichsrat. In 1908 Austria had annexed Bosnia-Herzegovina, and the minister of foreign affairs tried to defend Austrian policies in the Balkan countries by a show trial in Zagreb of fifty-three Croatians accused of high treason, conspiracy, and terrorism, and by the publication of documents (provided by a respected liberal scholar) showing the grip of the Slavic conspirators. Once again Masaryk was called on by his friends, or rather his former Prague students, to intervene; he traveled to Zagreb and Belgrade, where, on discovering a conspiracy of forgers within the Austrian diplomatic service, he immediately asked for a full parliamentary investigation. The result was that Emperor Franz Josef, citing "reasonable doubt" about the legal evidence in the case, quashed the Zagreb sentences, the scholar withdrew his documents, and Count Aehrenthal, the minister of foreign affairs, went on a long leave from which he did not return to office.

When war came in 1914, Masaryk did not hurry; he witnessed the German mobilization at Bad Schandau, in Saxony, where he was spending a vacation; enjoying his parliamentary passport, he went twice to Holland to strengthen his British contacts, and at home began to establish a secret organization, his *Mafie*, to provide him with political information. Warned of the police, he left with his daughter Olga for Italy on December 18, 1914. When an Italian stationmaster at the border tried to stop him, he jumped back on the rolling train. He traveled light: for four years, in Paris, London, New York, Moscow, Siberia, and Washington, he conferred with foreign correspondents, ambassadors, prime ministers, and presidents to organize a new republic, which, for a long time, existed only in the realm of his Platonic ideas.

Turbulent, Republican Prague

Taking over power from the imperial and royal authorities on October 28–30, 1918, in an orderly and almost ceremonial way was one matter, but the consolidation of the new state within its intended borders was another. If Masaryk said that he did not sleep on the first night in Hradčany Castle, it may have been only the first sleepless night of many yet to come. The new republic was to unify Czechs and Slovaks—as foreseen by the Pittsburgh agreement of June 30, 1918, with the Slovaks to enjoy an as yet unspecified autonomy, and even before Masaryk, the son of a Slovak father, had returned, Czech troops had started to push the Magyars out of Slovakia, and on February 14, 1919, Dr. Šrobár was able to set up an office in Bratislava; but in May, Red Army units of Béla Kun's Communist government in Budapest were trying to take back Slovakia (one of their political commissars at the Slovak front was the young philosopher George Lukács); after considerable military gains, they withdrew again under Allied pressure. The question of Bohemia's German regions was not easily solved either. Insisting on their own Wilsonian concept of self-determination, the Germans had established four autonomous provinces—Deutsch-Böhmen (German Bohemia, with Reichenberg as its capital), Sudetenland (referring only to northern Moravia and Silesia), Deutsch-Südmähren (German southern Moravia), and the Böhmerwaldgau (Bohemian Forest)—declaring that they were all integral parts of a (Socialist) Republic of German-Austria which would, in turn, join Socialist Germany. The Allies immediately intervened against this plan, and postponed an *Anschluss* between Austria and Germany for twenty years. Within six weeks three Czech regiments had occupied the German regions, but the Germans went on hoping that the Allies would allow a plebiscite and on March 4, 1919, demonstrated in many towns to show their allegiance to Deutsch-Österreich. Czech units were trigger-happy, and in the confrontations fifty-two Germans died and more than eighty were wounded, but by September 1919 the peace conference of St. Germain confirmed that the German regions of Bohemia would be part of the historical lands of the new Czechoslovak Republic. On June 15, German citizens participated in its first communal elections, showing that more than half of the German population favored the Social Democrats; parliamentary elections of April 18, 1920, from which the Czech Social Democrats, the National Liberals, and the Agrarians emerged victorious, also confirmed that Socialists, Agrarians, and Catholics were in a significant majority among the Germans (with fifty-five seats), clearly prevailing over the two German nationalist groups (seventeen) set irrevocably against the republic. Slowly, Czech and German Socialists and Agrarians began exploring the chances of working together, but it took many years before they actually did.

The spring and summer of 1920 were turbulent seasons, and by mid-November the disorders reached Prague again. Once again the national groups had a difficult time adjusting to each other; in the countryside, Czech soldiers, legionnaires, and Sokols, supported by nationalist journalists, were less than tolerant, and the Germans were unwilling or unable to grasp that they had grievously underrated the political potential of the Czechs, whom they had been looking down upon for so long. In late June, a legionnaire was found shot dead at Jihlava (Iglau), Czech soldiers and Sokols took over the town, disregarding the law, and all along the northern and western brim of Bohemia bitter fights erupted between Czechs wanting to do away with local German monuments, especially those to "the Germanizer," Joseph II, and German townspeople defending his imperial glory, possibly for the wrong reasons. When the poet J. S. Machar, by now inspector general of the Czechoslovak army, was asked about the matter, he told the new iconoclasts that Joseph II had been, really, a revolutionary acting from the top and had advanced new ideas with which republicans would certainly have to agree. He spoke in vain, of course, and Czechs and Germans went on fiercely disputing their monuments. In Asch, units fired into the crowd (killing and wounding people), in Podmokly (Bodenbach), a statue of Joseph II being absent, the Czechs wanted to vent their rage upon Friedrich Schiller of all people, and in Cheb (Eger), after the monument to Joseph was destroyed, Germans were said to have attacked a Czech school. In Prague, four Cheb schoolchildren, bandaged and looking miserable, were exhibited at the St. Wenceslas monument to stir up the people; on November 16, enraged demonstrators shouting "Revenge for Cheb!" began attacking the Jewish quarters, destroyed the archives of the Jewish town hall, burned Torah scrolls in front of the synagogue, and occupied the offices of Prague's German newspapers, including the liberal *Prager Tagblatt*; led by actors from the National Theater, who had long wanted another stage, they occupied by force the Theater of the Estates, established under the protection of Joseph II to reconcile nations through the joys of art. (My father, who happened to be dramaturge at the time, was rudely removed from his office and to my mother's surprise came home early for dinner.) Unfortunately, the crowds were encouraged by the strident newspapers and by Karel Baxa, Prague's mayor, who had risen to political power on the anti-Semitic wave at the time of the Hilsner affair, defending the idea of ritual murder, and it took a few years before the legal questions were sorted out by the hesitant courts. Yet there were intelligent people who did not yield to the demands of the street, among them Professor Emanuel Rádl, who declared that the crowds and their supporters "by occupying German institutions [and] the German theater and by persecuting Jews" acted against the fundamental ideas of the republic. Masaryk, as stubborn as ever, never again attended a performance at the Theater of the Estates because he did not want to seem to approve of any disrespect for the law, by whomsoever.

National conflicts became clashes of social interests, and in a city of rising prices and inflation, low wages, and unheated one-room apartments, after so many weeks of jubilation people were irritated, accusations were made easily, and riots were frequent, especially against the *ket'asy* (black marketeers) and *lichváři* (profiteers), who were held responsible for Prague's economic malaise. On May 21, 1919, industrial workers left the suburban factories and marched to the city center; thirty thousand people gathered in the Old Town Square to protest against the enemies of the people, shops and emporia were occupied, and people began to sell at prices set by themselves or simply plundered the shops until the police and the army intervened. The left radicals, or rather the Bolshevik faction of the Social Democrats, led by Bohumil Šmeral and Antonín Zápotocký (later president of the Socialist Republic in 1953–57), strained against the bounds of the Socialist organization and a year later occupied its Lidový Dům (People's House) and the editorial office of the party press. The government sent in the police, and the occupiers, barricaded behind office furniture, were turned out with only a few scratches. On December 10, 1920, the left faction responded with a general strike against the government, and, in its strike proclamation, went far beyond the party issues at hand, demanding that all industrial and agricultural production be controlled by workers' delegates, that wages rise 30 percent, and that all property be nationalized. For a few uncertain December days, strikers in Prague clashed with the police (one worker was killed), and though many but not all working people actively joined in the strike, the new government resolved not to yield. After five days the left radicals finally called the strike off; unlike Berlin, where during "Spartacus Week" working people and the army brutally fought each other in the streets, Prague was spared the bloody battles of a civil war. Six months later, in May 1921, the left Social Democrats joined the Third International, and in late October a unification congress of the new Communist Party met to gather Czechs, Slovaks, Germans, Hungarians, Ruthenians, and a few anarchists (who were to regret it) in a Bolshevik party of proletarian solidarity. In the election to the Prague city assembly in 1923, the Communists polled 18.18 percent, beating the Social Democrats down to 9.2 percent of the popular vote.

The turn of so many working people in Prague to the Communists may have been a signal to the Social Democrats and Agrarians to intensify their conversations with German comrades and colleagues; when the parliamentary election of 1925 again revealed much Communist strength, Prime Minister Švehla, acting in unison with Masaryk, negotiated with the German Agrarians (in the Bund der Landwirte) and Catholics, who were ready to test the possibilities of active participation in governing the republic; the first German ministers to be appointed, the ministers of public works and justice, were, respectively, Franz Spina, professor of Slavic studies at Prague University (he was to correct gently the bad Czech of his officials), and Robert Mayr-Harting, a distinguished lawyer. It was a time of slow consolidation and conciliation;

though German nationalists remained unforgiving, German "activists" tried to do their best to transform the Czechoslovak state (including a few minorities) into a republic of nationalities; when Masaryk was reelected president in 1927, their vote was indispensable in defeating his adversaries from the Communist Party, the Slovak Populists, and the Czech National Democrats, who were inexorably drifting to the right. In Prague, of German-speaking citizens (many may have been Jewish) 12,386 voted for the republican "activists" and 3,631 for the nationalist intransigents. Few people nowadays remember Spina, Mayr-Harting and his later colleague Dr. Ludwig Czech (the Socialist minister of public works and health, who died in a concentration camp), or Erwin Zajíček, German minister without portfolio, who died, a modest Austrian school principal, in 1976. The tragedy of the German "activists," Czechoslovakia's unsung heroes of national conciliation, deserves respect and recognition, even though their names do not appear in any of the travel guides. In the catastrophic elections of May 1935, when 1,249,531 Germans voted for the Sudeten Party, 605,122 German "activists" (Social Democrats, Christian Socialists, and Agrarians) held their own against Hitler; and in the Prague municipal election of 1938, 15,423 German-speaking citizens cast their ballot with the nationalists, and 4,849 voted, against all odds, for the German "activist" parties. Some German-speaking voters (I believe) may have cast their lot with the Czech Social Democrats and Communists, strongly internationalist at that time.

The Czechoslovak Republic recognized Jews as a nation, and as early as September 3, 1918, Masaryk asserted in the United States that Jews would enjoy the same rights as all other citizens; a month later, in *The New York Times*, he declared his respect for Zionism: "not a movement of political chauvinism" but one that "represents the moral rebirth of [the Jewish] people." Delegates of Jewish organizations in Prague presented a memorandum to the National Committee on October 28, and on December 31, 1918, delegates of the newly established Jewish National Council, one of them being Max Brod (Franz Kafka's closest friend), were received by the president at Hradčany Castle; he assured them that he looked with favor on their aims, though he delicately reminded them that Jews who felt close to Czech or German tradition should be free to assert their views. Assimilation, or rather acculturation, had advanced far in the western lands of the Czechoslovak Republic, and there was a significant gap between Jews who defined themselves by religion and those by nationality: in 1921, of all Bohemian Jews, nearly 80,000 in number, only 14.6 percent felt they belonged to a Jewish *nation*, and nine years later the situation had not much changed—of 76,301 only 16.6 percent declared Jewish *nationality*.

On January 6, 1919, a Jewish Party, claiming a right to self-determination based on Wilsonian principles, was established in Prague, but factional and ideological tensions continually ran high; in the elections, it failed to rally sufficient support to enter parliament and later succeeded in sending two delegates to parliament only by agreements with a Polish group in 1928 and in tandem with Socialists in 1935. In Prague, most middle-class Jews acculturated to the German tradition regularly voted for the German Democratic Freedom Party (Deutsche Demokratische Freiheitspartei), ably led by Dr. Bruno Kafka, a cousin of the writer; those closer to the Czechs more often than not voted Social Democratic (the record of the right-wing National Democrats was not inviting to either of them). The elections in the Prague Jewish community, reflecting the many Jewries of the republic, clearly revealed the polarity of options: of 31,751 Jews entitled to the ballot, less than one-third cared to vote at all in 1921, with the Jewish Party polling 1,968 votes, and, among other groups, the German Liberals 2,362, and the Union of Czech Jews nearly as many (2,344). Zionists, active in the Jewish Party and in many other organizations, were deeply divided between those who wanted to help build Eretz Israel here and now and the others, influenced by the theologian Martin Buber, who were committed to studying Jewish history and philosophy to increase Jewish religious and cultural self-consciousness. "Little mother Prague," as Franz Kafka well knew, did not let go of its people easily, and though Kafka's friend Hugo Bergmann and others left for Palestine early, Max Brod, personally committed to Jewish affairs, left on the last train from Prague to the Polish border (on March 15, 1939) and saw, through the windows, advance German units occupying Ostrava station. When he died, it is said, the 1939 Prague telephone directory was found on his desk.

The Cultures of Republican Prague

Punctually on October 28, 1918, a new committee, chaired by Přemysl Šámal, chief organizer of Masaryk's Mafie, took over Prague's city administration, but the discussion about how to reorganize the new capital of the republic dragged on for years; only on January 1, 1922, was Great Prague legally established. This new city consisted of the five towns that had been brought together in the mid-nineteenth century (Old Town, New Town, Hradčany, Vyšehrad, and Josefov), the five suburbs that joined subsequently, and thirty-eight towns and villages; the new metropolitan region incorporated nearly 700,000 citizens and was the sixth-largest city in Europe. At that time, 27.2 percent of all its apartments still consisted of only one room, and 81.3 percent lacked baths; it is not surprising, though patriots were astonished, that one-fifth of all votes in the municipal elections were Communist. Prague was distinctly behind in constructing affordable housing for the less privileged, and while in post-World War I Vienna, a Socialist city government had immediately employed outstanding architects to build apartments and swimming pools for the proletariat (or, rather, for loyal Social Democrats), in Prague funds and energies were invested in public office buildings and the new ministries. Prague architects had already broken with the past by 1911–12 (perhaps a little later than the painters who, after exhibitions of works by Edvard Munch and Paul Gauguin, formed the Czech-German Group of Eight), and František Kotěra had trained a remarkable group of disciples; from abroad came the Slovene Jože Plečnik, who made Hradčany Castle more habitable for Masaryk. Kotěra was fortunate to have patrons who did not interfere with his projects; his sternly playful Mozarteum, now a bit grimy and disfigured by a bazaar on the ground floor, the Koruna building on the lower left corner of Wenceslas Square, and, above all, the Lucerna complex of elegant shops, restaurants, theaters, and bars, built for Václav Havel's father, have become attractive elements of the modern cityscape. Younger members of the group tended to a Czech version of Cubism, which was among the most remarkable achievements of the Czech arts—e.g., Josef Gočár's house of the black Madonna (now, appropriately, a showplace of modern art) and Josef Chochol's ingenious apartment houses, hidden from the tourists in the gray streets under the Vyšehrad.

National and political demands have long burdened the free play of the arts in Central Europe and it can be argued that republican independence was a mixed blessing to the new architecture, requiring as it did that architects take on official tasks not necessarily consonant with avant-garde ideas. In Vienna, there was sufficient space for new offices in the old imperial palaces, but the new Czechoslovak Republic wanted its own ministries, not merely old Baroque shells for new files. State-sponsored competitions favored a massively modern tradition, as was evident in the ministries of transport and agriculture, and cubists began patriotically to play with Slavic folklore in which abstract and bright lines were softened

Social Topography of Prague 1930

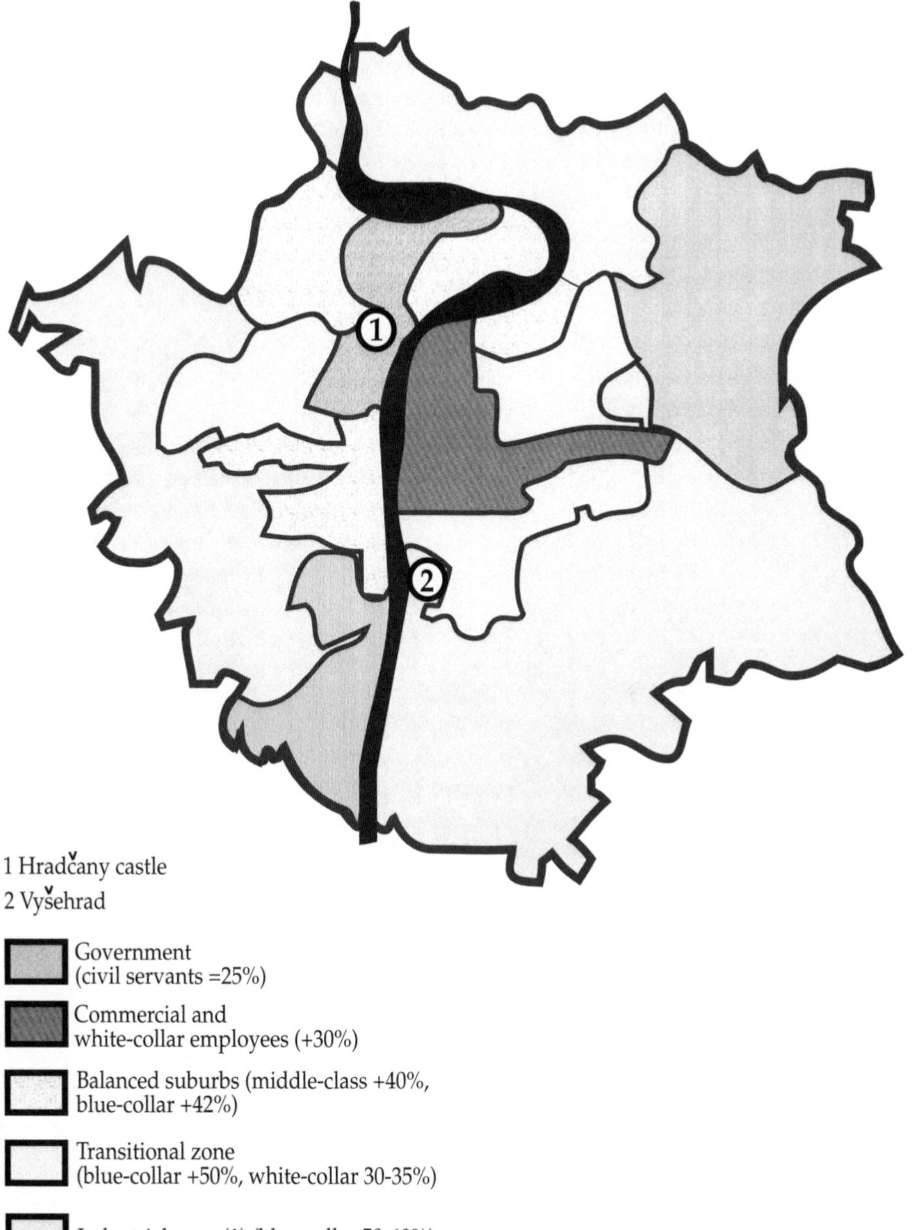

Source: Elizabeth Lichtenberger
Wien - Prag/Metropolenforschung.
Bőhlau Verlag Wien, 1993 (Sketch by M. Paal).
By permission.

in a "Rondocubism," exemplified by the bank of the Czechoslovak legions on Poříč Street, or compromised their radical principles with colorful facades and, possibly, ironic memories of the Italian Renaissance. (An Italian insurance company building on Jungmannova Street was called by visiting Le Corbusier a project of "Assyrian character," and he thought it showed Czech opposition to recent architecture.) By the end of the 1920s, pure lines and long glass fronts began to dominate in the new projects within the inner city; Josef Fuchs built the impressive Prague Fair Place (its history was spoiled by the Nazi order that Jews gather there to leave for the camps), and on Wenceslas Square constructivist norms determined the sober shape of the Štýblo Passage (now Alpha) and Hotel Juliš, unsure of its function today but in its time elegantly incorporating a cinema popular with chic young couples and a splendid café. Avant-garde architecture and the new film industry were bound to meet: functionalist principles prevailed at the Barrandov site on the south of Prague, incorporating the new film studios, a fashionable restaurant, U-shaped terraces, and a magnificent swimming pool at the bottom of a cliff. It was the meeting place of the *jeunesse dorée*—poets of uncertain income and great talent, starlets of the budding film industry—in the first republic's best years. Thanks to Václav Havel, Sr., father of the president, a rich and intelligent real estate mogul (perhaps the only one in Czech history), it was a far cry from the dark, self-centered Prague that international travelers nowadays want to discover at almost any price.

Among the soldiers who returned from the Siberian front to Prague in 1919 was the writer Jaroslav Hašek, but he did so halfheartedly at best. His picaresque novel *The Good Soldier Švejk* has been called by many of his contemporary colleagues a Dada enterprise, and his life was Dada even more. At home (when he did not roam on foot through Central Europe), the young man stylized himself as a Prague Maxim Gorki, worked for a while for a periodical specializing in zoological questions (among others, he contributed an article suggesting that elephants like gramophone music whereas tigers do not), and organized with his beer-guzzling friends a Party of Moderate Progress According to the Law, demanding a more severe supervision of the poor, the nationalization of sextons, and the transfer of all credit institutions into the hands of the clergy. When war broke out, he enlisted as a cadet officer; on August 13, 1915, he was awarded an imperial and royal silver medal for valor. A few months later, when the Russians broke through the Austrian positions, he used his chance, as did thousands of Czechs, and changed sides. The fraternal Russians put him first into a camp (where everyone suffered from hunger and typhoid fever), and from there he joined Czechoslovak legions fighting on the eastern front.

Politically, Hašek developed rather fast, to say the least; early in 1916 he declared in a soldiers' newspaper that Bohemia should be ruled by Romanovs, but a year later he defended parliamentary democracy (and Masaryk), in February 1918 he joined the left Social Democrats, and in May was among Bolsheviks, who sent him to Samara, on the Volga River, to do propaganda work there. Promoted to chair the party committee of the Fifth Soviet Army in April 1920, he edited a revolutionary newspaper in Irkutsk and married his assistant, Comrade Shura, a former aristocrat; somehow he forgot to tell her about his wife and son in Prague. He felt quite comfortable in Siberia, and the Prague party committee had to ask Moscow to send him home to Prague, where he was urgently needed. But when he finally arrived with Shura, the Communists had just lost their first battle against the parliamentary government and most of their leaders were in prison. Hašek was nearly lynched in the street when Czech legionnaires recognized the "commissar" who had deserted to the Bolshevik enemy, and the police suspected him, rightly, of bigamy. His idea was to write a novel that would end all his struggles, and he withdrew to a Bohemian village, where he wrote, or rather dictated, the first volumes of his *Švejk*, slowly drinking himself to death. Members of the Sokol, whom he had always ridiculed, were honor guards at his lonely village funeral, and the novel, which his publisher issued in installments on bad paper, was the first book in the new republic to attract international attention.

Most Czech intellectuals of recent generations have been proud to be able to quote Švejk's cunning folk wisdom in all possible and impossible situations, but few readers ever went beyond the third volume or the first part of the fourth to the continuations, written by Hašek's friend Karel Vaněk, who tried his best to continue in Hašek's way. In his own volumes, Hašek tends to repeat a few basic situations about Švejk versus the bureaucrats, and he offers a gallery of striking portraits rather than an unusual plot, as the picaresque genre requires. Švejk, "the little man," makes a living selling dogs with false pedigrees, smokes his pipe, drinks his beer, and finds himself in constant trouble because he talks too much—and yet police officers, army doctors, and judges always send him back home or return him to his regiment because they believe that only a congenial idiot can show so much enthusiasm for the dynasty and the emperor. He is an artist of survival, serves as *pucflek* (orderly) to army chaplain Katz, a baptized Jew, and to First Lieutenant Lukáš, a Czech and a ladies' man, and is constantly picked up by the Austrian military police as a Russian spy. He is the master of "yes saying," forcing his triumphant adversaries to reveal their foolishness, but the trouble is that it is rather difficult to say whether Švejk is cunning enough to offer his resistance without resistance or whether he is a simple moron. Hašek rarely intervenes as narrator and leaves it to the helpless reader to decide—except in the episode in military prison, where the narrator definitely suggests that the chief of guards is wrong to believe that Švejk is merely naive. Among Czech critics, responses to Švejk were less than unanimous; the left was generally in favor, the liberals preferred mixed enthusiasm and skepticism, and conservative patriots despised him as an egotist who was merely intent upon saving his "stinking skin from the world massacre" (as Arne Novák put it). Even Julius Fučík, a star Communist critic who was later killed by the Nazis, tried to find his own way out of the critical dilemma, saying in 1929 that Švejk was "the type of the soldier [one finds] in all imperialist armies" and in 1939, when political dangers were more acute, assuring Czech readers that Švejk unmasked the power of reaction, developing an intense "political consciousness" all the way (this is certainly not in Hašek's text). It is another question entirely how many people during the Stalinist regime adopted Švejk's way of resisting without resistance and whether, in doing so, they really sabotaged the authorities or simply made life easier for the new bureaucrats, who knew Hašek's book as well as anybody else.

Only in schoolbooks do political and literary developments neatly coincide, but the history of the independent republic and the chronicle of the Czech avant-garde diverge only a little. In Prague in 1908–12, painters and architects moved first in perfect synchrony with developments in Milan, Paris, and Berlin; Czech writers followed at a distance of nearly ten years. It was not that voices of individual rebels, often of anarchist sympathies, were not heard but they too had to carry the burdens of tradition; although their language was that of daily use rather than a high and rare symbolist vocabulary, they still handled accepted forms and genres. They felt rebellious, but they lacked the new formal consciousness that emerged, elsewhere, from the radical social and technological transformations of Europe's great capitals; the enormously gifted young poets of the young republic paradoxically had to learn more about the idiom of Guillaume Apollinaire and his contemporaries before they could speak in their own voice.

Karel Čapek was well known beyond Prague as Masaryk's friend (in Čapek's garden in Vinohrady, the president had a chance to meet younger intellectuals on Friday for tea) and as the author of *R.U.R.* (1921), *Věc Makropulos* (*The Makropoulos Secret*, 1922) and *Bílá Nemoc* (*The White Plague*, 1937), much performed on European stages. But it was far less known that he worked for years on pioneering translations of modern French poetry; his version of Apollinaire's *Zone* was a key text for the Czech avant-garde in 1918 and his anthology of recent French poetry in 1920 revealed a totally new world to a younger generation. Later critics assert that a Soviet orientation should be taken into account as well; the avant-garde was certainly inclined to the radical left in Prague as much as in Germany or France. However, a serious knowledge of early Soviet aesthetic developments was rare, and it is not impossible that the linguist Roman Jakobson (coming to Prague originally with a Soviet delegation) was one of the few witnesses qualified to tell young people what was going on in Soviet art and literature.

The avant-garde group that called itself Devětsil (the name of the butterbur plant tells little of the word's Czech etymological force, combining the words "nine" and "strength") first gathered in Prague in October 1920. Depending on the sources, it was made up either of talented bourgeois students of the elite Křemencárna school or of class-conscious writers (among them Jaroslav Seifert, a future Nobel laureate) ready to advance the cause of the revolutionary masses just preparing the first general strike against the young republic. A few years later, Devětsil's attention shifted from *Proletkult* fever to a revolution of aesthetic sensibilities, taking its strength from Charlie Chaplin's movies, from clowns, circus riders, and acrobats, from red stars in the sky, and from jazz; the young poets began to celebrate the rush of life as enjoyed in the great European and American cities (never London, perhaps thought to be too conservative). It was an intoxicating time of Devětsil poeticism, of which the proletarian poets were suspicious, but for a productive decade (1920–30) it was articulated by Karel Teige, its theoretician, and the expansive young poet Vítězslav Nezval, who became the experimental master of Czech verse. Nezval once wrote that he and Teige had discovered poeticism, or whatever it was, just walking through Prague, "feeling the atmosphere of happiness, witnessed by spring fragrances, the stars, the rosary of street lanterns, vomiting drunks, begging old women, and the makeup of the prostitutes leaning against the railing of the quai." Fortunately, Teige's theory of poeticism, in itself a conglomerate of all the ideas of the European avant-garde, was wide open to new talent—a creed of joy, exhilaration, sensuality, and amplitude that appealed to most gifted writers. Even if they did not stay, they participated in the élan of creating surprising poems, as did Jiří Wolker, issuing manifestos, and disdaining the middle classes. (Milena Jesenská, Franz Kafka's onetime friend, joined Devětsil by marrying Jaromír Krejcar, a functionalist architect close to Teige.) Nezval was the white magician of Prague who glorified its lights, clouds, bars, *parapluies*, and kisses:

Prague of a hundred towers
with the fingers of all the saints
with the fingers of perjury . . .
with the burning fingers of women lying on their backs
with the fingers that touch the stars . . .
with the fingers of a windmill and a lilac bush . . .
with the fingers of the rain, cut off, and the Týn cathedral
on the glove of the dawns . . .

Karel Teige, who in the late 1920s taught at the Dessau Bauhaus, the institutional headquarters of the German avant-garde, and Nezval, a voracious reader with a photographic memory, were perfectly qualified to make fine distinctions between what was going on among avant-garde writers in west and east, and they provided poeticism with a program that was fully if critically aware of its early links to Italian futurism and European Dadaism. They had a more difficult time separating the Czech poeticists from the French surrealists who came, they said, only after Prague poeticists had articulated their views. Both Teige in his discussions (among them an early and remarkable analysis of the art of photography and the cinema) and Nezval in his lively essay entitled "The Parrot on the Motorcycle" (1925) believed that the poem should emancipate itself, asserting its independence as poem against philosophies and ideologies. The magnificent practitioner Nezval was particularly eloquent in praising the process of untrammeled association, "a woman-alchemist quicker than the radio," and the creative principle of assonance and rhyme; he was frank enough to admit that the French surrealists who had studied Freud (still unknown in Prague, Nezval wrongly believed) knew more about the subconscious sources of the imagination than their Czech colleagues, but he defended the Czech belief that the music of poetry triggered free association against the surrealist disdain for rhyme, which was understandable only in the context of the French tradition. The poeticists, it became increasingly clear, were but surrealists *in statu nascendi*, and when their group had run out of collective steam and the ideological cohabitation with the revolutionary left had turned difficult, Nezval established a

Czech Group of surrealists and invited the French masters to come to Prague.

It was a great and much remembered moment when André Breton and Paul Eluard arrived in Prague in the earliest spring days of 1935. Breton, the prince of surrealism, before lecturing on the "surrealist object" (on March 31) and the political situation of the arts (on April 1) glorified Prague, a city "of legendary seductions," saying that among cities which he had never visited, it was perhaps the least foreign to him. Pushing aside geographical, historical, and economic considerations, and seeing it from a distance, it was *la capital magique de la vieille Europe*, the magic capital of old Europe. For decades Czech surrealists and their later friends misquoted Breton by simply ignoring his qualifying adjective *vieille*, telling us that Breton declared magic Prague to be the capital of Europe; even Angelo Maria Ripellino, who should know better, sustains that self-congratulatory myth. To Breton, Prague was the capital of *old* Europe and Paris the first city of European modernity.

Breton wrote home about his triumphs in Prague, where he addressed hundreds of "comrades" (his term) and stayed longer than planned; it is interesting to speculate about what the Czech and the French expected from each other in political terms. Paradoxically, as Mark Polizzotti has shown in his recent biography of Breton, both expected better grades in the books of the Communist Party (the French being able to refer to their famous revolutionary comrades Teige and Nezval, and the Czechs, not untouched by the commands of socialist realism, hoping that an alliance with the French masters would give them more elbowroom). The left avant-garde in Czechoslovakia, as all over Europe, had to confront the question of how to reconcile aesthetic choice with the stern discipline demanded by increasingly Stalinist party organizations; these factions of the 1930s immediately reemerged at the end of World War II. Those who had been critical of the Moscow show trials in 1936 or flirted with cultural policies as defined by Trotsky were later driven to silence and suicide or were, like Záviš Kalandra, sentenced in Prague show trials and executed. Others who adjusted to party requirements more readily were rewarded with important positions in the cultural apparat and rose from honor to honor. Teige (who died in 1951) was condemned to silence after the war, only to be rediscovered by the generation of the 1960s; Nezval, who had broken with the Paris surrealists before it was too late, especially in view of Breton's admiration for Trotsky, in 1949 wrote a submissive lyrical-epic poem "Stalin," to repent his sins, and was appointed chief of the nationalized Czech film industry.

After sixty years or more, it has become clear that the Prague Devětsil created an ingenious and witty art of imagination and charm, and while some of its achievements, in particular those not bound to the printed page—for instance, the paintings by Jindřich Štýrský and Toyen (Marie Čermínková)—are becoming more widely known, Czech poeticist poetry still constitutes one of the most astonishing and wonderful secrets of Prague, precisely because it is so difficult to translate. Nevertheless, in their own way, Nezval's vicissitudes and literary achievements raise radical questions about imagination and politics in the service of a party.

Jiří Voskovec and Jan Werich, two students at the elite Křemencárna school, located just opposite the famous U Fleků brewery, were also often found among the habitués of Kino Konvikt, where Charlie Chaplin films were shown regularly. These young men were to create an avant-garde theater of Devětsil inspiration, unique in Prague and in Europe; though Voskovec was later sent to Dijon (France) to study, Werich remained in Prague, and the inseparable friends met again when they entered law school, though there is little evidence that they were serious about training to become lawyers. Voskovec was early involved in the ideas of the European avant-garde, and in his essays (which he must have written when he was seventeen or eighteen) he defended futurism and expressionism against Czech traditionalists who still believed in the charms of "fragrant meadows," rather than in the "mechanical beauty" professed by the younger generation everywhere. In 1926, the two for the first time performed at a student matinee, and a year later, scribbling away at the Národní Kavárna and at the family dacha, completed their *West Pocket Revue*, a witty sequence of satire and parody, which created a theatrical sensation.

In 1928 Voskovec and Werich, known as V&W forthwith, consolidated their Osvobozené Divadlo (Theater Unchained, using Tairov's expression) in a 1,000-seat auditorium on Vodičkova Street, in the center of Prague, hired the comic Ferenc Futurista, he of the enormous buck teeth, to play minor parts, and were immediately excommunicated by the avant-garde community for having capitalist aspirations. They were fortunate to work with gifted Jaroslav Ježek, half a nervous George Gershwin, half Kurt Weill, who took over the orchestra, strong in the saxophone section, and composed, apart from concerti, V&W songs and haunting blues that have not been forgotten. (Theater history has less to say about the six vivacious if rather muscular Jančík girls who provided the ballet.) In the early 1930s, Voskovec and Werich were able to attract František Zelenka, a functionalist architect of note, who did sets and posters for them (he later organized the theater at Theresienstadt and died, together with his son and his wife, in Auschwitz). The team of V&W, Ježek, and Zelenka created an extraordinary moment for Prague theater, resuscitating the tradition of the commedia dell'arte, as the Soviet producer Meyerhold noted when he came to visit, and combining it with Dada's disruptive wit, surrealist imagination, linguistic intelligence, and, increasingly, a joyous defense of beleaguered Prague democracy—though, they had, like many others, considerable illusions about the policies of the Soviet Union.

Their most effective plays and films were produced in the mid-1930s, including the anti-Nazi *Osel a Stín* (*The Donkey and the Shadow*, 1933, against which the German ambassador protested), *Balada z hadrů* (*A Ballad of Rags*, 1935), and *Rub a líc* (*Heads or Tails*, 1936), which became the film *Svět patří nám* (*The World Is Ours*, 1937). By that time, fights between rightist and leftist students often erupted in the auditorium, and in the fall of 1938, after the Munich conference, a new Czech minister of the interior ordered the theater closed. The V&W team left for New York, where unfortunate Jaroslav Ježek (now totally blind) died in a hospital; the two friends worked for the Czech section of the Voice of America. They both returned to Prague in 1945, Werich first and Voskovec later, a little hesitatingly, but times had changed, and the Communist Party knew all too well what it wanted to tolerate and what to exploit. Werich stayed on and became a popular television personality; Voskovec left again and made his way as a serious actor in Chekhov and Shakespearean plays and in Hollywood. Werich died in Prague in 1980 and his friend Voskovec of cancer in California a year later. In Prague, CDs of their original repertory, edited in six installments, are among the hot items on the electronic market.

It is deplorable that we have to satisfy our nostalgia for the avant-garde of the past, certainly more exciting than that of the present, by listening to CDs and by reading in libraries. But the old glory places are gone: the Café Union at Perštýn Corner, lovingly called Unionka, in a shabby building marked by a strange edge-stone (with a grinning flat face, which I feared when I walked by it as a boy), was long the principal home for artists and intellectuals. Here Pan Dávidek, the owner, played his gramophone, mostly for his own entertainment, and the headwaiter, Patera, a mythical baldhead, provided newspapers (he had to pay for them out of his own pocket), remembered for years who owed him for a cup of coffee, and benevolently functioned as a kind of one-man credit institute, lending money to young painters, chess players, and anarchists.

Architects, editors, and critics sat here in the warrenlike little rooms or went from table to table—from the architect Gočár to the brothers Karel and Josef Čapek, from Jaroslav Hašek (who had his headquarters at the Zvěřina Pub) to Richard Weiner, interested in all things French. The German counterpart to the Unionka was the Arco, between the stock exchange and the old railway station, which was mostly frequented by traveling salesman, businesspeople, and bank clerks yet, for reasons difficult to fathom, attracted the most important German-writing authors and their artist friends; the headwaiter was weaselly Pan Počta. Kafka, Brod, and Franz Werfel, whenever he was in town, as well as the painters Friedrich Feigl and Willy Novak met here in a convenient extra room; occasionally, a Czech leftist turned up to demonstrate for Socialist solidarity; and, among the few women, Milena Jesenská was seen, to be close not to Kafka but to Ernst Pollak, a minor bank manager of a shrewdly critical mind, one of her future husbands. Hanging out at the Arco, she at least had a good chance to spite her father, an upright Czech nationalist who heartily disliked her German and Jewish acquaintances.

In the first years of the republic, Prague's housing shortage was catastrophic, and rather than freeze in their rented rooms, young writers, and many of the older people, assembled at the Národní Kavárna (National Café), exactly midway between the river and the Unionka; radicals, enamored of the Soviet habit of abbreviations, called it their Nárkav—though the regulars were of at least three different persuasions: the Devětsil people crowded in the back corner, the progressive Catholics in front, and the more sedate liberal journalists on the banquettes along the wall. In a separate room, the famous scholars of the Linguistic Circle, among its members professors Jan Mukařovský, Vilém Mathésius, Jakobson, and young René Wellek, later to establish the modern study of comparative literature in the United States, met to discuss recent literary theory. Only if the place was too crowded or the Devětsil writers became too noisy did people move down to the Slavia, a Prague showplace often visited by Albert Einstein and Thomas Mann. For a long time, the Slavia had been second home to people from the National Theater, across the street, but after the demise of the Unionka and the Národní Kavárna it became a (last) literary meeting place, especially in the 1970s and 1980s, when the dissidents had their regular tables here and the police agents (nearby) too.

In the 1920s and 1930s, Prague's cafés constituted an entire planetary system; though Czechs would rarely venture to the Café Continental (it was elegant and German), the frontiers of language were honored more by habit than by resolve, and writers also liked to sit at the Tůmovka, the

Deminka (among retired civil servants), or the Akademická Kavárna (Academic Café) on Vodičkova Street, now Prague's McDonald's #1. Other places catered to more specific inclinations and intents—for instance, the Café Rococo for the film industry or the Štěrba for ladies of the afternoon. Generations differed in their habits; Unionka regulars usually went, after hours, to the raunchy Montmartre in the Old Town, while the young Devětsil people preferred the chic bars, including the Chapeau Rouge, the Sect Pavillon, and the Pigalle.

The Nazi occupation and the long years of Communist Party rule did away with most of Prague's coffeehouses, but the new capitalism does not exactly favor comfortable places, either, where impecunious intellectuals can sip cups of coffee for hours and young people can hold hands (under the table, as they did at the Unionka). Since mid-century, the coffeehouse subculture has shifted to the writers' weekend *chatas*, or dachas, or to local pubs where regulars have held the fort for decades. The octogenarian writer Bohumil Hrabal was rightly famous for loyally dwelling at U zlatého tygra (At the Golden Tiger), near the Dominican Church, and when President Clinton visited Prague and wanted to see the sights, his colleague Václav Havel obligingly took him there, after the joint had been cased by the Secret Service, much to the dismay of Hrabal and the other regulars. Many tourists like to gather at the new Café Milena, run by the enterprising Franz Kafka Society, and members of the society are privileged to have coffee in the extra room, where they can catch a glimpse of roving Kafka experts from Duke or Yale in search of an authentic Prague café.

For thirty years now, the Czech intellectuals of the 1968 generation have celebrated "the world of Franz Kafka," or Prague German-Jewish literature, and it is difficult not to respond to their innocent generalizations with weary questions about history and its oddities. International tourists cannot complain that the Prague travel industry does not pander to their literary needs by offering Kafka T-shirts, ad hoc exhibitions, and Kafka pantomimes in every Old Town nook and cranny, but travelers have few opportunities to learn about the continuities and disjunctions of Prague's Jewish literary developments, which began well before 1848, if not before Emperor Joseph. They were, step by step, strengthened by the liberalization of rules and regulations concerning Jewish life and education, by a productive accord with German writing by non-Jewish authors (often under the pressure of Czech nationalists who brought together Prague Germans and German-speaking Jews), and the emergence of at least three generations obsessed, in the absence of political options, with literature and the arts. The Austrian Robert Musil, author of the *The Man Without Qualities*, was not entirely foolish when he remarked that in Prague true genius *refuses* to write. German-speaking Prague was too small and cliquish to guarantee spontaneity and fresh air, and as soon as young people in a new and talented cohort looked around, they decided to go elsewhere, to a place perhaps less magic but abounding with publishers, newspapers, and many divergent, clashing opinions.

The scholar Kurt Krolop (perhaps against his intentions) has shown that the brain drain was continuous: even before the revolution of 1848, young writers in Prague, whether German or Jewish-German, left for more challenging editorial jobs in Leipzig and Vienna and, beginning in the 1890s, went to Munich and Berlin. There were great departures in 1911–12 and in 1920 and after; even Kafka left for Berlin. Rilke, Werfel, Paul Kornfeld, and Ernst Weiss, deeply offended by the excesses of Czech nationalism, chose to go, and of the more important writers of German and Jewish-German Prague only four or five remained throughout the years of the republic—among them Max Brod (who died in 1968 in Tel Aviv), Paul Leppin (who died in 1945 back in Prague), Johannes Urzidil (who died in 1970 in Rome), and Ludwig Winder (who died in 1946 in London); it is a more melancholy than cynical observation that the only ones who remained had excellent, prestigious newspaper jobs, were incurably ill, or were too old to move. Few readers are aware that another young generation of writers grew up in republican Prague—my friend the poet H. W. Kolben (who died in 1942 at the Mauthausen concentration camp), the studious Orientalist Franz Baerman Steiner (who lived until 1952 in Oxford), the novelist and poet H. G. Adler (who died in 1988 in London), and the playwright and poet Franz Wurm, still living and working as a psychotherapist in Zurich, the last of the Prague Mohicans.

Even well-meant celebrations are not a good substitute for literary criticism, and the question was not often raised whether Prague German writers moved only in the modern mainstream of classical, neoromantic, or symbolist literature, or whether at least some of them contributed to the achievements of the European avant-garde. From the perspective of the Devětsil people, the intentions of their German-writing colleagues seemed a little old-fashioned and their continued admiration of Goethe, Heinrich von Kleist, or Adalbert Stifter (all high even in Kafka's canon) rather odd. Yet quite apart from Kafka, other writers resisted tradition and advanced new ways of writing. First among them was Franz Werfel, who in his early poetry—*Der Weltfreund* (*The World's Friend*, 1911), *Wir sind* (*We Are*, 1913), and *Einander* (*To Each Other*, 1915)—was among those who initiated the expressionist revolt even to Berlin readers and audiences (never mind the Hollywood best-sellers of his later years). His long, harsh lines breaking through neoromantic stanzas were no less astonishing than his sweeping gestures of love for earth, heaven, and all his fellow beings:

> I am a *corso* in a sunny town,
> A summer fete with lawns where women glide,
> My eye is dazed by too much brilliancy,
>
> Upon the twilight grass I will sit down,
> And with the earth into the evening ride . . .
> Oh Earth, oh Evening, Joy, Oh in the world to be!
>
> *(trans. by Edith Abercrombie Snow)*

Only a few experts remember Werfel's young Prague disciple Karl Brandt, who was too sick to fulfill his promise, or Melchior Vischer, the only Prague Dadaist, who later moved with his Jewish wife to Berlin, where he published a book on Jan Hus in 1940 that was immediately destroyed by the Nazi authorities. Literary history rarely recalls that Prague's expressionist playwrights, among them Kornfeld and Weiss, gave the German stage an entire repertory of plays far into the 1920s and early 1930s. Most of Prague's early nonconformists published in the Berlin avant-garde periodical *Der Sturm* (where Max Brod developed his idea that true poetry was based on the importance of the individual word) or in *Die Aktion*, edited by the anarchist Franz Pfempfert, committed to discover art and literature in radical opposition to its time and place. One of the interesting writers contributing from Prague was Marie Holzer, who in her own way anticipated Milena Jesenská by about a generation. Holzer had a sharp eye for changing mores, unveiled the sham relationships between men and women, called loyalty in traditional marriage "a drug," refused to submit to "nationalist egotism," and acknowledged not without pain that the Czechs, in 1915 a people certain of victory, had "poets of a wonderful force and of an unerring formal power." Mrs. Holzer was shot by her husband in a marital dispute, and her courage has yet to be honored in our memory.

Prague German-writing Jews, not much liked by the Czech nationalists, did their best, especially during the years before World War I and between the wars, to make the achievements of Czech art and literature widely known outside Bohemia. Czech writers tended to look to Paris, which rarely responded to their love, while their German-speaking friends were busy in Leipzig and Berlin triggering interest in Czech Prague. Max Brod had a certain inclination to see himself at the center of a Prague "circle" which actually consisted of many circles within circles, but I do not want to dispute his long and caring efforts to have the works of his German and Czech friends published in Germany and to attract attention to Czech literature and art. He was responsible for bringing Hašek's Švejk to the attention of the Berlin theater (and, indirectly, to Brecht) and he was instrumental in having Leoš Janáček's operas performed in European opera houses.

Prague Germans and German-writing Jews had long been active translating from contemporary Czech. In 1837–48, Rudolf Glaser had edited the courageous periodical *Ost und West* (*East and West*), cultivating German-Slavic togetherness. Siegfried Kapper was among the first translators of K. H. Mácha, and in the following generation Friedrich Adler rendered Jaroslav Vrchlický, a master of formal versatility, into German. During World War I, Pfempfert, in his *Aktion*, published German versions of Czech authors persecuted by the Austrian authorities, yet passed Prussian war censorship without much difficulty; he even printed three special Prague issues, dedicated to the expressionist Franz Werfel, the Czech artist Josef Čapek (brother of Karel), and the architect Vlastimil Hoffman. The trouble was that German and Czech poetic idioms had ceased to run close to each other; and as soon as Czechs relied, in a revolt of their own, on the spoken word of the family, the street, the pub, and the workplace, Prague German translators were immediately handicapped, for their literary as well as their spoken language was bookish and it lacked popular dialect or plebeian terms. Werfel's translation of the Czech visionary Otokar Březina (done with the support of Erik Saudek) was perfect, because both the Czech original and the German used rare and artful words, but translators had a far more difficult time in tackling Petr Bezruč, spokesman of the oppressed Silesian miners, or playful Vítězslav Nezval; it is not surprising that the best translations of Bezruč and Nezval were often undertaken by outsiders (the Bezruč translator Georg Mannheimer, for instance, came to Prague from Vienna before going to Israel). In the years of the republic and until mid-century, Paul/Pavel Eisner was the most productive literary mediator between the two languages, and he devoted so much loving effort and sympathy to Czech that he had become for all practical purposes a writer of the Czech tradition himself. During World War I he translated recent Czech poetry into German, often with expressionist overtones, but by 1930 he turned around and translated German into Czech. Eisner survived the Nazi occupation hidden in his room in Prague and, after the liberation, emerged as a Czech writer; in a widely read book he praised the strength and courage of Czech. His Czech translation of Thomas Mann's *Doktor Faustus* was published in 1948, linguistically congenial to the original text and an irreplaceable monument to the translator's art.

As the Prague philologist Emil Skála has shown, many elements appeared and disappeared in the long history of Prague German; if, in early centuries, northern and central German idioms combined, the events of 1620 and the Hapsburg centralization brought about an "Austrianization" of the Prague idiom; the scene was thoroughly provincial. The nineteenth and early twentieth centuries offered a late, uneasy stage; Yiddish had gone underground and was spoken with ambivalent feelings by family patriarchs (Kafka's father, for instance); when Czechs and Germans met in everyday situations, curious constructions with many interferences and fusions could be heard. Czechs spoke *Kucheldeutsch* (kitchen German) with German employers and superiors; middle-class German housewives used *Kuchelböhmisch* (kitchen Czech) to discuss culinary matters with their Czech cooks and servant girls. *Mauscheldeutsch* (the term used by the Jewish-German nationalist Fritz Mauthner, which suggests "kinky" German) denotes the last traces of ancient Jewish-German stubbornly defying the rules of polite German conversation. Phonetically, spoken German in Prague was part of an equally complicated situation: Whether Jew or gentile, Prague speakers of German immediately revealed to German listeners that they were "different," using the consonants *p, t, k* for *b, d, g,* simplifying all diphthongs in a uniform *ai,* and relying on Czech prepositions where German would have been appropriate. Johannes Urzidil renewed the romantic belief that Prague German was the purest of them all, going back to Johannes Noviforensis, chancellor to Emperor Charles IV—a defensive myth that compensates for the idiosyncrasies of speech and the literary abstractions of a middle-class idiom largely out of sync with the everyday speech of small-town Bohemian and Moravian Germans.

It may be misleading to regard Kafka as incarnating "Kafka's world" or Prague German writing (he was not even representative of himself, he would say), but he was one of the few writers who wrote about writing, and he did not avoid even the most painful, if not self-destructive, reflections about the language he was doomed to use in a city he wanted to leave. Kafka wrote little about Prague, and his early prose, as in *Beschreibung eines Kampfes* (*Description of a Fight,* 1909), combines literary considerations with rare allusions to Prague's streets, churches, and monuments, all unhesitatingly named; a similar combination can be found only in his late *Das Stadtwappen* (*The City Escutcheon*), though there in a more impersonal mode of narration. In the first part of the early text, a Prague flaneur who knows his Hugo von Hofmannsthal talks to a chance companion who turns out to be a writer too, characterized in a lively way by his theatrical manners as an actor and a thorough solipsist (I hesitate to think of Franz Werfel, who is chronologically wrong for the part, but the thought persists). The flaneur does not have a high opinion of his colleague's writings; they are too exalted, restless, "this fever, this seasickness on the firm earth." Unfortunately, the fellow writer is not content to call a poplar tree a poplar tree; he is not satisfied, in his "utter heat" to use "the truthful names of these things," and pours out words, in striking impatience, over things. He does not even want to know what kind of a tree a poplar is, speaking of it as "the tower of Babel," and the critic ironically adds he could have called the tree, swaying in the wind, "Noah as he drank." Such metaphors, though biblical and of high seriousness, hardly yield valid insights into matters as they are, though they do reveal good or bad writing; mobilizing metaphors, refusing to call a tree a tree, turns into a central indication of bad style. Good writing, the Prague flaneur assumes, would be unadorned, free of ornament, like Adolf Loos's architecture, and confident of a language of untroubled reference.

In their splendid and chaotic essay classifying Prague Jewish-German writing among the "minor" literatures of strong political potential, Gilles Deleuze and Félix Guattari have suggested that Kafka, trying to solve his authorial problems, did not opt for Czech—as if it had been an option to leave or take. Kafka's knowledge of Czech was better than Rilke's, who knew deplorably little Czech (as emerges from his as yet unpublished correspondence with Valerie David-Rhonfeld, his first Prague love), but, after a completely German education from elementary school to his law degree, he never mastered it. He read it with great philological empathy, shown in his German letters to Milena, born and bred Czech, but his difficulties are revealed in letters he had to write to his superiors at the Labor Insurance Company (1908–24); as Josef Čermák has shown, he found himself in dire language straits when the company after 1918 switched to functioning solely in Czech; Kafka, when writing to his director, had to enlist the services of his "family translation office," as he put it, consisting of his sister Ottla and her Czech husband, Josef. Kafka himself wrote about the "gorgeous lie about [his] knowledge of Czech" to his sister, and, when he went on writing in Czech to Josef, he curiously mixed spoken and literary idioms, ordered his sentences according to German syntactical rules, and stumbled over vocabulary and morphology, particularly difficult for anybody educated in German schools. Yet he could not escape to Yiddish either, which powerfully attracted him when he attended the performances of a Jewish traveling theater group in the shabby Café Savoy; he even arranged an evening of Yiddish recitations for his acculturated Prague Jewish audience, who truly feared, he believed, a language that had been spoken in Prague two generations ago. He felt, in one of his romantic moods, that Yiddish was the vital and lustful language of an authentic and proud community of Jews, but he, son of his father and member of a German acculturated society, had gone too far the other way. More clearly than anyone else, he recognized himself as one of the young Jews who resolved to write in German, though "with their hind legs . . . still glued to their father's Jewishness and with their waving front legs they found no new ground," who made their despair their inspiration. (His story of the young man who awakes one morning in the shape of an ugly insect may be a linguistic self-portrait.) In his search for pure and simple words, Kafka was, among all the impossibilities of writing (including the one *not* to write), condemned to German; he believed that the product of his despair "could not be German literature, though outwardly it seemed to be so." In his self-flagellation, he used images current in the vocabulary of contemporary German anti-Semites, as the historian Christoph Stölzl has reminded us, and asserted in 1921 that he was producing "a gypsy literature which had stolen the German child out of its cradle and in great haste put it through some kind of training, for someone has to dance on the tightrope." His anxieties were a far cry from the joy and exultation that brought together his Czech contemporaries, blissfully walking under his dark windows.

Prague, September 21, 1937

The sad news of T. G. Masaryk's demise did not come suddenly. He had been elected president of the republic four times, the last time in May 1934, but a year later decided that he should relinquish the office for reasons of health and age, and parliament voted to offer him his Lány residence and all his emoluments for life. He walked in the park, read, and welcomed a few visitors; his son Jan, an avid musician, said that his life went "from forte to fortissimo and then to pianissimo." In mid-September 1937, symptoms of a stroke combined with an inflammation of the lungs, and on September 12, the attending physicians notified the family and the government that the inevitable end was near. Masaryk died peacefully, on September 14, at 3:29 a.m., being eighty-seven years, six months, and seven days old. It was not an easy moment for the republic or for European democracy. Hitler had gone from success to success; in the Spanish Civil War there was heavy fighting around Oviedo and a new government offensive against Franco, the Prague newspapers reported; and when it was decided that Masaryk's funeral should be conducted by the army, people felt it was the right gesture of resolve and dignity in the face of increasing dangers. Citizens began to travel to Prague from all corners of Czechoslovakia, and the trains were crowded. His coffin was first placed in the Plečnik Hall of Hradčany Castle, and people lined up for days and nights to pay their respects. Nobody prodded them, and yet they came, 600,000 strong, a silent and dark column slowly moving ahead.

On September 21, the funeral was to proceed from Hradčany Castle to the Old Town and up Wenceslas Square to the railroad station (actually reversing the path Masaryk had taken when he triumphantly entered the city after his exile), and people put up chairs and little stools in the streets the evening before, to be there in the morning. By 10 a.m., after the family members had a last chance to take their leave, the casket was carried by six generals to the courtyard of the castle, where, on black-clad tribunes, the official guests gathered, on three sides, row after row. After President Beneš's funeral oration (which makes melancholy reading today, considering the development of his policies later), the old Hussite battle hymn, sung by a famous chorus of Prague schoolteachers, sounded out, and the procession formed while an air force squadron (later that air force was handed over to the Nazis plane by plane) crossed the sky. First in the procession was General Syrový on his horse, steel helmet and saber drawn; he was followed by representatives of all the Czechoslovak regiments, legions, and Sokols, carrying army flags and standards. The casket, placed on a howitzer gun carriage, was covered by the tricolor of the republic and accompanied by six soldiers who (a thought that might have pleased Masaryk) represented the six language groups serving in the army—Czechs, Slovaks, Germans, Hungarians, Ruthenians, and Poles. Behind the gun carriage walked Jan Masaryk and two grandsons (daughters and granddaughters waited at the railroad station), and behind them President Beneš, all alone, and his staff of presidential advisers at some distance. I was in the crowd, a fifteen-year-old kid, and we all were especially excited to see the many foreign representatives, ministers, generals, and diplomats, among them Léon Blum of France (of the government of the French Popular Front) with his shaggy head; Constantine Stojadinović, chief of the Yugoslav government; Norwegians, Americans, Albanians, British, Romanians, and dozens of others. I can see from newspaper clippings that Ambassador Eisenlohr of Germany was also there with two Wehrmacht attachés, and a first secretary of the Soviet embassy (actually a diplomatic snub, but the Soviets and Masaryk, who had financed a university of Russian émigrés in Prague from his own pocket, never liked each other very much). Konrad Henlein, *Führer* of the victorious Sudeten Party, called in sick at the last moment like a schoolboy, and he was represented by none other than Karl Hermann Frank, an ardent National Socialist, SS general (later), and Germany's last state minister in Prague before the Reich collapsed (he was executed immediately after the war). Massive units of legionnaires concluded the procession; twenty-five thousand of the Russian legions, joined by units who had fought in France and Italy, marched together for the last time under a clear autumn sky. I remember the eerie silence of the day; one million people lined the streets, but you heard only the muffled sound of the horses' hooves, the clink of wheels and weapons, the infantry boots on the cobbled streets, and quiet sobbing in the crowds.

Shortly after 3 p.m. the funeral procession arrived at the railroad station, and the small group that would accompany the casket to Lány County Cemetery was joined by Masaryk's entire family, including his daughters Alice and Olga, granddaughters Herberta and Anna, his niece Ludmila, as well as Hana Benešová, wife of the president. Two trains were readied, and all along the short route people waited and many of them threw flowers on the rails. Railroad workers took the coffin from the train at 6:45 p.m., and the final ceremony in the peaceful cemetery was private and brief. A preacher of the Czechoslovak Brethren read a psalm and a page from the Revelation of John, so dear to Emperor Charles IV, and while the hymn of the republic was intoned, the coffin was lowered into the grave, where Masaryk's mortal remains came to rest near his unhappy and courageous wife, Charlotte. Many poems and eulogies were published the next day, but none was more fair and moving than a short meditative piece written by Masaryk's friend Karel Čapek. He tried to grasp the many strains of his personality at a moment when legend had already begun to prevail, and in simple words suggested that Masaryk had been a "Greek Platonic" but also a man of science and reason and a believer in Christ's example. Čapek clearly explained what many had felt that day in a diffuse and anxious way. In Europe, new forces were emerging, of blood and collective instincts, and Masaryk had embodied, without strain and in living deeds, the most powerful counter-forces to these new threats: classical individualism coming to us from antiquity, sober reason in guiding the world, and, above all, a pristine Christian moral ideal of love for all your fellow people. Čapek was a student of American pragmatism, and it may have been his disinclination to accept metaphysical norms that made him particularly sensitive to what Masaryk had thought and done, in his own contradictory ways.

POSTCRIPT

A DIFFICULT RETURN TO PRAGUE

"When the express train rolled over the Smíchov bridge, which leads from the west into the main railway station of Prague, he stood at the corridor window and looked at the walls and the rocky slopes of the Vyšehrad. If I turn around now, he thought, and look through the compartment window, I am bound to see Hradčany Castle. At that point the castle and St. Vitus Cathedral came into view, as always, but they were even darker and thinner than he had expected. The train passed the Vyšehrad suburban station, a ruin, and its wheels rolled through a tunnel into the big hall built of steel and glass. Suddenly it seemed shabby and bare to him."

This is what I wrote on the evening of my return to Prague, in a thick notebook I had been careful to take along. By the next morning, however, I was already laughing at the way I had arranged my experience into dignified sentences that one might expect to find in a sentimental little novella. Literature for the last time! Crossing the border at Cheb (Eger) had been rather grotesque: a female passenger leaning against a window said, "I thought I'd have a stroke if I ever returned here," and as though summoned by her words, a stocky nurse wearing a starched uniform and carrying a medical bag appeared by the track and walked up and down alongside the train as though she expected whole clusters of sick homecomers to come tumbling out. A battalion of border guards in green uniforms with wolfhound insignia fanned out to check the train. The grim-faced captain, a good officer, seeing the notation "Born in Czechoslovakia" in my U.S. passport, stamped my visa and left the compartment as if inwardly goose-stepping, whereupon a lieutenant in Adidas shoes with his uniform gave me a Švejk-like look, handed me a customs form, and said that all this wasn't so important.

I had escaped in 1949 through the Bohemian Forest with the assistance of a knowledgeable Boy Scout (whose organization the Stalinists had already banned), in the company of H. and a group of students. I have dreamed about that journey for years. One of our group was wearing a new leather jacket that made crackling noises in the quiet forest, and at a crossroads we all had to lie flat in the underbrush because our Scout thought he heard border guards. Now, more than forty years later, I was crossing Wenceslas Square again. The March sun was shining, and even though I was in the midst of things, I saw everything as if through a glass wall. People looked so very different: passersby in shoddy jeans and leisure jackets, pale young girls with almost diaphanous skin, too many men with beer bellies hanging over their belts. My mother had always complained of agoraphobia, particularly when traveling, and that is what I felt now in the face of the incomprehensible strangeness of the people and houses, which, like the settings in an old UFA film, seemed to be crowding in upon me. I sought refuge in a hotel, the old Golden Goose, but I did not know what to say. In what idiom does one order a cup of coffee after forty years? The waiter, unmoved, recognized immediately that I came from the West, for I was wearing a jacket and tie, said *prosím* (please) and *děkuji* (thank you), and desperately stirred the viscous coffee (ground beans and hot water), which, I learned later, was served that way throughout the republic.

Whenever I opened my mouth, I realized I also lacked the more modern vernacular intonations—a singsong that had earlier been characteristic in the suburbs and now, after the passing of the old bourgeoisie, had penetrated to the inner cities. Old women working as doorkeepers in the many old state institutions, sitting by their little iron stoves, were the only ones who responded in a friendly way when they heard me speak the antiquated language of *Gymnasium* students and solid citizens, an idiom untouched by their experience in the collective.

On my walks I told myself that it was high time for me to be moved, as homecomers are in works of fiction, and I caught myself watching for an opportunity to shed tears at last. The tears did come, but at a wholly unexpected and almost comical moment. I had climbed up to Hradčany Castle in order to stand by the low wall on the castle square again and look out at the smoke curling over Prague's rooftops, where it had always belonged. Only the television tower was new. Groups of tourists—Japanese and Italians as well as Slovak school groups—were flooding the inner courtyards of the castle. Suddenly the windows opened and revealed festively clad woodwind and brass players who seemed to be waiting for a conductor. And then there was President Havel, wearing a blue suit and a reddish tie that matched his hair, along with his entourage, one of them in a leather jacket with an American flag on the back. While he made his way through the crowd to take up a position near the castle gate, plainclothesmen tried to clear a wider path, for it was high noon, time for a changing of the castle guards. "*Prosím Vás, lidičky, couvněte, tady se bude cvičit*" (Please, folks, we need a little room, we have to have exercise here), said one of the officers—and now my eyes finally filled with tears, not out of patriotism, but because I understood his tone, that of a policeman a bit embarrassed at being the guardian of order who wanted to do his duty without abridging people's right to rubberneck. I remembered other times and other policemen. In February 1948, on the day of the Communist putsch, I was among the two thousand students who marched to the castle to prevent President Eduard Beneš from accepting the Communist regime, but because we were foolish enough to march up narrow Neruda Street, we found ourselves caught between the police and the goons of the party's workers' militia. Today it was all different; a new chapter of Bohemian history was beginning here and now, and I wiped my eyes dry. The castle guards came marching along, and it turned out that this was only a dress rehearsal. President Havel, an experienced theatrical director, had had new uniforms designed by Theodor Pištěk, Jr. (whose father had once been a famous movie actor, playing father roles), and the young men looked as if they had stepped out of *The Music Man*.

So they restored the Royal Road, which Bohemia's rulers ascended when they came from the Old Town via the Charles Bridge to Hradčany Castle, and this is now the route taken by tourists and foreign currency. Everything is spic-and-span architecturally, but on the right and the left, to the north and the south, Prague is crumbling: on entire streets people move under primitive wooden boards that catch falling plaster and fragments from window ledges. The *sidliště*, the mighty housing developments on the city outskirts, precisely where the first Bronze Age people lived in the Prague area, were built with cheap prefabricated parts; the balconies are decaying and the nameplates disintegrating. The tenants call these bedroom communities, once the pride of the working class, their "rabbit hutches." What comes as a surprise is that the facades of Prague's houses, whether prefab or Renaissance, reveal nothing about their interiors. The exteriors may rot, but the rooms and apartments are clean and ingenious. People have furnished them individually, preserving and defending their own taste—older people with bric-a-brac and old carpets, the younger ones with bookshelves, artwork, and electronic gear obtained in one way or another.

The new customs require that one remove one's shoes before entering an apartment and leave them in the hall or in a niche (in the prefabricated houses, even outside the door), and Prague bedroom slippers get their historical due. This rule also applies at our old flat, kept in wonderful order, as though forty years of history out there meant nothing, by my stepmother, an amiable and vigorously sensible lady, a former dancer whom my widowed father married. When I entered, it was literally as if I had just come back from a quick errand in the city (that is, before I looked at myself in the hall mirror). Even the ashtray made of violet glass that I suddenly remembered was still on the desk. I fell asleep on the same sofa as in the past, and in an envelope I found faded family photos that were very familiar to me: of Father, Mother, my aunts and uncles, of vacations in Marienbad or in Silesian Karlsbrunn, and of me wearing the velvet suit with a white collar that my mother had made herself.

My father first caught sight of my mother at eight in the morning on a fine April day in 1913 or 1914, at the corner of Štěpánská and Wenceslas Square, and he was "hooked right away." On the next day he waited at the same corner, and she again showed up punctually, for she was a seamstress and had to hurry to work. Later the two strolled along the Vltava, and it turned out that they both came from immigrant families. He, Hans (his artistic name; his real name was Franz), came from a poor Ladin peasant family in the South Tyrol (ethnically related to the Swiss Romansh: I wonder in what language they conversed) that could no longer survive on the farm and therefore had migrated north, first to Linz, then to the Prague Týn, where my grandfather hoped to earn a living by selling wooden toys carved in the Groedner Valley; when metal toys appeared on the market he went bankrupt. She, Anna, came from a Jewish family in Poděbrady, a small town in central Bohemia, where her father was a textile merchant, but they had not wanted to stay there because their Czech fellow citizens displayed a certain tendency to demolish Jewish shops on the main square. In both Ladin and Jewish families old notions lived on unchanged. When the wedding carriage stopped in front of my father's house (I can picture the Czech coachman stopping the horses with a mighty *Prrr*), my paternal grandfather asked the bridegroom, "Do you really want to marry that Jewish sow?" and my mother's family shrugged their shoulders at the goyish cavalier, whose South Tyrolean mother was said to carry a rosary in her belt and speak Ladin while cooking. It sounded like old Provençal.

Like so many young people, my father had his heart set on becoming a Prague poet and dramaturge, and he studied the Berlin avant-garde periodicals. On Sundays the young betrothed would take the paddle steamer to Zbraslav—an obligatory excursion that Franz Werfel described in his early poem "Moldaufahrt im Vorfrühling" ("Voyage on the Moldau in Early Spring"): *"Oh Tanzlokale am Ufer, oh Brüder, oh Dampfer, Fährhaus, Erd- und Himmelsgeleit"* (O dance halls at the shore, o steamer, ferry house, escort of earth and heaven!). They strolled through the sparse woods and fortified themselves with beer and coffee at a garden restaurant, where they listened to a *K.u.K.* (imperial and royal) band. On Monday my father would write his weekly love poem for Mama, which would appear in the *Prager Tagblatt* the following Sunday. At first these verses were a bit neo-romantic ("Tonight, Madonna, when the first stars . . ."), but later they displayed expressionist boldness ("In the distance the organ tones of a toilet"). Thanks to German literary scholarship, they are all neatly preserved in the files of a research institute for Prague German literature in Wuppertal in the west of Germany.

The situation was not simple for these young people, for they were moving across invisible boundaries. The goyim spoke German, and Jews from small towns in Bohemia spoke Czech (though my Czech-Jewish grandmother lulled me to sleep by singing Heine's romance about the two grenadiers in German). There were other conflicts as well, for in both groups the older people, who valued business matters, were in conflict with the younger people, who defended pure intellect against their materialistic fathers. That was the case with the Kafkas and with the glove manufacturer Werfel, but they were not the only ones. Using terms from a satire by Karl Kraus, on one side there was *tachles*, the resourceful business mentality, and on the other *shmontses*, the creative values, though the *tachles* faction frequently dismissed these in the cultural section of the newspaper as *shmontsetten* (trifles). Oh, well, even the most important writers sometimes began with *shmontsetten* (for example, Franz Kafka in *Bohemia*), although fifty years later my father was still unable to comprehend that "Frankie" Kafka was a great writer, like Goethe or Dante.

I did not learn for some time what it meant to be a half-Jew, half-goy making his way between languages and nations, but at the age of fourteen or fifteen I certainly realized that my life was tied to T. G. Masaryk's republic and its liberal principles. Even later, when I was a prisoner of the Gestapo, did forced labor in a camp for half-Jews, and studied at the Charles University of Prague, I saw no reason to change my views. During my childhood in the late 1920s, all that was indistinct and remote.

I grew up on St. Peter's Square, with a view of the old church, and I remember visiting old shops with long fishing poles in a corner, for the Vltava was nearby. My mother liked to take me, unfortunately in the aforementioned velvet suit, to the Stadtpark (now destroyed by a new superhighway, despite Franz Werfel's poetry and Hermann Grab's beautiful prose), or to Žofín Island, from which one had a view of a "swimming school" (a Prague specialty: public baths on rafts), or, in winter, to the bumpy improvised skating rink below the National Theater. In the afternoon lady friends would visit my mother. They clinked the teacups with the little silver spoons that were part of the Poděbrady dowry, and speculated on the maiden name of one society lady or another. Only when the conversation turned to my aunts or uncles was I sent out of the room to read something educational (Egon Erwin Kisch).

Ah, yes, the aunts and uncles! My father's sister, Aunt Fritta, was the problem child of the family. No sooner had she memorized the monologues from Schiller's *Maid of Orleans* than she made off for the theaters of Frankfurt and Berlin, where she played leading roles; one of her partners was the star actor Heinrich George (of all people, for he turned to the Nazis later). Her first husband was the expressionist dramatist Paul Kornfeld, who later perished in the Lodz ghetto. Her visits to Prague caused great excitement, but my mama refused to stroll on the boulevard Na Příkopech with her because Tante Fritta, like Marlene Dietrich, wore pants. I liked her very much; she always paid me a handful of copper coins for an hour of golden silence, for she was *etepetete* (persnickety), as my father put it, and could not abide my Prague German with its Slavic consonants. Twenty years later, after an exile in Oxford, she told me that my German had still not improved all that much.

The ladies might also have gossiped about my uncle Karl (the Christian side and yet a member of the *shmontses* faction), but unfortunately he was *unter allem Niveau* (absolutely substandard). Karl, a graphic artist and draftsman, had a small studio not far from the Hradčany; family moralists disapproved of his taste in women, which tended toward the plebeian and the buxom (Café Štěrba). Karl was talented but not clever, for one evening in 1940, when he was drinking coffee in a hotel lobby, he declared to a man at his table that despite all the special communiqués the war was already lost for the Germans. That man was an official of the Gestapo; Uncle Karl was charged with high treason and promptly sentenced to twenty years in prison. At first he was incarcerated in the fortress Terezín, where sadistic *Kapos* tortured political prisoners to death, but then he was lucky enough to be transferred to a prison in Dresden, where he was rescued by the Allied air raids that destroyed it; he made his way through forests and across rivers to Prague, hid out in his father's apartment in the Týn, and did not leave the house again until the days of liberation came, in early May 1945. He helped build barricades, but a neighbor recognized him as German, he was removed from his post, and if he had not been saved by the testimony of former fellow prisoners, he would have gone to prison again, this time as a German.

My father had a rather low opinion of the pitiful poems and dubious novels of his Prague fellow writers, and it was some time before I realized that all these were famous people who later were the subjects of dissertations. My father thought very highly of Ludwig Winder, loved reciting from Paul Leppin's poetic collection *Glocken, die im Dunkeln läuten* (*Bells That Peal in the Dark*), and enjoyed his friendship with Hans Regina von Nack, who tended to cultivate the lighter muse, and Louis Weinert, who wrote dramas and popular detective novels (the Prague Edgar Wallace). He had no use for the young Rilke, and about Max Brod, of whom he was secretly jealous, he mainly told anecdotes, among them, according to him, about Brod corrupting the driver at the Čedok travel bureau with an annual Christmas goose and a driver always stopping the tourist bus in front of Max's apartment and calling out through his megaphone, "This is the home of the German poet Max Brod!" They (especially the ladies) "knew all about" Johannes Urzidil, later an ally of Adalbert Stifter, because he had addressed his expressionistic primal screams (published by the well-known Munich publisher Kurt Wolff) to my Aunt Fritta, who had, however, given him the cold shoulder, and later to my mother, who had had her fill of expressionist poetry. (Decades later Urzidil told me this in his apartment in his New York exile.) Live and let live—even when a nationalist mob occupied the old Ständetheater for the Czech nation in November 1920 and threw my father out of his office and down the stairs, he accepted this, as he later told me, as a traffic accident of Bohemian history. I also remember a borrowed frock coat that was ironed at home (to be exact, our Czech servant girl did the pressing and my mother the supervising) when my father was invited to an audience, at Hradčany Castle, with President T. G. Masaryk, who awarded him a scholarship from his private fund.

In my youth Prague did not attract as many tourists as it does today. The city was not particularly chic, and the palaces, churches, gardens, and bridges were open to the strollers, old people, lovers, and poets—all of them, Prague poets who wrote in German and surrealists who wrote in Czech.

Prague . . . I am the tongue of your bells and your rain
I am the tongue of the grapes and also that of the shelters
I am the tongue of boredom on Sundays and also of the water
over the weirs.

(Vítězslav Nezval)

In the cafés and wine taverns people gossiped about the latest scandals of Milena Jesenská or discussed the latest play of Karel Čapek, but today this would no longer be so simple. The Café Unionka, where Prague modernism happened under the care of that mythical headwaiter, long ago gave way to a dull glass palace in which government-approved children's books were produced, and the Café Slavia, where even dissidents of the 1970s and 1980s had a regular table under police surveillance, was claimed after the Velvet Revolution of 1989 by international tourist groups and European youths with alternative lifestyles, including "punks." (It is closed today, pending the legal resolution of difficult restitution problems.) In the evening a two-man band that Billy Wilder might have invented played there. The little wine tavern U Šupů, where surrealist poets used to discuss Trotsky, now serves Chinese food, and a waiter takes reservations three days in advance in a leather-bound red book. When I let it be known that I planned to visit the Arco Café, once the headquarters of the so-called Prague Circle, everyone repeatedly warned me that this was now the hangout of pickpockets, swindlers, and purse snatchers whom President Havel amnestied when he assumed office (and who are popularly known as "Havel's children"). At first they met in the buffet of the Ernest-Denis railroad station, but when the station management closed the buffet, they moved across the street to the venerable Arco. I went there anyway; the new picaresque element was, if anything, petit bourgeois, and the chairs were standard Prague café furniture from the Third Five-Year Plan. Retirees and lovers waiting for trains to the provinces were drinking Red River, the local Bohemian tonic water; I began to develop a taste for it too.

In my youth even the Charles Bridge was virtually deserted, and I had a trysting place there—on the left bank, under the bridge, down the steps in the direction of the Minor Town. There, near the sloshing old rental boats, was a little bench, and overhead the outlines of the saints' statues on the bridge and the stars. There it was easy to recite a poem and boldly undo a button on a blouse. My Italian friend Paola, who had read her compatriot Angelo Maria Ripellino's book about magic Prague, now wanted to sit on the bench with me, but I discovered that it now abutted a concrete-covered playground and crowds of tourists were passing by overhead. I had to content myself with telling her how I had sat there fifty years ago—with W. (no kisses, for she had a steady boyfriend), R. (Mondays), and C. (Wednesdays), when the Prague May nights with the streets filled with blossoming chestnuts worked their magic; failing that, we went to an outdoor restaurant, the Golden Well (Zlatá Studně), from which we could see the entire city (*ganz Prag in weiter Runde,* as Rilke put it), and finally we would ascend the Petřín Hill to the monument of Karel Hynek Mácha, the first Czech romantic poet, and, as tradition required, place a small bunch of violets on the pedestal as an offering to the spirit of love.

It is easy to avoid the international masses that push their way across the bridge; all you have to do is change direction and proceed upstream. After all, Prague has a second castle mountain, the Vyšehrad. For a long time the Přemyslid dynasty was not certain where it should reside, but once it decided on the Hradčany, the Vyšehrad with its chapels and churches began to lead a shadow existence. Now it is very quiet there, and the strollers are of a different kind: retired women lingering in the sunshine, high school kids smoking their first cigarettes, learned connoisseurs bent on knowing everything exactly. After all, Prague has always been a dual or triple city, and its topography has changed with the language that was spoken and the religion that was espoused. On Sundays, German residents went to the shady Stromovka, on the left bank, near the curve in the river, while the Czechs were more attracted to the old Vyšehrad cemetery, where the most important daughters and sons of the Czech nation are buried. I sat for a long time on a bench over the old bastions, where it was absolutely quiet, and then walked through the rows of crowded graves. Antonín Dvořák's grave is not far from the entrance, and by the other exterior wall is the tomb of Božena Němcová. In front of her grave were two gangly schoolgirls, who looked as their kind had looked forty years ago, and when one said earnestly to the other, "Here lies our Božena," I felt melancholy again.

I thought I would adjust soon, but then I saw an old friend, whom we shall call Vladimír, and realized I could never hope to feel at home again in Prague. The first moment of our reunion was noisily cheerful, an attempt to conceal our insecurity, and slowly I began to see the young Vladimír in the oldish man, especially in his high forehead and shining blue eyes that had wreaked such havoc among the ladies. Vladimír did not stay at the university for long; he did not want to collaborate, like many others, and found shelter in a school of languages, together with other politically unaffiliated people. There he taught for four decades, without being able to publish his scholarly writings. A few years before the Velvet Revolution, the powers that be decided to publish a scholarly study of his. I asked him whether it hadn't been hard for him to watch his colleagues who were active in the party rise to prominence, and he replied quite calmly that the careers of others had never affected him; he added that he was grateful for the chance to teach so many young and inquisitive pupils. For the rest, he had preserved his parents' house and filled it with old furniture, pictures, and books; furthermore, his poems (written in a regional Moravian dialect acceptable to the Party) had long ago found a readership. In a city in which everything still seemed to be up in the air I was facing a happy person. But I also realized I lacked his infinite patience; in the West I had been trained for competition and competitiveness, and I felt vividly that even though we had done similar things, our experiences had separated us once and for all.

My friends in the West envy me my excursions to "magic" or "mysterious" Prague, and the worst thing is that these clichés about the city are already beginning to implant themselves in the minds of my Czech friends. For a long time they were cut off from the outside world, but now they are discovering that they are more likely to be understood if they talk about the golem than if they discuss the metaphysical poet František Halas, known to only a very few Western visitors. Even the learned Milan Kundera seems compelled to refer to the Kabbalah and Rudolf II in his "Central European" essays. With all due respect for Prague's history, two dirty backyards do not add up to anything magic or mystical. In the famous Alchemists' Lane lived honest lackeys, grooms of the chamber; and Rabbi Loew, a great moralist, was not connected with the legend of the golem until two hundred years after his death—because a good rabbi needed a golem and because later Jewish sectarians in Prague insisted on claiming him as one of their own (roughly as Paul Wegener's film portrays him). More mystics lived in medieval monasteries of the central Rhineland than ever did in Prague, and in Safed, in Upper Galilee, there were more Kabbalists in the seventeenth century than ever lived in the shadow of Prague's Old New Synagogue.

I am waiting for someone, at long last, to start speaking of Prague as the city of analytic minds and rationalists: the pragmatic administrator Charles IV (his personal piety notwithstanding); the Hussites and their social theology; Rudolf II, who built a modern observatory for astronomers; the Czech philologists Dobrovský, Gebauer, and Goll, who unmasked historical misrepresentations; the logician Bernard Bolzano; the sociologist T. G. Masaryk (who, to be sure, preserved his evangelical piety); the Prague group of Franz Brentano's disciples; the Prague Linguistic Circle; or the dramatist Václav Havel, who acknowledged having learned much from his brother, a mathematician and linguist.

In the Czech tradition, Prague has always been a "golden" and "motherly" city, and mystical and magical elements did not begin to creep into literature until the nineteenth century, when traveling British and American authors strolled through the old streets of the ghetto with chills running down their spines, followed by Czech and German *fin de siècle* writers, from Karásek of Lvovic to Gustav Meyrink and Paul Leppin, all of whom peopled the city with eccentrics, sex killers, and vampire women. Anyone who doubts my view is invited to go to Žižkov, Smíchov, Nusle, or Vršovice to visit the old industrial sections, where textile workers went on strike as early as 1844, the same year as the Silesian weavers. However, the travel bureaus would not have much use for such excursions.

When I walk through the streets of Prague in the morning when the light is bright, I almost feel at home, but it takes only a moment, a shadow over the pavement, for everything to collapse again and for me to know I do not belong here anymore. I know Prague, and do not know it. It has continued to exist, and so have I, but somewhere else. I am sad that my shoes left no trace on the sidewalk, that my eyes have burned no holes in the stones. Nothing that is not inside me still reminds me of myself, and everything that seems familiar to me I have brought along with me—even the feeling in my fingertips when I am in my old apartment and stroke the wood of the white kitchen cupboard, whose drawers I used to open when I was seven or eight to look for nuts and raisins. I mingle with the living, but the dead and the killed push their way in between—my mother, my mother's mother, and others as well: Paul Kisch, Egon Erwin's brother, who on the eve of his deportation to the death camps greeted me in the full regalia of German fraternity students of the past; Waldtraut W., a German medical student from the northern Bohemian mountains whom I was crazy about, killed in front of the Jesuit church by an aerial mine dropped over Prague by Allied bombers on their return from Dresden; our neighbor the Catholic poet Josef Kostohryz, whom the Communist courts of terror sentenced to a long prison term and who subsequently vegetated and died penniless.

On the express train to Vienna that leaves Prague's main railroad station at 2:50 p.m., I shared a compartment with three American college kids who spent twelve hours in "wonderful Prague" and are on their way to Venice and two Viennese girls who worry whether the train will arrive in time for them to visit their favorite disco. As the train leaves the station, I tell myself that this cannot have been all, but we are already moving past open fields, and I see dilapidated signs at whistle stops bearing the names of places that were once our destination on summer Sunday excursions, and I know that I shall come back again, that I want to try it once more.

BIBLIOGRAPHY
INDEX

Bibliography

There are ancient chronicles of Bohemian events that tell of many Prague developments, but the first person to undertake a historical study from documents and records was the conservative city archivist Václav Vladivoj Tomek, in his *Dějepis města Prahy* (Prague, 1855–1901), 12 vols. This magnificent fragment reaches up to the early seventeenth century, and all later writers and historians remain indebted to their predecessor, who also compiled a city topography, *Základy starého místopisu Pražského* (Prague, 1866–72); he was followed by Josef Teige (ed.), *Základy starého místopisu Pražského: 1437–1602* (Prague, 1910–15), 2 vols. In our century the art historian Oskar Schürer published a widely read volume, *Prag: Kultur/Kunst/Geschichte* (Munich, 1930, 2nd ed. 1934, 3rd ed. 1939), often almost expressionist in tone and particularly attentive to the arts (I prefer the first edition). Other topographies, both old and more modern, include Jaroslav Schaller, *Beschreibung der königlichen Haupt- und Residenzstadt Prag* (1794–97), 4 vols.; Max Julius Schottky, *Prag, wie es war und wie es ist* (Prague, 1830–32), 2 vols.; and František Ekert, *Posvátná místa hlav. král. města Prahy* (1883–84), 2 vols., a treasure trove of information about churches and monasteries. Hugo Rokyta has reedited his topographical description, *Prag* (2nd ed. 1995), rich in literary associations. *Prague: Eleven Centuries of Architecture: A Historical Guide* (Prague, 1992), also available in German and French, was written by a group of learned architects and should please the educated traveler.

Dějiny Prahy (1964), under the general editorship of Josef Janáček, shows all the virtues and problems of official Czechoslovak publications of the early 1960s; the historical chapters are instructive, but later segments, covering events after 1900, change into a chronicle of the dominant party; in the short chronology *Dějiny Prahy v datech* (1988) similar reductions can be observed. Other interesting volumes on Prague include, e.g., Valentin Count Lützow, *The Story of Prague* (London, 1902), and, after World War II and the "Prague Spring" of 1968, Hans Tramer, *Prague: City of Three People* (New York, 1956), rightly stressing the Jewish heritage; Karel Krejčí, *Praha legend a skutečností* (Prague, 1981); Joseph Wechsberg, *Prague: The Mystical City* (New York, 1971); and, of course, Angelo Maria Ripellino, *Praga Magica* (Turin, 1973), which I have discussed in the text. The first Prague tourist guide was written by none other than František Palacký for the noble guests expected to attend the coronation of Ferdinand V (1836). It was edited by Amadeo Molnár and republished, with illustrations, as *Skizze einer Geschichte von Prag* (1983). Excellent for the siesta, Paul Wilson (ed.), *Prague: A Traveller's Literary Companion* (San Francisco, 1995), includes a few classical tales and notable contributions by our contemporaries Ivan Diviš, Ota Pavel, Josef Škvorecký, and Ivan Klíma.

Bibliography

HISTORIES, HANDBOOKS, ANTHOLOGIES

Karl Bosl (ed.), *Handbuch der Geschichte der böhmischen Länder* (Stuttgart, 1966–70), 4 vols.

Ingeborg Fiala-Fürst, *Prag: Ein jüdisches Städtebild* (Frankfurt, 1992), an anthology of Prague Jewish authors through the ages.

Jörg K. Hoensch, *Geschichte Böhmens* (Munich, 1987), balanced, with an excellent bibliography.

Wilma Iggers, *Die Juden in Böhmen und Mähren: Ein historisches Lesebuch* (Munich, 1986).

Zdeněk Kalista, *Stručné dějiny československé* (Prague, 1992), a voice long silenced for political reasons.

Antonín Měštan, *Geschichte der tschechischen Literatur im 19. und 20. Jahrhundert* (Vienna and Cologne, 1984) – *Bausteine zur Geschichte der Literatur bei den Slawen*, vol. 20.

Josef Mühlberger, *Geschichte der deutschen Literatur in Böhmen 1900–1939* (Munich, 1981).

Jan Mukařovský (ed. in chief), *Dějiny české literatury* (Prague, 1959–61), 3 vols., comprehensive and official.

František Palacký, *Dějiny národu českého* (Prague, 5th ed. 1965), 5 vols. The quintessential Czech history, and a literary masterpiece that has provided all the following generations with a guiding myth of national self-interpretation.

Tomáš Pěkný, *Historie židů Čechách a na Moravě* (Prague, 1993), the first comprehensive history in a long time of the Prague and Bohemian/Moravian Jewish communities.

Friedrich Prinz, *Deutsche Geschichte im Osten Europas: Böhmen und Mähren* (Berlin, 1994).

Robert William Seton-Watson, *A History of Czechs and Slovaks* (Hamden, Conn., 2nd ed. 1965).

Samuel Harrison Thompson, *Czechoslovakia in European History* (Hamden, Conn., 1965).

Rudolf Wolkan, *Geschichte der deutschen Literatur in Böhmen und in den Sudetenländern* (Augsburg, 1925).

My favorite discussions of national problems include Eva Hahnová, *Sudetoněmecký problem: Obtížné loučení s minulostí* (Prague, 1996); Jan Křen, *Konfliktní Společenství: Češi a Němci 1780–1918* (Prague, 2nd ed. 1990); Podiven (- Milan Otáhal, Petr Pithart, and Petr Príhoda), *Češi v dějinách nové doby* (Prague, n.d.); Emanuel Rádl, *Válka Čechů s Němci* (Prague, 1928), German translation 1928; Christian Willars, *Die böhmische Zitadelle* (Munich, 1965); Ferdinand Seibt, *Deutschland und die Tschechen* (Munich, 2nd ed. 1995); and Elizabeth Wiskemann, *Czechs and Germans* (Oxford, 1938, 2nd ed., 1967).

1. LIBUSSA, OR VERSIONS OF ORIGIN

What the Schoolchildren Learn

Alois Jirásek's novels were part of the socialist realist canon just a few years ago and available in many translations, e.g., *Böhmens alte Sagen*, trans. by Hans Gaertner (Prague, 1957, 2nd ed. 1975). More recently, *Old Czech Legends*, trans. by Marie K. Holeček (London, 1972), with a useful introduction. Important general information in Jaroslava Janáčková, *Alois Jirásek* (Prague, 1987), especially on the legends, pp. 237–43.

What Archaeologists and Historians Believe

With rare exceptions, archaeological literature about Prague has been published in Czech or German (occasionally with summaries in English or Russian).

Ivan Borkovský, *Levý Hradec* (Prague, 1965), and *Pražský Hrad* (Prague, 1969), both authoritative, with illustrations and German summary.

Francis Dvorník, *The Making of Central and Eastern Europe* (Gulf Breeze, Fla., 1974), and *The Slavs: Their Early History and Civilization* (Boston, 1956), are magisterial exceptions.

Jan Filip, *Pravěké Československo* (Prague, 1948), an older Czech standard text.

Ladislav Hrdlička, "Nástin vývoje reliéfu historického jádra Prahy ve středověku," *Archaeologica Pragensia*, 5 (1984), 197–209.

Jiří Neústupný, *Czechoslovakia Before the Slavs* (London, 1961).

Luboš Pok, *Fraganeo* (Prague, 1990), challenging.

Hellmut Preidel, *Die Anfänge der slawischen Besiedlung Böhmens und Mährens* (Gräfelfing, 1954–57), 2 vols., is the standard German text.

Reinhold Trautmann, *Die slawischen Völker und ihre Sprachen* (Göttingen, 1947), pp. 21–26, still highly instructive.

Rudolf Turek, *Čechy na úsvitě dějin* (Prague, 1963), German edition: *Böhmen im Morgengrauen der Geschichte* (Wiesbaden, 1974).

The Fortunes of Libussa

Bertold Bretholz (ed.), *Cosmae Pragensis Chronaca Bohemorum*, (Berlin, 1923) – *Monumenta Germaniae Historica, Scriptores rerum Germanicarum*, N.S., t. II.

Commentaries on Cosmas: Dušan Třeštík, *Kosmas* (Prague, 1966), and Josef Hemmerle, "Cosmas von Prag," in *Lebensbilder zur Geschichte der böhmischen Länder*, 4 (Munich, 1981), 23–48.

František Graus, *Lebendige Vergangenheit: Überlieferung im Mittelalter und in den Vorstellungen vom Mittelalter* (Cologne and Vienna, 1985).

Thomas M. Greene, *Besieging the Castle of the Ladies*, Medieval and Renaissance Texts and Studies (Binghamton and New York, 1995), Occasional Papers, No. 4.

Vladimír Karbusický, *Anfänge der historischen Überlieferung in Böhmen* (Cologne and Vienna, 1980). The new Czech edition, 1995, is still rejected by the old establishment and its young allies.

Plays

Clemens Brentano, "Die Gründung Prags," in *Sämtliche Werke und Briefe*, 14 (Stuttgart, 1980), 501–82, up-to-date critical edition of the text, including important autobiographical comments.

Franz Grillparzer, "Libussa," in *Sämtliche Werke*, 2 (Munich, 1961), 257–333, excellent edition, with notes.

2. OTAKAR'S PRAGUE, 880–1278

From Trading Post to Royal Residence

Zdeněk Fiala, *Přemyslovské Čechy: 995–1310* (Prague, 1975). Also "Die Anfänge Prags. Eine Quellenanalyse zur Ortsterminologie bis zum Jahre 1235," in *Giessener Abhandlungen zur Agrar- und Wirtschaftsforschung des europäischen Ostens*, vol. 40 (Wiesbaden, 1967), fortunately with an extensive English summary.

František Hoffmann, *Česká města ve středověku* (Prague, 1992), especially pp. 14–61.

Dušan Třeštik, *Počátky Přemyslovců* (Prague, 1981).

The Rise of a King

František Graus, "Přemysl Ottokar II. Sein Ruhm und sein Nachleben," in *Mitteilungen des Instituts für Österreichische Geschichte*, 79 (1991), 57–110.

Jörg K. Hoensch, *Přemysl Otakar von Böhmen* (Graz, 1989), judicious and readable.

Jiři Kuthan, *Přemysl Otakar II* (Prague, 1993), gives particular attention to architecture and the arts.

Václav Novotný, *Rozmach české moci za Přemysla Otakara. 1253–1271 / České dějiny* 1/4 (Prague, 1937), essential and still valuable.

Friedrich Prinz, *Böhmen im mittelalterlichen Europa* (Munich, 1963), pp. 7–22.

Josef Žemlička, *Století posledních Přemyslovců* (Prague, 1986).

Franz Grillparzer, "König Ottokars Glück und Ende," in *Sämtliche Werke*, 1 (Munich, 1961), 996–1083.

Bibliography

The Early Jewish Community and the Prague Tosafists

Bohumil Bondy and František Dvorský (eds.), *K historii židů v Čechách, na Moravě a ve Slezku: 906–1620* (Prague, 1906), early anthology of historical documents, including a full version of the *Statuta Judaeorum.*

Wilfried Brosche, "Das Ghetto von Prag," in Ferdinand Seibt (ed.), *Die Juden in den böhmischen Ländern* (Munich, 1983), pp. 87–122, ingenious reconstruction, topographically and sociologically.

H. Gross, "R. Isaak ben Mose Or Zarua aus Wien," in *Monatsschrift für die Geschichte und Wissenschaft vom Judentum*, 20 (1871), 241–64.

Peter Hilsch, "Die Juden in Böhmen und Mähren im Mittelalter," in Ferdinand Seibt (ed.), *Die Juden in den böhmischen Ländern* (Munich, 1983), pp. 13–26.

Roman Jakobson, "Řeč a písemnictví českých židů v době přemyslovské," in Ladislav Matějka (ed.), *Rok* (New York, 1957), pp. 47–58, provocative in the best sense.

Jiřina Šedinová, "Alttschechische Glossen in mittelalterlichen hebräischen Schriften und die ältesten Denkmäler der tschechischen Literatur," in *Judaica Bohemiae*, 17/2 (1981), 73–89.

H. Tykoczinsky, "Lebenszeit und Heimat des Isaaks Or Zarua," in *Monatsschrift für die Geschichte und Wissenschaft vom Judentum*, 55 (1911), 478–500.

Hana Volavková, *Zmizelá Praha* (Prague, 1947), vol. 3: *Židovské město pražské*, an important monograph.

J. Wellesz, "Isaak ben Mose Or Zarua," in *Monatsschrift für die Geschichte und Wissenschaft vom Judentum*, 48 (1904), 129–44, 209–13, 361–71, 440–56, 710–12.

Czech Saints, Italian Rhetoricians, and German Poets

Anežka Merhautová and Karel Stejskal, *Das St. Georgs-Stift auf der Prager Burg* (Prague, 1991).

Josef (Cardinal) Beran, *Blahoslavená Anežka česká* (Rome, 1974), is a biography based on full historical research.

Alfonso Marini and Paola Ungarelli, *Agnese di Boemia* (Rome, 1991).

Jaroslav Polc, *Agnes von Böhmen: 1211–1283* (Munich, 1989).

Kajetán Vyskočil, *Legenda Blahoslavené Anežky a čtyři listy sv. Kláře* (Prague, 1982) is the original text of the legend and four letters to Clara, including philogical commentary.

Patrizia Maria Costa, *Guglielma "l'heretica" di Chiaravalle* (Milan, 1985).

Ludovica Muraro, *Guglielma e Maifreda. Storia di un'eresia femminista* (Milan, 1985), ignored by Czech scholars and feminists.

S. C. Wessley, "The Thirteenth-Century Guglielmites," in Derek Baker (ed.), *Medieval Women* (Oxford, 1978), pp. 289–303.

J. Novák, "Henricus Italicus und Henricus de Isernia," in *Mitteilungen des Instituts für Österreichische Geschichte*, 20 (1899), 253–75.

Hans Joachim Bahr, *Literatur und Machlegitimation. Studien zur Funktion der deutschsprachigen Dichtung am böhmischen Königshof des 13. Jahrhunderts* (Munich, 1987), a pioneering analysis.

Winfried Baumann, *Die Literatur des Mittelalters in Böhmen. Deutsch-lateinisch-tschechische Literatur vom 10. bis zum 15. Jahrhundert* (Munich and Vienna, 1978).

Joachim Bumke, *Mäzene im Mittelalter. Die Gönner und Auftraggeber der höfischen Literatur in Deutschland* (Munich, 1979).

3. THE CAROLINIAN MOMENT

Burghers, Markets, and Cobbled Streets

František Graus, *Chudina městská v době předhusitské* (Prague, 1949), appropriately ideological, according to date of publication.

Jaroslav Mezník, *Praha před husitskou revolucí* (Prague, 1990), instructive and substantial, German summary.

———, "Der ökonomische Charakter Prags im 14. Jahrhundert," in *Historica*, 17 (1969), 5–30.

Prince Václav or, Rather, Charles

Bede Jarrett, *The Emperor Charles IV* (London, 1935), Catholic viewpoint, readable.

Zdeněk Kalista, *Karel IV—jeho duchovní tvář* (Prague, 1971), the emperor's spiritual profile by a historian long imprisoned by the Stalinist regime.

František Kavka, *Vláda Karla IV za jeho císařství: 1346–1378* (Prague, 1993–95), 2 vols., diplomatic history.

Ferdinand Seibt, *Karl IV: Ein Kaiser in Europa* (Munich, 1978), judicious recent German standard biography.

Jiři Spěváček, *Karel IV—život a dílo* (Prague, 1980), magisterial view, in fulfillment of State Research Plan VIII-7-214, as the writer says.

Heinz Stroob, *Kaiser Karl IV und seine Zeit* (Graz, 1990), German counterpart to Kavka (above).

Josef Šusta, *Karel IV* (Prague, 1946–48), 2 vols., essential reading.

Gerald Groveland Walsh, *The Emperor Charles IV* (Oxford, 1924).

Emil Werunsky, *Geschichte Karls IV und seiner Zeit* (Innsbruck, 1892; recent reprint, New York, 1961), 3 vols.

King Charles, Father of His Motherland/The Founding of the New Town/Charles Establishes His University

Zdeněk Bouše and Josef Myslivec, "Sakrální prostory na Karlštejně," in *Uměni*, 19 (1971), 280–93.

Antonín Matějček and Jaroslav Pěšina, *Czech Gothic Painting: 1350–1450* (Prague, 1950).

Karl Maria Swoboda (ed.), *Gotik in Böhmen* (Munich, 1969), extensively reviewed by Jaroslav Pěšina and four other Czech experts, in *Umění*, 19 (1971), 358–401.

Karel Stejskal, *L'emperor Charles IV: L'art en Europe en XIVe siècle* (Paris, 1980).

Vilém Lorenc, *Das Prag Karls IV: Die Prager Neustadt* (Stuttgart, 1982), German edition of Czech version (Prague, 1973), essential.

Emanuel Poche (ed.), *Praha středověká* (Prague, 1983).

Renate Dix, *Die Frühzeit der Prager Universität* (Diss., Bonn, 1988).

Jan Havránek and Michal Svatoš, "University Colleges at Prague from the 14th to the 18th Century," in *I collegi universitari in Europa tra il XIV e il XVIII secolo* (Milan, 1991), pp. 143–54.

Peter Moraw, "Die Universität Prag im Mittelalter," in *Die Universität zu Prag* (Munich, 1986), pp. 10–134.

V. V. Tomek, *Geschichte der Prager Universität* (Prague, 1849), also in Czech.

Otakar Odložilík, *Karlova Universita: 1348–1948* (Prague, 1948), completed before the author left the country.

Michal Svatoš (ed.), *Dějiny Univerzity Karlovy: 1347/8–1622* (Prague, 1995), most recent and representative publication, especially important contributions by František Šmahel and Jaroslav Kadlec.

Bibliography

The King's Kitchen Cabinet and the Italian Connection

C. C. Bayley, "Petrarch, Charles IV, and the 'Renovatio Imperi,' " *Speculum*, 17 (1942), 323–41.

František Michálek Bartoš, "Dantova monarchie, Cola di Rienzo, Petrarka, a počátky reformace u nás," *Věstník společnosti náuk*, 5 (Prague, 1951), 23.

Thomas G. Bergin, *Petrarch* (New York, 1970), essential.

Heinrich Friedjung, *Kaiser Karl und sein Anteil am geistigen Leben seiner Zeit* (Vienna, 1876), early and productive study.

Joseph Klapper, *Johann von Neumarkt: Bischof und Hofkanzler* (Leipzig, 1964) – *Erfurter Theologische Studien*, vol. 17.

Paul Piur (ed.), *Briefwechsel des Cola di Rienzo* (Berlin, 1912–28), 5 vols., grand undertaking, Konrad Burdach collaborating.

———, *Cola di Rienzo* (Vienna, 1931).

——— (ed.), *Petrarcas Briefwechsel mit deutschen Zeitgenossen* (Berlin, 1933), under the general editorship of Konrad Burdach.

Ugo Reale, *Cola di Rienzo* (Rome, 1991).

Carlo Salinari, *Francesco Petrarca* (Naples, 1969).

Ernst Schwarz, "Johann von Neumarkt," in *Lebensbilder aus den böhmischen Ländern*, ed. by Karl Bos (Munich, 1974), pp. 27–48, important article by older philologist.

Ferdinand Tadra, *Kulturní, styky Čech s cizinou až do válek husitský ch* (Prague, 1897).

Samuel Harrison Thomson, "Learning at the Court of Charles IV," *Speculum*, 25 (1950), 1–20, excellent panorama.

Charles Builds His Myth

Anton Blaschka, *Die St. Wenzelslegende Kaiser Karls IV. Einleitung, Text, Kommentar* (Prague, 1934).

———, *Kaiser Karls Jugendleben und die St. Wenzelslegende* (Weimar, 1956).

Jakub Pavel, *Životopis Karla IV* (Prague, 1970), complements Blaschka.

Otakar Odložilík, "The Terenzo Dream of Charles IV. A Critical Examination of the Available Sources," in *Orbis Mediaevalis*, Festgabe für Anton Blaschka (Weimar 1970), pp. 163–73.

New Writing in Carolinian Prague

Guillaume de Machault, *The Judgement of the King of Bohemia*, ed. and trans. by R. Barton Palmer (New York, 1984).

Heinrich von Mügeln, *Der Meide Kranz*, ed. by W. Jahr (Leipzig, 1908).

Antonin Hrubý, *Der "Ackermann" und seine Vorlage* (Munich, 1971).

Hynek Hrubý and František Šimek (eds.), *Tkadleček* (Prague, 1923).

Günther Jungblut (ed.), *Der Ackermann aus Böhmen des Johann von Tepl* (Heidelberg, 1969).

Ernst Schwarz, *Der Ackermann aus Böhmen des Johann von Tepl und seine Zeit* (Darmstadt, 1968) – Wege der Forschung, vol. 143.

Josef Hrabák (ed.), *Staročeské satiry* (Prague, 1962), pp. 115–28.

"Mastičkár," in Bohuslav Havránek and Josef Hrabák (eds.), *Výbor z české literatury od počátků po dobu Husovu* (Prague, 1957), pp. 248–61.

"Podkoní a žák," in *Výbor*, pp. 335–47.

Jan Vilikovský (ed.), *Legenda o Svaté Kateřině* (Prague, 1946).

Cracks in the Facade

Chronicon Aulae Regiae [Peter of Zittau], in J. Emler (ed.), *Fontes rerum Bohemicarum* (Prague, 1884), vol. 5.

František Michálek Bartoš, "Waldhauser a ohlas jeho díla u nás," in *Knihy a zápasy* (Prague, 1948), pp. 40–44.

Vilém Herold and Milan Mráz, "Jan Milič z Kroměříže a husitské revoluční myšlení," in *Filosofický časopis*, 22 (1974), 765–85, German version in *Mediaevalia Philosophica Polonorum*, 21 (1975), 27–52.

Otakar Odložilík, "Vláda Václava IV. Počátky opravného hnutí," in *Československá vlastivěda*, 4 (Prague, 1922), 114–62.

František Palacký, *Die Vorläufer des Hussitenthums in Böhmen* (Prague, 2nd ed. 1869).

Karl Richter, "Konrad Waldhauser," in Ferdinand Seibt (ed.), *Lebensbilder zur Geschichte der böhmischen Länder*, 3 (Munich, 1978), 159–74.

Samuel Harrison Thomson, "Prehussite Heresy in Bohemia," in *English Historical Review*, 48 (1932), 23–42.

The Carolinian Jewish Town and the Massacre of 1389

Ruth Bork, "Zur Politik der Zentralgewalt gegenüber den Juden im Kampf Ludwigs des Bayern um das Reichsrecht und Karls IV um die Durchsetzung des Königtums," in Annamaria Engel (ed.), *Karl IV: Politik und Ideologie* (Weimar, 1982), pp. 30–73, an East German scholar presenting tough evidence of the king's anti-Semitic policies in the Reich, possibly, an answer to Eckert (1978).

Willehad Paul Eckert, "Die Juden im Zeitalter Karls IV," in Ferdinand Seibt (ed.), *Kaiser Karl IV: Staatsmann und Mäzen* (Munich, 1978), tries to assuage our doubts.

František Graus, *Pest, Geissler, Judenmorde: das 14. Jahrhundert als Krisenzeit* (Göttingen, 1987).

Paul Lehmann, *Die Parodie im Mittelalter* (Stuttgart, 2nd ed. 1963), includes analysis of Prague Latin satire about the 1389 pogrom.

David Podiebrad, *Althertümer der Prager Judenstadt*, Neu bearbeitet von Benedikt Foges (Prague, 2nd ed. 1862), rare, presents moving translation of Rabbi Avigdor's elegy.

4. THE HUSSITE REVOLUTION, 1415–22

The King and the Vicar-General

Johanna von Herzogenberg and F. Matsche, *Johannes von Nepomuk* (Passau, 1971), important exhibition catalogue.

Wilhelm Hanisch, "Wenzel IV," in Ferdinand Seibt (ed.), *Lebensbilder zur Geschichte der böhmischen Länder* 3 (Munich, 1978), 251–79.

Jiří Spěváček, *Václav IV: 1361–1419* (Prague, 1986), important and learned synthesis, excellent bibliography.

František Stejskal, *Zbynek Zajíc z Hasenberka* (Prague, 1914).

Vít Vlnas, *Jan Nepomucký: Česká legenda* (Prague, 1993), a splendid revisionist analysis.

Ruben Ernest Weltsch, *Archbishop John of Jenstein: Papalism, Humanism, and Reform in Pre-Hussite Prague* (The Hague, 1968).

Eduard Winter, *Frühhumanismus* (Berlin, 1964), thoughtful and balanced.

The Advance of the Religious Reformers

Reginald Robert Betts, "The Regulae Veteris et Novi Testamenti of Matěj of Janov," *Journal of Theological Studies*, 22 (1931), 334–51.

Jan Gebauer, *O životě a spisích Tomáše ze Štítného* (Prague, 1923), especially introduction.

Howard Kaminsky, *A History of the Hussite Revolution* (Berkeley and Los Angeles, 1967), on Milič, pp. 5–23.

Miloslav Kaňák, *Milič z Kroměříže* (Prague, 1975).

Kamil Krofta, "Bohemia in the 14th Century," in *Cambridge Medieval History*, 7 (1932), 155–82.

Alois Kubíček, *Betlemská kaple* (Prague, 1962).

Vlastimil Kybal, *M. Matěj z Janova* (Prague, 1926), especially chs. 4 and 5.

Otakar Odložilík, "The Chapel of Bethlehem in Prague. Remarks on Its Founding Chapter," in *Studien zur älteren Geschichte Osteuropas*, ed. by G. Stökl, 1 (Graz, 1956), 125–41.

Jan Hus at Bethlehem and at Constance

František Michálek Bartoš, *Čechy v době Husově: 1378–1415* (Prague, 1947).

Remigius Bäumer, *Das Konstanzer Konzil* (Darmstadt, 1977) – Wege der Forschung, vol. 415.

Howard Kaminsky, *A History of the Hussite Revolution* (Berkeley and Los Angeles, 1967), especially pp. 5–96, excellent history of ideas.

Amadeo Molnár, *Jan Hus: témoin de la vérité* (Paris and Lausanne, 1978).

Fontes rerum Bohemicarum (Prague, 1932), vol. 8 (includes Petr of Mladenovice, "Relatio de Magistro Johanne Hus").

Václav Novotný and V. Kybal, *M. Jan Hus: život o učení* (Prague, 1919–31), 5 vols., fundamental study.

Ferdinand Seibt, *Hussitica: Zur Struktur einer Revolution* (Cologne and Graz, 1965).

Matthew Spinka, *John Hus and the Czech Reform* (Chicago, 1941).

———, *John Hus' Concept of the Church* (Princeton, 1966).

———, *John Hus at the Council of Constance* (New York, 1965); all three are eminently reliable and thoughtful.

Paul de Vooght, *L'hérésie de Jean Hus* (Louvain, 1960), a Catholic attempt at legal rehabilitation.

Ernst Werner, *Jan Hus* (Cologne, Graz, and Weimar, 1991).

Melchior Vischer, *Jan Hus: Sein Leben und seine Zeit* (Frankfurt, 1940, 2nd ed. 1958), first edition destroyed by Nazi authorities.

Eva Kantůrková, *Jan Hus* (Prague, 1991), interprets Hus against the neo-Stalinist "normalization" of the 1970s and 1980s, admirable.

The Decree of Kutná Hora

Reginald Robert Betts, "Jeroným of Prague," *University of Birmingham Historical Journal*, 1 (1947), 51–91.

Dekret kutnohorský. Prednášky a stati V. Novotného, K. Krofty, J. Šusty a G. Friedricha (Prague, 1909), and the continued discussion in *Dekret kutnohorský a jeho místo v dějinách* (Prague, 1959) – *Acta Universitatis. Phil. e hist.*, 2, official point of view.

Vilém Herold, *Pražská univerzita a Wyclif* (Prague, 1985).

Howard Kaminsky, "The University of Prague in the Hussite Revolution and the Role of the Masters," in *University and Politics* (Baltimore and London, 1972), pp. 79–106.

Jiří Kejr, *Husitský právník Jan z Jesenice* (Prague, 1965).

Ernst Lemberg, *Nationalismus* (Reinbek bei Hamburg, 1964), important study.

Ferdinand Seibt, "Jan Hus und der Abzug der deutschen Studenten aus Prag," in *Hussitenstudien* (Munich, 1987), pp. 1–5.

František Šmahel, *Idea národa v husitských Čechách* (České Budějovice, 1971), excellent analysis from the sources.

Milan Svatoš (ed.), *Dějiny univerzity Karlovy* (Prague, 1995), especially pp. 87–100 (by editor), and ch. 2 by František Šmahel.

John Adam Robson, *Wyclif and the Oxford Schools* (Cambridge, 1966).

Herbert Brook Workman, *John Wyclif* (Oxford, 1926), 2 vols.

Prague Attracts the European Dissidents/The Revolt of the Prague Radicals/The Crusaders Arrive/The Battles for Prague

František Michálek Bartoš, "Žižka a pikarti," *Kalich*, 8 (1924), 97–108.

———, *Literární činnost M. Petra Payna* (Prague, 1928).

Howard Kaminsky, *Hussite Revolution*, especially ch. 4.

——— et al., *Master Nicholas of Dresden: The Old Color and the New* (Philadelphia, 1965) – *Transactions of the American Philosophical Society*, N.S., vol. 55, part 1.

Horst Köpfstein, "Über den deutschen Hussiten Friedrich Reiser," *Zeitschrift für Geschichtswissenschaft*, 7 (1959), 1068–82.

———, "Über die Teilnahme der Deutschen an der hussitischen revolutionären Bewegung," *Zeitschrift für Geschichtswissenschaft*, 11 (1963), 116–45.

Amadeo Molnár, *Valdenští* (Prague, 1991), important study.

Božena Auštecká, *Jan Želivský jako politik* (Prague, 1925).

Wilhelm Baum, *Kaiser Sigismund* (Graz, 1993).

Frederick G. Heymann, *John Žižka and the Hussite Revolution* (Princeton, 1955), an essential study of the wars.

Howard Kaminsky, *Hussite Revolution*, chs. 7 and 8, and pp. 136–40 (the Battle of Vitkov Hill), pp. 175–79 (the Battle of the Vyšehrad).

Howard Kaminsky, "The Prague Insurrection of 30 July 1419," *Medievalia et Humanistica*, 17 (1966), pp. 106–26.

John Martin Klaasen, *The Nobility and the Making of the Hussite Revolution* (Boulder, Colo., 1978).

Amadeo Molnár, "Želivský, prédicateur de la révolution," *Communio Viatorum* (1959), pp. 324–34.

Josef Pekař, *Žižka a jeho doba* (Prague, 1927–33), 4 vols., by a master of Czech historiography.

František Šmahel, *Husitská revoluce* (Prague, 1993–95), 4 vols., a recent classic. Unfortunately, for financial reasons, published only in a limited number of copies by the Czech Academy.

Karel Vladislav Zapa, *Vypsání husitské války* (Prague, 2nd ed. 1893), popular, battle-by-battle narrative.

Hussites and Jews

František Michálek Bartoš, "Židé v Čechách v době Husově," in *Kalendár česko-židovský*, 35 (Prague, 1915–16), 154–63.

Ruth Kestenberg-Gladstein, "Hussiten und Judentum," *Jahrbücher der Gesellschaft für Geschichte der Juden in der tschechoslowakischen Republik*, 8 (1936), 1–25, essential.

Tomáš Pěkný, *Dějiny Židů v Čechách a na Moravě* (Prague, 1993), pp. 38–42.

Maria Tischler, "Böhmische Judengemeinden 1340–1519," in Ferdinand Seibt (ed.), *Die Juden in den böhmischen Ländern* (Munich, 1938), pp. 73–86.

Valentin Urfus, *Právo, úvěr, a lichva v minulosti* (Brno, 1975).

Laurentius (Vavřinec) of Březová, *Chronicon* (Hussite Chronicle), in the original Latin, together with a Czech translation, in *Fontes rerum Bohemicarum* (Prague, 1898), vol. 5.

5. RUDOLF II AND THE REVOLT OF 1618

Praga Mystica?

Jan Bechyňka, *Praga Mystica*, ed. by Amadeo Molnár (Prague, 1993), *Acta Reformationem Bohemican Illustrantia*, III.

After the Polish Kings, the Hapsburgs Again

Viktor Bibl, *Maximilian II, der rätselhafte Kaiser* (Vienna, 1929).

Peter Brock, *The Political and Social Doctrines of the Unity of Czech Brethren in the Fifteenth and Early Sixteenth Centuries* (The Hague, 1957).

Ernest Denis, *Fin de l'indépendance bohème* (Paris, 1930), a famous study.

Kenneth Dillon, *King and Estates in the Bohemian Lands* (Brussels, 1976).

Winfried Eberhard, *Monarchie und Widerstand: Zur ständischen Oppositionsbildung im Herrschaftssystem Ferdinands I in Böhmen* (Munich, 1985), an important analysis.

Bibliography

Friedrich Edelmayer and Alfred Kotrba, *Kaiser Maximilian II: Kultur und Politik im 16. Jahrhundert* (Munich, 1972) – *Wiener Beiträge zur Geschichte der Neuzeit*, vol. 19, new researches by D. J. Jansen on Jacopo Strada, pp. 182–202.

Robert John Weston Evans, *The Making of the Habsburg Monarchy 1550–1700: An Interpretation* (Oxford, 1979), learned and balanced.

Anton Gindely, *Geschichte der böhmischen Brüder* (Prague, 1868), 2 vols.

Josef Janáček, *České dějiny doby předbělohorské: 1526–1547* (Prague, 1968), 2 vols., almost encyclopedic.

Thomas DaCosta Kaufmann, *Court, Cloister and City: The Art and Culture of Central Europe: 1450–1800* (Chicago, 1995), instructive and truly cosmopolitan.

Pavel Preiss, *Italští umělci v Praze* (Prague, 1986), here especially ch. 1.

Rudolf Říčan, *Die böhmischen Brüder: Ihr Ursprung und ihre Geschichte* (Berlin, 1961), shortened version of Czech study (Prague, 1957).

Helmut Teufel, "Juden im Ständestaat: 1526–1620," in Ferdinand Seibt (ed.), *Die Juden in den böhmischen Ländern* (Munich, 1938), pp. 57–72.

Rudolf II

Bohdan Chudoba, *Spain and the Empire* (Chicago, 2nd ed. 1969).

Robert John Weston Evans, *Rudolf II and His World: A Study in Intellectual History* (Oxford, 2nd ed. 1982), essential and enormously learned.

Anton Gindely, *Rudolf II und seine Zeit* (Prague, 1862–65), 2 vols., by the tutor of crown prince Rudolf, the suicide of Mayerling.

Josef Janáček, *Pád Rudolfa II* (Prague, 1973).

Gertrude von Schwarzenfeld, *Rudolf II, der saturnische Kaiser* (Munich, 1961), a popular biography.

Karl Vocelka, *Rudolf II und seine Zeit* (Vienna and Cologne, 1985), instructive cultural history.

Franz Grillparzer, *Ein Bruderzwist in Habsburg. Ein Trauerspiel in fünf Aufzügen*, in *Sämtliche Werke*, 2 (Munich, 1961), 345–448, an excellent edition with full commentary.

Thomas DaCosta Kaufmann, *The School of Prague: Painting at the Court of Rudolf II* (Chicago, 1988), inclusive and magisterial, with useful bibliography.

Eliška Fučíková, "The Collections of Rudolf II at Prague: Cabinet of Curiosities or Scientific Museum?" in Oliver Impey and Arthur MacGregor (eds.), *The Origin of Museums* (Oxford, 1985), pp. 47–53.

Jaromir Neumann, *Obrazárna pražského hradu* (Prague, 1964).

Prag um 1600: Kunst und Kultur am Hofe Rudolf II, catalogue of exhibition presented by Kulturstiftung Ruhr (Villa Hügel), (Freren, 1988), with distinguished contributions by R. J. W. Evans, Erich Trunz, Zdeněk Horský, Ivan Muchka, and others.

Pavel Preiss, *Giuseppe Arcimboldi* (Praha, 1947).

Elisabeth Schleicher, *Die Kunst- und Wunderkammern der Habsburger* (Vienna, 1979).

Josef Svátek, "Poslední dnové rudolfínských sbírek v Praze" and "Strádové z Rosenbergu," in *Obrazy z kulturních dějin českých* (Prague, 1891), pp. 49–67 and 103–31, anecdotal and informative.

Scientists and Alchemists

Carola Baumgardt, *Johann Kepler: Life and Letters* (New York, 1951), readable and informative.

Max Caspar, *Kepler* (London and New York, 1959), standard work.

John Allyne Gade, *The Life and Times of Tycho Brahe* (Princeton, 1947), useful and entertaining.

Josef von Hasner, *Tycho Brahe und Johannes Kepler in Prag* (Prague, 1872).

Zdeněk Horský, *Kepler v Praze* (Prague, 1980), distinguished expert on Prague sciences.

Arthur Koestler, *The Watershed: A Biography of Johann Kepler* (New York, 1960), critical analysis.

Franz Pick, *Johannes Jessenius de Magna Jessen* (Leipzig, 1926), fundamental study.

Josef V. Polišenský, *Jan Jesenský-Jessenius* (Prague, 1965).

Bibliography

Richard Deacon, *John Dee, Scientist, Geographer, Astrologer and Secret Agent of Elizabeth I* (London, 1968).

John Dee, *Private Diary*, ed. by J. O. Halliwell (London, 1842).

Peter J. French, *John Dee: The World of an Elizabethan Magus* (London, 1972), instructive biography.

Jiljí V. Jahn, *Alchemie v Čechách* (Prague, 1993), synopsis.

Donald C. Laycock, *The Complete Enochian Dictionary: A Dictionary of the Angelic Language as Revealed to Dr. John Dee and Edward Kelley* (New York, 1978), for the connoisseur.

Josef Svátek, "Alchemie v Čechách za doby Rudolfovy," in *Obrazy z kulturních dějin českých* (Prague, 1891), pp. 39–75.

The "Golden Age" of Prague's Jewish Community

Isaac Eisenstein-Barzilay, *Yoseph Shlomo Delmedigo, Yashar of Candia* (Leiden, 1974).

Isidore Fishman, *The History of Jewish Education in Central Europe from the End of the Sixteenth Century to the Eighteenth Century* (London, 1944).

Arnold L. Goldsmith, *The Golem Remembered, 1909–1980* (Detroit, 1981), variations of the legend analyzed, ancient and modern.

Nathan Grün, *Der hohe Rabbi Loew und sein Sagenkreis* (Prague, 1855).

Moshe Idel, *Kabbalah: New Perspectives* (New Haven, 1988), in which Prague does not figure prominently.

Otto Muneles (ed.), *The Prague Ghetto in the Renaissance Period* (Prague, 1965), fundamental research instrument.

André Neher, *Le puits de l'éxil: la théologie dialectique du Maharal de Prague* (Paris, 1966).

———, *Jewish Thought and the Scientific Revolution of the Sixteenth Century: David Gans and His Times* (Oxford, 1986); two pathbreaking studies.

———, *Faust and the Maharal de Prague: Le myth et le réel* (Paris, 1987), unfortunately more myth than *réel*.

Gershom Scholem, *Major Trends in Jewish Mysticism* (New York, 1941), a classical study.

———, *Kabbalah* (New York, 1974), from the sources.

———, "Prague and Rehovot. A Tale of Two Golems," in *Commentary*, 41 (1966), 62–65, a timely reminder of the golem and cybernetics.

Byron L. Sherwin, *Mystical Theology and Social Dissent: The Life and Work of Judah Loew of Prague* (Rutherford, N.J., 1982), sober and well-written analysis.

Sippurim: Geschichten aus dem alten Prag, ed. by Peter Demetz (Frankfurt, 1994) – Insel Taschenbuch 1519; rationalist stories about Rabbi Loew, pp. 44–47 and 100–10.

Picaresque Prague

Journal de ma vie. Memoirs du Maréchal de Bassompierre (première édition, conforme au manuscrit original publiée avec fragments inédits), M. de Chantérac (ed.), (Paris, 1870), 4 vols., here particularly vol. 1, pp. 132–44.

"Hermann Christoph Graf von Russwurm," in *Allgemeine deutsche Biographie*, 30 (Berlin, 2nd ed. 1970), 12–19.

Pierre Bergeron, Jacques Esprinchard, and François Bassompierre, *Tři francouzští kavalíři v rudolfinské Praze*, preface by Eliška Fučíková and notes by Josef Jánaček (Prague, 1989).

Egon Erwin Kisch, "Zwei Kavaliere exzedieren," in Bodo Uhse and Gisela Kisch (eds.), *Gesammelte Werke in Einzelausgaben* 2:2 (Berlin and Weimar, 1969), 104–16, readable, as usual.

Niklas Ulenhart, *Sonderbare Geschichte von Isaak Winckelfelder und Jobst von der Schneidt*, newly edited by Gutta Veidl (Munich, 1941).

The Revolt of 1618 and the Battle of the White Mountain

Bohdan Chudoba, *Španělé na Bílé Hoře* (Prague, 1945); the author died in exile.

Ernst Denis, *La Bohème depuis la Montagne-Blanche* (Paris, 1903), a pro-Czech classic.

Anton Gindely, *Friedrich V. von der Pfalz* (Prague, 1884), still usable.

Josef Janáček, *Ženy české renesance* (Prague, 1977), on the women of the Bohemian seventeenth century, including Polyxena of Pernštejn (Lobkovic).

Josef Pekař, *Bílá Hora* (Prague, 1921), important study.

Josef Petráň, *Staroměstské exekuce* (Prague, 1971), narrative account of 1621 executions.

Josef V. Polišenký, *Třicetiletá válka a český národ* (Prague, 1960).

Josephine Rose, *The Winter Queen: The Story of Elizabeth Stuart* (New York, 1979).

Hans Sturmberger, *Georg Erasmus von Tschernembl* (Graz and Cologne, 1953).

———, *Aufstand in Böhmen* (Vienna, 1959); both important monographs.

Josef Forbelský, Jan Royt, and Mojmír Horyna, *Pražké Jezulátko* (Prague, 1992).

Zdeněk Kalista, *Tvář baroka* (Prague, 1982); a conservative point of view.

———, *Ctihodná Maria Elekta Ježíšova: Po stopách španělské mystiky v českém baroku* (Rome, 1975); pioneering study.

Václav Vilém Stěch, *Barockskulptur in Böhmen* (Prague, 1959).

Karl Maria Swoboda (ed.), *Barock in Böhmen* (Munich, 1964).

6. MOZART IN PRAGUE

Gli Italiani a Praga

Italians have shown surprisingly little systematic interest in the community life of their compatriots in Prague between 1550 and 1900, but many details can be found in Pavel Preiss, *Italští umělci v Praze* (Prague, 1986), a masterful study of Italian artists in Prague and their lives. Also: Josef Janáček, "Italové v předbělohorské Praze," in *Pražský historický sbornik*, 16 (1983), 77–118, on economic relationships.

Ettore LaGatto, *Civiltà italiana nel mondo* (Rome, 1939), chapter on Bohemia.

Enrico Marpurgo, *Gli artisti italiani in Austria* (Rome, 1937), vol. 1.

Karel Šmrha, "Vlaššti stavitelé v Praze a jejich druzi," *Umění*, 24 (1974), 159–84.

A Third-Rate Place/The Age of Reforms

R. J. W. Evans, "The Hapsburg Monarchy and Bohemia," in Mark Greengrass (ed.), *Conquest and Coalescence: The Shaping of the State in Early Modern Europe* (London, 1991), pp. 134–54.

Eila Hassenpflug-Elzholz, *Böhmen und die böhmischen Stände in der Zeit des bürgerlichen Zentralismus* (Vienna, 1982) – *Veröffentlichungen des Collegium Carolinum*, vol. 30.

Charles Ingrao, *The Habsburg Monarchy 1618–1815* (Cambridge, 1994), excellent.

Zdenka Pelikánová-Nová, "Lidnatost Prahy v 18. und v první části 19. století," *Pražký sborník historický*, 68 (1967), 5–43.

Oswald Redlich, *Das Werden einer Grossmacht: Österreich von 1700–1740* (Vienna, 4th ed. 1962), fundamental analysis.

Alfred von Arneth, *Geschichte Maria Theresias* (Vienna, 1863–79), 10 vols., older standard and reference work.

Edward Crankshaw, *Maria Theresa* (New York, 1970).

Jana Janusová, *Maria Teresie: Legendy a skutečnost* (Ostrava, 1991), judicious analysis.

Arnošt Klíma, *Manufakturní období v Čechách* (Prague, 1955).

Carlile Aylmer Macartney, *Maria Theresa and the House of Austria* (Mystic, Conn., 1969).

Gustav Otruba, *Die Wirtschaftspolitik Maria Theresias* (Vienna, 1963).

Karl A. Roider, Jr. (ed.), *Maria Theresa* (Englewood Cliffs, N.J., 1973), good introduction, with excerpts from important monographs.

Derek Beales, *Joseph II* (Cambridge, 1987), vol. 1: *In the Shadow of Maria Theresa*, best analysis in English.

T. C. W. Blanning, *Joseph II* (London and New York, 1994), excellent introduction.

François Fejtö, *Un Habsbourg révolutionnaire: Joseph II/Portrait d'un despot éclairé* (Paris, 1953).

Hans Magenschab, *Joseph II, Revolutionär von Gottes Gnaden* (Graz and Cologne, 2nd ed. 1980), important on religious questions.

Saul Padover, *The Revolutionary Emperor Joseph the Second* (Hamden, Ct. 2nd ed. 1967).

Fritz Valjavec, *Der Josephinismus* (Brünn, 1944), standard analysis.

Eduard Winter, *Der Josefinismus. Die Geschichte des österreichischen Reformkatholizismus* (Berlin, 2nd ed. 1962), written from the point of view of an enlightened Catholic.

Vladimir Lipscher, "Jüdische Gemeinden in den böhmischen Ländern zur Zeit des landesfürstlichen Absolutismus," Eila Hassenpflug-Elzholz, "Toleranzedikt und Emanzipation," and Anna M. Drabek, "Die Juden in den böhmischen Ländern zur Zeit des landesfürstlichen Absolutismus," in Ferdinand Seibt (ed.), *Die Juden in den böhmischen Ländern* (Munich, 1938), pp. 73–86 (Lipscher), pp. 144–60 (Hassenpflug-Elzholz), and pp. 123–44 (Drabek).

Ruth Kestenberg-Gladstein, *Neuere Geschichte der Juden in den böhmischen Ländern 1780–1830* (Tübingen, 1969), fundamental study from the archival sources, unfortunately not continued into the later period.

Josef Prokeš, *Úřední antisemitismus a pražské ghetto v době pobělohorské* (Prague, 1929).

Divadlo v Kotcích: 1739–1783 (Prague, 1992), instructive studies by various hands.

Derek Beales, *Mozart and the Hapsburgs* (Stanton Lecture, University of Reading, 1993).

Volkmar Braunbehrens, *Mozart: Ein Lebensbild* (Munich, 1994), useful introduction.

———, *Malignant Maestro: The Real Story of Antonio Salieri*, trans. by Eveline S. Kanes (New York, 1992), to counteract the movie.

Sheila Hodges, *Lorenzo da Ponte: The Life and Times of Mozart's Librettist* (New York, 1985).

Rudolf von Procházka, *Mozart in Prag* (Prague, 1892), written by an amateur collector and admirer, a wonderful treasury of contemporary anecdotes and reports, revised and enlarged by Paul Nettl, *Mozart in Böhmen* (Prague, 1938).

Jan Vondráček, *Dějiny českého divadla: doba obrozenecká 1771–1824* (Prague, 1956).

Eduard Mörike, *Mozart auf der Reise nach Prag*, ed. by Karl Pörnbacher (Stuttgart, 1976) – UB 8153, includes documents and commentary. English version by Walter and Catherine Alison Philips, *Mozart on His Way to Prague* (New York, 1947).

Jaroslav Seifert, *Mozart v Praze/Mozart in Prague*, bilingual edition, with translations from the Czech by Paul Jagavich and Tom O'Grady (Iowa City, 1985).

7. 1848 AND THE COUNTERREVOLUTION

The Travelers

Miroslav Ivanov, *Důvěrná zpráva o Karlu Hynku Máchovi* (Prague, 1977), impressive biographical reevaluation.

Ruth Kestenberg-Gladstein, *Neuere Geschichte de Juden in den böhmischen Ländern 1780–1830* (Tübingen, 1969), here especially pp. 115–309.

Ernst Nittner, "Volk, Nation und Vaterland in der Sozialethik Bernard Bolzanos," in Ferdinand Seibt (ed.), *Die böhmischen Länder zwischen Ost und West* (Munich and Vienna, 1983), pp. 149–74 [Festschrift Karl Bosl].

Albert Pražák, *České obrození* (Prague, 1948), valuable.

Hans Raupach, *Der tschechische Frühnationalismus* (Darmstadt, 2nd ed. 1969).

Walter Schamschula, *Die Anfänge der tschechischen Erneuerung und das deutsche Geistesleben* (Munich, 1973), distinguished study, excellent bibliography.

Vincy Schwarz (ed.), *Město vidím veliké: Cizinci v Praze* (Prague, 1940), admirable collection of what foreign travelers ever said about Prague (the editor was killed by the Gestapo).

Johannes Urzidil, *Goethe in Böhmen* (Zurich and Stuttgart, 2nd ed. 1962), inexhaustible on Goetheana and the cultural problems of Bohemia.

Eduard Winter, *Die Sozial- und Ethnoethik Bernard Bolzanos* (Vienna, 1977).

Karel Hynek Mácha, *Máj. Necenzurovaný deník z roku 1835* (Paris, 1986).

K. H. Mácha, "May," trans. by William E. Harkins in *Cross-Currents: A Yearbook of Central European Culture*, 6 (1987), 479–504.

1844–48

Václav Čejchan, *Bakunin v Praze* (Prague, 1928).

Karel Kazbunda, *České hnutí roku 1848* (Prague, 1929), fundamental study.

Arnošt Klima, *Češi a Němci v revoluci 1848–49* (Prague, 2nd ed. 1994).

Hans Kohn, *Pan-Slavism: Its History and Ideology* (New York, 2nd ed. 1960).

Karel Kosík, *Čeští radikální demokraté* (Prague, 1958).

Arnošt Kraus, "Böhmisch nebo tschechisch," *Naše Doba*, 24 (1916–17), 341–48, 429–36, 521–28, 601–8, revealing history of the terms "Bohemian" and "Czech."

Oldrich Mahler and Miroslav Broft, *Události pražské v červnu 1848* (Prague, 1989), a chronicle, richly illustrated.

Hermann Münch, *Böhmische Tragödie* (Braunschweig, 1949), illuminating views of a German conservative.

Lawrence Orten, *The Prague Slav Congress of 1848* (Boulder, Colo., 1978).

Josef V. Polišenský, *Aristocrats and the Crowds in the Revolutionary Year 1848* (Albany, 1980), an American edition of a Czech monograph (1975).

Stanley Z. Peck, *The Czech Revolution of 1848* (Chapel Hill, 1964), informative and judicious.

———, "The Czech Working Class in 1848," *Canadian Slavonic Papers*, 9 (1967), 60–73.

Otto Urban, *Die tschechische Gesellschaft 1848–1918* (Vienna, 1994), 2 vols., detailed and learned, Czech original 1992.

Karel Havlíček

Karel Havlíček Borovský, *Dílo* (Prague, 1986), 2 vols. Convenient edition by Jiří Kořejčík and Alexander Stich.

Milena Beránková, *Karl Havlíček Borovský* (Prague, 1980).

Manfred Jähnichen, *Zwischen Diffamierung und Widerhall: Tschechische Poesie im deutschen Spiegelbild 1815–1867* (Berlin, 1967).

Jiří Morava, *C. k. disident Karel Havlíček* (Prague, 1991), bravely demythologizing, from a study of the police records.

T. G. Masaryk, *Karel Havlíček* (Prague, 1875), portrait of a moderate national liberal.

Siegfried Kapper

Siegfried Kapper's writings, whether in German or in Czech, have never been collected or selectively reedited.

Natalia Bergerová (ed.), *Na križovatce kultur. Historie československých židů* (Prague, 1992), excellent individual contributions.

Oskar Donath, "Siegfried Kapper," in *Jahrbuch der Gesellschaft für Geschichte der Juden in der tschechoslowakischen Republik*, 6 (1939), 323–442, by the father of all Kapper research.

Fw (– František Weiner), "První pokus o česko-židovské hnutí: Siegfried Kapper," in *Kalendář* (Prague, 1989), samizdat.

Hillel J. Kieval, *The Making of Czech Jewry: National Conflict and Jewish Society in Bohemia 1870–1918* (New York and Oxford, 1988), best historical-sociological analysis.

———, "The social vision of Bohemian Jews: Intellectuals and community in the 1840s," in Jonathan Frankel /Steven J. Zipperstein (eds.), *Assimilation and community: The Jews in nineteenth-century Europe* (Cambridge, 1992), 246–83

Božena Němcová

Božena Němcová, *Granny*, trans. by Edith Pargeter (Westport, Conn., 1977).

———, *Die Grossmutter*, trans. by Peter and Hana Demetz (Zurich, 6th ed. 1993).

Václav Černý, *Knížka o Babičce* (Toronto, 2nd ed. 1982).

Alexander Guski (ed.), *Zur Poetik und Rezeption von Božena Němcovás "Babička"* (Berlin, 1991).

Georg J. Morava, *Sehnsucht meiner Seele: Božena Němcová, Dichterin/Ein Frauenschicksal in Alt-Österreich* (Innsbruck, 1995), excellent new biography.

Helena Sobková, *Tajemství Barunky Panklové* (Prague, 1992), genealogical speculations.

Václav Tille, *Božena Němcová* (Prague, 1969), older standard biography.

8. T. G. MASARYK'S PRAGUE

A Modernized City

G. B. Cohen, *The Politics of Ethnic Survival: Germans in Prague 1861–1914* (Princeton, 1981), important sociological study, from the city records.

Norman Cohn, *Warrant for Genocide: The Myth of the Jewish World Conspiracy and the "Protocols of the Elders of Zion"* (New York, 1967).

Elfriede Ledig, *Paul Wegener's Golem-Filme im Kontext fantastischer Literatur* (Munich, 1989).

Pražská asanace, by various contributors (Prague, 1993) – *Acta Musei Pragensis*, vol. 93, with extensive summaries in English and German.

Jeffrey L. Sammons, "The Literary Origins of the 'Protocols of the Elders of Zion,'" *A Jewish Journal at Yale*, 2/1 (Fall 1984), 8–12.

Rudolf M. Wlaschek, *Juden in Böhmen* (Munich, 1990) – *Veröffentlichungen des Collegium Carolinum*, vol. 66.

Francis Marion Crawford, *The Witch of Prague* (London, 3rd ed. 1892).

George Eliot, *The Lifted Veil* (London, 1985), with a new afterword by Beryl Gray.

Wilhelm Raabe, "Hollunderblüte," in *Sämtliche Werke*, ed. Karl Hoppe (Freiburg, 1951–), 9/1, 85–120.

Sir John Retcliffe (– Hermann Goedsche), *Biarritz* (historisch-politischer Roman in acht Bänden) (Berlin, 1868, 2nd ed. 1876).

Peter Demetz, "Die Legende vom magischen Prag," *Transit*, 7 (1994), 142–62, reprinted in Peter Demetz, *Böhmische Sonne/Mährischer Mond: Essays und Erinnerungen* (Vienna, 1996), pp. 143–67.

Republican Prague

Karl Bosl (ed.), *Die erste tschechoslowakische Republik als multinationaler Parteienstaat* (Munich, 1979).

J. W. Bruegel, *Czechoslovakia Before Munich* (Cambridge, 1973), brittle analysis of national problems and British appeasement policies.

Václav Čada, *28 října 1918: Skutečnost, sny, iluse* (Prague, 1988), popular reading, with an official slant.

Jörg K. Hoensch, *Geschichte der Tschechoslowakei* (Stuttgart, 1992), the best recent German story of the republic.

Egon Hostovský, "The Czech-Jewish Movement," in *The Jews of Czechoslovakia*, 2 (New York, 1971), 148–54, written by the prominent novelist.

Victor S. Mamatey and Radomír Luža (eds.), *A History of Czechoslovakia: 1918–1945* (Princeton, 1973), by various hands, important and instructive.

Ferdinand Peroutka, *Budování státu* (Prague, 1933–36), 4 vols. in 5, admirably ironic and sharp analysis by a distinguished writer and essayist.

Miloslav Rechcígl, Jr. (ed.), *Czechoslovakia—Past and Present* (London, 1969).

Emil Strauss, *Die Entstehung der tschechoslowakischen Republik* (Prague, 1934), by a German Social Democrat who died in a concentration camp.

Zdeněk Zeman, *The Break-up of the Habsburg Empire* (Oxford, 1963).

T. G. Masaryk

Karl Čapek (ed.), *Masaryk Tells His Story* (London, 1951); the earlier German edition is *Masaryk erzählt sein Leben* (Prague, 1936).

Jan Herben, *T. G. Masaryk* (Prague, 1926–27), 3 vols., takes the story of Masaryk's life up to 1921.

Roland J. Hoffmann, *T. G. Masaryk und die tschechische Frage* (Munich, 1988).

Jiří Kovtun, *Tajemná vražda: Případ Leopolda Hilsnera* (Prague, 1994), careful report on Hilsner trial.

Charlotta G. Masaryková, *Listy do vězení* (Prague, 1948), Masaryk's wife writes to her daughter imprisoned by the Austrian authorities (letters originally in German).

T. G. Masaryk and the Jews: A Collection of Essays, trans. by Benjamin R. Epstein (New York, 1941), contributions by Max Brod, Felix Weltsch, Oskar Donath, and others.

Zdeněk Nejedlý, *T. G. Masaryk* (Prague, 1930–37), 5 vols., detailed biography up to 1885.

Jaroslav Opat, *Filozof a politik T. G. Masaryk: 1882–1893* (Prague, 1990), a study of ideas.

Paul Selver, *Masaryk: A Biography* (London, 1949), eminently readable.

Zdeněk Zeman, *The Masaryks* (London, 1976), on the entire family.

The Cultures of Republican Prague

Jaromír Krejcar, *L'architecture contemporaine en Tchéchoslovaquie* (Prague, 1928), by Milena Jesenká's second husband.

Vladimír Šlapeta, *Praha 1900–1978: Průvodce po moderní architektuře* (Prague, 1978).

Alexander Vegesack (ed.), *Czech Cubism: 1910–1925* (New York, 1992), richly documented.

Gustav Janouch, *Jaroslav Hašek* (Bern, 1966), to be read with caution.

Cecil Perrot, *The Bad Bohemian* (London, 1978), best book in English, written by former British Ambassador to Prague.

Jaroslav Krížek, *Jaroslav Hašek v revolučním Rusku* (Prague, 1957), full story of Hašek, the adventurous Bolshevik.

Radko Pytlík, *Jaroslav Hašek a dobrý voják Švejk* (Prague, 1983).

Markéta Brousek, *Der Poetismus: die Lehrjahre der tschechischen Avantgarde und ihrer marxistischen Kritiker* (Munich, 1975).

Květoslav Chvatík, *Die Prager Moderne* (Frankfurt, 1991), with an introduction by Milan Kundera.

———, and Zdeněk Posat, *Poetismus* (Prague, 1967), illuminating anthology, amply illustrated.

Marie and Václav Kubín, *Magické zrcadlo: Anthologie poetismu* (Prague, 1982).

Vítězslav Nezval, *Moderní básnické směry* (Prague, 1964), his views of contemporary poetry.

Jiří Voskovec and Jan Werich, *Máme za to* (Prague, 1990), the old songs live on.

Karl-Heinz Jahn (ed.), *Das Prager Kaffeehaus* (Berlin, 1988), East German nostalgia for the old Prague cafés.

Jürgen Born (ed.), *Deutschsprachige Literatur Prags und Böhmens im ersten Viertel des 20. Jahrhunderts: Tabellarische Übersicht und Bibliographie* (Wuppertal, 2nd ed. 1988).

Max Brod, *Der Prager Kreis* (Frankfurt, 1979) with a (skeptical) postscript by Peter Demetz.

Bibliography

Gilles Deleuze and Félix Guattari, "What Is a Minor Literature?" in Mark Anderson (ed.) *Reading Kafka: Prague, Politics, and the Fin de Siècle* (New York, 1989), pp. 80–94.

Ingeborg Fiala-Fürst, *Der Beitrag der Prager deutschen Literatur zum deutschen literarischen Expressionismus* (St. Ingbert, 1996), comprehensive, with excellent bibliography.

Marino Freschi, *Saggi di letteratura Pragese* (Naples, 1987).

———, *La Praga di Kafka* (Naples, 1990).

Eduard Goldstücker (ed.), *Weltfreunde: Konferenz über die Prager deutsche Literatur* (Prague, 1967), within the limits of the (then) possibilities.

Helena Kanyar-Becker, "Eine verhängnisvolle Liebe: Zur Pragerdeutschen Literatur," in *Leben der Grenze/Theorie der Grenze* (Würzburg, 1995), pp. 67–88.

Milan Tvrdík, "Paul Eisner-Vermittler deutschsprachiger Literatur der böhmischen Länder," in *Dokumente: Germanistentreffen BRD-ČSFR* (Bonn, 1992), pp. 47–57.

Giuliano Baioni, *Kafka: letteratura ed hebraismo* (Turin, 1984), valuable discussion of Kafka and the Jewish tradition.

Hartmut Binder (ed.), *Kafka Handbuch* (Stuttgart, 1979), 2 vols., everything you ever wanted to know about Kafka, and more, by distinguished European and American scholars and critics.

Josef Čermák, "Franz Kafkas Sorgen mit der tschechischen Sprache," in Kurt Krolop und Hans Dieter Zimmermann (eds.), *Kafka und Prag*, Colloquium im Goethe Institut, November 24–27, 1992 (Berlin and New York, 1994), pp. 59–66.

Eduard Goldstücker (ed.), *Kafka aus Prager Sicht* (Prague, 1965), papers read at a Prague Conference rescuing Kafka for the Communist world; retrospectively, Jiří Stromšík, "Ein Rückblick von 1991," in Norbert Wiener and Wolfgang Kraus (eds.), *Franz Kafka in der kommunistischen Welt*, (Vienna and Cologne, 1993), pp. 120–43 – *Schriftenreihe der österreichischen Kafka-Gesellschaft*, 5.

Kurt Krolop, "Hinweis auf eine verschollene Rundfrage: Wann haben Sie Prag verlassen?" *Germanistica Pragensia*, 4 (1966), 47–64.

———, and Hans Dieter Zimmermann (eds.), *Kafka und Prag* (Frankfurt, 1987); contributors include Margarita Pazi, Rio Preisner, and others.

Marta Marková-Motyková, *Mýtus Milena* (Prague, 1993), demythologizing the icon Milena Jesenská.

Antonio Pasinato, *Praga: Mito e letteratura: 1900–39* (Florence, 1993).

Christoph Stölzl, *Kafkas böses Böhmen: Zur Sozialgeschichte eines Prager Juden* (Munich, 1975).

Alena Wagnerová, *Milena Jesenská: Eine Biographie* (Mannheim, 1994).

Index

Index

Index

Index

Index

Index

Index